MODERN MACROECONOMICS

second edition

Michael Parkin
Robin Bade

Prentice-Hall Canada Inc., Scarborough, Ontario

Canadian Cataloguing in Publication Data

Parkin, Michael, 1939–
    Modern macroeconomics

Includes bibliographical references and index.

ISBN 0-13-595224-7.

1. Macroeconomics. I. Bade, Robin. II. Title.

HB172.5.P37 1985   339   C85-099508-6

Prentice-Hall Inc., Englewood Cliffs, *New Jersey*
Prentice-Hall International, Inc., *London*
Prentice-Hall of Australia, Pty., Ltd., *Sydney*
Prentice-Hall of India Pvt., Ltd., *New Delhi*
Prentice-Hall of Japan Inc., *Tokyo*
Prentice-Hall of Southeast Asia (Pte.) Ltd., *Singapore*
Editora Prentice-Hall do Brasil Ltda., *Rio de Janeiro*
Prentice-Hall Hispanoamericana, S.A., *Mexico*
Whitehall Books Ltd., Wellington, *New Zealand*

ISBN 0-13-595224-7

Project Editor: Marta Tomins
Production Editors: Maura Brown, Sharyn Rosart
Layout: Janet Eidt
Manufacturing Co-ordinator: Sheldon Fischer
Cover Design: Brian Bean

Composition: Q Composition Inc.
Printed and bound in Canada by John Deyell Company

1 2 3 4 5   JD   90 89 88 87 86

To Catherine, Richard and Ann

Contents

Preface to the First Edition

This book presents a comprehensive and up-to-date account of macro-economics—that branch of economics that seeks to understand and explain inflation, unemployment, interest rates, foreign exchange rates, the balance of payments, and other related phenomena. Unlike any other book currently available at this level, a considerable amount of space and attention is devoted to developments that have taken place in the subject in the past ten years. The chief of these is the incorporation into macroeconomics of the rational expectations hypothesis. This hypothesis is explained in simple, intuitive terms, and its implications for the determination of inflation, unemployment and for the assessment of economic stabilization policies are analyzed. The book does not deal exclusively with developments in macro-economics that have taken place in the past ten years. It also provides an account of the mainstream Keynesian and pre-Keynesian theories from which the modern macroeconomic theories have grown. In addition, attention is paid to the interrelations between the domestic economy and the rest of the world (open economy macroeconomics) and to the design and conduct of macroeconomic policy.

Modern Macroeconomics attempts to avoid the extremes of dry theory and passionate policy advocacy. It presents the various theories in such a way that the reader may quickly and easily see their predictive content—the facts which each theory seeks to explain. It also checks the predictions of each theory against the facts, revealing in the process what that theory is capable of explaining well and what its main shortcomings are. Policy is treated by analyzing the implications of pursuing the policy recommendations of different schools of thought in such a way that the reader may see clearly why it is that different economists reach different conclusions on important questions.

The central purpose of the book is to make modern macro-economics accessible to beginning and intermediate students as well as to the serious, general reader. The book is pitched at a level which is appropriate for intermediate undergraduate students in Canadian universities. It uses the simplest available analytic techniques, intuitive explanations and, wherever possible, illustrations drawn from Canadian experience. *Modern Macroeconomics* will also be found helpful both by readers who have not reached the intermediate stage of study and by those who have already moved well beyond that stage. Indeed, in view of the lack of any alternative treatment of much of the material that is presented here, this book will be useful even for beginning graduate students who are looking for a broad overview of material which they will study in greater depth in their post-graduate courses. And finally, *Modern Macroeconomics* will be of interest to those whose formal study of economics was completed before the rational expectations revolution hit macroeconomics, and who are now in positions as professional economists in government, industry and commerce.

The book is organized around three main themes—facts, theories and policies. The two introductory sections set out the facts that macroeconomics seeks to explain and also give an account of the ways in which macroeconomics phenomena are observed and measured. The core of the book deals with theory. It is organized around a series of progressively more comprehensive models of the economy, each of which has some merits in explaining a limited set of facts, but each of which also has some shortcomings which are pointed out. Following this section discussing alternative theories, macroeconomic policy—the attempt to actively deal with the problem of stabilizing output, employment and prices—is discussed at considerable length. Then, in the last five chapters, the linkages between the Canadian economy and the rest of the world are dealt with.

Macroeconomics is a controversial subject and economists often disagree vehemently on policy issues. Despite this, there is a considerable measure of agreement on most matters. There do, however, remain crucial issues that divide economists and, although it is a slight caricature, it seems reasonably accurate to divide macroeconomists into two camps—Monetarists and Keynesians. I am widely regarded as being a monetarist and, as descriptive matter, cannot seriously quarrel with that label. I have nevertheless tried to write a book which avoids falling into the trap of being a monetarist tract. Some, no doubt, will conclude that I have failed. I have certainly not shied away from presenting alternative views on macroeconomic policy in the sharpest possible focus. I have attempted to do justice to the positions of each view and explain precisely what it is that each group believes and why. Acceptance of the hypothesis that expectations are formed rationally is often regarded as being synonymous with monetarism. The fact that this book, unlike any other at this level, presents an account of rational expectations, will, no doubt, lead some to conclude, for that reason alone that this book is a monetarist tract. Such a view will be seen, on careful reflection, to be incorrect. There are rational expectations Keynesians (usually referred to as New Keynesians) as well as monetarists (usually referred to as New Classicals). Both of these strands in the recent literature are presented and explained.

*   *   *

This book would not have been completed without the help of a large number of people. First and foremost, I owe an enormous debt to Robin Bade. From the outset of this project she has been a constant source of help, guidance and criticism. She has read the manuscript almost as many times as I have (possibly even more), drafted all the diagrams, dreamt up many of the review questions, corrected my grammar and caught many inconsistencies and errors. Michael Cox (of the Virginia Polytechnic Institute) has also read and commented upon substantial parts of the manuscript and provided many of the review questions. Michael Sumner (of the University of Salford, England) and my colleagues David Laidler and Stephen Margolis provided extensive comments on the entire manuscript. I also benefitted from the comments of what were, at the time, anonymous referees, but whom I now know to have been Brian Scarfe of the University of Alberta and James Pesando of the University of Toronto. Several generations of undergraduate students and graduate teaching assistants at the University of Western Ontario have been of considerable help in providing comments and criticisms upon various parts of the book at different stages of its development. I am especially grateful to Rosalind Wong, Monica van Huystee and David Abramson. Jane McAndrew provided expert library and clerical assistance and research assistance was provided by Eddie McDonnell. The many drafts and revisions have been typed with great skill by Marg Gower, Yvonne Adams, Leslie Farrant and Brenda Campbell. I am indebted to them all.

Michael Parkin
London, Ontario
December 1981

Preface to the Second Edition

This second edition is a substantially revised version of *Modern Macroeconomics*. All the chapters have been revised and rethought to reflect new data, new research, readers' comments and suggestions, as well as our own ideas and efforts to improve the exposition and content of the book.

The single most important change in this edition is one of structure. In the first edition the body of macroeconomic theory was organized around the historical development of the subject—the Classical, Keynesian, and Modern Rational Expectations approaches. This revision organizes its presentation of theory around the three great concepts of aggregate demand, aggregate supply, and macroeconomic equilibrium. This broad way of thinking about the functioning economy in aggregate is itself relatively uncontroversial. Also, the theory of aggregate demand is in a relatively settled state. As a consequence, we are able to move quickly through the uncontroversial parts of macroeconomics and also present the alternative and competing theories of aggregate supply and macroeconomic equilibrium. Thus we can present a more streamlined and less taxonomic development of macroeconomic theory than was possible in the first edition. We can also focus more clearly on areas that are controversial and bring the nature of the controversies to the attention of the reader. Yet this organization permits us to cover the entire body of macroeconomic theory all the way through to the new rational expectations models, in a half-year course.

In addition to organizing our presentation of macroeconomic theory in a more streamlined way, we have provided a more unified and coherent series of chapters that seek to use macroeconomic theory to understand the key facts about macroeconomic performance. Four chapters, dealing with inflation, unemployment, output growth, and cycles, draw out the implications of economic theories and show how they account for the facts. The output growth chapter is new. The other chapters represent significant reworking, reorganization and updating of material that was scattered throughout the first edition. The chapter on unemployment has been substantially updated to reflect some interesting and potentially far-reaching new ideas.

The open economy material comes earlier in the new edition than it did in the first—before the discussion of macroeconomic policy. The instructor wishing to leave the open economy to the end can, however, still perform that reorganization with little cost.

The policy chapters are now in the final section of the book and these have been substantially expanded. In particular, a new chapter on supply-side policies has been included as well as two additional chapters on the labour market, one investigating the implications of tax-based incomes policies (TIPS), a popular and often advocated approach to directly influencing wage developments, and one analyzing the macroeconomic effects of wage indexation.

In developing this second edition we have been greatly helped by the many readers both of the first edition of this work as well as of the United Kingdom and United States versions that grew out of the first edition. We are especially grateful to Ben Benanke (Stanford University); Ronald Bodkin (University of Ottawa); Paul Boothe (University of Alberta); Don Daly (York University); Evan Douglas (Bentley College); Laura Finestone (University of Rochester); David Gordon (University of Rochester); Gary Grant (Acadia University); Jeremy Greenwood (University of Western Ontario); Herschel Grossman (Brown University); Joseph Guerin (St. Joseph's University); Geoffrey Kingston (University of Queensland); John Lapp (North Carolina State University); David Laidler (University of Western Ontario); Fred Lazar (York University); Dominic Li (University of Guelph); Glenn MacDonald (University of Western Ontario); Andrea Maneschi (Vanderbilt University); Stephen Margolis (North Carolina State University); Bob Nobay (University of Liverpool); Andrew Policano (University of Iowa); Nicholas Rowe (Carleton University); Michael Sumner (University of Sussex); Randall Wigle (University of Western Ontario); Ian Wooton (University of Western Ontario).

We have prepared a totally revised version of the Instructor's Manual which is available on request from the publisher. Also, a Study Guide has been prepared by Robin Bade to accompany this edition. It provides a wide range of questions of progressively increasing difficulty. It also provides worked examples to sample problems, as well as answers to all questions.

In preparing this second edition we have been greatly assisted by Catherine Parkin and Laura Noble. The numerous drafts of revisions have been handled with cheerfulness and skill by Yvonne Adams, Leslie Farrant and Nancy Joslin. We are deeply indebted to them all.

Robin Bade
Michael Parkin
London, Ontario
January, 1986

I

INTRODUCTION

1
Macroeconomic Questions

This book is going to help you to get abreast of the current state of knowledge in macroeconomics. Five tasks in this introductory chapter will start you out on that process. These tasks are to:

a) Know the questions which macroeconomics seeks to answer.
b) Know the macroeconomic problems facing Canada in the middle 1980s.
c) Understand the distinction between macroeconomic science, policy and popular debate.
d) Know the macroeconomic policy issues on which economists disagree.
e) Know the views of the leading "schools of thought."

A. Macroeconomic Questions

Macroeconomic questions have changed over the years and have usually been motivated by a concern to understand the economic problems of the day.

(i) Inflation

The oldest macroeconomic question is, what determines the general level of prices? A very closely related question is, what determines the rate of inflation (or the rate of deflation)? Concern over this issue goes back at least to the late Roman Empire, when rampant inflation was experienced. In more modern times the world has had a checkered inflationary history. Following the period of European (particularly Spanish) colonization of the Americas and the influx into Europe of vast quantities of gold, there was a substantial rise in the general level of prices in Europe and North America. This went on well into the early seventeenth century. There then followed a period of price stability, which in turn was followed (from about 1750 to the early nineteenth century) by further very strong inflation. In the early part of the nineteenth century, following the Napoleonic wars, there was a period of falling prices. The next hundred years saw alternating periods of rising and falling prices, but over the century as a whole there was remarkable price stability. Since the 1930s, prices have persistently risen and especially strongly so between the late 1960s and the early 1980s.[1] By the middle 1980s, more moderate inflation rates have returned to most of the developed countries.

The questions for macroeconomics are: why have there been periods of prolonged inflation and deflation? What has caused these major movements in the general level of prices? Can we predict future price level movements? How can we control inflation?

(ii) Unemployment

The second major question for macroeconomics is, what determines the percentage of the labor force that is unemployed? This problem became particularly acute in the late 1920s and 1930s when high and persistent unemployment dominated the entire world economy. In many countries unemployment hardly fell below 20 percent for almost fifteen years. In the period immediately following World War II unemployment was, throughout the whole world, remarkably low. Its rate began to rise, however, during the 1960s and, in the 1970s and especially in the 1980s unemployment has again emerged as a major concern.

The questions for macroeconomics are: what determines the level of unemployment? Why does its rate fluctuate, and why at certain times does unemployment remain persistently high? What actions, if any, can governments take to smooth out fluctuations in unemployment and lower its average rate?

(iii) Aggregate Output — GNP

What determines a country's level of aggregate output — or level of Gross National Product — or GNP? The precise meaning of GNP will be given in Chapter 3. For now, and loosely speaking, you may think of GNP as a measure of the volume of the goods and services that can be bought with the income of all the individuals in the economy.

---

[1] An excellent account of the long-term movements in prices may be found in Anna J. Schwartz, "Secular Price Change in Historical Perspective," *Journal of Money, Credit and Banking*, V, no.1, pt II (February 1973) 243-69.

Fluctuations in GNP give rise to fluctuations in the standard of living, and differences in average growth rates of GNP between countries produce large intercountry differences in living standards. Macro-economics seeks to understand the reasons why there are persistent differences in GNP growth rates between countries and why there are fluctuations in GNP around its trend growth rate. Macro-economics also seeks to understand how policy actions that governments might take may influence the growth and fluctuations in GNP.

(iv) Interest Rates

A fourth question which macroeconomics addresses is, what determines the level of interest rates? There are, of course, many rates of interest in a modern economy. In the study of macroeconomics it is customary to study average levels of interest rates but also to distinguish between short-term and long-term rates of interest. *Short-term* rates (or more simply, *short rates*) are the rates of interest paid and received on loans of a short term or temporary nature — up to five years. *Long-term rates* are those on loans of more than five years — and could be on loans that run indefinitely. There is a tendency for all interest rates to move up and down together, but for short rates to fluctuate more strongly than long rates. An essential problem for macroeconomics is to understand what determines the general ups and downs in interest rates and why short-term rates fluctuate more than long-term rates. Macroeconomics also seeks to understand how actions of the government — such as, for example, financing government spending by borrowing — by creating a large deficit — affects interest rates.

(v) Balance of Payments and Foreign Exchange Rate

A fifth question is, what determines a country's balance of payments with the rest of the world? and a sixth, related question is, what determines the value of one country's currency in relation to that of another country? — that is, what determines the foreign exchange rate? These questions have a long history. Countries have been concerned with their balance of payments for as long as there has been international trade. In recent years fluctuations in foreign exchange rates have become a major issue.

Macroeconomics seeks to understand why foreign exchange rates and balance of payments fluctuate and also to determine the influence of government policy actions on these variables.

B. Canada's Macroeconomic Questions in the 1980s

It is evident that although some of the macroeconomic questions posed above have been more important at certain stages in history than at others, in recent years they have all taken on a considerable importance — not least in Canada.[2]

(i) Inflation

As the 1980s opened Canada's inflation was running at about 10 percent per annum. At first it rose to a little more than 12 percent but then, by mid-decade dropped to less than 4 percent. The rise in inflation — which began in the 1970s — had caught most people by surprise. By around 1982, however, when inflation in excess of 10 percent had become entrenched, rates of this magnitude came to be regarded by most people as "normal" and likely to continue into the indefinite future. As a consequence, the fall in inflation in 1983 and 1984 was, for most people, simply astonishing.[3] These unexpected and large variations in the rate of inflation have generated enormous problems. For example, many people, especially farmers and others operating small businesses, borrowed at high rates of interest in the late 1970s and early 1980s expecting to be able to repay their loans and pay the interest on them with a rising revenue from the sale of products whose prices would rise in line with an ongoing inflation of 10 percent or more. When inflation collapsed and revenues did not grow as quickly as they had been expected to, loans could not be repaid and a massive wave of business failure and bankruptcy ensued.

(ii) Unemployment

Unemployment, which in 1980 had stood at the then alarming rate of $7^1/_2$ percent rose dramatically to 13 percent in the winter of 1982-83. It persisted in excess of 11 percent all the way through to the middle of the decade. When unemployment rises its incidence is not evenly spread across the population. The most notable and serious feature of an economy experiencing high unemployment is the tendency for the unemployment to be concentrated (although not exclusively of course) among the younger segments of the work force. This has been a feature of unemployment in Canada which has given rise to great concern.

(iii) Aggregate Output — GNP

Aggregate output, GNP, grew slightly in the first two years of the 1980s but then declined dramatically in 1982 with the result that by

---

[2] A good, up-to-date and comprehensive source for facts about Canada's macroeconomic condition is the *Bank of Canada Review*, published monthly by the Bank of Canada, Ottawa K1A 0G9.

[3] Although most people were astonished by the fall in inflation that occurred in 1983-84, we were not! You may find it interesting to read Michael Parkin, "Watch Out for Falling Inflation!" in *The Canadian Business Review*, 8 no. 3 (Autumn 1981), pp. 18-22.

the end of 1982, total output in Canada was virtually unchanged from its value in 1980. The years 1983 and 1984 saw a return to the more usual state of affairs in which total output grows at a moderate rate each year. The failure of total output to grow in the early years of the 1980s combined with a continually growing population resulted in a gradual (though only slight) decline in the total volume of goods and services available, on the average, for each individual Canadian. This state of affairs, though far from calamitous, stands in marked contrast to the one that Canadians had become accustomed to — a situation in which per capita consumption grows year after year.

(iv) Interest Rates

Interest rate movements have been of major concern for Canadians during the 1980s. For most of the decade, rates have been well into the teens and, on occasion, have exceeded 20 percent. Such high interest rates have been welcomed, of course, by those doing the lending but have been greeted with alarm by borrowers. Businessmen and farmers as well as homeowners with mortgages have experienced serious financial hardship as a result of interest rate fluctuations. Also, Canada's largest borrower — the government — has found its own deficit growing year after year largely as a consequence of having to meet ever-increasing interest payments on its outstanding debt.

(v) Balance of Payments and (vi) Exchange Rate

Canada's overall balance of payments has fluctuated massively during the decade of the 1980s. On the average, however, the balance has been approximately zero. The major external problem for Canada has not been its balance of payments but the movement in the value of the Canadian dollar. The exchange rate that Canadians notice most is that between the Canadian and U.S. dollars. Viewed in that light, the Canadian dollar has been declining in value and quite dramatically so. On the average, in 1980, a U.S. dollar could be bought for $1.17 Canadian. By 1985 that same U.S. dollar cost $1.30 Canadian. The decline in the value of the Canadian dollar against the U.S. dollar has been steady and persistent.

Although the Canadian dollar has been losing ground against its U.S. counterpart it has not been declining in value against most currencies. What has been happening in the 1980s is that the U.S. dollar has been particularly strong, gaining in value on the average against all currencies.

Movements in foreign exchange rates, like movements in inflation rates and interest rates, have important effects on individuals and businesses. Exporters, and those competing with foreign imports, usually make short-term gains when there is an unexpected drop in the value of a currency, but those consuming imported goods — including the consumers of foreign vacations — suffer a short-term loss in such a situation.

You have now reviewed Canada's major macroeconomic problems in the 1980s. You have reviewed a half-decade in which inflation dramatically collapsed; unemployment increased to, and persisted at, high levels; real income growth was very low; interest rates were high and volatile; and the external value of the Canadian dollar against its U.S. counterpart declined dramatically. Thus in the middle 1980s, the macroeconomic questions for Canada are: Why did we have so much inflation at the beginning of the decade and why did its rate collapse after 1983? Why has unemployment increased to, and persisted at, such high levels? Why has aggregate output grown at such a slow rate? Why have interest rates been so high and volatile and why has the U.S. dollar value of the Canadian currency declined so sharply?

A related, more important, and yet much harder to answer set of questions are: What are the effects on inflation, unemployment, aggregate output growth, interest rates and the foreign exchange rate of the policies which the Canadian government — and the Bank of Canada — might adopt and how might policy be arranged so as to achieve steadier and more predictable inflation, lower unemployment, higher output growth, lower interest rates and a more stable and predictable value of the Canadian dollar? To what extent must Canada live with the market forces that influence and drive these variables and to what extent can policy enable Canada to steer an independent and steadier course?

The questions set out in Part A, and the manifestation of those questions in Canada's recent economic experience, provide the subject matter of macroeconomics.

C. Macroeconomic Science, Policy, and the Popular Debate

We have seen in the two previous sections of this chapter that macroeconomics deals with things that people care about and that affect their well-being. As a result a great deal of macroeconomics features in the contemporary policy debate. Politicians offer their favored solutions to the whole range of macroeconomic policy problems. Journalists, both in print and on the airwaves, add their voices to the chorus. Labor union leaders, prominent businessmen, public servants, and academics (whether trained in economics or not) all provide an endless stream of views on current macroeconomic problems. The contemporary macroeconomic policy debate is so important and, at times, so exciting that it becomes difficult for students of economics, whether they are just embarking on the subject or are seasoned professionals, to pursue their science with objectivity and untrammelled logic.

It is also difficult at times, especially when discussing policy issues that are of major contemporary importance, to keep firmly in mind that the science of macroeconomics is a very young one whose body of theory, though extensive, is not sufficiently reliable to deliver solutions to all of the perceived macroeconomic problems of the day.

The purpose of this book is to give an account of the *science* of macroeconomics. That is, the book presents an account of the current state of knowledge on macroeconomic *theory*. In order to help you to see the relevance of particular pieces of theory, examples drawn from Canada's macroeconomic experience will be presented. These examples are intended as nothing more than illustrations of a particular piece of theory in action. They are emphatically not offered as a commentary on, or as a contribution to, Canada's contemporary macroeconomic policy debate.

We find it helpful to try to keep three activities clearly distinguished. They are:

a) macroeconomic science

b) macroeconomic policy recommendations, and

c) macroeconomic policy debates.

Macroeconomic science is the body of knowledge — incomplete and imperfect — that seeks to *understand* the macroeconomic phenomena that we have set out above.

Macroeconomic policy proposals are recommendations concerning how government policy should be pursued and are usually accompanied by predictions as to what the effects of those policies on macroeconomic performance will be. Macroeconomic policy proposals may or may not make use of macroeconomic science. Clearly, policy proposals that achieve their desired objectives will be based on macroeconomic science (assuming that the science has developed to an appropriate level of reliability). There is no logical reason, however, why someone should not make macroeconomic policy recommendations even in the absence of a reliable body of economic science capable of generating predictions concerning the effects of pursuing the recommended policies.

Macroeconomic policy debates are attempts to persuade a sufficient number of people that a particular policy should be pursued. Macroeconomic science clearly can be one ingredient in that debate. The argument that some particular policy should be pursued because a particular body of science predicts that the policy will have certain well-defined and desired effects is often a compelling one. There is, however, no restriction on the rules of debate requiring that some underlying science be invoked to legitimize the proposed policy. Debaters, even those who are macroeconomic specialists, often stray outside the limits of their science in order to score a point!

This book tries very hard to stay within the confines of the science of macroeconomics, to pursue the activity of seeking to understand macroeconomic phenomena and to make statements about macroeconomic policy that are implied by — that are in line with — the current state of macroeconomic theory.

Although it appears to aid clear thinking to make a sharp distinction between the three activities of science, policy advice, and policy debate there are, of course, important connections between them. These connections were identified and reflected on in a manner that we believe is particularly relevant and illuminating for our present purposes by Professor George J. Stigler of the University of Chicago in his Nobel Lecture. In that lecture Stigler remarked that:

> The central task of an empirical science such as economics is to provide general understanding of events in the real world, and ultimately all of its theories and techniques must be instrumental to that task. That is very different from saying, however, that it must be responsive to the contemporaneous conditions and problems of the society in which it is situated . . . .
>
> The responsiveness of economics to environmental problems will naturally be more complete and more prompt the more urgent the problems of the day. The response will also be more complete, the less developed the relevant body of economic analysis. The responsiveness of macroeconomics to contemporary events is notorious. Keynes's conquest in the 1930s was due to the fact that the neoclassical theory could not account for the persistent unemployment of that decade. A generation later, persistent inflation even with less than full employment was equally decisive in ending Keynes's supremacy. If and when macroecnomics produces a good theory of the business cycle, its responsiveness to environmental changes will diminish sharply.
>
> A viable and healthy science requires both the persistent and almost timeless theories that naturally ignore the changing conditions of their society and the unsettled theories that encounter much difficulty in attempting to explain current events. Without the base of persistent theory, there would be no body of slowly evolving knowledge to constitute the science. Without the challenge of unsolved, important problems, the science would become sterile.[4]

Macroeconomics is, we believe, "a viable and healthy science." It is, however, one that has very little danger of running out of "challenges of unsolved, important problems, [likely to make] the science . . . become sterile." The policy problem and the policy debate that fuels macroeconomic science is too important, exciting, and durable for that to happen.

Let us now turn our attention more fully to some macroeconomic policy issues.

D. Macroeconomic Policy Issues

There is, as you know, a widespread belief that the government can and should take actions designed to influence key economic variables such as inflation and unemployment. Economists do not agree among themselves, however, on what measures will achieve the desired results. The main reason why there is disagreement is that we still lack a deep enough understanding of macroeconomic phenomena. Another way of saying this is that we lack good theories; that is, no one particular theory fits the facts so exactly that it is compelling. This means

---

[4]George J. Stigler, Nobel Lecture: The Process and Progress of Economics, *Journal of Political Economy*, Vol. 91, No. 4, 1983, pp. 529-544. The quotation came from pp. 534-5.

that each of us tends to subscribe to that theory that best supports our predisposition (or perhaps even our prejudices). This should not be taken to mean that macroeconomics is just a matter of opinion. On the contrary, there exists a solid "core" of theory that commands widespread support among economists regardless of the policy view that they adopt. There are, however, some areas where agreement on the relevant theoretical approach is still lacking. Even in these cases, there is general agreement among economists on the way to proceed to resolve conflicts of view.

There is also virtually complete agreement among economists that many of the popular explanations for macroeconomic problems are simply too shallow to be useful. The most common sources of such explanations are the media and politicians. Pay attention the next time your favorite newscaster is telling you about the latest figures on inflation or unemployment or interest rates. You will usually hear something like this:

Inflation has risen this month *because* of sharp rises in the prices of fuel and food.

or

Unemployment rose in April *because* of massive layoffs in the auto industry.

or

Interest rates have eased *because* of a return of investor confidence. You are going to discover that these answers to macroeconomic questions are too superficial or shallow to be of any value. In effect they are simply descriptions of the phenomenon that needs to be understood or explained.

Although we know that many popular so-called explanations of macroeconomic phenomena are not really explanations at all and provide no basis for the conduct of macroeconomic policy, we are not able to provide a satisfactory explanation using what Stigler called "almost timeless theories" that are sufficiently reliable to provide unambiguous and uncontroversial direction to the design and conduct of macroeconomic policy. This means that as macroeconomic scientists, we have to maintain due humility when asked for advice on contemporary policy problems. It does not mean, however, that we have nothing to say. Although we do not know all of the answers we certainly *do* know that some of the proposed answers are wrong. A fine story that will give you the flavor of what we mean by this was told recently by Robert E. Lucas, Jr.

> The archaeologist Heinrich Schliemann, the discoverer of Troy, became convinced, we are told, that a particular skull unearthed in a later excavation was the head of Agamemnon. To the frustration of this creative and productive scientist, his associates confronted him with one devastating argument after another to the effect that this could not possibly be the case. Exhausted, Schliemann took up the skull and

thrust it in the faces of his unconstructive critics: "All right then, if he is not Agamemnon, who is he?"[5]

Just as the science of archaeology is incapable of answering Schliemann's question, so the science of macroeconomics is incapable of answering equivalent questions such as, for example, why is Canada's unemployment rate in the middle 1980s so much higher than it was in the 1970s? Just as the science of archaeology *is* capable of saying whose skull Schliemann had *not* found so the science of macroeconomics is capable of demonstrating that some of the alleged explanations for the rise in unemployment (and the policy implications of such an explanation) simply cannot be correct.

The lack of complete agreement and the lack of a close enough correspondence between the currently available theories and the facts will be highlighted and emphasized throughout this book. You will come to know and understand the existing theories; you will also learn the facts, both those that the theories "fit" or explain and those that they do not. It is the as yet unexplained facts that provide much of the agenda for future research.

This book, unlike any of the others that are currently available, is not going to shortchange you by neglecting to bring to your attention some of the new theories in macroeconomics. On the contrary, it is going to present a comprehensive account of *all* the alternative theories that have been advanced to explain macroeconomic phenomena. It is going to be bold in showing where particular theories fail. The most recently advanced theories have not yet been shown to fail. Because of that, you may gain the false impression that we are asserting that all the "old" theories of macroeconomics are wrong and the "new" theories are right. We are indeed going to assert, and as far as we can in the confines of a book of this level, we are going to demonstrate, that some features of the "old" theories are indeed failing. We are not going to assert, however, that the new theories are correct. It is still too soon to tell. They are, for the moment, the best that are available. It would be surprising, however, if they were to survive unscathed when subjected to the test of fitting all future circumstances.

Let us turn now to the final task of this introductory chapter and examine some of the leading alternative views of economists concerning macroeconomic policy questions.

E. Leading Schools of Thought

There are almost as many alternative positions on macroeconomic policy questions as there are macroeconomists. (There might even be

---

[5]Robert E. Lucas, Jr., "Tobin and Monetarism: A Review Article", *The Journal of Economic Literature*, Vol. 19, No. 2, June 1981, pp. 558-567.

more opinions than economists since one of the occupational hazards of this business is indecisiveness — you have probably heard of the three-handed economist: "on the one hand . . . , on the other hand . . . , and . . ."!)

Despite this tremendous diversity of opinion some classification and grouping can be illuminating. We find it useful to focus on two broad macroeconomic policy questions on which economists disagree among themselves. They are: (i) Should macroeconomic policy be global or should it be detailed? And (ii) should policy be governed by a set of rules or be active and responsive to the current economic situation?

(i) Should macroeconomic policy be global or detailed?

Global policies are those which are directed at influencing the values of a small number of aggregate variables such as the money supply, the foreign exchange rate, the overall level of government expenditure, the overall level of taxes, and the size of the government's budget deficit. Those who take the view that a small number of aggregate policy instruments should be the central concern of macroeconomic policy generally believe that it is desirable to leave as much scope as possible for individual initiative to be coordinated through the market mechanism.

Detailed policies are directed at controlling the prices of, or other terms concerning the exchange of, a large number of specific goods and services. Such policies are too numerous to list in full. Some examples are: wage and price controls that regulate the wages and prices of a large number of types of worker and individual products; minimum wage policies; interest rate ceilings or other regulations on banks, savings and loan institutions, and insurance companies; regional policies in the form of special subsidies to particular regions; investment incentives; regulation and control of private manufacturing industry; regulation of international trade by the use of tariffs and quotas; and regulation of international capital flows. Those economists (and others) who favor detailed policies generally take the view that there are a large number of important areas in which markets fail to achieve a desirable economic outcome. They believe that detailed government intervention is needed to modify the outcome of the market process.

Often the disagreement between those advocating detailed intervention and those arguing against it is not so much a disagreement about the existence of a problem which the free market is having trouble solving, but rather about whether or not the government can solve the problem better than the market can.

(ii) Should macroeconomic policy be governed by a set of rules or be active and responsive to the current economic situation?

Those economists favoring rules are not unanimously agreed upon what the rules should be. They are agreed, however, on one crucial point — that controlling an economy is fundamentally different from controlling a mechanical (or electrical, or electronic) system, such as, for example, the heating/cooling system in a building. What makes controlling the economy different is that it is people who are being controlled, and unlike machines, people know that they are being controlled and are capable of learning the procedures that are being employed by the controllers — the government — and of organizing their affairs so as to take best advantage of the situation created by policy. A policy based on fixed rules minimizes the uncertainty that people have to face and thus enables a better economic performance.

Those who favor active intervention argue that if new information becomes available, it is foolish not to use it. By committing itself to a set of rules, the government ties its hands and bars itself from being in a position to exploit the new information.

The key difference between the advocates of rules and activism is a judgment as to whether individuals acting in their own interests, coordinated by markets, are capable of reacting to, and taking account of, new information without the need for government assistance in the matter.

In view of the major source of the disagreement on global versus detailed policies and rules versus discretion, you will not be surprised to be told that, on the whole, those economists who favor global policies also favor rules, while those who favor detailed policies also favor active intervention.

Broadly speaking, economists fall into two schools of thought on macroeconomic policy. There are no widely accepted, neat labels for identifying these two schools; however, the term *monetarist* is often applied to one group, and the term *Keynesian* to the other. Monetarists advocate fixed rules whereas Keynesians favor active intervention. These labels give flavor to, but sometimes fail to do full justice to, some of the subtleties of the distinctions between the two broad schools of thought. Nevertheless, in this book, the terms will be used to identify the two schools[6].

(iii) The Monetarist View

Monetarists advocate that governments have policies towards a limited number of global macroeconomic variables such as money supply growth, government expenditure, taxes, and/or the government deficit. They advocate the adoption of fixed rules for the behavior of these variables. A well-known example is the rule that the money supply should grow at a certain fixed percentage rate year in and year out. Another proposed rule is that the government budget should be balanced, on the average, over a period of four to five years. More

---

[6]An excellent, though demanding, discussion of the identifying characteristics of the different schools may be found in Douglas D. Purvis, "Monetarism: A Review," *The Canadian Journal of Economics*, 13, no. 1 (February 1980), 96-122. The twofold classification suggested here is qualified in many subtle ways by Purvis.

strongly, some monetarists urge the introduction of a constitutional amendment mandating the government to balance its budget and limiting the fraction of peoples' incomes that government may take in taxes. In any event, monetarists argue, the policy interventions that do occur should be announced as far ahead as possible so as to enable people to take account of them in planning and ordering their own economic affairs.

The intellectual leaders of this school are Milton Friedman (formerly of the University of Chicago and now working at the Hoover Institution at Stanford University), Karl Brunner (University of Rochester) who is credited with coining the term "monetarist," and Robert E. Lucas Jr., (University of Chicago).

(iv) The Keynesian View

Keynesians advocate detailed intervention to "fine tune" the economy in the neighborhood of full employment and low inflation. They would, if necessary, attempt to control inflation by direct controls of wages and prices and to control unemployment by stimulating demand, using monetary and fiscal policy. They would use discretion in seeking to stimulate the economy in a depression and holding it back in a boom, modifying their policy in the light of the current situation. In their view, policy changes are best not pre-announced so as to deter speculation.

The intellectual leaders of this group of macroeconomists are Franco Modigliani (Massachusetts Institute of Technology) and James Tobin (Yale University).

An Analogy

Imagine that you are listening to an FM radio station in a crowded part of the wave band. The signals are repeatedly and randomly drifting, so that from time to time your station drifts out of hearing and a neighboring station in which you have no interest comes through loud and clear. What should you do to get a stronger and more persistent signal from the station you want to hear?

The Keynesian says, "Hang on to the tuning knob and whenever the signal begins to fade, fiddle with the knob attempting, as best you can, to stay with the signal."

The monetarist says, "Get yourself an AFC (Automatic Frequency Control) tuner; set it on the station you wish to hear; sit back; relax and enjoy your music. Do not fiddle with the tuner knob; your reception will not be perfect; but on the average you will not be able to do any better than the AFC."

Although we have identified two groups — monetarists and Keynesians — these labels are becoming increasingly inadequate to describe the divisions of opinion among economists. They also neglect to emphasize the fact that many macroeconomists have very little interest in policy and very little to say about it. They see their job as getting on with the business of understanding macroeconomic phenomena and not of applying the fruits of that understanding directly to designing macroeconomic policy. This kind of division of labor is much like that which occurs in the natural sciences and engineering. Some people specialize in better understanding the properties of materials, for example, while others get on with the business of applying that understanding in a variety of practical situations. This specialization and division of labor within macroeconomics seems to be on the increase and is a natural consequence of the increasing technical requirements of macroeconomic research.

Summary

A. Macroeconomic Questions

There are six main questions in macroeconomics. They are, what determines:

(i) the rate of *inflation?*
(ii) the *unemployment* rate?
(iii) the level of *real national income?*
(iv) the *rate of interest?*
(v) the *balance of payments?*
(vi) the *foreign exchange rate?*

B. Canada's Macroeconomic Problems in the 1980s

Inflation ran at more than 10 percent for the first three years of the 1980s but fell to less than 4 percent by mid-decade. Unemployment has gradually increased from $7^1/_2$ percent in 1980 to more than 10 percent by mid-decade and reached 13 percent at its height. Output growth was virtually nil for the first three years of the 1980s, but by mid-decade had become more normal. Interest rates have been very high and volatile. The external value of the Canadian dollar — foreign exchange rate — has declined against the U.S. dollar though increased against many other currencies.

C. Macroeconomic Science, Policy, and the Popular Debate

Macroeconomic science is the body of knowledge that seeks to *understand* macroeconomic phenomena. Macroeconomic policy proposals or recommendations concerning our government policy should be pursued to achieve particular objectives. Macroeconomic policy debates are attempts to persuade a sufficient number of people that a particular policy should be pursued. This book is about macroeconomic science. It also analyzes macroeconomic policy, evaluating alternative policies in the light of the current state of macroeconomic theory.

D. Macroeconomic Policy Issues

Economists do not agree among themselves concerning all macroeconomic policy issues. A major reason for disagreement arises from a lack of good theories.

There are two major disagreements among economists concerning macroeconomic policy. One concerns whether policy should use *global* instruments or whether it should involve *detailed* intervention in individual markets. The second concerns whether policy should be governed by fixed *rules* or whether it should be varied from time to time at the *discretion* of the government in the light of current economic conditions.

E. Leading Schools of Thought

There are two major schools of thought: (1) *Monetarists* who advocate *global* instrument setting under fixed *rules*, and (2) *Keynesians*, who advocate *detailed* intervention in a large number of individual markets with *discretion* to vary that intervention from time to time.

Review Questions

The following statements were made by the Honorable Michael H. Wilson in his Budget Speech of May 23, 1985 and printed in *The Budget Speech*, Department of Finance. Each statement concerns some aspect or other of Canadian economic policy. Read the statements carefully and then classify them according to whether:

    (i) they deal with *macro*economic issues or not

    (ii) they deal with *detailed* or *global* policy

    (iii) they are talking about *rules* or *discretion* in the conduct of policy.

1. "The actions I am proposing . . . are designed to deal with the two major problems facing Canada today: high unemployment and our spiralling national debt." (p. 5.)

2. "We will encourage growth and job creation by encouraging private initiative, improving government effectiveness and controlling our national debt." (p. 5.)

3. "I am announcing measures to encourage greater investment in smaller businesses by pension funds." (p. 7.)

4. "I am proposing a major change in the taxation of capital gains." (p. 6.)

5. "The government will monitor the situation closely and . . . [take] action to protect the purchasing power of pensions." (p. 13.)

6. "If I believed that higher deficits . . . would help create . . . jobs, I would gladly increase the deficit to achieve that goal." (p. 21.)

7. "[O]ld age security payments . . . will be indexed only for the annual increase in the consumer price index greater than 3 per cent. . . . any increase in inflation above 3 per cent will be fully compensated." (p. 17.)

2

Canada's Macroeconomic History Since 1920

Too often in the past, economists have disagreed with each other about theory while paying little or no attention to the basic questions: What are the facts? and which, if any, of the theories being advanced are capable of explaining the facts? All useful theories begin with *some* facts in need of explanation. Theories are, in effect, "rigged" to explain a limited set of facts. They are subsequently tested by checking their ability to explain other facts, either not known, or not explicitly taken into account, when "rigging" the theory. The theories of macroeconomics that are presented in this book have been designed to explain some aspect or other of the facts about inflation, unemployment, real income, interest rates, the foreign exchange rate, and the balance of payments. The evolution of these variables over time may be called the macroeconomic history of a country. This chapter is designed to give you a "broad brush" picture of the macroeconomic history of Canada. It should be thought of as a first quick look at some of the facts which macroeconomics seeks to explain. It presents the facts in the most direct, uncluttered manner possible and in no way tries to begin the task of explaining the facts. The chapter will serve two main purposes. First, it will provide you with some basic equipment that will enable you to reject some of the more obviously incorrect theories that you may come across. Second, it will provide you with a quick reference source — especially the appendix to this chapter and the data sources listed therein — in the event that you want to pursue a more systematic testing of macroeconomic theories.

The chapter pursues two tasks, which are to:

a) Know the main features of the evolution of the key macro-economic variables in Canadian (i) inflation, (ii) unemployment, (iii) real income, (iv) interest rates, (v) balance of payments, and (vi) exchange rate, since 1920.

b) Know the main macroeconomic characteristics of Canada in each decade since 1920.

A. Evolution of Macroeconomic Variables

(i) Inflation

Look at Figure 2.1. It shows two measures of Canadian inflation. One measure is the annual rate of change of the Consumer Price Index and some earlier related index numbers, which charts the course of inflation since 1920. The other measure is known as the GNE Deflator,

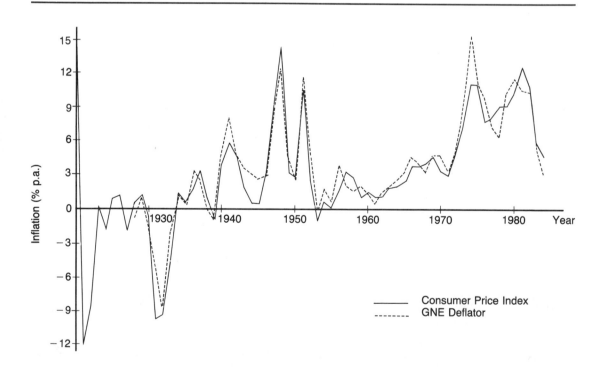

Figure 2.1
Inflation: 1920-1984

Two measures of inflation (the Consumer Price Index and the Gross National Expenditure Deflator) show similar paths. Inflation has trended upwards. Extremes of falling prices occurred in the early 1920s and 1930s. The strongest bursts of rising prices occurred during and immediately after World War II and in the 1970s and early 1980s.

Source: Appendix to this chapter.

and it runs from 1926 to 1984. Chapter 5 will explain precisely how these inflation rates are calculated and measured. For now, it is sufficient if you think of inflation as being simply the rate at which prices, on the average, are rising. Notice that although the two measures of inflation are not identical, they do, nevertheless, tend to move up and down together. What do they tell us about Canadian inflation?

The first thing that we learn is that the average inflation rate in Canada has been on a *rising trend* in the period since the early 1920s. In the 1920s and 1930s, there were several years in which prices were falling, on the average (inflation measured negatively). After 1934, however, with the exceptions of 1939 and 1953, prices rose every year. Furthermore, since the early 1950s at least, inflation seems to have been becoming progressively more severe.

The second thing that we learn about Canada's inflation history is that it has been erratic. There are some distinct *cycles* in the inflation rate, but the up and down movements could not be described as following a regular cycle.

Third, the *range* of Canada's inflation experience as measured by consumer prices goes from a maximum of 15.7 percent, which occurred in 1920, down to a minimum of minus 11.8 percent (prices falling at 11.8 percent a year), which was experienced in 1921. As measured by the GNE Deflator, the range is from 15.3 percent in 1974 to minus 9.3 percent in 1932. These extreme values are uncommon, as you can see from Figure 2.1.

The biggest bursts of inflation (rising prices) occurred in the early years of World War II (1940-1942), in the years immediately following World War II (1947 and 1948), at the time of the Korean War (1951), and in the decade 1973-83. With the exception of the post-1973 period, all the strong outbursts of inflation in Canada have been associated with war or post-war activity. The years of strongest falling prices occurred in the early 1920s (1921-22) and in the early 1930s (1931-33).

Aside from these extreme experiences of strongly rising or strongly falling prices, Canada's inflation rate has been close to zero. Through the second half of the 1920s up to 1930 prices rose some years and fell other years, but on the average were remarkably stable, and in the period from 1952 to the middle 1960s, inflation was present each and every year, but at a very modest rate of between 2 and 3 percent per annum.

(ii) Unemployment

Next, look at Figure 2.2, which shows the unemployment rate in Canada since 1921. As with inflation, the precise definition of, and method of measuring, unemployment will be dealt with in Chapter 5. For the present you may simply think of unemployment as measuring the extent to which people who have indicated that they wish to work are not able to find a job.

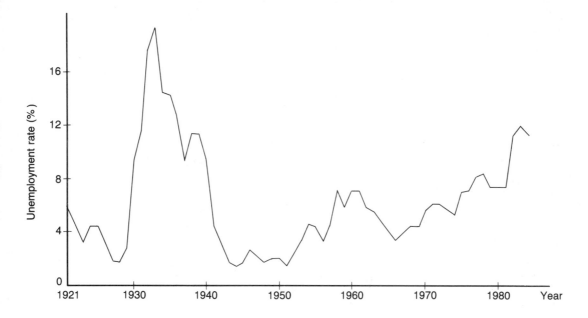

Figure 2.2
Unemployment: 1921-1984

Massive and prolonged unemployment dominated the 1930s. The war years of the 1940s saw the lowest unemployment in Canada's history. Since the early 1950s, unemployment has cycled. Since 1966 there has been a trend rise in unemployment.

Source: Appendix to this chapter.

The most striking feature about the behavior of unemployment in Canada since the early 1920s is its persistently high level from 1930 all the way through to 1940. These were the years of the Great Depression and its aftermath.

In addition to the massive unemployment experienced during the Great Depression years, you will perhaps also be struck by the rather clear long cycles in unemployment. The first of these has a trough in the unemployment rate in 1927-28 and then climbs quickly to a peak of almost 20 percent by 1933. There is then a long period of persistently falling unemployment, down to 1944. From that year, for almost a decade, there is virtually no trend in the unemployment rate. It wobbles around but stays very close to 2 percent per annum. Starting in 1953, however, there is a clear tendency for the unemployment rate to trend upwards and to reach a new peak in 1960-61. From there, the rate falls through 1966, but then from 1966 to 1984 continues to trend upwards again. Thus, there are three long cycles in the unemployment rate since 1920. The first has a trough in 1928 and a peak in 1933; the second starts in 1933, has a long flat trough that lasts for almost ten years (from 1943 to 1952) and then peaks in 1960; and the third starts in 1960, has a trough in 1966, and peaks in 1983.

Superimposed upon the long cycles in unemployment are some distinct shorter cycles. There are several of these, and it would not be very instructive simply to catalogue them. You may, by carefully inspecting Figure 2.2, observe some of the shorter ups and downs in the unemployment rate that are distinctly present but much less striking than the three long cycles just identified.

The range of Canada's unemployment goes all the way from a peak of 19.3 percent in 1933 to a trough of 1.4 percent in 1944. The average unemployment rate over this whole period has been 6.2 percent.

(iii) Real Income

There are two ways in which the evolution of real income can be examined. One fairly natural thing to do is to look at the behavior of its growth rate. Another is to look at the percentage deviations of its level from trend. Let us do both of these things.

Figure 2.3 sets out the behavior of the growth rate of real national income in Canada since 1927. We do not have data prior to that, and even the data from 1927 through 1947 are not as reliable as the subsequent figures. (Chapter 3 will describe exactly how national income is measured.)

The first thing that immediately strikes the eye when inspecting Figure 2.3 is the erratic nature of the path of real income growth. It seems to bounce around all over the place and, to a large degree, at random. The range of the apparently random fluctuations in real income growth seems to have narrowed in recent years. To some extent that is probably an illusion that arises from the fact that we have been able to measure real income more accurately in recent years than we were in earlier years. It is probably not, however, entirely illusory. Certainly there were some big reductions in real income in the Great Depression years of the 1930s, as shown in the chart. Real income growth became remarkably strong during the second half of the 1930s and into the years of World War II. Towards the end of World War II, and in the second half of the 1940s, real income growth was modest. It then fluctuated rather markedly in the 1950s (though less so than it had done in the 1930s). After 1960, real income growth was positive each and every year until 1982. Also, with the exception of the early 1980s, the fluctuations in real income growth have been much smaller than in previous decades.

The range of real income growth has been substantial. The maximum positive growth rate was 18.6 percent and occurred in 1942. The biggest fall in real income occurred in 1931, when a drop of almost 13 percent was recorded. The trend real income growth rate over the entire period since 1926 has been 3.9 percent.

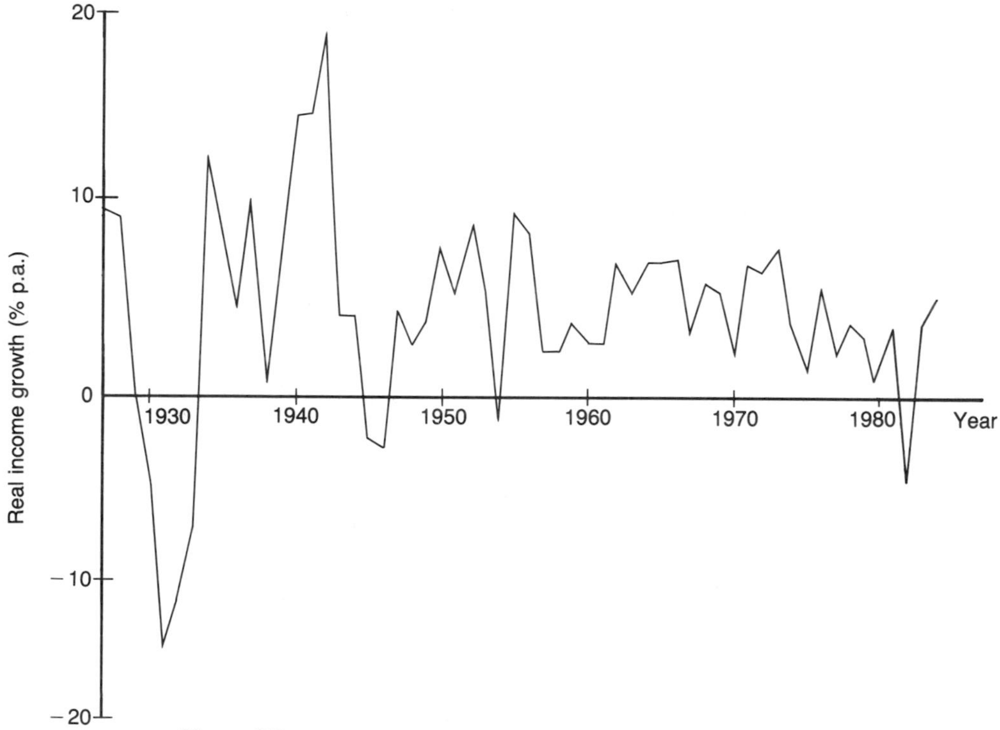

Figure 2.3
Real Income Growth: 1927-1984

Real income growth in Canada fluctuated wildly between the late 1920s and the beginning of World War II. Since then fluctuations have been much less pronounced. Rarely has real income fallen in any year.

Source: Appendix to this chapter.

Figure 2.4 sets out the deviations of real income from trend. (The trend level of real income has been calculated by passing a line having a constant growth rate of 3.9 percent per annum through the centre of the line that describes the actual path of real income, making the deviations about the line over the time period from 1926 to 1984 sum to zero.)

It is striking that the ups and downs in real income, viewed as deviations from trend, are less erratic than the growth rates of real income appear. A second striking feature of the data presented in Figure 2.4 is the enormity of the swing in economic activity during the late 1920s and 1930s. Real income was strongly ahead of its trend value for the final years of the 1920s, but then sank to 31 percent

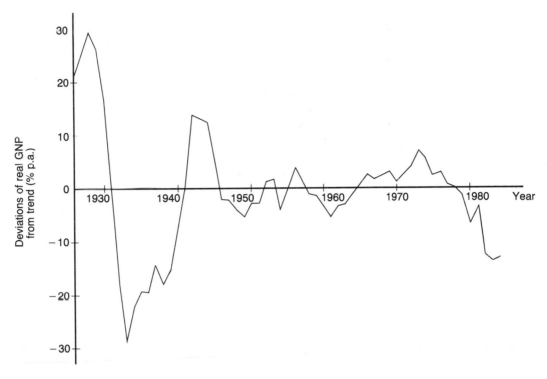

Figure 2.4
Deviations of Real Income From Trend: 1926-1984

As in the case of income growth, deviations of income from trend were the most violent in the 1920s, 1930s and early 1940s. There are pronounced peaks in the cycle of real income deviations in 1928, 1942, 1956 and 1973 and troughs in 1933, 1949, 1961 and 1982-83.

Source: Appendix to this chapter.

below trend by 1933. Although there was a long persistent recovery from that deep depression, it was not until into the 1940s that real income moved back to above its trend level. The history of real income deviations from trend from the 1940s through the 1970s is, by comparison with the 1920s and 1930s, very mild. There have, nevertheless, been some interesting fluctuations throughout that period. During the years of World War II, income was above its trend and on the average it stayed very close to trend during the 1950s. From 1964 to 1979 real income stayed above trend, but in the early 1980s it fell substantially short of its trend values. Indeed, the depressed state of output in 1982-83 is comparable with the 1930s.

(iv) Rates of Interest

Figure 2.5 sets out the behavior of two rates of interest. One of them, the rate on a representative long-term government of Canada bond, runs from 1920 to 1984, and the other, the rate on three-month finance company Bills of Exchange, runs only from the middle 1950s.

It is evident that the long-term rate is remarkably smooth in its movements, both in comparison with the short-term rate, and with the other macroeconomic variables that we have already examined. Both rates follow a rising trend from the middle 1950s and both follow cycles but the up and down swings in the short rate are much more pronounced than those in the long rate.

Over the long period going back to 1920, it is clear that interest rates (as reflected in the long-term rate) were on a falling trend, at least until the middle 1940s. The upward trend, shown by both rates

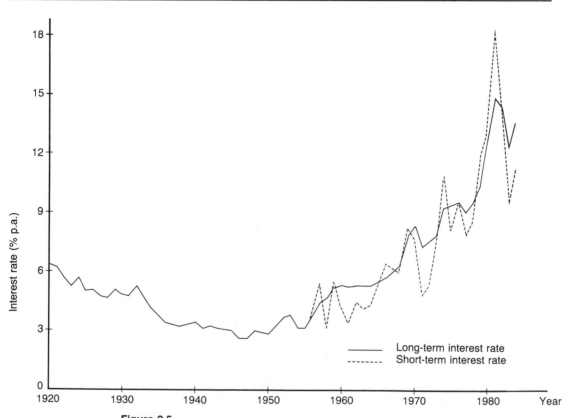

Figure 2.5
Interest Rates: 1920-1984

Long-term interest rates are very smooth in their behavior. They fell from 1920 into the war years of the 1940s and since then have trended upwards, steadily so at first but strongly in the 1970s. Short-term interest rates (shown since 1956) tend to follow long-term rates but are more volatile.

Source: Appendix to this chapter.

from the middle 1950s, clearly began around the end of the Second World War. In the early 1980s, interest rates were higher than ever before in Canadian history. By mid-decade they had moderated somewhat though were still very high by historical standards.

(v) The Balance of Payments

Let us now turn our attention to Canada's balance of payments. The precise way in which the balance of payments is measured will not be dealt with until Chapter 24 of this book.

For now, you may think of it as a measure of the net payments to, or receipts from, the rest of the world by Canadian residents in aggregate. If, in their economic relations with the rest of the world, aggregate Canadian sales of goods and services plus borrowing exceeds Canadian purchases of goods and services plus lending, then the balance of payments will be in surplus. The reverse situation, in which Canadian residents sell less than they buy and borrow less than they lend, is referred to as a deficit.

Figure 2.6 shows the history of the balance of payments. The most striking thing about the balance of payments is its extreme volatility during the 1940s. There were fairly sizeable fluctuations also in the 1970s, late 1920s and early 1930s. Although the balance of payments has fluctuated considerably there is no general tendency for the balance to move persistently in one direction or the other. The decade of the 1970s was, however, a period during which there was a general movement from a strong surplus to a sizeable deficit. The 1980s, however, look much more stable in this regard.

(vi) The Exchange Rate

The exchange rate is the value of the Canadian dollar in terms of foreign currencies. Figure 2.7 shows one method of measuring the exchange rate. The Canadian dollar against the U.S. dollar exchange rate runs all the way from 1920 to the middle 1980s.

The history of the value of the Canadian dollar, measured as the number of U.S. dollars that you would have to pay for one Canadian dollar, is set out in the Figure. Some parts of this history record Canada as being on a flexible exchange rate (a situation in which the exchange rate is free to fluctuate, much like the prices of ordinary goods), and other parts, on a fixed exchange rate (a situation in which the government pegs the exchange rate). The flexible exchange rate periods are the most common. Fixed exchange rates were in operation between 1925 and 1928, 1940 and 1950, and 1962 to 1969. Between 1925 and 1928 the Canadian dollar was pegged at one U.S. dollar per Canadian dollar. During World War II the Canadian dollar was pegged at 90.9 U.S. cents, but in 1946, it was revalued to parity with the U.S. dollar. In 1949 the Canadian dollar was devalued and pegged at 90 U.S. cents. In the 1960s, the Canadian dollar was pegged at 92.5 U.S. cents.

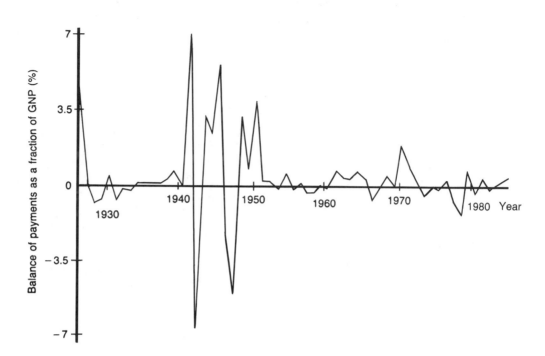

Figure 2.6
The Balance of Payments: 1920-1984

The Canadian balance of payments has usually been in a slight surplus. The balance of payments was particularly volatile during the war years of the 1940s and in the 1970s.

Source: Appendix to this chapter.

During the remaining periods since 1921, the Canadian dollar has fluctuated in value from day to day, week to week, and year to year against the U.S. dollar. The Canadian dollar was relatively cheap in the early 1920s and again during the Great Depression years, reaching an all-time low value in the Great Depression. The Canadian dollar again dipped against the U.S. dollar in 1950 and 1951 and then rose to be more valuable than the U.S. dollar through the 1950s all the way to 1960. In the most recent flexible exchange rate period, the Canadian dollar rose back to equality with the U.S. dollar in the early 1970s and then, for a few years, stood at a higher value than the U.S. dollar. Since 1976, however, the Canadian dollar has plummeted against the U.S. dollar and now stands close to its historically low level. At the time of writing the Canadian dollar stands at 72 U.S. cents.

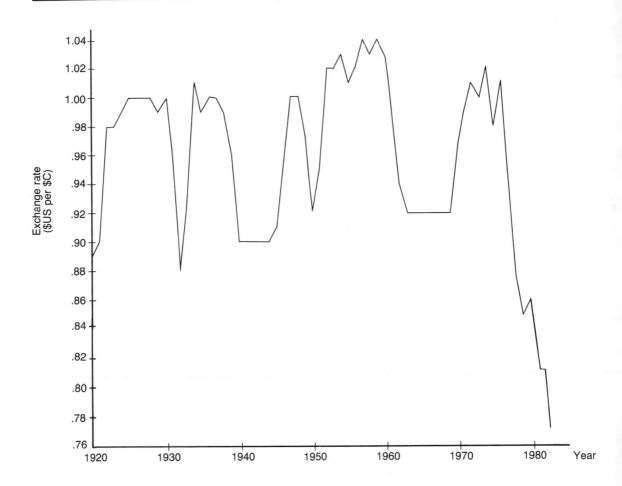

Figure 2.7
The Canadian Exchange Rate ($U.S. per $C): 1920-1984

With brief exceptions, the Canadian dollar has been worth slightly less than the U.S. dollar. During World War II (1941-1944) and the 1960s (1962-1969) the exchange rate was fixed by the government. At other times the rate has been flexible. During the period since the middle 1970s, the exchange rate has plummeted.

Source: Appendix to this chapter.

B. Decade Summaries

In order to present Canada's macroeconomic history in a slightly more compact manner, this section focusses on the decade averages of the variables since 1920. Their course is set out in Table 2.1. The figures for the 1980s cover just the first four years of the decade. For comparison purposes the average from 1920 to 1984 is presented in the last row of that table.

TABLE 2.1
The Decade Averages

	INFLATION		UNEMPLOY-MENT RATE (%)	REAL INCOME		LONG-TERM INTEREST RATES (% p.a.)	BALANCE OF PAYMENTS (% of GNP)	EXCHANGE RATE $US per $C
DECADE	CPI (% p.a.)	GNE DEFLATOR (% p.a.)		GROWTH RATE (% p.a.)	DEVIATIONS FROM TREND (%)			
1920s	−0.6	−0.2ᶜ	3.5ᵃ	6.2ᶜ	12.2ᶜ	5.2	0.72ᶜ	0.97
1930s	−1.8	−1.4	13.1	0.5	−15.4	3.9	0.11	0.97
1940s	4.7	5.4	2.9	5.9	4.2	2.9	0.83	0.93
1950s	2.4	2.9	3.9	5.1	0.5	3.7	0.46	1.01
1960s	2.5	2.7	5.0	5.2	1.8	5.8	0.31	0.94
1970s	7.4	8.1	6.8	4.2	4.5	8.5	0.15	0.96
1980-84	8.7	3.7	9.8	1.6	−9.8	13.2	−0.08	0.82
Average 1920-84	2.8	3.7ᵈ	6.2ᵇ	4.0ᵈ	0ᵉ	5.6	0.37ᵈ	0.95

Notes: ᵃ1921-29 ᵇ1921-84 ᶜ1926-29 ᵈ1926-84
ᵉdefined to be zero by the method of construction of the series.

The first decade is incompletely recorded in the table. The unemployment figures don't begin until 1921, and output, until 1926. That part-decade was obviously a very successful one in macroeconomic terms. Output was booming (averaging 25 percent positive deviations above trend), with real growth rates of an average of 6.2 percent. Prices fell slightly, unemployment was modest, and interest rates on long-term debt averaged just over 5 percent. The balance of payments was in a surplus, and the Canadian dollar stood at just below $1.00 U.S.

The 1930s present a marked contrast to the boom years of the 1920s. Output collapsed to an average of almost 15 percent below trend for the decade as a whole, and real growth averaged only a half a percent a year. Unemployment stayed in the teens for most of the decade. This disastrous output and unemployment performance went along with fairly stable prices (actually falling slightly), and equilibrium in the external payments, and a virtually constant exchange rate for the dollar. This was the decade that gave birth to Keynesian macroeconomics.

The 1940s were dominated by World War II. During that decade, prices began to rise at almost 5 percent per annum on the average. The Canadian dollar slipped in value to average 93 U.S. cents. Interest rates were maintained at low levels throughout the war. Real economic activity boomed, however, with output growing at almost its late-1920s rate, although the extent to which the trend output rate was bettered was only an average of 4.2 percent. Unemployment fell to historically low levels, to average the entire decade at less than 3 percent.

The 1950s were placid years. Inflation was mild, unemployment low, output growth strong, interest rates modest, the Canadian dollar strong (standing at slightly more than $1.00 U.S.), and the external payments were in a slight surplus. The 1960s remained much like the 1950s. The only blemishes were a tendency for unemployment to rise (though still only to average 5 percent) and for the dollar to slip (down to 94 U.S. cents). Interest rates also rose, but only slightly. These two decades were the background against which the post-Keynesian orthodoxy — what came to be called the neoclassical synthesis — in macroeconomics flourished.

The 1970s became a decade of inflation, unemployment, slowing growth, and increased balance of payments deficits. On the average in the 1970s, output was bigger than its trend value by slightly more than 4 1/2 percent. This occurred despite the fact that the trend growth rate in the 1970s was slightly below its long-term average. The combination of these two events arose from the fact that output growth was very strong in the first part of the 1970s and weak in the second part. This meant that the slow-trend output growth started out from a fairly high level, relative to its longer-term trend value. The facts of the 1970s constituted the single most serious challenge to the post-Keynesian orthodoxy and gave impetus to important new developments in macroeconomics.

As the 1980s opened, the early signs were ominous. Inflation, unemployment, and interest rates were all higher than they had ever been in any decade average since 1920. Output growth was lower than ever before, the dollar cheaper, and the external deficit bigger. As the decade has progressed, however, inflation, interest rates and unemployment have all begun to fall and output growth has started to pick up. Even so, by mid-decade, the unemployment rate remained at historically high levels as did interest rates.

This description of Canada's economic condition in the mid-1980s gives urgency to the task of improving our understanding of the functioning of the economy as a whole, and certainly attests to the importance of the study of macroeconomics.

You have now reviewed the behavior of the six key macroeconomic variables in Canada and have looked at the main macroeconomic characteristics of each decade since the 1920s. Many questions will be occurring to you:

On inflation Why are there some periods when the inflation rate is very high, others when it is moderate, and yet others when prices are falling? Can the ups and downs in inflation be controlled and perhaps eliminated, or do we have to live with them? What has caused the apparent upward trend in Canada's inflation? Is there anything that can be done to stop it?

We do not know the full answers to any of these questions. We know substantial parts of the answers to all of them, however, and explaining what we know constitutes one of the prime tasks of this book.

On unemployment Why was there such an enormous and prolonged burst of unemployment during the 1930s? You will discover that important though this question is, a satisfactory answer still eludes us. Part IV of the book deals with the most comprehensive and systematic attempt to answer this question and explains why we are still searching for a fully satisfactory answer. Why have there been such marked movements in the unemployment rate, characterized by the long cycles that we identified? In particular, why has there been a tendency for unemployment to rise persistently since the middle 1960s? Why does unemployment fluctuate so markedly in shorter, yet very clear, cycles? Finally, can unemployment be controlled so that the fluctuations in its rate can be removed? These questions also will occupy the center of our attention in what follows.

On output Why does real income grow in a cyclical but erratic fashion? Why has real income deviated from trend, severely negatively so in the 1930s and positively in the 1940s and 1970s? What can be done to eradicate the fluctuations in real income?

On interest rates Why are long-term interest rate movements relatively smooth? Why did interest rates gradually fall from 1920 through to the middle 1940s and then gradually rise again? Why did interest rates move to all-time high levels in the early 1980s? Why do short-term interest rates fluctuate more than long-term rates?

On the balance of payments and the exchange rate Why has Canada's balance of payments fluctuated so violently? Why have the fluctuations become bigger in more recent years? What can the government of Canada do to correct the balance of payments deficit and return the Canadian economy to an equilibrium comparable to that experienced in the 1950s?

Why is it that sometimes the Canadian dollar has a fixed value and at other times a fluctuating value? How is it possible for the Canadian government to hold the dollar fixed as it did between 1925 and 1928, during World War II, and again in the 1960s? What is it that occasionally makes the Canadian dollar more valuable than the U.S. dollar, as it was in the 1950s and middle 1970s, but usually makes it cheaper than the U.S. dollar, as it was in the Great Depression and as it is at the present time?

These questions concerning Canada's external macroeconomic relations are examined in the final part of this book.

It would not be sensible or useful to attempt a more detailed mapping out of the specific parts of the book that deal with each of these questions than that just given. Many of the questions turn out to be intimately related to each other in a way that you will find hard to appreciate if you have little or no knowledge of macroeconomics, but that will seem obvious and natural once you have made some progress with your study of the subject. To help you see some of the connections between the questions, after explaining in more detail how the macroeconomic variables are defined, observed and measured, but before embarking on the task of *explanation* of macroeconomic phenomena, Chapter 6 will explore some of the connections among the macroeconomic variables by defining and describing the business cycle. In the final section of that chapter you will have a further opportunity to return to the features of the six variables described here and to gain some further insights into the way they behave.

Summary

A. Evolution of Macroeconomic Variables

The main feature of *inflation* has been a distinctly rising trend. There have also been clear, but irregular, cycles in inflation. The range of inflation runs from falling prices of 11.8 percent per annum (in 1921) to rising prices of 15.7 percent per annum (in 1920). The average rate of inflation (as measured by consumer prices) between 1920 and 1984 has been 2.8 percent per annum.

Unemployment has displayed three very long cyclical swings and has had shorter cycles superimposed upon those. Unemployment was at its worst in the 1930s (1933 being the worst single year, when unemployment reached 19.3 percent). In the 1940s unemployment was at its lowest levels (reaching 1.4 percent in 1944).

Real income growth has been trendless. It has been characterized by a high degree of randomness. The worst year for real income growth was 1931, when income fell by almost 13 percent and the strongest boom year was 1942, when real income grew by 18.6 percent. These are most unusual extremes, however. Normally, real income has fluctuated between about zero and 8 percent per annum. *Deviations of real income from trend* provide an alternative measure to the evolution of real income. Real income was strongly above trend in the 1920s, deeply depressed relative to trend in the 1930s, slightly ahead of trend during the war years, and in the period since then, has fluctuated in a mild cycle.

The *long-term rate of interest* has been the smoothest of the major macroeconomic variables in Canadian history. It has displayed a long cycle, with a tendency to fall gradually from 1920 to 1940 and to rise gradually in the period since then. Short-term rates move in the same general way as long-term rates, but have bigger fluctuations.

The *balance of payments* as a fraction of GNP has tended to fluctuate around zero — deficit years and surplus years have tended roughly to offset each other. Extreme volatility in the balance of payments occurred in the 1940s. There were fairly sizeable fluctuations in the late 1920s, early 1930s and in the 1970s.

The *exchange rate* has sometimes been fixed against the U.S. dollar and sometimes has been flexible. Usually, the Canadian dollar has been less valuable than, or valued at par with, the U.S. dollar.

B. Decade Summaries

The averages of the macroeconomic variables in each decade since the 1920s are set out in Table 2.1 and should be studied carefully. The 1920s were years of falling prices, high employment, and strong output growth, with modest interest rates and external surplus. The 1930s were the years of the Great Depression. The 1940s saw mildly rising prices with strong output growth and very low unemployment. The 1950s and 1960s were years of macroeconomic tranquillity. Prices inflated at 2 1/2 percent per annum, unemployment was between 4 and 5 percent, output grew at more than 5 percent, interest rates were modest, and there was a strong external value to the dollar and the balance of payments position. The 1970s saw the onset of macroeconomic problems in all dimensions: inflation, unemployment, and interest rates all rose; output growth fell; and the balance of payments moved into deficit. As the 1980s opened, all these problems remained, but in accentuated form. By mid-decade, there had been some improvements, especially on the inflation front, but unemployment and interest rates remained historically high.

Review Questions

1. Briefly describe the history of each of the following macroeconomic variables in Canada since 1945: (i) inflation; (ii) unemployment; (iii) real income; (iv) interest rates; (v) the balance of payments; and (vi) the exchange rate.

2. Briefly describe the history of each of the above macroeconomic variables in Canada in the "inter-war years" — 1920 to 1940.

3. Using later editions of the sources given at the foot of the table in the Appendix to Chapter 2, update the table for each of the variables. Describe how each of these variables has evolved so far in the 1980s.

4. One of these six macroeconomic variables has at some time been fixed by the government. Which variable is this, and for what periods has it been fixed?

5. In which decade was inflation Canada's major macroeconomic problem? Was it associated with any other major macroeconomic problems?

6. What were Canada's major macroeconomic problems of the 1930s?

7. In which decade since 1920 has Canada suffered the highest average unemployment rate? Compare this average with that so far in the 1980s.

8. In which decade of Canadian history since 1920 has the average long-term interest rate been highest? Compare this with the average long-term interest rate so far for the 1980s.

9. Has Canada's balance of payments, on the average, been in deficit in any decade since 1920? Would you deduce from this that Canada has had balance of payment problems?

10. Looking at decade averages of the history of the exchange rate and the balance of payments, does there appear to be a relationship between them? If so, what is the relationship?

11. What are the major economic problems of Canada in the eighties (thus far)?

12. Assume that you are employed as an economic speech writer by Mr. Turner. Write a short speech which argues as strongly as possible that Canada's macroeconomic performance in the 1970s compares favorably with that of earlier decades and is a credit to the economic management of the government.

13. Assume that you are employed as an economic speech writer by Mr. Mulroney. Write a short speech which argues as strongly as possible that Canada's macroeconomic performance in the 1970s compares unfavorably with that of earlier decades and discredits the government's economic management.

APPENDIX
Canadian Macroeconomic Variables 1920–1984

| YEAR | INFLATION | | UN-EMPLOY-MENT RATE (%) | REAL INCOME (GNP) | | INTEREST RATES | | BALANCE OF PAYMENTS (% of GNP) | EXCHANGE RATE ($US per $C) |
	CPI (% p.a.)	GNE DEFLATOR (% p.a.)		GROWTH RATE (% p.a.)	DEVIATION FROM TREND (%)	LONG TERM (% p.a.)	SHORT TERM (% p.a.)		
1920	15.7	—	—	—	—	6.1	—	—	0.89
1921	−11.8	—	5.8	—	—	6.0	—	—	0.90
1922	−8.4	—	4.4	—	—	5.4	—	—	0.98
1923	0.0	—	3.2	—	—	5.1	—	—	0.98
1924	0.0	—	4.5	—	—	5.5	—	—	0.99
1925	0.5	—	4.4	—	—	4.9	—	—	1.00
1926	1.1	—	3.0	—	14.2	4.9	—	4.2	1.00
1927	−1.6	−1.1	1.8	9.5	19.4	4.6	—	0.1	1.00
1928	0.0	−0.6	1.7	9.1	24.2	4.5	—	−0.8	1.00
1929	1.6	1.1	2.9	0.4	20.6	4.9	—	−0.6	0.99
1930	1.1	−2.5	9.1	−4.3	12.3	4.7	—	0.6	1.00
1931	−9.8	−6.2	11.6	−12.7	−5.2	4.6	—	−0.7	0.96
1932	−9.0	−9.3	17.6	−10.4	20.1	5.1	—	−0.1	0.88
1933	−4.6	−1.7	19.3	−6.7	−30.9	4.6	—	−0.2	0.92
1934	1.4	1.4	14.5	12.1	−23.4	4.0	—	0.1	1.01
1935	0.7	0.3	14.2	7.8	−19.8	3.6	—	0.1	0.99
1936	2.0	3.3	12.8	4.4	−19.4	3.3	—	0.1	1.00
1937	2.7	2.6	9.1	10.0	−13.8	3.2	—	0.1	1.00
1938	1.3	0.0	11.4	8.2	−16.8	3.1	—	0.3	0.99
1939	−0.6	−0.9	11.4	7.4	−13.6	3.2	—	0.7	0.96
1940	3.9	4.7	9.2	13.8	−4.6	3.3	—	0.0	0.90
1941	5.6	7.9	4.4	14.6	5.1	3.1	—	6.9	0.90
1942	5.3	4.5	3.0	18.6	18.2	3.1	—	−6.6	0.90
1943	1.7	3.5	1.7	4.0	18.2	3.0	—	3.3	0.90
1944	0.5	3.1	1.4	4.0	18.2	3.0	—	2.3	0.90
1945	0.5	2.5	1.6	−2.2	12.0	2.9	—	5.6	0.91
1946	3.3	2.9	2.6	−2.7	5.3	2.6	—	−2.2	0.95
1947	9.5	8.8	1.9	4.3	−3.0	2.6	—	−5.0	1.00
1948	13.9	12.3	1.6	2.5	−5.1	2.9	—	3.2	1.00
1949	3.4	4.3	2.0	3.8	−5.9	2.8	—	0.8	0.97
1950	2.9	2.4	2.0	7.6	−3.0	2.8	—	3.9	0.92
1951	10.7	11.3	1.5	5.0	−2.7	3.2	—	0.3	0.95
1952	2.2	4.4	2.0	8.9	1.4	3.6	—	0.2	1.02
1953	−0.7	−0.2	3.0	5.1	1.9	3.7	—	−0.1	1.02
1954	0.7	1.6	4.6	−1.2	−3.9	3.1	—	0.5	1.03
1955	0.0	0.6	4.4	9.4	0.7	3.1	—	−0.2	1.01
1956	1.4	3.7	3.4	8.4	4.2	3.6	3.7	0.1	1.02
1957	3.1	2.1	4.6	2.4	2.1	4.2	5.3	−0.3	1.04
1958	2.7	1.5	7.0	2.3	−0.2	4.5	3.2	0.3	1.03
1959	1.3	2.0	6.0	3.8	−0.9	5.0	5.2	0.0	1.04
1960	1.3	1.3	7.0	2.9	−2.6	5.1	4.0	−0.1	1.03
1961	0.6	0.4	7.1	2.8	−4.3	5.0	3.4	0.7	0.99
1962	1.2	1.4	5.9	6.8	−2.2	5.1	4.4	0.4	0.94
1963	1.9	1.9	5.5	5.2	−1.7	5.1	4.0	0.3	0.92
1964	1.8	2.4	4.7	6.7	0.3	5.1	4.2	0.7	0.92
1965	2.4	3.3	3.9	6.7	2.2	5.3	5.0	0.3	0.92
1966	3.5	4.4	3.4	6.9	4.4	5.7	6.3	−0.6	0.92

Year									
1967	3.7	4.0	3.8	3.3	3.2	6.0	5.8	0.0	0.92
1968	4.1	3.3	4.5	5.8	4.3	6.7	6.8	0.5	0.92
1969	4.5	4.4	4.4	5.3	5.0	7.6	7.8	0.0	0.92
1970	3.3	4.6	5.7	2.5	3.0	8.0	7.3	1.9	0.96
1971	2.4	3.2	6.2	6.9	5.1	7.0	4.5	0.9	0.99
1972	5.2	5.0	6.2	6.1	6.6	7.2	5.1	0.3	1.01
1973	7.6	9.1	5.5	7.5	9.3	7.6	7.5	−0.4	1.00
1974	10.9	15.3	5.3	3.6	0.3	8.9	10.5	0.0	1.02
1975	10.8	10.7	6.9	1.2	5.0	9.0	7.9	−0.2	0.98
1976	7.5	9.6	7.1	5.8	6.2	9.2	9.2	0.3	1.01
1977	8.0	7.4	8.1	2.0	3.6	8.7	7.5	−0.7	0.94
1978	8.8	6.7	8.4	3.6	2.6	9.2	8.5	−1.4	0.88
1979	9.2	10.3	7.5	3.2	1.3	10.2	11.8	0.7	0.85
1980	10.2	11.4	7.5	1.1	−2.2	12.3	12.9	−0.4	0.86
1981	12.5	10.6	7.5	3.3	−3.5	15.0	18.3	−0.4	0.83
1982	10.8	10.3	11.1	−4.4	−12.5	14.4	14.2	−0.2	0.81
1983	5.8	5.3	11.9	3.3	−13.8	11.8	9.5	0.1	0.81
1984	4.4	2.8	11.3	5.0	−13.4	12.7	11.2	−0.3	0.77

Sources and Methods:
Urquhart, M.C., and K.A.H. Buckley, eds., *Historical Statistics of Canada*, (Toronto: The Macmillan Company of Canada Ltd., 1965) (referred to below as U and B).

1. Inflation — (a) CPI; Cansim Series D49400, *Consumer Prices and Price Indexes*, Cat. 62-010, Statistics Canada. The figures in the table are percentage changes in the index over the previous year.
   (b) GNE Deflator; Cansim Series D40672 *National Income and Expenditure Accounts*. Cat. 13-531, Statistics Canada. The figures in the table are percentage changes in the index over the previous year.

2. Unemployment: 1921–1952; U and B, Series C54 divided by Series C50 expressed as a percentage, p. 61.
   1953–1965; Cansim Series D755041, *Monthly Labour Force Survey, Statistics Canada.*
   1966–1984; Cansim Series D767611, *Revised Monthly Labour Force Survey*, Statistics Canada. The figures in the table are annual averages of monthly data.

3. Real Income: GNP in constant (1971) dollars (real GNP); Cansim Series D40646, *National Income and Expenditure Accounts*, Cat. 13-531, Statistics Canada.
   (a) Growth Rate is the percentage change in real GNP over the previous year.
   (b) Deviation from Trend is the precentage deviation of real GNP from a logarithmic trend fitted to real GNP 1926–1984. The trend line is log (real GNP) = 9.297 + 0.046 (year-1925) indicating a trend growth rate of real GNP of 4.6 percent per annum.

4. Interest Rates: (a) Long-term; market rate of interest on long-term (15 years and over) bonds.

1920–1936: U and B, Series H605, p. 275.
1937–1959: U and B, Series H614, p. 275.
1960–1963: *Bank of Canada Statistical Summary*, 1963, Table VIII, pp. 69, 73, 79, 85.
1964; *Bank of Canada Statistical Summary*, 1965, Table VIII, p. 67.
1965; *Bank of Canada Statistical Summary*, 1966, Table VIII, p. 69.
1966; *Bank of Canada Statistical Summary*, 1967, Table VIII, p. 75. The figure in the table for the years 1960–1966 is the average of weekly yields on Government of Canada 1966–1998 bonds.
1967, *Bank of Canada Statistical Summary*, 1968, p. 75. The figure in the table is the average of weekly long-term average yield on Government of Canada Bonds.
1968–1984; *Bank of Canada Review*, Table 1, Column 33, April 1980 and July 1985.
(b) Short-term; 90-day finance company paper rate; Cansim Series B14017, *Bank of Canada Review*. Annual average of monthly data.

5. Balance of Payments:
1920–1926; U and B, Series F56 (with sign reversed), p. 159.
1927–1960; *The Canadian Balance of International Payments*, Cat 67-201, Statistics Canada, p. 89.
1961–1984; Cansim Series D50212, *The Canadian Balance of International Payments*, Cat 67-201, Statistics Canada. The figure in the table represents the overall "official settlements" balance.

6. Exchange Rate: 1920–1960; U and B, Series H627 (inverted), p. 276.
1961–1984; Cansim Series B3400 (inverted), *Bank of Canada Review*.

II

MEASURING MACROECONOMIC ACTIVITY

3

Aggregate Income Accounting

Aggregate income accounting provides one of the major sources of data that are needed in order to do macroeconomic analysis. The other major data needs are met by aggregate balance sheet accounting — which provides a statement of what people in the economy owe and own — and the measurement of inflation and unemployment. This chapter deals with aggregate income accounting, Chapter 4 with aggregate balance sheet accounting, and Chapter 5 with the measurement of inflation and unemployment. As a preliminary to examining aggregate income and balance sheet accounts, this chapter also deals with the distinction between flows and stocks. You have six specific tasks in this chapter; these are to:

a) Understand the distinction between flows and stocks.
b) Know the definitions of: output (or product), income and expenditure; domestic and national; gross and net; market price and factor cost; nominal and real.
c) Understand the concepts of aggregate output, income (or product), and expenditure.
d) Know how aggregate income is measured, using: the expenditure approach; the factor incomes approach; the output approach.
e) Know how aggregate income in constant (real) dollars is measured.
f) Know how to read the national income accounts of Canada.

A. Flows and Stocks

A macroeconomic variable that measures a *flow* measures a rate per unit of time. In contrast, a *stock* is a value at a point in time. Examples of flows are income and expenditures. The dimension of these variables is dollars per unit of time, for example, dollars per month or dollars per year. Examples of stocks are: money in the bank, the value of a car or a house, the value of the airplanes owned by Wardair, and the value of the telephone lines and exchange switching equipment owned by Bell Canada. All these variables are measured in dollars on a given day.

Although such items as cars, houses, and physical plant and equipment are stocks, the purchase of additional equipment and the physical wearing out of plant and equipment are flows. Stocks of physical plant and equipment are called *capital*. Additions to capital are called *investment*. The reduction in the value of equipment as a result of wear and tear and/or the passage of time is known as *depreciation*. Let us illustrate this with something concrete. Imagine that on the first of June 1981, you had a 1975 car that had a current market value of $2000. In the year from the first of June 1981 to the first of June 1982, the market value of the car fell to $1600. The value of the car on the first of June each year is a stock. That stock has fallen from $2000 in 1981 to $1600 in 1982. The depreciation (the loss in the value of the car) is a flow. That flow is $400 per year (or, equivalently, $33.63 per month). If, in May 1982, you sold your 1975 car and replaced it with a 1978 car, the value of which is $3000, your capital stock in June of 1982 would, of course, be the same $3000. In that case you would have *invested* a total of $1400. (The $1400 is the difference between the $3000 that your newer car is worth and the $1600 that your old car would have been worth, had you kept it.) The change in your capital stock from June 1981 to June 1982 is, of course, not $1400 but $1000. This is made up of an investment in a new car known as a *gross* investment of $1400, minus the depreciation of the old car of $400. The difference between your gross investment and the depreciation of your capital is known as *net* investment.

A useful analogy to illustrate the distinction between flows and stocks is a physical one involving a bathtub, a faucet, and a drain. Suppose a bathtub has some water in it, the faucet is turned on, and there is no plug in the drain, so that water is flowing into the bathtub and flowing out of it. The water in the tub is a stock, the water entering the tub through the faucet and the water leaving the tub through the drain are flows. If the flow through the faucet is greater than the flow through the drain, the stock will be rising. If, conversely, the flow through the drain is greater than the flow through the faucet, the stock will be falling. In this example there are two flows and one stock, and the stock is determined by the flows. Suppose that the rate of outflow through the drain is a constant which cannot be controlled. The stock can be increased by opening the faucet so that the inflow exceeds the outflow, and the stock can be decreased by closing the faucet so that the outflow exceeds the inflow.

In terms of the capital stock, investment and depreciation concepts illustrated earlier with reference to transactions in used cars, you can think of the water in the bathtub as the capital stock, the outflow through the drain as depreciation, and the inflow through the faucet as gross investment. The difference between the outflow and inflow is net investment, which may, of course, be positive (if the water level is rising) or negative (if the water level is falling).

Suppose that we introduce a human element into the story. Imagine that someone wants to maintain the water level in the tub at a particular depth. That is, they have a desired stock of water. If the actual stock exceeds the desired stock, the corrective action would be to slow down the rate of inflow. If the actual stock was less than the desired stock, the corrective action would be to speed up the rate of inflow. You can see that in this extended story, the stock determines the flow in the sense that individual actions that adjust the flow are triggered by the level of the stock. In the economic analysis that you will be doing shortly, flows (such as national income and expenditure) will be determined by stocks (such as the supply of money).

The remaining tasks in this and the next chapter are a necessary prelude to conducting such economic analyses. The rest of this chapter explains how the national income and expenditure flows are measured and Chapter 4 deals with the measurement of the stocks of assets and liabilities in the economy. Let us begin by reviewing some of the definitions of the main aggregate income and expenditure flows.

B. Some Frequently Used Terms

You have almost certainly encountered in newspapers or on television current affairs programs, terms like *gross domestic product* or *gross national income*, or, perhaps *gross national product in constant dollars*. This section will enable you to know what these and a few other important terms mean. Following are five groups of words among which you need to be able to distinguish.

(i) Output (or Product), Income, and Expenditure

Three concepts of aggregate economic activity are commonly used. These are dealt with in some detail in the next section. For now, all that you need to know are the definitions of these terms: *output* (or *product*) means the value of the output of the economy; *income* means the sum of the incomes of all the factors of production (labor, capital, and land) employed in the economy; *expenditure* means the sum of all the expenditures in the economy on final goods and services. (*Note:*

See below for the distinction between expenditure on *final* goods and services and expenditure on *intermediate* goods and services).

(ii) Domestic and National

In the preceding paragraph the term *the economy* is used as if it is unambiguous. There is ambiguity, however, as to what is meant by "the economy." What is the "Canadian economy"? There are two possible answers. One involves the *domestic* economy, which is all economic activity taking place in the geographical domain of Canada. The other involves the *national* economy, which is all economic activity of the residents of Canada wherever in the world that activity happens to be performed.

Thus, *domestic* output (or product), income, and expenditure refers to the aggregate of output, income, and expenditure in the geographical domain of Canada. And the concept of *national* output (or product), income, and expenditure refers to the output produced by, the income earned by, or expenditure made on goods produced by Canadian residents, no matter where in the world the economic activity takes place.

The difference between these two aggregates is known as "net property income from (or paid) abroad." It is not large for most countries and is very small for Canada. Thus, since no special purpose is served by the distinction between the two concepts, this book will use the term *aggregate product, income,* and *expenditure* to refer to either or both the national and domestic concepts.

(iii) Gross and Net

Gross national (or domestic) product (or income or expenditure) means that the aggregate is measured *before* deducting the value of the assets of the economy which have been used up or depreciated in the production process during the year.

Net national (or domestic) product (or income or expenditure) means that the aggregate is measured *after* deducting the value of the assets of the economy which have been used up or depreciated in the production process during the year. Macroeconomics is concerned with explaining the overall scale of economic activity and uses the gross concept. The net concept is of use in measuring standards of living, a topic outside the scope of macroeconomics.

(iv) Market Price and Factor Cost

In most modern economies (and certainly in Canada) the government taxes expenditure on some goods and subsidizes expenditure on others. Examples of taxes on expenditure are the excise duties on liquor and tobacco. An example of a subsidy is the sale of milk at less than cost. There are two ways of measuring the value of a good or service. One is based on the prices paid by the final user (consumer) and is known as the *market price* valuation. The other is based on the cost of all the factors of production, including the profits made. This is known as the *factor cost* valuation. Market prices include taxes on expenditure and are net of subsidies. Factor costs exclude taxes on expenditure but do not have subsidies netted out.

The various aggregates defined above can be measured on either the market price or factor cost basis. If sales taxes were increased and income taxes cut by equal amounts, nothing (as a first approximation) would happen to the level of aggregate economic activity. The market price concept of national income, however, would rise. The factor cost concept would not change. Macroeconomics is concerned with measuring the scale of economic activity and, ideally, would use the factor cost concept. In practice, provided care is taken to interpret any large changes in indirect taxes and subsidies, the market price concept is used.

(v) Nominal and Real

The various aggregates defined above can be measured either in current dollars (nominal) or in constant dollars (real).The *nominal* valuation uses prices of goods or factors of production prevailing in the *current* period to value the current period's output or expenditure. The *real* valuation uses prices of goods or factors that prevailed in a *base* period to value the current period's output or expenditure. Real values are the appropriate ones for measuring the level of economic activity. Since macroeconomics is concerned with both the scale of activity and prices (and inflation), both of these concepts are of importance and will appear again later in this chapter and in Chapter 5.

It is now time to go beyond learning definitions and to develop a deeper understanding of the central concepts of output (or product), income and expenditure.

C. Aggregate Output (or Product), Income, and Expenditure

In order to help you *understand* the central concepts of aggregate output (or product), income, and expenditure, it will be convenient to begin by considering an economy that is much simpler than the one in which you live. We will then successively add various features of the economy until we have a picture which corresponds quite closely to the world that we inhabit.

(i) The Simplest Economy

Let us suppose that the economy is one which has no transactions with the rest of the world; that is, no one exports anything to foreigners or imports anything from them. No borrowing or lending takes place across the national borders, either. Indeed, no communications of any kind occur between the domestic economy and the rest of the world.

Next, suppose that there is no government; that is, no one pays taxes; all expenditures by households are voluntary; and all the goods and services that firms produce are bought by households, rather than some of them being bought by governments or their agencies.

The economy consists of just two kinds of economic institutions or *agents*: households and firms. A *household* is an agent that:

(1) Owns factors of production.

(2) Buys all final consumer goods.

A firm is an agent which:

(1) Owns nothing.

(2) Hires factors of production from households.

(3) Sells the goods which it produces to households.

(4) Pays any profits that it makes on its activities to households.

This economy can be visualized more clearly by considering Figure 3.1. The households in this economy are represented by the circle labelled *H*, and the firms are represented by the circle labelled *F*. Two kinds of flows take place between households and firms. First, real things are supplied by households to firms and by firms to households. Second, money passes between households and firms in exchange for these real things. The real flows are shown with the dashed

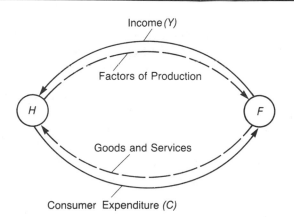

Figure 3.1
Real Flows and Money Flows in the Simplest Economy

Income *(Y)*

Factors of Production

H   *F*

Goods and Services

Consumer Expenditure *(C)*

The flow of factors of production from households (*H*) to firms (*F*) and the flow of goods and services from firms to households (clockwise dashed lines) are matched by equivalent flows of money — firms paying income to households (*Y*) and households paying firms (*C*) for consumer goods and services (counterclockwise continuous lines).

lines, and the money flows are shown with the continuous lines. Households are shown as supplying factors of production to firms, and firms are shown as supplying goods and services to households. Moving in the opposite direction to these real flows are the money flows. Firms pay income to households, and households spend their income on consumer goods. The aggregate income payment will be denoted by Y and aggregate consumer expenditure by C.

It is evident that in this economy the value of the income that households receive from firms must be equal to the value of the expenditure which households make on consumer goods. If this were not so, firms would be making either gains or losses that they would not be passing on to the households, who are the ultimate suppliers of factor services. It will also be evident that the *value* of the goods and services produced by the firms — the value of output of the firms — is also equal to the value of the expenditure on those goods and services by the households. In other words,

$$\text{expenditure} = \text{income} = \text{value of output.} \qquad (3.1)$$

This very simple economy, which abstracts from much of the detail of the actual world in which we live, has enabled us to establish the equality of income, expenditure, and output, which follows purely from the definitions of the terms involved. We now want to go on to see that this equality also applies to the more complicated world in which we live.

(ii) Some More Realistic Economies

There are three features of the "real world" which are not captured in the story above and in Figure 3.1. They are:
  (1) Households typically do not spend all their incomes on consumer goods — they also save some of their income.
  (2) Governments are large (and indeed growing) institutions in the modern world that tax individual incomes and use their tax proceeds to buy large quantities of goods and services from firms.
  (3) Economic activity is not restricted to trading with other domestic residents. International trade, travel, and capital movements are commonplace.

These three characteristics of the world in which we live will be introduced one by one, rather than all at once.

(iii) Savings by Households

Since households typically do not spend all their income on consumer goods, but also do some saving, it looks as if Figure 3.1 has a serious defect. If households save some of their income, then consumer expenditure must be less than income, and, therefore, the flow of expenditure from households to firms shown in Figure 3.1 must be smaller than the flow of income received by households from firms. This would mean that firms are continually short of cash because they are paying out more than they are receiving. How does this complicating factor affect the concepts of national income, expenditure and output and their equality?

The easiest way of dealing with this is to consider a still slightly fictitious (but less fictitious than previously) representation of the economy in which we think of there being two kinds of firms — those that produce consumer goods and those that produce capital goods. (Denote consumer goods firms by the letters F_c, and capital goods firms by the letters F_k.) You can think of F_c firms as being, for example, those that produce food, clothing, and the thousands of commodities that households typically consume; and you can think of F_k firms as those that produce, for example, steel mills, highways, generating stations, and the like. (Of course, in the real world there isn't a clean-cut, hard-and-fast division.)

Figure 3.2 illustrates the real flows and the money flows between the various kinds of firms and households. Households supply factors of production to both consumer goods producers and capital goods

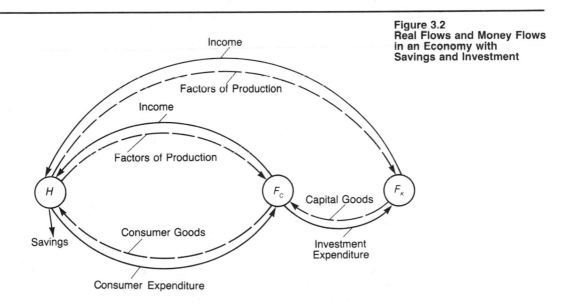

Figure 3.2
Real Flows and Money Flows in an Economy with Savings and Investment

Households (*H*) supply factor services to producers of consumer goods (*F_c*) and capital goods (*F_k*). Consumer goods producers supply households, and capital goods producers supply consumer goods producers with new equipment. These real flows (clockwise dashed lines) are matched by equivalent money flows (counterclockwise continuous lines). Income is paid to households equal in value to the production of both consumer and capital goods. Households pay firms for the purchase of consumer goods. Consumer goods producers pay capital goods producers for their purchases of new equipment. These payments are known as investment expenditure.

producers. These are shown as the two continuous lines representing flows from households to the two kinds of firms. The consumer goods producers, F_c, supply consumer goods to households, and the capital goods producers, F_k, supply capital goods to the producers of consumer goods. (Two further fictions that we will maintain are first, that capital goods firms do not themselves buy capital goods and second, that households do not buy capital goods. We could easily relax these assumptions, although it would make the pictorial representation of what is going on more complicated.)

To summarize: The real flows in the economy are the two sets of factor services flowing from households to the two kinds of firms, and real goods flowing in the opposite directions, with capital goods flowing from capital goods producers to consumer goods producers, and consumer goods flowing from consumer goods producers to households.

Financial flows move in a direction opposite to the goods and factor flows. Two kinds of firms pay income to households. Households make consumer expenditures, which represent the flow of money from households to consumer goods producers, and consumer goods producers make investment expenditures by paying money to capital goods producers in exchange for the capital goods supplied. In addition, households save some of their income. This is shown as the flow going *from* households (H). Households' savings is not a payment to either capital goods or consumer goods producers directly and therefore is not shown as a flow into either of these two institutions, but simply as a flow out of households.

In order to make the picture of the economy simpler, let us now add together the two kinds of firms (F_c and F_k) into a single, aggregate firms sector (F). This is done in Figure 3.3. Now, instead of having two income flows from firms to households, there is one, and this represents the sum of the two flows in Figure 3.2. Also, instead of there being two flows of factor services to firms, there is one, and this also represents the sum of the two flows shown in Figure 3.2. The expenditure by households on goods and services to firms is exactly the same as before, namely, the expenditure on consumer goods. Also, the flow of goods and services from firms to households is the same as the flow from the consumer goods firms to households. By aggregating all the firms in the economy into a single sector, the flow of capital goods from one kind of firm to another and the flow of investment expenditure on those goods have been lost, so to speak, in the aggregation. That is, by only looking at the aggregate of firms and the transactions that they have with households, we are not able to "see" in the picture the flow of investment expenditure between the firms and the flow of capital goods between firms. As a substitute for this, and so that we do not forget that it is there, Figure 3.3 shows the flow of investment expenditure as a net receipt by firms.

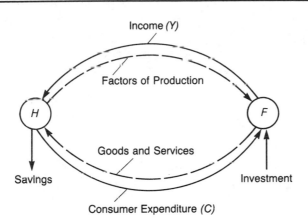

**Figure 3.3
Real Flows and Money Flows
in an Economy with
Savings and Investment
— Simplified**

Consumer and capital goods producers are consolidated into an aggregate firm sector (*F*). Firms in total buy factor services from households (*H*) in exchange for income. Households buy consumer goods and services in exchange for the money flow of consumer expenditure. What households do not spend on consumer goods they save. Households' savings are equal in value to firms' investment expenditure.

To simplify things further and to make it easier to move on to the next two stages of complexity, Figure 3.4 reproduces Figure 3.3, but leaves out the flows of factors of production and real goods and services, showing only the financial flows. Also, it uses only the symbolic names for the flows rather than their full names. Let us now focus on Figure 3.4. What this figure shows us is that income (*Y*) is paid by firms to households; households' consumption expenditure (*C*) is received by firms; households also save (*S*). This latter activity simply represents the non-spending of income by households and does not represent *direct* transfers of resources to firms. In addition, firms make investment (*I*) expenditure on new capital goods.

The savings which households make out of their income and the investment that firms make in new capital goods clearly are in some sense related to each other. It is capital markets — markets in which people borrow and lend — that provide the mechanism whereby these two variables are linked. Households place their savings in various kinds of financial assets, and firms borrow in a variety of ways from households in order to undertake their investment activity. Thus, it is the capital markets that provide the financial flow linkage between savings and investment.

Let us now return to Figure 3.4 and look again at the concepts of income, output, and expenditure embodied in this more complicated representation of the world. To highlight matters, focus first of all upon the firms (the circle labelled *F*). We have put an extra circle

Figure 3.4
Money Flows in an
Economy with Savings
and Investment — A More
Abstract Representation

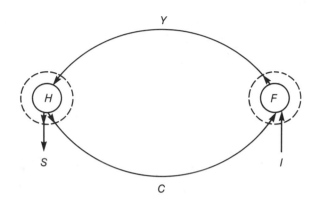

The money flows only are shown, with symbols denoting: income (*Y*), consumer expenditure (*C*), savings (*S*), investment (*I*). The broken circles around the households (*H*) and firms (*F*) contain arrows going to or from households and firms. An arrow leading into a sector represents a receipt. An arrow leaving a sector represents a payment. Total receipts by a sector equal total payments. Thus, for households, *Y* = *C* + *S*. For firms, *Y* = *C* + *I*. It follows directly that *S* = *I*.

(dotted) around *F* that contains three arrows — two leading into the *F*, and one going from the *F*. Recall that everything a firm receives it also has to pay out. Firms do not own anything, and the profits they make are paid out to households as factor income. Given this fact, it is clear that the incomes paid out by firms must be equal to the expenditure by households on consumer goods and the expenditure by firms on investment goods; that is

$$Y = C + I \qquad (3.2)$$

Next, focus on households (*H*) and on the dotted circle surrounding *H* in Figure 3.4. This circle also has three arrows, one leading to *H* and two leading from *H*. Since households must, in some way, dispose of their incomes, either by consuming or saving, it is evident that consumption plus savings (the outflows from households) must be equal to households' incomes, i.e.,

$$Y = C + S \qquad (3.3)$$

Equation 3.2 above tells us that the value of all income in the economy is equal to the value of all expenditure. The expenditure is now broader than it was in the first example and includes investment expenditure as well as consumer expenditure.

Further, just as it was in the simpler example, the value of output in the economy is also equal to income or expenditure. To see this, all you have to do is to recognize that the value of the goods and services produced is equal to the value placed upon them by the final demanders of those goods and services. That value is the value of consumer expenditure plus investment expenditure. Thus, income, expenditure, and output are equal again in this more "realistic" representation of the world.

You must be careful to distinguish between expenditure on final goods and services, payment to factors of production, and expenditure on intermediate goods and services. These distinctions are easier to see in this simplified economy, but apply to all the more complicated economies described later.

The distinction between expenditure on final goods and services, payment to factors of production, and expenditure on intermediate goods and services is most easily understood with the aid of an example. Suppose you buy a chocolate bar from the local university store for 50¢. The university store bought that chocolate bar from its wholesale supplier for 40¢; the wholesaler bought it from the manufacturer for 36¢; the manufacturer bought milk for 2¢, cocoa beans for 4¢, sugar for 4¢ and, electricity for 6¢; it paid wages to its workers of 14¢ and made a 6¢ profit which it paid to its stockholders. The total expenditure in the story of the chocolate bar is 50 + 40 + 36 + 2 + 4 + 4 + 6 + 14 + 6 = \$1.62. Of this \$1.62, only 50¢ represents expenditure on final goods and services. The rest is expenditure on intermediate goods and services or payment to factors of production. The expenditure can be classified as shown in Table 3.1.

Notice that the first column gives the value of expenditure (expenditure on final goods and services) on a chocolate bar, the second column total gives the incomes earned by all those who had a hand in producing the chocolate bar, and the final column simply records

TABLE 3.1
Intermediate and Final Expenditures and Factor Incomes

ITEM	EXPENDITURE ON FINAL GOODS AND SERVICES	FACTOR INCOMES	EXPENDITURE ON INTERMEDIATE GOODS AND SERVICES
Purchase price of chocolate bar	50¢	—	—
Wholesaler's selling price	—	—	40¢
Manufacturer's selling price	—	—	36¢
Farmer's income (milk)	—	2¢	—
Farmer's income (cocoa beans)	—	4¢	—
Farmer's income (sugar)	—	4¢	—
Electricity producers' incomes	—	6¢	—
Chocolate producers' wages	—	14¢	—
Chocolate producers' profits	—	6¢	—
Wholesaler's profit	—	4¢	—
Retailer's profit	—	10¢	—
Total	50¢	50¢	

some intermediate transactions. From the viewpoint of macro-economics, these last items are irrelevant. They arise from a particular form of industrial structure and would change if the industrial structure changed. For example, if the manufacturer sold directly to the retailer (for the 40¢ charged by the wholesaler in the above example), the expenditure on intermediate goods and services would fall by 36¢. Nothing important, however, would have changed. Total expenditure on final goods and services would still be 50¢. Also, factor incomes would still be 50¢; the profit of the wholesaler would have been eliminated and transferred to the manufacturer (by assumption in the above story). To count the expenditure on intermediate goods and services as well as the expenditure on final goods and services involves counting the same thing twice (or more than twice if there are several intermediate stages) and is known as "double counting."

(iv) Government Expenditure and Taxes

Now let us consider a yet more complicated world — one in which government economic activity plays a role. Figure 3.5 illustrates this type of economy. In addition to households (H) and firms (F), we also have government (denoted as GOV). Figure 3.5, which shows the relationship between households, firms, and government is drawn on the simplified basis introduced in Figure 3.4. That is, we do not show

**Figure 3.5
Money Flows in an
Economy with Savings,
Investment and Government
Economic Activity**

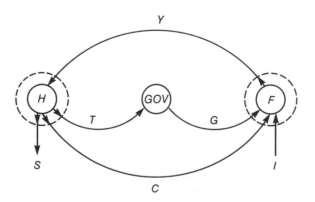

Government (GOV) taxes households (H) and buys goods and services produced by firms (F) — government expenditure on goods and services are shown by (G), and government revenue — taxes — are shown by T. When these flows are added to those shown (and defined) in the previous figures, the households' income and expenditure account is modified to become $Y = C + S + T$. The firms' income and expenditure account is modified to become $Y = C + I + G$. It follows directly from these last two statements that $S + T = I + G$. There is no reason why government expenditure should equal taxes. The government may run a surplus ($T > G$) or a deficit ($T < G$).

both the real flows and the money flows. We show only the money flows. Also, we only label the various flows with their symbolic rather than their full names. There are two new symbols: T stands for taxes and G stands for government expenditure on goods and services.

In this more complicated world, households receive incomes (Y) from firms. They dispose of that income either by buying consumer goods (C), paying taxes (T), or saving (S). Firms, as before, receive households' consumption expenditure (C) as well as investment expenditure (I) (financed by various capital market operations). They also have receipts from the government in exchange for its purchase of goods and services (G). The government itself simply receives taxes (net of any transfers that it makes to households) and makes expenditure on goods and services.

Now, to see the national income accounts that emerge from this more complex world, focus again, first of all, on firms (F) and on the arrows in the broken circle surrounding (F). Notice that now firms pay out income (Y) and receive consumer expenditure (C), government expenditure (G), and investment expenditure (I). Since, as before, they have no ultimate ownership of resources, everything that they receive is paid out to households. Hence,

$$Y = C + I + G \tag{3.4}$$

Next, focus on households (H). They receive income and dispose of that income in the activities of consuming (C), saving (S) and paying taxes (T). Hence,

$$Y = C + S + T \tag{3.5}$$

In this economy, expenditure is still equal to income, but expenditure now incorporates consumer expenditure, firms' investment expenditure, and in addition, government expenditure on goods and services.

It is important that you understand that government payments to households, such as, for example, unemployment insurance compensation, are *not* government expenditure on goods and services; they are the transfer of money from the government to households and are called *transfer payments*. You can think of these as negative taxes, so that total tax payments (denoted as T), need to be thought of as being *net* taxes equal to the gross taxes paid by households minus the transfers from government to households.

As in the two simpler economies considered above, not only are income and expenditure equal to each other, but output is also equal to income and expenditure. The value of the goods and services bought by households (C), firms (I), and government (G) represents the value of the goods and services produced in the economy — the output of the economy. Hence, even in this more complex economy, aggregate income, expenditure, and output are one and the same.

(v) The Rest of the World

Now consider the final complication arising from the fact that economic agents do business with their counterparts in the rest of the world. Figure 3.6 will illustrate the story here. Now we have households (H), firms (F), government (GOV), and the rest of the world (R). All the flows are as before, except for some additional flows between the rest of the world and the domestic economy. The left-hand part of Figure 3.6 is identical to Figure 3.5. and does not need to be described again. The additional activities in Figure 3.6 are imports and exports of goods and services. Foreigners buy goods from domestic firms, and, therefore, there is a flow of money from the rest of the world to those firms (EX) for exports. In addition, domestic firms buy goods from the rest of the world, transferring money to foreigners in exchange for those goods — imports (IM). From the way the figure has been drawn, it looks as if only firms do the importing. We know, of course, that sometimes households import goods directly. This could easily be shown in the picture, but it would not add anything of substance.

Figure 3.6
Money Flows in an Economy
with Savings, Investment,
Government Economic
Activity and Trans-
actions with the
Rest of the World

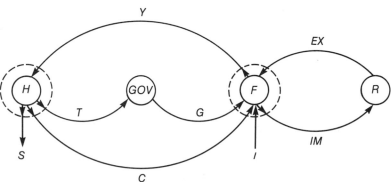

The flow transactions with the rest of the world are exports that give rise to a receipt by the firms doing the exporting (EX) and imports that give rise to payments by firms doing the importing (IM). These receipts and payments run between firms (F) and the rest of the world (R). Extending the flows to include those with the rest of world leaves the households' income and expenditure unchanged. They remain $Y = C + S + T$. The firms' account now becomes $Y = C + I + G + EX - IM$. There is no requirement that exports (EX) equal imports (IM). There may be a trade surplus ($EX > IM$) or a trade deficit ($EX < IM$) with the rest of the world.

Let us see how the national income accounts will now look in this economy. There is no change in the flows into and out of households. It is true that households now buy consumer goods, some of which have been imported from the rest of the world by the firms from whom they buy them. That, however, will not show up directly in the households' accounts. Their accounts still say that income (Y) is equal to consumption (C), plus savings (S), plus taxes (T).

We get a slightly different picture, however, when we look at firms. We now have two arrows leading out of the F circle — flows of money from firms to other agents — and four arrows flowing into F. Firms pay factor incomes to households (Y) and pay foreigners for the value of goods and services that have been imported from them (IM). They receive from foreigners the value of exports (EX), from government the value of goods and services purchased by government (G), and from households the value of consumer goods purchased (C). There is also a net inflow of funds to finance the firms' investment expenditures (I). Thus, considering all the arrows showing flows into and out from the firms, it is clear that

$$Y = C + I + G + EX - IM \qquad (3.6)$$

The items on the right-hand side of Equation (3.6) are total *net* expenditures on domestic output. Hence, the equality between income and expenditure is retained in the world pictured in Figure 3.6. Income is the flow of money from firms to households, and it represents the value of the factor services supplied by households to firms. Expenditure is equal to the consumption expenditure of households (C), the value of purchases of capital equipment by firms (I), government expenditure on goods and services (G), and the net value of foreigners' expenditure on domestic output. By *net* value we mean the difference between the gross purchases by foreign residents (exports) and the purchase of foreign goods by domestic residents (imports). Also, the value of output is equal to income (and expenditure).

There is an additional interesting implication in the national income accounts in this more "realistic" picture of the world. It follows immediately from the equality between income and expenditure and the fact that income is allocated by households to consumption, savings and taxes. If you begin by considering Equations (3.5) and (3.6), it will be immediately apparent to you that

$$I + G + EX = S + T + IM \qquad (3.7)$$

Now, deduct savings, taxes, and imports from both sides of this equation and rearrange the order of the terms so that we obtain:

$$(I-S) + (G-T) + (EX-IM) = 0 \qquad (3.8)$$

The three terms in brackets in Equation (3.8) have a very natural interpretation. The first term ($I-S$) is the excess of investment over savings by the private sector of the economy. The second term $(G - T)$ is the government's budget deficit. The third term $(EX - IM)$ is the surplus on the balance of trade with the rest of the world.

What Equation (3.8) says is that the sum of these three items must always be zero. There are various alternative ways in which this could be put. One way, which is perhaps helpful, is to notice that Equation (3.8) implies that if firms are investing more than households are saving, then either it is necessary for there to be a balance of trade deficit — that is, for imports to exceed exports — so that the extra investment goods may indeed be acquired by firms; or it is going to be necessary for government expenditure to be less than taxes, so that, in effect, the government is doing some of the saving that is enabling capital goods to be accumulated by firms. Another way of putting the same thing would be to say that if the government insists on spending more than it generates in taxes — if there is a government budget deficit — then there must either be a shortfall of investment as compared with savings or there must be a balance of trade deficit with the rest of the world to enable the government to acquire the resources in excess of the value of the taxes that it is levying.

D. Measuring Aggregate Income

(i) The Expenditure Approach

In order to measure national income (or expenditure or output), it is necessary to record and add together the appropriate flows that are taking place in the economy. The three most common methods of measuring national income will now be discussed. The first is the *expenditure approach*. You can think of the expenditure approach as an attempt by the national income statisticians to measure the total value of consumer expenditure on goods and services (C), firms' investment expenditure, government expenditure on goods and services (G), as well as exports (EX), and imports (IM). When these are combined in accordance with Equation (3.6), they provide one estimate of the value of national income, expenditure or output.

These items can be measured with varying degrees of accuracy. Consumer expenditure is measured partly by taking surveys of what households are spending and partly by observing the value of the sales of consumer goods by producers. Government expenditure is measured directly from the accounts of government itself. Investment expenditure is measured by surveying firms' capital spending programs and inventories. Finally, foreign trade is monitored through the official documentation required to conduct that trade. Most countries have some form of control over international movements of goods and services, and in some cases, these items are subject either to quotas or tariffs. In order to implement these arrangements, governments automatically collect data on the volume of international trade flows.

Thus, by measuring these items, C, I, G, EX and IM, it is possible to obtain a measure of aggregate income, expenditure or output by using the previous formula

$$Y = C + I + G + EX - IM \qquad (3.6)$$

By adding the values of expenditure, the aggregate that results will be based on market prices and will include taxes on expenditure less subsidies. To convert this to the factor cost measure needed for macro-economic analysis, it is necessary to deduct taxes on expenditure and add subsidies to give aggregate income (output or expenditure) at factor cost.

(ii) The Factor Incomes Approach

A second method of measuring national income is to measure factor incomes directly. The major sources of such measurements are the returns which individuals and firms make to the tax-collecting branch of government — in Canada, Revenue Canada. Since most taxes are collected as a levy on incomes earned, the reporting of those incomes for the purpose of tax calculations provides the major input for the *factor incomes approach* to the measurement of aggregate income. By using these sources it is possible to arrive at an estimate of aggregate income. This measure of aggregate income (output or expenditure) is automatically on a factor cost basis and needs no further adjustment.

The two measures of aggregate income — the expenditure approach (adjusted to the factor cost basis) and the factor incomes approach — never quite agree with each other. There is always a statistical discrepancy since it is simply too costly to devote the necessary resources to obtain precise values of these variables.

(iii) The Output Approach

A third method of measuring national income is to measure the value of output of each industry and then aggregate those output measures to arrive at an estimate of aggregate output. The major sources of direct output measurement are surveys of production and sales by firms. By using data collected from such surveys, it is possible to arrive at estimates of aggregate output by what is known as the *output approach*. In addition to providing a third way of arriving at an estimate of aggregate of economic activity, this approach also provides estimates of the output of each major sector of the economy.

E. Measuring Aggregate Income in Constant Dollars (Real)

The *expenditure approach* to measuring aggregate income provides the basis for the measurement of aggregate income (output or expenditure) in constant dollars, or real terms. A base period is chosen. At the moment, in Canada, that base period is 1971. The average level of prices prevailing in the base period is defined to be equal to 100.

The expenditures of a particular year are revalued using the prices prevailing in the base year. They are then aggregated using the formula in Equation (3.6) above to arrive at real income, output or expenditure.

F. Reading the National Income Accounts of Canada

Canada's aggregate income accounts are assembled by Statistics Canada. The accounts are drawn up on a quarterly and annual basis and are published in the *National Income and Expenditure Accounts*. Long historical runs of data are provided in the *Historical Statistics of Canada*, F. H. Leacy (ed.) (Ottawa: Statistics Canada, 1983); and *National Income and Expenditure Accounts, 1969-83*. The detailed definitions, concepts, sources, and methods are described (with immense attention being paid to the intricacies involved) in a publication called *A Guide to the National Income and Expenditure Accounts: Definitions, Concepts, Sources, Methods*, Catalogue 13-549E (Ottawa: Statistics Canada, September 1975).

Reading the Canadian national income accounts and translating them into the aggregate concepts that you have become familiar with in the preceding sections of this chapter is a relatively straightforward business. You may, nevertheless, need some guidance in that task.

If you look at Statistics Canada's *National Income and Expenditure Accounts* (you will find a copy in any university library and in the business/economics section of many public libraries), the first thing that will strike you (probably with mild alarm) is the immense detail presented. There are sixty tables covering eighty-eight pages. It is hard to know where to begin. Fortunately, for the purposes of macroeconomic analysis, four tables contain most of what is needed. They are Table 2, which gives the details of expenditure on gross national product; Table 6, which gives the same information but in constant dollars; Table 3, which shows the relation between the "national" and "domestic" concepts of aggregate income; Table 1, which gives the information needed to calculate the "factor cost" concepts, together with capital consumption.

The contents of the aggregate income accounts are brought together in Table 3.2 in a form that will enable you to see the relationships among the variables, using the concepts developed earlier in this chapter. The name (or names) of the items given in parentheses beneath each major item refer to the details contained in the officially reported national income and product accounts tables. There is little to be gained from committing all this detail to memory. You may, however, find it a useful reference in the event that you want to construct your own accounts for a year, or years other than 1984, the example used here.

Looking at the major items in Table 3.2, you will see that consumption (*C*), *plus* investment (*I*), *plus* government expenditure (*G*), *plus* exports (*EX*) *less* imports (*IM*) with a small residual error adds up to gross national product (GNP) at market prices. By adding net property income paid to non-residents, the total of gross domestic

TABLE 3.2
Canada's National Income and Expenditure in 1984

		$ millions
	CONSUMPTION (*C*) (personal expenditure on consumer goods and services Table 2, line1)	247 113
add	INVESTMENT (*I*) (gross fixed capital formation, business, $66 783 mill.; value of physical change in inventories, business, nonfarm $2592 mill., and farm $1048 mill., Table 2, lines 8, 14 and 15)	68 327
add	GOVERNMENT EXPENDITURE (*G*) (government current expenditure on goods and services $90 861 mill.; gross fixed capital formation; government, $11 706 mill.; value of physical changes in inventories; government $20 mill.; Table 2, lines 2, 4 and 13)	102 587
add	EXPORTS (*EX*) (exports of goods and services, Table 2, line 16)	131 311
deduct	IMPORTS (*IM*) (imports of goods and services, Table 2, line 17)	−129 694
deduct	Residual error (residual error of the estimate, Table 2, line 18)	1 226
equals	GROSS NATIONAL PRODUCT AT MARKET PRICES (gross national product, Table 1, line 13)	420 870
add	NET PROPERTY INCOME PAID TO NON-RESIDENTS (investment income paid to non-residents $20 103 mill. less investment income received from non-residents $5097 mill., Table 3, lines 4 and 5)	15 006
equals	GROSS DOMESTIC PRODUCT AT MARKET PRICES (not shown in official tables)	435 876
deduct	INDIRECT TAXES LESS SUBSIDIES (Table 3, line 3)	44 150
deduct	Residual error (resudial error of the estimate, Table 3, line 2)	−1 227
equals	GROSS DOMESTIC PRODUCT AT FACTOR COST (*Y*) (gross domestic product at factor cost, Table 3, line 6)	392 953
	CAPITAL CONSUMPTION (Table 1, line 11)	51 744

Note: The note in parentheses below each item in the Table gives the exact name of the item used in the source cited here as well as the table and line numbers where the item may be located.
Source: National Income and Expenditure Accounts, Catalogue 13-001 (Ottawa: Statistics Canada, July 1985). Tables 1, 2, and 3.

product (GDP) at market prices is arrived at. By deducting from that total the value of indirect taxes less subsidies, the factor cost definition of GDP is arrived at.

The bottom of the table notes the amount of capital consumption — that is, depreciation of fixed capital. By subtracting that amount from any of the other *gross* figures, you may arrive at the corresponding *net* national income, expenditure or product; or *net* domestic income, expenditure or product. Gross domestic product at factor cost (Y) is the aggregate income variable which macroeconomics seeks to explain.

Summary

A. Flows and Stocks

A flow is a rate per unit of time such as income per annum or expenditure per month. A stock is the value of a variable at a point in time such as the amount of money you have in the bank on a particular day.

B. Some Frequently Used Terms

  (i) Output (or product), Income and Expenditure
    — *output* (or *product*) is the value of the goods and services produced in the economy.
    — *income* is the sum of all the incomes earned in producing the output of the economy.
    — *expenditure* is the sum of all expenditures on final goods and services in the economy.

  (ii) Domestic and National
    — *domestic* refers to an aggregation of economic activity taking place in a particular country.
    — *national* refers to an aggregation of the economic activity of all residents no matter in which country the activity takes place.

  (iii) Gross and Net
    — *gross* is before deducting the depreciation of assets.
    — *net* is after deducting the depreciation of assets.

  (iv) Market Price and Factor Cost
    — *market price* valuations are based on the prices paid by consumers and include taxes on expenditure and are net of subsidies.
    — *factor cost* valuations are based on the amounts paid to the factors of production, including profits, and exclude taxes on expenditures and are gross of subsidies.

  (v) Nominal and Real
    — *nominal* valuation uses prices prevailing in the current period.
    — *real* valuation uses prices that prevailed in a base period.

C. Aggregate Output (or Product), Income, and Expenditure

Aggregate output is the value of all the goods and services produced in the economy. Aggregate income is the sum of all the incomes of all the individuals in the economy. Aggregate expenditure is the sum of all the expenditures on *final* goods and services produced by the economy. The values of aggregate output, income, and expenditure are equal to each other.

D. Measuring Aggregate Income

The *expenditure approach* to aggregate income measurement samples the expenditures of households, firms, government, and foreigners and makes an estimate of the sum of those expenditures. From the fact that income, expenditure and output are equal to each other, this estimate of expenditure is also an estimate of income and output.

The *factor incomes approach* samples the incomes of individuals and from this forms an estimate of aggregate income. From the conceptual equality of income, expenditure, and output, this provides an alternative estimate of aggregate expenditure and output as well as income.

The *output approach* samples the production of individual firms and from this forms an estimate of the value of output in each sector of the economy and in aggregate.

The three approaches never produce identically the same estimate, but provide a good approximation to the value of aggregate income, expenditure, and output.

E. Measuring Aggregate income in Constant Dollars (Real)

To measure real income (output and expenditure), the expenditure approach is used. The final goods and services bought in each year are valued at the prices which prevailed in the base year.

F. Reading the National Income Accounts of Canada

Canada's national income and product accounts are published by Statistics Canada in *National Income and Expenditure Accounts*. The way in which the detailed items supplied in the published tables aggregate into the concepts employed in macroeconomics are set out in Table 3.2, and that table should be used as a reference guide.

Review Questions
1. Indicate which of the following are flows and which are stocks:
    (a) the amount of water that flows over the Niagara Falls in a day
    (b) the amount of water in Lake Ontario
    (c) gross domestic product
    (d) real national income
    (e) the value of the airplanes owned by Air Canada

2. Review the definition of each of the following terms:
   (a) gross domestic product
   (b) gross domestic product at market price
   (c) gross national product at factor cost
   (d) real national income

3. Give examples which illustrate the differences between the following terms:
   (a) nominal and real
   (b) gross and net
   (c) national and domestic
   (d) factor cost and market price

4. What are the units of measurement of (a) a nominal variable and (b) a real variable?

5. Using the latest available data from the *National Income and Expenditure Accounts*, calculate the latest year values of (a) aggregate income, (b) aggregate expenditure, and (c) aggregate output.

6. Using the latest *National Income and Expenditure Accounts*, calculate aggregate income for 1985 using (a) the expenditure approach, and (b) the factor incomes approach. Is your measure of aggregate income a gross or a net measure? What is the difference between gross aggregate income and net aggregate income in 1985?

7. Using gross aggregate income for 1985 (calculated in Question 6) and other relevant data from the *National Income and Expenditure Accounts*, calculate 1985 aggregate income in constant 1971 dollars.

8. Suppose that you want to describe the pattern of aggregate output in Canada during the 1970s. Which of the following would be the best series to use, and why?
   (a) aggregate expenditure at market prices
   (b) aggregate output at factor cost
   (c) gross domestic product in constant dollars
   (d) gross domestic product
   Say exactly what *all* the faults are with *all* the series that you would *not* use.

9. The following activities took place in an imaginary economy last year:

	$ millions
Wages paid to labor	800 000
Consumer expenditure	650 000
Taxes paid on wages	200 000
Government payments to support the unemployed, sick, and aged	50 000
Firms' profits	200 000
Investment	250 000
Taxes paid on profits	50 000
Government purchases of goods and services	200 000
Exports	250 000

Note: There was no property income paid to or received from non-residents.

  (a) Calculate:

     gross domestic income

     gross national expenditure

     savings

     imports

     the government budget surplus/deficit

  (b) What extra information do you need in order to calculate net national income?

10. A troupe of Russian dancers tours Canada. The dancers fly to Montreal on an *Aeroflot* (Soviet airline) flight at a total round trip cost of $200 000. They travel inside Canada on domestic airlines at a total cost of $185 000. Their hotel and food bills in Canada amount to $150 000. The receipts from ticket sales for performances of the troupe amounts to $1 000 000. The cost of renting theatres is $100 000, hiring Canadian musicians is $200 000, and advertising is $350 000. The Russian dancers wages amounted to $75 000 for the period of the visit. The dancers bought Canadian-made souvenirs worth a total of $2500. Any profit or loss on the visit accrued to or was borne by the Soviet government. Show where each of the economic activities described here appears in the national income accounts of Canada.

4

Aggregate Balance Sheet Accounting

This is an unusual topic to appear in an intermediate macroeconomics text, and it reflects the unusual nature of the book with which you are working. Keynesian macroeconomics places a great deal of emphasis on the national income accounts and on aggregate income and expenditure flows, and the last chapter dealt with the concepts that lie behind that accounting framework. If you were working with a conventional Keynesian-oriented macroeconomics book you would now be reading the first "theory" chapter. That chapter would present a theory about how national income is determined, and the theory would be based purely on the items from national income flow accounts. It would postulate hypothetical relationships between various flows — hypotheses that one flow depends in some behavioral way on another flow — and from that it would develop a predictive theory of the determination of national income.

That route is not taken here. The kind of macroeconomics that you are studying in this book is built on the presumption that the most important behavioral relationships are not only those between various flows, but also those between flows and stocks. Accordingly, as a prelude to studying macroeconomic theory, this chapter explains the connections between the main stocks (the assets and liabilities in the economy) and also explains how those stocks are measured.

You have four tasks. These are to:

a) Understand the meaning of "asset," "liability," and "balance sheet."

b) Know the definition of money and understand the nature of money.
c) Know the main items in the balance sheets of households, firms, chartered banks, the central bank, government, and the rest of the world.
d) Know the main sources of information about aggregate balance sheets in Canada.

A. Asset, Liability, and Balance Sheet

(i) Asset and Liability

An *asset* is simply something which someone owns. A *liability* is what someone owes.

There are two types of assets: financial and real. A *real asset* is concrete, tangible, a real piece of nuts and bolts. Examples of real assets are the desks and tables at which you sit and study; your stereo and records; your car, motorcycle, skis, surfboard, etc. Other examples are highways, steel mills, coal mines, power stations, and airplanes.

There is one special real asset which you probably do not ordinarily think of as an asset — that is yourself (and everyone else). The value of that asset in the economy as a whole is the value of all the work that human beings are capable of doing now and in the future. This asset is called human capital. Of course, in societies such as our own where slavery is prohibited, it is not possible to buy and sell human capital. It is possible, however, to borrow from a bank against a promise to commit future income (i.e., human capital) to the repayment of the loan.

Financial assets are different from real assets. They are pieces of paper which constitute an asset to one economic agent and a liability to another. That is, they *define a debt relationship* between two agents. Examples of financial assets (which are also someone else's financial liabilities) are: (a) your savings account at the local bank — from your point of view that is a financial asset (you *own* the deposit) while from the point of view of your bank it is a liability (the bank *owes* you the deposit); (b) an IBM bond — this is an asset to the person who owns it, but a liability to stockholders of IBM; (c) a Bank of Canada one dollar bill — this is an asset to you, but is it anyone's liability? Yes it is: It is a liability of the Bank of Canada — this country's central bank. Of course, since everyone is willing to accept your dollar bill in exchange for goods and services, the Bank of Canada never has to honor its debt to you.

All financial assets are like the three examples in the above paragraph. Each financial asset has a financial liability that goes with it. It is a piece of paper that specifies that someone X has a claim on someone else Y; that is, a financial asset is an asset to X and a liability to Y.

(ii) Balance Sheet

A balance sheet is a statement about what is owned by (is an asset of) and what is owed by (is a liability of) a particular individual or agency. It could be an individual like yourself, or it could be an agency like the Bank of Canada, a chartered bank like the Bank of Montreal, the government of Canada, or IBM. The best way to get a feel for a balance sheet is to consider the balance sheet of an individual like yourself.

Table 4.1 sets out an example of what an individual student's balance sheet might look like. The balance sheet shown in Table 4.1 lists the assets in the first column and the liabilities in the second column. The assets are divided between financial items (in the top part of the balance sheet) and real items (in the bottom part of the balance sheet). The person whose balance sheet is shown here has some bank notes and coins, $25 (item 1); a savings account, $150 (item 2); and Canada savings bonds, $200 (item 3). These are the person's financial assets. The individual has two financial liabilities: a bank loan, $1000 (item 4); and an outstanding balance of $200 with a credit card company — Mastercard (item 5). Item 6 totals the financial assets and liabilities. You will see that this person owes more (has bigger liabilities) than he/she owns (has assets).

The next items are real assets. The individual has a car worth $1500 dollars and a stereo and records worth $1000 giving a total of real assets (item 9) of $2500. The total assets and liabilities are shown in item 10. This individual has assets of $2875 and liabilities of $1200.

It is a feature of a balance sheet that it must balance. Clearly, as depicted in item 10, the assets of this individual exceed the liabilities.

TABLE 4.1
An Individual's Balance Sheet

	Assets $	Liabilities $
1. Bank notes and coins	25	
2. Savings account	150	
3. Canada savings bonds	200	
4. Bank loan		1,000
5. Mastercard account		200
6. TOTAL FINANCIAL ASSETS AND LIABILITIES	375	1,200
7. Car	1,500	
8. Stereo and records	1,000	
9. TOTAL REAL ASSETS	$2,500	
10. TOTAL ASSETS AND LIABILITIES	2,875	1,200
11. Wealth		1,675
12. Totals	$2,875	$2,875

The amount by which the assets exceed the liabilities is $1675. This amount of money is the wealth of this individual. *Wealth* is defined to be a "fictitious" liability (yes, liability) and is shown in item 11 as a liability of $1675. If you add the wealth of the individual to the other liabilities you see that total liabilities (item 12) are equal to total assets, $2875. In order to feel more comfortable with the idea of wealth as a liability, you may like to think of it as the amount which is owed by an individual to himself. Another equivalent way of defining wealth, which is perhaps more appealing, is simply: Wealth equals total assets less total liabilities. In the example:

$$\begin{aligned} \text{Total assets} &= \$2875 \\ less \quad \text{total liabilities} &= \underline{\$1200} \\ equals \quad \text{wealth} &= \underline{\$1675} \end{aligned}$$

Wealth is commonly referred to by the alternative name "*net worth.*"

B. Definition and Nature of Money

Money is anything which is generally acceptable as a medium of exchange. A medium of exchange is anything which is acceptable in exchange for goods and services. Which precise assets constitute the medium of exchange varies from one society to another and has varied over the years. Gold has commonly served as a medium of exchange; so has silver and so have other metals. In some prisoner-of-war camps in World War II, cigarettes circulated as a medium of exchange. These are all examples of commodity money.

In modern societies, money is a financial asset that is the financial liability either of the central bank or of other banks. There are two widely used alternative measures of the money supply in Canada today. One is sometimes called "narrow money" or M1, and the other is referred to as "broad-money" or M3.

Narrow money (M1) consists of currency (Bank of Canada notes and coins) in circulation, plus demand deposits (checking account balances), at chartered banks.

Broad money (M3) is M1 plus other checkable, notice and term deposits.

Notice and term deposits, which are included in the M3 definition of money but excluded from the M1 measure, are not directly transferable from one person to another by writing a check, and although it is customary to think of such deposits as "money in the bank," it is important to recognize that only M1 is money in the strict sense that it is a means of payment.

In recent years, innovations in the banking sector made possible by the advance of computer technology have begun to blur the distinction between M1 and M3. Some of the accounts which banks make available to their customers have some of the properties of a means of payment and therefore ought to be regarded as M1, although in other respects they have the properties of savings accounts — which would put them in the M3 category. A good example of such arrangements are the so called daily interest checking accounts. Bank customers operating with daily interest checking accounts are, in effect, able to earn interest on bank deposits while at the same time keeping those deposits available for active transactions use. These relatively new forms of bank accounts, although, in effect, identical to regular checking accounts from the point of view of the holder are not counted as part of M1. They are included in the slightly broader aggregate called M1(A). (A particular example serves to highlight the fact that there is no precision in the M1 measure of money). Ideally the Bank of Canada would be constantly monitoring the definition of the aggregate that serves as the means of payment and be constantly revising that aggregate so as to take account of innovations that occur in the financial sector to ensure that the measured aggregate is as close as possible to the total stock of the means of payment in the economy.

Although there are some imprecise borderline cases between money and non-money, there is no doubt at all that money does not include credit cards, such as a Mastercard or Visa card. These cards are convenient identification tags that enable you to create two debts simultaneously. One debt is between yourself and the credit card company and the other is between the credit card company and the seller. These debts are settled when you pay the credit card company and the credit card company pays the seller.

Money in the modern world stands in sharp contrast to commodity money in that it is a financial asset not backed by any commodities and not exchangeable by the issuer for anything other than another unit of itself. Its value arises from the fact that it is universally acceptable by all in exchange for goods and services.

C. Main Balance Sheet Items

We are going to look at the balance sheets of six agents:

Households	H
Firms	F
Chartered Banks	B
Bank of Canada	BOC
Government of Canada	GOV
Rest of World	R

You will identify this as an extension of the agents whose flow activities we analyzed when dealing with the aggregate income accounts in the previous chapter. There we examined households, firms, government and the rest of the world. We did not deal with chartered banks or the Bank of Canada because these institutions are not major actors in the flow of goods and services. They are, however, major actors in the monetary and balance sheet structure of the economy.

(i) Financial Assets and Liabilities

Table 4.2 records the main financial items in the balance sheets of these six agents (or sectors). A + denotes an asset and a − denotes a liability. Additional explanations for the items and diagrams in Table 4.2 are given below.

(a) CHARTERED BANK DEPOSITS WITH THE BANK OF CANADA

Chartered banks maintain checking accounts just as individuals do. The banker to the chartered banks is the central bank — the Bank of Canada. As far as the banks are concerned, their deposits with the Bank of Canada are like money and are part of their assets. These deposits are a liability of the Bank of Canada. A bank can convert its deposits with the Bank of Canada into notes and coins, or vice versa, as it chooses.

(b) CURRENCY

Currency consists of all Bank of Canada notes and coins held by (and therefore assets of) households, firms and banks. The notes are a liability of the Bank of Canada, but the coins are issued by the Royal Canadian Mint, a government agency (to be precise, a Crown corporation located in Winnipeg), and are therefore shown in Table 4.2 as a liability of the government.

TABLE 4.2
The Structure of Financial Indebtedness

ITEM	SECTOR					
	H	F	B	BOC	GOV	R
Chartered bank deposits with the Bank of Canada			+	−		
Currency (Notes and coins)	+	+	+	−	−	
Demand deposits	+	+	−		+	
Other checkable, notice and term deposits	+	+	−	+		
Government securities	+	+	+	+ −	+	
Bank loans	−	−	+			
Corporate bonds	+	−				+
Equities	+	−				+
Foreign securities	+	+	+			−
Foreign exchange				+	+	−
Net financial assets	+	−	0	0	−	±

Notes: (+) denotes assets;
(−) denotes liabilities.

The sectors are: Households (*H*); Firms (*F*); Chartered Banks (*B*); the Bank of Canada (*BOC*); Government (*GOV*); the Rest of the World (*R*). The boxes show the items included in the alternative definitions of the money supply: M1 and M3. The triangle shows the items included in the monetary base.

(c) MONETARY BASE (MB)

All the liabilities of the Bank of Canada added together, plus the currency liabilities of the government, make up what is known as the *monetary base*. This is shown in the triangle in Table 4.2.

(d) DEMAND DEPOSITS

Demand deposits are bank accounts from which funds may be withdrawn on demand, typically by writing a check. They are liabilities of banks and assets of households, firms, government, and foreigners.

(e) NARROW MONEY (M1)

The total of currency held by households and firms and demand deposits is "narrow money" or M1. The dotted box in Table 4.2 shows the total of M1. Notice that M1 does *not* include the currency held inside the banking system, nor does it include chartered bank deposits with the Bank of Canada. Further, M1 does not include the demand deposits at the chartered banks owned by government.

(f) OTHER CHECKABLE, NOTICE AND TERM DEPOSITS

These are interest-bearing deposits held at chartered banks by households and firms and typically may only be withdrawn on demand by incurring an interest penalty. Thus, they are not quite as useful as demand deposits as a means of payment.

(g) BROAD MONEY (M3)

If we add other checkable, notice and term deposits to M1, we obtain M3, which is shown as the dashed box in Table 4.2.

(h) GOVERNMENT SECURITIES

Next there is a whole class of financial assets called *government securities*. Very many different types of assets are in this category. Examples are : Canada savings bonds, long-term government of Canada bonds and Treasury bills. These items are a liability of the government of Canada and are held by (are assets of) all of the other sectors. The government securities held by the Bank of Canada are the assets that provide the backing for the monetary base. In order to raise the size of the monetary base, the Bank of Canada buys government securities with newly created money.

(i) BANK LOANS

The next major item to consider in the sectoral balance sheets is bank loans. These include the personal and business loans that are assets as far as the chartered banks are concerned and are liabilities of the households and firms that have borrowed the money.

(j) CORPORATE BONDS

Corporations raise money to buy capital equipment by selling bonds. A corporate bond holder, unlike an equity holder (see next item), is not an owner of the company. Rather, such a person has made a loan to the company. All that a corporate bond holder is entitled to is the pre-agreed interest payment on the bond. In contrast, an equity holder is entitled to his share of any residual profits earned by the firm. In terms of balance sheet accounting, a corporate bond appears as a liability to firms and is an asset of households and the rest of the world.

(k) EQUITIES

In addition to raising funds to buy capital equipment by selling bonds, corporations also issue equities. An equity holder in a corporation is in fact a part owner of the corporation. That is, the households and foreigners that own equities really own a share of the firm's physical capital stock. In legal terms, of course, the owner of a share in a firm can only sell the share. The owner of a share cannot decide to sell the whole of (or even that individual's share of) the physical plant itself. Thus in legal terms there is an indebtedness between households and foreigners who own firms and the firm itself. The firm has a liability, and the households and foreigners own the corresponding asset.

(l) FOREIGN SECURITIES

There are various securities issued by foreign governments and foreign companies which are held by Canadian households, firms, and banks.

(m) FOREIGN EXCHANGE RESERVES

The final item in Table 4.2 is the foreign exchange reserves of the country. These constitute an asset to the Bank of Canada and to the government, which hold (and own) the country's foreign exchange reserves. These reserves are in the form of deposits and other short-term securities issued by foreign governments, central banks, and chartered banks. You can think of this item as representing Canada's bank account with the rest of the world.

(ii) Net Financial Assets

If we add up all ten items in Table 4.2, we arrive at the net financial assets of each of the major sectors in the economy. The net assets for the chartered banks and for the Bank of Canada will approximately add up to zero, reflecting the fact that these institutions have comparatively small holdings of real assets. (They do, of course, have large *absolute* holdings of real assets. For example, they own quite a large amount of real estate and office space. However, compared with their financial assets and liabilities, such items are relatively insignificant and, for our purposes, can be ignored.)

Typically, households and firms, which together constitute what is called the *non-bank private sector*, have positive net financial assets. That is, they own financial assets in excess of the liabilities which they have issued. The government, on the other hand, typically has a net financial liability. That liability is sometimes referred to as the *national debt*. The net financial asset position of the country vis-à-vis the rest of the world may be positive or negative. That is, the rest of the world may have a net financial claim on Canada (if Canada has a net liability, it is referred to as a *net debtor*) or Canada may have a net financial claim on the rest of the world (if Canada has a net financial asset, it is referred to as a *net creditor*). As a matter of fact, Canada is a fairly sizeable net debtor.

(iii) Real and Financial Assets

Table 4.3 shows the net financial assets of the six sectors. It also shows some additional (non-financial) items that will be described below. Further, that table contains an extra column which shows the Canadian economy-wide total value of its five sectors' holdings of the various items.

For the world as a whole (not shown in Table 4.3), net financial assets are zero — someone's financial asset is someone else's liability. For Canada, however, net financial assets are negative since foreigners, not counted as part of the Canadian economy, hold the corresponding asset. Thus in the final "economy" column of Table 4.3 the entry "net claims of the rest of world" appears.

TABLE 4.3
Financial Assets and Liabilities and Real Assets

ITEM	SECTOR						
	H	*F*	*B*	*BOC*	*GOV*	*R*	*ECONOMY*
Net financial assets	+	−	0	0	−	±	
Net claims of the rest of world							
Real assets	+	+			+	(excluded)	Nonhuman wealth
Future tax liabilities	−	−			+		
Monetary base							
Undistributed profits	+	−	−	0			
Human wealth	+						Human wealth
Wealth	+	0	0	0	0	±	Wealth

Notes: (+) denotes an asset and (-) denotes a liability. The sectors are: Households (*H*), Firms (*F*), Chartered Banks (*B*), the Bank of Canada (*BOC*), Government (*GOV*), and the Rest of the World (*R*). The column headed Economy refers to the economy as a whole and is the sum of the first five sectors. A zero in the table denotes that the item in question *sums* to zero. A blank in the table denotes that the item in question does not appear (or appears negligibly) in a particular sector's balance sheet.

(a) REAL ASSETS

Real assets — plant, equipment, buildings, etc. — are owned by households, firms, and government. (As discussed earlier, the banks' holdings are very small in relation to the total and are ignored.) The "rest-of-world" holding of real assets is excluded from the table since these do not constitute part of the economy of the country with which we are dealing.

The total of all the real assets held by households, firms, and government constitute the *non-human wealth* of the economy.

(b) FUTURE TAX LIABILITIES

If the government has liabilities that exceed its real assets — which it typically does — then it is the households and firms that pay taxes that will be responsible for meeting those liabilities. The goverment will have to levy taxes on households and firms that equal in value the excess of its liabilities over its assets. This may be thought of as an *implicit* financial asset. It is implicit because no explicit paper claim exists to represent this item. It is an asset to the government and a liability to households and firms.

There is one important government sector liability that never has to be repaid and that does not even involve the government in having to raise taxes to make interest payments. This is the currency that the government has issued, together with the value of the government bonds that are held by the Bank of Canada as backing for its liabilities — chartered bank reserve deposits and Bank of Canada bank notes. That this currency never has to be redeemed by the government is obvious. That the government securities held by the Bank of Canada are in the same category is perhaps less obvious and needs explaining. The reasoning is as follows. First, the Bank of Canada is under no obligation to redeem its liabilities, and it does not have to pay any interest on them. Second, the income made by the Bank of Canada on its holdings of government securities is, except for having to cover some relatively small expenses, a profit which the Bank of Canada pays to the government. In effect, the government does not have to pay interest on that part of its debt held by the Bank of Canada because although it pays the interest, it gets nearly all of it back as profits of the Bank of Canada. Since the Bank of Canada does not have to redeem its liabilities and since the government gets a free loan that never has to be repaid equal to the value of the Bank of Canada's liabilities, those liabilities are exactly like currency in the sense that they do not attract any future tax liability.

The future tax liabilities of households and firms is less than the value of the corresponding asset of the government by the amount of currency and Bank of Canada liabilities that never have to be redeemed by the government. The sum of currency and the Bank of Canada's liabilities is the monetary base (see Table 4.2). Therefore, in Table 4.3, the sum of future tax liabilities for the economy as a whole is shown as being equal to the value of the monetary base.[1]

(c) UNDISTRIBUTED PROFITS

The government and firms are fundamentally different legal entities from households. Households (and the individuals which constitute them) are the ultimate wealth holders. Firms can be regarded as owing to households the net undistributed profits from their activities. These profits (or losses) are exactly equal to the difference between the firms' real assets and net financial liabilities and are shown as an asset to households and as a liability to firms. In the case of firms that have issued equity, undistributed profits are already taken into account (provided that the equity has been valued correctly).

As an example, consider two firms that are identical in all respects except that one of the firms has purchased some plant and equipment with undistributed profits, whereas another has purchased the equivalent amount of plant and equipment with the proceeds from a bond sale. The stock market value of the equity of the firm with undistributed profits will clearly be higher than that of the firm that has financed some of its planned acquisitions with the proceeds of a bond sale. For firms that do not issue equity (i.e., partnerships and other private firms) however, the undistributed profits need to be counted as a liability to the firm and as an asset to the owner or owners of the firm even though there is no explicit marketable security representing that asset and liability.

(d) HUMAN WEALTH

The value of the future income of the individuals in the economy constitutes the economy's human wealth (or human capital). You will probably understand the concept of human wealth most thoroughly if you consider the example of your own human wealth. Your human wealth is the sum of money which, if used here and now to buy an annuity, would provide an income each year for the rest of your life equal in value to the income that you will earn each year. It is an *implicit* asset (rather than an *actual* asset) in the sense that (at least since the abolition of slavery) human capital is not traded directly in markets. It is possible, however, for people to borrow using part of their human capital as collateral. This happens whenever an individual borrows purely for consumption purposes and promises to

---

[1] You may be thinking that the government is under no obligation to redeem (buy back) any of its debt and could go on issuing additional debt for ever, and further, could issue debt to pay interest on debt. This is certainly true. Nevertheless, each time the government sells a bond that it has no intention of redeeming (except for another like bond), it commits itself to the payment of an interest stream that has the same value as the funds raised by the bond rate and so may be thought of as establishing a *future* liability on households and firms. Chapter 31 will provide a more precise and thorough explanation of this.

repay the debt out of *future labor income*. Another, and more precise, definition of human capital is the present value of future labor income.

(c) WEALTH

The sum of all the net claims on the rest of the world, the non-human wealth, the monetary base, and human wealth is the economy's wealth. The household sector owns all the wealth because of the implicit asset/liability items that take account of future tax liabilities and undistributed profits. Government has no wealth on its own account. It owes any excess of assets over liabilities to the households, and the households are liable for its net debts. Similarly, firms have no net wealth because they owe (are liable for) to households any undistributed profits (and households have to stand any losses).

(iv) National Balance Sheets and National Income Accounts

Changes in the net financial asset position of the various sectors are related to flows in the national income accounts which we examined in Chapter 3. The change in the net financial assets of households and firms taken together represents the difference between savings (S) and investment (I) (shown in Table 4.4 as $S-I$). The reason for this is very natural. Savings constitute the difference between what is earned (the economy's income) and what is spent on consumer goods and paid in taxes. Some of that saving is used to buy physical capital goods. That is, it is invested in real assets. That which is not invested (i.e., not used to buy real assets) is used to buy financial assets. Therefore, the change in the net financial assets of households and firms is the same thing as savings minus investment.

Chartered banks and the Bank of Canada having zero net financial assets also, of course, have zero change in net financial assets.

The change in the government's financial assets is exactly equal to the difference between its current tax receipts (T) and its current expenditure (G). Thus, we show in Table 4.4 T-G as the change in net financial assets of the government.

TABLE 4.4
Change in Financial Assets and the National Income Flows

ITEM	SECTORS					
	H	*F*	*B*	*BOC*	*GOV*	*R*
Change in net financial assets	*S-I*		0	0	*T-G*	*IM-EX*

Note: The sectors are Households (*H*), Firms (*F*), Chartered Banks (*B*), the Bank of Canada (*BOC*), Government (*GOV*), and the Rest of the World (*R*). *S* is savings; *I* is investment; *T* is total taxes net of transfer payments; *G* is government expenditure on goods and services; *IM* is imports; and *EX* is exports.

The change in the net financial assets of the rest of the world is measured by the difference between the flow of expenditures by domestic residents on foreign goods (imports, *IM*) and the flow of foreign expenditures on domestic goods (exports, *EX*). We show the change in net financial assets of the rest of the world as being the difference between imports and exports (*IM-EX*).

It is evident that if we aggregate (add up) net financial assets across all the sectors then we wind up with zero. That is, what is issued as a liability by one sector is held as an asset by another sector, or sectors. If we add up the net financial asset changes, that is, savings minus investment $(S - I)$, plus taxes minus government expenditure $(T - G)$, plus imports minus exports $(IM - EX)$, then we also always come out with zero, reflecting a fact which we discovered when examining the national income accounts, namely, that savings plus taxes plus imports are equal to investment plus government expenditure plus exports.

(v) The Sectoral Balance Sheets

If you look at each column of Table 4.2 separately, you will see the financial aspects of the balance sheets of each of the six sectors. Usually in macroeconomics we do not separately analyze the balance sheets of households and firms but rather aggregate them together. If we aggregate the two items — currency and demand deposits — across both households and firms (unbroken box), the total of those items equals the narrow money supply, M1. If we aggregate the three items — currency, demand deposits, and other checkable, notice, and term deposits — across both households and firms, then the total (the dashed box) equals the broad measure of the money supply, M3. These magnitudes are of crucial importance in macroeconomic analysis.

Consider next the third column (*B*) of Table 4.2. This shows the balance sheet of the chartered banks. It is clear that the liabilities of this sector are the deposits that the chartered banks issue in the form of demand deposits, and other checkable, notice and term deposits. Their assets consist of reserve deposits at the Bank of Canada, currency, government securities, and loans to individuals and firms.

The Bank of Canada's balance sheet has a very simple structure. The liability of the Bank of Canada consists of all the Bank of Canada notes outstanding, plus the chartered banks' reserve deposits at the Bank of Canada. This aggregate, plus the coin issued by the Royal Canadian Mint, is the monetary base. The assets of the Bank of Canada that back that monetary base are government securities and foreign exchange reserves. The Bank of Canada can change the volume of the monetary base either by buying and selling government securities or by trading in the foreign exchange market. If the Bank of Canada wants to increase the monetary base, it will simply buy government securities, paying for the securities with newly created money. It could equivalently buy foreign exchange, that is, buy, say, U.S. dollars using newly created Canadian dollars. It could, of course, reduce the monetary base with the opposite operation.

The balance sheets of the government sector and the rest of the world do not in and of themselves have any intrinsic interest for our present purposes and have been presented here so that you can have a complete picture of the structure of indebtedness in the economy and the connection between changes in net financial assets and the flows in the national income accounts.

D. Measuring Aggregate Balance Sheets in Canada

The Bank of Canada and Statistics Canada are the main agencies responsible for coordinating and publishing information about aggregate balance sheets in Canada. In the monthly *Bank of Canada Review*, the bank publishes a large volume of monthly and quarterly data, as well as some annual data, on either complete or part items of the balance sheets of the bank itself, the chartered banks, the government of Canada, together with institutions dealing with the financing of real estate, consumer credit and corporations.

The flow of funds accounts are published quarterly by Statistics Canada in *Financial Flow Accounts*. These record the flows of funds between thirteen major sectors of the economy (representing a more detailed sectoral classification than that employed in Table 4.2 above). The flows themselves are classified according to the acquisitions of three different types of real assets (new fixed capital, inventories, and purchases of existing, i.e., [used] assets) and more than twenty financial assets. It is important to take careful note that the flow of funds accounts, although giving information about aggregate balance sheet movements, are not themselves balance sheets. Rather, they give information about changes in assets and liabilities. This means that there are some evaluation problems that are potentially quite difficult to solve. These arise from the fact that the flow of funds accounts show only the values of assets and liabilities acquired or disposed of during a particular period of time and do not give information about changes in the values of previously and remaining outstanding stocks of assets and liabilities.

The Bank of Canada also regularly publishes information on the magnitudes of the monetary aggregates M1 and M3 in the *Bank of Canada Review*.

A more comprehensive statement of the flow of funds accounts is published from time to time by Statistics Canada, giving a long historical run of both quarterly and annual data. These historical flows are published in *Financial Flow Accounts, Quarterly Flows* (catalogue 13-562) and *Financial Flow Accounts, Annual Flows and Year-end Financial Assets and Liabilities* (catalogue 13-563).

Our knowledge about aggregate balance sheets is more fragmentary than is our knowledge of the national income and expenditure flows. From the data collected and published by the Bank of Canada, we obtain frequent, reliable and up-to-date information on the bank itself, the chartered banks, and some key financial institutions. We do not, however, obtain much information from the Bank of Canada concerning the balance sheets of households and firms. The flow of funds accounts do, to some extent, help to fill that gap. The flow of funds information is not, however, a balance sheet since, as already noted, it does not allow for changes in the value of outstanding stocks of assets and liabilities.

In recent years Statistics Canada has devoted a good deal of effort to overcoming come of these problems and has, since 1977, been publishing estimated end of year values of assets and liabilities. In June 1985, this process of steady improvement in information about aggregate assets and liabilities took an important new step with the publication by Statistics Canada of *National Balance Sheet Accounts, 1961–1984*. This new publication provides aggregate and sectorial balance sheets on an annual basis back to 1961 and with similar detail to that presented in the Flow of Funds account.

Summary

A. Asset, Liability, and Balance Sheet

An asset is what someone owns. A liability is what someone owes. There are two types of assets, financial and real. A financial asset is always someone else's liability. An individual's wealth equals total financial and real assets less total liabilities. A balance sheet is a statement of assets and liabilities.

B. Definition and Nature of Money

Money is anything which is generally acceptable as a medium of exchange. In Canada today, money is narrowly defined (M1) as the sum of notes and coins in circulation plus demand deposits. Money is defined more broadly (M3) as M1 plus other (interest-bearing) bank deposits.

The monetary base is defined as the total liabilities of the Bank of Canada — notes outstanding plus chartered banks' reserve deposits with the Bank of Canada — together with the stock of coins in circulation with the public.

C. Main Balance Sheet Items

Main balance sheet items are summarized in Tables 4.2 and 4.3 above. The net value of financial assets in an economy is its net claims on the rest of the world. For Canada, that net values is negative. In other words, it is a net liability which is equal to the net claims of the rest of the world. The change in net financial assets of the economy equals savings minus investment (*S-I*), plus taxes minus government expenditure (*T-G*), plus imports minus exports (*IM-EX*), which is always zero.

The aggregate of net claims of the rest of the world, non-human wealth, monetary base, and human wealth is the wealth of the economy.

A major part of the macroeconomic analysis that we shall be doing centers on the relationships between stocks and flows. In particular, it centers on the connection between the stock of money and the flows of expenditure. The theory of aggregate demand which we shall be developing shortly builds on the concepts that have been defined and on the accounting frameworks that are dealt with in this and in the previous chapter.

D. Measuring Aggregate Balance Sheets in Canada

The main coordinator of information about aggregate balance sheets in Canada is the Bank of Canada and Statistics Canada. The Bank of Canada collects and publishes information about its own balance sheet, about those of the chartered banks, and about those of other financial institutions. Statistics Canada collects information on and publishes the *Flow of Funds Accounts*. These accounts give information about *changes* in stocks rather than stocks themselves and do not include information about valuation changes.

In 1985, Statistics Canada began publishing a comprehensive *National Balance Sheet Accounts*. The key stock variables needed for macroeconomic analysis are those concerning the monetary base and various definitions of the aggregate stock of money, all of which are collected frequently and reported in the *Bank of Canada Review*.

Review Questions

1. Which of the following are *stocks* and which are *flows?*
   (a) a pocket calculator worth $50
   (b) a bank deposit of $50
   (c) the *purchase* of a pocket calculator for $50
   (d) a car
   (e) the labor used to make a car
   (f) the consumption of gasoline by a car
   (g) the labor used to serve gasoline
   (h) an outstanding bank loan
   (i) the interest paid on a bank loan

2. Which items in a balance sheet are stocks and which are flows?

3. What is the difference between an asset and a liability?

4. Construct your own personal balance sheet. What are your total financial assets and liabilities? What are your real assets? What is your wealth?

5. Using the *Bank of Canada Review*, set out, for a recent date, the balance sheets of the Bank of Canada and of the chartered banks. What are the net financial assets, real assets, and wealth of the Bank of Canada and of the chartered banks?

6. Indicate how you would set about calculating the national debt of Canada.

7. How would you set about calculating the future tax liabilities of the government of Canada? Whose liabilities are these, and why?

8. Which of the following are "money" in Canada today?
  (a) Mastercard cards
  (b) deposits at Canada Trust
  (c) Federal Reserve $1 bills
  (d) Bank of England £1 notes
  (e) Bank of Canada $1 bills
  (f) demand deposits at chartered banks
  (g) savings accounts at trust companies
  (h) checks
  (i) bank loans
  (j) mortgages

9. Using data that you will find in the *Bank of Canada Review*, draw a time-series graph from 1970 to the present of: (a) M1 growth rate, and (b) M3 growth rate. Describe these two series. Highlight when each grew the fastest and the slowest. Compare and contrast the magnitude and the direction of change of each.

10. What are the links between aggregate balance sheets and aggregate income accounts? In describing the links, be explicit about flows and stocks.

11. Trace the effects on the balance sheets of the seven sectors of Table 4.2 of the following:

> You take a bank loan of $2000 from a chartered bank with which you buy a new computer costing $3000 from Radio Shack. You use your savings account to make up the difference between the bank loan and the purchase price. The Radio Shack computer is made in the United States with American-made component parts.

12. Show the effect of the above transaction on the aggregate income accounts. What are the effects on savings and investment? Show the effects also on the net changes in financial assets and show that these are consistent with the aggregate income accounts.

5
Measuring Inflation and Unemployment

Inflation and unemployment are two of the central variables which macroeconomic theory is designed to explain and that macroeconomic policy seeks to control. Your next preliminary tasks before embarking on a study of macroeconomic theory and policy are to:

a) Know the definition of inflation.
b) Understand the concept of a price index and its percentage rate of change.
c) Know how inflation is measured in Canada.
d) Know the definition of unemployment.
e) Know how unemployment is measured in Canada.

A. Definition of Inflation

Inflation may be defined, if somewhat loosely, as the percentage rate at which the general level of prices is changing. We refer to the "general level of prices" as the *price level*. You will notice that the dimension of inflation is the percentage rate of change per unit of time. The concept of the general level of prices is a little bit vague, and we will give more precision to that term below.

First of all, it is important to notice that inflation is an *on-going process* — that is, a process of prices rising on a more or less continuous basis rather than on a once-and-for-all basis. Figure 5.1 illustrates this distinction. The price level is measured on the vertical axis, and time is measured in years on the horizontal axis.

**Figure 5.1
The Distinction
Between Inflation
and a Once-and-for-All
Rise in the Price
Level**

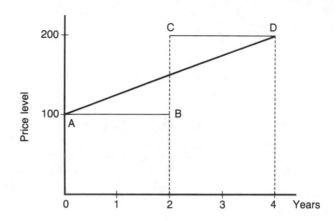

The economy that moves directly along the line AD is one which experiences inflation. The economy that moves along the line ABCD experiences a once-and-for-all rise in the price level in year 2.

Looking at Figure 5.1, suppose that the economy started out in year 0 with a price level equal to 100. If, over the four-year period shown, the price level rose gradually and continuously to the level 200 (as indicated by the continuous, upward-sloping straight line), then we would want to describe that four-year period as a period of inflation. In contrast, suppose that the economy started out at the price level 100 and had a stable level of prices, that is, with prices remaining at level 100 all the way through the first two years. Then suppose that at the beginning of year 2, there was a sudden jump in the price level, from 100 to 200. Suppose thereafter that prices remained at the level 200 and were stable at that level for the remaining two years. We would not normally want to describe this second economy as having had an inflationary four years. Indeed, prices would have been stable in that economy for the first two years at a level of 100 and stable for the second two years at a level of 200.

It is true that the price level starts out at 100 and finishes up at 200 in both cases. However, in the first case, inflation was present in the economy throughout the four-year period. In the second case, we could think of there having been a single instant of inflation when the price level doubled (from 100 to 200) at the beginning of year 2, whereas for the rest of the four-year period the economy was characterized by stable prices. That is, there was a once-and-for-all rise in the price level at the beginning of year 2. In practice, the distinction between a once-and-for-all rise in the price level and inflation may be somewhat blurred because it is possible that a shock to the economy that produces a once-and-for-all rise in prices may have effects that are somewhat drawn out. Thus, although the distinction between inflation and a once-and-for-all rise in prices is an important one in principle, it may in practice often be hard to distinguish one from the other.

The second feature of the phenomenon of inflation that is worth emphasizing at this stage is that it is a rise in the *general* level of prices and not a rise in some particular price or group of prices. The economy may, for example, be experiencing rapid increases in the prices of food and yet not be undergoing an inflation. The rapid increases in food prices may be offset by rapid decreases in prices of some other commodities such as, for example, electronic data processing equipment, video games, fuel-efficient cars, and the like. Such price movements, even though they may be very rapid and of great social consequence, are not inflation. They are changes in relative prices.

In order to give more precision to the meaning of inflation, it is now necessary to give more precision to the meaning of the term *the general level of prices* or *price level.*

B. Price Index and Its Percentage Rate of Change

There can be no unique measure of the price level. The prices of some commodities rise faster than others, and the prices of some things even fall. Movements in the price level can only be calculated once we have fixed *the basket of goods* to which the price level refers.

A price index measures the amount that would have to be paid for a specific basket of goods in the current period compared with what would have had to have been paid for that same basket in some previous period, known as the *base period*. The basket of goods used may be representative of typical consumption patterns in the base period or in the current period. The value of the index in the base period is defined to be 100. Percentage changes in the value of a price index from one year to the next measure the rate of inflation according to the particular index being used.

In order to gain a more concrete understanding of the ideas just set out in summary form, it will be best if we move straight to the next task and illustrate the above propositions.

C. Measuring Inflation in Canada

There are two widely used price indexes for measuring inflation in Canada today. One is known as the Consumer Price Index (CPI), and the other is known as the Gross National Expenditure (GNE) Deflator.

(i) The Consumer Price Index

The Consumer Price Index (which is calculated and published by Statistics Canada each month) is an index which attempts to measure movements in the prices of goods and services which are typically consumed by a group of urban Canadian families.

The index is a weighted average of price movements of approximately 490 items. The items themselves and the weights attached to them are chosen to be representative of the goods and services usually bought by urban families. The present basket of goods and services is based on data from the 1978 Family Expenditure Survey.

Each month, price statistics are collected from 64 urban centers. An urban center is defined as a main labor market area of continuously built-up centers of population of 30 000 or more inhabitants in 1978. Prices are collected from selected outlets with the average number of prices collected each month being greater than 130 000. An index is calculated using the following formula:

$$\frac{P_1^t Q_1^0 + P_2^t Q_2^0 + \ldots + P_{490}^t Q_{490}^0}{P_1^0 Q_1^0 + P_2^0 Q_2^0 + \ldots + P_{490}^0 Q_{490}^0} \times 100$$

Although this formula looks formidable, it is in fact very simple. Let us take it piece by piece. The numerator

$$P_1^t Q_1^0 + P_2^t Q_2^0 + \ldots + P_{490}^t Q_{490}^0$$

represents the total amount of money that it would cost in month t at the prices ruling in month t to buy the bundle of commodities which is being used to weight the prices. The term P_1^t is simply the price of commodity class one in a month t, and the number Q_1^0 is the number of units of commodity class one in the basket of goods that is being valued. If we simply add up the total outlay on each of the 490 commodity classes in the index, then we arrive at the number of dollars that would have to be spent to buy the basket of commodities at the prices prevailing in month t. (The dots in the middle of the expression stand for commodities 3 to 489.)

The denominator of the index number calculation

$$P_1^0 Q_1^0 + P_2^0 Q_2^0 + \ldots + P_{490}^0 Q_{490}^0$$

is the amount of money that would have had to have been spent in the base period to purchase the index basket of commodities valued at the prices ruling in the base period. The term P_1^0 is the price of commodity class one in the base period, period 0. So, $P_1^0 Q_1^0$ is the outlay on commodities in commodity class one in the base period. Adding the outlays on all commodities that make up the 490 commodity classes gives the dollar sum of money that would have had to have been spent purchasing the index bundle of commodities in the base period.

The ratio of the outlay in month t to the base period outlay multiplied by 100 gives the index number for the Consumer Price Index in month t. If that index number is 100, then prices have been constant. If the index is greater than 100, prices have risen; and if less than 100, prices have fallen.

Various subsidiary index numbers are available for food, all items excluding food, housing, clothing, transportation, health and personal care, recreation, reading and education, and tobacco and alcohol. In addition, separate CPIs are published for 15 urban centers.

A detailed description of the calculation of the Consumer Price Index is given in *The Consumer Price Index Reference Paper, Concepts and Procedures* (Ottawa: Statistics Canada, 1982).

(ii) Gross National Expenditure (GNE) Deflator

The Consumer Price Index seeks to measure movements in the prices of a basket of goods which would typically be consumed by an average urban Canadian family. In contrast, the GNE Deflator measures movements in the general level of prices of the entire basket of goods and services produced in the Canadian economy.

If you think of national income, measured by the expenditure approach, as being equal to the sum of the values of all the goods and services produced, then you have the starting point for the GNE Deflator. In order to calculate that total, it is necessary to take the quantity of each good, Q_i, and multiply it by its price, P_i. We then have to add up the resulting values over all the goods and services in the economy. This gives gross national expenditure in current dollars. That is, gross national expenditure in current dollars equals

$$P_1^t Q_1^t + P_2^t Q_2^t + \ldots + P_n^t Q_n^t$$

The P's and Q's in this formula stand for the prices and quantities of the entire production of final goods and services in the economy, and not simply for that typical urban consumer's basket that was referred to in the preceding section on the Consumer Price Index. It includes the typical urban consumer's expenditure as well as expenditure on all other consumer goods, capital goods (investment), government purchases of goods and services, exports and imports.

Now, instead of valuing gross national expenditure by multiplying the quantity of each good consumed in a given year by the price of the good in that year, we could multiply consumption in a given year by the prices that prevailed in some base year, for example, year 0. If we pursued such a calculation, we would calculate gross national expenditure in constant dollars equals

$$P_1^0 Q_1^t + P_2^0 Q_2^t + \ldots + P_n^0 Q_n^t$$

This is a measure of the value of gross national expenditure in year t but valued at the prices prevailing in the base year, year 0.

If we divide the constant price GNE figure into the current price figure, we obtain the GNE Deflator:

$$\text{GNE Deflator} = \frac{\text{GNE in current dollars}}{\text{GNE in constant dollars}} \times 100$$

The GNE Deflator is sometimes called the GNE *Implicit* Deflator. The deflator is implicit because we arrive at it from the evaluation of the gross national expenditure on the basis of two alternative sets of prices.

(iii) The Percentage Rate of Change in the Price Index as a Measure of Inflation

We can now define Canadian inflation precisely: Canadian inflation is the percentage rate of change over a specified unit of time (usually a year) in either the Consumer Price Index or GNE Deflator.

For example, in December 1984, the Consumer Price Index was 124.1. In December of the year earlier, 1983, the index was 119.6. To calculate the rate of inflation as measured by the Consumer Price Index for the year from December 1983 to December 1984, perform the following calculation:

$$\text{Inflation} = \frac{(124.1 - 119.6)}{119.6} \times 100$$
$$= 3.8\% \text{ per annum}$$

We could perform a similar calculation using the GNE Deflator.

The Consumer Price Index is available monthly and gives a continuous monitoring of the economy's inflation rate. The GNE Deflator is available quarterly. Movements in these indexes do not coincide, but they are not excessively divergent. The table in the appendix to Chapter 2 lists the rate of inflation in Canada each year from 1920 to 1984 as measured by these indexes, and Figure 2.1 of Chapter 2 shows how they behave.

For convenience, the inflation rates as measured by the two price indexes over the last ten years are reproduced here as Table 5.1. The broad picture presented by each of these two index numbers is of course the same. Inflation was at its strongest in 1974-1975 and again in 1979-1981. Inflation is lower in 1983-1984 than earlier. The detailed picture given by each index is, however, different. In particular, the Consumer Price Index seems to suggest a faster inflation rate than the GNE Deflator. There are several reasons for this, three of which are worth highlighting.

The first reason for the different measured inflation rates arises from the weights used to compile the index numbers. The Consumer Price Index uses fixed weights. This means that the attempts by consumers to substitute away from relatively more expensive items towards relatively less expensive items are not captured in the CPI.

TABLE 5.1
A Comparison of Inflation Rates as Measured by the Consumer Price Index (CPI) and Gross National Expenditure (GNE) Deflator

YEAR	CPI	GNE Deflator	CPI LESS GNE Deflator
1974	10.9	15.3	−4.4
1975	10.8	10.7	0.1
1976	7.5	9.6	−2.1
1977	8.0	7.4	0.6
1978	8.8	6.7	2.1
1979	9.2	10.3	−1.1
1980	10.2	11.4	−1.2
1981	12.5	10.6	1.9
1982	10.8	10.3	0.5
1983	5.8	5.3	0.5
1984	4.4	2.8	1.6

Source: Appendix to Chapter 2.

Perhaps an example will make this clearer. Suppose that oranges and apples were consumed in equal quantities in the base year. Suppose that between the base year and the current year, the prices of oranges have doubled, but the prices of apples have increased by only 20 percent. It would be expected that this would lead to a substitution away from oranges towards apples so that, in the current year, more apples and fewer oranges are consumed compared with the base year. If an index was calculated of the price of fruit that assumed that equal quantities of apples and oranges were consumed in both the base year and the current year, then that would tend to overstate the rise in expenditure (the rise in the average price of) fruit. If the weights attaching to oranges and apples were changed, however, in accordance with the changed spending patterns in the current year, then the substitution away from the now more expensive oranges towards the now less expensive apples would be captured. The CPI presumes unchanged weights, whereas the GNE Deflator allows for substitutions to take advantage of relatively less expensive items.

The second reason for the differences in the two indexes reflects difficulties that the Consumer Price Index has in coping with quality changes and with the introduction of new products. Again, an example will perhaps make this clear. Suppose that between 1983 and 1984 the price of cars rose by 10 percent. Suppose also, however, that improvements took place in the fuel efficiency of their engines so that their gas consumption was down by 5 percent on the average between the two years. How much have car prices really increased during that year? The answer is that they have increased by less than 10 percent.

But how much less? How can one allow adequately for quality improvements of that type? With sufficient ingenuity we could presumably figure out the exact answer to the question and allow for quality improvements in this case. There will be other cases, however, where allowance for quality improvements will be virtually impossible. For example, over the years the quality of the picture and sound delivered by a television set has improved dramatically. How should that be allowed for in calculating the true rate of inflation of television prices? This question (and similar ones in connection with many thousands of other products) are hard to answer and, as a result, there is a general presumption that the Consumer Price Index does not adequately allow for gradual improvements in product quality.

The third reason for the difference in the performance of these two indexes lies in the way in which each measures the cost of owner-occupied housing. Big movements in interest rates show up quickly in the Consumer Price Index but are allowed to be reflected in the GNE Deflator only to the extent that they change the rental rates on houses of comparable quality to owner-occupied houses.

The difference in the inflation rates of the CPI and the GNE Deflator is shown in column 3 of Table 5.1. Since 1974, this difference has ranged from − 4.4 in 1974 to 2.1 percentage points in 1978. The reason why the GNE Deflator inflation rate differs from that of the CPI lies mainly in the fact that it measures the prices of a much broader basket of goods, one that includes capital goods as well as those goods bought by government and net exports. The difference in the GNE Deflator and the Consumer Price Index, then, can be seen as reflecting changes in the relative price of consumer goods to all other goods.

We will be analyzing the determination of the rate of inflation as measured by the GNE Deflator in our theoretical analysis later in this book. However, since movements in the two index numbers are broadly in line with each other, you can, for most purposes, think of the analysis as relating to the Consumer Price Index as well, although there may be some specific exercises for which such a presumption would not be warranted.

Let us now turn our attention to the definition and measurement of unemployment.

D. Definition of Unemployment

A person is said to be unemployed when he or she is able and willing to work and is available for work (that is, the person is actively searching for employment) but does not have work. The number of people unemployed in an economy is the number of people whom that description fits. The unemployment rate in an economy is the number of unemployed expressed as a percentage of the total labor force. The total labor force is defined as the number of people employed plus the number of people unemployed.

You will notice that the definition of unemployment says nothing at all about the reasons for unemployment. It simply defines an aggregate or a percent rate based on an explicit and objective criterion for classifying individuals. Much economic analysis of the causes of unemployment and fluctuations in its rate uses terms such as *voluntary* and *involuntary* to describe different types of unemployment.

We shall not have any reason to use such definitions. It may be very interesting for some purposes to know whether a person is voluntarily or involuntarily unemployed. From our point of view, however, it is irrelevant. We are going to be concerned with an objective analysis of the factors that lead to variations in unemployment and to develop theories which will enable us to predict the consequences for unemployment of certain well-defined policies. It will not be necessary for us to enquire into the state of mind of the unemployed person concerning the voluntary or involuntary nature of the unemployment being experienced.

E. Measuring Unemployment in Canada

Unemployment figures are calculated by Statistics Canada, and are published each month in a publication called *The Labour Force*. A considerable amount of detail concerning the anatomy of unemployment is provided by Statistics Canada. Unemployment is classified by province, sex and age, industry and occupation, class of worker, duration of unemployment, type of job sought, activity prior to looking for work, job search methods used, reason for leaving last job, and whether the worker is looking or not looking for work.

All the unemployment figures are based on information generated from a sample survey of households known as the Labour Force Survey. Each month interviews are carried out in approximately 56 000 households across Canada. The Labour Force Survey began in November 1945 and has from time to time been upgraded and improved. A detailed account of the existing methods employed in the Labour Force Survey is published in *Methodology of the Canadian Labour Force Survey 1976*, Catalogue 71-526 (Ottawa: Statistics Canada, October 1977).

In order for a person to be recorded as unemployed in the Canadian Labour Force Survey, the following characteristics have to be satisfied. The unemployed persons are those who during a specific week (referred to as the reference week) (a) were without work, had actually looked for work in the last 4 weeks and were available for work; or (b) had not actively looked for work in the past 4 weeks but had been laid off for 26 weeks or less and were available for work; or (c) had not actively looked for work in the past 4 weeks but had a new job to start in 4 weeks or less from the reference week and were available for work.

To calculate the unemployment rate, the total number of persons that fit the above definition of unemployment are added to the total of employed to obtain an estimate of the total labor force, and then the unemployed are calculated as a percentage of the total labor force.

No questions are asked concerning the wages at which a person would be willing to work. Thus, although the Labour Force Survey counts the number of people who are able and willing to work and who are available for work, it does not check whether there was a willingness to work at any particular wage rate. Fairly clearly, if wages were "high enough," just about everyone would be willing to work, and in that case the entire population not in employment could be regarded as unemployed. Equally clearly, that would not be a very helpful definition of the concept of unemployment. What we really would like to know is the total number of people who are able and willing to work and available to work on terms and conditions currently available. There is a presumption, although there is no explicit means of checking it, that the respondents to the Labour Force Survey are implicitly indicating a willingness to work on currently available terms and conditions.

A further shortcoming of the measured unemployment rate arises from the way in which it treats so-called discouraged workers and those in part-time employment who would prefer to be in full-time employment. Discouraged workers are people who are unemployed in the sense that they would be willing to work on currently available terms and conditions, and are available to work but have given up the active search for work because of their discouraging experience. This type of (unmeasured) unemployment is likely to be most serious when the unemployment rate is high, as it has been for some time. Those in part-time employment who would ideally want to have full-time employment may be thought of as being partially unemployed. The measured unemployment rate misses the fraction of the work effort that such individuals would be willing to supply on current terms and conditions. Broader measures of unemployment than those calculated on the basis of the Labour Force Survey, which included discouraged workers and partial unemployment of part-time workers, clearly would show the unemployment rate to be higher than that actually measured. It is likely, however, that the broad up-and-down movements in the broader measure would be similar to those in the official measure.

Summary

A. Definition of Inflation
Inflation is defined as the percentage rate of change in a price index.

B. Price Index and its Percentage Rate of Change
A price index is calculated by valuing a specific basket of goods at the prices prevailing in a base period and at the prices prevailing in

a subsequent period. The price index is the ratio of the values of these two baskets multiplied by 100. The rate of inflation is measured as the percentage rate of change of the index.

C. Measuring Inflation in Canada

There are two commonly used price indexes in Canada: the Consumer Price Index (CPI), and the Gross National Expenditure (GNE) Deflator. The CPI is based on a fixed basket of goods and services typical of the consumption patterns of urban households. The GNE Deflator is calculated on the basis of a current basket of goods and services, and includes all consumption plus investment purchases and net exports.

D. Definition of Unemployment

Unemployment is defined as the number of people able and willing to work and available for work but not having work.

E. Measuring Unemployment in Canada

Unemployment is measured in Canada by the Labour Force Survey, conducted each month. The survey records as unemployed all those who did not work during the reference week, who made specific efforts to find a job within the preceding 4 weeks and who were available for work during the reference week. It also includes as unemployed those who were waiting to be called back to a job from which they had been laid off for 26 weeks or less as well as those waiting to start a new job within 4 weeks.

Review Questions

1. What is inflation?

2. What are the two commonly used measures of inflation in Canada?

3. How is the Consumer Price Index in Canada calculated? What is the Consumer Price Index designed to measure?

4. Using a recent *Bank of Canada Review*, find the Consumer Price Index (CPI) for the period from 1970 to the present. Be sure you are consistent and collect either mid-year (June) or end-of-year (December) figures.
   (a) What is the base year of the CPI that you have collected?
   (b) Calculate the percentage rate of change of the CPI each year since 1970 and explain exactly what it measures.

5. What does the GNE Deflator measure and how is it calculated? Why is it called an *implicit* deflator?

6. From a recent *Bank of Canada Review*, collect the GNE Deflator for the period from 1970 to the present. Calculate the percentage rate of change of the GNE Deflator. Explain exactly what this series measures.

7. The table in the appendix to Chapter 2 gives a comparison of inflation rates as measured by the CPI and the GNE Deflator. Plot these time-series graphs for the period since 1974. Describe these series. Highlight the higher measure of inflation. Compare and contrast inflation as measured by these two series.

8. What is unemployment?

9. Exactly how does Statistics Canada define unemployment?

10. How is unemployment in Canada measured?

11. The unemployment rate in Canada varies from province to province. Use the Statistics Canada publication *The Labour Force* to collect time-series data starting in 1967 on the unemployment rate of the province in which you live and for Canada as a whole. Plot these two time-series as graphs. Describe, compare, and contrast them. Does your province have higher or lower unemployment than Canada on the average? Try to think of reasons why your province differs in the way that it does from the national average.

12. What are the main problems with the way unemployment is measured in Canada?

6

Patterns
in the
Data

The final chapter of this section is different from the other three. It does not deal with the problem of measuring a single macroeconomic variable (or group of variables). Rather, it is concerned with the problem of observing and discerning patterns in the evolution of the economic aggregates and in the relationships among variables. In short, it is concerned with the business cycle.[1]

Until the middle 1930s, the term *business cycle* was used to describe the phenomenon which students of short-term movements in economic aggregates sought to explain and understand. Scholars saw their task as one of understanding the general recurrent ups and downs in economic activity *viewed as an ongoing process*. In 1936, however, with the publication by John Maynard Keynes of *The General Theory of Employment, Interest and Money*,[2] there was a fundamental redirection of research effort. What Keynes did was to change the question which students of aggregate economic phenomena tried to answer. Instead of trying to understand the recurrent ups and

---

[1] This chapter draws heavily on, and in places will be recognized as a paraphrase of, parts of the important paper "Understanding Business Cycles," by Robert E. Lucas, Jr., in *Stabilization of the Domestic and International Economy*, Carnegie-Rochester Conference Series on Public Policy, Vol. 5, Karl Brunner and Allan H. Meltzer, eds. (Amsterdam: North Holland Publishing Co., 1977.)

[2] John Maynard Keynes, *The General Theory of Employment, Interest and Money* (London: MacMillan & Co. Ltd., 1936).

downs of economic activity viewed as an ongoing process, Keynes redirected our research efforts to an apparently easier question, namely, that of the determination of output, employment, prices, interest rates, etc., viewed *at a point in time*, taking the past history of the economy and expectations about the future as given.

At about the same time as Keynes's simplification enabled scholars to direct their attention to the simpler question of the determination of the aggregate economic variables at a point in time, strides were being made in the mathematical formulation and statistical testing of economic theories, notably by the Dutch economist Jan Tinbergen. As a result of the pioneering efforts of Keynes and Tinbergen, subsequent scholars were able to develop a considerable refined body of knowledge which came to be known as *macroeconomics*. In this new macroeconomic analysis, there seemed to be no special place for business cycle theory. Indeed, as far as Keynes himself was concerned, the job of explaining what determined the values of economic variables at a moment in time is almost the same thing as explaining the business cycle (or *trade cycle* as it is known in Europe). Keynes said that

> since we claim to have shown . . . what determines the volume of employment at any time, it follows, if we are right, that our theory must be capable of explaining the phenomena of the Trade Cycle.[3]

Further, not only did it appear that there was no need for a special theory of the business cycle, it even seemed as if the earlier attempts to find a theory of the business cycle were hopelessly muddled and confused in comparison with the clarity that had been brought to the task of understanding the determination of the aggregate economic variables at a point in time.

It was not until the early 1970s, with the seminal work of Robert E. Lucas, Jr. of the University of Chicago, that attention was redirected to the problem of understanding more than what determines income, employment, prices, etc., at a point in time, given their past history. Lucas suggested that the bigger question of what *process* determines the evolution of the aggregate economic variables over time had to be tackled head on if we were to develop a deep enough understanding of aggregate economic phenomena for us to be able to design policy arrangements that would stand some chance of improving matters.

As Lucas sees things, and as will be elaborated more fully later in this book, the task of understanding what determines income, employment, and prices at a moment in time, given their past history,

---

[3] *Ibid.*, p. 313.

cannot be accomplished without *analyzing the entire ongoing cyclical process* that determines these aggregate economic variables. The key reason for this is that what people do today depends on their expectations of what is going to happen in the future. To formulate an expectation as to what is going to happen in the future, people have to do the best they can to assess how the economy will evolve in the future. This means that their current action will depend upon their expectations of future actions by themselves and others. Now it is evident that the only guide that is available concerning what will happen in the future is what has happened in the past. This means that if present actions depend on expectations of the future, they must also depend upon what has happened in the past. Only by analyzing an entire economic process — past, present and future — shall we be able to understand what is happening at any given moment.

The redirection of research effort in macroeconomics by Keynes was not, in our view, a blind alley. Rather, it was a necessary stage in the process of developing a satisfactory theory of the business cycle. Not until we had made a great deal of progress with the simpler question posed by Keynes were we able to go back to the harder question to which Lucas has now redirected us.

To progress through the subject matter of modern macroeconomics all the way to the new theories of the business cycle will take the next two parts of this book. Not until we get to Chapter 23 will it be possible to summarize our current understanding of what determines business cycles.

In order to pave the way, this chapter will take you through five tasks that are designed to enable you to understand what we mean by business cycles. These tasks are to:

a) Know the definition of the business cycle.
b) Understand the concept of autocorrelation.
c) Understand the concept of co-movement.
d) Know the properties of the business cycle.
e) Know the features of the Canadian business cycle.

A. Definition of the Business Cycle

Although business cycles have been studied for well over a hundred years, it was not until the 1940s that a clear definition of business cycles emerged, due to the efforts of a group of outstanding and careful observers of cycles working under the auspices of the National Bureau of Economic Research in New York. Wesley Clare Mitchell and Arthur F. Burns (Burns subsequently became Chairman of the Board of Governors of the Federal Reserve System) defined the business cycle as follows:

Business cycles are a type of fluctuation found in the aggregate economic activity of nations that organize their work mainly in business enterprises: A cycle consists of expansions occurring at about the same time in many economic activities, followed by similarly general recessions, contractions and revivals which merge into the expansion phase of the next cycle; this sequence of changes is recurrent but not periodic; in duration business cycles vary from more than one year to ten or twelve years; they are not divisible into shorter cycles of similar character with amplitudes approximating their own.[4]

Let us dissect this definition a little bit. Three aspects of the definition are worth highlighting. First, let us ask, What is a business cycle a cycle in? The answer to that is given in the first part of the definition: the business cycle is a cycle (or fluctuation) in aggregate economic activity. Although there are several alternative ways in which "aggregate economic activity" may be measured, the most natural comprehensive measure is the level of real income (output or expenditure) — real GNP. Such a measure summarizes all the many individual producing and spending activities in the economy. Because real GNP, on the average, grows from one year to the next, it is necessary in defining the cycle to abstract from that growth trend and define the cycle as "deviations of real GNP from trend." By regarding the deviations of real GNP from trend as defining the cycle, it is possible to examine the ups and downs of other aggregate variables in relation to or *with reference to* the cycle in real GNP.[5]

The second thing to notice about the definition of the cycle is that it involves two turning points, an upper turning point and a lower turning point; and two phases, an expansion phase and a contraction phase. In Table 6.1 deviations of real GNP from trend are calculated by subtracting the trend value from the actual value of real GNP. The trend growth rate is taken as 4 percent per year. The deviations from trend trace out a business cycle. Figure 6.1 illustrates that hypothetical business cycle. The upper turning point is often referred to as the *cyclical peak* and the lower turning point as the *cyclical trough*. The movement from the peak to the trough is the *contraction*, and the movement from trough back to peak is the *expansion*. If a contraction is particularly severe it is referred to as a *recession*. Technically, a recession is defined as occurring when real GNP falls for two successive quarters. An even more severe contraction and prolonged trough would be known as a *depression* or, if particularly

---

[4] This definition is from Arthur F. Burns and Wesley Clare Mitchell, *Measuring Business Cycles* (New York: National Bureau of Economic Research, 1946), p. 3.

[5] In their pioneering work on measuring the business cycle, the National Bureau of Economic Research economists (referred to above) developed a concept of the *reference cycle*, which was somewhat more general than simply using deviations of real GNP from trend. Their methods, however, to some degree involve judgment, and to describe them and fully appreciate them would divert us too far.

TABLE 6.1
Calculating Deviations of Real GNP from Trend

| YEAR | REAL GNP | | |
	ACTUAL VALUE	TREND VALUE	DEVIATION FROM TREND
0	101.2	100.0	+1.2
1	94.9	104.0	−9.1
2	101.4	108.2	−6.8
3	102.4	112.5	−10.1
4	109.4	117.0	−7.6
5	126.0	121.7	+4.3
6	134.7	126.5	+8.2
7	147.8	131.6	+16.2
8	144.0	136.9	+7.1
9	152.7	142.3	+10.4
10	150.8	148.0	+2.8
11	155.9	153.9	+2.0
12	151.7	160.1	−8.4

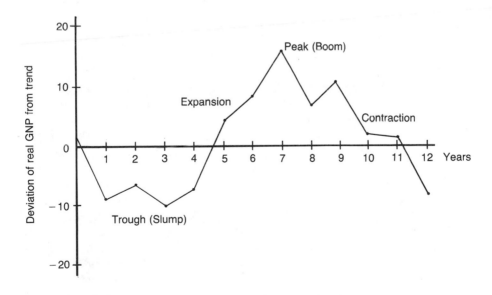

Figure 6.1
A Hypothetical Business Cycle

A cycle in the deviation of real GNP from trend begins in the contraction phase, reaches a trough (or slump), moves through an expansion to a peak (or boom) and then turns into a further contraction phase.

severe, the prefix *great* would be attached to it. The picture of the hypothetical business cycle shown in Figure 6.1 gives just one complete down-and-up movement in the deviation of real GNP from trend.

The third feature of the definition of the business cycle emphasizes the fact that cycles are not regular *periodic* ups and downs (such as the motion of a child's swing) but are *irregular* though *recurrent* ups and downs, the duration of which (measured from trough to trough) could run from something slightly more than one year to as long as ten or twelve years. To see how we might characterize this in a simple way involves introducing a technical idea which will be developed in the next section of this chapter — the concept of autocorrelation.

The fourth and final feature of the definition of the cycle given above — that "they are not divisible into shorter cycles of similar character with amplitudes approximating their own" — is simply designed to capture the idea that the cycle is a basic unit of observation and analysis. It is not divisible into smaller similar patterns.

Let us now turn to the first of the two technical tasks that face us in this chapter.

B. Autocorrelation

This section and the next one deal with technical matters. They do so, however, in a non-technical way.[6] It is worthwhile becoming familiar with the concept of autocorrelation because it will give you a more precise, and at the same time very simple, way of viewing a process that may be used to describe the recurrent but non-periodic ups and downs in economic activity that characterize the business cycle.

Two key ideas are combined in the concept of autocorrelation. First, *the present is influenced by the past*; second, *the present is not completely predictable from knowledge of the past*. An alternative way of capturing the same two ideas would be to say that the current value of some variable may be better predicted by knowledge of its past values but may not be exactly predicted on the basis of such knowledge.

There are many examples in everyday life of autocorrelation. One obvious one is the state of the weather. Wet days and dry days tend to go in runs. If you were to try predicting tomorrow's weather without using refined meterological observations and methods, one possible rule might be to predict that tomorrow will be much like today. If today is wet, you predict that tomorrow will also be wet. If today is dry you predict that tomorrow will be dry. Such a prediction will, of course, often be wrong. It turns out, however, that it will be right

---

[6] If you want a more technical though still simplified treatment of this topic you should work through the appendix to this chapter.

more often than it is wrong. It will certainly do better than flipping a coin and calling "dry" for heads and "wet" for tails. How much better it will do will depend in part on where you live and what the longer term climatic patterns are. Nevertheless, the basic idea of predicting tomorrow's weather on the basis of today's is a sound one (though not the best available) and one which exploits the auto-correlation in weather patterns.

Another example concerns the movements of waves on the ocean surface. Sitting at the ocean side you can predict the pattern and timing of the wave movements breaking on the shoreline by suppos-ing that the next wave will look much like the one that has just preceded it. You will not be exactly right because the wind patterns and the interaction of the waves ensure that no wave is exactly like its predecessor. There is, however, a strong resemblance.

A third example would be the movement of a child's swing or rocking horse. If you wanted to predict the extent of the movement of the horse or the height attained by the swing on a given movement, predicting an outcome similar to that which occurred on the previous rock or swing would be fairly accurate. It would not be exactly right because you wouldn't know exactly how much work the child was doing to keep the motion of the swing or horse at a constant level. An unpredictable surge of effort on the child's part would send the swing or horse on a more extreme course, whereas an unpredicted slackening off of effort would cause the horse or swing to come closer to a rest position.

These are all examples of the existence of autocorrelation in the behavior of variables that we commonly observe in the ordinary course of life. We need to be more precise, however, in specifying how the current value of some variable relates to its previous value or values. The simplest case would be where the value of a variable at a given point in time depends only on its own value at the previous point in time. (The units in which time is measured will vary from case to case and could be as short as an instant or as long as a decade. In economics we typically think of units of time as coming either in calendar quarters or years.) Such a case is given the special name *first-order autocorrelation*. If the current value of a variable depends on its own values at the previous point in time *and* at the time before that, then it is given the special name *second-order autocorrelation*. This idea clearly can be generalized to permit any degree of influence of the past on the present.

The aspect of autocorrelation having to do with imperfect pre-dictability simply reflects the obvious fact that the world is a fairly complicated place and is not capable of prediction by the application of simple (mechanical) rules linking current values of variables to their own past values. A different way of saying the same thing is that, to some extent, the world is *random* (or *stochastic*).

Let us now use the notion of autocorrelation to describe the evolution of the variable y from one year to the next. The variable y would be autocorrelated if next year's value of y could be better predicted, although not exactly predicted, from knowledge of the current (and perhaps some previous) year's value of y. We can capture this idea by writing an equation that says

$$y_t = 25 + 0.75y_{t-1} + e_t \qquad \textbf{(6.1)}$$

The variable y_t represents the value of y in year t. The same variable with the subscript $t - 1$ represents the value of y in the previous year. The variable e_t represents all the random unpredictable influences that affect y that are not predictable on the basis of knowledge of previous values of y. What this equation says (and it is of course just an example) is that the value of y in a given year will be equal to three-quarters of its previous year's value, plus 25, plus some unpredictable random amounts.

Such an equation, as we shall see in the final section of this chapter, fairly well describes the movements in the deviations of real GNP from its trend.

You have now discovered what autocorrelation is. Autocorrelation simply means that the value of some particular variable at some particular date is related to its own value at some earlier date. In the above example, y at date t is related to y at date t-1. The relationship is not perfect. There is a randomness that loosens the link between y at date t and at date t-1. In rough terms, an autocorrelated series is one that shows systematic, recurrent up-and-down movements.

It is important to realize that *describing* the path of deviations of real GNP from trend by a low-order stochastic difference equation is not the same thing as *understanding* what *causes* the movements in those deviations — that is, what causes the business cycle. The description is simply a neat and convenient way of thinking about the process. It also directs our attention to potential explanations in the sense that it alerts us to the idea that we shall have to find, in any theory of the business cycle, two things:

(1) A source of, or more generally, sources of, random disturbance to the economy.
(2) Systematic sources of inertia causing movements of the deviations of real GNP from trend (and other aggregates) from one period to another to be gradual — that is, to display autocorrelation.

Although you are now able to describe the recurrent ups and downs in the deviations of real GNP from trend in very simple terms, you need to be aware of some other technical language that will help you to talk about broader aspects of the business cycle. That is the next task.

C. Co-movement

In fully characterizing business cycles, it is going to be necessary to talk about the way in which different variables move in relation to each other. That is, we shall want to be able to say how employment and unemployment, prices and wages, money and interest rates all move in relationship to the movements in real income. In other words, we want to be able to characterize the co-movements of various pair-wise combinations of variables.

There are four features of co-movements among variables that may be identified. First, co-movements may be *procyclical* or *counter-cyclical*. A procyclical co-movement is a movement in a variable that has broadly the same cyclical pattern as the variable with which it is being compared. It tends to rise when the reference variable rises and to fall when the reference variable falls. Since the reference variable for the business cycle is deviations of GNP from trend, pro-cyclical variables are those that rise as GNP rises above trend and fall as GNP falls below trend.

A countercyclical co-movement is a movement in one variable that is in the opposite direction to the movement in the reference variable. Thus, a countercyclical variable is one that falls as real GNP rises above its trend and that rises as real GNP falls below its trend.

Usually, variables do not exactly move in a procyclical or counter-cyclical manner. They tend to either *lead* or *lag* the reference variable. This is the second feature of co-movement that we need to identify. Figure 6.2 illustrates leading and lagging procyclical variables. Suppose that the curve labelled (a) represents the cycle in deviations of real GNP from trend. Then the line (b) would represent a variable

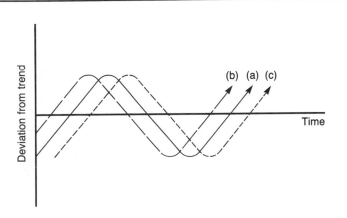

**Figure 6.2
Leading and Lagging
Procyclical
Co-Movements**

The three series plotted here have procyclical co-movements. If (a) describes the reference cycle of real income deviations from trend then the variable (b) leads the cycle in income and the variable (c) lags that cycle.

**Figure 6.3
Countercyclical
Co-Movements**

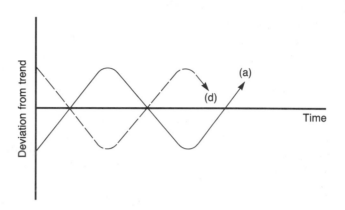

The variable marked (d) displays perfect countercyclical co-movement with the variable marked (a).

that leads the cycle, and (c) would represent a variable that lags the cycle. Both variables are generally procyclical. That is, they generally move up with rises in GNP above its trend and down with falls in GNP below its trend, but they don't move at exactly the same time. Figure 6.3 illustrates a countercyclical co-movement. If (a) again is the reference cycle then (d) would be the path of a variable which moves countercyclically.

You will recognize that there is a potential element of ambiguity as to whether a variable is countercyclical or procyclical if it leads or lags the reference variable by "too much." You could, as a matter of description, regard a variable that is exactly countercyclical as one that is procyclical but lagged by half a cycle. That would seem to be using language in an awkward way, however. We don't think of leads and lags as being as big as half a cycle.

A third feature of co-movement has to do with the *amplitude* of fluctuation in one variable relative to another. Roughly speaking, the amplitude of fluctuation in a variable is the distance from the average value to its peak value, or average value to its trough value. Figure 6.4 illustrates this. Suppose that the line labelled (a) measures the percentage deviation from trend of real GNP. The thin lines marked (b) and (c) are examples of variables that display smaller amplitude (b), and larger amplitude (c) than the fluctuations in real GNP about its trend (a). Of course, there has to be a unit-free method of comparing different variables. It would not do to measure deviations of real GNP from trend in billions of dollars and interest rates in percentages, for example. The most natural unit-free measure is the percentage deviation of each variable from its trend.

The fourth and final feature of a co-movement which we need to identify is the *conformity* between the two variables. We shall say

**Figure 6.4
Amplitude**

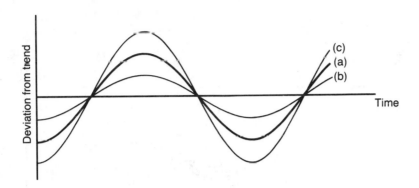

The cycle in (b) has smaller amplitude than the reference cycle (a), and the cycle in (c) has larger amplitude than the reference cycle.

that co-movement has a high degree of conformity if two series "look the same". For example, all the series graphed in Figures 6.2 and 6.3 have a high degree of conformity. A low degree of conformity would occur if one variable sometimes appeared to follow the same cyclical pattern as the reference variable, but did not always do so. Figure 6.5 illustrates. Suppose that (a) is the reference variable. We would describe the variable plotted with the broken line marked (b) as displaying a lower degree of conformity. There is obviously some rough procyclical relationship between (a) and (b), but it is by no means exact.

We may thus speak about the co-movements (joint movements, if you like) between two variables as being either procyclical or counter-cyclical, as involving a lead or a lag of one variable in relation to the other, as displaying greater or less amplitude of fluctuation, and as having a high or low degree of conformity. This is merely a language for describing business cycles. It is now possible to go on and use this language to address the more substantive tasks of this chapter. The first of these is to characterize the business cycle more fully.

D. Properties of the Business Cycle

The properties of the business cycle may now be set out more precisely, using the language that has been introduced to you in the previous two sections.

The first feature of business cycles has to do with the movements in the deviations of real GNP from trend.

> Technically, movements about trend in Gross National Product in any country can be well described by [a low order autocorrelation]. These movements do not exhibit uniformity of either period or amplitude,

**Figure 6.5
Conformity**

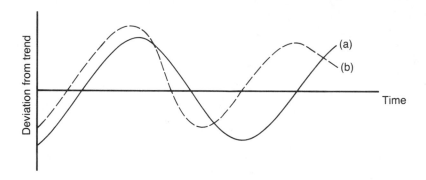

The series (a) and (b) display only a moderate degree of conformity. Series (b) follows the same general pattern as the reference cycle (a) in the first up- and down-swing but begins to lead the reference cycle in the second up-swing.

which is to say, they do not resemble the deterministic wave motions which sometimes arise in the natural sciences.[7]

The second feature of business cycles has to do with the co-movements among the various aggregates. The chief regularities which are observed are in the co-movements among different aggregate time series.

The principal among these are the following:[8]

1. Output movements across broadly defined sectors of the economy move together.
2. Production of durable goods exhibits much greater amplitude than production of non-durables.
3. Production and prices of agricultural goods and natural resources have lower than average conformity.
4. Business profits show high conformity and much greater amplitude than other series.
5. Prices generally are procyclical.
6. Short-term interest rates are procyclical; long-term rates slightly so.
7. Monetary aggregates and velocity measures are procyclical.

For the purpose of what will follow in this book, where the primary emphasis is on economic aggregates, we shall be concerned with four features of the cycle selected from those set out above. First, we shall be concerned to understand why it is that movements in real GNP about its trend can be described by a low-order autocorrelation process; second, we shall be concerned to understand why fluctuations

---

[7] Lucas, Jr., "Understanding Business Cycles," p. 9.

[8] *Ibid.*, with slight adjustments from the original.

in output of durable goods exhibit greater amplitude than that of non-durables; third, why prices are generally procyclical; and fourth, why interest rates are procyclical.

These are the central features of the business cycle which macro-economics seeks to understand. In addition, implicit in the charac-terization but need to be made explicit we shall be concerned to explain why unem ~~employment~~ employment pro-cyclical. If unemp ion) procyclical, in general there will be a negative relationship between inflation and unemployment.

Before moving on to begin these tasks, let us look at some of the broad facts about the Canadian business cycle.

E. The Canadian Business Cycle

(i) The Movements in Real GNP About its Trend

As you have already discovered in Chapter 2, real GNP (real income) in Canada has grown at an average rate of 4.4 percent over the period between 1926 and 1984. The deviations of real GNP from its growth trend were set out in Figure 2.4 (Chapter 2). Recall that the most dominant feature of those deviations was the large negative deviation during the Great Depression years and the rest of the 1930s and the large positive deviation during World War II (1942-45). There were also distinct but irregular smaller cycles visible in the data. Can this history of deviations of real GNP from trend in Canada be described by a low-order autocorrelation process? You are about to discover that, as a matter of fact, it can.

The fluctuations around trend in real GNP since 1926 are well described by the following equation:[9]

$$(y_t - y_t^*) = 0.88 \, (y_{t-1} - y_{t-1}^*) + e_t \qquad \textbf{(6.2)}$$

The way to read this is as follows: y_t represents real GNP in year t and y_t^* represents the trend value of real GNP in year t. Thus $(y_t - y_t^*)$ represents the deviation of real GNP from trend in year t. The same

---

[9]Equation (6.2) and Figure 6.6 were constructed in the following way. First, devia-tions of real GNP from trend were calculated by fitting a trend line to real GNP from 1926 to 1984. The deviations were then analyzed to determine their degree of auto-correlation and it was discovered that although not quite a perfectly satisfactory relationship, that shown as Equation (6.2) in the text could be regarded as a useful approximate description of the data. The random shock charted in frame (c) of the Figure 6.6 is the calculated residual movements in real GNP about its trend not ac-counted for by the previous year's value of that variable multiplied by the coefficient 0.88. As a matter of fact, a *second* order difference equation — one that says that the deviation of real GNP from trend in year t depends on the deviations in year t-1 and year t-2 as well as a random disturbance — describes the data best. The improvement in the description is not, however, so enormous as to render the first-order description misleading.

variable with the subscript t-1 represents deviations from trend in the previous year. As before, e_t represents a random disturbance. Notice that Equation (6.2) is very similar in the magnitude of the coefficient to the one that we used as an example in the section on autocorrelation above (and in the appendix to this chapter). It says that real GNP will deviate from its trend value by 0.88 of its previous deviation plus a random disturbance.

In interpreting Equation (6.2) recall that you discovered that this way of looking at the movements of real GNP about its trend simply involves breaking the actual movement into two components: (1) a source of (or, more generally, sources of) random disturbance to the economy, and (2) systematic sources of inertia. In the above equation, the inertia is represented by the term $0.88(y_{t-1} - y^*_{t-1})$ and the sources of random disturbance in any one year are represented by the term e_t.

To give you a better feel for what has been going on, Figure 6.6 plots the deviations of real GNP from trend and its two components — the systematic source of inertia and the random component. Frame (a) of the figure shows the deviations of real GNP from trend. [These are exactly the same as those shown in frame (b) of Figure 2.4, Chapter 2.] This cycle in real GNP is decomposed into a purely random element[10] and an inertia element in frames (c) and (b) of Figure 6.6. Frame (c) of the figure shows the purely random disturbances that have hit the Canadian economy over this time period. Those disturbances add up to zero over the entire period. Sometimes they have been as large as a negative shock of 16.1 and a positive shock of 13.7 (percent of GNP). Most of the time, however, the shocks have been small, 26 of them lying between $+2$ and -2, a further 19 lying between $+5$ and -5, a further 9 lying between $+10$ and -10 and only 4 being greater than $+10$ or -10 (percent of GNP). These shocks impact on the economy to produce the cycle in real GNP described by Equation 6.2 and plotted as frame (a) of Figure 6.6. Frame (b) of Figure 6.6 represents the contribution of inertia to the deviations of GNP from trend. The line in frame (a) of Figure 6.6 represents nothing other than the summation of the lines in frames (b) and (c).

To get a feel for how this works, consider a particular year. The year 1942 will illustrate the story well. According to this description of events, in 1942 there was a positive random shock of 13.7 percent of GNP — the biggest of the positive shocks recorded. The shocks from 1939 to 1941 had also been positive, and had accumulated over those years to produce a positive deviation of GNP from trend in 1941

---

[10] What we are calling a "purely random element" is, in fact, only approximately so. The movements in deviations of real GNP from trend not accounted for by a second-order difference equation are indistinguishable from purely random disturbances. The disturbances in Figure 6.5 could be reduced slightly and made "more random" by taking account of this. The broad picture would not, however, be changed by adding this complication.

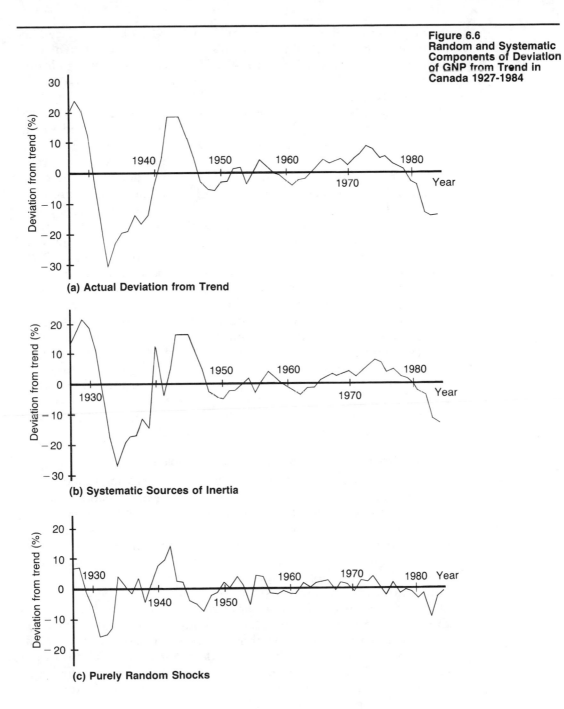

**Figure 6.6
Random and Systematic
Components of Deviation
of GNP from Trend in
Canada 1927-1984**

(a) Actual Deviation from Trend

(b) Systematic Sources of Inertia

(c) Purely Random Shocks

The actual deviations of real GNP from trend [frame (a)] are decomposed into a systematic source of inertia [frame (b)] and purely random shocks [frame (c)].

Source: Appendix to Chapter 2.

of 5.1 percent. You can read this off in frame (a) of Figure 6.6. This positive deviation in 1941, when multiplied by the coefficient 0.88 gave positive inertia to GNP in 1942 of 4.5 percent as shown in frame (b) of Figure 6.6. This inertia, other things remaining the same, would have put real GNP above trend by that same 4.5 percent in 1942. Other things, however, were not the same. In 1942 a large positive shock (13.7 percent of GNP) occurred. This has to be added to the positive inertia and moves the actual value of GNP to 18.2 percent above trend. Thus, the 18.2 percent deviation of GNP from trend in 1942 represents the sum of a large positive shock (13.7 percent) and inertia (4.5 percent) coming from the accumulation of previous positive shocks.

It cannot be emphasized sufficiently that this is merely *a way* of *describing* the movement of GNP. It does, however, provide us with a valuable way of thinking about what has been happening to GNP. The economy is bombarded by shocks as described in frame (c) of Figure 6.6, and those shocks affect the level of output (and other variables as well) in a manner which looks much less random than the shocks themselves. We can translate the random shocks into a more systematic up-and-down movement of output by the device of describing output as following a first-order difference equation which is stochastically (randomly) disturbed. The task for explanation is to figure out: (1) what causes the shocks shown in frame (c) of Figure 6.6, (2) what gives rise to the translation of those shocks into movements of output and other variables, and (3) what are the sources giving rise to inertia as described in frame (b).

(ii) The Production of Durables and Non-durables

The second feature of the business cycle that was identified above was the tendency for the production of durables (investment goods and consumer durables) to fluctuate with greater amplitude than the production of non-durables (consumer goods and services). This general feature of the business cycle is very evident in the the Canadian data, as Figure 6.7 shows. Data for the post-war years only have been used in this figure because the division of output into durables and non-durables was severely distorted in the war years (1942-1945) and obscures the basic peacetime pattern. Frame (a), which illustrates the movements in durables, shows fluctuations commonly ranging from as much as 10 percent above or below trend and, on several occasions, going above or below trend by almost 20 percent. In the early 1980s these fluctuations have increased to almost 26 percent. In contrast, the production of non-durables [frame (b)] rarely gets more than 5 percent away from its trend. The ups and downs in durable production also occur with greater frequency than those in non-durable production.

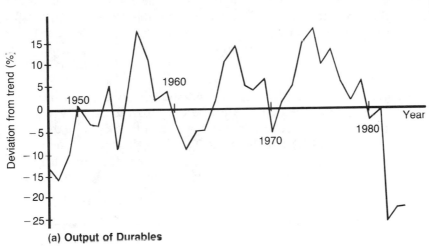

(a) Output of Durables

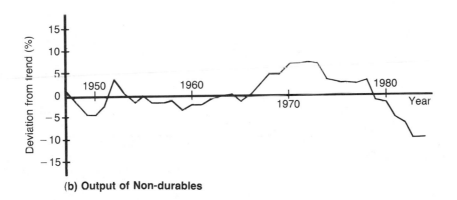

(b) Output of Non-durables

The production of durables [frame (a)] fluctuates with much greater amplitude than the production of non-durables [frame (b)].

Source: Durables is the sum of Cansim Series D40736, D40649, and D40661. Non-durables is the difference between real GNP and durables.

(iii) Output and Unemployment

A further general feature of the business cycle that was identified above was the tendency for output and employment to move together or, equivalently, for output and unemployment to move opposite each other. A useful way of exploring the co-movements among variables is to plot one variable against another in the same diagram, that is, to construct what is called a *scatter diagram*. Figure 6.8 does this for unemployment and deviations of real GNP from trend. Each point in Figure 6.8 represents a year and shows the levels of unemployment and of the deviation of real GNP from trend in a particular year. To be sure that you know how to read Figure 6.8, consider the point marked 33. This is in the bottom right-hand corner of the figure. It represents the observation for the year 1933. In 1933, unemployment was 19.3 percent (which you can read off on the horizontal axis of the diagram) and real GNP was 30.9 percent below trend (which you can read off on the vertical axis of the diagram). Evidently, there is a clear tendency for unemployment to move in the opposite direction to deviations of real GNP from trend. The relationship is by no means perfect, but is nevertheless very distinct. One year that evidently was considerably out of line with the generally observed relationship was

Figure 6.8
Unemployment and
the Deviation of Real GNP
From Trend

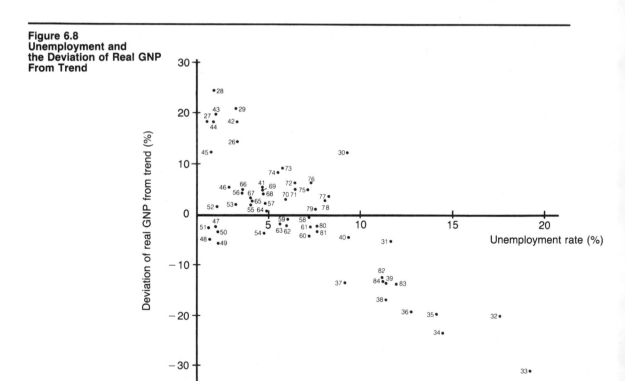

Each point shows the deviation of real GNP from trend and the unemployment rate occurring in a particular year. Years are identified by their last two digits — thus, for example, 1933 is shown as 33. There is a clear tendency for unemployment to be highest when real GNP is furthest below trend and lowest when real GNP is above trend.

Source: Appendix to Chapter 2.

1930. In that year unemployment was higher than usual (9.1 percent), but real GNP was, according to the figures presented here, 12.3 percent above trend. For the most part, however, there is a clear and systematic tendency for unemployment to move countercyclically with reference to deviations of real GNP from trend.

(iv) Price Movements

A general feature of the business cycle is that prices move procyclically. This means that inflation rates are strongest when output is deviating above trend and weakest when output deviates below trend. Equivalently, we could expect to find a negative association between inflation movements and unemployment movements. That is, inflation is generally at its highest when unemployment is at its lowest. Viewing the procyclical nature of inflation as a countercyclical relation between inflation and unemployment enables us to focus on a

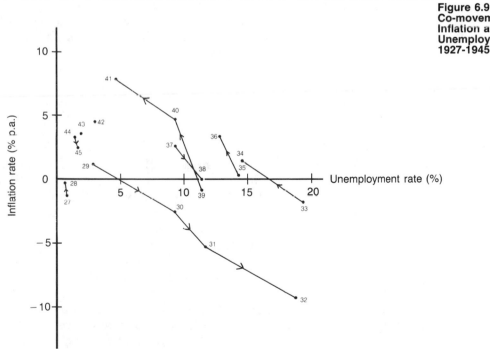

**Figure 6.9
Co-movements of
Inflation and
Unemployment
1927-1945**

Each point shows the inflation rate and the unemployment rate that occurred in a given year. Years are identified by their last two digits (e.g., 1933 is shown as 33). There have been long periods when inflation and unemployment moved in opposite directions (shown by the arrowed lines) and other periods when there is considerable independence in the movements of the two series.

Source: Appendix to Chapter 2.

relationship known as the Phillips relation (named for the New Zealand economist A.W. Phillips who popularized this relationship).[11]

Figures 6.9 and 6.10 show the co-movements of inflation and unemployment in Canada between 1927 and 1945 and between 1946 and 1983. (The reason for plotting these data on two separate figures is that the range of variation in the inter-war years is so gigantic that the actual variation in the post-war years would be lost in the corner of the diagram if we were to plot the points shown in Figure 6.10 on the scale used in Figure 6.9.)

Notice that there is, from time to time, a clear tendency for inflation and unemployment to move in opposite directions. This is visible between all the years marked with a line in both Figures 6.9 and 6.10. What is also clearly visible, however, is the fact that there is no single relationship that characterizes all the co-movements between inflation and unemployment. Two-thirds of the movements are *inverse* (i.e., when inflation rises, unemployment falls or when inflation falls, unemployment rises) but there are significant occasions on which both variables move in the same direction. Consideration of the Phillips relation in the Canadian data raises as many questions having to do with these simultaneous increases in inflation and unemployment (or simultaneous decreases) as it does concerning their negative co-movement. All of these stylized facts will have to be coped with by any viable theory concerning the causes of inflation and unemployment. It will be necessary to understand why, most of the time, the two variables move in opposite directions and why there are other periods when they move in the same direction as each other.

(v) Interest Rates

The general description of the business cycle is that short-term interest rates are procyclical and long-term rates only slightly so. A useful way of looking at the cyclical nature of short-term interest rates is to examine how they move with inflation. Since we know that inflation is generally procyclical, then if interest rates and inflation move together we shall know that interest rates also are procyclical. Figure 6.11 shows the relationship between short-term interest rates and inflation in Canada since 1956. The generally procyclical nature of short-term interest rates is visible in this figure. You can see that although there is not a perfect relationship between interest rates and inflation, there is nevertheless a tendency for these two variables to move in the same direction . This feature of interest rates and inflation rates to move together is also something which our theories are necessarily going to have to be able to account for.

---

[11] Phillips' original contribution is A.W. Phillips, "The Relation between Unemployment and the Rate of Change of Money Wage Rates in the United Kingdom, 1861-1957," *Economica*, 25 (November 1958), 283-99.

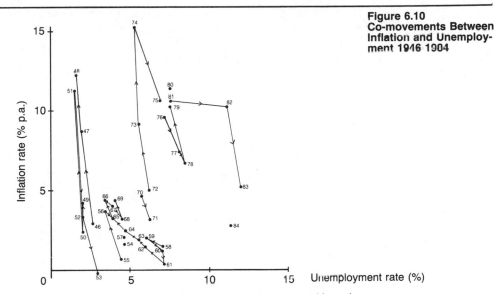

**Figure 6.10
Co-movements Between
Inflation and Unemployment 1946 1984**

Each point shows the inflation rate and the unemployment rate that occurred in a given year. Years are identified by their last two digits (e.g., 1949 is shown as 49). There have been several periods in which unemployment and inflation have moved in opposite directions to each other (shown by the arrowed lines). There have also, however, been sizeable and important positive co-movements of these two variables.

Source: Appendix to Chapter 2.

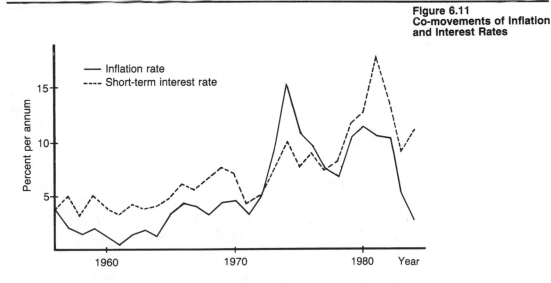

**Figure 6.11
Co-movements of Inflation
and Interest Rates**

The trends in these two variables are similar, but the movements in interest rates sometimes lag behind those in inflation.

Source: Appendix to Chapter 2.

There is no need to examine separately the movements of long-term interest rates. You know from Figure 2.4 that long-term interest rates are much smoother than short-term rates. You also know that there is a general tendency for long-term rates to move in the same broad direction as short-term rates. It immediately follows that long-term interest rates do have the general characteristic that they are procyclical, but only slightly so.

These, then, are the major features of the Canadian business cycle that macroeconomic theory needs to be able to explain. The next two parts of this book are concerned with the task of explanation.

Summary

A. Definition of the Business Cycle

Business cycles are recurrent but non-periodic fluctuations in aggregate economic activity as measured by fluctuations in real GNP about its trend.

B. Autocorrelation

Autocorrelation is a technical term which means that the value of some variable is related to itself at some earlier date (or dates). An autocorrelated variable is described by a difference equation which is stochastically or randomly disturbed.

C. Co-movement

The term *co-movement* is used in the description of the movement of one variable in relation to another. Co-movements may be procyclical, in which case two variables move up and down together; or countercyclical, in which case two variables move in the opposite direction to each other. The cycle in one variable may lead or lag the cycle in another. The cycle in one variable may display a greater or smaller amplitude than the cycle in the other. Co-movement may display high conformity, in which case the two variables move in a similar manner; or low conformity, in which case they do not move in close sympathy with each other.

D. Properties of the Business Cycle

Movements in real GNP about trend are well described by a simple difference equation which is stochastically disturbed. In general, employment, prices, and interest rates are procyclical. Unemployment is countercyclical.

E. The Canadian Business Cycle

The general features of the business cycle set out above apply precisely to the Canadian case, with the important observation that movements in inflation, while generally procyclical, are not universally so. There are important co-movements of inflation and unemployment which do not fit a simple pattern.

Review Questions

1. What are business cycles cycles in?

2. Describe the different phases of a cycle.

3. What is a "recession"?

4. Are all business cycles the same length? If not, why do we use the term *cycle* to describe the phenomenon of non-periodic economic fluctuations?

5. What is a difference equation? Can a difference equation describe the path followed by deviations of real GNP from trend?

6. Explain how random shocks combine with inertia to describe recurrent but non-periodic up-and-down movements in economic activity.

7. What is meant by the term *co-movement*?

8. What is meant by the term *conformity*?

9. Try to think of examples (not necessarily economic) of:
   (a) Procyclical co-movements which have high conformity or low conformity.
   (b) Countercyclical co-movements which have high conformity or low conformity.

10. Describe the general character of business cycles.

11. How might the deviation of real GNP from trend in Canada be described in the period since 1926?

12. What have been the co-movements between real GNP and inflation, unemployment, and interest rates in the period since 1960?

13. (You will only want to tackle this question if you have worked through the appendix to this chapter.) Reinforce your understanding of the concept of autocorrelation by conducting the following experiments:
   (a) Using the same "economic shocks" as set out in Table 6A.2 (in the appendix), generate a path for real income if it is described by the processes

   $$y_t = 90 + 0.1 \, y_{t-1} + e_t$$

   and

   $$y_t = 1 + 0.99 \, y_{t-1} + e_t$$

   (b) Compare the paths of y_t in the above two equations with each other and with that derived in the appendix using Equation (6A.2). How do the paths differ? What do you learn from this experiment?

Appendix

Autocorrelation

This appendix deals with the concept of autocorrelation in a slightly more technical way than was done in the preceding text. The appendix contains no fundamentally new ideas that are not treated in any intuitive way in the body of the chapter. It may, however, provide you with a better understanding of the concept of autocorrelation, and certainly the numerical example will provide you with an opportunity to review your understanding of the concept.

It is useful to approach the concept of autocorrelation in two steps. The first is to understand what is meant by a *difference equation*. A difference equation is nothing other than a statement that tells us how some variable evolves over time. We shall only deal with the simplest kind of difference equation and even then only with an example. Let us suppose that we want to describe the evolution of a variable called y over time. So that we are clear about the date that attaches to the variable, let us denote the value of y in some particular year, the tth year, as y_t. Let us suppose that y in year t is always related in some way to its own value in the previous year. Never mind why for the present. Specifically, let us suppose that the following equation describes the evolution of y from one year to the next:

$$y_t = 25 + 0.75\, y_{t-1} \qquad\qquad \textbf{(6A.1)}$$

Let us first of all satisfy ourselves that we can read this equation. What it says in words is that y in year t (yt) will be equal to 25, plus three-quarters (0.75) of the level of y in the previous year (year t-1), that is, (y_{t-1}). To get a feel for this, imagine that y in year t-1 was equal to 100. You can calculate 3/4 of 100 (equals 75), add 25 to that, and the result is the value of y in year t. The answer that you have obtained, of course, is that y in year t will be 100. Now imagine going forward to year $t+1$. At year $t+1$ the previous year becomes year t. Since y in year t is 100, in year $t+1$, by the same calculation, it will also be 100. You can quickly convince yourself that y will be 100 in each and every year if the above equation is true and if real GNP in year t-1 was equal to 100.

Now suppose that y in the previous year (y_{t-1}) was not 100 but 110. What does this imply about the value of y in year t? You can calculate that answer by finding 3/4 of 110 and adding 25 to that to give you the value of y in year t. You should get an answer of 107.5. In the next year, year $t+1$, y will be 25 plus 3/4 of 107.5. This will give a level of y of 105.6. By repeating the calculation, you will obtain for the next successive years values of 104.2, 103.2, 102.4, 101.8, 101.3, 101.0, 100.8. . . . Thus, in the indefinite future, y will converge to the level of 100. The value of 100 is known as the steady-state value of y. It is that value towards which the above equation always tends.

You are probably now saying to yourself, "Well that's all very simple but so what?" Clearly, neither of these paths that have just been calculated trace out a cycle. According to the first exercise that we did, if y starts out at 100, it always stays at 100; and according to the second exercise, if it starts out at something other than 100, it converges monotonically towards 100. How does this help us understand the movements of deviations of real GNP from trend such as those which occur in an actual economy like that of Canada? The answer is that on its own, it is of no help at all. With one tiny addition, however, the first-order difference equation [Equation (6A.1)] (*first-order* means that y today depends only on y yesterday) can be capable of producing patterns in the evolution of y which are similar in character to patterns that we observe in the deviations of real GNP from trend.

That simple addition is to make the difference equation above a *stochastic* difference equation. A stochastic difference equation is very similar to a difference equation. That is, it has all the properties of the equation that you have just looked at and become familiar with. In addition, however, it adds on to the above equation a *random* shock. In other words, instead of y in one year being uniquely determined, given knowledge of y in the previous year, there is an additional random element that will allow y in the current year to deviate from the prediction of the above equation by a random amount. We could write a stochastic difference equation comparable to the above equation as follows:

$$y_t = 25 + 0.75\, y_{t-1} + e_t \qquad \textbf{(6A.2)}$$

The term e_t at the end of the equation represents a random shock. On the average it will take on the value of 0. From time to time, however, it will take on different values than 0, sometimes positive and sometimes negative.

To keep things simple and concrete, let us generate an example of a random shock (or a series of random shocks) and then see how y evolves when the difference equation that describes its path is stochastically disturbed.

We have created a set of random shocks by conducting a simple experiment which you can conduct for yourself. The experiment involves rolling a die and assigning an economic shock depending on the score of the die roll. Table 6A.1 sets out the way that we have converted die scores into economic shocks. You will see that if the die came up 3 or 4, we scored an economic shock of 0, so that there is a 1 in 3 chance that there is no random disturbance to the economy. If the die came up 2, we scored a negative shock of 5 (think of that as a shock that is depressing the economy), and if the die scored 1, then we gave a bigger weight to the depressing effect on the economy

TABLE 6A.1
Converting Die Scores into Economic Shocks

DIE SCORE	ECONOMIC SHOCK
1	-10
2	-5
3	0
4	0
5	$+5$
6	$+10$

(-10). If the die came up 5 or 6, we scored a positive shock to the economy (a boom) assigning a shock of 5 for a die score of 5 and 10 for a die score of 6. Thus you can see that there is a 1 in 6 chance that the economy will be hit with any of the shocks $+10$, $+5$, -5, -10, and a 1 in 3 chance of no shock. The shocks, then, that will hit the economy are symmetrical and have an average value of 0 and a range of 20, ranging from $+10$ to -10.

We rolled the die 30 times, and Table 6A.2 records the scores of our 30 die rolls together with the value of the economic shock implied by the scoring scheme set out in Table 6A.1. You will notice that our 30 rolls turned out to have an average value that was greater than 0 (in fact our average was $+1$), indicating that we rolled rather more 5's and 6's than we did 1's and 2's. Nevertheless, if we had rolled, say, 1000 times, then it is certain that our average would have been very close to 0.

With the series of economic shocks shown in Table 6A.2, it is now possible to see how the variable y would evolve if the above stochastic difference equation describes its evolution. The calculation for the first ten values of y are set out in Table 6A.2. The first column shows the level of y in year t and the second column in year t-1. The third column records the value of the shock, e_t. The values of the shocks listed there are the first ten shocks from Table 6A.2. Imagine that in year 0, the variable started out in its steady state with y equal to 100 and with y in the previous year equal to 100 and with no random shock. The shocks then begin. In year 1 we need to take 3/4 of the previous y (75) and add 25 which gives 100 and then add the shock of 5 to get the value shown for y of 105. In year 2, year 1's value of 105 becomes the previous year's level y. To calculate year 2 y, we take 3/4 of 105 and add 25 to that; we then subtract 10, the current year's shock of -10, to give a value of 94 for y. This process is repeated

TABLE 6A.2
Thirty Random Shocks in an Imaginary Economy

DIE ROLL	DIE SCORE	ECONOMIC SHOCK
1	5	+5
2	1	−10
3	6	+10
4	6	+10
5	4	0
6	4	0
7	6	+10
8	4	0
9	2	−5
10	3	0
11	3	0
12	4	0
13	4	0
14	6	+10
15	5	+5
16	5	+5
17	1	−10
18	1	−10
19	3	0
20	2	−5
21	3	0
22	6	+10
23	5	+5
24	6	+10
25	2	−5
26	5	+5
27	2	−5
28	4	0
29	1	−10
30	5	+5

throughout the table. Check that you can reproduce the figures listed in column 1 of Table 6A.3 by applying the above-described formula. (The figures given in the table are rounded. To calculate the correct values you should carry the unrounded figures in the memory of your calculator.)

Figure 6A.1 illustrates the values of *y* over the full thirty-year experiment that is described in Tables 6A.2 and 6A.3. The graph of the ups and downs of this imaginary variable looks remarkably as if it could have been generated from plotting actual figures for the deviation of real GNP from trend, such as those shown in Chapter 2. Notice that there is certainly a recurrent up-and-down movement, but there

TABLE 6A.3
Calculation of Evolution of an Imaginary Variable y
(periods 0 to 10 only)

$y_t = 25 + 0.75\,y_{t-1} + shock$

YEAR	y_t	y_{t-1}	SHOCK
0	100	100	0
1	105	100	+5
2	94	105	−10
3	105	94	+10
4	114	105	+10
5	111	114	0
6	108	111	0
7	116	108	+10
8	112	116	0
9	104	112	−5
10	103	104	0

is no exact periodicity. The timing from the trough of observation 2 to the next trough (year 13) is eleven years . The next trough occurs at year 20 — a seven-year cycle. The next trough occurs at year 29 — a nine-year cycle. Thus, the cycle lengths in this example, as measured from trough to trough, vary from a short cycle of seven years to a long cycle of eleven years. Notice too that the severity of the down phase varies. The downturn that begins in year 8 continues throughout year 13 but never gets very deep. The next downturn that begins in year 17 only runs for four years, but it goes all the way to 10 points below the steady-state value.

The particular path of the variable *y* generated by a stochastic difference equation depends in an important way on the strength of the inertia in the process — that is, on the magnitude of the effect of previous income on current income. In our example, that effect is 3/4. If, instead of current income depending on previous income with a weight of 3/4, we were to lower that weight almost to zero, then *y* would no longer display much systematic movement but would be purely random (completely unpredictable) like the random shocks, e_t, that are bombarding the variable. At the other extreme, if we were to raise the weight on previous income from 3/4 to almost 1, then the cyclical swings in *y* would be much longer (the time from the peak of one cycle to the peak of the next one would be longer).

The key point to take careful note of is that a very simple process — a stochastically disturbed, first-order difference equation — is capable of generating a path for a variable that is very similar in its characteristics to the recurrent but non-periodic ups and downs of

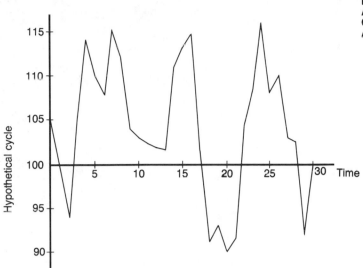

The simple randomly disturbed difference equation $yt = 25 + 0.75\ yt\text{-}1 + et$ generates nonperiodic but recurrent fluctuations that could easily be taken to be real world deviations of real GNP from trend.

deviations of real GNP from trend (and other variables) over the course of the business cycle. Of course, the specific path of actual movements of GNP about trend will only be capable of description by specific shocks and a specific difference equation.

III

MACROECONOMIC THEORY

Overview

7

Aggregate Demand and Aggregate Supply: an Overview

You have now reviewed the questions that macroeconomics seeks to answer; the key macroeconomic facts; the way in which the macroeconomic variables are measured; and the characteristics of the business cycle. It is now time to move on to the more challenging — and more interesting and exciting — problem of *explanation* of macroeconomic phenomena. Macroeconomic phenomena are explained, or understood, by using *macroeconomic theory*. Unlike many areas of the natural sciences, and indeed unlike some areas of economics, macroeconomic theory is still in a state of controversy and rapid development. As a consequence, there is no single, universally accepted theory capable of explaining macroeconomic phenomena. Instead there is a variety of competing and conflicting theories. In such a state of affairs it is necessary to become familiar with *all* the alternative theories and to develop procedures for choosing among the alternatives so that ultimately, we may reject all of them except one.

Although macroeconomic theory is not in a settled and uncontroversial state, there are some basic tools of analysis that are common to all theories. This chapter will introduce you to these tools. Central among them are the tools of aggregate demand, aggregate supply, and macroeconomic equilibrium.

The chapter will take you through four tasks, which are to:
a) Understand the concept of aggregate demand.
b) Understand the concept of aggregate supply.
c) Understand the concept of macroeconomic equilibrium.
d) Understand how shifts in aggregate demand and aggregate supply generate movements in aggregate output and the price level.

A. Aggregate Demand

Aggregate demand is the demand for goods and services in total. It is the demand for aggregate output of the economy. The *aggregate demand curve* is defined as the relationship between the aggregate quantity of goods and services which people are willing to buy in a given period of time and the price level.

The questions that we shall be interested in concerning the aggregate demand curve, are:

(1) What is the shape of the aggregate demand curve? Does it slope downwards? That is, would the level of aggregate demand rise if the price level fell?

(2) What variables cause the aggregate demand curve to shift? That is, what variables, other than the price level, cause aggregate demand to vary?

Before we tackle these questions directly, it will be useful to recall some familiar ideas about *demand* in the *micro*economic study of demand for a particular good or service.

You are familiar, from your study of microeconomics, with the concept of *demand* when it is applied to individual goods or services — the demand for orange juice, the demand for hamburgers, etc. You are also familiar, in such a context, with the notion of a *demand curve* — the relationship between the quantity of orange juice demanded and the price of orange juice. You are also familiar with the idea of the *elasticity of demand* — that is, with the responsiveness of the quantity demanded of a good to a change in its price. That is, you are accustomed to talking about demand being: (a) *elastic* if a one percent change in the price of the good leads to a more than one percent change in the quantity demanded; (b) *inelastic* if a one percent change in the price of the good leads to a less than one percent change in quantity demanded; and (c) *unit elastic* in the case where a one percent change in the price of the good leads to a one percent change in the quantity demanded. Finally, you are accustomed to thinking about *shifts* in the *demand* curve for a particular good (such as orange juice) as arising from changes in all those factors that influence the quantity demanded of the good other than the price of the good itself.

When we talk about the *demand* for orange juice, we do not mean the same thing as the quantity of orange juice that people *actually purchase*. Rather, we mean the quantity of orange juice that would be purchased at a particular price of orange juice and at particular prices for grapefruit juice, apple juice, etc., and at a given level of income.

It is a good idea to think of demand (and supply) as *decision rules*. Decision rules are schedules that set a person's prior calculation of his/her best response in all conceivable situations. That is, a person decides upon rules of behavior for all conceivable circumstances, and then, in any given situation, implements the previously chosen rule.

Decision rules can be stated in a variety of alternative, but equivalent, ways. For example, a decision rule could be represented as a
table that lists the alternative prices of orange juice and, opposite
each price, states the quantity of orange juice that an individual
would choose to consume. An equivalent way of representing a decision rule is in the form of a diagram in which the quantity that
would be purchased is shown on one axis and the price on the other.
This is the standard way in which we represent decision rules about
quantities that individuals would choose to purchase in economics.
Such a representation is called the demand curve. Of course, the
decision rule concerning how much orange juice to consume is not
completely described by the two variables — the quantity of orange
juice consumed and its price. Many things other than the price of the
good affect the quantity demanded of it, and a complete statement
of the decision rule about how much to buy requires that all those
other factors be taken into account. We represent changes in those
other factors — factors other than the price of the good — as shifts
in the demand curve. Thus, for example, if an individual's income
was to rise, that would trigger a rise in the demand for orange juice
at each different orange juice price.

We can apply these same ideas that are familiar from the study of
microeconomics to the macroeconomic analysis of *aggregate* demand.
In doing so, however, we need to exercise some care.

As noted at the beginning of this section, aggregate demand is the
demand for goods and services in total — the demand for the real
Gross National Product. No one individual demands in equal pro-
portions the many different goods and services that make up the Gross
National Product. The variety of items in the gross national product
is immense — orange juice, haircuts, video shows, plane rides, new
orange juice production plants, new TV studios, new airplanes, new
tanks, new submarines, new satellites, etc. Some of these things are
demanded by households, some by the firms, some by government
and some by foreigners. Aggregate demand is the total of the demands
for goods and services of all these different agents — of households,
firms, government, and the rest of the world.

Just as we are careful to distinguish between the quantity demanded and the quantity actually purchased when talking about an
individual good so we must also be careful when dealing with aggregate demand. *Aggregate demand* is *not* the same thing as the *total
volume of goods and services actually purchased*. Rather, it is the schedule of the aggregate quantities of goods and services that would be
bought at each particular price level and in each of the particular
circumstances that could prevail. In other words, aggregate demand,
like the demand for an individual good, is a schedule of plans.

Just as it is helpful to think of an individual's demand for orange
juice as a decision rule, so it is also helpful to think of aggregate
demand as the aggregate of the decision rules of all the individual

agents in the economy concerning expenditures on all goods and services. Just as the demand curve for orange juice tells us the quantities of orange juice that will be demanded as the price of orange juice changes, so the aggregate demand curve tells us the quantities of goods and services in total that will be demanded as the general price level varies. Figure 7.1 illustrates an aggregate demand curve.

Why is the aggregate demand curve shown as a downward-sloping curve? We shall be exploring the precise reasons why this is so in Chapters 13 and 26. For now we shall content ourselves with some intuition on why the demand curve may be presumed to slope downwards.

We know that the demand curve for an individual good slopes downwards primarily because of the *substitution effect*. As the price of one good falls *relative to the prices of other goods*, people will reallocate their income and substitute the good that has become relatively inexpensive for goods that have become relatively more expensive. This factor is part of the reason why the aggregate demand curve slopes downwards. If the average price of goods and services produced in the domestic economy declines while the prices of goods produced in other countries remain constant there will be a tendency for people both in the domestic economy and in the rest of the world to substitute in favor of the goods and services produced in the domestic economy. This international substitution of demand is, then, one reason why the aggregate demand curve slopes downwards.

A second reason why the aggregate demand curve may be presumed to slope downwards has to do with what is called the *wealth effect*. At any given moment there is a certain stock of real and fi-

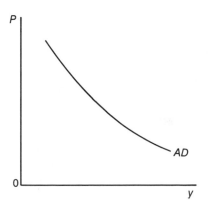

**Figure 7.1
Aggregate Demand**

The aggregate demand curve slopes downwards. At lower price levels: (a) there is substitution away from rest-of-world goods to domestic goods and (b) as wealth rises because the real value of the financial assets in the economy rises, additional demand for goods and services is generated.

nancial assets that constitutes the wealth of all the agents in the economy. As the price level varies nothing happens to the real value of the stock of real assets. There is, though, a change in the real value of the stock of financial assets. The higher the price level, the smaller the real value of the stock of financial assets. Thus at a higher price level, people would feel less well off than at a low price level and may be presumed to demand a smaller quantity of goods and services.

This intuitive reasoning that suggests a downward-sloping aggregate demand curve does not provide us with any insights into the elasticity of aggregate demand. Aggregate demand could be highly elastic or highly inelastic. You will pursue a deeper study of the factors influencing aggregate demand that will shed some light on this matter later in Chapter 13 for a closed economy and in Chapter 26 for an open economy.

One of the key ingredients in the theory of demand for an individual good concerns an analysis of the factors that shift the demand curve. That is also an important matter for macroeconomics. Many things can, in principle, change the level of aggregate demand at a particular price level, thereby shifting the aggregate demand curve. Some examples are the total population, the wealth of the economy, the level of real income and wealth of the rest of the world (which influences the demand by foreigners for domestic goods and services), the level of government demand for goods and services (which, in turn, is determined by a large number of social and political considerations), the rate at which firms are seeking to add to their stock of capital equipment (which, in turn, depends on the pace of technical change, business confidence, and a variety of other factors).

The above list of things that can make the aggregate demand curve shift should be seen at this point as purely illustrative. Your subsequent, more detailed study of the theory of aggregate demand will make much more precise and sharp statements about how these potential influences upon aggregate demand have their effects. You will also discover that in certain cases some of the factors which we have listed above as having a possible effect on aggregate demand in fact have no effect at all.

You now have a fairly clear notion as to what is meant by the concept of aggregate demand, the aggregate demand curve, and have some rough notion as to why the aggregate demand curve is downward sloping and also some idea as to what sorts of things might make the aggregate demand curve shift over time.

Let us now turn our attention to aggregate supply.

B. Aggregate Supply

Aggregate supply is the quantity of goods and services that all the producers in the economy would wish to supply at each given price level.

You will probably find it helpful to begin considering aggregate supply in the same way as we began our consideration of aggregate demand, by considering the case of an individual commodity. You are already familiar with the notion of the supply curve of, say, orange juice. In general, the quantity of orange juice willingly supplied rises as the price of orange juice rises relative to the prices of other things.

The concept of aggregate supply applies these same considerations to the supply of aggregate output or real GNP. Aggregate supply is the total quantity of goods and services that all producers would like to supply in any given circumstances. To use the same language as we used before, it is the aggregation of the *decision rules* of all the individual producers in the economy. We know that the supply of orange juice rises when the price of orange juice rises. Is the same true of the supply of goods and services in total? That is, does the level of aggregate supply rise as the general price level rises? There seem to be two interesting possibilities that can be explored. The orange juice example will help to get things straight.

Imagine that a competitive producer of orange juice experiences a 10 percent rise in the price of orange juice. Further, imagine that nothing else happens to the orange juice producer's costs and technology. He is using the same production techniques, hiring the same labor, and paying out the same wages. In that case, the producer will slide up his marginal cost (supply) curve, thereby increasing the total supply of orange juice.

Consider a second case. This time, when the price of orange juice rises by 10 percent so do the wages of the orange juice workers and so also do all the other costs of production. In this situation the firm's cost curves will rise by 10 percent. The combination of a 10 percent rise in price with a 10 percent rise in all costs will leave the profit-maximizing quantity of orange juice exactly the same as it was before. That is, there is no change in the supply of orange juice.

Now extend the reasoning from the case of orange juice producers to that of all goods and services. If the prices of all final outputs were to rise but the prices of all factors of production were to remain constant, then the producers of all goods and services would seek to raise their output so that aggregate output would rise. In this case aggregate supply would rise as the price level rises.

Consider the second case. This time the prices of all final goods and services rise and the prices of all inputs — labor, capital and all other factors of production — rise by the same percentage amount. In such a situation there would be no incentive for producers to change their output so that, as the price level rises, aggregate supply remains constant.

Figure 7.2 illustrates these two cases. The curve labelled AS_1 illustrates the first case where, as the price level rises, the cost of production does not rise. That is, as the price level rises the prices of all the factors of production remain constant. In this case, a higher

Figure 7.2
Aggregate Supply

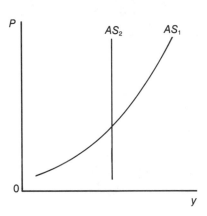

If, as the price level rises, the prices of factors of production remain constant (or do not rise as quickly as the price level) producers will raise output and aggregate output will rise. The aggregate supply curve is AS_1. If, as the price level rises, the prices of all inputs into production rise by the same percentage amount, producers will not change the quantity they supply and aggregate output will be constant. The aggregate supply curve is AS_2.

price level induces a higher level of aggregate supply. The curve labelled AS_2 illustrates the second case. That is a situation in which, as the price level rises, so the prices of all inputs to the production process also rise by the same percentage amount. In this case there is no change in aggregate supply as the price level varies.

Many factors can generate shifts in the supply curve of orange juice. Favorable growing conditions will produce a rise in supply; unseasonal frost will produce a fall in supply. Improvements in orange tree varieties can generate higher yields and increase supply. The application of improved fertilizers can also increase supply. Further, the application of capital in the form of irrigation schemes could increase supply.

Similar considerations apply to aggregate supply. Aggregate supply can be affected by major climatic factors; by improved technologies; and by increased investment in capital equipment that raises productivity and also by investment in human capital through improved education and training of the labor force. Each or any of these types of factors can produce shifts in the aggregate supply curve.

Let us now go on to consider the interaction between supply and demand at the level of the economy as a whole.

C. Macroeconomic Equilibrium

Macroeconomic equilibrium is a situation in which aggregate demand is equal to aggregate supply. Figure 7.3 illustrates a state of macroeconomic equilibrium. When the price level is P_0, the level of aggregate demand is equal to y_0 and the level of aggregate supply is also equal to y_0. The price level P_0 and the output level y_0 are called equilibrium values.

It is a feature of macroeconomic equilibrium that the plans of individual agents in the economy are compatible with each other. People are implementing their decision rules — that is, they are doing what they said they would do in a given set of circumstances. There is nothing particularly "good" about equilibrium. The equilibrium output level could be a very low one and the equilibrium price level could be a very high one. The equilibrium output and price levels are simply the values of those variables determined by a particular theory.

Notice that an important implication of this is that every actual state of affairs that has any predictive content is an equilibrium *by definition*. Equilibrium and disequilibrium are not states of affairs in the actual world. They are propositions about a model. We can talk about disequilibrium and we can hypothesize disequilibrium states within a model. That is, we can conjecture about what would happen if the conditions of equilibrium were not satisfied. In effect, we can conduct *thought experiments* about what would happen in a state of dis-equilibrium. These thought experiments do not, however, say anything about the world. When we conduct such thought experiments we are imagining how some particular agents would adjust their behavior in a situation in which their decision rules could not be implemented. If the decision rules of agents could not be implemented then a theory that only says what happens when those decision rules

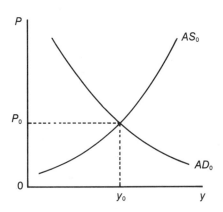

Figure 7.3
Macroeconomic Equilibrium

Macroeconomic equilibrium occurs when aggregate demand equals aggregate supply. The price and output levels (P_0, y_0) represent an equilibrium if aggregate supply is AS_0 and aggregate demand is AD_0.

are implemented would be of no value in making predictions about the world. Thus, only equilibrium statements are statements about the world.

These points can be made more vivid by considering Figure 7.4. This figure shows an equilibrium level of output at y_0 and price level of P_0. What would happen if the price level was, for some reason, stuck at P_0'? The answer is that we cannot say. The model does not tell us what happens in a situation such as that. It only tells us what happens when agents' decision rules can be implemented. If those decision rules are correctly summarized in the supply curve AS_0 and the demand curve AD_0 then, at the price level P_0', plans are incompatible and cannot be carried out. Either the price level cannot be P_0' or the aggregate demand and aggregate supply curves cannot be correct representations of agents' decision rules. If the aggregate demand and aggregate supply curves are in fact correct representations of decision rules then the price level has to be P_0 and the output level y_0.

D. Price and Output Changes

Your final task in this chapter is to see how you can put the basic framework of aggregate supply, aggregate demand, and macroeconomic equilibrium to work in understanding movements of output and the price level. Figure 7.5 provides the vehicle for the analysis.

Figure 7.4
Disequilibrium?

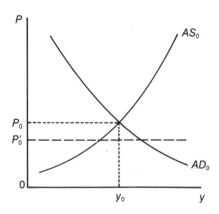

Disequilibrium cannot be a state predicted by a model. It can only be a state that is conjectured about in a thought experiment. If agents' decision rules are correctly summarized in the supply curve AS_0 and demand curve AD_0 then, at the price level P_0', agents plans are incompatible and cannot be carried out. Either the price level cannot be P_0' or the decision rules cannot be correct. If the decision rules are correct, the price level has to be P_0 and the output level y_0.

Focus first on the aggregate demand curve AD_0 and the aggregate supply curve AS_0. Where those curves intersect the macroeconomic equilibrium is determined at the price level P_0 and the output level y_0.

It the level of aggregate demand was to rise for some reason to AD_1, what would happen? The answer is that output would rise to y_1 and the price level would rise to P_1. Thus, a rise in aggregate demand raises both the output level and the price level. You can easily conduct the reverse experiment of considering what happens when there is a drop in aggregate demand. To do this, imagine that the economy starts out at P_1, y_1 where the aggregate demand curve AD_1 cuts the aggregate supply curve AS_0. Then imagine that there is a drop in aggregate demand to AD_0. In this case the price level falls to P_0 and output falls to y_0. Thus, a drop in aggregate demand lowers both the output level and the price level.

Next consider the case of a shift in the aggregate supply curve. Figure 7.6 illustrates this case. Suppose, again, that the economy starts out at P_0, y_0 where the curves AD_0 and AS_0 intersect. Then suppose that aggregate supply was to shift from AS_0 to AS_1 with aggregate demand remaining at AD_0. In this case the price level rises to P_1 but output now falls to y_1. As you can see a shift of the aggregate supply curve to the left raises the price level and lowers output. Again you can consider the reverse experiment. To do this imagine that the economy starts out at P_1, y_1 — the intersection point of the curves AD_0 and AS_1. Now imagine that aggregate supply increases from AS_1 to

---

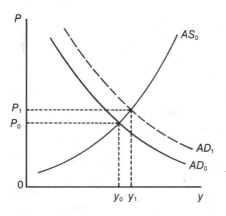

Shifts in the aggregate demand curve generate changes in the same direction in both the level of output and the price level. A rise in aggregate demand (from AD_0 to AD_1) raises both output and the price level; a drop in aggregate demand (from AD_1 to AD_0) lowers both output and the price level.

Figure 7.6
Shifts in Aggregate Supply

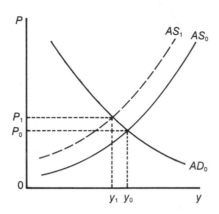

Shifts in the aggregate supply curve generate movements in output and the price level that are in opposite directions. A drop in aggregate supply (from AS_0 to AS_1) lowers the level of output and raises the price level. A rise in aggregate supply (from AS_1 to AS_0) raises output and lowers the price level.

AS_0. In this event output rises to y_0 and the price level falls to P_0. Thus, a rise in aggregate supply raises the level of output but lowers the price level.

To summarize: a change in aggregate demand changes both output and the price level in the same direction. If aggregate demand rises both output and the price level rise; if aggregate demand falls both output and the price level fall. In contrast, a shift in the aggregate supply curve generates movements in output and the price level in opposite directions. A fall in aggregate supply lowers output and raises the price level and a rise in aggregate supply raises output and lowers the price level.

It will be evident to you that this basic framework is capable of tracking macroeconomic events both when output and the price level move in the same direction as each other and when they move in opposite directions.

You have now studied the basic framework of aggregate demand and aggregate supply analysis and have a general understanding of the concepts of aggregate supply and aggregate demand and, more importantly, a clear view of the nature of macroeconomic equilibrium and the place of the equilibrium analysis in making predictions. You will now to go on to explore in greater depth and detail some particular theories of aggregate demand and aggregate supply that enable us to make clear-cut predictions about movements in output and prices (and other variables as well).

The next six chapters are going to take you through a detailed development of the theory of aggregate demand. This theory is relatively uncontroversial. After that, there will be three chapters on the theory of aggregate supply. There is less agreement in this area, and three alternative theories of aggregate supply will be presented. We shall then go on to consider macroeconomic equilibrium and the crucial role of expectations about the price level in determining that equilibrium. After we have completed these chapters (Part III of the book) we shall then return to the facts and see how the theories of macroeconomics help us to understand the macroeconomic facts that are described in Chapters 2 and 6.

Summary

A. Aggregate Demand

Aggregate demand is the demand for all goods and services — the demand for aggregate output. The aggregate demand curve is the relationship between the price level and the quantity demanded of all goods and services. The aggregate demand curve summarizes the aggregate of the expenditure decision rules of all the agents in the economy.

B. Aggregate Supply

Aggregate supply is the supply of all goods and services — the supply of aggregate output. The aggregate supply curve is the relationship between the price level and the total quantity of goods and services supplied. The aggregate supply curve summarizes the aggregate of the output decision rules of all agents in the economy.

C. Macroeconomic Equilibrium

Macroeconomic equilibrium occurs when aggregate demand equals aggregate supply. The equilibrium point is the only point that has empirical content. Disequilibrium points can be conjectured about and be the subject of thought experiments but not the subject of predictions about the world. This is not an empirical matter. It is an axiom — a matter of principle.

D. Price and Output Changes

Shifts in aggregate demand produce positive co-movements of output and the price level. Shifts in aggregate supply produce negative co-movements between output and the price level.

Review Questions

1. What is meant by aggregate demand?
2. What is the difference between aggregate demand and the quantity of goods and services bought?

3. Why would we expect the aggregate demand curve to be downward-sloping?

4. List some of the things that might shift the aggregate demand curve.

5. What is the key difference between the theory of demand for orange juice and the theory of aggregate demand? (*Hint*: What kind of a price is the price of orange juice and what kind of a price is the price level?)

6. What do we mean by aggregate supply?

7. Why might the aggregate supply curve slope upwards?

8. In what circumstances would it make sense to suppose that the aggregate supply curve is vertical?

9. List some of the things that might shift the aggregate supply curve.

10. What is meant by macroeconomic equilibrium?

11. Why is disequilibrium only a state of mind and not the prediction of a theory?

12. Suppose there was a rise in aggregate demand and a fall (shift to the left) in aggregate supply. What would happen to (a) the price level and (b) the level of output?

8

Aggregate Demand and Consumption

The subject matter of this and the next five chapters was, for the twenty years from the late 1950s through to the late 1970s, the heart of macroeconomics. Several generations of intermediate textbooks on the subject, many important research monographs, and literally thousands of important articles in learned journals deal with various aspects of the material presented here. It is the theory of aggregate demand that has grown out of the work of John Maynard Keynes. You should be aware that the material presented here covers only the essential features of that theory. As a result of the developments in macroeconomics in the past ten to fifteen years — developments that will be explained in some detail in Chapters 15 to 19 — we now have a much better perspective than ever before on the Keynesian theory of aggregate demand. It no longer stands as the whole of macroeconomics. It does not even provide the centerpiece of the explanation for macroeconomic fluctuations. That is not to say, however, that the Keynesian theory of aggregate demand is wrong. There is nothing wrong with an analysis that is but one part of the complete story. The part of the story that Keynesian analysis contains is the determination of aggregate demand at a given price level.

To embark upon your study of the theory of aggregate demand, you have six tasks, which are to:

a) Know the components of aggregate demand.
b) Know the theories of the consumption function proposed by Keynes, Friedman, and Modigliani.

    c) Understand the connection between wealth and income and why current income is a major determinant of consumption.

    d) Know how to represent the consumption and savings functions in simple equations and diagrams.

    e) Know the main features of the consumption function in Canada.

    f) Understand the Keynesian cross model.

First, it will be useful to know the components into which aggregate demand is divided.

A. Components of Aggregate Demand

Just as a matter of arithmetic, aggregate demand could be divided up in an infinite number of different ways. It would be possible to distinguish between the demand for beer, for pretzels, for steak, for ketchup, for power stations, for nuclear submarines, and so on. For some purposes, such a detailed disaggregation of the total volume of demand in the economy is essential. For the purpose of the questions addressed in macroeconomics, however, such a detailed classification of the components of aggregate demand appears to be unnecessary. It has turned out to be useful, nevertheless, to divide aggregate demand into a small number of key components, the determination of each of which involves different considerations. Specifically, for the purpose of doing macroeconomic analysis, aggregate demand is divided into four components. They are:

    (1) Consumption demand

    (2) Investment demand

    (3) Government demand

    (4) Net foreign demand.

These four components of aggregate demand are closely related to the components of aggregate expenditure dealt with in Chapter 3. [For example, see Equation (3.6)]. There are, however, two important distinctions between the components of aggregate expenditure and the components of aggregate demand. One of these distinctions will be explained now and the other reserved until we have examined the components of aggregate demand.

One distinction between the components of aggregate expenditure and those of aggregate demand turns on the distinction between the terms *expenditure* and *demand*. *Expenditure* refers to what people have actually *spent*. *Demand* refers to what people *plan* to spend — to their *decision rules*. Expenditure is an actual *quantity*. Demand is a *schedule* — a statement about how much would be spent under certain specified conditions. Always keep this distinction in mind.

Let us now go on to briefly describe the four components of aggregate demand. When we have completed our description of consumption and investment demand, it will be possible to come back and emphasize another distinction between the components of aggregate demand and those of aggregate expenditure.

(i) Consumption Demand

Consumption demand is the aggregate demand by households for goods and services to be used up for current consumption purposes. Examples of consumption demand would be the demand for beer and pretzels and for steak and ketchup. Other examples would be the demand for vacations, travel, movies and entertainment; the demand for houses and apartments; the demand for electricty, gas or oil; the demand for haircuts, skiing lessons, etc., indeed, the demand for any of the many thousands and thousands of activities on which we plan to spend our income.

(ii) Investment Demand

Investment demand is distinguished from consumption demand by the fact that an *investment is the purchase of a capital good*, defined as a new piece of equipment that is durable and that provides services over a number of years. Sometimes the services will be in the form of consumption services, and sometimes they will be production services. Both households and firms make investment expenditures. Examples of investment expenditures made by households are the purchase of a new house, a new car, a new refrigerator, or any of the other many thousands of new consumer durable goods. Examples of investment expenditures by firms are the purchase of a new steel mill, a hydroelectric generating plant, a car assembly line, a computer, or again, any of the many thousands of different types of new capital goods used in the production process.

It is important that you clearly understand the distinction between consumption and investment. *Consumption* is the purchase of goods and services for current use. *Investment* is the purchase of goods and services for current and future use. When you buy a consumption good, you buy a current flow of services. When you invest, you buy a capital good that is a stock of new equipment that gives rise to a current and future flow of either production or consumption services.

It is also important to distinguish clearly between the term investment in the sense in which economists use it when doing macroeconomic analysis and the way in which the term is used in everyday speech. In everyday usage, investment often means the purchase of a stock or a share or a bond. That is not investment in macroeconomic analysis. Such an activity is a portfolio reallocation and has very different causes and consequences from the purchase of newly produced capital equipment.

Before going on to deal with the other components of aggregate demand, let us also notice a further distinction between the components of aggregate demand and the components of aggregate expenditure set out in Chapter 3. We are here distinguishing between consumption and investment in terms of the *durability* of the goods purchased. Consumption is the purchase of goods and services that are going to be used up in the current period regardless of whether they are bought by households or firms. Investment is the purchase of goods that are more durable than a single period and that will provide either productive or consumption services into the future.

In Chapter 3, we did not make that distinction. Rather, we talked of consumer expenditure as being the purchase of all goods and services by households regardless of whether they were durable or not, and we referred to investment as the purchases of capital equipment by firms only. There are two reasons why Chapter 3 used the definitions that it did. First, that is the way the National Income Accounts are put together. Second, the flow diagrams used in that chapter would have been more cumbersome if we had allowed both households and firms to invest or buy new capital equipment. (You may find it beneficial to go back to Chapter 3 and develop for yourself some flow charts that take into account this additional investment activity.) Now that we are about to embark upon an analysis of the determination of the demand for consumer and capital goods, it becomes necessary to be more careful in distinguishing between the demand for consumption services and the demand for capital goods.

Let us now go on to consider the remaining two components of aggregate demand.

(iii) Government Demand

The third component of aggregate demand is the government demand for goods and services. Much of government demand represents the demand by the government for goods and services produced by the private sector of the economy. Examples are the demand for a nuclear submarine, for a highway, for a new administrative building, or for paper clips and paper. Notice that the examples just given include both capital and consumption goods. No distinction is made between what might be termed government investment demand (demand for nuclear submarines, highways, and buildings) and what might be termed government consumption demand (demand for paper clips and paper).

For the purpose of macroeconomic analysis, there is no advantage to be gained from dividing government expenditure into its investment and consumption components. Indeed, such a decision is, to a large extent, arbitrary. For example, two of the big items of expenditure by the government, health and education expenditure, could be regarded as either consumption or investment. They are consumption in the sense that they provide an immediate flow of services — of good health and knowledge. They are also interpretable as investment expenditure because a healthy and educated person has an asset — human capital — which is capable of generating an income stream not just at the present but in the future as well. For some purposes it is crucial to be able to correctly distinguish the investment from the consumption component of government expenditure. For present purposes, however, there is no gain from pursuing that distinction.

In addition to buying goods and services produced by the private sector, the government also demands goods and services that it supplies itself. Examples are administrative services, police and law enforcement services, and military services. In its undertaking of these activities, you may think of the government as being like a firm. It hires labor from households (soldiers, sailors, bureaucrats, judges, and so on) and produces goods and services — goods and services that it uses itself.

Government demand for goods and services is treated as being exogenous. That is, the quantity of goods and services demanded by the government is treated as something that it is not our task to explain and that can be determined by the government at whatever level the government so chooses, independently of the values of any of the other variables in our macroeconomic model.[1]

Much of government expenditure in the modern world is excluded from the above definition of government demand. For example, government social security expenditure on pensions and welfare programs and subsidies to various industries, although vast in volume, do not represent government expenditure on goods and services. Rather, they are transfers of money — of purchasing power — from the government to private individuals and firms. These expenditures are called *transfer payments*. Their effects on aggregate demand are analyzed by examining their effects on private consumption and investment demand. They are not ignored, therefore, but they are not treated as direct demands for goods and services by the government.

(iv) Net Foreign Demand

Net foreign demand for goods and services is the difference between the demands for exports and imports. Foreigners place demands on the domestic economy by demanding those goods and services that are exported from the domestic economy. Residents of the domestic

---

[1] As a matter of fact, in some very elaborate statistical models of the economy, government demand for goods and services is broken into two parts, that which is exogenous and that which responds to the state of the economy. Such a dichotomization of government demand is important for some purposes, but not essential to the task upon which you are currently embarked.

economy place demands on the rest of the world, and these are measured by the demand for imported goods and services. The difference between these two magnitudes represents net foreign demand. For the purposes of what follows, it will be assumed that net foreign demand is always exactly zero. This, of course, does not correspond with the facts. By making the assumption, it turns out to be possible to considerably simplify the task of understanding the main elements of the theory of aggregate demand. In Chapter 25, the theory of aggregate demand is modified to take explicit account of international trade and investment.

Aggregate demand has been divided into four components — consumption, investment, government, and net foreign demand for goods and services. The last item is being ignored for the present, and government demand is being treated as exogenous and therefore does not have to be explained. The other two items, however, do need explanation. The rest of this chapter deals with the determinants of consumption demand, and the next chapter, with investment demand.

B. Theories of the Consumption Function proposed by Keynes, Friedman and Modigliani

In his analysis of the determination of aggregate demand, the so-called theory of the consumption function was regarded by Keynes as the centerpiece of his new theory of income and employment. We now suspect that Keynes had an exaggerated opinion of the importance of this innovation. It is, nevertheless, an important ingredient in the theory of aggregate demand.

(i) Keynes's Theory of the Consumption Function

Keynes's theory of the determinants of consumption was that, of the many possible factors that influence the level of consumption demand, the most important is the level of real disposable income.[2] By real disposable income is meant real income (real GNP) minus the real value of taxes levied by the government. The way in which consumption demand is influenced by real disposable income is, according to Keynes, based on what he called "the fundamental psychological law upon which we are entitled to depend with great confidence." That law, Keynes went on to outline, is the proposition "that men are disposed, as a rule and on the average, to increase their con-

---

[2] Keynes set out his theory of the consumption function in Chapters 8 and 9 of the *General Theory of Employment, Interest and Money* (London: Macmillan & Co. Ltd., 1936). The two quotations in this paragraph are taken from p. 96 of this source.

sumption as their income increases, but not by as much as the increase in their income." What Keynes is saying is that consumption depends on income such that, for a given rise in income, consumption will rise by some fraction of the rise in income.

Following the first statement of Keynes's consumption function hypothesis, a great deal of statistical work was undertaken that sought to test Keynes's theory with the newly available national income accounting data. It was discovered as a result of this work that although Keynes's basic ideas seemed well founded, there was an important difference in the relationship between consumption and income in the short run (year by year) as compared with the long run (decade by decade). The long-run data revealed that consumption was proportional to income. The short-run data revealed that although consumption and income move in the same direction, the relationship between the two is non-proportional. Furthermore, when individual consumption and income data were examined, it was discovered that although people with higher incomes consumed more, the variations in consumption were much smaller in proportionate terms than variations in income. Also, these individual variations in income and consumption were less than those observed for variations in aggregate income and consumption over time.

These puzzles and problems revealed by the data led to a more refined formulation of the theory of the consumption function. The two leading architects of the refining were Milton Friedman, who developed the permanent income hypothesis[3] and Franco Modigliani, who developed the life-cycle hypothesis.[4] These two contributions have more similarities than differences and hark back to the work of one of the greatest pre-Keynesian economists, Irving Fisher. They can be conveniently summarized by treating them as if they are a single theory.

(ii) Friedman's and Modigliani's Theory of the Consumption Function

Friedman and Modigliani reasoned as follows. If people can borrow and lend freely through financial institutions, then their consumption in any one particular period will not be constrained by their income

---

[3] Milton Friedman, *A Theory of the Consumption Function* (Princeton, N.J.: Princeton University Press, 1957).

[4] Franco Modigliani gave a useful and comprehensive appraisal of his work in his paper "The Life-Cycle Hypothesis of Saving Twenty-five Years Later," in *Contemporary Issues in Economics*, Michael Parkin and A. R. Nobay, eds. (Manchester, England: Manchester University Press, 1975), pp. 2-36. This paper also contains a fairly comprehensive bibliography on the consumption function.

in that particular period. If for some reason income is *temporarily* high, it wili be possible to save a larger than normal fraction of that temporarily high income, so that consumption would be a low fraction of income. If, in some other year, income was temporarily low, it would be possible to consume the whole of income and perhaps also to consume some previous savings (or, if previous savings were inadequate, to borrow against future income).

Recognizing the possibility of breaking the direct link between income and consumption through borrowing and lending, Modigliani and Friedman suggested that the ultimate constraint upon how much consumption an individual can undertake is the amount of that individual's wealth. They proposed the hypothesis that the wealthier an individual is, on the average, the more will that individual consume. In Modigliani's version of the theory (called the *life-cycle* hypothesis), the individual would attempt to smooth out the path of consumption over the life span, even though income received would vary from year to year. In Friedman's version of the theory (called the *permanent income* hypothesis), families are assumed to live forever and seek to smooth consumption both over lifetimes of individual family members and across the generations.

Upon careful investigation of the data, it turns out that both the *permanent income* hypothesis and *life-cycle* hypothesis, which say that consumption depends on wealth, are theories that fit the facts better than the Keynes's hypothesis that consumption depends primarily on disposable income.

C. Connection Between Wealth and Income and Why Current Income is a Major Determinant of Consumption

Wealth and income are related to each other in a simple way. As you already know, wealth is a stock and income is a flow. The relationship between income and wealth can be put in terms of stocks and flows. Income is the flow that is generated by the stock of wealth.

You have already seen in Chapters 3 and 4 how the main macroeconomic flows and stocks are defined and measured. You are now going to be able to deepen your understanding of the relationship between these stocks and flows. The easiest way to see the connection is in the case of a financial asset. Suppose that you own a savings deposit in a bank that has a value of $1000 and pays interest at the rate of 15 percent per annum. Evidently, if you have a deposit of $1000 yielding a rate of return of 15 percent per annum, you will receive an income from that deposit of $150 per annum. The deposit of $1000 is a *stock* and is part of your *wealth*. The income of $150 per annum is a *flow* and is part of your *income*. The rate of interest is what converts the stock of wealth into the flow of income.

In calculating the flow of income generated by a stock of wealth it is necessary to be careful to take proper account of inflation. Suppose, in the example that we have just worked through, that the economy is experiencing inflation with prices rising at 5 percent per annum. This means that your $1000 bank deposit will only buy you $950 worth of goods at the end of the year. Thus, you have suffered a loss of $50 worth of goods as a result of your bank deposit falling in real value. This $50 loss has to be subtracted from your $150 interest income in order to arrive at your *real income*. Thus, your *real income* is only $100. This is equivalent to a 10% rate of return.

To keep all this clear we need to be more precise in our use of terms. Let us call the rate of interest received on the bank deposit the *market rate of interest*. Let us call the rate of return obtained after allowance has been made for the losses caused by inflation the *real rate of interest*. Thus,

market rate of interest = real rate of interest + rate of inflation

The rate of interest that converts a stock of wealth into a flow of income (real income) is the real rate of interest. We can write an equation to describe this, which reads:

Wealth × Real Rate of Interest = Real Income.

This same type of relationship holds between *all* forms of wealth and all forms of income. For example, the stocks of physical assets held — plant and equipment — and their rate of return generate an income. Also, the stock of human capital (see Chapter 4) and its rate of return generate a labor income. That is:

Human Wealth × Real Rate of Interest = Real Labor Income.

Of course, financial assets are traded in markets and pay an explicit rate of interest. Human wealth is unlike other forms of wealth in that it does not (at least in societies that do not have slavery) trade directly in markets. Nevertheless, conceptually the relationship between human wealth and labor income is identical to that between other forms of wealth and the income stream that they generate.

If we were to add up all the forms of wealth owned by an individual, the individual's total wealth would be obtained. The rate of return on that total wealth would generate the individual's total income.

The concept of *permanent income*, which gives the name to Milton Friedman's theory of the consumption function, can now be understood. It is the level of income that would be sustained on the average through the infinite future, while maintaining a constant stock of wealth. It could be thought of as the stock of wealth multiplied by the normal, long-run, average real rate of return. Actual income will fluctuate from year to year as a result of random fluctuations in the actual rate of return.

So far we have talked about how to convert wealth into income. We do this by multiplying the relevant wealth stock by a rate of return. We could equivalently convert a future stream of income into its equivalent current stock of wealth. In performing such a calculation it is important to notice that the value today (today's wealth) of $1 of income earned in the future depends on how far in the future that income is earned. One dollar earned in the next 5 minutes is worth much more than $1 earned in the last 5 minutes of your life. The reason for this is easy to see. One dollar earned in the next 5 minutes could be used to buy an interest-bearing security that would lead to the accumulation of more dollars in the future from interest receipts. One dollar earned 50 years in the future would be worth less than $1 earned in the next 5 minutes simply because it would be incapable of earning interest for you over the next 50 years. To calculate the wealth equivalent of future income, the future income stream has to be converted to a common valuation basis.

The most useful common valuation basis is known as the *present value*. The present value of a future sum of money is simply that sum of money that if you were to receive it today, would, when invested at the average rate of interest, accumulate to the pre-stated future value. For example, if the rate of interest is 10 percent, $100 invested today would accumulate in 1 year to $110. It would be said, therefore, that the present value of $110 to be received 1 year hence, at a 10 percent rate of interest, is equal to $100. The sum of $100 invested today at a rate of interest of 10 percent for 2 years would, at the end of that period, accumulate to $121 — $10 interest in the first year accumulating to $110, plus $11 in the second year ($10 interest on the principal and $1 interest on the $10 of interest earned in the first year). It would be said, therefore, that the present value of $121 to be received 2 years hence, at a 10 percent rate of interest is equal to $100.

It is important that you keep clear the distinction between real and nominal or market interest rates when performing present value calculations. The purpose in calculating a present value is not simply to cancel out the effects of inflation. It would be necessary to calculate a present value even in a world in which there was no inflation.

The arithmetic example given in the preceding paragraph, where the rate of interest is 10 percent, could be thought of as applying to a world in which there is no inflation (and in which the real rate of interest is 10 percent). What is being said in that example is that $110 received 1 year hence would be worth less to someone today than would $110 received today, even though one year from now it would have the same purchasing power in terms of goods as $110 would today. The reason for this is that if the individual had $110 today, it would be possible to use that money and earn a real rate of interest so that in 1 year from now more goods than $110 worth could be bought. With constant prices and a real rate of interest of 10 percent, $100 today is the equivalent of (would be regarded by anyone as being just as good as) $110 to be delivered 1 year from today. The calculation of a present value, therefore, is a *real* calculation. It is the conversion of a real stream of future income into a present value.

If we add up the present values of the incomes that an individual will (or expects to) receive each year in the future, we arrive at a total that is the individual's wealth. That is, we arrive at a sum of money that is a present stock and that has an equivalent value to the future (discounted) income flow.

Now that you understand the connection between income and wealth, you will be aware that the life-cycle and permanent income hypotheses of consumption are, in effect, generalizations of the Keynesian theory of consumption. They both say that consumption will depend on today's disposable income and on all future (discounted) disposable income. Other things being equal, the larger that today's disposable income is, the larger wealth is, and the greater will be the level of consumption. The larger that future disposable income is, other things being equal, the larger wealth is, and the greater will be today's consumption.

There are two lines of reasoning that lead to the proposition that the most important factor determining current consumption is current disposable income. The first follows directly from the discussion above concerning the relationship between wealth and income. Although it is true that if borrowing and lending in free capital markets is possible, then it is wealth rather than income which is the ultimate constraint on consumption. There is nevertheless good reason for elevating the level of current disposable income to a more important status than wealth.

As you saw above, wealth can be equivalently thought of as current disposable income plus all future disposable income converted to its present value. There is an important distinction, however, between the present and future that arises from the information that we have about them. The present is known and certain, whereas the future is unknown and probabilistic. It is very likely that what is happening in the present to an individual's disposable income is going to be treated as a signal concerning what is likely to happen in the future. It seems sensible to hypothesize, therefore, that wealth, as perceived by an individual, is positively related to current disposable income. If that is so, it is current disposable income rather than wealth that is, from an operational or observational point of view, the major determinant of current consumption.

Another way of putting this would be to say that to a large extent wealth is not a directly observable and measurable variable. It contains, in part, future expected income flows that are not yet known. Those future expected income flows must be forecasted on the basis of things that are known, one important ingredient of which is current disposable income.

There is a second reason why current disposable income will be an important determinant of consumption. The permanent income and life-cycle hypotheses both reach the conclusion that consumption will depend on wealth by assuming that individuals may borrow and lend unlimited amounts in order to smooth out consumption over their lifetime. However, there are good reasons why this will not, in general, be possible. It is difficult to borrow unlimited funds against future labor income. It may be possible, therefore, that an individual is constrained in the amount of consumption that can be undertaken by the amount of current disposable income, since that amount will be used as an indication to a potential lender concerning the individual's ability to repay the loan and pay the interest on it.

For two reasons, then, (1) because current income provides good information to an individual about future income and therefore about wealth, and (2) because current disposable income provides good information to potential lenders, it seems reasonable to suppose that it is current disposable income that is the most important single factor determining current consumption demand.[5]

D. Consumption and Savings Functions in Simple Equations and Diagrams

The discussion and analysis that has been conducted above may now be summarized in a very compact form by writing a simple equation to describe the determination of consumption demand. Such an equation would be

$$c = a + b(y - t) \qquad a > 0, 1 > b > 0. \tag{8.1}$$

The value of aggregate real consumption demand is represented by c, real income (real gross national product) is represented by y, the

---

[5] The account of the theory of the consumption function given in this chapter has been highly condensed and selective. The best, lengthy textbook treatment of the subject that will fill in a lot of the detail for you is Gardner Ackley, *Macroeconomic Theory* (New York: The Macmillan Publishing Co. Inc., 1961), Chaps. 10-12.

An up-to-date survey of the empirical issues, but using U.S. data, is Walter Dolde, "Issues and Models in Empirical Research on Aggregate Consumer Expenditure," in *On the State of Macro-Economics*, Karl Brunner and Allan H. Meltzer, eds., 12 (Spring 1980), 161-206, Carnegie-Rochester Conference Series on Public Policy.

total collection of taxes by the government net of transfer payments is represented by t, and a and b are *constants* or *parameters*. According to Keynes's "fundamental psychological law," the parameter b will be a positive fraction; an example would be, say, 3/4. The parameter a captures the effects of all these things that influence consumption other than disposable income. These other factors will include such things as demographic trends and tastes. There are, of course, many such things. The assumption being made, however, is that all the other influences upon consumption have effects that may be ignored either because their effects are slight or because they are factors which are themselves changing slowly. The parameter a will presumably be positive, indicating that if people had very low current income, they would seek to consume more than their income, thereby using up part of their past accumulated savings.

The consumption function written as an equation above may be shown in a simple diagram. Figure 8.1 illustrates the consumption function. The vertical axis measures real consumption, and the horizontal axis measures real income. In order to show the relationship between consumption and income on a diagram, it is necessary to be precise about how taxes vary as income varies. For present purposes, it will be assumed that taxes are set by the government to yield a certain total amount of revenue, t, independently of what the level of income is. In other words, taxes will be treated as a constant. This is not the only assumption that could have been made, nor is it necessarily the most natural one. Permitting taxes to vary with income would be more natural, but it makes the presentation of the analysis slightly more cumbersome and does not modify the results that we shall get in any qualitative way.

Proceeding then with the assumption that taxes are constant, we can now illustrate the relationship between real consumption and real income in Figure 8.1. The continuous line labelled $c = a + by$ represents the consumption demand or consumption function in an economy in which taxes and transfer payments sum to zero. The dashed line labelled $c = a + by - bt$ represents the consumption function in an economy that has net taxes at the level t. The other line in the diagram is a 45° line and can be read as telling you that at each point on that line consumption would be exactly equal to income. You may use this as a reference line, therefore, to figure out whether or not consumption will exceed, equal, or fall short of current income. You see, for example, that at the income level y_1 and the level of net taxes t, consumption exactly equals income. At income levels above y_1, consumption is less than income, and at income levels below y_1, consumption exceeds income.

This equation and diagram summarize the theory of the determinants of consumption demand. The slope of this line (represented

Figure 8.1
The Consumption
Function

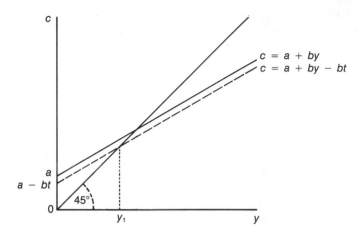

Consumption is a function of disposable income. When consumption (c) is graphed against real income (y), the consumption function slopes upwards at the rate of the marginal propensity to consume (the parameter b). If the level of taxes (t) is zero, the intercept of the consumption function, the continuous line, on the vertical axis is equal to a. If the level of taxes is non-zero, the intercept of the consumption function, the dashed line, on the vertical axis is equal to a minus the marginal propensity to consume (b) times the level of taxes (t).

by the parameter b) is given a name, and that name is the *marginal propensity to consume.* If the marginal propensity to consume is high (close to 1), the consumption function will be steep (almost as steep as the 45° line). The lower is the marginal propensity to consume, the flatter is the consumption function.

Notice that the consumption function as drawn in Figure 8.1 will shift each time there is a different level of taxes. You can see this directly in Figure 8.1 by comparing the continuous line drawn for zero taxes with the dashed line drawn for a tax level of t. This tells you that the higher the level of taxes, the further downwards the consumption function shifts. What this means is that the higher the tax level, the lower the level of disposable income, and therefore, the lower the level of consumption associated with each level of real income or gross national product. The amount by which the consumption function shifts down for a \$1 rise in taxes is the fraction b. The reason why the consumption function shifts down by only the fraction b and not by the whole amount of the increase in taxes is that some of the increase in taxes comes from a reduction in savings, and only fraction b of the increase in taxes comes from a reduction in consumption. You will be able to see this more clearly by considering the relationship between consumption, savings, and taxes, which is the next and final task in what has been a long section of this chapter.

A household can do only three things with its income: it can (1) consume, (2) save, or (3) pay taxes. This can be written as an equation, namely

$$y = c + s + t \tag{8.2}$$

Savings are what are left over after meeting consumption expenditures and paying taxes. Clearly, in planning its consumption, the household is also implicitly planning how much saving to undertake. If planned consumption is determined by Equation (8.1) above, that is, if $c = a + b(y - t)$, it must be the case that the household is planning to save an amount given by another equation, namely

$$s = -a + (1 - b)(y - t) \tag{8.3}$$

How do we know that Equation (8.3) tells us about the household's savings plans? The answer is simply that if we add together the household's consumption plan, Equation (8.1), and its savings plan, Equation (8.3), we get the proposition that

$$c + s = y - t \tag{8.4}$$

namely, that planned consumption plus savings is equal to disposable income. You will recognize this as simply a rearrangement of Equation (8.2) above. Equation (8.3) is usually referred to as the *savings function*, and the slope of the savings function $(1 - b)$ is the *marginal propensity to save*. The marginal propensity to save plus the marginal propensity to consume always add up to unity.

You may find it helpful to represent the consumption function and the savings function in a diagram that shows how the two are related. Figure 8.2 does just this. Frame (a) shows consumption plotted against income, and frame (b) shows savings plotted against income. Indeed, frame (a) is nothing other than Figure 8.1. Adopt the convention that the units of measurement are the same on both horizontal axes. That being the case, the two frames are related to each other in the following way. Look first at the continuous lines that represent an economy with no taxes, so that disposable income and aggregate income are the same number. In that case, the vertical distance between the consumption function and the 45° line in frame (a) is equal to the vertical distance between the horizontal axis and the savings function in frame (b). As an example, at the income level y_2, consumption exactly equals income, and savings exactly equals zero. At an income level above y_2, for example, y_h, savings can be represented on frame (a) by the vertical line marked h and equivalently in frame (b) by the vertical distance h.

Next, consider the economy in which taxes are not zero. In that case the consumption function has shifted downwards by an amount equal to b times taxes. The savings function has also shifted down,

Figure 8.2
The Consumption and
Savings Functions

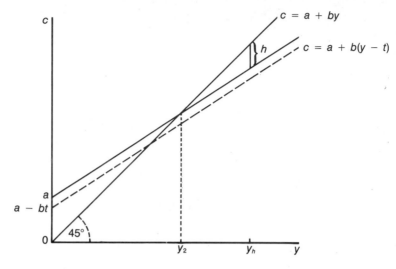

(a) Consumption Function

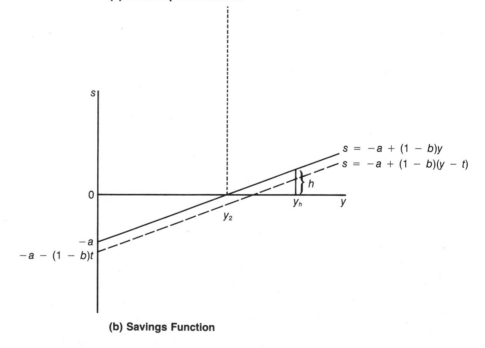

(b) Savings Function

Since income must be disposed of either by consuming, saving, or paying taxes, the consumption function implies a savings function. When saving and consumption plans are added together they exactly exhaust disposable income. For example, if taxes are zero (the continuous lines) and if income is y_h, then the amount saved, h, may be read off directly from the savings function in frame (b) or as the distance marked h in frame (a). When taxes are t the consumption function is lower by bt [the dashed line in frame (a)] and the savings function is lower by $(1 - b)t$ [the dashed line in frame (b)].

but this time by an amount equal to $(1 - b)$ times taxes. What does this mean? It means simply that for a \$1 rise in taxes, planned consumption drops by fraction b of a dollar, and savings drop by fraction $1 - b$ of a dollar — the drop in savings and planned consumption taken together being enough to make up the \$1 of taxes. The after-tax consumption and savings functions are parallel to the pre-tax functions.

Adding the consumption function and the savings function together gives a number equal to disposable income; that is, a number equal to income minus taxes.

You have now covered the major aspects of the theory of consumption demand and the related theory of savings. Let us now turn to the task of examining the actual data on consumption in Canada and discover the properties of Canada's consumption function.

E. Canadian Consumption Function

What does the Canadian consumption function look like? We cannot answer this question precisely because we do not have a precise measure of the *consumption* of durables. We know how much people spend on durables each year. We do not, however, have a good measure of the rate at which the stock of durables is being used up — is being depreciated — and therefore, consumed. There are two ways that we can proceed in taking a look at the actual consumption function. One is to pretend that expenditure on durable goods gives us a good indication as to the actual consumption of the stock of durable goods. In other words we could treat total consumer expenditure as a proxy measure for actual consumption. An alternative would be to look only at expenditure on non-durables. This would understate total consumption for it would ignore the consumption services yielded by the stock of durable goods. The first method of attempting to approximate the value of consumption seems to be the more desirable one.

Using total consumer expenditure as a measure of consumption, Figure 8.3 gives a plot of Canada's consumption function. Each point in that diagram represents a single year and the year is indicated by the two-digit number so that, for example, 1982 appears as the dot marked 82.

Notice that the Canadian consumption function shown in Figure 8.3 looks remarkably like the theoretical consumption function shown in Figure 8.1. Consumption rises as income rises but by a smaller amount than the rise in income. As a matter of fact the marginal propensity to consume implied by these data is 0.855.

Notice that, like the theoretical consumption function in Figure 8.1, the actual consumption function shows that when income is very low, consumption exceeds income. This is a situation in which people

Figure 8.3
The Canadian
Consumption Function

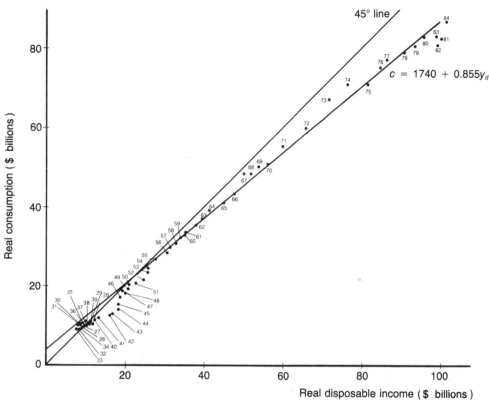

The relationship between real consumer expenditure and real disposable income in Canada is a close one and is similar to the theoretical consumption function proposed by Keynes. The marginal propensity to consume is 0.855 and the equation describing real consumption expenditure is $c = 1740 + 0.855y_d$.

Source: Real consumption is Cansim Series D40735. Real disposable income is personal disposable income, Cansim Series D30848, deflated by the personal consumption expenditure deflator, Cansim Series D40626.

are running down the values of their assets by temporarily spending more than they are earning.

If, instead of measuring consumption as total consumer expenditure, we focussed only on expenditure on non-durables, the consumption function would look similar to that shown in Figure 8.3 but it would have a flatter slope and would be lower down. The marginal propensity to consume on non-durables only in the Canadian data is about 2/3.

You have now covered not only the major aspects of the theory of consumption demand and the related theory of savings, but also have examined Canada's consumption function. It is now possible to move on to explore the simplest theory of income determination, the Keynesian cross model.

F. Keynesian Cross Model

The essence of the Keynesian theory of aggregate demand — what has come to be called the *Keynesian cross model* — may now be understood.

This simplest theory of income determination applies to an economy in which there is a considerable amount of underutilization of labor and capital resources so that output can fluctuate independently of the capacity of the economy to produce goods and services. It also applies only in the special circumstances in which the aggregate supply curve (introduced in Chapter 7) is perfectly elastic — that is, is horizontal. You should be suspicious that these are pretty unusual and not very likely circumstances. To fit the real world such circumstances would require that all producers face a technology that enables them to produce output at a constant cost regardless of the scale of output, and we should also require a situation in which the costs of all factors of production remain constant as output (and employment of factors of production) varies. Such circumstances (unlikely though they are) would, were they to occur in the world, give rise to a horizontal aggregate supply curve.

If the aggregate supply curve did happen to be horizontal, then the quantity of output demanded would determine the actual level of output. That is the situation visualized in this simplest Keynesian cross theory of the determination of output. Let us now proceed to see how the theory works.

In Figure 8.1 you have already become familiar with a diagram in which output is measured on the horizontal axis (recalling that output and real income are equal to each other), and one of the major components of aggregate demand (consumption) is measured on the vertical axis. We don't have to move very far from the content of Figure 8.1 to determine the level of aggregate demand and aggregate output (real income) in the simplest Keynesian cross framework. We can do this by broadening our view slightly, as we do in Figure 8.4, and measure on the vertical axis of the diagram not just consumption but all the components of aggregate demand added together; that is, y^d. We continue to measure actual output, y, on the horizontal axis.

The first thing to understand about the diagram in this slightly modified form is the meaning of the 45° line. That line has been labelled $y = y^d$ and states that actual output, y, is equal to the quantity of output demanded, y^d.

The consumption function, the line labelled $c = a + b(y - t)$, already introduced in Figure 8.1, is reproduced in Figure 8.4. Con-

**Figure 8.4
The Keynesian
Cross Model**

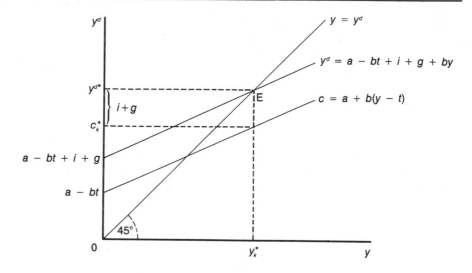

The Keynesian cross model is the essence of the Keynesian theory of output determination. Actual output (y) is equal to aggregate demand (the 45° line). Aggregate demand is the sum of consumption demand (c) and autonomous expenditure ($i + g$). The point where the aggregate demand line ($y^d = a - bt + i + g + by$) cuts the 45° line determines the equilibrium level of real income (y_k^*).

sumption demand is only part of total demand. The other elements of aggregate demand (ignoring net foreign demand) are investment demand and government demand for goods and services. We have already agreed to treat government demand as exogenous so that government expenditure is fixed. Let us, for the moment, treat investment demand in the same way. That is, let us suppose that the level of investment is fixed. (The next chapter actually goes on to discuss the factors that determine investment demand.) Aggregate demand, then, can be written

$$y^d = c + i + g \qquad (8.5)$$

where i and g are real investment and real government expenditure on goods and services, respectively. In order to graph aggregate demand y^d in Figure 8.4, all that we have to do is to add the fixed amount of investment and government expenditure to the consumption function. That is, we need to displace the consumption function upwards by an amount equal to investment plus government expenditure. This is done in the diagram and represented by the line labelled

$$y^d = a - bt + i + g + by$$

This curve tells us what the level of total demand will be at each level of income. Total demand will rise as income rises. It will not, however, rise by as much as income since the consumption function itself has a slope of less than 1. At low income levels, total demand would exceed income, and at high income levels, total demand would fall short of income. There is only one income level, y_k^*, that generates a level of aggregate demand equal to itself. This is the equilibrium level of aggregate demand in the Keynesian cross model.

Income is the variable that adjusts to achieve the equilibrium. To see how this happened, consider hypothetically what would occur if income was greater than y_k^*. This is a purely hypothetical experiment which could not actually happen in the world described in Figure 8.4. In such a case, the level of aggregate demand would be less than the level of income. You can see this is true because the curve labelled y^d is lower than the 45° line at all points to the right of y_k^*. This would mean that total spending (gross national product) was less than income. However, you know this to be impossible. Hence, the conjectured income level greater than y_k^* could not occur. Similarly, income levels below y_k^* could not occur. There is one, and only one, income level that is compatible with the relationships hypothesized here, and that is the income level y_k^*, or the point E at which the aggregate demand curve cuts the 45° line.

The analysis that you have just gone through is the essence of Keynes's general theory.[6] (Keynes himself was explicit about this on page 29 of *The General Theory of Employment, Interest and Money*.)

An important and interesting implication of this analysis is the simple, so-called autonomous expenditure multiplier. Investment and government expenditure (and taxes) are all variables that change their values autonomously with respect to (independently of) the level of real income. Only consumption changes as income changes. If there is a change in the level of taxes, investment, or government expenditure, there will be induced changes in consumption and income, and the change in income will be larger than the initial change in autonomous expenditure.

To see this, consider by way of an example the effects of a rise in the level of investment. Suppose that taxes and government spending are held constant, but investment rises. We know that any change in income that occurs will be equal to the change in investment plus any induced change in consumption. That is, using the symbol "Δ" to denote "change in," we have

$$\Delta y = \Delta c + \Delta i \qquad (8.6)$$

---

[6] The presentation of this model on pp. 28 and 29 of the *General Theory* is slightly disguised by the fact that Keynes uses the level of employment rather than the level of output (income) as the variable determined by the analysis, but if you work carefully through these two pages of Keynes's book, you will find the above model there.

But we know from the theory of the consumption function that the change in consumption will be equal to the change in income multiplied by b, the marginal propensity to consume: that is,

$$\Delta c = b\Delta y \tag{8.7}$$

Substituting this equation into the previous one tells us that the change in income will be equal to b times the change in income plus the change in investment. That is,

$$\Delta y = b\Delta y + \Delta i \tag{8.8}$$

Rearranging this equation by taking the term $b\Delta y$ to the left-hand side and then dividing through by (1-b) gives

$$\Delta y = \frac{1}{1-b}\Delta i \tag{8.9}$$

You have just worked out the famous Keynesian multiplier. The change in income that is induced by a change in autonomous expenditure (investment in this case) is equal to 1 divided by the marginal propensity to save, times the initial change in autonomous

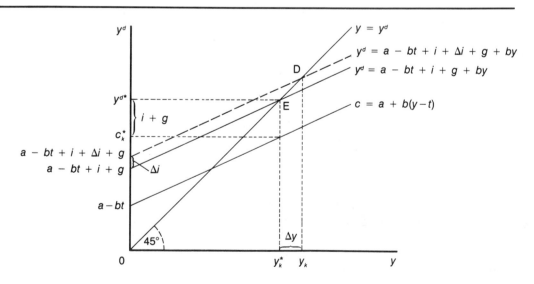

Figure 8.5
The Multiplier in the Keynesian Cross Model

A rise in autonomous expenditure (for example, a rise in investment by Δi) raises aggregate demand from the continuous line y^d to the dashed line y^d. The equilibrium is now at D, not E. Equilibrium income (output) has increased by Δy, an amount equal to $[1/(1-b)]\Delta i$.

expenditure. If the propensity to consume was, for example, 0.855 (the value obtained from the Canadian data in Section E above), then the multiplier would be 7.

Figure 8.5 illustrates the multiplier. It is possible to mark the rise in investment (Δi) on the vertical axis of the figure, thereby generating a new aggregate demand curve — the dashed curve labelled

$$y^d = a - bt + i + \Delta i + g + by$$

The new equilibrium level of income is at point D at an income level y_k. The rise in income is marked in the figure as Δy. A change in government expenditure induces a change in income that is identical to that induced by a change in investment expenditure and shown in Equation 8.9.

A change in taxes, however, induces a change in income that has a different multiplier from that on investment and government spending. Why is that? There are two reasons: first, a rise in taxes will lower income, whereas a rise in investment and a rise in government spending will raise income. This occurs because when taxes rise, disposable income and therefore consumption fall. However, a rise in taxes of $1 will in part be paid out of lower savings. Savings will be cut by $1 times the marginal propensity to save (by $1 - b$), and consumption will only be cut by b. Thus, a $1 rise in taxes leads to a fraction b of $1 cut in consumption. It is this number that has to be scaled up by the standard multiplier so that the change in income induced by a tax change is

$$\Delta y = \frac{-b}{1 - b} \Delta t \qquad (8.10)$$

Continuing with the example of a marginal propensity to consume of 0.855, the multiplier for a tax change would be -5.9. Thus a $1 rise in taxes would cut income by $5.9.

You have now discovered that in the simplest version of the Keynesian theory of aggregate demand, the level of demand (which equals the level of actual income and output) is determined by the level of autonomous expenditure. Change taxes, government spending, or investment and there will be a change in income that is bigger than the initial change in autonomous expenditure.

Summary

A. Components of Aggregate Demand

The components of aggregate demand are consumption demand, investment demand, government demand for goods and services, and the demand for net exports.

B. Theories of the Consumption Function Proposed by Keynes, Friedman and Modigilani

Keynes hypothesized that the major determinant of consumption was current disposable income. Keynes supposed that the level of consumption would rise as income rose, but the fraction of income consumed would decline. Friedman and Modigliani developed the permanent income and life-cycle hypotheses, which emphasized the role of wealth as the ultimate constraint upon consumption.

C. Connection Between Wealth and Income and Why Current Income is a Major Determinant of Consumption

Wealth is the present value of current and future income. By borrowing and lending, it is possible to break the direct connection between current income and current consumption. Nevertheless, current income is an important indicator of potential future income and therefore will influence the extent to which an individual can borrow against future labor income and will influence the individual's own assessment of what represents a desirable, sustainable consumption and savings plan. Therefore, current income is a major determinant of consumption.

D. Consumption and Savings Functions in Simple Equations and Diagrams

The consumption function may be written as

$$c = a + b(y-t)$$

Since savings plus consumption must equal disposable income, it follows that the savings function must be

$$s = -a + (1-b)(y-t)$$

If savings and consumption are added together, they always add up to disposable income $(y-t)$.

E. Canadian Consumption Function

The Canadian consumption function looks almost identical to the theoretical consumption function set out in Figure 8.1. The marginal propensity to consume (defining consumption as total consumer expenditure) is 0.855. There is a close and linear relationship between real consumer expenditure and real disposable income.

F. Keynesian Cross Model

The essence of the simple Keynesian theory of aggregate demand can be summarized in the Keynesian cross diagram. Aggregate demand is measured on the vertical axis and actual output on the horizontal axis. The 45° line says that the level of actual output will equal the quantity demanded. The aggregate demand curve plotted in the diagram shows the consumption function plus the assumed fixed level of investment and government expenditure. The point where the aggregate demand line cuts the 45° line determines the equilibrium level of income. It is an equilibrium in the sense that it is the only income level that generates a level of consumption that, when added to investment and government spending, equals that same level of income.

A rise in investment or government spending shifts the aggregate demand curve upwards and produces a higher equilibrium income level. The rise in income equals the rise in investment or government expenditure multiplied by $1/(1-b)$, where b is the marginal propensity to consume. A rise in taxes changes income by $-b/(1-b)$ times the rise in taxes (i.e., a tax rise lowers income).

Review Questions

1. What are the components into which aggregate demand is separated in order to study the determination of aggregate demand?

2. Classify the following according to whether they are consumption (c), investment (i), government expenditure (g), none of these and not part of aggregate expenditure (n), or, not enough information to say ($?$):

   (a) your purchase of lunch today
   (b) the purchase of a new car
   (c) the purchase of a used car
   (d) the purchase of a new office block by the government of Quebec
   (e) the payment of unemployment compensation by the governments of Canada
   (f) the purchase by Air Canada of a Boeing 747 airplane
   (g) the purchase by Air Canada of food for in-flight service (*Hint:* Be careful — look at Chapter 3 on the distincion between final and intermediate expenditure.)
   (h) your purchase of a ticket on an Air Canada flight
   (i) the purchase of a computer by the Bank of Montreal
   (j) your income tax payments to the government of Canada

3. What is Keynes's theory of the consumption function?

4. What, according to the permanent income and life-cycle hypotheses, is the fundamental constraint on consumption?

5. What is the connection between income and wealth?

6. If a person's income was to rise in 1987 by $1000, but thereafter to return to its original path, and if the rate of interest was 10 percent, by how much would that person's wealth rise in 1986?

7. Why is it that despite the fact that wealth is the fundamental constraint on consumption, disposable income is regarded as the major determinant of consumption?

8. What is the meaning of the term *marginal propensity to consume* (*b*)? Why is the *b* less than one?

9. What is the savings function? What is the relationship between the savings function and the consumption function?

10. You are given the following information about a hypothetical economy:

$$c = 100 + 0.8(y - t)$$
$$i = 500$$
$$g = 400$$
$$t = 400$$

(*c* = consumption, *i* = investment, *g* = government expenditure on goods and services, *y* = real income, *t* = taxes).

(a) Calculate the equilibrium level of output and consumption.

(b) If government expenditure is cut to 300, what is the *change* in income and the *change* in consumption?

(c) What is the size of the government expenditure multiplier on output?

9

Investment
Demand

You already know from the definitions given at the beginning of the last chapter that investment demand is the demand for durable goods by both households and firms. You also know from your examination of the characteristics of the business cycle in Chapter 6 that the fluctuations in the output of durables have much greater amplitude than those in non-durables. Understanding what determines investment demand is, therefore, of crucial importance in understanding some of the major sources of fluctuations in aggregate demand. What determines investment demand, and why does it fluctuate so much? These are the principal questions for this chapter.[1] Answering these questions is a fairly big task and one that is going to be more easily approached by breaking it up into a series of specific subtasks, which are to:

a) Understand the distinction between investment and the capital stock.

b) Understand what determines the demand for capital.

c) Understand what is meant by the rental rate of capital.

d) Understand how investment demand is related to the demand for capital.

e) Know how to represent the investment demand function in a simple equation and diagram.

f) Know the properties of the investment demand function in Canada.

---

[1] The development of the theory of investment presented in this chapter is based very closely on Dale W. Jorgensen, "Capital Theory and Investment Behavior," *American Economic Review Papers and Proceedings*, 53 (1963), 247-59.

A. Distinction Between Investment and Capital Stock

Investment demand is the demand for capital goods for use in production or consumption-yielding activities. Investment may be undertaken for two purposes:

(1) To add to the existing stock of capital.

(2) To replace capital equipment that has depreciated.

You already know that investment is a flow. It is the flow of additions to the capital stock or replacements for worn-out capital. In any one year, the amount of investment is small relative to the size of the capital stock. For example, in Canada in 1984, gross investment was 68 billion dollars. Of this, 44 billion dollars was replacement investment, so that the rate of net investment (addition to the capital stock) was 24 billion dollars. The capital stock at the end of 1983 was estimated to be 1097 billion dollars so that net investment in 1984 was 2.2 percent of the capital stock.

To summarize: the capital stock is the total value of the capital equipment located in the economy at a particular point in time. The level of investment is the rate of flow of additions to that capital stock, plus the rate of flow of expenditure on capital goods to replace worn-out capital equipment.

What determines the rate of investment? This question is best answered in a slightly roundabout manner. Rather than answering it directly, we are going to approach it by asking first of all, what determines the amount of capital stock that, in the aggregate, the agents in the economy want to hold? Let us now examine that question.

B. Demand for Capital

In any productive or consumption-yielding activity, there is a range of choice of techniques available. For example, it will be possible to undertake almost any imaginable task by using only labor as the resource and using no capital at all. At the other extreme, it would be possible to undertake almost any imaginable task by using a very capital-intensive technology, that is, a technology that involves very little labor and large amounts of capital. (It is true, of course, that there are some tasks that one could not imagine doing in any way other than by using large amounts of capital — for example, putting a satellite into earth orbit.) Nevertheless, over a very large range of economic activities, it is possible to visualize differing degrees of intensity of use of capital. A classical example would be the building of a dam, which could be undertaken with massive earth-moving equipment and a small amount of labor or by masses of labor working by hand or using small wooden shovels, themselves made by hand. A technology that uses a lot of capital and a small amount of labor is called a *capital-intensive technology*. The opposite, which uses large amounts of labor and very little capital is called a *labor-intensive technology*.

What determines the extent to which a capital-intensive technology will be used rather than a labor-intensive technology? A moment's reflection suggests that the choice will depend on the relative costs of the alternative techniques of production, which in turn will depend on the relative costs of capital and labor. If capital is cheap relative to labor, then it would seem efficient to use a capital-intensive technology. If, on the other hand, labor is cheap relative to capital, then a labor-intensive technology would seem to be indicated.

All this seems obvious enough until one reflects a little further and begins to wonder how to calculate whether or not capital was cheap relative to labor. After all, buying a piece of equipment is buying something that is durable and that is going to be usable over a long period of time, whereas hiring labor is something that is more in the nature of a consumption activity. How can we compare the price of capital and the price of labor in order to know whether capital is cheap or not? The answer lies in a concept called the *rental rate* of capital. By comparing the rental rate of capital with the wage rate of labor we can establish the relative price of capital and labor.

The term rental rate of capital suggests the notion of a price that has to be paid for the *use* of a piece of capital and not the price that has to be paid to *buy* a piece of capital. Most capital equipment is not, however, rented at all; it is bought and used as needed. It is convenient to think of the owner of a piece of capital equipment as wearing two hats; one hat is that of the owner, the other is the hat of the user. Put differently, the owner rents the equipment and is the renter of the equipment. We call the rent *implicit* because no actual rent is explicitly paid.

There are, of course, many examples of explicit renting — when the owner and user of a piece of capital are different people. Examples include the rental of a car at an airport, or more commonly, the rental of an apartment or a house. Firms often rent equipment, for example, the rental of heavy earth-moving and other specialized equipment by civil engineering contractors.

Whether capital equipment is explicitly rented by its user from its owner or implicitly rented by its owner from himself for his own use makes no difference to the general concept of the rental rate of capital.

You will be aware from your study of microeconomics that, in order to maximize profits, the producer sets the marginal cost (MC) of production equal to the price of output (P). In other words,

$$MC = P \qquad\qquad (9.1)$$

When this condition is satisfied the firm is making maximum profit (provided that the marginal cost curve is rising at this point). To calculate marginal cost we have to determine the factor of production whose rate of use is being varied in order to vary output. For present purposes we want to consider the effects on marginal cost of varying the input of capital. When varying the input of capital the marginal cost of publication will be equal to the rental rate of the marginal unit of capital divided by its marginal product (*MP(k)*). That is,

$$MC = \frac{R}{MP(k)} \tag{9.2}$$

For example, if the rental rate of capital was $10 an hour and if a machine hour could produce 100 units of output, the marginal cost (the cost of the last unit of output) would be $10 ÷ 100 = 10¢. Now, replacing marginal cost in Equation (9.3) with the price of output (from Equation (9.1)) it is clear that

$$\frac{R}{MP(k)} = P \tag{9.3}$$

If we divide both sides of this equation by *P* and multiply both sides by *MP*, we obtain

$$MP(k) = \frac{R}{P} \tag{9.4}$$

Let us call *R/P* the real rental rate — *RR*, so that

$$MP(k) = RR \tag{9.5}$$

Now the marginal product of capital declines as the quantity of capital employed rises — the law of diminishing marginal product. It follows from this law together with Equation (9.5) that the demand for capital rises as the real rental rate falls. That is, if the real rental rate falls, producers use a larger capital stock so that the marginal product of the larger capital stock declines to come into equality with the lower real rental rate.

Let us now go on to explore more fully how the real rental rate is determined.

C. Rental Rate of Capital

The best way of understanding what is meant by the rental rate of capital is to proceed by example. How much would you be willing to pay each year to rent a house that you could otherwise buy for $60 000? To answer that question, you need to know a little bit more information than you have just been given. Let's supply some more pieces of information.

The house will last for 50 years, so that if you bought the house, it would wear out at a rate of 2 percent a year.[2] The interest rate that

---

[2] Actually, to say that a house will last 50 years and that it will wear out at the rate of 2 percent a year is slightly contradictory. The two statements are approximately equivalent, however. If a house wore out in 50 years at exactly a rate of 1/50 of the initial house each year, then the depreciation expressed as a percentage of the remaining value of the house would rise. If we express the depreciation rate as a constant percent each year, what we are really saying is that the asset will never finally wear out. This is known as radioactive depreciation. It makes the arithmetic easier and is approximately the same as a constant absolute amount of depreciation.

you would face is 15 percent per annum. That means that you would have to pay 15 percent per annum for any money that you borrowed (any mortgage money) to buy the house. Equivalently, if you sold some existing securities to buy the house, you would have to forego a 15 percent rate of interest on those securities. Either way, the opportunity cost of funds that you used to buy the house is going to be 15 percent. House prices are rising and are expected to rise indefinitely through the future at a rate of 10 percent per annum.

You now have enough information with which to answer the question. How much would you pay each year to rent a house that you could otherwise buy for $60 000? The answer is you wouldn't pay any more rent than the amount that you would implicitly have to pay to yourself if you were to buy the house and live in it for as long as you needed it and thereafter sell the house. How much is that amount? To figure it out, consider the following three costs of owning the house and renting it to yourself. First, there is a cost in the form of physical depreciation on the house; second, there is a cost in the form of the interest that you would have to pay in order to acquire the $60 000 needed to buy the house; and third, there is a negative cost, the gain that arises from the fact that the value of the house on the housing market will rise at a rate at which house prices are expected to rise (in the example, 10 percent per annum).

If you are going to buy a $60 000 house, the depreciation of 2 percent per annum would cost you $1200 a year. The interest payment at 15 percent would cost a further $9000 a year. Thus your total cost so far is $10 200. However, offset against this is the fact that the house value will appreciate by 10 percent a year, which will give you a capital gain of $6000. This has to be offset against the $10 200 to give a net annual cost of $4200. Ignoring tax considerations and ignoring the costs of searching for a house and of transacting to buy and sell a house — abstracting from all those things — $4200 per annum is the implicit rental rate that you would have to pay to yourself if you were to buy the house. If houses actually rented for less than $4200 a year, it would pay you to rent rather than buy. If houses of this type rented for more than $4200 a year, it would pay you to buy rather than rent.

Since everyone is capable of doing the kinds of calculations that you have just performed, it might be expected that there would be some equilibrating forces at work in the marketplace ensuring that the actual rental rates on houses did not stray too far away from the implicit rental rate that we have just calculated. That is, if the implicit rental rate was less than the actual market rent, there would be a rise in the demand for houses to buy and a fall in the demand for houses to rent. This would tend to raise the purchase price of houses and lower house rental rates. The process would continue until people were indifferent between owning and renting. The same considerations apply in the opposite case. If the implicit rental rate was greater than the market rental rate on houses, then there would be a drop in the demand for houses to buy and a rise in the demand for houses to rent. This would have the reverse effect on rents and purchase prices and, again, would bring about an equality between the actual and implicit rental rates. Thus, the actual rent of capital goods (a house in this example) and the implicit rent may be regarded as the same.

You have now calculated a formula that can be stated in general terms; namely, the rental rate of a piece of capital equipment is equal to the price of the capital multiplied by the sum of the rate of depreciation plus the market rate of interest minus the expected rate of change of the price of the piece of capital equipment. Let us write that as an equation, defining P_k as the price of capital, δ as the depreciation rate, r_m as the market rate of interest, and $\Delta P_k^e/P_k$ as the rate at which the price of capital is expected to rise. The formula for the rental rate becomes:

$$P_k \left[(\delta + r_m) - \left(\frac{\Delta P_k^e}{P_k} \right) \right] \qquad (9.5)$$

Let us check that this formula gives us the right answer for the annual rental rate of a house. Using the numbers introduced above, P_k equals $60\,000$, and δ is 2 percent per annum, expressed in proportionate terms as .02. The interest rate, r_m (again expressed as a proportion), is 0.15, and the expected rate of increase of house prices, $\Delta P_k^e/P_k$ (also expressed as a proportion) is 0.10. Putting these numbers into the formula, we have:

Rent = $60\,000 (0.02 + 0.15 - 0.10)$
     = $60\,000 \times 0.07$
     = 4200 per annum.

Evidently the formula works.

Now that you have got the basic idea of how to calculate the rental rate on a piece of capital equipment, let us return to the task of figuring out how a producer will choose how much capital and labor to employ in the production process. You already know that in order to maximize profits, a producer will set the marginal product of capital equal to the *real* rental rate. What we have just calculated above is the nominal rental rate. The real rental rate (RR) is obtained by dividing the nominal rental rate by the price level (P) to give:

$$RR = \frac{P_k}{P} \left[(\delta + r_m) - \left(\frac{\Delta P_k^e}{P_k} \right) \right] \qquad (9.6)$$

Since we are interested in aggregate economic phenomena we are interested in the economy average real rental rate. In terms of the above equation, this means that we want to interpret P_k/P as the relative price of capital goods to goods and services in general. It is a reasonable approximation to regard that ratio as constant. (During the period between 1926 and 1984 in Canada, capital goods prices increased by 0.3 of a percent per annum relative to consumer goods prices.) By calculating a price index for capital goods (P_k) and for consumer goods in general (P) with the same base, we can regard the relative price as being equal to one. Further, since capital goods prices inflate at approximately the same rate as prices in general, we can replace the term $\Delta P_k^e/P_k$ with the expected rate of inflation, π^e. This enables us to write the formula for the real rental rate of capital in a simpler way as:

$$RR = (\delta + r_m - \pi^e) \tag{9.7}$$

Notice that the expected change in the price of capital now becomes π^e, the expected rate of inflation.

The term $r_m - \pi^e$ is very important and is given a special name. It is the *expected real rate of interest*. In what follows, we shall suppose that the expected rate of inflation, π^e, and the actual rate of inflation, π, are equal so that the expected real rate of interest is equal to the actual real rate of interest. Let us denote the real rate of interest as r. Using this we may simplify the formula for the real capital rental rate as:

$$RR = \delta + r \tag{9.8}$$

If the rate of depreciation is a technologically given constant, it is clear that the only *variable* that affects the real capital rental rate is the real rate of interest. Thus, the higher the real rate of interest, the higher is the real capital rental rate.

If producers utilize capital and labor resources in an efficient way, at a lower real rate of interest they will seek to use a more capital-intensive technology. Figure 9.1 illustrates the relationship between the desired capital stock (K) and the real rate of interest (r), the demand for capital. If the real rate of interest was the level r_0, then the capital stock that producers would wish to have is shown as K_0. If the interest rate was lower, at r_1, then the higher capital stock K_1 would be desired.

Now that you understand the relationship between the real rate of interest and the real rental rate of capital and also the relationship between the real rate of interest and the demand for capital stock, it is possible to take the next step and see how the rate of investment is determined.

D. Investment and the Demand for Capital

As already stated earlier in this chapter, investment demand is the demand for capital goods for use in productive (or consumption-yielding) activities. Investment is a flow that represents either ad-

**Figure 9.1
The Demand for
Capital Stock**

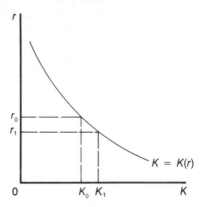

The demand for capital stock (K) will depend inversely on the real rental rate of capital. The real rental rate will be equal to the technologically given rate of depreciation plus the difference between the money rate of interest and the rate of inflation of asset prices The difference between the money rate of interest and the rate of inflation of asset prices is the real rate of interest (r). The demand for capital (K) will therefore depend inversely on the real rate of interest (r). If the real rate of interest falls from r_0 to r_1 the demand for capital would rise from K_0 to K_1.

ditions to the existing stock of capital or replacement of worn-out (depreciated) pieces of capital equipment. Capital equipment that is wearing out will be proportional to the stock of capital in existence, and from the discussion that we had above concerning the rental rate of capital, the depreciation rate, denoted there as δ, implies that the rate at which capital stock is being worn out is equal to δK. The rate at which the capital stock is changing is equal to ΔK. Therefore, investment, i, is the sum of these two things; that is,

$$i = \delta K + \Delta K \qquad (9.9)$$

There are some very elaborate theories that explain the speed with which firms will seek to add to their capital stock. For our purposes, it seems sufficient to remark that if firms added to their capital stock too quickly, they would incur a variety of high costs in the form of organizational problems and planning bottlenecks. If, on the other hand, they added to their capital stock too slowly, then they would have to put up with having too little equipment for too long. There would seem to be some optimum rate at which to add to the capital stock, which might be thought of as depending on the extent to which the capital stock currently in place falls short of (or exceeds) the desired capital stock.

We know what the preferred capital stock is. It is shown in Figure 9.1 and depends on the real rate of interest. If the change in the capital stock proceeds at some rate that depends on the gap between this preferred capital stock and the actual capital stock, then the rate of investment will depend on two things: first, the real rate of interest, since this determines the desired capital stock; and second, the existing capital stock, since this affects how much capital shortage or surplus there is. How do these two variables, the real rate of interest and the stock of capital, affect the investment rate? A moment's reflection will reveal, other things being constant, that they each have a negative effect on investment. We have already seen that the higher the real rate of interest, the smaller will be the desired capital stock. The bigger the actual capital stock, the smaller, other things being equal, will be the gap between the desired and the actual capital stock that firms seek to close. Both of these forces, then, would work to reduce the rate of investment.

To summarize, then, the rate of investment will depend on the real rate of interest and the existing capital stock. The higher is either of those two variables, the lower will be the rate of investment.

There is one final simplification that will be useful to introduce into the analysis, and this concerns the approximation arising from the fact that investment is a small number relative to the capital stock, so that even though positive investment is being undertaken at all times, the capital stock is a very slowly changing variable and may be regarded as approximately constant. This being so, it is possible to simplify the theory of investment still further by ignoring, at least for short-run purposes, the effect of the capital stock on the rate of investment. Thus, the theory of investment used in short-run macroeconomic models is one that supposes that investment depends only on the real rate of interest.

In developing the proposition that investment depends only on the real rate of interest, a great deal has been set aside. Indeed, it would not be an exaggeration to say that the major sources of fluctuation in investment are ignored by focussing exclusively on the real rate of interest as a determinant of investment. There are obviously many things other than the real rate of interest that will influence the pace of investment. Such things as taxes; changes in technology that make some types of equipment outmoded and stimulate massive demand for new, previously unknown types of capital; changes in population (both in terms of its size, age, and sex distributions); and changes in entrepreneurs' perceptions of profit opportunities as well, of course, as the slowly changing capital stock itself, are all examples of things that undoubtedly exert a major influence upon investment.

Furthermore, because investment is the *flow* by means of which the *stock* of capital is changed, anything that changes the desired stock of capital will have a magnified effect on the flow of investment. When the demand for capital (a stock demand) rises, the flow of investment will jump. When the stock of capital reaches its desired level, the pace of investment will slacken off to a rate consistent with replacing worn-out capital.

The bathtub analogy that we have used before illustrates this phenomenon well. The desire to soak in a tub leads to a rise in the demand for a *stock* of water. This results in opening the tap to maximum pressure — a *flow* — for as long as necessary to achieve the desired water level. Then the tap is closed and the flow stops — although the stock remains. Thus, a flow rises from zero to its maximum rate and back to zero very quickly. The flow displays large fluctuations. It is exactly the same with the variables that lead to changes in the desired capital stock. These variables result in large fluctuations in investment. This, indeed, is the reason why the cycles in the output of durables have greater amplitude than those in non-durables.

The key to understanding the theory of investment as used in macroeconomic analysis is the realization that all the factors that influence investment, other than the real rate of interest, may as a reasonable approximation, be taken to be independent of all the other variables that a macroeconomic model determines. This means that when such factors change, a shift occurs in the investment demand curve, and this sets up repercussions for income, prices, interest rates, and other macroeconomic variables. It is assumed, however, that there are no significant feedbacks onto the rate of investment itself other than those that go through the real rate of interest.

E. The Investment Demand Function

The entire discussion in this chapter can now be summarized very compactly. The investment demand function implied by the previous discussion may be written as a simple equation, which is

$$i = i_0 - hr \qquad i_0, h > 0 \qquad \textbf{(9.10)}$$

This equation says that the level of investment will be equal to some amount that is independent of all the other variables in our macroeconomic model, i_0, and, over and above that, will vary inversely with the real rate of interest. The way that the equation is specified makes the relationship linear. A one percentage point rise in the real rate of interest would produce an h-million dollar drop in the rate of investment. The same relationship as appears in Equation (9.10) is shown in Figure 9.2. Here, however, we are measuring the rate of interest on the vertical axis and investment on the horizontal axis.

Thus, the slope of the line in Figure 9.2 is not $-h$ but $-\left(\frac{1}{h}\right)$. You

should think of the volatility of investment as being reflected in shifts in the investment function as shown in Figure 9.2, or equivalently, in exogenous changes in the intercept of the investment function, i_0. These changes would arise from the many factors, such as changes in taxes, technology, population size and composition, entrepreneur-

Figure 9.2
The Investment Function

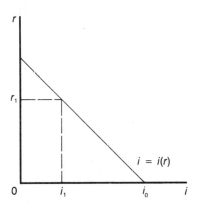

Investment (*i*) will be undertaken to replace existing capital and to close the gap between the desired and actual capital stock. Since the desired capital stock depends inversely on the real rate of interest (*r*), and since the actual capital stock changes only slowly over time, investment (*i*) itself will be a function, $[i(r)]$, of the real rate of interest (*r*). Many other factors, summarized in the intercept i_0, will influence investment. None of the variables that influence the position of the investment demand function, i_0, is determined in the macroeconomic model. Rather, shifts in the investment demand function may be important exogenous sources of fluctuation in aggregate demand. At the real rate of interest r_1 investment demand is i_1.

ial perceptions of profit opportunities, and the (slowly evolving) capital stock itself.[3]

F. Canadian Investment Demand Function

Let us now turn from the theory of investment to an examination of the facts about investment in Canada. Does investment in Canada vary inversely with the real rate of interest as predicted by the theory of investment? Is investment volatile? That is, are there massive fluctuations in investment that are independent of movements in the rate of interest? Another way of asking this same question is: does the intercept in the investment equation, i_0 fluctuate as the theory of investment would predict?

To answer these questions we need to examine the facts about investment and about the real rate of interest. We know from our

---

[3]As in the case of the consumption function, the theory of investment presented here is highly condensed and selective. A superb treatment of the subject at a more advanced level, however, may be found in Frank Brechling, *Investment and Employment Decisions* (Manchester: Manchester University Press, 1975). A good, up-to-date, though again fairly demanding survey is Andrew B. Abel "Empirical Investment Equations: An Integrative Framework," in *On the State of Macro-Economics*, Karl Brunner and Allan H. Meltzer, eds., Carnegie-Rochester Conference Series, 12 (Spring 1980), 39-92.

study of Canada's macroeconomic history in Chapter 2 that interest rates fluctuate and that the trend in interest rates is quite similar to the trend in inflation. The timing of the ups and downs in interest rates are not quite the same, however, as the timing of the ups and downs in inflation. Since the expected real rate of interest is the difference between the market rate of interest and the expected rate of inflation we might suspect expect that the expected real rate of interest would fluctuate fairly markedly but that it would not display any major trend.

We also know, from our study of Canada's macroeconomic history, that aggregate income has been dominated by its trend growth path. The same is true of investment. That is, although investment fluctuates as a fraction of gross national product it is dominated by an upward trend over the long term.

If we wish to study the relationship between investment and the expected real rate of interest we are, inevitably, looking at the relationship between a variable that is dominated by its upward trend (investment) and one that fluctuates and does not show any major trend (the expected real rate of interest). In order to take the trend out of investment it is convenient to look, not at the level of investment, but at the fraction of GNP represented by investment. That is, we look at the ratio i/y.

One further preliminary matter has to be mentioned. The expected real rate of interest is the difference between the market rate of interest and the expected rate of inflation. We know what the market rate of interest is. It is a number that is recorded on a regular basis and reported in the financial columns of the daily newspaper. We have charted some of its history in Chapter 2. We know what the actual rate of inflation is. We have also examined its behavior in Chapter 2. We do not, however, know what the *expected* rate of inflation is. When we get to Chapter 18 we shall have a great deal to say about expectations, how they are formed, and how they fluctuate. For present purposes we are going to suppose that we can measure the expected rate of inflation by making it equal to the actual rate of inflation. In other words, to approximate the expected real rate of interest we are going to calculate what is sometimes called the *ex post* real rate of interest — the difference between the market rate of interest and the actual rate of inflation.

Figure 9.3 provides a summary statement of the facts about the relationship between the real rate of interest (*ex post*) and the fraction of GNP invested (i/y). Each point in that figure represents a year. Thus, for example, the point marked 32 at the top of the figure represents the year 1932.

The first thing that immediately becomes apparent from the data shown in Figure 9.3 is that both the real rate of interest and the fraction of GNP invested vary enormously. Real rates of interest range

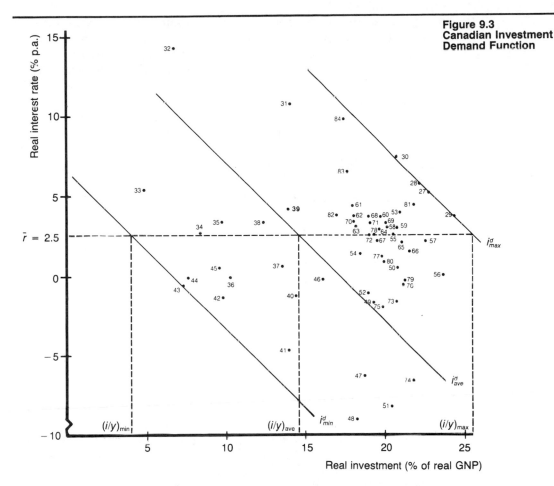

**Figure 9.3
Canadian Investment
Demand Function**

The vertical axis shows the *ex post* real rate of interest. The horizontal axis shows investment as a percentage of GNP. Evidently there are large fluctuations in the fraction of GNP invested and in the real rate of interest. The data may be interpreted (as just one possibility) as being generated by an investment demand curve that has a slope of −1 and that fluctuates between i^d_{max} and i^d_{min}.

Source: Real investment is the sum of Cansim Series D40655 and D40661 less D40662. Real GNP is Cansim Series D40646. The real rate of interest is the long-term interest rate less the inflation rate as measured by the GNE Deflator. See appendix to Chapter 2.

from a high of almost 15 percent to a low of almost −10 percent. Investment fluctuates from almost 25 percent of GNP down to as little as 5 percent. Real rates of interest between 0 and 5 percent are the most common and investment rates of around 20 percent are the most common.

In addition to the points in Figure 9.3, you will observe three downward-sloping lines. The particular slope of those lines has no scientific status. They are arbitrarily determined such that the parameter *h* in Equation (9.10) is equal to one. In other words, the lines represent a particular example of an investment demand function in which a 1 percent point drop in the real rate of interest produces a rise in investment of 1 percent of GNP. It is certainly possible to imagine that these data were generated by such an equation. The intercept of the equation, i_0, will fluctuate between a low level as shown in the case of the curve labelled i^d_{min} and a high level as shown in the case of the curve labelled i^d_{max}. On the average investment demand is as indicated by the line labelled i^d_{ave}. Thus, at a real rate of interest of 2.5 percent marked $\bar{r}$ (an average real rate of interest) investment represents 15 percent of GNP. At that average interest rate of 2.5 percent, however, the investment demand function, as shown in Figure 9.3, fluctuates between investment levels of less than 5 percent of GNP and more than 25 percent of GNP. (Marked $(i/y)_{min}$, and $(i/y)_{max}$).

It is evident from this review of the Canadian data on investment that the data may be interpreted using the simple theory of investment developed earlier in this chapter.

Summary

A. Distinction Between Investment and Capital Stock

Investment demand is the demand for capital goods for use in production or consumption-yielding activities. It represents additions to the stock of capital or replacement of depreciated capital. Thus, investment is the *flow* that augments or maintains the *stock* of capital.

B. Demand for Capital

The demand for capital is determined by cost-minimizing or profit-maximizing considerations. Capital will be demanded up to the point at which its marginal product equals its real rental rate.

C. Rental Rate of Capital

Where capital equipment is explicitly rented, as is often the case with houses, and occasionally with cars, TV sets, and industrial equipment, the rental rate of capital is simply the rate per hour that has to be paid for the use of a particular type of equipment. Most capital is not rented explicitly but is owned by the individual or firm that uses it. In such a case, the rental rate on capital is *implicit*. The individual implicity rents the equipment from him/herself. That implicit rental rate will be equal to the price of capital multiplied by the sum of the rate of depreciation and the real rate of interest.

D. Investment and the Demand for Capital

The rate of investment will be determined by the size of the capital stock relative to the profit-maximizing capital stock. The bigger the stock of capital relative to the desired stock, the slower will be the rate of investment. Since the capital stock is a slowly changing variable, as an approximation, the rate of investment may be presumed to depend only upon the real rental rate of capital. The real rental rate will in turn depend primarily upon the real rate of interest. Thus, the simple macroeconomic theory of investment is that it depends on the real rate of interest. A higher real rate of interest will induce a lower rate of investment. This theory leaves out more than it includes. What is left out, however, may be presumed to be independent of (exogenous with respect to) the other variables that macroeconomics seeks to understand. It is fluctuations in those other variables, however, that are responsible for some of the major swings in investment activity.

E. Investment Demand Function

The investment demand function can be written in a simple equation

$$i = i_0 - hr$$

This equation states that as the real rate of interest, r, rises, the level of investment, i, falls. The constant, h, is the degree of responsiveness of investment to interest rate changes. When plotting the investment demand function with the rate of interest on the vertical axis, the slope of the curve is $-\left(\dfrac{1}{h}\right)$. Volatility of investment is reflected in changes in i_0 that shift the investment demand function.

F. Canadian Investment Demand Function

The Canadian data on investment and real interest rates can be readily interpreted using the theory of investment demand developed in this chapter. Figure 9.3 shows the relationship between investment (as a fraction of GNP) and the real rate of interest (*ex post*). The data may be interpreted by imagining large swings in an investment demand function that has a slope of -1.

Review Questions

1. What is the difference between investment and the capital stock?

2. What is the difference between a change in investment and a change in the capital stock?

3. How do firms decide on the size of the desired capital stock?

4. What is the rental rate of capital? How does it relate to the price of capital goods?

5. A car that you are thinking of buying costs $6000 and will, after one year, have a resale value of $5000. The rate of interest on the bank loan that you would take if you did buy the car is 15 percent. A friend who already owns an identical car offers to lease you that car for one year for $1800 (you buy the gas and pay for maintenance). Should you accept the offer from your friend or should you buy the car? What is the rental rate that your friend is asking? What is the implicit rental rate if you buy?

6. What determines the rate of investment?

7. What is the investment demand function? What is being held constant, and what is varying as we move along the investment demand function?

8. What causes shifts in the investment demand function?

10

The *IS* Curve

There are various stages in the process of learning economics that involve mastering certain steps of analysis that seem, at the time, completely pointless. It is as if analysis is being mastered for its own sake, rather than to achieve some objective in terms of having greater insights or better understanding of how the economy works. It is not until a later stage in the learning process that the point of a particular piece of analysis becomes fully apparent. You are about to embark on such a piece of analysis in this chapter. The objective toward which you are working is to have an understanding of what determines aggregate demand and how aggregate demand is affected by such things as government expenditure, taxes, and the money supply.

Achieving a level of expertise and understanding that is worthwhile involves mastering a body of analysis that, in its entirety, is hard to grasp the first time through (and even the second or third time for some of us). It is easier to grasp and understand if it is broken down into a series of individually easy-to-manage steps. This makes the process of comprehension and understanding easier. At the same time, it does give rise to the problem that we describe above; namely, that while a series of small intermediate steps are being taken, the final objective, the point to where it is all leading, may be lost from sight.

Try to keep in mind where you are going. You are going to end up, by the time you get to Chapter 13, with a clear understanding of the theory of aggregate demand. You are going to see how the various bits and pieces, one of which is now going to be developed in this chapter, all fit together.

The part of the aggregate demand story that you are going to master in this chapter involves a relationship called the *IS* curve. *I* stands for investment and *S* for savings. You are going to undertake four tasks, which are to:

a) Know the definition of the *IS* curve.
b) Know how to derive the *IS* curve.
c) Understand what determines the slope of the *IS* curve.
d) Understand what makes the *IS* curve shift and by how much.

A. Definition of the *IS* Curve

The *IS* curve is a relationship between the level of output and the real rate of interest. It is the relationship that links the level of income and the real rate of interest when the goods market is in flow equilibrium. Flow equilibrium occurs when investment demand plus government demand equals savings plus taxes.[1] Equivalently, it is the relationship between the level of real income and the real rate of interest that ensures that aggregate demand (consumption demand plus investment demand plus government demand) is equal to the level of real income.

It might be helpful to put this slightly differently and more long windedly. Since consumption depends on income, different levels of income will bring forth different levels of consumption. When consumption is added to investment and government spending, the result is a particular level of total demand for output (real income). The *IS* curve traces the relationship between the level of output (real income) and the real rate of interest when the level of aggregate demand is equal to the level of real income that generates that level of aggregate demand.

The *IS* curve is not a description of the desires or decisions of any single agent or group of agents. Rather, it is the same kind of relationship as the aggregate demand curve that you have already met. It is an equilibrium locus. It traces the locus of points that give an equality between the aggregate demand for goods and services and the level of output of goods and services. Indeed, you can think of the *IS* curve as a kind of aggregate demand curve. The aggregate demand curve as we defined it in Chapter 7 is a relationship between the total demand for goods and services and the price level. That meaning of the term aggregate demand curve is a useful one, and we shall reserve

---

[1] You may think that the *IS* curve is peculiarly named since it is a curve that describes the equality of investment (*I*) plus government spending (*G*), and savings (*S*) plus taxes (*T*). Aside from *IGST* being a clumsy name, when the analysis presented here was first invented by Sir John Hicks in 1936, he illustrated the analysis for an economy in which government spending and taxes were assumed to be zero; hence the name *IS*.

it for something other than the *IS* curve. Nevertheless, the *IS* curve tells us what the total demand for goods and services is as we vary, not the price level, but the real rate of interest.

It is important not to interpret the *IS* curve as implying anything about causality. The *IS* curve emphatically does not say that different levels of aggregate demand are caused by different levels of the real rate of interest. All that it is telling us is that the real rate of interest and the level of real income cannot be just any values that they like. They must be restricted to lie on the *IS* curve. The two variables will be determined simultaneously (by a procedure that we shall get to in Chapter 13).

What you are going to be looking at next, then, is the way in which the *IS* curve is derived.

B. Derivation of the *IS* Curve

The easiest way to learn how to derive the *IS* curve is to begin by refreshing your memory about the components of aggregate demand for goods and services and the ways in which aggregate income may be allocated by households. Recall that aggregate income may be allocated in three ways. It may be spent on consumption, saved, or paid in taxes, that is,

$$y = c + s + t \qquad \textbf{(10.1)}$$

[Recall that c is consumption demand, s is savings, t is taxes, and y is real income (output).] Also recall that aggregate demand is decomposed into three components — consumption demand, investment demand, and government demand for goods and services. That is,

$$y^d = c + i + g \qquad \textbf{(10.2)}$$

You subtract c from both sides of Equation (10.1) to obtain

$$y - c = s + t \qquad \textbf{(10.3)}$$

This simply says that income minus consumption demand must be equal to savings-plus-taxes. This does not say anything about behavior, of course. It is simply a statement about the necessary relationship between income and expenditure. It is nothing other than the household sector's budget constraint.

Next, subtract c from both sides of Equation (10.2) to obtain

$$y^d - c = i + g \qquad \textbf{(10.4)}$$

What this says is that the difference between aggregate demand and consumption demand is equal to investment-plus-government spending. Equation (10.1) says exactly the same thing as Equation (10.3), and Equation (10.2) says the same thing as Equation (10.4). They are simply different ways of looking at the same thing.

The *IS* curve, the derivation of which you are now embarking upon, traces the relationship between the level of aggregate demand and the real rate of interest when the level of aggregate demand is equal to the level of real income. In other words, the *IS* curve has to be derived satisfying the condition

$$y = y^d \qquad (10.5)$$

This says that points on the *IS* curve are points such that aggregate demand is equal to aggregate real income (output).

You will notice, if you replace y with y^d in Equation (10.3), that the left-hand side of Equation (10.3) is exactly the same as the left-hand side of Equation (10.4). It follows, therefore, that the right-hand side of Equation (10.3) must be equal to the right-hand side of Equation (10.4) when we are on the *IS* curve. That is,

$$s + t = i + g \qquad (10.6)$$

Equation (10.6) says that planned savings-plus-taxes must equal investment-plus-government spending at all points on the *IS* curve. It is Equation (10.6) that gives the name to the *IS* curve. If there was no government, so that t and g were equal to zero, it would simply say that to be on the *IS* curve, savings plans must equal investment demand. With government spending and taxes not being zero, these have to be added to private savings and investment to obtain the equivalent flow equilibrium condition in the goods market that underlies the *IS* curve.

With this background it is now possible to proceed to derive the *IS* curve. It will be helpful to proceed in easy stages, however, and first to examine the right-hand side of Equation (10.6) — investment-plus-government spending. Figure 10.1 illustrates this aspect of the demand for goods and services. The real interest rate is measured on the vertical axis, and investment is measured on the horizontal axis. The thin curve labelled $i = i_0 - hr$ is the investment demand function, the derivation of which was discussed in Chapter 9. It shows that the level of investment demand increases as the real rate of interest falls. For example, at the interest rate r_1, the level of investment demand will be i_1. At higher interest rates, the level of investment demand will be less than i_1.

The thicker line in the figure, which is drawn parallel to the investment demand curve, is the level of investment demand plus the level of government demand for goods and services. You will recall that the level of government demand is assumed to be exogenous. It is determined independently of the level of the interest rate or of any other of the variables in the model. The horizontal distance between the investment demand curve and the curve labelled $i + g$ is the fixed level of government demand. It is illustrated by the horizontal line g at the interest rate r_1. You can see, however, that the distance be-

Figure 10.1
Investment-plus-
Government Spending

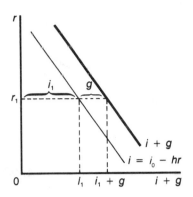

Investment (the thin line) varies inversely with the real rate of interest. Government spending is fixed independently of the rate of interest. Investment-plus-government spending (the thick line) has the same slope as the investment line but is shifted to the right by the amount of government spending (*g*). For example, at the real interest rate r_1, investment is i_1 and investment-plus-government spending is $i_1 + g$.

tween i and $i + g$ is the same at all rates of interest. The thick line $i + g$ represents the total amount of investment demand and the total demand for goods and services by the government added together — investment-plus-government spending. This diagram will be returned to later.

Next, consider the other side of Equation (10.6), savings-plus-taxes. This is slightly trickier than the previous analysis. The reason that it is trickier is that savings depend on *disposable* income. Disposable income, in turn, depends in part on taxes, so taxes have a double influence on the volume of savings-plus-taxes. That is, higher taxes mean lower savings, but higher taxes also mean bigger savings-*plus*-taxes all taken together. You need to be careful, therefore, in sorting out the relationships involved here. Figure 10.2 illustrates what goes on. Looking at Figure 10.2, first focus on the middle line. This line shows the level of savings that would be forthcoming at each level of income if taxes were equal to zero. It is simply describing the equation $s = -a + (1 - b)y$. This is the savings relation implied by the consumption function that was discussed in Chapter 8. Now, focus on the income level y_1 and notice that if taxes were indeed zero, savings would be equal to s_0 at the income level y_1.

Now, drop the assumption that taxes are zero and allow taxes to be some positive number, t. You will recall, from the discussion in Chapter 8, that with taxes at level t, the savings function will shift downwards by an amount equal to $(1 - b)$ times the level of taxes. This is because when taxes go up, consumption and savings must fall

Figure 10.2
Savings-plus-Taxes

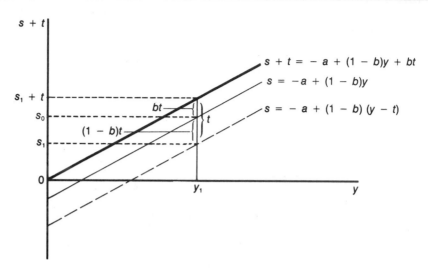

In the absence of taxes, savings would be s, the center line. With taxes at level t, the savings function is the dashed line. It is displaced downwards by the propensity to save $(1 - b)$ times taxes. Taxes are treated as constant. The savings-plus-taxes function, therefore, lies above the savings function by the amount of taxes and is shown as the thick line. If taxes rise, the savings-plus-taxes line rises by the marginal propensity to consume (b) times the rise in taxes.

by an amount equal to the tax rise. Fraction b of the taxes is paid for by reducing consumption, and fraction $1 - b$ is paid for by reducing savings. The bottom line in Figure 10.2 illustrates the savings function, allowing for taxes at level t. With taxes at level t and income at y_1, savings will be equal to s_1. The vertical distance between the line labelled $s = -a + (1 - b)y$ and the line $s = -a + (1 - b)(y - t)$ is equal to $(1 - b)t$.

Now, according to Equation (10.6), it is savings-plus-taxes that must be equal to investment-plus-government spending, and it is therefore the total of savings-plus-taxes that we are interested in. The top line of Figure 10.2 is a graph of savings-plus-taxes. It is nothing other than the level of taxes, t, added (vertically) to the lowest of the three lines in the diagram. This is illustrated at the income level y_1 by the distance indicated by t.

You are now in a position to understand the nature of the relationship between savings-plus-taxes and income. This relationship is similar to the relationship between savings and income. If you start from the curve describing the relationship between savings and income when taxes are zero, the savings-plus-taxes curve is equal to that original savings curve, plus taxes times the marginal propensity to consume. What this says is that a rise in taxes does not raise

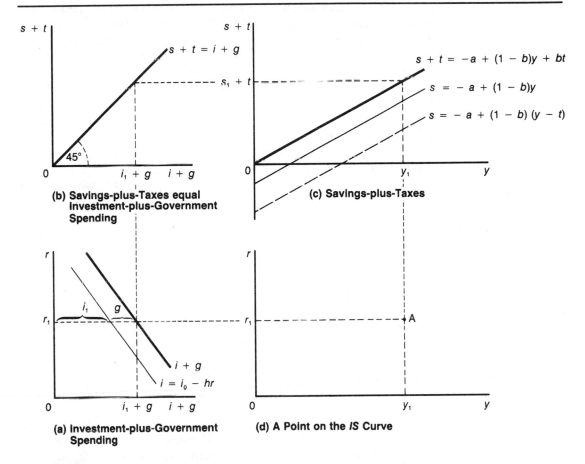

Figure 10.3
The Derivation of a Point on the *IS* Curve

The *IS* curve traces the relationship between the real rate of interest and the level of real income at which investment-plus-government spending equals savings-plus-taxes. Point A is a point on the *IS* curve. At point A, real income is y_1 [horizontal axis of frames (d) and (c)], so that savings-plus-taxes are $s_1 + t$. At A, the interest rate is r_1 [vertical axis of frames (d) and (a)], so that investment-plus-government spending is $i_1 + g$. Looking at frame (b), you see that $s_1 + t$ equals $i_1 + g$, so that point A satisfies the definition of the *IS* curve.

savings-plus-taxes one-for-one. A rise in taxes raises savings-plus-taxes by less than the rise in taxes because there is going to be a drop in savings in order to meet part of the tax payments.

You are now in a position to derive the *IS* curve graphically. Figure 10.3 is the source of the derivation. It looks much more formidable than it is, so try not to be put off by your first glance at that figure. Just follow the text carefully and slowly as it leads you through what, as you will soon see, is a straightforward derivation.

Frame (a) is nothing other than Figure 10.1 — investment-plus-government spending. The interest rate r_1, the investment level i_1, and the government spending level g shown in that frame are the same as the values shown in Figure 10.1. Frame (c) is exactly the same as Figure 10.2 — savings-plus-taxes. Again, the income level y_1, the savings level s_1, and the tax level t are the same in frame (c) as those shown and already discussed in Figure 10.2. The new frames of Figure 10.3 are frames (b) and (d). Frame (b) of the figure is just a graphical representation of the equilibrium condition that defines the *IS* curve. It is a 45° line. You will readily verify that measuring investment-plus-government spending on the horizontal axis in the same units as savings-plus-taxes are measured on the vertical axis implies that at each point on that 45° line, savings-plus-taxes are equal to investment-plus-government spending.

You can think of the *IS* curve now as being a relationship between the level of real income and the real rate of interest such that the economy is located on each of the three curves depicted in frames (a), (b), and (c). One point on the *IS* curve is the point A depicted in frame (d). Notice that the axes of frame (d) measure the real rate of interest and real income. Opposite this real interest rate axis, in frame (a), the real interest rate is also measured. Transferring the real interest rate r_1 across from frame (a) to frame (d) takes us horizontally across to point A. You will also notice that the level of real income on the horizontal axis of frame (d) is the same as the horizontal axis of frame (c) immediately above it. Transferring the income level y_1 down from frame (c) to frame (d), we shall reach the same point A. Notice that the level of savings-plus-taxes generated by the income level y_1 is exactly equal to the level of investment-plus-government spending generated by the interest rate r_1. You can verify this by tracking up vertically from frame (a) to frame (b) and across horizontally from frame (c) to frame (b). Point A, then, is a point on the *IS* curve.

Let us complete the derivation of the *IS* curve in a slightly less cluttered-up diagram but one that is in every respect identical to Figure 10.3 except that it has some of the lines removed for clarity. Figure 10.4 reproduces the curves $i + g$ and $s + t$ from Figure 10.3. First of all, familiarize yourself with Figure 10.4 and satisfy yourself it is identical to Figure 10.3 except that some lines have been left off to give the diagram a fresher and clearer appearance.

Now choose a higher interest rate than r_1, such as r_2. Notice that at r_2, the level of investment-plus-government spending is $i_2 + g$, which is less than $i_1 + g$. Then track up from frame (a) to frame (b) and record the level of investment-plus-government spending $i_2 + g$ on the horizontal axis of frame (b). Notice that if investment-plus-government spending is equal to savings-plus-taxes (if we are going to be at a point on the *IS* curve), the level of savings-plus-taxes must

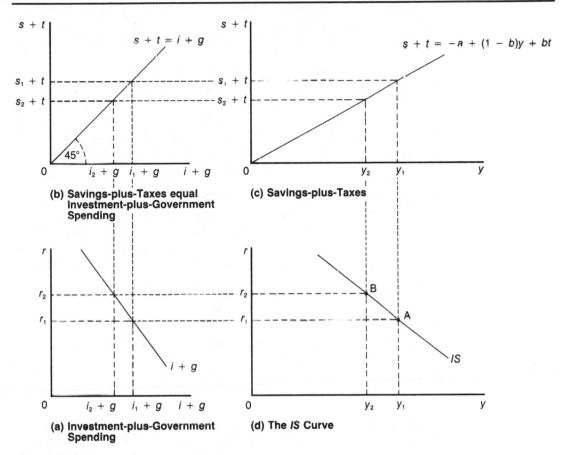

Figure 10.4
The Derivation of the *IS* **Curve**

This figure is exactly like Figure 10.3 except that in frames (a) and (c), only the $i + g$ and $s + t$ curves are plotted. Point A in this figure is the same as point A in Figure 10.3. Point B [in frame (d)] is equivalent to point A but relates to the income level y_2 and the interest rate r_2. At point B the income level is y_2 and savings-plus-taxes are $s_2 + t$. The interest rate at point B is r_2, so that investment-plus-government spending is $i_2 + g$. By looking at frame (b), you can see that $i_2 + g$ equals $s_2 + t$, so that B is also a point on an *IS* curve. Joining up A and B and extending the line beyond those points traces out the *IS* curve.

equal $s_2 + t$ as shown on the vertical axis of frame (b). Now transfer that amount of savings-plus-taxes horizontally across to frame (c). You may now read off from frame (c) the level of real income that is necessary to ensure that the volume of savings-plus-taxes equals $s_2 + t$. That level of income is given by y_2. Now transfer the income level y_2 down to the horizontal axis of frame (d) and transfer the interest rate level r_2 horizontally across from frame (a) to frame (d). Where these two lines join, labelled B, is another point on the *IS* curve. Joining together points A and B with other intermediate points traces out the *IS* curve.

You will probably find it helpful to derive an *IS* curve for yourself by setting up the diagrams shown as frames (a), (b), and (c), and then deriving explicitly points on the *IS* curve for a series of interest rates such as r_1, r_2, and other intermediate rates. Be sure that you are thoroughly conversant with the way in which the *IS* curve is derived before moving on to the next two sections of this chapter.

C. Determinants of the *IS* Curve Slope

You already know that the *IS* curve slopes downward. You can see this simply from frame (d) of Figure 10.4 in which you have derived an *IS* curve. You can also see from inspecting Figure 10.4 and comparing frame (d) with frame (a) that the *IS* curve is flatter than the slope of the investment demand curve. What does this mean? It means that as the interest rate falls from, say, r_2 to r_1, the investment rise from i_2 to i_1 is less than the amount by which income rises from y_2 to y_1. Call the change in interest rates Δr, the change in investment Δi and the change in income Δy. What is the relationship between the change in income and the change in investment when the interest rate is (hypothetically) allowed to drop from r_2 to r_1 i.e., change by Δr? Figure 10.5 illustrates this relationship.

You can figure this out by using a small amount of high-school geometry. A thickened triangle is shown in frame (c). What are the properties of that triangle? Its base clearly has length Δy, and its height equals the change in savings which, from frame (b) has length Δi. You also know that the hypotenuse of that triangle has a slope equal to $1 - b$, the marginal propensity to save or, equivalently, one minus the marginal propensity to consume. Now recall your high-school geometry. The proposition that you need is the one that goes "slope equals rise over run." The "slope" in this case is $1 - b$, the "rise" is Δi, and the "run" is Δy. Translating "slope equals rise over run" into the numbers that represent the "slope," "rise," and "run" of the triangle in frame (c), we have:

$$\text{"slope"} = 1 - b$$
$$\text{"rise"} = \Delta i$$
$$\text{"run"} = \Delta y$$

so that

$$1 - b = \frac{\Delta i}{\Delta y}$$

Now multiply both sides of this equation by the change in income (Δy) to give

$$\Delta y(1 - b) = \Delta i$$

Then divide both sides of the equation by the marginal propensity to save $(1 - b)$, to give

$$\Delta y - \frac{1}{(1 - b)} (\Delta i) \qquad\qquad (10.7)$$

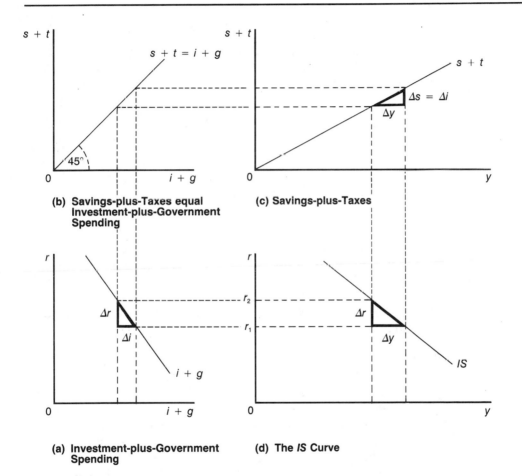

(b) Savings-plus-Taxes equal Investment-plus-Government Spending

(c) Savings-plus-Taxes

(a) Investment-plus-Government Spending

(d) The IS Curve

Figure 10.5
The Slope of the IS Curve

The IS curve slopes downwards. The lower the real rate of interest, the higher the level of investment [frame (a)], and since investment-plus-government spending must equal savings-plus-taxes, the higher too must be the level of savings [frame (c)]. Since savings depend on income, higher savings will require higher income levels. Hence, to be on the IS curve, the lower rate of interest will have to be associated with a higher level of income [frame (d)]. The slope of the IS curve is the fraction $(1 - b)$ of the slope of the investment curve. That is, the slope of the IS curve is $-(1 - b)/h$.

This is the famous Keynesian multiplier that you have already met in Chapter 8. It says that the change in income will be related to the change in investment by the amount $1/(1 - b)$. Clearly, since b is a fraction, $1 - b$ is also a fraction, and $1/(1 - b)$ is a number bigger than one, a multiple giving rise to the name *multiplier*.

To determine the slope of the *IS* curve, divide Equation (10.7) by Δr and then invert it. This gives

$$\frac{\Delta r}{\Delta y} = (1 - b)\frac{\Delta r}{\Delta i} \qquad (10.8)$$

Now look at the left-hand side of Equation (10.8) and then look at the thickened triangle in Frame (d). The left-hand side of this equation is the "rise over run" of the thickened triangle in frame (d). This is the slope of the *IS* curve. Now look at the right-hand side of Equation (10.8). What is $\frac{\Delta r}{\Delta i}$? From frame (a) you can see that $\frac{\Delta r}{\Delta i}$ is the slope of the investment curve. In Chapter 7 we established that the slope of the investment curve is $-\frac{1}{h}$. If we substitute $-\frac{1}{h}$ for $\frac{\Delta r}{\Delta i}$ in Equation (10.8), this equation now tells us that the slope of the *IS* curve is equal to $\frac{-(1 - b)}{h}$.

You have now discovered that the slope of the *IS* curve is negative and that it is flatter than the slope of the investment demand curve. The slope of the investment demand curve is $-1/h$. The slope of the *IS* curve is equal to the slope of the investment demand curve multiplied by the marginal propensity to save, or one minus the marginal propensity to consume.

D. Shifts in the *IS* Curve

The *IS* curve will shift if government spending changes, if taxes change, and if autonomous investment expenditure, i_0, changes. Notice that this implies that the *IS* curve will shift due to a change in any of its determinants that is not itself induced by a change in either real income or the rate of interest. We shall focus only on changes in government spending and taxes. Changes in i_0 have identical effects on the *IS* curve to changes in government spending, as you will readily be able to verify for yourself once you are familiar with the analysis.

First, let us look at the effects of a change in government spending. Figure 10.6 will illustrate the analysis. The continuous curves simply reproduce the curves already introduced here and used in Figures 10.4 and 10.5. Now suppose that there is a rise in government spending by an amount that will be called Δg. What does that do to this diagram? The answer is shown in frame (a). The curve labelled $i + g$, which shows investment-plus-government spending, shifts to

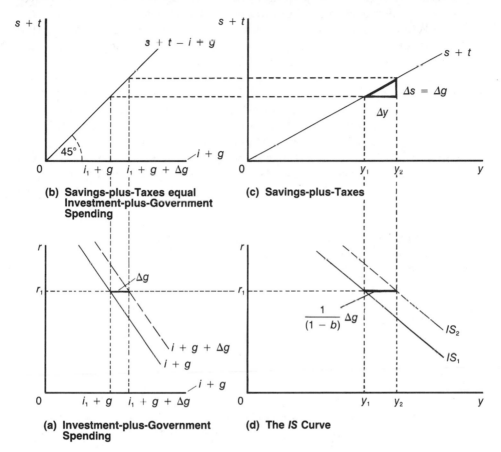

Figure 10.6
A Change in Government Spending Shifts the *IS* Curve

A rise in government spending of Δg shifts the investment-plus-government spending function to the right by the amount Δg. The *IS* curve is shifted to the right as a result of this by an amount equal to $[1/(1 - b)]\Delta g$.

the right by an amount equal to the rise in government spending. This is illustrated by the dashed line in frame (a) that is displaced horizontally to the right from the original $i + g$ line by an amount indicated as Δg.

Holding taxes constant for the moment, there are no changes to be recorded in frame (c). All that remains is to work out the implications of the shift in the curve $i + g$ for the *IS* curve. You can do that by deriving a new *IS* curve, using the new $i + g + \Delta g$ line in frame (a). Applying the method that you have learned in the previous section on derivation of the *IS* curve, you will discover that the new *IS* curve is the one labelled IS_2 in frame (d). (If you are not sure how to derive the *IS* curve, you should go back to that section and reinforce your understanding of how to derive the *IS* curve.)

What is the effect on the *IS* curve of the rise in Δg? Suppose that *g* rises by an amount that will be called Δg. You can see by inspecting Figure 10.6 what happens to the *IS* curve. It shifts to the right. At the interest rate r_1 the shift is equal to $y_2 - y_1$. Further, the *IS* curve shifts to the right by more than the rise in government spending (Δg). You can see this by visual inspection of frames (a) and (d).

How far to the right has the *IS* curve shifted? We can find the answer to this question from the thickened triangle in frame (c). The magnitude of the shift of the *IS* curve is $(y_2 - y_1)$ from frame (d) and this is the same as the base, Δy, of the triangle in frame (c). The height of the triangle is the change in savings necessary to maintain flow equilibrium in the goods market — that is, the change in savings necessary to raise savings-plus-taxes by the amount Δg. Using the formula that "slope equals rise over run" you can work out the relationship between Δg and Δy. It is

$$\frac{\Delta g}{\Delta y} = (1 - b)$$

Dividing both sides of this equation by Δg and then inverting the equation gives

$$\Delta y = \frac{1}{1 - b} \Delta g$$

Thus, you have established that the rise in income at a given rate of interest — the shift in the *IS* curve — induced by a rise in government expenditure is equal to the rise in government expenditure Δg multiplied by $1/(1 - b)$.

A rise in government spending shifts the $i + g$ curve in frame (a) by the amount that government spending rises (Δg). This results in a shift of the *IS* curve in frame (d) of $\left[\frac{1}{(1 - b)}\right] \Delta g$. The coefficient $\frac{1}{(1 - b)}$ is the autonomous spending multiplier which we met in Chapter 8. The marginal propensity to consume *b* is a fraction so $\frac{1}{(1 - b)}$ is greater than one. That is, an increase in government spending shifts the *IS* curve further to the right than the $i + g$ curve.

Now let us turn to an analysis of the effects of a rise in taxes on the *IS* curve. This is slightly more complicated, and the extra complexity arises from the fact that the savings-plus-taxes schedule is a slightly more tricky relationship than the investment-plus-government spending schedule. Figure 10.7 will illustrate the analysis. Let us again familiarize ourselves with the setup by noting that the continuous curves in Figure 10.7 are identical to those used in Figure

10.4. The *IS* curve labelled IS_1 is the *IS* curve that would be derived under the conditions prevailing in Figure 10.4.

We now want to ask what happens to the *IS* curve if taxes rise by an amount that will be called Δt. The impact effect of the rise in taxes is to be seen in frame (c). You know from the material that you have already mastered earlier in this chapter that if taxes rise, this will raise the savings-plus-taxes schedule but not by the full amount of the tax rise. This is because savings themselves will fall somewhat. If taxes rise by Δt, the savings-plus-taxes schedule will move to the schedule labelled $s' + t + \Delta t$. You should satisfy yourself that this new schedule is higher than the original schedule by an amount equal to $b\Delta t$. Savings will have dropped to s', which is $(1 - b)\Delta t$ lower than originally. The total rise in taxes is the distance between the top line and the bottom line in frame (c).

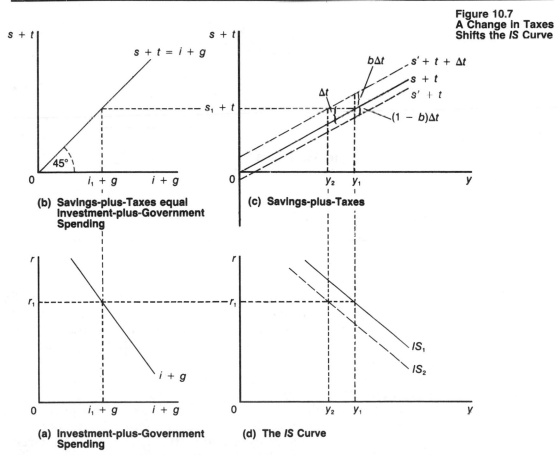

Figure 10.7
A Change in Taxes Shifts the IS Curve

A rise in taxes of Δt will raise the savings-plus-taxes curve by $b\Delta t$. This results in a *leftward* shift in the *IS* curve.

**Figure 10.8
The Size of the Shift
in the *IS* Curve Resulting
from a Change in Taxes**

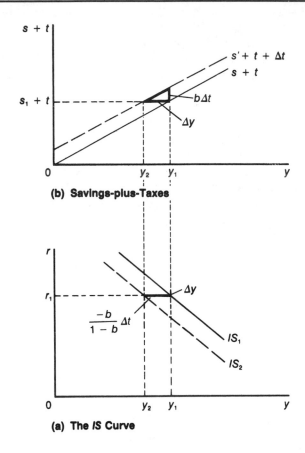

(b) Savings-plus-Taxes

(a) The *IS* Curve

A tax rise of Δt will raise the savings-plus-taxes curve by $b\Delta t$. This shifts the *IS* curve by $[-b/(1-b)]\Delta t$. That is, the *IS* curve shifts to the left by an amount equal to $[b/(1-b)]\Delta t$.

Now let us figure out what this change in taxes has done to the *IS* curve. Derive a new *IS* curve, using exactly the same technique as before but using the curve labelled $s' + t + \Delta t$, the new savings-plus-taxes curve in frame (c). This *IS* curve, you will discover, is the one labelled IS_2 in frame (d).

How does this *IS* curve compare with the curve IS_1? First, you will notice that a rise in taxes leads to a leftward shift in the *IS* curve. By how much does the *IS* curve shift leftwards when the level of taxes is increased? This question is answered in Figure 10.8. Figure 10.8 reproduces frames (c) and (d) of Figure 10.7. Focus on the interest rate at r_1 with the income level at y_1. Notice that at the interest rate r_1, the tax rise shifts the *IS* curve such that, if the interest rate was to remain constant at r_1, income would fall to y_2. Call the change in income from y_1 to y_2, Δy. That income change is labelled Δy in frame (a). Transferring that income change up to frame (b), you see that it forms the base of a triangle whose height is given by b times the change in taxes. Again, use the formula "slope equals rise over run" to figure out what the change in income is in this case. You know that the "slope" of the hypotenuse of this triangle is $1 - b$, the "rise" is $b\Delta t$, and the "run" is $(-\Delta y)$, so you may establish that "slope equals rise over run" becomes

$$1 - b = \frac{b\Delta t}{(-\Delta y)}$$

(Why have we put a minus sign in front of Δy? Because income *falls* as taxes *rise*, so they move in opposite directions.) Now multiply both sides of this equation by the change in income (Δy) to give

$$\Delta y(1 - b) = -b\Delta t$$

Then divide both sides of this equation by $1 - b$, the marginal propensity to save, and obtain

$$\Delta y = \left(\frac{-b}{1 - b}\right) \Delta t$$

What does this say? It says that a change in taxes changes income in the opposite direction and by an amount that is equal to the marginal propensity to consume divided by the marginal propensity to save, times the change in taxes.

You have now discovered that a rise in government expenditure shifts the IS curve to the right by an amount equal to $1/(1 - b)$ times the rise in government spending. That is,

$$\Delta y = \frac{1}{1 - b} \Delta g$$

You have also discovered that a rise in taxes shifts the IS curve to the left and by an amount equal to $-b/(1 - b)$ times the rise in taxes. In other words,

$$\Delta y = \frac{-b}{1 - b} \Delta t$$

What would happen to the IS curve if government spending and taxes were simultaneously increased and by the same amount? You can very easily figure out the answer to this question by combining the two effects that we have just calculated. If the change in taxes equals the change in government spending then

$$\Delta g = \Delta t$$

It must be the case, therefore, that income rises by $1/(1 - b)$ times the rise in g and falls by $b/(1 - b)$ times the rise in g. In other words,

$$\Delta y = \frac{1}{1-b} \Delta g - \frac{b}{1-b} \Delta g$$

Bringing these two terms together it is evident that

$$\Delta y = \left(\frac{1}{1-b} - \frac{b}{1-b} \right) \Delta g$$

or, more simply,

$$\Delta y = \left(\frac{1-b}{1-b} \right) \Delta g$$

which is,

$$\Delta y = \Delta g$$

You have just discovered that a balance budget rise in taxes and government spending shifts the *IS* curve to the right by exactly the same amount as the rise in government spending.

Summary

A. The Definition of the *IS* Curve

The *IS* curve is the relationship between the aggregate demand for goods and services and the real rate of interest when flow equilibrium prevails in the goods market, that is, when investment-plus-government spending is equal to planned savings-plus-taxes.

B. Derivation of the *IS* Curve

The *IS* curve is derived from the investment-plus-government spending curve, the planned savings-plus-taxes curve, and the equality of investment-plus-government spending and savings-plus-taxes. Figures 10.1 through 10.4 illustrate this and should be thoroughly understood.

C. Determination of the *IS* Curve Slope

The *IS* curve slopes downwards. That is, at lower real interest rates, higher levels of real income are required to maintain flow equilibrium in the goods market. This arises because at lower interest rates there is more investment spending, and with higher investment there needs to be higher savings to maintain equilibrium. Higher savings require a higher level of income, so that lower interest rates require higher income levels to maintain flow equilibrium in the goods market. More precisely, the slope of the *IS* curve is equal to the slope of the investment demand curve multiplied by $(1 - b)$, where b is the marginal propensity to consume.

D. Shifts in the *IS* Curve

The *IS* curve shifts when government spending or taxes change. A rise in government spending will lead to a rightward shift in the *IS* curve by an amount equal to $1/(1 - b)$ times the change in government spending. A rise in taxes will cause the *IS* curve to shift leftwards. The amount of the shift will be equal to the rise in taxes times $b/(1 - b)$. A simultaneous rise in government spending and taxes of the same amount shifts the *IS* curve to the right by the same amount as the rise in government spending.

Review Questions

1. What is the *IS* curve?

2. Which markets are in equilibrium along the *IS* curve?

3. Why does the *IS* curve slope downwards?

4. Why is the *IS* curve flatter than the investment demand curve?

5. What happens to the position of the *IS* curve if there is a $1 million rise in government expenditure on goods and services?

6. What happens to the position of the *IS* curve if there is a $1 million rise in government transfers to individuals in the form of increased pensions and unemployment benefits?

7. What happens to the position of the *IS* curve if the government cuts pensions and raises defence spending by $1 million?

8. You are given the following information about a hypothetical economy:

$$c = 100 + 0.8(y - t)$$
$$i = 500 - 50r$$
$$g = 400$$
$$t = 400$$

(c = consumption; i = investment; g = government spending on goods and services; t = taxes; r = real rate of interest)

(a) Find the equation for the *IS* curve.

(b) Show that the slope of the *IS* curve is the same as the slope of the investment demand curve multiplied by the marginal propensity to save.

(c) Show that a rise in g shifts the *IS* curve to the right by five times the rise in g.

(d) Show that a rise in t shifts the *IS* curve to the left by four times the rise in t.

Appendix

The Algebra of the *IS* Curve

This appendix sets out the algebra of the *IS* curve. The material presented here is simply another way of looking at the derivation given in the body of the chapter. For those who prefer an algebraic treatment, this may be found to be more compact and straightforward. It does not, however, contain anything of substance that is not stated in words and diagrams in the chapter.

Aggregate demand for goods and services is shown by

$$y^d = c + i + g \qquad \text{(10A.1)}$$

Consumption demand is determined by

$$c = a + b(y - t) \qquad a > 0, 0 < b < 1 \qquad \text{(10A.2)}$$

and investment demand is determined by

$$i = i_0 - hr \qquad i_0, h > 0 \qquad \text{(10A.3)}$$

Substituting c and i from Equations (10A.2) and (10A.3) into Equation (10A.1) gives

$$y^d = a + b\,(y - t) + i_0 - hr + g \qquad \text{(10A.4)}$$

To be on the *IS* curve,

$$y = y^d \qquad \text{(10A.5)}$$

so replacing y^d with y in Equation (10A.4) gives

$$y = a + b(y - t) + i_0 - hr + g \qquad \text{(10A.6)}$$

which may be rearranged as

$$(1 - b)y = a + i_0 + g - bt - hr \qquad \text{(10A.7)}$$

and dividing both sides by $1 - b$, we have

$$y = \frac{1}{1 - b}(a + i_0 + g - bt - hr) \qquad \text{(10A.8)}$$

or, equivalently,

$$y = \frac{a + i_0}{1 - b} + \frac{1}{1 - b}(g) - \frac{b}{1 - b}(t) - \frac{h}{1 - b}(r) \qquad \textbf{(10A.9)}$$

Equations (10A.8) and (10A.9) are alternative ways of writing the equation for the *IS* curve. The second of these is perhaps the clearest way of writing the *IS* curve and the one that makes interpretation of it most straightforward. The variables that enter the *IS* curve are government spending (g), taxes (t), and the rate of interest (r). The parameters that affect the *IS* curve are the constant in the consumption function (a), the constant in the investment demand function (i_0), the responsiveness of investment to a change in the rate of interest ($-h$), and the marginal propensity to consume (b). The way in which these various parameters enter the *IS* curve is made very precise in Equation (10A.9). First, the level of output that would obtain, even if government spending, taxes, and the rate of interest were all zero, is the first term in Equation (10A.9); that is,

$$\frac{a + i_0}{1 - b}$$

The slope of the *IS* curve (the change in the rate of interest that occurs when income changes) is given by the inverse of the coefficient in front of the rate of interest, namely,

$$\frac{-(1 - b)}{h}$$

Since $-1/h$ is the slope of the investment curve, you can immediately verify the proposition derived in the text that the slope of the *IS* curve is equal to the slope of the investment curve multiplied by $1 - b$.

A change in government spending shifts the *IS* curve by an amount indicated by the coefficient that multiplies g in Equation (10A.9). That coefficient is $1/(1 - b)$ and agrees with the derivation in the chapter.

A rise in taxes lowers the level of income (shifts the *IS* curve leftwards) since the coefficient in front of taxes has a minus sign attached to it. The size of the change in income that results from a rise in taxes will be equal to $b/(1 - b)$ times the change in taxes. This also agrees with the derivation in the chapter.

If government spending and taxes are increased together, and by the same amount, then the *IS* curve shifts to the right by $\frac{1}{(1 - b)}$ and to the left by $\dfrac{b}{(1 - b)}$ times the rise in government spending, that is

or
$$\Delta y = \left(\frac{1}{1 - b} - \frac{b}{1 - b} \right) \Delta g$$

$$\Delta y = \Delta g$$

This too agrees with the derivation in the chapter.

11

The Demand
For Money

The three preceding chapters have taken you through an analysis of
the determination of equilibrium between the *flows* of consumption,
savings, investment, and income. That analysis is built on the flow
accounts — the aggregate income and expenditure accounts — that
you studied in Chapter 3. The next part of the story of the determination of aggregate demand concerns equilibrium in the markets for
assets. The accounts for these asset markets are the ones that you
studied in Chapter 4. Although we set out in that chapter a fairly
elaborate set of inter-related balance sheets, the way in which macroeconomics uses those balance sheets is to aggregate them to consider
a single aggregate private sector and to distinguish between just two
classes of assets — money on the one hand and everything else on
the other. We study equilibrium in the asset markets by considering
how the equilibrium allocation of wealth between money and all
other non-money forms of holding wealth are determined. It is interesting to note, however, that we have already studied one aspect
of the way in which people will want to allocate their wealth — our
study of the demand for capital. We are now going to go on to apply
similar reasoning to an investigation of the way in which people
allocate their wealth between money and all other forms of wealth
holding. The chapter will take you through five tasks. They are to:

a) Understand what is meant by the demand for money.
b) Understand what determines the demand for money.
c) Understand why the market rate of interest is the opportunity
cost of holding money.
d) Know how to represent the demand for money function in a
simple equation and diagram.
e) Know the properties of the demand for money function in Canada.

A. Demand for Money

First, what do we mean by the demand for money?[1] You already know what money is: it is the *stock* of currency and demand deposits[2] in existence at a given point in time. Most of us acquire money as a *flow* of income which, typically, is received at either weekly or monthly intervals. At the beginning of payday, the amount of money that we are holding is at a minimum, and just after we have been paid, it is at a maximum. In the period between the moment that we have been paid through to the next payday, we typically spend our income gradually, thereby running down our money balances.

Figure 11.1 illustrates the pattern of money holdings for an individual who receives an income of $1000 per month at monthly intervals and who spends that $1000 in equal daily amounts through the month. The saw-tooth line shows the actual money holdings of that individual. Those money holdings are $1000 at the beginning of each month and zero at the end of each month. The broken line through the middle of the diagram shows the average money holding of this individual, which, in this case, is $500. It is the average money holding that we refer to as the individual's *demand* for money. The amount of money demanded is an average *stock*, and the income is a *flow*. Call the quantity of money demanded M^d (the superscript d on the M is to remind you that M^d is the *demand* for money), and call money income Py — the price level (P) multiplied by real income (y). Then let us define the ratio of money demanded (M^d) to money income (Py) as k. That is,

$$k = \frac{M^d}{Py} \tag{11.1}$$

The individual in the above example has an annual income of $12 000 ($1000 each month) and a demand for money $500. For this individual, therefore, the ratio of average money holdings to annual money income is

$$k = \frac{\$500}{\$12\ 000} = \frac{1}{24}$$

An alternative way of writing Equation (11.1) would be (by multiplying both sides of the equation by Py) as

$$M^d = kPy \tag{11.2}$$

This says that the demand for money is some fraction k of money income. Let us give a name to k: we will call it the *propensity to hold money*.

---

[1] The analysis of the demand for money presented here is highly simplified. A comprehensive treatment of this topic may be found in David Laidler, *The Demand for Money: Theories and Evidence*, 2nd ed. (New York: Harper and Row, 1978).

[2] This is the definition of money known as M1 (see Chapter 4).

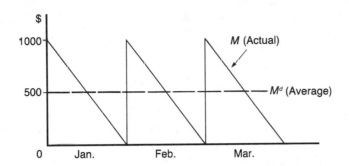

Figure 11.1
Money Balances

Actual money balances are at their peak at the beginning of each month and are gradually run down to their minimum as expenditure takes place throughout the month. The demand for money refers to the average money holdings (indicated in the diagram by the dashed line).

B. Determinants of the Demand for Money

The determinants of the demand for money and the determinants of k, the propensity to hold money, are identical. What determines the propensity to hold money? Will it be constant or will it vary in some systematic way? Put slightly differently, would it make sense for individuals to mechanically hold money balances equal, on the average, to one-half of their periodic income? That is, would it make sense for an individual paid weekly to hold money balances equal, on the average, to one-half a week's income; a person paid monthly to hold money balances equal, on the average, to one-half a month's income; and so on? The answer, in general, is that it would not. Rather it would be sensible to attempt to *economize* on money holdings.

Consider the example of a person who receives $12 000 a year, paid at quarterly intervals. Specifically, suppose a person receives $3000 on the first of January, April, July, and October. Would it make sense for such a person to run down his money balances at an even rate over each quarter? Notice that if such a person did spread his outlays evenly, the propensity to hold money would be one-eighth. That is, on the average, one-eighth of a year's income would be held in the form of money. The average money holding of such a person would be $1500. What could such a person do to economize on his money holdings? There are two possibilities: (1) He could make a loan by buying and holding some financial asset other than money, an asset that unlike money, pays interest; or (2) He could bunch the purchase of goods towards the beginning of the income period, thereby holding less money, on the average, and having a higher average inventory of goods.

Under what circumstances would an individual attempt to use one or both of these devices for economizing on money holdings? Obviously, the higher the rate of interest, the more will an individual be losing by holding money rather than buying interest — earning financial assets. Equally obviously, the higher is the rate of inflation, the more will an individual be losing by holding money rather than buying and holding inventories of goods. It seems reasonable to suppose, therefore, that the higher the rate of interest, the more will individuals seek to switch out of money holdings and into the holdings of financial assets that earn a return. This action will lower an individual's propensity to hold money.

It also seems reasonable to suppose that the faster prices are rising or, equivalently, the higher the rate of inflation, the more it would pay an individual to bunch purchases of goods so that most goods are bought soon after payday. There is, however, an important difference between the interest rate that an individual can earn on a financial asset and the consequences of inflation that can be avoided by buying goods earlier rather than later. When an individual buys a financial asset, the interest rate that will be paid on that financial asset is known at the time of the purchase. But when an individual seeks to avoid losses from inflation by buying goods early, he does not know with any certainty what the inflation rate will in fact turn out to be over some relevant future period. Thus, what will determine the decision to economize on money holdings and buy bigger inventories of goods is not the actual, but the *expected*, rate of inflation.

In the example that we have just worked through, we dealt with an individual whose income was received at quarterly intervals. This meant that the individual received a fairly sizeable amount of money on each payday and therefore would be able to earn a substantial amount of interest income (or avoid losses from inflation) by taking economizing actions of the type discussed. However, the more frequently a person is paid, the less the incentive to take advantage of these economizing actions. In fact, for people paid at very frequent intervals, such as a week, it may well be that the best they can do is to hold money balances that roughly equal one-half a week's income. This is because the interest that could be earned on a half a week's income would not be sufficient to justify the costs of moving between money and interest-earning securities and back again into money all within a week. For these individuals, the propensity to hold money (k) would be $1/104$. For such individuals, then, the propensity to hold money would indeed be a constant.

There is another factor working in the direction of reducing the incentive to economize on money holdings and that is the increasing tendency for certain types of bank deposits that are themselves part of the stock of money to bear interest. If all forms of money received interest at a rate that moved up and down in line with movements in other interest rates, then there would be no tendency for the incentive to economize on money holdings to vary with the level of interest rates. In a situation, however, in which not all components of the stock of money bear interest (such as in today's world), there will remain an incentive to economize on money holdings as interest rates and inflation fluctuate.

Let us now summarize the above. There are two ways of economizing on money holdings — (1) by buying financial assets, and (2) by buying real goods. Buying financial assets is a way of earning interest, and buying goods is a way of avoiding some of the loss in the value of money resulting from expected inflation. The higher interest rates and the higher the expected rate of inflation, the more that people will seek to economize on money holdings and the lower will be the propensity to hold money.

C. Opportunity Cost of Holding Money

The next step in developing the theory of the demand for money is to show that the opportunity cost of holding money is nothing other than the market rate of interest. At first this seems surprising because in the previous section we discovered that there are *two* ways of economizing on money holdings. One of these ways, buying financial assets, results in a rate of return equal to the market rate of interest. The other method of economizing, buying real goods, avoids money balances losing value as a result of inflation. It thus appears as if there should be two distinct opportunity costs of holding money — the rate of inflation and the market rate of interest. There is, however, a connection between these two that we are now going to explore.

Let us begin by refreshing our understanding (briefly introduced in Chapter 9) of the link between the market rate of interest and the real rate of interest.

The rate of interest actually paid and received is the *money* (or, equivalently, *nominal*) rate of interest. This is to emphasize its distinction from the *real* rate of interest. The distinction between real and money (or nominal) interest is a vital and natural one. In an economy in which prices are expected to rise by, say, 10 percent a year, money that is borrowed and lent will be expected to lose value at the rate of 10 percent a year. This means that someone who lends money for a year will expect to be repaid at the end of the year in dollars that are worth 10 percent less than the dollars that were lent. Similarly, the borrower will expect to repay the loan with cheaper dollars. This expected fall in the value of money — *expected inflation* — must be subtracted from the rate of interest — the *money rate of interest* — in order to calculate the interest rate that people expect they will *really* pay and receive.

All this can be summarized in a simple equation. Call the money rate of interest r_m and the real rate of interest r. Then, the real rate of interest is the difference between the money rate of interest and the expected rate of inflation, i.e.,

$$r = r_m - \pi^e \tag{11.3}$$

Equation 11.3 tells us the rate of return that people will *really* obtain if they place their wealth in interest-earning assets. What will they *really* earn if, instead of placing their wealth in interest-earning assets, they hang on to their money balances? A moment's reflection will lead you to the conclusion that the real rate of return from holding money is equal to minus the rate of inflation, that is $(-\pi)$. Holding money delivers a rate of return equal to minus the rate of inflation because the goods and services that can be purchased in the future will be less than what can be purchased at the present when inflation is positive and by a percentage amount that is related one to one with the rate of inflation.

You can think of the opportunity cost of holding money as being the difference between the real rate of return on holding money and the real rate of return on placing wealth in the form of interest-bearing assets. What is that opportunity cost? Define opportunity cost as the difference between the real rate of return on assets and the real rate of return on holding money (minus the rate of inflation). Thus we would have:

$$\text{Opportunity Cost of Holding Money} = r - (-\pi)$$

Of course, when people make decisions about how much money to hold they do not know what the future rate of inflation is going to be and have to base their decisions upon expectations of its rate. That is, they base their decision upon the expected opportunity cost of holding money. The expected opportunity cost of holding money is given by:

$$\text{Expected Opportunity Cost of Holding Money} = r - (-\pi^e)$$

We already know from Equation 11.3 that the real rate of interest is equal to the market rate of interest minus the expected rate of inflation. Thus, using this in the above equation gives:

$$\text{Expected Opportunity Cost of Holding Money} = r_m - \pi^e - (-\pi^e)$$

Recording that the negative of a negative number is positive you will immediately see that the above equation implies that:

$$\text{Expected Opportunity Cost of Holding Money} = r_m$$

In effect, what you have discovered is that movements in the market rate of interest, r_m, capture movements in the real rate of interest and movements in the expected rate of inflation. The higher the market rate of interest, the more people will seek to economize on their money holdings and the lower will be their marginal propensity to hold money.

Let us now go on to summarize these ideas in a simple representation of the demand for money function.

D. The Demand for Money Function

The entire discussion of the previous sections can now be summarized in some very simple propositions. We have discovered that the propensity to hold money will vary inversely with the market (or nominal) rate of interest.

We can write this as an equation, which says

$$\frac{M^d}{Py} = k(r_m) \qquad (11.4)$$
$$(-)$$

where $k(r_m)$ stands for "the propensity to hold money, k, is a function of — or depends on — r_m, the rate of interest." The minus sign $(-)$ below the equation is there to remind you that as the rate of interest *rises*, the propensity to hold money *falls*.

We can also illustrate the proposition with Figure 11.2. The downward-sloping line shows how k rises as r_m falls. If the rate of interest was as high as r'_m, people would no longer want to use money, and trade would be undertaken with barter or some commodity means of exchange. If the rate of interest was zero, then k would equal k'.

Equivalently, we can write Equation (11.4) in the form of Equation (11.2), as

$$M^d = k(r_m)Py \qquad (11.5)$$
$$(-)$$

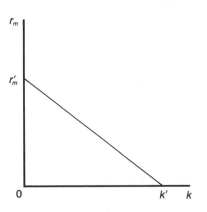

Figure 11.2
The Propensity
to Hold Money

The opportunity cost of holding money is the market rate of interest, r_m. It is the difference between the real rate of return on other assets and the real rate of return on money (the negative of the expected inflation rate, π^e). The higher the market rate of interest the lower will be the propensity to hold money.

Recalling that the market rate of interest is the sum of the real rate of interest and the expected rate of inflation enables us to write the demand for money function equivalently as

$$M^d = k(r + \pi^e)Py \qquad (11.6)$$

This states that the demand for money (M^d) depends on the level of money income (Py), the *real* rate of interest and the expected rate of inflation (π^e). Writing the demand for money function in this way enables us to focus on a crucial distinction between the effects on the demand for money of *inflation* and the effects of the *price level*.

If the price level doubled overnight, and if everything else (including the rate of inflation) remained the same,[3] then the amount of money that people would want to hold would also double. Thus, the demand for money is proportional to the level of prices. This idea, that the amount of money demanded is proportional to the price level, enables us to make use of a simpler statement about the demand for money based on a definition of real money. Real money is the quantity of money (M) divided by the price level (P). That is,

$$\text{Real money} = \frac{M}{P}$$

In contrast, if the rate of inflation was to rise, raising with it the market rate of interest, the demand for money — the demand for real money — would decline.

We may therefore express the demand for money function as a demand for real money balances. The demand for real money balances depends on the level of real income and on the rate of interest. The higher the level of real income, the more real money balances will be demanded; and the higher the rate of interest, the less real money balances will be demanded.

We may represent this in terms of a simple equation derived directly from Equation (11.5), which says:

$$\frac{M^d}{P} = k(r_m)y \qquad (11.7)$$
$$(-)$$

E. Canadian Demand for Money Function

What does the Canadian demand for money function look like? Is the theoretical formulation of the propensity to hold money, shown in Figure 11.2, anything like a representation of the facts about the propensity to hold money in Canada?

---

[3]If the idea of the price level doubling overnight and the rate of inflation remaining constant seems puzzling, recall the distinction between a once-and-for-all change in the price level and inflation — Figure 5.1.

Figure 11.3 contains the answer. In that figure, we have plotted the short-term rate of interest (from Chapter 2) on the vertical axis and on the horizontal axis we have plotted a measure of k. The particular measure of k that we have used is one based on the M1 measure of the money stock. Recall that $k - \frac{M}{Py}$. Now Py is *nominal* income, or more precisely, nominal GNP. The amount of M1 held, expressed as a fraction of GNP is the propensity to hold M1. That is the measure of k plotted on the horizontal axis of Figure 11.3. The data is shown

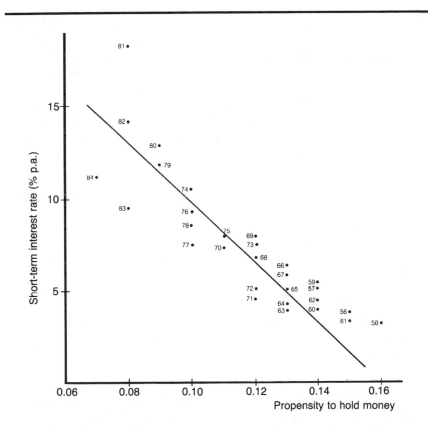

**Figure 11.3
Canadian Demand
for Money**

Each point shows the short-term interest rate and the propensity to hold money in a particular year. Years are identified by their last two digits — thus, for example, 1958 is shown as 58. The relationship between the short-term rate of interest and the propensity to hold money in Canada is remarkably similar to the theoretical relationship between those two variables shown in Figure 11.2. There were some discrepancies in 1981, 1983 and 1984 but for the most part the relationship is a close one — most points lie close to the line.

Source: The short-term interest rate is given in the Appendix to Chapter 2. The propensity to hold money is Cansim Series D92866 + D92870 as a proportion of Cansim Series D30013.

for the period between 1956 and 1984. Each point represents a year identified by its last two digits. As you can see the propensity to hold money varies inversely with the short-term nominal rate of interest in exactly the way that the theory predicts. With the exceptions of two years, 1981 and 1983, the "fit" between the theory and the facts is very close. At a zero nominal rate of interest the propensity to hold money would be about 16 percent of GNP. For each 1 percentage point rise in the rate of interest the percentage of GNP held in the form of M1 money would decline, according to the figures presented here, by a little more than one-half a percent point.

The rather large divergences from the systematic inverse relationship between the short-term rate of interest and the propensity to hold money that are apparent in 1981 and 1983 reveal that there are other forces than the short-term rate of interest that can influence the propensity to hold money. Changes in banking system practices, the offering of new types of checking accounts — the sorts of things that we discussed in Chapter 4 — clearly are at work, and in years such as the early 1980s may have been especially important.

Despite these brief aberrations, it is clear that the basic theory of the demand for money provides a good rationalization of the facts about the relationship between short-term interest rates and the propensity to hold money.

Summary

A. Demand for Money

The demand for money is a demand for an average stock of money to hold.

B. What Determines the Demand for Money

The demand for money depends on the level of real income and (inversely) on the market rate of interest. The demand for money is the demand for real money.

C. Opportunity Cost of Holding Money

The market rate of interest is the difference between the real rate of return on interest–earning assets and the real rate of return on money. The real rate of return on money is the negative of the expected rate of inflation.

D. Demand for Money Function

The demand for money function may be represented as a simple equation such as Equation (11.7) or in the form of a simple diagram such as Figure 11.2.

E. Canadian Demand for Money Function

The theory of the demand for money fits the Canadian facts remarkably well. This is illustrated in Figure 11.3.

Review Questions

1. What does the term *demand for money* mean?

2. Calculate your own average holding of money. What are the units of this quantity? Is it a stock or a flow?

3. Calculate your own demand for money.

4. Calculate your own propensity to hold money. What are the units of this quantity?

5. If the interval between when you are paid is lengthened (i.e., multiplied by 2 or 4) would your demand for money change? Explain why or why not.

6. Some people "economize" on their money holdings. What does this mean? Explain why they would "economize."

7. If the inflation rate dropped to zero tomorrow and remained there, would your demand for money change? Explain why or why not.

8. If the inflation rate doubled tomorrow and remained at that level, would you "economize" on your money holdings? Explain why or why not.

9. The propensity to hold money is related to the expected inflation rate. What is this relationship? Draw a diagram to illustrate this relationship.

10. What is the relationship between the demand for money and money income?

11. What is the relationship between the demand for money and the price level?

12. What is the relationship between the demand for money and real income?

13. What is the relationship between the demand for money and the market rate of interest?

12

The
LM Curve

The subject matter of this chapter is very similar to that of Chapter 10. In that chapter we studied the way in which the *IS* curve summarizes *flow equilibrium* in the market for goods and services. *Stock equilibrium* in the markets for money (and assets) may be similarly summarized by an equivalent relation called the *LM* curve. This chapter deals with the *LM* curve. You have four tasks ahead of you in this chapter, which are to:

a) Know the definition of the *LM* curve.
b) Know how to derive the *LM* curve.
c) Understand what determines the slope of the *LM* curve.
d) Understand what makes the *LM* curve shift and by how much.

A. Definition of the *LM* Curve

Like the *IS* curve that you studied in Chapter 10, the *LM* curve is also a relationship between the rate of interest and the level of real income. Specifically, the *LM* curve is that relationship between the rate of interest and the level of real income that makes the demand for money equal to the supply of money.[1] Thus, like the *IS* curve, the *LM* curve is an equilibrium locus. It is worth emphasizing again that the *LM*

---

[1] You may be wondering why the *LM* curve is so called. The name was first used by Sir John Hicks who invented the *IS-LM* analysis. The letter *L* stands for "Liquidity Preference," the name that Keynes gave to the demand for money (what we are calling M^d). The letter *M* stands for the supply of money. Thus, the label *LM* reminds us that this curve depicts values of the rate of interest and the level of income at which the demand for money (*L*) equals the supply of money (*M*).

curve does not imply any causal relationship from the rate of interest to the level of income or in the reverse direction. Like the *IS* curve, it places further restrictions on the values that these two variables may take on. Let us now proceed to see how the *LM* curve is derived.

B. Derivation of the *LM* Curve

The starting point for the derivation of the *LM* curve is to recall the theory of the demand for money.[2] This theory, set out in the previous chapter, says that the amount of real money balances that people will want to hold in the aggregate will vary directly with the level of real income and inversely with the level of the market or *money* rate of interest.

Purely for convenience we will treat the demand for money function as *linear* in real income and the rate of interest.[3] Specifically, we shall suppose that the demand for money is determined by the equation

$$\frac{M^d}{P} = ky + m_0 - \ell r_m \tag{12.1}$$

M^d stands for the quantity of nominal money balances demanded, P is the price level, y is real income, r_m is the market rate of interest, and k, m_0 and ℓ are constants. This equation says that the demand for real balances (M^d/P) depends on the level of real income and the market rate of interest. For each extra dollar of real income in the economy, k dollars of extra real balances will be demanded. For every 1 percentage point rise in the market rate of interest on bonds, the demand for bonds would rise and the demand for real balances would drop by ℓ dollars. Even at a zero level of income and a zero rate of interest, there would be some rock-bottom level of real balances demanded equal to m_0.

The market rate of interest will be equal to the real rate of interest plus the inflation rate. That is,

$$r_m = r + \pi \tag{12.2}$$

---

[2] There are several excellent discussions of the theory of, and empirical evidence on, the demand for money function. In our view, you can do no better than study David Laidler's *The Demand for Money: Theories and Evidence*, 2nd ed. (New York: Harper & Row, 1978). An excellent and even more up-to-date study is David Laidler, "The Demand for Money in the United States—Yet Again," in *On the State of Macro-Economics*, Karl Brunner and Allan H. Meltzer, eds., 12 (Spring 1980), 219-71, Carnegie-Rochester Conference Series on Public Policy.

[3] The precise functional form of the demand for money that best fits the facts is a logarithmic function that says that the logarithm of real money demanded is a linear function of the logarithm of real income and the level (not logarithm) of the rate of interest. The different forms of the function used in Chapter 11 and here are selected for analytical convenience and may be regarded as holding approximately for small enough movements in the variables.

The *LM* curve depicts a relationship between the level of income and the rate of interest when the supply of money is equal to the demand for money. Evidently the demand for money depends on the level of income, the real rate of interest, the rate of inflation and the price level. To define the *LM* curve we treat the price level as being given at some fixed number, P_0, and the rate of inflation, π, as zero. We can write the demand for real money as follows:

$$\frac{M^d}{P_0} = ky + m_0 - \ell r \qquad (12.3)$$

This equation incorporates the fact that the amount of nominal money demanded is deflated by the particular fixed price level, the price level called P_0, and the market rate of interest, r_m, is exactly the same as r, the real rate of interest, since with a fixed price level the inflation rate, π, is equal to zero.

Equilibrium in the money market requires the demand for money to be equal to the supply of money. Calling the supply of money that is determined by the actions of the monetary authorities M, the equilibrium condition in the money market may be written as:

$$M^d = M \qquad (12.4)$$

Just as in Chapter 10 government spending and taxes were regarded as exogenous, so in this chapter, M is treated as being exogenous. That is, the money supply, M, does not respond directly to the values of any of the variables in the model, but rather is determined externally to the model and influences the values of those variables. In fact, the supply of money is determined by the actions of the central bank and the banking system, and this process will be analyzed in some detail in Chapter 31. In treating the supply of money as being determined exogenously we are bypassing that process.[4]

Making the assumption that the supply of money (M) is exogenous, enables us to move on to examine how money market equilibrium determines the level of aggregate demand for goods and services.

---

[4]When proper account is taken of the linkages between the domestic economy and the rest of the world, it is not always possible to regard the supply of money as being determined exogenously. If the economy has a floating exchange rate, such an assumption may be in order. In the case of an economy with a fixed exchange rate, however, it is inappropriate to regard the money supply as being determined exogenously. For present purposes, therefore, you should regard the exercise that is being conducted as one that applies to an economy that does not have any trading links with the rest of the world, or as applying to an economy that has a floating exchange rate. (The world as a whole is the only interesting example of an economy that does not have trading links with the rest of the world.) Chapter 25 will introduce the explicit modifications that have to be made to this analysis in order to allow for international transactions.

If M^d is replaced in Equation (12.3) with M, we obtain

$$\frac{M}{P_0} = ky + m_0 - \ell r \qquad \textbf{(12.5)}$$

which is the equation for the *LM* curve. Notice that there are two variables in this equation, y and r. All the other terms in the equation are constants. The money supply, M, is a constant determined by the monetary authorities; P_0 is being treated as a constant (because we are studying the determinants of aggregate demand at a given price level); and m_0, ℓ and k are constants, being parameters of the demand for money function.

Figure 12.1 illustrates the derivation of the *LM* curve. To draw Figure 12.1, first break the demand for real balances into two parts.

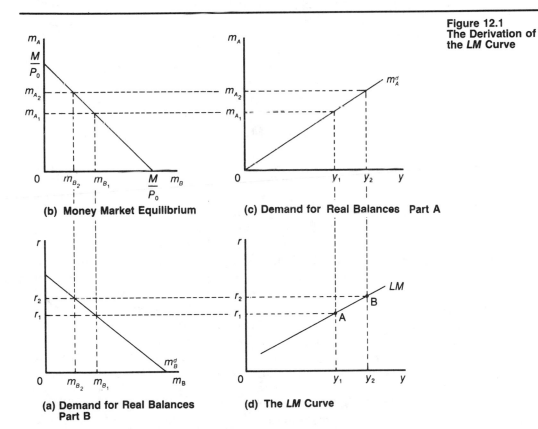

**Figure 12.1
The Derivation of
the *LM* Curve**

(b) Money Market Equilibrium

(c) Demand for Real Balances Part A

**(a) Demand for Real Balances
Part B**

(d) The *LM* Curve

The *LM* curve traces the relationship between the real rate of interest, r, and the level of real income, y, which ensures that the demand for real balances, $m_A^d + m_B^d$, equals the supply of real balances M/P_0. The *LM* curve slopes upwards. For a given supply of real balances, a higher level of real income (which gives rise to a higher demand for real balances) can only be sustained if there is more economizing on money balances. A higher rate of interest is needed to induce such economizing.

Define the first part, ky, as m_A^d and the second part, $(m_0 - \ell r)$ as m_B^d. The demand for real balances may be written as:

$$\frac{M^d}{P_0} = m_A^d + m_B^d$$

Now turn to Figure 12.1. The figure has four parts. Frame (c) contains a graph of the part of the demand for real balances m_A^d. As real income rises m_A^d (or ky) rises. Frame (a) contains the other part of the demand for real balances m_B^d. Notice that frame (a) is very similar to Figure 11.2 which you studied in Chapter 11. As the real interest rate rises m_B^d (or $m_0 - \ell r$) falls. Frame (b) measures m_B^d on the horizontal axis and m_A^d on the vertical axis. The line drawn in frame (b) slopes at "minus one" and is located in the following way. Measure on the horizontal axis the total exogenously given amount of money divided by the price level P_0, the supply of real balances; then measure the same distance on the vertical axis, and join together the two points. What that line tells us is the amount of real balances that is in existence and that must be held and "allocated" to either m_A^d or m_B^d. In effect, it is the supply of real balances. The *LM* curve, derived in frame (d), is a relationship such that the supply of real balances depicted in frame (b) is held and is demanded in accordance with the two-part demand function plotted in frames (a) and (c).

To derive the *LM* curve, proceed as follows. First, pick an interest rate — say, r_1. Focus on frame (a) and notice that at the interest rate r_1 the amount of real balances demanded under part B of the demand for real balances is m_{B_1}. Transfer that level of real balances demanded up to frame (b) and notice that if m_{B_1} is demanded under part B, then under part A, m_{A_1} real balances must be demanded ($m_{B_1} + m_{A_1}$ exactly equals the supply of real balances available). Then transfer m_{A_1} across to the vertical axis of frame (c) and using the curve drawn in that frame, work out the level of income that is necessary to ensure that m_{A_1} is demanded. That level of income is y_1. Now transfer the initially selected interest rate r_1 rightwards across to frame (d) and transfer the income level y_1 vertically downwards from frame (c) to frame (d). These two lines meet at point A indicating that with the interest rate r_1 the income level y_1 will generate a sufficient demand for real balances to ensure that the quantity of real balances in existence is willingly held.

Now repeat the above experiment with the interest rate r_2. At the interest rate r_2, m_{B_2} real balances are demanded in part B. That leaves m_{A_2} real balances to be demanded in part A of the demand for real balances. According to frame (c), in order that m_{A_2} real balances be demanded, the income level would have to be y_2. Thus, the interest rate r_2 and the income level y_2, taken together, would lead to a demand for real balances equal to the supply of real balances. This gives point B in frame (d). The points A and B are both points on the *LM* curve as defined above. Joining those points together and extending the curve beyond those points plots the *LM* curve.

The *LM* curve that you have just derived graphically can be derived by a simple piece of algebra that involves nothing more than a slight rearrangement of Equation (12.5). By dividing through Equation (12.5) by k, the equation for the *LM* curve can be written with real income, y, on the left-hand side as

$$y = \frac{1}{k}\left(\frac{M}{P_0}\right) - \frac{m_0}{k} + \left(\frac{\ell}{k}\right)r \qquad \textbf{(12.6)}$$

Alternatively, by dividing Equation (12.5) through by P and rearranging things slightly, the equation for the *LM* curve can be written as

$$r = -\frac{1}{\ell}\left(\frac{M}{P_0}\right) + \frac{m_0}{\ell} + \left(\frac{k}{\ell}\right)y \qquad \textbf{(12.7)}$$

which is an equation relating y to r. Equations (12.6) and (12.7) are identical and, indeed, are identical to Equation (12.5).

You have now seen how the *LM* curve may be derived graphically and you have seen how it can be represented in a simple equation. Equation (12.7) is a direct representation of the *LM* curve shown in frame (d) of Figure 12.1. Let us now go on to explore more thoroughly the properties of the *LM* curve.

C. Determinants of the *LM* Curve Slope

The slope of the *LM* curve has considerable importance for the relative effectiveness of changes in the money supply and changes in government spending and taxes on the level of aggregate demand. You will see this in the next chapter. For now, let us focus on the factors that determine the slope of the *LM* curve. You can see from inspecting frame (d) in Figure 12.1 that the *LM* curve slopes upwards. What determines how steep or flat the *LM* curves will be? There are only two things that underlie the slope of the *LM* curve — the parameters k and ℓ. These determine the sensitivity of the demand for money or the demand for real balances with respect to changes in the level of real income and the rate of interest.

Figure 12.2 illustrates the effects on the *LM* curve of changing the sensitivity of the demand for real balances to changes in the rate of interest, by changing the parameter ℓ. The curve LM_2 is derived from the steeper demand for real balances plotted in frame (a). Notice that the steeper demand for real balances makes the *LM* curve steeper. That is, the less sensitive the demand for real balances to changes in the interest rate (the smaller the value of ℓ), the steeper will be the *LM* curve. In the limit, if the demand for real balances became perfectly elastic with respect to the rate of interest, the *LM* curve would

Figure 12.2
The Interest Sensitivity of the Demand for Money and the Slope of the *LM* Curve

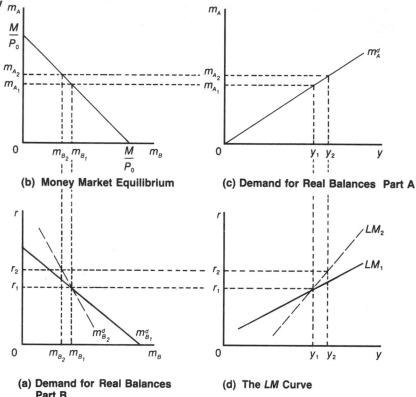

(b) Money Market Equilibrium

(c) Demand for Real Balances   Part A

(a) Demand for Real Balances Part B

(d) The *LM* Curve

The less sensitive the demand for money to interest rate changes, the steeper will be the slope of the *LM* curve. The less sensitive the demand for money to changes in the interest rate, the steeper becomes the demand for real balances, part B in frame (a), and the steeper becomes the *LM* curve in frame (d). In the extreme, if the demand for money was completely elastic [horizontal demand for real balances in frame (a)], the *LM* curve would be horizontal; whereas, if the demand for money was totally inelastic [vertical demand for real balances in frame (a)], then the *LM* curve would become vertical.

become horizontal; and if the demand for real balances became completely inelastic with respect to the rate of interest, the *LM* curve would become vertical. Check that you can derive those two extreme cases.

Figure 12.3 illustrates the effects of changing the sensitivity of the demand for money or the demand for real balances to changes in real income, by changing the parameter k. Again, LM_1 is identical to the *LM* curve in Figure 12.1. The curve LM_2 is derived for the steeper m_A^d curve in frame (c). Notice that the more sensitive the demand for real balances to changes in real income (the bigger the value of k), the steeper is the *LM* curve.

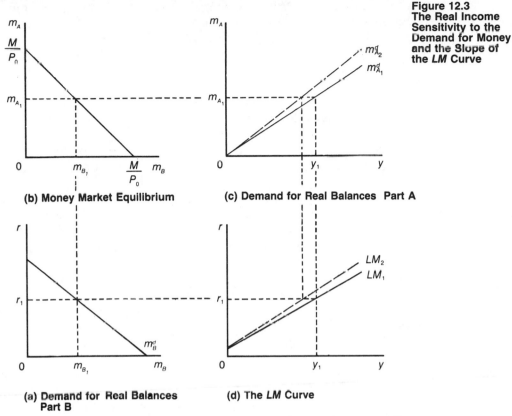

Figure 12.3
The Real Income
Sensitivity to the
Demand for Money
and the Slope of
the LM Curve

(b) Money Market Equilibrium

(c) Demand for Real Balances   Part A

(a) Demand for Real Balances
Part B

(d) The LM Curve

The more sensitive the demand for money to a change in real income, the steeper will be the slope of the LM curve. As the demand for money becomes more sensitive to the level of real income the demand for real balances part A in frame (c) becomes steeper and so does the LM curve in frame (d).

You can obtain these results that we have just derived directly from Equation (12.7), the equation to the LM curve. Notice that the LM curve equation says that the rate of interest is equal to some constants that involve only the money supply, the price level, and the parameters ℓ and m_0, plus a term equal to $(k/\ell)y$. Clearly, the ratio k/ℓ measures the slope of the LM curve. The bigger that k is, the steeper the LM curve; and the bigger that ℓ is, the flatter the LM curve.

What this all means is very simple. If money is a poor substitute for other assets, so that the demand for money is inelastic with respect to the rate of interest (ℓ is very small), then the LM curve will be very steep. Thus small changes in real income will require big changes in the rate of interest in order to preserve money market equilibrium. Conversely, if money and other assets are very close substitutes for each other so that the demand for money is elastic with respect to the rate of interest (ℓ is very large), big variations in real income will be possible with only small variations in the rate of interest, while maintaining money market equilibrium.

D. Shifts in the *LM* Curve

There are three things that can make the *LM* curve shift. One is a shift in the demand for money (a change in one of the parameters, m_0, ℓ, or k), another is a change in the money supply, and the third is a change in the price level. We shall focus attention on the second and third factors. Notice that in the equation that defines the *LM* curve, the money supply is divided by the price level. In other words, the position of the *LM* curve depends upon the real money supply. It follows immediately from this that a 1 percent rise in the money supply will have exactly the same effect on the position of the *LM* curve as a 1 percent cut in the price level. It is possible, therefore, to discuss both these factors that shift the *LM* curve by considering what would happen to the *LM* curve if the money supply changed. Once you know how the *LM* curve shifts when the money supply changes, you also know, by implication, how the *LM* curve shifts in response to price level changes.

Figure 12.4 illustrates the effects on the *LM* curve of a rise in the money supply. The continuous curves in Figure 12.4 are identical to those in Figure 12.1. Now suppose that there is a rise in the money supply from M_1 to M_2, an amount ΔM. This is shown in the diagram in frame (b) by the parallel shift of the real money supply curve. Notice that it is shifted horizontally by an amount $\Delta M/P_0$, indicating that at all interest rates and income levels there is an extra $\Delta M/P_0$ of real money balances to be held. You can derive the new *LM* curve for this new higher quantity of real balances in exactly the same manner as the original *LM* curve, LM_1, was derived. You will notice that this new *LM* curve, LM_2, is to the right of LM_1. Thus, a rise in the quantity of money shifts the *LM* curve to the right. The amount by which the *LM* curve shifts to the right is evidently equal to $(1/k)$ times the rise in the quantity of real money balances. How do we know this? We know it by looking at frame (c). Notice that the thickened triangle in frame (c) provides the detailed calculation of the amount of the shift, Δy, in the *LM* curve. The rise in the real money supply $\Delta M/P_0$ measures the height of that triangle. We know that its slope is equal to k, and we know that its base is the change in income that would occur at a given interest rate, $y_2 - y_1$ or Δy. Using the formula "slope equals rise over run," we can see that

$$k = \frac{\Delta M/P_0}{\Delta y}$$

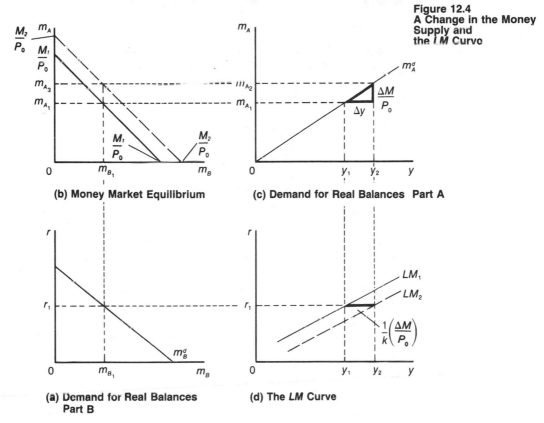

Figure 12.4
A Change in the Money Supply and the *LM* Curve

(b) Money Market Equilibrium

(c) Demand for Real Balances Part A

(a) Demand for Real Balances Part B

(d) The *LM* Curve

A rise in the supply of money shifts the *LM* curve to the right. The rise in the money supply from M_1 to M_2 (ΔM) shifts the real money supply curve in frame (b). This shifts the *LM* curve from LM_1 to LM_2 in frame (d). The *LM* curve shifts by an amount equal to $(1/k)$ times the rise in the real money supply, $\dfrac{\Delta M}{P_0}$, as shown by the triangle in frame (c).

Dividing both sides of that equation by k and multiplying both sides by Δy gives

$$\Delta y = \frac{1}{k}\left(\frac{\Delta M}{P_0}\right)$$

That is, the size of the shift of the *LM* curve to the right, Δy, equals $(1/k)$ times the rise in real money supply, $\Delta M/P_0$.

A percentage fall in the price level equal to the rise in the money supply just considered would shift the *LM* curve in exactly the same way.

Summary

A. Definition of the *LM* Curve

The *LM* curve is defined as an equilibrium locus that traces out the relationship between the real rate of interest and the level of real income when the money supply is equal to the amount of money demanded.

B. Derivation of the *LM* Curve

The *LM* curve is derived graphically in Figure 12.1. This derivation should be thoroughly understood.

C. Determinants of the *LM* Curve Slope

The *LM* curve slopes upwards. This is because as interest rates rise, people economize on their holdings of money. With a given quantity of money in existence the only way that monetary equilibrium can be maintained at higher interest rates is for there to be a higher level of real income to induce a rise in the demand for money to offset the economizing on money holdings. The less elastic the demand for real balances with respect to the rate of interest, the steeper will be the *LM* curve. Also, the more responsive the demand for real balances to real income changes, the steeper will be the *LM* curve. The slope of the *LM* curve is (k/ℓ).

D. Shifts in the *LM* Curve

The *LM* curve will shift if the money supply changes or if the price level changes. A rise in the supply of money will make the *LM* curve shift to the right by an amount equal to $(1/k)$ times the rise in the real money supply. A rise in the price level will have an equivalent but opposite effect on the *LM* curve to that of a rise in the money supply.

Review Questions

1. What is the *LM* curve?

2. Which markets are in equilibrium along the *LM* curve?

3. Why does the *LM* curve slope upwards?

4. If money was a perfect substitute for bonds, what would be the slope of the *LM* curve?

5. If money and bonds were completely non-substitutable, what would be the slope of the *LM* curve?

6. What happens to the position of the *LM* curve when the money supply rises?

7. What happens to the position of the *LM* curve when the price level rises?

8. What happens to the position of the *LM* curve if the money supply grows at a constant rate?

9. Why does the demand for money depend on the money rate of interest rather than on the real rate of interest?

13

The
IS-LM Analysis
of Aggregate
Demand

It is now possible to see the light at the end of the aggregate demand tunnel![1] You may feel that you have been groping in the darkness of that tunnel for the last few chapters. Very soon you should be able to see the light. You are going to do five things in this chapter. They are as follows:

a) Understand why the intersection of the *IS* and *LM* curves determines the equilibrium levels of output and the interest rate, at a given price level.

b) Know the properties of the *IS-LM* equilibrium.

c) Understand the effects of changes in government expenditure and taxes at a given price level.

d) Understand the effects of a change in the money supply at a given price level.

e) Understand how the *IS-LM* analysis generates the theory of aggregate demand.

---

[1] This chapter presents the analysis developed by J.R. (now Sir John) Hicks in "Mr. Keynes and the 'Classics': A Suggested Interpretation," *Econometrica*, 5 (April 1937), 147-59. The sheer brilliance of John Hicks is displayed in this paper which managed to cut through the complexities of the *General Theory* so soon after the work appeared.

A. Equilibrium at the *IS-LM* Intersection

You will have noticed in the statement of the "tasks" the repetition of the phrase "at a given price level." What does that phrase mean? It means that we are going to study what would happen to real income and the (real) rate of interest when certain things are changed, *if* the price level was to remain constant. It does not mean that some of the exogenous changes that we shall analyze will not, in fact, lead to a change in the price level. A different way of saying the same thing is that in this chapter we are going to study *only* aggregate demand and not the interaction of aggregate demand and aggregate supply.

The basis of the analysis that we are now going to perform has already been established in Chapters 10 and 12. In Chapter 10 we set out the theory of the *IS* curve which tells us what the level of real income will be at each level of the rate of interest such that the goods market is in equilibrium. In Chapter 12 we studied the *LM* curve, which tells us the relationship between the level of real income and the level of the rate of interest at which the amount of money demanded will equal the amount supplied. In effect, the *IS* curve and the *LM* curve give us two equations in two unknown variables — the level of real income and the rate of interest. When the economy is on both the *IS* curve and the *LM* curve, a unique level of real income and of the rate of interest is determined.

According to the *IS-LM* analysis, we shall never observe the economy "off" either of these two curves. If the economy was, in an imaginary sense, "off" the *IS* curve, investment-plus-government spending would not be equal to savings-plus-taxes. Equilibrating forces (which will be described below) would be set up that would produce an equality between these two variables. If the economy was "off" the *LM* curve, the demand for money would not be equal to the supply of money. Again, equilibrating forces would be set up to bring about this equality. Only when the demand for money and the supply of money are equal, and savings-plus-taxes are equal to investment-plus-government spending, will individuals' plans be compatible with each other, and will the economy be in equilibrium.

An analogy may be useful here. Suppose that Lake Ontario was arbitrarily divided by a straight line running north-south midway along its length. Now ask the question, what would happen if the water level on the left-hand side of this line was 10 feet higher than the water level on the right-hand side? This is a perfectly sensible question to ask. The answer is that the molecular structure of the water is such that the force of gravity would very quickly act upon the higher level to reduce it to equality with that of the lower level. In the ordinary course of events we would never observe such an inequality, although the theory that explains why the lake surface is flat involves conceptually letting the level be temporarily and hypothetically perturbed. It is the same in the goods or money market. The very forces that would lead to goods or money market equilibrium will, in the ordinary course of events, prevent the goods or money market from ever straying very far away from such an equilibrium.[2]

Let us now go on to characterize the equilibrium level of real income and the interest rate in the *IS-LM* analysis.

B. Properties of the *IS-LM* Equilibrium

(i) Equilibrium

The *IS* curve derived in Figure 10.4 and the *LM* curve derived in Figure 12.1 are brought together and shown in the same diagram in Figure 13.1. Since the *IS* curve slopes downwards and the *LM* curve slopes upwards, these two curves cut in just one place. Label this point y_1, r_1. It is a property of the interest rate r_1 and the income level y_1 that two sets of equilibrium conditions are simultaneously satisfied. First, planned savings-plus-taxes are equal to planned investment-plus-government spending. Second, the stock of money demanded is

Figure 13.1
***IS-LM* Equilibrium**

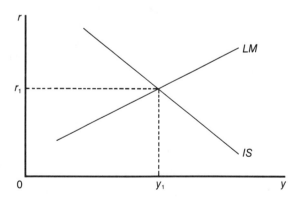

When investment-plus-government spending equals savings-plus-taxes (the economy is on the *IS* curve), and when the demand for money equals the supply of money (the economy is on the *LM* curve), then the economy is in equilibrium. Such an equilibrium is shown as y_1, r_1 in the diagram.

---

[2] David Hume first suggested this water-level analogy. See his essay "Of the Balance of Trade" in *Essays: Moral, Political and Literary* (London: Oxford University Press, 1963), p. 319.

equal to the stock of money in existence. The point at which the income level is y_1 and interest rate is r_1 is the only point at which these two equilibrium conditions are simultaneously satisfied. This position is the equilibrium level of real income and the interest rate in the *IS-LM* analysis.

To determine the values of the other variables in the economy — the level of investment and savings — all that is necessary is to use a diagram like Figure 10.4 and work backwards from the quadrant that displays the *IS* and *LM* curves. Figure 13.2 illustrates the equilibrium values of investment and savings. In frame (d), the *IS* and

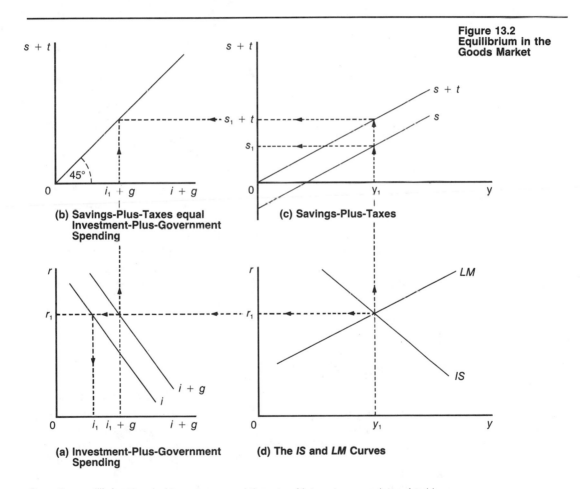

**Figure 13.2
Equilibrium in the
Goods Market**

**(b) Savings-Plus-Taxes equal
Investment-Plus-Government
Spending**

(c) Savings-Plus-Taxes

**(a) Investment-Plus-Government
Spending**

(d) The *IS* and *LM* Curves

Once the equilibrium level of income, y_1, and the rate of interest, r_1, are determined by the intersection of the *IS* and *LM* curves [frame (d)], it is possible to trace backwards to establish the equilibrium levels of savings, s_1, [frame (c)] and investment, i_1, [frame (a)]. When taxes are added to savings, $s_1 + t$, and government spending to investment, $i_1 + g$, as frame (b) shows, investment-plus-government spending is equal to savings-plus-taxes.

LM curves from Figure 13.1 are reproduced. The *IS* curve itself is derived from the underlying savings and investment decisions that are shown in frames (a) and (c). By working backwards from frame (d), we can work out the equilibrium levels of savings and investment. Transfer the equilibrium income level y_1 from frame (d) to frame (c), and you can read off immediately the equilibrium level of savings in the economy, s_1. Tracking leftwards across to frame (a), you can read off the equilibrium level of investment, i_1, that is generated by the equilibrium interest rate r_1. By tracking this level of investment-plus-government spending vertically upwards to frame (b) and by tracking the level of savings-plus-taxes horizontally leftwards across from frame (c) to (b) you can see that the position depicted is indeed in equilibrium, for the two lines meet on the 45° line that describes the equality of $i + g$ with $s + t$.

(ii) Convergence to Equilibrium

Just what are the forces that bring about the equilibrium between investment-plus-government spending and savings-plus-taxes on the one hand and the supply of and demand for money on the other? To answer this question it is necessary to perform a conceptual experiment just like the lake water analogy. Suppose, in a hypothetical sense, that the economy was "off" the *IS* curve. Frame (a) of Figure 13.3 can be used to illustrate the discussion. If the economy was "off" the *IS* curve and to its right, investment-plus-government spending would be less than savings-plus-taxes. That is, you could view the interest rate as being too high, thereby depressing investment to too low a level, or income too high, raising savings to too high a level. Either way, savings-plus-taxes would exceed investment-plus-government spending. On the left side of the *IS* curve, the reverse inequality will hold. The interest rate is too low and is stimulating too much investment, or conversely, income is too low and is generating too little saving. Either way, investment-plus-government spending exceeds savings-plus-taxes.

Suppose the economy is in this second situation of too much investment-plus-government spending relative to the amount of savings-plus-taxes. What would happen? According to this analysis income would not be at its equilibrium level and therefore would not be stationary, but rising. The reason why income would be rising is that the total amount of spending that individuals are attempting to undertake exceeds the level of income out of which they are attempting to undertake that spending. To see this, recall that consumption is simply income minus savings minus taxes; this means that if savings-plus-taxes are less than investment-plus-government spending, the sum of consumption and investment-plus-government spending must be a bigger number than income. Such a situation clearly cannot be because we know that, as a matter of fact, income is equal to con-

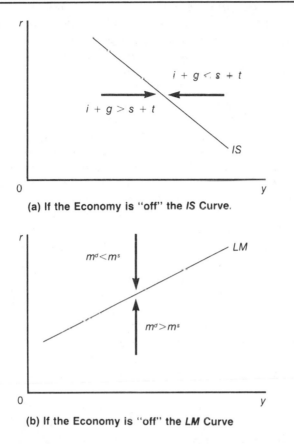

Figure 13.3
Equilibrating Forces

(a) If the Economy is "off" the *IS* Curve.

(b) If the Economy is "off" the *LM* Curve

If the economy is "off" the *IS* curve, the demand for goods will differ from income [frame (a)]. In such a case, income rises if $i + g > s + t$ or falls if $i + g < s + t$. The movement in income would be rapid, and the economy quickly would be brought to a point on the *IS* curve. If the demand for money was not equal to the supply of money, the economy would be "off" the *LM* curve [frame (b)]. This would lead to the buying or selling of securities, which would produce a rise or fall in the interest rate, so that money market equilibrium was achieved. These equilibrating forces are assumed to operate quickly, so that the economy is not, in the normal course of events, observed to be "off" either the *IS* or the *LM* curves.

sumption plus investment-plus-government spending. We can illustrate this point with a story (analogous to the story told above about different levels of water in Lake Ontario). The story would go like this. As people *tried* to spend more than current income, income would rise and keep on rising until it had reached a high enough level to be equal to the total level of spending that individuals were undertaking. We know where that point is. For any given interest rate, it is the point at which income is read off from the *IS* curve.

To reinforce your understanding, consider the reverse situation. Suppose the economy was to the right of the *IS* curve, with savings-plus-taxes bigger than investment-plus-government spending. In that case, total spending plans would add up to a number less than income, and would be falling and would continue to fall until it had reached a low enough level for spending plans to have reached equality with income. Again, that is a point on the *IS* curve.

Thus, one part of the equilibrating force is a change in income that ensures that investment-plus-government spending is equal to savings-plus-taxes. In other words, income adjusts to put the economy on its *IS* curve. Income, not the price level or the interest rate, is the equilibrating variable at work in this case.[3]

Next, consider a conceptual experiment in the money market. Suppose the economy is "off" the *LM* curve, as shown in frame (b) of Figure 13.3. If it was below the *LM* curve, then the demand for money would exceed the supply of money. That is, the interest rate would be too low or income would be too high, generating a larger demand for money than the amount of money available. If the economy was above the *LM* curve, the demand for money would be less than the supply of money. That is, the interest rate would be too high and/or the income level too low, making the amount of money demanded fall short of the amount available to be held.

What would happen if the economy was in one of these situations? Imagine that it is in a situation in which the demand for money was less than the supply of money. Obviously, since the supply of money is physically present in the economy, even though the amount demanded is less than the amount supplied, the amount supplied would have to be the same as the amount being held. In other words, individuals would have in their pockets, purses, and bank accounts more money than they would want to be holding in current conditions. What would they do in such a situation? The answer is they would try to get rid of the excess money.

This analysis assumes that in order to lower their money holdings, people would buy bonds and other kinds of financial assets. Of course, each individual can get rid of unwanted excess money holdings by buying bonds. Individuals in aggregate, however, cannot do this be-

---

[3] Don Patinkin (of the Hebrew University in Jerusalem), the world's leading Keynes scholar, believes that the essential originality in Keynes' *General Theory* was this idea — that income rather than prices plays the equilibrating role in the economy. If you wish to pursue this matter in greater depth and also get some experience of how a first-rate historian of economic thought works, you can do no better than read two of Don Patinkin's pieces on this subject. They are: "A Study of Keynes' Theory of Effective Demand," *Economic Inquiry*, 17 (April 1979), 155-76; and "The Process of Writing the *General Theory*, A Critical Survey" in *Keynes, Cambridge, and the General Theory*, eds., D. Patinkin and J. C. Leith (London: Macmillan, 1977) pp. 3-24.

cause there is a certain fixed amount of money in existence in the economy. One individual's purchase of bonds is another individual's sale of bonds. The reduction in one individual's holdings of money will be matched by an increase in someone else's. For the economy as a whole, then, the attempts by individuals to rid themselves of excess money balances cannot result in a drop in the amount of money being held. Something else has to do the adjusting. What is it that adjusts? The answer is the rate of interest. The effect of buying bonds is to raise the demand for bonds and bid up their prices. Bidding up the price of a bond has the effect of bidding down its rate of return — the rate of interest.

You might find it helpful to have this spelled out. Suppose a bond pays $5 a year in interest in perpetuity, and suppose that the bond has a current market price of $50. The rate of interest clearly, then, is 10 percent — $5 divided by $50 expressed as a percent. Now suppose that instead of being $50, the bond price is $25. The interest payment is still $5 a year, but now the interest rate has increased to 20 percent ($5 divided by $25). Yet again, suppose that instead of being $50, the bond price is $100. In this case, with an interest payment of $5 a year, the interest rate would be 5 percent ($5 divided by $100). You see, then, that the rate of interest on a bond (the market rate of interest in the economy) is inversely related to the price of a bond.

Continuing now with the story: as people try to get rid of their unwanted excess money balances by buying bonds, they would bid up the price of bonds and bid down the rate of interest. This process would continue until a situation arose in which the excess supply of money was eliminated. The interest rate would fall far enough to eliminate the excess supply of money because people would continue to buy bonds, bidding up their price and bidding down the interest rate, until they were satisfied that the money they were holding was equal to the amount that they wanted to hold.

The same mechanism would work in the opposite direction. If the demand for money exceeded the amount of money in existence, individuals would seek to add to their money balances. They would do this by selling bonds. As they sold bonds, the price of bonds would fall, and the interest rate on them would rise. This process would continue until the interest rate had risen sufficiently to make the amount of money in existence enough to satisfy people's demand for money. Either way, then, an excess demand or excess supply in the money market would lead to a movement in the rate of interest by an amount sufficient to place the economy on the *LM* curve.

Now bring these two stories together. If the economy was "off" the *IS* curve, income would adjust to bring about an equality between savings-plus-taxes and investment-plus-government spending. If the economy was "off" the *LM* curve, the interest rate would adjust to bring about an equality between the demand for money and the supply of money. These two forces, operating simultaneously, ensure that both the stock equilibrium in the money market and the flow equilibrium between investment-plus-government spending and savings-plus-taxes are simultaneously achieved. It is an assumption of the *IS-LM* analysis that these forces are sufficiently strong that the economy is observed only at the point of intersection of the *IS* and *LM* curves.

C. Changes in Government Spending and Taxes

You have now studied all the key ingredients of the *IS-LM* analysis and are in a position to work out, in a fairly straightforward manner, the effects of changes in government spending, taxes and the money supply on the level of real income and the rate of interest. You should not confuse such an exercise with an analysis of macroeconomic policy. Properly understood, it is just one ingredient in a full policy analysis — the ingredient that tells us how changes in the government's monetary and fiscal policies influence the level of aggregate demand. A comprehensive analysis of macroeconomic policy cannot be performed using only the aggregate demand side of the economy. We shall conduct a thorough analysis of macroeconomic policy in Part VI of this book. Nevertheless, this is a useful stage of your study at which to analyze the effects of changes in government macroeconomic policy variables on the level of aggregate demand. Let us now turn to that task.

(i) Changes in Government Spending

First, let us analyze the effects of a change in government spending. You already know that a change in government spending leads to a shift in the *IS* curve. Specifically, you know that a rise in government spending leads to a rightward shift of the *IS* curve by an amount equal to the change in government spending multiplied by one over one minus the marginal propensity to consume. What is the effect of the change in government spending, not on the shift in the *IS* curve, but on the equilibrium level of income and rate of interest? Figure 13.4 provides the basis for answering this question. Assume that initially the level of government spending is such that the *IS* curve is represented by IS_1. This intersects the *LM* curve at the interest rate r_1 and the income level y_1. Now imagine that there is a rise in government spending by an amount sufficient to shift the *IS* curve from IS_1 to IS_2. By inspecting Figure 13.4 you can discover that the effect on the equilibrium levels of income and the rate of interest of this shift in the *IS* curve is to raise the interest rate from r_1 to r_2 and to raise income from y_1 to y_2. This result, depicted in Figure 13.4, is a general result. A rise in government spending raises both real income and the rate of interest.

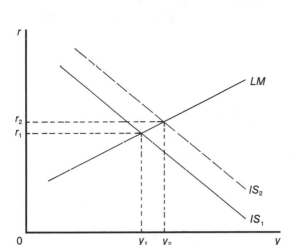

Figure 13.4
The Effect of
Government Spending
on the Interest Rate
and Real Income

A rise in government spending will shift the *IS* curve from IS_1 to IS_2. The result will be a higher income level (y_1 to y_2) and a higher interest rate (r_1 to r_2).

The amounts by which income and the interest rate rise depend on the slopes of both the *LM* and *IS* curves. To see how the slope of the *LM* curve affects the outcome, consider Figure 13.5. In this figure are shown two extreme slopes for the *LM* curve. The curve labelled LM_A is horizontal. This would be one limiting case of the slope of the *LM* curve — the case in which money and non-money assets are such perfect substitutes for each other that people really don't care how much money they are holding, relative to other assets. If the interest rate was slightly above r_1, they would want to hold entirely non-money assets. If the interest rate was slightly below r_1, they would want to hold nothing but money. So r_1 represents the interest rate at which people are entirely indifferent as to whether they want to hold money and other assets. This is a pretty unlikely case, but one that serves to illustrate one of the extreme outcomes of a change in government spending. In this particular case, you can see that the effect of a rise in government spending would be to raise income and leave the interest rate unchanged. The rise in income would be equal to the full amount of the horizontal shift of the *IS* curve. That is, it would be equal to the rise in government spending multiplied by one over one minus the marginal propensity to consume.

The other extreme case illustrated in Figure 13.5 is that of the *LM* curve labelled LM_B. The *LM* curve would be vertical if the demand for real balances did not depend on the interest rate at all. This would

Figure 13.5
Government Spending
and the Steepness
of the *LM* Curve

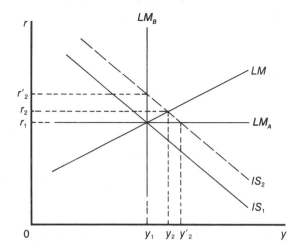

The flatter is the *LM* curve, the bigger is the effect of a change in government spending on income, and the smaller will be its effect on the interest rate. A rise in government spending shifts the *IS* curve from *IS*$_1$ to *IS*$_2$ raising income to y_2 and the interest rate to r_2. In the extremes, with a horizontal *LM* curve (*LM*$_A$) income will rise from y_1 to y'_2, and the interest rate stays constant; and with a vertical *LM* curve (*LM*$_B$), the interest rate will rise from r_1 to r'_2, and real income will remain unchanged at y_1.

be the case if people regarded non-money assets as completely useless as substitutes for money, so that regardless of the opportunity cost of holding money, there would be a certain amount of money that they felt it absolutely necessary to hold. In that not so unlikely but nevertheless exaggerated case, the rise in government spending that shifts the *IS* curve to *IS*$_2$ would raise the interest rate to r_2 but would leave the level of real income unaffected. What is going on here is that the amount of money which people want to hold is a rigid fraction of the level of income. Since the amount of money in the economy has not been changed, then neither can the level of income change. Any change in government spending is fully "crowded out" by a rise in the interest rate choking off an equal amount of investment demand.

The analysis in Figure 13.5 serves to illustrate two propositions: (1) The effect of a change in government spending on real income is larger, the flatter the *LM* curve or the more interest elastic the demand for real balances. (2) The effect of a change in government spending on the rate of interest is larger, the steeper the *LM* curve or the less interest elastic the demand for real balances.

The amounts by which income and the interest rate rise when government spending rises depend also on the slope of the *IS* curve. This is illustrated in Figure 13.6.

**Figure 13.6
Government Spending
and the Steepness
of the IS Curve**

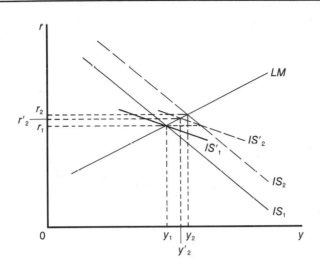

The flatter the *IS* curve, the smaller will be the effect of a change in government spending on both interest rates and income. When the *IS* curve is IS_1, a rise in government spending shifts the *IS* curve to IS_2, raising income from y_1 to y_2 and interest rates from r_1 to r_2. If the *IS* curve is flatter, IS'_1, a rise in government spending shifts the *IS* curve to IS'_2 raising income and interest rates to y'_2 and r'_2.

Consider first the *IS* curve labelled IS_1, and the equilibrium r_1, y_1. Now imagine that government spending increases, shifting the *IS* curve to IS_2. This produces a change in income to y_2 and a change in the interest rate to r_2. Now imagine that the *IS* curve is flatter than those depicted as IS_1, IS_2. In particular, let the initial *IS* curve be IS'_1. Now conduct the same experiment of raising government spending. Raise it by exactly the same amount as before. We know that the new *IS* curve will be parallel to the original one and will shift to the right by the same absolute amount, so that at the interest rate r_1 the curve IS'_2 intersects the curve IS_2. Now the new equilibrium income level is y'_2 and the interest rate level is r'_2. Notice that y'_1 is lower than y_2 and r'_2 is lower than r_2.

The analysis in Figure 13.6 shows that the flatter the *IS* curve, the smaller will be the effect of a change in government spending on income and on the rate of interest. When the *IS* curve is flatter, so is the investment demand curve or the more interest elastic the investment demand.

The consequences of the slopes of the *LM* and *IS* curves may now be summarized succinctly. The smaller the interest elasticity of the demand for real balances and the greater the interest elasticity of investment demand, the smaller will be the effect of a change in government spending on the level of real income. The smaller the interest elasticity of demand for real balances and the smaller the interest elasticity of investment demand, the larger will be the effect of a change in government spending on the interest rate.

(ii) Changes in Taxes

Considering the effects of a tax change is a straightforward extension of the exercise that you have just conducted. You already know from Chapter 10 that a rise in taxes shifts the *IS* curve in the *opposite* direction to that of a rise in government spending. That is, a rise in taxes will shift the *IS* curve to the left, whereas a rise in government spending will shift the *IS* curve to the right. You also know that the distance of the shift is fraction b (marginal propensity to consume) of the shift for an equivalent change in government spending. The differences between the effects of changes in government spending and taxes end here. The other effects of each of the two changes are identical in the *IS-LM* analysis. All the remarks made above concerning the effects of the slopes of the *LM* and *IS* curves on the amounts by which real income and the interest rate change as a result of a change in government spending apply identically to a tax change. The effects of a tax rise on income and the rate of interest are *opposite* in direction and fraction b of the magnitude of the effects of changes in government spending.

Figure 13.7
The Effects of Monetary
Policy on Real Income
and the Rate of Interest

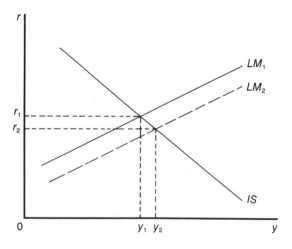

A rise in the money supply shifts the *LM* curve to the right from LM_1 to LM_2. This lowers the rate of interest from r_1 to r_2 and raises the level of real income from y_1 to y_2.

D. Change in the Money Supply

You already know that a change in the money supply will shift the *LM* curve. The effects of an *LM* curve shift on the equilibrium level of real income and the interest rate will, like the effects of the *IS* curve shift just analyzed, depend on the slopes of both the *IS* and *LM* curves. Let us consider first the general case. Figure 13.7 illustrates the effects of a change in money supply on the equilibrium level of real income and the rate of interest. The economy is initially in equilibrium, with the *IS* curve intersecting LM_1 at the interest rate r_1 and real income y_1. Now imagine the money supply is increased, so that the *LM* curve moves rightward to LM_2. The new intersection of the *IS* and LM_2 curves is at the income level y_2 and the interest rate r_2. You can see by inspection of Figure 13.7 that the rise in the money supply leads to a rise in real income and a fall in the rate of interest. This is the general prediction of the *IS-LM* analysis.

Now consider what happens to these effects when the slope of the *IS* curve is allowed to vary. The relationship between the effects of a change in monetary policy and the slope of the *IS* curve is illustrated in Figure 13.8. Just as in the previous case, two extreme slopes for the *IS* curve are shown. If the *IS* curve is the horizontal curve IS_A, a rise in the money supply raises real income by the full amount of the

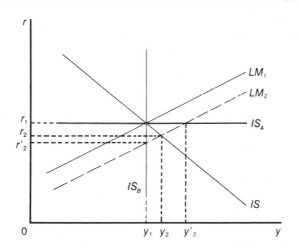

Figure 13.8
Monetary Policy and the Steepness of the *IS* Curve

The flatter the *IS* curve, the bigger is the effect of a change in the money supply on the level of real income and the smaller is its effect on the rate of interest. If the *IS* curve was horizontal (IS_A) the shift in *LM* from LM_1 to LM_2 raises real income from y_1 to y'_2 and leaves the interest rate unchanged. If the *IS* curve was vertical (IS_B), a rise in the money supply that shifts the *LM* curve from LM_1 to LM_2 lowers the interest rate from r_1 to r'_2 and leaves real income unchanged.

horizontal shift of the *LM* curve, from y_1 to y_2'. The interest rate remains unchanged at r_1. This result would arise if the marginal product of capital was completely constant, independent of the size of the capital stock. The opposite case, depicted as the vertical curve IS_B, leads to the prediction that a rise in the money supply lowers the interest rate from r_1 to r_2', but income would remain unchanged at y_1. This would arise if, no matter how much the rate of interest changed, firms saw no reason to change their capital stock.

What is going on in these two cases is straightforward to interpret. With a horizontal *IS* curve (with a fixed rate of interest), the level of real income moves one-for-one with the level of the money supply. In the case of a vertical *IS* curve, the change in the money supply merely changes the rate of interest, leaving the level of real income unaffected. This arises because, with investment being completely insensitive to interest rates, the level of investment will remain unchanged no matter what the interest rate is. Since the level of government spending is also constant (by assumption), and since consumption demand depends only on income, there is nothing being altered on the demand side of the economy to produce any change in real income. All the adjustment, therefore, has to come out in a lower interest rate.

What Figure 13.8 illustrates is the general proposition that the more elastic the investment demand with respect to the rate of interest, the bigger is the effect of a change in the money supply on income, and the smaller is the effect of a change in the money supply on the rate of interest.

Next, consider the effect of the slope of the *LM* curve on the size of the change in the real income and the rate of interest resulting from a change in the money supply. This is illustrated in Figure 13.9. Again, let the economy initially be in an equilibrium where the *IS* curve intersects the curve LM_1 at the interest rate r_1 and the income level y_1. Now let the money stock increase, so that the *LM* curve shifts rightwards to LM_2. This produces a rise in income to y_2 and a drop in the interest rate to r_2. Now imagine that instead of the *LM* curve being $LM_1(LM_2)$, it is steeper than that, indicating a less elastic demand for real balances with respect to the rate of interest. Specifically, suppose the *LM* curve initially is LM_1'. When the money supply is increased, the *LM* curve will shift to LM_2'. (Remember that the horizontal shift at a given interest rate, in this case r_1, is independent of the steepness of the *LM* curve.) What is the effect of an equivalent change in the money supply in this case? It is to raise income to y_2' and lower the interest rate to r_2'. Notice that the change in both income and the interest rate is bigger in this case than it was in the previous case. This serves to illustrate the general proposition that the smaller is the interest elasticity of the demand for real balances, the bigger

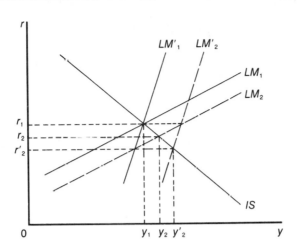

Figure 13.9
Monetary Policy and
the Steepness of the
LM Curve

The steeper the *LM* curve, the bigger are the effects of a change in the money supply on both the level of real income and the rate of interest. If the money supply rises so that the *LM* curve shifts from *LM'*₁ to *LM'*₂, then the changes in real income and the rate of interest are from y_1 to y'_2 and r_1 to r'_2. These are larger than the changes arising in the case of the increased money supply shifting the flatter *LM* curve from *LM*₁ to *LM*₂.

will be the effect of a change in the money supply on both the rate of interest and the level of income.

You have now completed your investigation of the properties of the *IS-LM* analysis. The final section of this chapter is designed to help you see how the *IS-LM* analysis may be seen as a theory of aggregate demand.

E. Theory of Aggregate Demand

Just as there are various stages in the process of learning economics that involve mastering some steps of analysis that seem completely pointless at the time, so also there are times when everything seems to be falling into place. You have now reached one such point. It is as if a major section of a complicated jigsaw puzzle is just about to have the final piece put in, and a single pattern connecting previous seemingly distinct sections is revealed. Specifically, you are now going to be able to see not only the *IS-LM* analysis in its entirety but also how this the analysis generates the theory of aggregate demand.

Begin by recalling the concept of the aggregate demand curve. As set out in Chapter 7, the aggregate demand curve is defined as the relationship between the aggregate quantity of goods and services that people want to buy in a given period of time and the general price level. This definition (and concept) is sufficiently general to embrace all conceivable theoretical frameworks and certainly that of the *IS-LM* analysis.

It is easy to derive the aggregate demand curve in the *IS-LM* analysis by using the two-part diagram set out in Figure 13.10. Frame (a) shows the rate of interest on the vertical axis and real income on the horizontal axis. Frame (b) shows the price level on the vertical axis and real income on the horizontal axis. In frame (a) are shown an *IS* curve and an *LM* curve when the price level is P_0, labelled $LM(P_0)$. These two curves intersect at the income level y_1 and interest rate r_1.

**Figure 13.10
Derivation of the
Aggregate Demand
Curve**

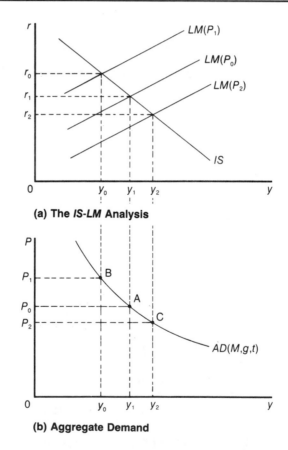

(a) The *IS-LM* Analysis

(b) Aggregate Demand

By hypothetically allowing the price level to vary from P_0 to P_1 and P_2, the *LM* curve shifts [frame (a)], generating different equilibrium interest rate and income levels. Each equilibrium income level is also the level of aggregate demand at the relevant price level. These combinations of the price level and level of aggregate demand give us points A, B and C on the aggregate demand curve in frame (b). In general, aggregate demand will depend on the money supply, government spending, and taxes.

This is exactly the solution that we have been working with throughout this chapter. That solution point can also be characterized in frame (b). It is point A. We know that it is point A because we know that we have been treating the price level as predetermined at P_0. Also we know that the model has determined for us a level of real income or of aggregate demand of y_1. Point A is therefore one point on the aggregate demand curve.

It is possible to ask, hypothetically, what the level of aggregate demand would be in the *IS-LM* analysis if the price level was different from P_0. Suppose the price level was higher than P_0, say, at P_1. What then would be the quantity of goods and services demanded if everything else was the same? From the analysis of the *IS* curve in Chapter 10 you can quickly verify that the position of the *IS* curve is independent of the price level. It is entirely a real curve that relates real income to the rate of interest and depends only on other real variables, namely, real taxes and real government spending. The *LM* curve, in contrast, is not independent of the price level. You can quickly verify from its definition and derivation that a change in the price level has the same type of effect (but opposite in direction) on the *LM* curve as does a change in the money supply. If we *lower* the money supply, we shift the *LM* curve to the left. If we *raise* the price level to P_1, we know that the *LM* curve will also shift to the left. Let us suppose that it shifts to become the curve $LM(P_1)$ in frame (a).

This new *LM* curve intersects the *IS* curve at the interest rate r_0 and the real income level y_1. Since we know the price level that gave rise to that *LM* curve is P_1, we can read off from frame (b) the point at which the real income level y_0 is associated with the price level P_1. That point is B. Point B is, like point A, another point on the aggregate demand curve. Next, imagine that the price level is at some lower level than P_0, say, P_2, as shown on the vertical axis of frame (b). With a lower price level we know that the *LM* curve would shift to the right (equivalent to a rise in the money supply). Suppose, in fact, that the *LM* curve shifts to the curve labelled $LM(P_2)$, which generates the real income level y_2 and the interest rate r_2. Transferring this level of income or aggregate demand y_2 down to frame (b) gives us point C. Point C is also a point on the aggregate demand curve. Joining up points B, A, C and extrapolating to points beyond B and C traces out the *aggregate demand curve*.

In conducting the *IS-LM* analysis of the determination of real income, it was possible, of course, to focus only on point A. By looking at what happens to the *IS-LM* intersection at the given price level, P_0, we are simply examining how the point A travels horizontally. You can now see, however, that the same analysis applies at each and every possible price level and tells us how the aggregate demand curve shifts as the levels of taxes, government spending and the money supply are varied.

This is the key thing to understand about the theory of aggregate demand that we have conducted in the *IS-LM* analysis. The analysis tells us about the factors that cause horizontal shifts in the aggregate demand curve. Anything that shifts point A will also shift point B and point C in the same horizontal direction. Thus, a rise in government spending or a cut in taxes or a rise in the money supply will all produce a rightward shift of the aggregate demand curve.

The aggregate demand curve *AD* in frame (b) in Figure 13.10 is labelled *AD(M,g,t)* to remind us of this. The size of that shift will depend on the slopes of the *IS* and *LM* curves. Those slopes will in turn depend on the slopes of the demand for money function and the investment demand function. In general, the steeper the demand for money function with respect to the interest rate and/or the flatter the investment demand function with respect to the interest rate, the bigger will be the effect of a change in the money supply on the horizontal shift of the aggregate demand curve, and the smaller will be the effect of a change in government spending or taxes.

In the limiting case where the *IS* curve is horizontal (the interest rate is fixed) or where the *LM* curve is vertical (money is completely non-substitutable for other assets), then only changes in the money supply will lead to changes in the aggregate demand curve, and changes in government spending and taxes will leave the aggregate demand curve unaffected.

At the other extreme, if money is a perfect substitute for other assets so that the *LM* curve is horizontal, or if investment demand is completely unresponsive to interest rate changes so that the *IS* curve is vertical, then only changes in government spending and taxes will lead to shifts in the aggregate demand curve, and changes in the money supply will leave the aggregate demand curve unaffected. This is the special case of the Keynesian cross model that we examined in Chapter 8.

In general, none of these extremes will be a relevant description of an actual economy, and the aggregate demand curve will shift both because of changes in the money supply and because of changes in the levels of government spending and taxes.

Summary

A. Equilibrium at the *IS-LM* Intersection

The *IS* curve shows at each level of the interest rate the level of real income that equates savings-plus-taxes with investment-plus-government spending. The *LM* curve gives another relationship between real income and the interest rate, that equates the supply of and the demand for money. There is just one level of the interest rate and of real income at which both of these relationships are simultaneously satisfied. This point is the equilibrium of the *IS-LM* analysis.

B. Properties of the *IS-LM* Equilibrium

The *IS-LM* equilibrium occurs when both the demand for money equals the supply of money and savings-plus-taxes equal investment-plus-government spending. It is assumed that the forces making for equality of both these sets of magnitudes are strong enough to ensure that the economy is never observed away from equilibrium. If saving-plus-taxes were to exceed investment-plus-government spending, real income would fall to restore the equality. If the demand for money exceeded the supply of money, the act of attempting to reduce money balances and acquire bonds would put downward pressure on interest rates to the point at which the amount of money in existence was willingly held. Both sets of forces have sufficient strength for the economy never to be observed "off" either the *IS* or *LM* curves. Thus, the intersection point of the *IS* and *LM* curves is the point that describes the state of the economy.

C. Changes in Government Spending and Taxes

In general, a rise in government spending or a cut in taxes will raise the level of real income and the rate of interest. The steeper the *IS* curve the greater will be the rise in both variables. The flatter the *LM* curve the greater will be the rise in real income and the smaller will be the rise in the interest rate.

D. Change in the Money Supply

In general, a rise in the money supply will lead to a rise in real income and a fall in the rate of interest. The steeper the *LM* curve the larger will be the change in both variables. The flatter the *IS* curve the greater will be the change in real income and the smaller will be the change in the interest rate.

E. Theory of Aggregate Demand

By using the *IS-LM* analysis to find the equilibrium levels of real income for a variety of different price levels, an aggregate demand curve may be traced out. That aggregate demand curve will be downward sloping. In general, the aggregate demand curve will shift when the money supply changes, when government spending changes, or when taxes change. There are special extreme cases in which some of the variables under government control have no effect on the aggregate demand curve. If the *IS* curve is vertical or if the *LM* curve is horizontal, only government spending and taxes will shift the aggregate demand curve; changes in the money supply will leave the curve unaffected. (This is the Keynesian cross model of Chapter 8.) At the other extreme, if the *IS* curve is horizontal or if the *LM* curve is vertical, then changes in the money supply will shift the aggregate demand curve, but changes in government spending and taxes will leave it unaffected.

Review Questions

1. Which markets are in equilibrium at the point of intersection of the *IS* and *LM* curves?

2. What would be happening if the economy was "off" its *IS* curve?

3. What would be happening if the economy was "off" its *LM* curve?

4. Show the effects in the *IS-LM* analysis of a rise in government spending on the level of real income and the rate of interest. What conditions would lead to only the rate of interest changing? What conditions would lead to only real income changing?

5. Suppose there was a rise in the government's budget deficit (g rises relative to t). What does the *IS-LM* analysis predict will happen to the rate of interest?

6. Could your answer to Question 5 be part of the reason for high interest rates in Canada in recent years? (Be careful to distinguish between real and money rates of interest in your answer to this question.)

7. Show the effect in the *IS-LM* analysis of a rise in the money supply on the rate of interest and the level of real income. What conditions would lead to only the level of real income changing?

8. What is the aggregate demand curve? Which markets are in equilibrium along that aggregate demand curve? What is being held constant along the aggregate demand curve? Why does the aggregate demand curve slope downwards? Are there any conditions that would make the aggregate demand curve vertical?

9. You are given the following information about a hypothetical economy:

$$c = 100 + 0.8(y\text{-}t)$$
$$i = 500 - 50r$$
$$g = 400$$
$$t = 400$$
$$M^d/P = 0.2y + 500 - 25r$$

The price level is fixed at 1.
The money supply is 520.

(c = consumption; i = investment; g = government expenditure; t = taxes; r = rate of interest; M^d = demand for money; P = price level; y = real income)
(a) Find the equilibrium values of real income, consumption, investment, and the rate of interest.
(b) Find the effect on these equilibrium values of a unit rise in the money supply, government expenditure and taxes.

Appendix:

The Algebra of the *IS-LM* Model

This appendix takes you through the algebra of the determination of the equilibrium levels of real income and the rate of interest when the price level is fixed at P_0. Like the Appendix to Chapter 10, it contains nothing of substance that is not explained in words and diagrams in the body of the chapter. It does, however, determine the precise magnitudes of the changes in real income and the interest rate. It may, nevertheless, provided that you feel comfortable with algebraic formulations, give you a clearer picture of how the *IS-LM* analysis works.

Aggregate demand is determined by the sum of consumption demand, investment demand, and government demand. That is

$$y^d = c + i + g \tag{13A.1}$$

Consumption demand is determined by the consumption function, which is

$$c = a + b(y - t), \qquad a > 0, 0 < b < 1 \tag{13A.2}$$

Investment demand is determined by

$$i = i_0 - hr, \qquad i_0, h > 0 \tag{13A.3}$$

Flow equilibrium prevails in the goods market when aggregate demand equals actual income. That is

$$y^d = y \tag{13A.4}$$

The above four equations taken together constitute the equation for the *IS* curve. That equation may be derived by using Equations (13A.1), (13A.2), and (13A.3) together with Equation (13A.4) to give

$$y = a + b(y - t) + i_0 - hr + g \tag{13A.5}$$

This may be rearranged or "solved" for real income as

$$y = \frac{1}{1 - b}(a + i_0 + g - bt - hr) \tag{13A.6}$$

Equation (13A.6) is the equation for the *IS* curve.

The demand for money function, M^d, is given by

$$\frac{M^d}{P_0} = m_0 + ky - \ell r, \qquad k > 0, \ell > 0 \tag{13.A.7}$$

Monetary equilibrium requires that the demand for money be equal to the supply of money; that is,

$$M^d = M \tag{13A.8}$$

Substituting Equation (13A.7) into Equation (13A.8) yields an equation for the *LM* curve which may be "solved" for real income as

$$y = \frac{1}{k}\left[\frac{M}{P_0} - (m_u + \ell r)\right]$$ (13.A9)

Equation (13A.9) describes the *LM* relation.

Equations (13A.6) and (13A.9), the equations for the *IS* and *LM* curves, contain two unknowns — real income and the rate of interest. By setting the real income level in Equation (13A.6) equal to the real income level in Equation (13A.9) and solving for the rate of interest, you readily obtain

$$r = \frac{1}{1 - b + kh/\ell}\left[\frac{k}{\ell}(a + i_0 + g - bt) - \frac{(1 - b)}{\ell}\left(\frac{M}{P_0} - m_0\right)\right]$$ (13A.10)

Equation (13A.10) is an algebraic expression for the equilibrium value of the rate of interest in the *IS-LM* analysis. By substituting Equation (13A.10) back into Equation (13A.9) to eliminate the rate of interest, you may obtain an expression for the level of real income. It is possible to "tidy up" the expression to give

$$y = \frac{1}{1 - b + (kh/\ell)}\left[(a + i_0 + g - bt) + \frac{h}{\ell}\left(\frac{M}{P_0} - m_0\right)\right]$$ (13A.11)

Equation (13A.11) is the solution of the *IS-LM* analysis for the equilibrium level of real income.

In order to obtain a better understanding of what those equations are saying, let us examine Equations (13A.10) and (13A.11) to see how the interest rate and the level of income vary as we vary the three policy instruments — government spending, taxes, and the money supply. Imagine that each of those three policy variables took on a different value from *g*, *t*, and *M*. Specifically, suppose that *g* was to increase to *g'* and *t* to *t'*, and *M* to *M'*. In that case, we know that the solutions for the interest rate and the level of income could be expressed as

$$r' = \frac{1}{1 - b + (kh/\ell)}\left[\frac{k}{\ell}(a + i_0 + g' - bt') - \frac{1 - b}{\ell}\left(\frac{M'}{P_0} - m_0\right)\right]$$

$$\text{(13A.12)}$$

$$y' = \frac{1}{1 - b + (kh/\ell)}\left[(a + i_0 + g' - bt') + \frac{h}{\ell}\left(\frac{M'}{P_0} - m_0\right)\right]$$ (13A.13)

Equations (13A.12) and (13A.13) are, of course, identical to Equations (13A.10) and (13A.11) except that the values of the variables (r and y on the left-hand side and g, t, and M on the right-hand side) have all changed from their original values to their new (primed) values.

Now subtract Equation (13A.10) from Equation (13A.12) to obtain Equation (13A.14). Also subtract Equation (13A.11) from Equation (13A.13) to obtain Equation (13A.15). Notice that in Equations (13A.14) and (13A.15) the terms a, i_0 and m_0 have disappeared since they are common to both the original solutions and the new solutions for y and r. Thus,

$$r' - r = \frac{1}{1 - b + (kh/\ell)} \left[\frac{k}{\ell}(g' - g) \right.$$
$$\left. - \frac{bk}{\ell}(t' - (t' - t)) - \frac{1 - b}{\ell}\left(\frac{M'}{P_0} - \frac{M}{P_0}\right) \right] \qquad \textbf{(13A.14)}$$

and

$$y' - y = \frac{1}{1 - b + (kh/\ell)} \left[(g' - g) - b(t' - t) + \frac{h}{\ell}\left(\frac{M'}{P_0} - \frac{M}{P_0}\right) \right]$$
$$\textbf{(13A.15)}$$

Now call the gap between y' and y the change in y and label it Δy. Similarly, call the gap between r' and r, Δr, and likewise for the policy variables. That is, $g'-g$ is Δg, $t'-t$ is Δt, and $M'-M$ is ΔM. Using this convention, you can write Equations (13A.14) and (13A.15) slightly more compactly as Equations (13A.16) and (13A.17); that is

$$\Delta r = \frac{1}{1 - b + (kh/\ell)} \left[\frac{k}{\ell}\Delta g - \frac{bk}{\ell}\Delta t - \frac{(1 - b)}{\ell P_0}\Delta M \right] \qquad \textbf{(13A.16)}$$

$$\Delta y = \frac{1}{1 - b + (kh/\ell)} \left[\Delta g - b\Delta t + \frac{h}{\ell P_0}\Delta M \right] \qquad \textbf{(13A.17)}$$

You can now interpret Equations (13A.16) and (13A.17) very directly. Notice that the expression

$$\frac{1}{1 - b + (kh/\ell)}$$

will be a positive coefficient relating the changes in the policy variables to the changes in the rate of interest and the level of real income. (You know that this expression will be positive since b is a positive fraction, $1 - b$ is also a positive fraction, and k, h and ℓ are all positive parameters.) You can see that, in general, Equation (13A.16) says a rise in *g* will raise the interest rate, whereas a rise in *t* and a rise in *M* will cut the interest rate. From Equation (13A.17) you can see that in general, a rise in *g* or a rise in *M* will raise income, but a rise in *t* will cut income. Equations (13A.16) and (13A.17) are nothing other than algebraic expressions for the equivalent propositions obtained in Chapter 13 by direct inspection of the diagrammatic solution for equilibrium income and the interest rate.

The relationship between an endogenous variable such as real income or the rate of interest and an exogenous variable such as government expenditure, taxes or the money supply is called a multiplier. It is the number that multiplies a change in an exogenous variable in order to provide the magintude of the change in the endogenous variable. The multipliers can be read off from Equations (13A.16) and (13A.17). For example, the government expenditure multiplier on the interest rate is the coefficient on Δg in the equation that determines Δr, Equation (13A.16), which is

$$\frac{k/\ell}{1 - b + (hk/\ell)}.$$

In this chapter some extreme cases were presented, and the way in which the changes in policy instruments affected by the slopes of the *IS* and *LM* curves was examined. This can now be done more precisely with the algebraic solutions in Equations (13A.16) and (13A.17). Let us now look at this.

Some Special Cases

First, suppose that the parameter *h* became infinitely big. An infinitely big *h* means that the investment demand curve and, hence, the *IS* curve is horizontal; it also means that the rate of interest remains constant. What are the changes in the interest rate and real income when *h* is infinitely big? By inspecting Equations (13A.16) and (13A.17), you can establish that the changes are as follows:

$$\Delta r = 0 \qquad\qquad \textbf{(13A.18)}$$

$$\Delta y = \frac{1}{kP_0} \Delta M \qquad\qquad \textbf{(13A.19)}$$

What this says is that the aggregate demand curve will shift (*y* will change by Δy) only as a result of a change in the money supply. The shift will be equal to $1/(kP_0)$ times the change in the money supply. Changes in government spending and taxes will have no effect on aggregate demand in this special case.

Consider as the next special case that in which $\ell = 0$. This would be where the demand for money (real balances) is completely insensitive to interest rates. You can think of this situation as arising when money is such a unique asset that it is completely non-substitutable for any other assets. In this case, by inspection of Equations (13A.16) and (13A.17), you will discover that the changes in the interest rate and real income become

$$\Delta r = \frac{1}{h}\left(\Delta g - b\Delta t - \frac{1-b}{kP_0}\,\Delta M\right) \qquad \text{(13A.20)}$$

and

$$\Delta y = \frac{1}{kP_0}\,\Delta M \qquad \text{(13A.21)}$$

In this case, the interest rate will change when government spending, taxes, or the money supply changes. It will rise with a rise in government spending, and it will fall with a rise in taxes or the money supply. The change in y will be exactly the same as in the previous special case.

Now consider the opposite special case to the first one, where instead of h being infinitely big, it becomes infinitely small, specifically, zero. This would be the case where firms' investment plans were completely unresponsive to interest rates. In this case, the changes in the rate of interest and in the real income level will be given by

$$\Delta r = \frac{1}{1-b}\left(\frac{k}{\ell}\Delta g - \frac{kb}{\ell}\Delta t - \frac{(1-b)}{\ell P_0}\Delta M\right) \qquad \text{(13A.22)}$$

$$\Delta y = \frac{1}{1-b}(\Delta g - b\Delta t) \qquad \text{(13A.23)}$$

This tells you that in this case, a rise in government spending will raise the interest rate, and a rise in taxes or the money supply will cut the interest rate. Unlike the two previous special cases, a rise in government spending or a cut in taxes will raise real income, but a change in the money supply will leave real income unaffected. Equation (13A.23) says that in the special case of $h = 0$, aggregate demand will change only as a result of changes in fiscal policy variables and will remain unchanged when the money supply changes.

Now consider the opposite special case to the second one, in which we let the parameter ℓ become infinitely big. This would be the case where money is regarded as a perfect substitute for other non-money assets. Substituting an infinite value for ℓ in Equations (13A.16) and (13A.17) gives the solutions for the change in interest rate and the change in income as

$$\Delta r = 0 \qquad \text{(13A.24)}$$

$$\Delta y = \frac{1}{1-b}(\Delta g - b\Delta t) \qquad \text{(13A.25)}$$

This time the interest rate is entirely unaffected by changes in any of the variables. Real income changes, however, as a result of changing government spending or taxes (rises when government spending rises and falls when taxes rise) but is unaffected by a change in the money supply.

Notice that Equations (13A.23) and (13A.25) are identical, just as Equations (13A.19) and (13A.21) are identical. Equations (13A.19) and (13A.21) say that the only money supply affects aggregate demand, whereas Equations (13A.23) and (13A.25) say that only fiscal policy variables affect aggregate demand.

These two sets of results are the two extreme cases that arise as the parameter values ℓ and h are allowed to vary. The effect of a change in government spending, taxes, and the money supply on real income actually only depends upon the ratio of h to ℓ. As this ratio goes from zero to infinity so the value of the government spending multipliers falls from $1/(1 - b)$ to 0, and that of the money multipliers, normalizing the price level equal to 1, rises from 0 to $1/k$.

14

Aggregate Supply and the Labor Market

It is now time to embark on the study of aggregate supply. This will be the subject of this and the following two chapters. The theory of aggregate supply, in contrast to the theory of aggregate demand, remains in an unsettled and controversial state. There are three leading theories. The first, *classical*, will be presented in this chapter. A second, *new classical*, will be developed in Chapter 15 and a third, *new Keynesian*, will be presented in Chapter 16. You have four tasks ahead of you in this chapter which, are to:

a) Understand the concept of the short-run aggregate production function.

b) Understand how a competitive aggregate labor market works.

c) Understand the basic model of aggregate supply.

d) Understand why aggregate supply grows and fluctuates.

A. Short-Run Aggregate Production Function

A useful starting point in explaining the concept of the short-run *aggregate* production function is with the production function of an individual producer. A production function is simply a statement about the maximum output that can be produced with a given list of inputs, and more than that, a statement of how that maximum level of output will vary as the inputs themselves are varied.

The maximum output of some particular good that can be produced will depend on the amount of capital employed, the state of technology, the amount of land resources used, and the number and skill of the workers employed. Over time, all the inputs used in a production process can be varied. Capital equipment can be purchased, technology can be changed, land use can be modified, and workers can acquire new skills. These ongoing changes are the source of the long-term growth in output.[1] At any given moment, however, these four factors are fixed. The input, which can be varied quickly, is the quantity of labor employed. The short-run production function shows the relationship between the maximum amount of output that can be produced as the quantity of labor employed is varied while holding constant the other inputs into the production process.

What you have just reviewed is the analysis of the short-run production function that is used in microeconomic theory. It is possible to use this microeconomic analysis to derive an *aggregate* short-run production function. The aggregate short-run production function relates the *aggregate* output to the total number of workers employed. (Recall from Chapter 3 that aggregate output is equal to real expenditure and real income — that is, real GNP.)

Define output as y, and also define number employed as n. Then, the aggregate short-run production function can be written as

$$y = \phi(n) \tag{14.1}$$

The symbol $\phi(\ \ )$ should be read as "is a function of" or, more simply, "is determined by." Thus, Equation (14.1) states that the maximum value of y that can be produced is determined by the level of n and that it varies as n is varied.

The properties of the short-run production function are most easily described by plotting a specific example. This is done in Figure 14.1. The label on the curve, $\phi(n)$, is just a shorthand way of saying that output (y) depends on (or is a function of) the amount of labor employed (n). The short-run production function depicted in Figure 14.1 reflects a common technological fact: as the number of workers employed is increased, the output of the marginal worker — marginal product — declines.

There is a problem concerning the labor input of which you should take note. It concerns the role of "hours per worker" in the definition of the labor input. Normally, labor is measured in terms of *manhours*. For example, three people each working for 4 hours a day can produce a similar output to two people working 6 hours a day each. Macroeconomics is more concerned with explaining variation in the *number of people employed* than with explaining the average number of *hours* worked *per worker*. As the economy goes through a cycle of activity from boom to slump, it may be that output drops by, say, 10 percent.

---

[1] Chapter 22 deals with the determination of the long-term growth trend.

Figure 14.1
The Aggregate Short-
Run Production
Function

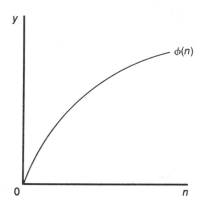

The production function, $\phi(n)$, shows the maximum attainable output level (y) as the level of labor input (n) is varied. The employment of more units of labor produces more units of output. However, each additional unit of labor produces less additional output than did the previous unit — there is diminishing marginal product.

That output drop could be accommodated by a cut of 10 percent in the average hours worked by each worker with no one becoming fully unemployed. Typically, however, this does not happen. Average hours per worker employed remains relatively constant, while the number of workers employed declines. It is possible to develop an explanation as to why it is that employment rather than average hours per worker varies with the level of economic activity. Rather than pursue such an explanation, however, we are simply going to assume that each worker works a fairly constant average number of hours, and as economic activity varies, the number of workers employed varies. The variable n will, therefore, throughout this book, be taken to mean the number of workers employed. It will reflect the number of manhours employed, provided the number of hours per man is constant, which we will assume to be the case.

This completes the definition of the short-run aggregate production function.

B. Competitive Aggregate Labor Market

(i) The Demand for Labor

First consider the demand side of the labor market. Each competitive firm will demand labor and produce output up to the point at which the price of its output is equal to the marginal cost of its production. Let us call the output price of an individual firm P_i and its marginal cost of production MC_i. The subscript i is to remind us that we are dealing with an *individual* firm. Thus,

$$P_i = MC_i \tag{14.2}$$

If this condition is satisfied, the firm is making maximum profits (provided that the marginal cost curve is rising at this point).

Marginal cost is easy to calculate. Recall that in the short run, the only input that can be varied is labor. The cost of hiring one extra worker is equal to the money wage per worker (W). However, the money wage is not the marginal cost. The amount produced by the marginal worker is known as the marginal product (MP_i). The marginal cost is the cost of the marginal worker (W) divided by the output that that marginal worker can produce (MP_i). That is,

$$MC_i = \frac{W}{MP_i} \tag{14.3}$$

For example, if the wage rate was \$10 an hour and if a worker could produce 100 units of output in an hour, the marginal cost (the cost of the last unit of output) would be \$10 ÷ 100 = 10¢. Now, replacing the marginal cost in Equation (14.3) with the price from Equation (14.2), it is clear that

$$P_i = \frac{W}{MP_i} \tag{14.4}$$

If we divide both sides of this equation by P_i and multiply both sides by MP_i, we obtain

$$MP_i = \frac{W}{P_i} \tag{14.5}$$

The Equation (14.5) says that the marginal product of some particular firm will be equal to the money wage (W) divided by the price of the output of that firm (P_i). To see how this condition leads directly to the demand for labor function, consider Figure 14.2, which plots the marginal product of labor of the ith firm against the number of workers employed in that firm. Call this downward-sloping relation the marginal product curve.

You have seen that a condition for profit maximizing (Equation 14.5) is that the marginal product of labor must equal the ratio of the money wage to the price level. This ratio is the real wage. You can therefore equivalently measure the real wage on the vertical axis of Figure 14.2. The marginal product curve then automatically becomes the demand for labor curve when thought of as being drawn against the real wage.

So far we have talked only about an individual firm's demand for labor. We now want to move on to consider the economy-wide or

Figure 14.2
The Marginal Product
Curve—The Demand
for Labor in a
Competitive Industry

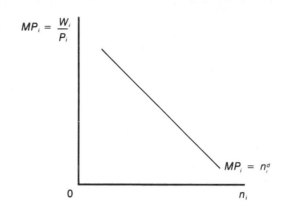

Marginal product (MP_i) declines as labor input (n_i) increases. Profits are maximized when the marginal product is equal to the real wage (W_i/P_i). The marginal product curve and the demand for labor curve of a competitive firm are, therefore, the same curve.

aggregate demand for labor. We can obtain this by adding the individual demand for labor curves across all the firms in the economy. There is no difficulty in adding up the quantities of labor demanded across all the firms. The result is the total quantity of labor demanded in the economy as a whole. We have to be careful, however, in interpreting the aggregate demand for labor curve because, on the vertical axis of the diagram describing an individual firm's demand for labor, the real wage that appears is specific to the individual firm. It is the money wage rate divided by the individual firm's output price. If we take an average of the output prices of all the firms in the economy, then what we obtain is simply the economy-wide average price level. In effect, we obtain the GNE Deflator. The economy-wide demand for labor curve, therefore, shows the total quantity of labor demanded in the economy plotted against the economy average real wage, which is the same thing as the money wage divided by the average price level. Such a demand for labor curve is shown in Figure 14.3.

(ii) The Supply of Labor

Consider next the supply of labor. The theory of household behavior predicts that utility-maximizing households will supply more hours of labor as the real wage increases up to some maximum. Thereafter, as the real wage rises, the number of hours supplied will decline since a higher income will lead the household to want to consume more leisure along with other goods. Thus, the supply of hours per individual household would be represented by a supply curve which in-

Figure 14.3
The Demand for Labor

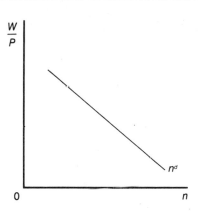

The demand for labor in the economy as a whole n^d is obtained by aggregating the demand for labor in all the individual industries. Like the industry demand curves, the lower the real wage (W/P), the greater the quantity of labor (n) demanded.

creases with the real wage up to some maximum and then begins to fall off.

For our purposes we are interested in developing a theory of the aggregate supply, not of hours per worker but of the number of workers. In effect, we are interested in analyzing the outcome of an all-or-nothing choice. That is, the potential worker has to evaluate how much utility he would derive from not working at all and compare that with the utility that he would derive from working for a fixed number of hours per week and consuming his real wage. If the utility from working exceeds that from not working, the individual will make the decision to be in the labor force and therefore be part of the labor supply. In general, as the real wage rises, more and more people will evaluate the prospect of working as yielding more utility than the prospect of not working. Let us suppose that this is the case and that as a consequence, the aggregate supply of labor increases as the real wage increases. Figure 14.4 shows such a relation.

(iii) Competitive Equilibrium

Next, consider the competitive equilibrium in the labor market. Figure 14.5 brings together the demand curve from Figure 14.3 and the supply curve from Figure 14.4. It is supposed that the economy generates sufficient information about supply and demand in the labor market for the real wage to achieve a market-clearing equilibrium value. The economy settles down at the real wage $(W/P)^*$, and at the level of employment n^*. The real wage is the ratio of the *money* wage

Figure 14.4
The Supply of Labor

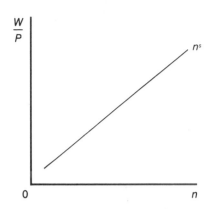

Households choose whether to enter the labor force by comparing the utility they would get from working a fixed number of hours at a certain wage rate with the utility they would derive from taking leisure. The higher the real wage, the larger the number of households that will regard working as yielding superior utility to consuming leisure. Thus the supply of labor (n^s) will rise as the real wage (W/P) rises.

to the *price level*, and it is the money wage which will adjust in the labor market to ensure that for a given price level, the equilibrium real wage is attained.

We have now determined equilibrium values of the real wage and the level of employment. You can think of the employment level as the aggregate number employed in the economy and the real wage as the economy's average real wage. Individuals' real wages will be highly variable, depending on individual skills and other factors. If relative wages are fairly stable, however, movements in the average real wage in the economy will also reflect movements in each individual's real wage.

The way in which the analysis has been developed has ignored the phenomenon of unemployment. That is not to say that unemployment cannot exist in this model. It is simply to say that at the present time we are not discussing the implications of the model for the rate of unemployment. This will be the subject of Chapter 21. Furthermore, monopolistic elements in the labor market, such as, for example, the operation of labor unions, have been ignored. This, too, will be dealt with in Chapter 21.

C. Aggregate Supply Curve

First, recall the definition of the aggregate supply curve: the aggregate supply curve shows the amount of output that the economy will sup-

**Figure 14.5
Labor Market
Equilibrium**

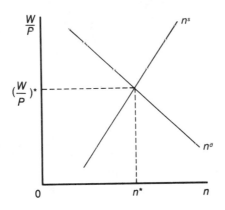

The line labelled n^d is the demand for labor curve and the line labelled n^s is the supply curve of labor. The labor market is in equilibrium when households are maximizing utility (are on their supply of labor curve) and firms are maximizing profits (are on their demand for labor curve). The only such point is where the supply and demand curves cut at the real wage $(W/P)^*$ and the employment level n^*.

ply at each different price level. It is a curve that is drawn in a diagram with the price level on one axis and output on the other. In the classical model, the aggregate supply curve shows the amount of output that will be supplied at each price level *given that firms are maximizing profits, households are maximizing utility,* and the *labor market is in equilibrium.*

To derive the aggregate supply curve, it is necessary to bring together the two components of analysis developed above, namely, the short-run production function and the competitive equilibrium in the labor market. This is done in Figure 14.6.

First notice that there are four parts to Figure 14.6. Frame (a) is nothing other than Figure 14.5, which you have just been studying. It shows a labor market in competitive equilibrium with the real wage equal to $(W/P)^*$ and the level of employment, n^*.

The second part of the figure, frame (b), is exactly the same as Figure 14.1, namely, a short-run production function. Notice that the horizontal axes of frames (a) and (b) both measure the same thing — the volume of employment. You can immediately read off from the horizontal axis of frame (b) the same equilibrium level of employment, n^*, as is determined in frame (a). The dotted line and arrow indicate this.

With the level of employment equal to n^*, the short-run production function in frame (b) determines the level of output y^* as shown on the vertical axis.

**Figure 14.6
Derivation of the
Aggregate Supply
Curve**

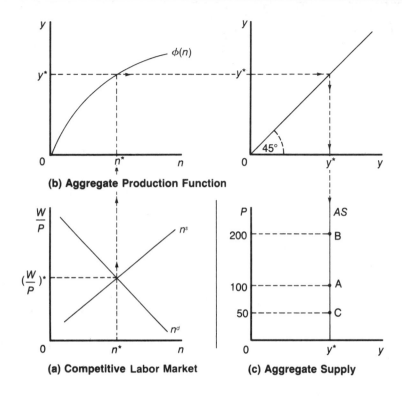

(b) Aggregate Production Function

(a) Competitive Labor Market

(c) Aggregate Supply

Frame (a) is identical to Figure 14.5 and frame (b) is identical to Figure 14.1. Frame (c) shows the aggregate supply curve (*AS*). This curve shows the amount of output which will be supplied as the price level varies when firms are hiring the profit-maximizing quantity of labor and households are supplying the utility-maximizing quantity of labor. There is a unique level of output y^* that will be produced by the equilibrium level of labor input (n^*) at the equilibrium real wage $(W/P)^*$. That level of supply will be independent of the price level, so that the aggregate supply curve is vertical.

So far, you have used frames (a) and (b) to determine the equilibrium values of the real wage, the level of employment, and the level of output.

To complete the derivation of the aggregate supply curve, the question that has to be answered is: how does the equilibrium level of output vary as the price level varies? The answer to this question (and the aggregate supply curve) will be discovered in frame (c). This part of the figure measures the price level on the vertical axis and the level of output on the horizontal axis. Notice that the vertical axis of frame (b) and the horizontal axis of frame (c) measure the same thing — output. The top right part of the diagram has output on both axes and a 45° line. It is just a pictorial device to enable you to read off from the horizontal axis of frame (c) the same quantity as is shown on the vertical axis of frame (b). Notice, by the way, that the vertical axis of frame (c) *does not* measure the same thing as the vertical axis of frame (a) — there are no arrowed lines going from frame (c) directly to frame (a). The arrows (and the analysis) start in frame (a) and go clockwise to finish in frame (c).

Now go back to the question: how does equilibrium output vary as the price level varies? Suppose that the price level initially is equal to 100. We can arbitrarily define our units so that is true. This would mean that there is a point at 100 on an aggregate supply curve, which is identified by the letter A in frame (c). Suppose now that the price level was doubled from 100 to 200. What would happen to the amount of output which firms would be willing to supply? The answer is quickly seen — nothing would happen to it.

If the price level doubled to 200, then the money wage would also have to double to preserve labor market equilibrium [frame (a)]. To see that this is so, suppose that after the price level had increased, the money wage remained fixed. In such a case, the real wage would have fallen, and the demand for labor would exceed the supply of labor. Such a situation would force the money wage to rise until the labor market was again in equilibrium. The only real wage consistent with equilibrium is the original one. Thus, the money wage must rise by the same percentage amount as does the price level. In this case, following a doubling of the price level, the money wage would also have to double in order to keep the real wage constant. With the labor market remaining at its original equilibrium, the quantity of employment would remain unchanged as would the amount of output supplied. The economy would move, therefore, to the point identified with the letter B in frame (c).

Next, suppose the price level halved from 100 to 50. The effects of this on the amount of output that the economy would produce are exactly the same as the effects of the doubling of the price level. In this case, the money wage would have to fall to one-half of its previous level in order to maintain the real wage at its market equilibrium value, and employment and output would remain constant at n^* and y^*. The economy would thus move to the point identified with the letter C in frame (c). These three points (and all the other points above, below, and between them) trace an aggregate supply curve for this economy.

The classical aggregate supply curve is perfectly inelastic. The level of output will be equal to y^* no matter what the price level.

D. Growth and Fluctuations in Aggregate Supply

In thinking about the factors that make aggregate supply vary it is convenient to distinguish between those things that generate *long-term growth* of output and those that produce *fluctuations* around the trend increase. Chapter 22 of this book will examine in greater detail the long-term growth process. Most of what you will study in this book abstracts from long-term growth and concentrates on fluctuations in aggregate economic activity around the growth trend.

There are three major sources of long-term growth in the economy — capital accumulation, technical progress, and population growth. Trends in these factors will generate an upward trend in aggregate output.

Fluctuations in output occur for two types of reasons. First, and very importantly, the rate of capital accumulation and the rate of technical progress, although trending upwards, are by no means smooth and steady. There are periods in which there is rapid technical change associated with a very high rate of capital accumulation. There are other periods when technical progress is slow and when hardly any new techniques are being applied to increase output. To some extent the timing of inventions and the application of new techniques is the outcome of rational economic choices. There is always, though, going to be an element of randomness or unpredictability in the timing of such events.

A good example of such randomness concerns the basis of the existing wave of economic growth — the invention and application of the silicon chip. It became obvious in the 1960s that although bigger and more powerful computers could be built simply by stringing together larger and larger circuits of transistors, the labor cost of handling all the connections, ensuring that they were properly made, and checking out the circuits, would be such as to make the cost of very large-scale computers so high that their application would be limited to a small number of activities. The gain from being able to build circuitry that did not involve separately joining together large numbers of individual transistors was obvious to many people working in the field. How to achieve circuits that did not involve that process was, however, far from obvious. Many people worked on the problem from a variety of angles. Then, in the middle 1950s, scientists came up with the idea of introducing impurities into a piece of common sand which, if arranged in appropriate patterns, would replicate the work not just of one transistor but of a whole array of them connected together in a particular way. The basis for very low-cost large-scale computing power was in place. In the period since then, advances on that basic idea and, more importantly, the exploitation of that idea in an incredibly wide array of activities are leading to a rise in capital accumulation and an increase in output potential.

This modern example also serves to illustrate another very important fact. The invention of something new does not necessarily — indeed does not usually — lead immediately to its rapid deployment or to a rapid increase in the stock of capital equipment — plant and machinery — and rise in output. At first, a new invention creates a more uncertain environment. People using old techniques to achieve given tasks become aware that a new technique has been discovered. They are not sure how the application of that new technique will affect what they are doing, nor are they sure as to the best time for them to switch from the old to the new way of doing things. An initial period of uncertainty can lead to a fall in investment. For example, a firm that was just about to replace an old worn-out machine with a new version of the same thing might very well delay its investment if a new technique is known to be just around the corner.

The key point to notice is that the invention of new techniques is, to a large degree, a random process over which no one has precise control. As new inventions come along they influence the profitability of existing methods of producing goods and services and influence the pace with which firms will seek to replace their existing plant and machinery with either similar or new technologies. The ebbs and flows in the pace of both the invention and application of new techniques will lead to fluctuations in the total amount of output that the economy can produce.

You can think of these fluctuations using the device that you have studied earlier in this chapter — the short-run production function. At times when the economy is undergoing a rapid expansion because of the application of new productivity-increasing technologies, the short-run production function will be moving upwards quickly. Thus, any given amount of labor force will produce a rapidly growing amount of aggregate output. At times when there is a low level of activity in the exploiting of new technologies and a low rate of capital accumulation, the production function will be moving upwards but at a pace slower than its overall longer-term growth rate.

There is another set of factors that can lead to fluctuations in aggregate output and that sometimes have been important. These are random shocks either to the natural environment — climate related — or to the political environment — war and conflict related. A good example of the latter type of shock occurred in 1973 when the oil producing countries (OPEC) imposed a massive oil embargo, lowering the shipments of oil to the developed countries and massively raising the price of those shipments. This large cut in the availability of a key input into the production process in effect shifted the aggregate short-run production function in a downward direction making it possible for a given amount of labor to produce a smaller amount of aggregate output than previously. The first type of shock — climate related — has also been important in recent years. Rainfall is the major variable at work here and has its biggest impact upon economies that have a very large agricultural sector. Low rainfall typically produces low harvests, especially in the grain (and grain-related) product classes. Low grain harvests do not only directly lower aggregate output, they have secondary effects. Low grain output raises grain prices and lowers the efficient output of grain-eating animals. Thus, food production in total tends to decline. Shocks of this kind can have important impacts upon the aggregate economy.

All of the types of shocks that have just been discussed can be summarized as things that shift the short-run production function. They will, therefore, also shift the aggregate supply curve. The way in which they will shift the aggregate supply curve needs a little

**Figure 14.7
Shifts in the
Aggregate Supply
Curve**

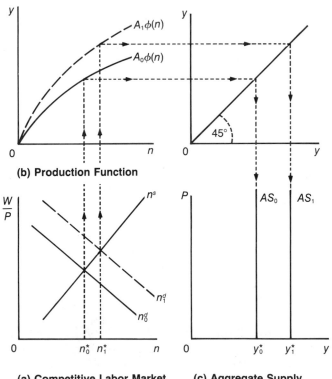

(b) Production Function

(a) Competitive Labor Market   (c) Aggregate Supply

A technology shock that shifts the production function from $A_0\phi(n)$ to $A_1\phi(n)$ will raise the marginal product of labor and the demand for labor curve. This increases the level of employment from n_0^* to n_1^* and raises output from y_0^* to y_1^*. The aggregate supply curve shifts from AS_0 to AS_1.

analysis. Figure 14.7 is going to provide you with the vehicle for investigating this. Let us begin to work through Figure 14.7. First of all notice that it is arranged in exactly the same way as Figure 14.6 — frame (a) shows a competitive labor market, frame (b) an aggregate production function, and frame (c) aggregate supply. Focus first of all on the production function [frame (b)]. Here we have shown two production functions, one labelled $A_0\phi(n)$ and another, higher short-run production function, labelled $A_1\phi(n)$. You can think of these two short-run production functions as representing the range over which the production function might fluctuate as a result of the various shocks that were discussed above.

Next look at frame (a) and first, in that frame, focus on the demand for labor curves. Associated with each production function is a marginal product curve. If the production function is the lower one, then the demand for labor curve (the marginal product of labor) will be the line labelled n_0^d. If the production function is the higher of the two then the marginal product curve — and demand for labor curve — will be the higher one, namely, n_1^d. So far we have just looked at the production function and demand for labor curve and summarized the way in which shocks to the production function, usually called technology shocks, move those curves. Frame (c) shows the impact of technology shocks on the aggregate supply curve. Shocks that raise the production function, and along with it the demand for labor curve, shift the aggregate supply curve to the right. The bigger the shocks to the production function, the larger the shift of the aggregate supply curve.

Next, let us consider the supply of labor. We have not studied the factors that underly the supply of labor curve in any detail. Some considerations might lead us to suppose that the supply of labor would be very unresponsive to real wages — would be inelastic. Casual reasoning would lead us to suppose that this might be the relevant case. It is conceivable, however, that the supply of labor at any given moment in time is highly elastic. Some lines of reasoning would lead to the presumption that this is the normal case. Taking account of the possibility of working harder at a given point in time and then taking more leisure at a later time — substituting leisure over time — is one of the arguments that would lead to this presumption. The amount by which the aggregate supply curve shifts as a result of technology shocks is influenced by the elasticity of the supply of labor.

Figure 14.8 illustrates the effect of the elasticity of the supply of labor on the magnitude of the shift of the aggregate supply curve that results from a technology shock. An inelastic supply of labor curve is the steep curve labelled n_I^s in frame (a); whereas an elastic labor supply is shown by the flat curve n_E^s. We can work out the implications of both alternative cases by deriving the shift in the aggregate supply curve that would occur if the production function moved from its lower to its higher level and for each of the two alternative assumptions about the elasticity of labor supply. First, derive the aggregate supply curve for the original position where the production function is at the lower level. This generates an equilibrium that is identical to that depicted in Figure 14.6. Where the demand for labor curve n_0^d cuts the supply of labor curve (both supply curves are at the same point here) an equilibrium real wage $(W/P)_0^*$ and employment level

Figure 14.8
Shifts in the Aggregate Supply Curve and the Elasticity of the Supply of Labor

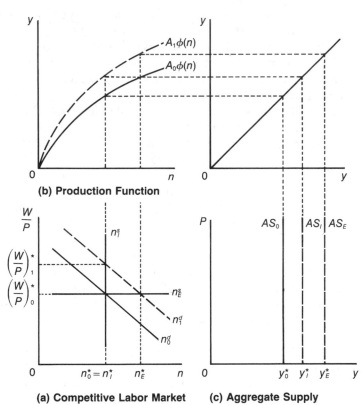

(b) Production Function

(a) Competitive Labor Market   **(c) Aggregate Supply**

A technology shock that shifts the production function from $A_0\phi(n)$ to $A_1\phi(n)$ raises the demand for labor from n_0^d to n_1^d. If the supply of labor is inelastic (n_I^s) the real wage rises to $\left(\dfrac{W}{P}\right)_1^*$, employment remains constant and the aggregate supply curve shifts from AS_0

to AS_1. If the supply of labor is elastic (n_E^s) the real wage remains constant, employment rises to n_E^* and the aggregate supply curve shifts from AS_0 to AS_E. That is, the more elastic the aggregate supply of labor, the smaller the rise in real wages and the larger the rise in both employment and output.

n_0^* are determined. At that employment level, and using the lower production function, we can determine the level of output at y_0^*. This level of output will be produced regardless of the price level and so the aggregate supply curve is the vertical line AS_0 in frame (c). Now consider what happens when the production function shifts to $A_1\phi(n)$. The marginal product of labor — the demand for labor — rises to n_1^d. If the supply of labor is inelastic then the real wage rises very sharply to $(W/P)_I^*$. Employment rises very little to n_I^*. Output rises however, to y_I^* and the aggregate supply curve shifts to become the curve AS_I.

If the supply of labor is very elastic we get a much bigger change in both employment and output. In such a case the real wage does not rise and employment will rise very sharply to n_E^*. Output will rise to y_E^* and the aggregate supply curve will shift to that labelled AS_E in frame (c). The shift of the aggregate supply curve is larger the more elastic the supply of labor.

A comparable analysis could be performed for a drop in the production function. You can easily work that case out for yourselves simply by reversing the example that we have just taken you through here.

Summary

A. Short-Run Aggregate Production Function

The short-run aggregate production function shows how the maximum amount of output will vary as the number of workers employed varies, holding constant the stock of capital, the state of technology, and the skills of labor. Its properties are the same as the short-run production function of an individual firm in that it displays diminishing marginal productivity.

B. Competitive Aggregate Labor Market

A competitive aggregate labor market will determine an equilibrium real wage and level of employment where the downward-sloping demand curve (derived from the marginal product curve) cuts an upward-sloping supply curve (derived from utility-maximizing decisions of households.)

C. Aggregate Supply Curve

The aggregate supply curve shows how output varies as the price level varies when firms are maximizing profits, households are maximizing utility, and the labor market is in equilibrium. In the basic model developed in this chapter, aggregate supply is perfectly inelastic with respect to the price level.

D. Growth and Fluctuations in Aggregate Supply

Aggregate supply will grow over time as a result of trends in technical progress, population growth and capital accumulation. Aggregate supply will fluctuate around its trend partly because technical change and capital accumulation do not proceed smoothly and partly because of random shocks caused by such things as variations in the climate and political instability. Such shocks to the production function — called technology shocks — will shift the aggregate supply curve. The amount by which the aggregate supply curve shifts and the effect of such shocks on the level of employment and real wages depends on the elasticity of aggregate labor supply. The more elastic the supply of labor the smaller the fluctuations in the real wage, the larger the movements in the level of employment and the larger the shifts in the aggregate supply curve.

Review Questions

1. A firm produces a good from inputs of labor and capital. Labor is measured by the number of workers employed. Use the following data to draw the firm's short-run production function.

No. of men	1	2	3	4	5	6	7	8	9	10
Output	10	21	33	45	56	66	75	83	90	96

If the money wage is $18 and the firm sells the good it produces for $2, how many workers will the firm employ?

2. If the economy consisted of 1000 firms, all identical and all exactly like the firm described in Question 1, show in a diagram the shape and position of the *aggregate* short-run production function. Also show the aggregate demand for labor curve. If the aggregate labor supply curve is

$$n^s = 2000(W/P) - 2000$$

how many workers will be employed and what will be the economy-wide average real wage?

3. What is an aggregate supply curve?

4. Use your answer to Question 2 to derive the aggregate supply curve for the hypothetical economy described in that question.

5. In drawing the aggregate supply curve, several assumptions have been made. List these assumptions.

6. Labor allocates its time between work and leisure in order to maximize its utility. Along which curve in Figure 14.6 is utility maximized?

7. Firms produce that output which maximizes profit. Along which curve in Figure 14.6 are all firms maximizing profit?

8. Is the aggregate supply curve fixed in position forever, or does it shift from time to time? If it does shift, list some of the things that would cause it to do so.

9. Review the factors that lead to long-term trend increases in aggregate supply.

10. Review the factors that can make the aggregate supply curve shift about its long-term trend.

11. Show how the effect of a technology shock on the aggregate supply curve depends on the elasticity of aggregate labor supply.

Appendix A:

Monopoly and the Demand for Labor

You may be thinking that the analysis presented in this chapter is fine for a competitive industry but not for a monopoly. You may also have been taught that we simply *know* that there are no competitive industries in the actual world. If so, you will be regarding the preceding analysis as being about as useful for the task in hand as the flat earth theory would be for charting an air route from Toronto to Tokyo! Leaving aside the deep question of whether or not it is possible *simply to know* whether or not competitive industries exist, it is perhaps of some interest to notice that for the task at hand, it simply doesn't matter whether the economy is competitive or monopolistic. To see this, consider how the analysis would go for a monopolist.

Now in order to maximize profits, a monopolist will set marginal cost equal, not to price, but to marginal revenue (MR_i). That is

$$MC_i = MR_i \qquad \text{(14A.1)}$$

Just as in the case of a competitive firm, the monopolist's marginal cost will be equal to the wage rate divided by the marginal product of labor; that is,

$$MC_i = \frac{W}{MP_i} \qquad \text{(14A.2)}$$

The monopolist's marginal revenue will be related to price by the formula

$$MR_i = \left(1 + \frac{1}{\eta}\right)P_i, \quad \eta < -1 \qquad \text{(14A.3)}$$

where η is the elasticity of the monopolist's demand curve. (See Appendix B to this chapter). To get a feel for how the relationship between marginal revenue and price [Equation (14A.3)] works, notice that if the elasticity of demand (η) was infinite, then MR_i would equal P_i. This, of course, is exactly the case of perfect competition. If η was equal to -1, the demand for the monopolist's output would be unit elastic and the demand curve would be a rectangular hyperbola. In that case, the monopolist's marginal revenue would be zero and the monopolist would not be in business.

In general, the monopolist's marginal revenue will be less than price but a stable fraction of the price.

Using Equations (14A.3) and (14A.2) in (14A.l) enables us to obtain

$$\left(1 + \frac{1}{\eta}\right)P_i = \frac{W}{MP_i} \qquad \text{(14A.4)}$$

Proceeding as we did in the case of the competitive firm, dividing both sides of Equation (14A.4) by P_i, and multiplying both sides by MP_i, we obtain:

$$\left(1 + \frac{1}{\eta}\right)MP_i = \frac{W}{P_i} \tag{14A.5}$$

This says that some fraction (the fraction $\left(1 + \frac{1}{\eta}\right)$) of the marginal product of a monopolistic firm will be equal to the real wage. The monopolist's demand for labor will therefore be *less* than that of a competitive producer (assuming that they have identical production functions) but will still have the crucial property that as the real wage rises, so the demand for labor falls. By aggregating across all producers, whether competitive or monopolistic, we shall still end up with an aggregate demand for labor that looks like that shown in Figure 14.3.

Appendix B:

Elasticity of Demand, Marginal Revenue, and Price

Elasticity is a measure of responsiveness. The elasticity of demand measures, in a precise way, the responsiveness of the quantity demanded to a change in the price. The higher the elasticity the more responsive is the quantity demanded to a price change. Elasticity is a unit-free measure of responsiveness. To be precise, it is the percentage change in the quantity demanded divided by the percentage change in price or, equivalently, the proportionate change of quantity demanded divided by the proportionate change in price. Calling the elasticity η, the change in the quantity demanded ΔQ, the change in price ΔP, the quantity demanded Q, and the price P, the elasticity is measured as

$$\eta = \frac{\Delta Q}{Q} \div \frac{\Delta P}{P} \qquad (14A.6)$$

This may equivalently be written as

$$\eta = \frac{\Delta Q}{Q} \cdot \frac{P}{\Delta P} \qquad (14A.7)$$

For future reference it is useful to notice that one over the elasticity (the inverse of the elasticity) is

$$\frac{1}{\eta} = \frac{\Delta P}{\Delta Q} \cdot \frac{Q}{P} \qquad (14A.8)$$

To obtain the formula used in Appendix A, notice that total revenue (R) is equal to price (P) multiplied by quantity (Q); that is

$$R = PQ \qquad (14A.9)$$

Now suppose that there was a change in the price that induced a change in quantity and a change in revenue. Then the new revenue that we could call $R + \Delta R$ will be determined as

$$R + \Delta R = (P + \Delta P)(Q + \Delta Q) \qquad (14A.10)$$

Multiplying out Equation (14A.10) gives

$$R + \Delta R = PQ + P\Delta Q + \Delta PQ + \Delta P\Delta Q \qquad (14A.11)$$

If the change in price (ΔP) is very very small, then Equation (14A.11) is approximately

$$R + \Delta R \approx PQ + P\Delta Q + Q\Delta P \qquad (14A.12)$$

(You see that we are treating the last term in Equation (14A.12) as if it was zero.) Now subtract Equation (14A.9) from Equation (14A.12) to give

$$\Delta R \approx P\Delta Q + Q\Delta P \qquad (14A.13)$$

This can be manipulated by multiplying and dividing the second term on the right-hand side by P to give

$$\Delta R \approx \left[\Delta Q + \frac{Q}{P}(\Delta P)\right]P \qquad \textbf{(14A.14)}$$

Dividing this equation through by ΔQ gives

$$\frac{\Delta R}{\Delta Q} \approx \left[\frac{\Delta Q}{\Delta Q} + \frac{Q}{P}\left(\frac{\Delta P}{\Delta Q}\right)\right]P \qquad \textbf{(14A.15)}$$

The left-hand side of Equation (14A.15) $(\Delta R/\Delta Q)$ is what is called *marginal revenue* — the change in revenue induced by a change in the quantity sold. Obviously, the first term in brackets — $\Delta Q/\Delta Q$ — in Equation (14A.15) is equal to one. You can also see, by referring back to Equation (14A.8), that the second term in brackets — $(Q/P)(\Delta P/\Delta Q)$ — in Equation (14A.15) is the inverse of the elasticity of demand. Equation (14A.15) may therefore be written more simply as:

$$\frac{\Delta R}{\Delta Q} \approx \left(1 + \frac{1}{\eta}\right)P \qquad \textbf{(14A.16)}$$

This is the relationship used in Appendix A. In words, it states that marginal revenue equals one plus one over the elasticity of demand all multiplied by the price. Clearly if the elasticity of demand is infinitely big (the case of perfect competition), price and marginal revenue are the same as each other.

Another interesting special case is when the elasticity of demand is minus one (the case of a rectangular hyperbola demand curve). In that case, you can verify from Equation (14A.16) that marginal revenue is equal to zero. Notice that, in general, marginal revenue is positive but less than the price since η, in general, is negative and lies between minus infinity (perfect competition) and minus one.

15

The New Classical Theory of Aggregate Supply

This chapter explains the *new classical* theory of aggregate supply[1] and derives the expectations-augmented aggregate supply curve. The chapter has four tasks, which are to:

a) Understand how incomplete information affects the supply of, and demand for, labor.

b) Understand how the money wage and level of employment (and unemployment) are affected by wrong expectations.

c) Know the definition of the expectations-augmented aggregate supply curve.

d) Know how to derive the expectations-augmented aggregate supply curve.

A. Incomplete Information and the Labor Market

In the classical model of the labor market presented in the previous chapter, the demand for labor, the supply of labor and the market equilibrating process paid no attention to any special characteristics of labor. We could have been talking about stocks and shares, wheat, futures contracts in gold, or just about any competitive market for

---

[1] The theory of aggregate supply presented in this chapter had its origins in Milton Friedman, "The Role of Monetary Policy," *The American Economic Review*, 58 (March 1968), 1-17. It is also similar to that developed by Robert E. Lucas, Jr. in "Some International Evidence on Output-Inflation Tradeoffs," *The American Economic Review*, 63, 3 (1973), 326-34.

any commodity at all. There are, however, some features of labor that make it unlike many other commodities. One important feature concerns the scale of the costs that individuals (both suppliers and demanders of labor) have to incur in order to find someone with whom to do business. From the household side, there is a heavy search cost — the cost of finding a job that is attractive enough, well paid enough, and satisfactory in other dimensions. From the point of view of the firm demanding labor, there are recruiting costs — the costs of finding potential employees with the required skills and personal attributes.

The fact that there are heavy search and recruiting costs in the labor market implies that labor will typically be traded in a way that is very different from the way in which shares and goods are traded. Instead of being traded on a market that works like a continuous auction, labor generally is traded in markets dominated by medium-term contracts. Individuals enter into arrangements with each other for a specified period of time, often for a year or more ahead.

The contracts that govern labor-trading arrangements could, in principal, be very complex documents that incorporate hundreds (perhaps thousands) of contingency clauses specifying the wages and other employment conditions contingent on a variety of potential future events. The costs of negotiating, writing, monitoring, and enforcing such contracts would, however, be very high. To avoid these costs, most labor market contracts are relatively simple. They specify a *money wage* (and other non-wage terms) that will be paid for a certain type of labor over a specified future period. If the contract is to run for more than a year, it will also typically specify an adjustment in the money wage, either in money terms or as some pre-agreed fraction of the change in the cost of living as measured by the Consumer Price Index.

The typical labor market contract is one in which the worker and the employer agree to trade labor services for a certain money wage, for a certain period of time into the future, but they make no commitments concerning the quantity of employment. The employer will typically *not* undertake to guarantee employment at the agreed wage and will be free to vary the number of workers hired. Individual workers will also be free to quit their jobs if they can find better ones with other firms.

How will firms decide how much labor to hire, and how will households decide how much labor to supply? Recall that a firm will hire labor up to the point at which the marginal product of that labor equals the real wage paid. In order to calculate the real wage, the firm simply has to divide the money wage by the *price of the firm's own output*. The firm will then hire labor up to the point at which its marginal product equals that firm-specific real wage. On the other side of the labor market, the amount of labor that a household will want to supply at any particular point in time will depend *not* on the real wage as calculated by the firm for the purpose of figuring out how much labor to demand but rather the real basket of goods and services that the household can consume with its wage. It will depend on the money wage divided by a general index of prices such as the Consumer Price Index. Thus, there is an asymmetry in the labor market concerning the price level that is relevant for calculating the real wage on the two sides of the market. As far as the firm is concerned, what matters is the ratio of the money wage to the price of the output produced by that firm. What matters on the supply side is the ratio of the money wage to an index of prices of all the goods and services from which households will choose their consumption. This asymmetry is the basis of the new theories of aggregate supply.

Let us consider the information that firms and households will need in order to make decisions about how much labor to demand and supply. Firms will need to know the money wage and the price of their own output. Households will need to know the money wage and the prices of all the goods and services from which they will choose their consumption bundle. A moment's reflection will lead you to a very important conclusion concerning these variables. Nobody has any difficulty in knowing the money wage (this will be specified when workers and firms are contemplating doing business together). Further, there will be very little problem in figuring out the price of the output of the firm. For some multi-product firms this might not be a totally straightforward matter, but it may be presumed that the firm's own accounting procedures are capable of generating accurate up-to-date information on the prices of the firm's output and that that information is readily available both to the firm and its workers.

However, in contrast to these two bits of information, knowledge of the prices of all the goods and services from which individuals will choose their consumption bundle will be very imperfect and incomplete. It is true that general price indexes, such as the Consumer Price Index, are calculated and published. It is also a fact, however, that they are published with a time lag; that is, they refer to the past, not to the present or the immediate future. Furthermore, they refer to a basket of goods that the mythical average household consumes and that no particular household consumes. From the perspective of any one individual household, what matters is the average level of prices of all the goods and services from which the final consumption bundle will be chosen. To actually know these prices would involve a process of searching and observing prices, a process that is so expensive that by the time the individual had amassed all the relevant information, there would be no time left either for work or consumption!

The implication of all this is that households cannot know everything that they would need to know if they were to make their labor supply decisions on the basis of the ratio of the money wage to the general level of prices. Put more directly, the notion that the supply of labor depends on the real wage cannot be given operational content since no one can know the relevant real wage at the time that a labor supply decision is being made. Thus, in the absence of information about the general level of prices, it becomes necessary for households to make their supply decision on the basis of some other criterion. The most natural criterion is the expected real wage. Since there is no difficulty about knowing the money wage component of the real wage, the only problem remaining is to figure out an expectation of the level of prices.

We can summarize the discussion so far in the following way: firms will decide how much labor to demand by figuring out the real wage on the basis of two known bits of information — the money wage and the price of the firm's own output. Households will decide how much labor to supply by calculating the expected real wage based on the known money wage and their expectation of the average level of prices prevailing in the markets for all the goods and services from which they will choose their consumption bundle. It is worth emphasizing that the price expectation that households will have to form in order to make a labor supply decision refers not to past prices but to current and future prices. Any labor supply decision made at a given moment in time, even if it was made on the basis of complete information about prices prevailing at that moment, would still have to be made on the basis of expectations of prices that will prevail at some future point in time when the proceeds from the work are eventually spent.

You may be thinking that it ought to be possible for people to figure out what the general level of prices is simply from knowing the prices in the sector of the economy in which they work, and perhaps knowing the prices of a few goods and services that they are consuming on a regular, almost daily basis. A moment's reflection will convince you, however, that although there is *some* information to be had from such sources, it is not sufficient. The economy is constantly undergoing change that results in constantly changing relative prices. Some relative price changes are, of course, predictable, but many, perhaps most, are not. They are in the nature of random events that arise from a multitude of forces. That being so, it will be very hard for people to figure out what is happening to the overall general level of prices simply from knowing the prices of one or two things. Therefore, in the rest of this chapter we shall make the extreme (and obviously slightly wrong) assumption that people get no help at all in figuring out the general level of prices from knowing the price of the output in their own sector of the economy. This extreme assumption could be modified, but the result of doing so would be to make our analysis a good deal more complicated without producing any change of substance in the conclusions that we should reach. We shall return to this matter in the next section.

The final thing to notice is that the asymmetry that has been discussed above is not an asymmetry between firms and households concerning the amount of information that each has. Firms are not being supposed to be smarter, in some sense, than households. Rather, the asymmetry arises from the fact that firms sell a small number of goods, so they and their workers are specialized in information concerning the prices of those goods. In contrast, households buy a large number of goods and services and are not specialized in information concerning the prices in all those markets. It is that asymmetry, and not an asymmetry in the amount of information that households and firms have, that provides the basis for a modified theory of aggregate supply.

The starting point for developing this theory is an extended analysis of the labor market that builds on the above remarks.

B. Wrong Expectations and the Labor Market

(i) The Labor Market and Money Wages

Recall the classical model of the labor market as shown below in frame (a) of Figure 15.1. This figure shows a competitive labor market in equilibrium at a real wage of $(W/P_0)^*$ and an employment level n^*. The demand for labor increases as the real wage falls because of profit-maximizing labor demand decisions by firms (marginal product equals the real wage); the supply of labor increases as real wages rise since more households will enter the labor force, the higher the real bundle of goods that they will be able to buy in exchange for their work.

Suppose for a moment that the price level is equal to one, i.e., $P_0 = 1$. With the price level equal to one, we may simply rename the vertical axis of Figure 15.1 to measure the money wage. If the price level is fixed at one, and we plot the demand and supply curves against the money wage, this is exactly the same as plotting them against the real wage. Frame (b) reproduces the demand and supply curves, n^d and n^s, and shows the same employment equilibrium, n^*, and the equilibrium money wage, W^*.

Next, notice that the equilibrium real wage $(W/P_0)^*$ [shown in frame (a)] could be attained at *any* money wage. All that is necessary is that the money wage and the price level stand in the appropriate relationship to each other: if the price level doubled, the money wage would have to double; if the price level rose by x percent, the money wage would have to rise by x percent. In frame (a) where we draw the demand and supply curves against the real wage, changes in the price level are not visible. The equilibrium determined in frame (a) is a real equilibrium and is independent of the price level.

Is the same true of the equilibrium in frame (b)? Is the equilibrium depicted in this frame independent of the price level? The answer is

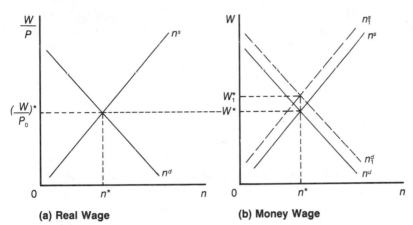

**Figure 15.1
The Labor Market and
the Money Wage**

(a) Real Wage

(b) Money Wage

The supply and demand curves in the labor market that are drawn against the real wage [frame (a)] may equivalently be drawn against the money wage [frame (b)]. In that case, there is a separate supply and demand curve for each price level. Both curves move vertically one-for-one as the price level varies.

that the *real* equilibrium — real wage and employment level — is independent of the price level, but the money wage, measured on the vertical axis of frame (b), is not. Since in frame (b) the money wage is measured on the vertical axis, it is necessary to be aware that the demand and supply curves can only be drawn for a *given* level of prices. The supply and demand curves, illustrated as n^d and n^s, are drawn for a price level equal to one.

Suppose the price level was to increase to P_1, which is higher than P_0 by x percent, i.e.,

$$P_1 = (1 + x)P_0$$

You may find some numbers helpful: if $x = 5$ percent, i.e., 5/100, then the equation

$$P_1 = (1 + x)P_0 \text{ is } P_1 = (1 + 5/100)P_0 \text{ or } P_1 = (1.05)1 = 1.05$$

If the price level rose by x percent, how would the demand and supply curves in frame (b) move? It is clear that the money wages that firms would now be willing to pay for each quantity of labor would be higher by the same x percent as the price level has increased by. Since the firm is only interested in the real wage, an x percent rise in the price level means that at a money wage x percent higher, the firm would be willing to hire the same number of workers as it would be at the lower price level and lower money wage. Thus, the demand for labor curve will shift upwards by the same x percent as the price level has risen by. This is shown as the dashed curve n_1^d in frame (b) of Figure 15.1.

What happens on the supply side? Precisely the same as on the demand side: the quantity of labor that households are willing to supply depends on the real wage. Therefore, if the price level rises by x percent, the money wage will have to rise by x percent if the quantity of labor supplied is to remain unchanged. Thus, the dashed curve n_1^s shows the supply of labor at the price level P_1. That is, the supply curve moves upwards by x percent in exactly the same way as the demand curve does.

It is now a simple matter to see that since the two curves have both moved upwards by the same percentage amount, they must cut at the same employment level as before and at a money wage that is x percent higher than before. This new equilibrium *money wage* is shown in frame (b) as W_1^* and is equal to $(1+x)W^*$. The equilibrium level of employment remains unchanged at n^*.

So far, nothing new has been introduced other than the idea that the labor market can be analyzed so as to determine the equilibrium wage and employment in the classical model, with the money wage on the vertical axis of the supply and demand diagram instead of the real wage. With the money wage on the vertical axis, the demand and supply curves shift when the price level changes. With the real wage on the vertical axis, the curves are fixed independently of the price level.

How the labor market works with incomplete information will now be analyzed.

(ii) Incomplete Information and Expectations

First, recall the information assumptions that we have made. Firms and households are presumed to know the price at which the firm will be able to sell its output, but neither firms nor households are presumed to have complete knowledge of the prices of all the goods and services from which households will choose their consumption bundles. Labor supply decisions will be made on the basis of the best available estimate or expectation of those prices. Call the price level that consumers expect to have to pay to buy their basket of consumer goods the *expected price level*, and denote it as P^e.

Next, recall the above discussion about the demand for labor by an individual firm. Each firm will demand labor up to the point at which the real wage that it faces equals the marginal product of labor. The real wage facing any individual firm will be the money wage divided by the price of the individual firm's output. If we add up all the demands of all the individual firms and take an average of the real wages faced by each firm, we would obtain the aggregate or economy-wide demand for labor curve. This aggregate demand for labor would depend on the *actual* economy average real wage, W/P.

This may seem puzzling because we have assumed that nobody knows the average price level. A moment's reflection will reveal, however, that nobody needs to know the actual price level for the economy aggregate demand for labor to depend on the actual real wage. The aggregate demand curve itself is simply arrived at by adding up the individual demands of all the individual firms. Not only does nobody know the average price level, but nobody knows the aggregate demand for labor, and nobody needs to. All that each individual firm needs to know is the price of its own output and its own demand for labor. The aggregate demand for labor and the aggregate price level are constructs of our theory and are not things that are in the minds of the individual firms whose behavior we are analyzing and studying.

The supply of labor by each individual household depends, as we have seen, on the expected real wage, that is, on W/P^e. We can obtain the economy-wide aggregate supply of labor by adding all the supply curves of all the households together. Since the supply of each household depends on the expected real wage, so the aggregate supply of labor will also depend on the expected real wage. There is thus a crucial difference between the demand and supply curves once we take account of the information that households and firms have concerning price information.

The final thing that we need to do before we can figure out the implications of our assumptions is to make some proposition about the interaction between households and firms in the labor market. We have already noted, as a descriptive matter, that most labor markets work on the basis of there being a precommitment to a particular money wage, with households and firms then making decisions about how much labor to supply and demand at that money wage, given actual selling prices of output and expectations of the purchase prices of consumer goods. This seems to suggest that we ought to assume that money wages are rigid and that labor markets do not necessarily achieve equilibrium. This is *not* the assumption of the new classical theory. On the contrary, the theory assumes that there is sufficient flexibility in the money wage for the average money wage to continuously adjust to maintain labor market equilibrium. This is a crucial assumption of the *new classical* analysis, which distinguishes it from the *new Keynesian* analysis that you will look at in the next chapter.

Although most firms and households do business with each other on the basis of pre-agreed wage schedules, there are in fact many ways in which you could think of the effective real wage adjusting so as to continuously maintain labor market equilibrium. One possibility is that the contracted wages themselves build in some automatic variation in the average hourly wage rate as a result of overtime schedules. Another possibility is that the intensity of work could be varied so as to vary the wage per unit of effort supplied as opposed to per hour supplied. (You probably know from your own labor market experience, and certainly from your experience as a student, that some hours of work are more intense than others. They range all the way from pure leisure to unadulterated drudgery!)

A further source of flexibility in the average wage paid arises from the heterogeneity of labor and the existence of different wages for different types of labor. This makes it possible for firms to change the quality mix of their labor force, perhaps using a higher proportion of higher paid and more highly skilled labor in times of high demand than in times of low demand. This would lead to an automatic variation in the average rates of wages paid, even though the pre-agreed wage schedules remain unchanged.

The key point to take from these "stories" is not that wages *do in fact* always adjust to achieve labor market equilibrium. Rather, it is that the *assumption* that labor markets always achieve equilibrium is not absurd, and is not contradicted by the commonly observed fact that labor is traded on contracts that specify a money wage. Let us now summarize the three assumptions that we have made:

(1) The demand for labor depends on the *actual* real wage.
(2) The supply of labor depends on the *expected* real wage.
(3) The *average* money wage adjusts continuously to achieve labor market equilibrium.

Let us now see what these assumptions imply.

Figure 15.2 will be the main vehicle for following the analysis. The vertical axis measures the money wage, and the horizontal axis measures the level of employment. The curve $n^d(P_0)$ is the demand curve for labor when the price level is fixed at P_0. The supply curve of labor is plotted for a given *expected* level of prices. The supply curve, marked $n^s(P^e = P_0)$, is for a level of expected prices that equals the actual price level P_0. Thus, the supply curve $n^s(P^e = P_0)$ and the demand curve $n^d(P_0)$ can be thought of as representing the original curves n^d and n^s, in frame (b) of Figure 15.l. They determine an equilibrium money wage W^* and an employment level n^*, which will now be called the *full-employment values*. The full-employment values of employment and the real wage are identical to those determined in the classical model.

Now consider what would happen if the price level was higher than P_0, while the expected price level remained at $P^e = P_0$. In particular, consider what would happen if the actual price level increased by x percent to P_1, where P_1 equals $(1 + x)P_0$. Each firm, knowing that its own selling price had risen by x percent, would now be willing to pay a higher money wage for its labor. That is, the demand for labor curve would shift upwards. The new demand curve that would result is shown as $n^d(P_1)$.

Recall that we are conducting a conceptual experiment in which the general price level *expected* by households does not change. Since

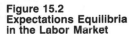

**Figure 15.2
Expectations Equilibria
in the Labor Market**

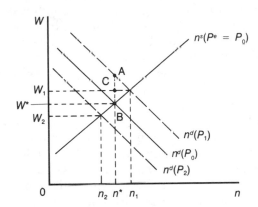

The demand for labor by each firm depends upon the firm's own output price. This means that the aggregate demand for labor depends on the actual price level. The supply of labor depends on the expected price level. The equilibrium wage and employment level will be different at each different price level. At the price level P_0 there is full-employment equilibrium; at the price level P_1 there is over-full employment (wage W_1, employment n_1); and at the price level P_2 there is unemployment (wage W_2, employment n_2).

the *expected* price level has not changed, the supply curve is not affected by the change in the actual price level and remains in its original position.[2]

The labor market will now attain an equilibrium at the money wage W_1 and the employment level n_1. That is, with the actual price level higher than the expected price level, the money wage will be higher than its full-employment value, and the level of employment will be higher than its full-employment value. The real wage, however, will be lower than its full-employment value. This can be seen in Figure 15.2. The price level increase is measured by the full vertical shift of the labor demand curve, for example, the distance AB. The

---

[2] Strictly speaking, there is an inconsistency in the treatment here. Everybody knows the price in the market for the commodity that they are concerned with the production of, and yet they do not seem to take this information into account in forming an expectation of the general price level. This is wasteful of information. A more complete, but more difficult, treatment would extract information from the known price of a particular commodity to obtain a better inference about the general price level. The essence of the new classical theory of aggregate supply is not affected, however, by ignoring this piece of information. For the reader able to follow statistical analysis, the paper by Robert E. Lucas, Jr., "Some International Evidence on Output-Inflation Tradeoffs," *The American Economic Review*, 63, 3 (1973), 326-34, and the Appendix to Chapter 18 deal with this problem. This Lucas paper is probably the most important, accessible, original presentation of the new classical theory of aggregate supply.

money wage, however, rises by a smaller distance, BC. You see, therefore, that the price level rise is greater than the money wage rise, and therefore the real wage has fallen. This fall in the real wage has induced firms to hire more labor and has generated the increase in employment from n^* to n_1. Households expect the price level to be P_0, and therefore as the money wage rises, households expect the real wage to be (W_1/P_0). This encourages households to supply the extra amount of labor n^* to n_1.

In this situation and while they are doing business with each other, households and firms are in equilibrium. Both households and firms are happy, and there is nothing that either could do to improve their situation. However, as they look backwards to a previous period, households will realize that they have made a mistake. They will realize that they did too much work and at too low a real wage. Of course, bygones are bygones, and there will be nothing that can be done about that. All that households can do the next time around is again to use all the information that is available to them and make the best deal that they can. The situation just analyzed is called one of *over-full employment*.

Next, consider the opposite experiment, of a fall in the price level below P_0, while the expected price level remains constant at $P^e = P_0$. In particular, let us suppose that the price level falls by x percent from P_0 to P_2, but that the expected price level remains at P_0. The demand for labor curve will now shift downwards and is illustrated by the new demand curve, $n^d(P_2)$. The supply curve does not shift because the expected price level has not changed. What happens in this event? Again, the answer is clear and is contained in the diagram (Figure 15.2). This time the labor market will come to what is called an *unemployment equilibrium*. The equilibrium wage will be W_2 and the employment level n_2. Thus, with a lower price level than that expected, employment and the money wage will fall below their full-employment levels. The real wage, in this case, will rise above its full-employment level. The real wage rises because the price level falls by more than the fall in the money wage. The demand curve falls by the full percentage amount of the fall in the price level, but as you can see, the money wage falls by only a fraction of that. It is the higher real wage that creates the fall in employment, inducing firms to hire fewer workers. The expected real wage falls, however, because households do not expect the fall in the price level, and when they see a fall in the money wage, they read this as being a fall in the real wage.

There is, therefore, no inconsistency between the behavior of households and firms concerning the drop in employment and the change in the money wage. Households willingly reduce their employment to n_2 in the face of an expected fall in the real wage, while firms willingly cut their hiring to n_2 since they are facing a higher real wage.

While households and firms are trading labor, everyone is happy; both firms and households are doing the best they can for themselves. The workers $n^* - n_2$ will choose not to be employed, and their decision to be unemployed is correct in the light of their expectation of a low real wage. They expect a low real wage because although the money wage has fallen, their expectation is that the price level will remain constant. Each firm, on the other hand, knowing its own output price, regards the drop in the money wage as insufficient to compensate for the drop in its own price, and so the resulting higher actual real wage induces them to hire less labor.

You see, then, that if the price level that is expected actually comes about, the economy will settle down at an equilibrium that is the same as the equilibrium in the classical model. That equilibrium is called *full employment*. If the price level is higher than expected, the labor market will equilibrate at a higher level of employment and a lower level of the real wage than the full-employment levels. In this case there will be *over-full employment*. If the price level turns out to be lower than that which is expected, then there will be a cut in the employment level and a higher real wage — there will be *unemployment*.

In the institutional setting of Canada, such a cut in unemployment will usually be recorded as a rise in unemployment since the individuals involved will be "available for" and "able and willing to" work. They are not, however, willing to work at the wage that is available. The unemployment survey does not ask questions in sufficient detail to establish that fact. It does not distinguish between people who are willing to work at the wage currently prevailing but cannot find such work and those who are unwilling to work at the prevailing wage but would like to work for a higher wage than is available.

Once expectations are introduced, there is no single unique equilibrium in the labor market The equilibrium level of employment and the real wage will be influenced by the actual price level relative to its expected level. The higher the actual price level relative to its expected level, the higher will be the level of employment and the money wage, and the lower will be the level of unemployment and the real wage.

C. Definition of the Expectations-Augmented Aggregate Supply Curve

The expectations-augmented aggregate supply curve shows the maximum amount of output that the economy will supply at each different price level but with a fixed expected price level.

This is an extension of the classical aggregate supply curve that was derived in Chapter 14. The classical aggregate supply curve can be thought of as showing the maximum amount of output that the economy will supply when there is no difference between the actual and the expected price levels. That is, the classical aggregate supply curve is the same as the expectations-augmented aggregate supply curve when everyone has full information and everyone knows the actual price level.

D. Derivation of the Expectations-Augmented Aggregate Supply Curve

It is a straightforward matter to derive the expectations- augmented aggregate supply curve from the analysis that you have already conducted. Figure 15.3 illustrates how this is done. Frame (a) simply reproduces Figure 15.2. If you have understood Figure 15.2, you will understand frame (a) because it contains nothing new. The demand for labor curve drawn for the price level P_1 is $n^d(P_1)$, the curve for the price level P_0 is $n^d(P_0)$, and the curve for the price level P_2 is $n^d(P_2)$. The supply curve is drawn for a fixed expected price level P^e equal to P_0.

Figure 15.3 is used to do something with which you are already familiar. It is used to derive the classical aggregate supply curve. This is done by reading off the equilibrium level of output for which the expected price level equals the actual price level. In this case, everyone has full information — no one is misled. The equilibrium in the labor market is where the demand for labor curve $n^d(P_0)$ cuts the supply of labor curve $n^s(P^e = P_0)$. At this point, employment is n^* and the money wage is W^*.

Transferring this employment level up to frame (b), you can read off from the production function the equilibrium level of output that will be supplied at full-employment equilibrium. This is y^*. Transfer that level of output (following the dotted line) round to frame (c), and plot the level of output that will be produced in full-employment equilibrium against the price level P_0, point E. Point E is one point on the classical aggregate supply curve. Now, as the price level is varied, *and* provided we also vary the expected price level — so that actual and expected prices are always equal to each other [recall frame (b) of Figure 15.l] — nothing would happen to the equilibrium level of employment or the real wage. The money wage would change proportionately with the price level, and the real equilibrium in the labor market would be undisturbed. This is essentially the exercise we performed when deriving the classical aggregate supply curve: as the price level is varied and as the expected price level is varied so as to always equal the actual price level, the equilibrium level of employment remains constant, and from frame (b), the equilibrium level of output also remains constant. This traces out the classical aggregate supply curve, *AS*, in frame (c).

Next consider what happens when the expected price level is held constant, but the actual price level changes. First, suppose the actual

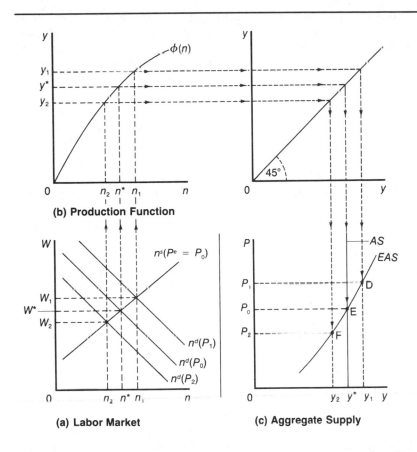

**Figure 15.3
Derivation of the
Expectations-Augmented
Aggregate Supply
Curve**

(b) Production Function

(a) Labor Market

(c) Aggregate Supply

Frame (a) is the same as Figure 15.2. At each different price level there is a different labor market equilibrium. The employment levels associated with these different equilibria translate into different output levels [frame (b)]. By associating the initially assumed different price levels with the output levels generated [frame (c)] the expectations-augmented aggregate supply curve is derived. Position E is the same full-employment equilibrium in the basic model. The expectations-augmented aggregate supply curve cuts the classical aggregate supply curve at the expected price level.

price level rises from P_0 to P_1, while the expected price level stays at P_0. This higher price level is shown on the vertical axis of frame (c) as P_1. What is the level of output that profit-maximizing producers would want to supply at that price level? The answer is obtained by starting in the labor market. You know that the demand for labor curve will shift upwards to $n^d(P_1)$. You also know that the supply curve of labor will not move because its position depends on the expected price level, and this has not changed. The labor market will clear at a higher money wage W_1 and a higher level of employment n_1. At this higher level of employment, firms will produce a higher level of output y_1, which is read off from the production function in frame (b). If we transfer this level of output (by following the dotted line) to frame (c), we generate the new point D in frame (c). Point D shows the output level y_1 which profit-maximizing firms are willing to supply if the actal price level is P_1 and the expected price level is P_0.

Next, consider what would happen if the actual price level fell below P_0. Such a price level is shown on the vertical axis of frame (c) as P_2. What is the profit-maximizing supply of output in this case? The answer is again obtained by starting in the labor market. You know that the demand for labor curve falls to $n^d(P_2)$, so that the equilibrium level of employment and the money wage fall to n_2 and W_2, respectively. At this lower level of employment, firms will produce the lower level of output y_2, read off from frame (b). Now transferring this output level y_2 (following the dotted line) to frame (c) shows that profit-maximizing firms are willing to supply the level of output y_2 at the price level P_2. That is, the economy would operate at point F. Point F says that if the actual price level is P_2 but the expected actual price level is P_0, firms will choose to supply y_2 as their profit-maximizing output.

If we join together the points D, E, and F and all other points in between and beyond these, we will generate the expectations-augmented aggregate supply curve, labelled *EAS*.

The expectations-augmented aggregate supply curve shows how the profit-maximizing and utility-maximizing quantity of supply varies as the price level varies — when the expected price level is fixed. Notice that the expectations-augmented aggregate supply curve (*EAS*) cuts the aggregate supply curve (*AS*) at the point at which the actual price level is equal to the expected price level. In the example in frame (c), this is at the price level P_0. This is not a coincidence. It happens because only when expectations turn out to be correct do we get the same aggregate supply as we would if everyone always had complete information.

This new aggregate supply analysis will be combined with the theory of aggregate demand in Chapter 17 to reexamine the effects of a change in aggregate demand on the level of output and prices.

Summary

A. Incomplete Information and the Labor Market

Because it is costly for workers to find suitable jobs and because it is costly for firms to find suitable employees, labor is not traded as if in a continuous auction market. Rather, contracts are entered into that run for a year or more. Because contracts last for a sizeable length of time and because it is expensive to write complicated contracts with detailed contingency clauses, it is typically the case that firms and households fix the price at which they will buy and sell labor services in money units — i.e., they fix a money wage. However, because their decisions to buy and sell labor services are influenced by the real wage, it is necessary for both households and firms to form an expectation about the price level that will prevail over a wage contract period.

Firms and households can do a better job of forming a reliable expectation about the prices in their own sector of the economy than they can about prices in general. Firms typically sell a small number of commodities and have a large amount of information about the markets in which they operate. In contrast, households buy a very large range of commodities and are not typically well informed about future prices in those markets. As a first approximation, everyone knows the prices at which the output of their sector will be selling over the future wage contract period; however, no one knows *all* the prices that they will be facing when buying goods, so it is necessary to form an expectation of those commodity prices based on incomplete information.

B. Wrong Expectations and the Labor Market

For a given expectation of the price level, a rise in the money wage will be read by households as a rise in the real wage and they will increase their supply of labor. A cut in the money wage will be read as a cut in the real wage, and they will decrease their supply of labor. However, each firm, knowing the prices of its own limited range of commodities will not be misinformed about the real wage it is paying, and the demand for labor will depend on the *actual* real wage. The higher the actual price level relative to the expected price level, the lower will be the real wage, the greater will be the amount of labor that firms hire, the higher will be the expected real wage, and the greater will be the amount of labor that households supply. There are many equilibrium levels of the real wage and employment. The only equilibrium that corresponds to the classical one is the equilibrium in which the expected price level is equal to the actual price level. This occurs when everyone's expectation is correct.

C. Definition of the Expectations-Augmented Aggregate Supply Curve

The expectations-augmented aggregate supply curve traces out the quantities of aggregate output that firms will be willing to supply as the price level varies, at a given expected price level.

D. Derivation of the Expectations-Augmented Aggregate Supply Curve

The derivation is done in Figure 15.3. You should review Figure 15.3 as many times as necessary until you are thoroughly familiar with the derivation of the expectations-augmented aggregate supply curve.

Review Questions

1. What are the key assumptions of the new classical theory of the labor market?

2. What is the asymmetry in the labor market on which the new classical theory of aggregate supply is based? Does it imply that workers are more ignorant than their employers about prices?

3. What are the ways in which firms can vary the wage rate, independently of negotiating a new contract?

4. Why does the aggregate demand for labor in the new classical model depend on the *actual* real wage? How can it do so, when, by the assumptions of the model, no one knows the actual real wage?

5. Why, despite the fact there is never any involuntary unemployment in the new classical model, might there be concern about unemployment even in the context of that model?

6. What markets are in equilibrium along the new classical *EAS* curve? Is there any involuntary unemployment?

7. What determines the slope of the new classical expectations- augmented aggregate supply curve? Show how the slope of the *EAS* curve changes as the supply of the labor curve becomes more elastic.

16

The New Keynesian Theory of Aggregate Supply

There has recently emerged a new Keynesian theory of aggregate supply that differs in subtle but important ways from the new classical theory. The principal architects of the new Keynesian theory are Stanley Fischer of the Massachusetts Institute of Technology, Edmund Phelps of Columbia University, and John Taylor of Stanford University.[1] The approach had its origins, however, in an interesting paper by JoAnna Gray[2] dealing, not with the theory of aggregate supply, but with a related matter that will be dealt with in chapter 37, the linking of wages to the cost of living. The treatment of the new Keynesian theory that will be presented in this chapter is in some respects closer to that of Jo Anna Gray than to those of Fischer, Phelps, and Taylor. The work of these three scholars, in fact, has interesting differences, some of which will be noted later.

---

[1] The main contributions to what we are calling the *new Keynesian theory* of aggregate supply are Stanley Fischer, "Long-Term Contracts, Rational Expectations and the Optimal Money Supply Rule," *Journal of Political Economy*, 85 (February 1977), 191-206; Edmund S. Phelps and John B. Taylor, "Stabilizing Powers of Monetary Policy under Rational Expectations," *Journal of Political Economy*, 85 (February 1977), 163-90; and John B. Taylor, "Staggered Wage Setting in a Macro Model," *The American Economic Review, Papers and Proceedings*, May 1979, pp. 108-13. The first two papers cited deal with a much broader range of issues than this chapter does and extend into the policy questions that are dealt with in Chapters 32 and 33.

[2] Jo Anna Gray, "Wage Indexation: A Macroeconomic Approach," *Journal of Monetary Economics*, 2, no. 2 (April 1976), 221-35.

The point of departure of the new Keynesian theory is the description of the institutional arrangements in the labor market presented in the first section of the previous chapter. A key aspect of that institutional description is the general prevalence in labor markets of contracts that specify an agreed and, for a predetermined period, fixed money wage rate. The new classical theory assumes that there remains sufficient flexibility in the labor market for the average money wage to be in a state of continuous adjustment so as to achieve continuous labor market clearing. It is this assumption of the new classical theory that the new Keynesian theory replaces.

The new Keynesian theory regards the contractual fixing of money wages as being such a crucial feature of the labor market that it must figure prominently in any theory of how the labor market works. According to the new Keynesian theory, labor markets do not act like markets that are in a state of continuous auction, with prices (wages) being frequently adjusted to achieve an ongoing equality between supply and demand. Rather, supply equals demand only on the average. At any particular moment in time, demand may exceed or fall short of supply. Taking explicit account of the institutional fact of contractually fixed money wages has important implications for the specification of the aggregate supply curve. This chapter explores these implications. Four specific tasks will help you in that objective. They are to:

  a) Know the key assumptions of the new Keynesian analysis.
  b) Understand how money wages are determined in the new Keynesian theory of aggregate supply.
  c) Understand the implications of the new Keynesian theory of wage determination for the expectations-augmented aggregate supply curve.
  d) Understand the implications of overlapping labor market contracts.

A. Assumptions of the New Keynesian Analysis

There are four key assumptions in the new Keynesian theory of aggregate supply. The first of these is that wages are set in money terms for a fixed contractual period before the quantity of labor supplied and demanded is known. Wages are not continuously adjusted so as to equate the *actual* supply of labor with the *actual* demand for labor. No explicit theory of maximizing behavior on the part of labor suppliers and demanders is set out that rationalizes a contract like this, although the developers of the new Keynesian theories do have in mind some underlying optimization by individuals that involve trading-off the costs of collecting information and negotiating changes in wages against the losses that arise when wages fail to adjust continuously to achieve market clearing. It is asserted that, for whatever reason, the real world so obviously is characterized by such arrangements in labor markets that it is inappropriate to develop an analysis of the labor market that ignores the contractual fixity of money wages.

The second key assumption of the new Keynesian analysis is that the actual quantity of labor traded is equal to the quantity demanded. After wages are set, the actual supply and demand conditions become known. Once those conditions are known, both suppliers and demanders in the labor market are tied into a labor contract. There has to be some rule for determining the quantity that will be traded. This rule could be that the short side of the market dominates. What this means is that if demand is less than supply, the quantity traded is the quantity demanded, but if demand exceeds supply, the quantity traded is the quantity supplied. However, this is *not* the assumption employed in the new Keynesian analysis. Instead, it is assumed that the demand side always dominates. The suppliers of labor are assumed to stand ready to supply whatever labor is demanded in exchange for the certainty of a fixed money wage over the duration of the existing contract.

The third assumption of the new Keynesian theory concerns the objectives that govern the setting of the money wage rate at the beginning of a contract. Here, the different scholars who have contributed to this approach each make their own special assumptions. Phelps and Taylor propose that wages of a given group of workers will be set at a level that takes account of:

(1) Any wage changes that have occured among other groups in the period since the previous wage contract date.
(2) Any expected wage and price changes that are going to take place over the interval for which wages are now being agreed.
(3) The state of excess demand (or supply) of labor.

Wages will increase faster the faster the wages of other groups of workers have recently increased, the faster are prices and the wages of the others expected to rise over the term of the contract, and the greater is the state of excess demand for the particular group of labor in question.

Stanley Fischer makes a simpler assumption that ignores the effect of excess demand on the level of wages. He proposes wages will be set so as to achieve a *fixed* real wage rate. This assumption makes a great deal of sense for a world in which there are never any changes in technology that would shift the demand for labor curve and change the equilibrium real wage. If, however, technology does keep changing and equilibrium real wages change as a result, then any wage-setting behavior that seeks to fix the real wage will inject into the labor market a barrier that prevents the supply of labor from ever equalling the demand for labor even on the average. It is very hard to see why people would want to be parties to contracts that have such a feature. Furthermore, we know from simple observation of the behavior of real wages that, in fact, they do vary from time to time. This assumption of Fischer's, then, although a useful one for his purposes, is too restrictive.

It seems more appropriate to adopt the Phelps and Taylor approach and assume that money wages not only respond to expectations of changes in the wages of others and prices but also respond to the state of supply and demand in the labor market. One way of allowing for the effects of supply and demand on wages that can be viewed as a special case of the Phelps and Taylor assumption is to assume that money wages are set so as to achieve an equality between the expected supply and expected demand for labor over the duration of the labor contract. This, in fact, is the assumption employed by Jo Anna Gray (referred to above) and it is the assumption that we shall use in order to derive a new Keynesian theory of aggregate supply.

Before going on to do that, however, let us be sure that we understand exactly what this assumption is and how it relates to but also differs from the assumptions made by Phelps and Taylor and Fischer. We are going to assume that the money wage is set at the beginning of a contract and is held constant throughout the contract period so as to achieve an equality between the *expected supply* and *expected demand* for labor. It will be immediately clear that if there are no expected changes in supply and demand in the labor market then the expected real wage will be constant, and the money wage will be set so as to achieve this expected constant real wage. Thus, provided there are no expected labor market shocks, the assumption that we are making is equivalent to that made by Stanley Fischer. If, however, there are expected changes in supply and demand in the labor market, there will be an expected change in the real wage, and the money wage will be set to reflect that expectation. To this extent the assumption that we are making is more general than that made by Fischer.

Next compare our assumption with that of Phelps and Taylor. They propose that when there is an excess demand for labor, money wages will rise faster than they otherwise would do. Our assumption agrees with that. If there is an excess demand for labor (which is expected to continue into the future), then money wages will increase by more than they otherwise would have done but by a very specific amount — the amount that produces an expected equality between supply and demand for labor. Phelps and Taylor are not quite as precise as that: they simply say that if there is excess demand for labor, money wages will rise faster than they otherwise would do. They will not necessarily rise by an amount that will completely close the gap between supply and demand in a given contract period. To this extent the assumption that we are making is slightly more restrictive than that of Phelps and Taylor.

The fourth key assumption of the new Keynesian theory of aggregate supply is that labor market contracts last for a longer term than the frequency with which the economy is being bombarded by various kinds of random and policy shocks. This means that workers and their employers often become aware of the fact that the contractually agreed-upon wage, based on information that was available at the time the agreement was drawn up, may now be in some sense inappropriate for the new conditions. Nevertheless, being tied into an agreement, both sides of the market have to live with the pre-committed money wage until the next review date. Taken on its own, this would imply that any shocks occurring after a wage contract has been written will have effects that could persist to some future date on which the existing contract with the longest term is to be reviewed.

There is, however, a further consideration that generates even more persistence in the effects of shocks than that. It arises from the fact that not all labor market contracts are signed on the same day to run for the same duration. Rather, they are signed on different dates for different durations (although the differences in durations are not so important as the differences in the dates on which the contracts are signed). The fact that contracts overlap or are "staggered" rather than bunched to the same date and time interval has important implications that will be discussed later in this chapter. The next two sections will not take account of the overlapping nature of labor market contracts, but for simplicity will proceed as if all contracts are signed on the same day and run for the same duration.

B. Determination of Money Wages

The process whereby the money wage is determined in the new Keynesian theory is illustrated in Figure 16.1; it is analogous to the diagram used in Figure 15.2. The level of employment is measured on the horizontal axis, and the money wage rate is measured on the vertical axis. The supply curve of labor $n^s(P^e = P_0)$ is drawn for a fixed expected price level equal to P_0. It is assumed that the labor market convenes and negotiations take place and that the money wage contract is signed prior to the commencement of the period for which the labor will be supplied and demanded. The price level at which the demanders of labor will sell their output is, therefore, unknown at the time that the labor market contract is signed.

The demand for labor that is relevant for the determination of the wage contract is that based on the expected price level. Such a demand function is drawn in Figure 16.1 as the curve labelled $n^d(P^e = P_0)$. This is the expected demand for labor curve, given the expected price level equal to P_0. Where the expected demand curve cuts the expected supply curve determines the expected labor market equilibrium. The level of employment n_0^e is the expected equilibrium level of employment, and the wage W_0 is the expected market-clearing money wage.

Figure 16.1
The New Keynesian
Labor Market

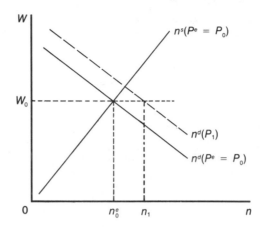

The labor market meets and a money wage is set before the actual price level is known. That wage rate, W_0, is set to achieve an equilibrium in the labor market based on the expected price level (P_0). When the actual price level (P_1) is revealed, the quantity of labor traded will equal the quantity demanded (n_1).

The contractually determined money wage will be set equal to this expected market-clearing money wage. Once the money wage is determined, nothing is allowed to change it until the next bargaining date at some time in the future. In the meantime, the actual level of employment will be determined at the contracted money wage by the *actual* demand for labor curve. Suppose that the actual price level turns out to be P_1, so the actual demand for labor curve is $n^d(P_1)$. In this case, the wage rate remains at W_0 and the quantity of labor employed is n_1. The real wage will have fallen because the price level P_1 is higher than the expected price level, P_0, on which the fixed money wage rate W_0 is based.

C. The New Keynesian Expectations-Augmented Aggregate Supply Curve

The new Keynesian theory of aggregate supply implied by the theory of wage determination just presented is very similar, in qualitative terms, to the new classical theory. The derivation of the new Keynesian expectations-augmented aggregate supply curve is presented in Figure 16.2. It will be recognized that this figure is almost identical to Figure 15.3, which was used to derive the new classical expectations-augmented aggregate supply curve. The labor market analysis presented above in Figure 16.1 is repeated in frame (a). The production function appears in frame (b), and the aggregate supply curve is generated in frame (c). As described above, the money wage is determined at W_0, which is the money wage that achieves an expected equilibrium in the labor market. That is, it achieves an equality between the expected supply of labor and the expected demand for labor with the expected price level P_0. If the actual price level turned out to be P_1 so that the demand for labor curve was in fact $n^d(P_1)$ then the quantity of labor demanded would be n_1 in frame (a). The quantity of labor n_1 would, from the production function in frame (b), generate a level of output equal to y_1. Transferring output level y_1 through the 45° quadrant to the aggregate supply diagram in frame (c), gives the

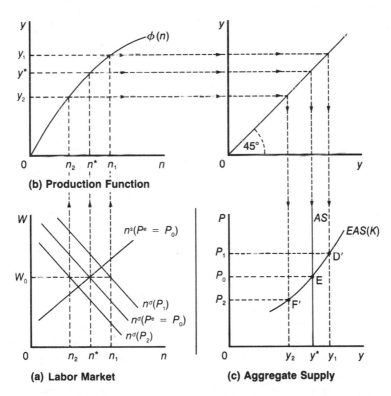

Figure 16.2
Derivation of the Expectations-Augmented Aggregate Supply Curve in the New Keynesian Model

The development in this diagram parallels that of Figure 15.3. In frame (a), the labor market sets a money wage at W_0 based on the expected price level P_0. Full-employment equilibrium would be at n^*. Different actual price levels (P_0, P_1, P_2) generate different demand curves. The quantity traded is read off from the demand curve (n_1 at price level P_1 and n_2 at price level P_2). The output levels produced by these different labor inputs are read off from the production function in frame (b). The resulting new Keynesian expectations-augmented aggregate supply curve is traced out as F′ED′. The aggregate supply curve based on correct information is the classical aggregate supply curve, AS.

output level y_1 on the horizontal axis of frame (c). This output level y_1 is, associated with the price level P_1 so that point D′ is a point on the expectations-augmented aggregate supply curve of the new Keynesian analysis.

If, conversely, the price level was lower than P_0 at, say, P_2 so that the demand for labor curve dropped to the curve $n^d(P_2)$, then the quantity of labor demanded would become the quantity n_2 on the horizontal axis of frame (a). This level of employment would generate an output level y_2 read off from the vertical axis of frame (b). Transferring the output level y_2 through the 45° quadrant to the aggregate supply diagram in frame (c) shows that the output level y_2 is associated with the price level P_2 at point F′. If the price level turned out to be that which was expected, namely, P_0 then the quantity of labor employed would be n^* [frame (a)] and the output level would be y^* [frame (b)], generating a point on the aggregate supply curve, point E. Joining together points F′, E, and D′ and extrapolating beyond those points traces out the new Keynesian expectations-augmented aggregate supply curve, labelled *EAS(K)* in frame (c).

So that you can see clearly the relationship between the new Keynesian expectations-augmented aggregate supply curve and the new classical aggregate supply curve, Figure 16.3 superimposes the two analyses on top of each other. You can easily verify that Figure 16.3 contains everything that is in Figure 16.2 that generates the curve *EAS(K)* (the new Keynesian aggregate supply curve) and also everything that is in Figure 15.3 that generates the new classical aggregate supply curve, the curve *EAS(C)*. Notice that the new Keynesian aggregate supply curve is flatter than the new classical curve. In a sense, this says that the new Keynesian analysis gives rise to more pessimistic predictions than the new classical analysis about the effects on output of a cut in aggregate demand, but it also gives more optimistic predictions concerning the inflationary consequences of stimulating aggregate demand.

Aside from the slopes of the two curves, the two theories as presented so far look very similar. There is, however, a crucial difference between the two that has not yet been revealed as fully as it needs to be, and that arises from the fact that the contractually determined wages are not all set on the same date but rather overlap each other. Let us now turn to an examination of the implications of this factor.

D. Overlapping Wage Contracts

The new Keynesian theory of aggregate supply developed above is based on the idea that at the beginning of each period of time, workers and employers sit down together, form an expectation of what the price level will be over the coming period (say a year), agree on a money wage that will achieve an expected equilibrium in the labor market, and then agree to trade at that wage for the coming year.

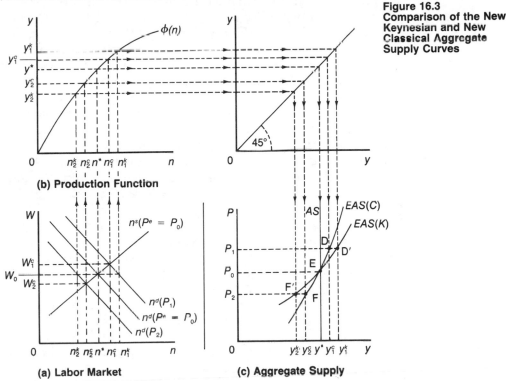

**Figure 16.3
Comparison of the New Keynesian and New Classical Aggregate Supply Curves**

This diagram superimposes Figure 15.3 upon Figure 16.3. The key differences between the new Keynesian and new classical theories are seen in frames (a) and (c). In the new Keynesian analysis, the money wage is fixed at W_0 so that as the price level varies between P_1 and P_2 the quantity of labor traded varies between n_1^k and n_2^k and output between y_1^k and y_2^k. In the new classical analysis, as the price level varies between P_1 and P_2 shifting the demand for labor curve between $n^d(P_1)$ and $n^d(P_2)$ so the money wage fluctuates between W_1^c and W_2^c. These fluctuations in the wage dampen off fluctuations in the quantity of labor demanded so that employment and output fluctuate between n_1^c and n_2^c and output fluctuates between y_1^c and y_2^c. The two expectations-augmented supply curves cut the classical aggregate supply curve at the expected price level, point E. The new classical curve is steeper than the new Keynesian curve.

The amount of labor that they trade will be determined by the actual demand for labor once the general price level is revealed.

The assumption that all contracts start and end at the same time as each other is obviously a fiction used purely to simplify the diagrammatic analysis. Let us now get rid of that assumption. Suppose, instead, that one-half of the labor force sits down at the beginning of January each year and negotiates a wage that is to prevail, not for one year, but for two years. The other half of the labor force will negotiate a wage on the alternate January, again for a period of two years. The analysis contained in Figures 16.1 and 16.2 still applies, but now it only applies to one-half of the labor force. The other half of the labor force has already performed that same exercise one year earlier and will be performing it one year later. Thus, the actual wage rate that is observed at any one point in time in the economy will be an average of the wages that have been set at various dates in the past on contracts that are still current. In the example, if one-half of the labor force sets its wages in January of one year and the other one-half in January of the alternate year, then the wage that prevails in any one year will be equal to one-half of the wage determined at the beginning of January of the year in question plus one-half of the wage determined at the beginning of the preceding January. This wage will be based on expectations of the general price level that were formed at two different dates in the past.

This being so, the expectations-augmented aggregate supply curve will depend not only on current expectations of the current price level but also on older (and perhaps by now known to be wrong) expectations of the current price level. Once agents are locked into a money wage decision based on an old, and perhaps falsified, expectation of the price level, by the hypothesis embodied in the new Keynesian analysis there is nothing they can do about it until the next wage review date comes along.

It would be incorrect, however, to jump to the conclusion that the effects of expectations that are now known to be wrong would be eliminated once a new contract was written. The fact that contracts overlap means also that they influence each other in a persistent manner. To see this, consider a group of workers setting their wage in the current period. One of the things that they will want to do in determining the money wage is to take a view of the expected behavior of prices over their own contract period. Another thing that will influence them is the levels of wages that have already been set by other workers. To move their own wages too far out of line with those earlier wages could cause employers to find ways of substituting among different types of labor. Thus, the money wage being negotiated today is not going to be entirely independent of money wages that have been negotiated in the past. A forecasting error made by those whose wage contract was written in the previous period will influence the wages that are going to be set in the current period, and these effects will persist (although in diminishing form) into the indefinite future.

The fact that labor market contracts are long-term and overlapping has very important implications for the analysis of economic policy, as you will see in subsequent chapters in this book.

This new Keynesian analysis is a way of rationalizing "sticky money wages." Money wages are sticky not because of some mysterious downward rigidity as in Keynes's analysis, but because contractual commitments prevent people from adjusting money wages in the light of new information. In effect, workers and firms have said to each other, "These are the terms on which we are willing to do business *come what may* until the next time we sit down two years from now."

There is a lively debate in the current literature concerning the efficiency of the labor market contracts that the new Keynesian economists use in their theory of aggregate supply. New classical economists such as Robert Barro insist that such contracts are inefficient and cannot be rationalized as the kinds of contracts that rational profit-maximizing and utility-maximizing agents would enter into.[3] The new Keynesians agree that it is hard to think of convincing reasons why people would enter into contracts such as these. They insist, however, that we do observe such contracts as commonplace, and in the absence of a firm understanding as to why, they argue that we have no alternative but to incorporate them into our macroeconomic analysis.

Summary

A. Assumptions of the New Keynesian Analysis

There are four key assumptions of the new Keynesian analysis:
  (1) Money wages are set for an agreed period and do not continuously adjust.
  (2) The actual quantity of labor traded is determined by the quantity demanded.
  (3) Money wages are set so as to achieve equality between the expected supply and expected demand for labor.
  (4) Wage contracts last for a longer term than the frequency with which the economy is hit by shocks and overlap in time.

B. Determination of Money Wages

Money wages are determined in the new Keynesian theory of aggregate supply by equating the supply of labor that is expected on the basis of the expected price level with the demand for labor that is expected on the basis of the expected price level. Figure 16.1 illustrates this relationship and should be thoroughly understood.

---

[3] Robert J. Barro, "Long-Term Contracting, Sticky Prices, and Monetary Policy," *Journal of Monetary Economics*, 3 (July 1977), 305-16.

C. New Keynesian Expectations-Augmented Aggregate Supply Curve

The new Keynesian theory of wage determination implies that the expectations-augmented aggregate supply curve will have the same basic shape as the new classical expectations-augmented aggregate supply curve. The new Keynesian aggregate supply curve will, however, be flatter than the new classical curve. This arises because, when the demand for labor function shifts because of changes in the actual price level, there are no partially compensating adjustments in the money wage rate to dampen off some of the effects of the shift in demand function on the quantity demanded. The quantity of labor demanded adjusts fully to reflect shifts in the demand function at the fixed money wage, and the level of output therefore fluctuates by a larger amount than otherwise would be the case.

D. Overlapping Wage Contracts

The fact that not all labor market contracts are signed on the same date, but overlap each other, has fundamental implications for the aggregate supply curve. Instead of the position of the aggregate supply curve depending only on *current* expectations of the price level, it will also depend on previous expectations of the current period's price level. Expectations formed in the past and now known to be wrong will be embodied in the position of the Keynesian expectations-augmented aggregate supply curve.

Review Questions

1. What are the four key assumptions of the new Keynesian theory of the labor market?

2. Why is the new Keynesian expectations-augmented aggregate supply curve flatter than the new classical curve?

3. Why do the new Keynesian, new classical, and the classical aggregate supply curves all intersect at full-employment output and the expected price level?

4. The new Keynesian theory of the labor market assumes that households can be "off" their supply curves. How might firms induce households to behave in such a way? Could households be induced to be permanently "off" their supply curves?

5. What are the implications of overlapping labor market contracts?

6. An economy is described by the following equations: the marginal product of labor is described by the equation

$$MP = 5 - 5n$$

The supply of labor is given by

$$n^s = W/P$$

(a) What is the equilibrium level of employment and the real wage, given complete information? That is, what is the full-employment equilibrium?

(b) If the production function is $y = 5n - 2.5n^2$, calculate and plot an equation for the new classical expectations-augmented aggregate supply curve, assuming that the expected price level is unity.

(c) Calculate and plot an equation for the new Keynesian expectations-augmented aggregate supply curve assuming that the expected price level is unity. (*Hint:* Try actual price levels of 1/2, 1, and 2 for the purpose of this exercise.)

17
Equilibrium with Fixed Expectations

You are now getting to the point at which you can pull together the various strands in the macroeconomic theory that you have been studying. In Chapters 8 through 13 you have studied the theory of aggregate demand. In the last three chapters you have studied three alternative approaches to the theory of aggregate supply. We are now going to take the next natural step and study macroeconomic equilibrium. In studying macroeconomic equilibrium we are going to work on the presumption that one of the two "new" theories of aggregate supply is the relevant one. That is, we shall study equilibrium in an economy in which the expected price level is not always equal to the actual price level so that the aggregate supply curve is of either the new classical or new Keynesian variety.

Throughout this and the next two chapters which deal with the predictions and policy implications of rational expectations models, the analysis will be conducted for an economy whose trend inflation rate is zero. This is a convenient simplification which makes it possible to conduct all the analysis in diagrammatic terms. It is not a limitation of the analysis. The theories that are to be reviewed are equally applicable at *any* trend rate of inflation. You may therefore conveniently regard the analysis presented as representing deviations from the trend rate of inflation. Thus, when we talk about a rise in the price level or a fall in the price level you may, provided you are careful to remember what is going on, interpret that as a temporary rise in the inflation rate above its trend or a temporary fall in inflation below its trend. In making that interpretation you need to be constantly on guard to maintain the sharp analytical distinction introduced earlier concerning the difference between inflation and a once-and-for-all change in the price level.

This chapter employs the expectations-augmented aggregate supply curve and analyzes what happens when aggregate demand changes but the expected price level is fixed. However, before embarking on this analysis, there are two preliminary tasks that need attention. Overall, then, you have four tasks in this chapter, which are to:

a) Know the definition of *full-employment equlibrium*.
b) Know how to characterize full-employment equilibrium in a simple diagram.
c) Understand how output, employment, the real wage, the price level, and the money wage are affected by a rise or fall in aggregate demand when the expected price level is fixed.
d) Understand how output, employment, the real wage, the price level, and the money wage are affected by a rise or fall in the expected price level when aggregate demand is fixed.

A. Full-Employment Equilibrium

Full-employment equilibrium is a situation in which the actual price level is equal to the expected price level. The full-employment equilibrium levels of output, employment, and the real wage are the levels of those variables that occur when the actual price level is equal to the expected price level.

Although the name *full-employment equilibrium* is used to describe a situation in which the price level is equal to the expected price level, this does not mean that there is no unemployment in full-employment equilibrium. This may seem like a contradiction of terms, but it really is nothing more than a convenient use of language. In Chapter 21 we shall study in some detail a variety of factors that can give rise to unemployment. Such things as minimum wages that raise the economy average real wage above the equilibrium real wage, or an economy-wide labor union that raises the real wage above the equilibrium real wage, or the presence of generous unemployment insurance benefits, or unusually large reallocations of labor across sectors or regions will be shown to be factors that could generate unemployment — and sizeable amounts of it. Such unemployment is sometimes called *natural unemployment*. At full-employment equilibrium, the unemployment rate is equal to the natural unemployment rate.

As a matter of definition, then, when the unemployment rate is equal to the natural unemployment rate, the term *full employment* is used to describe the condition of the labor market.

In what follows in the rest of this and the next two chapters, the analysis abstracts from the natural rate of unemployment. That does not mean that the natural rate of unemployment is ignored or assumed not to exist. Rather, the analysis will be thought of as determining the level of unemployment relative to the natural rate of unemployment. In the formal analysis, the natural rate of unemployment will be treated as if it was zero. That is only an analytical convenience. The reason for making this abstraction is that the natural unemployment rate itself is not affected by the factors that are being considered. Conversely, the natural unemployment rate does not affect the factors that will be considered. It is possible, therefore, to analyze fluctuations of unemployment around the natural rate independently of what the natural rate of unemployment is.

To summarize: full-employment equilibrium values of real income, employment, and the real wage occur when the price level is equal to its expected level. There will be some unemployment in that situation, determined by the real factors (that will be discussed in Chapter 21) that determine the natural rate of unemployment.

B. A Simple Diagram to Characterize Full-Employment Equilibrium

It is important to characterize full-employment equilibrium before moving on to analyzing the effects of a change in the money supply on the levels of output, employment, and prices. Figure 17.1 illustrates a full-employment equilibrium, and the text in this section guides you through that figure.

Notice that the diagram is similar to Figures 14.6 and 15.3. Frame (a) shows the labor market with the money wage on the vertical axis and employment on the horizontal axis. Frame (b) shows the production function — the relationship between the maximum amount of output that can be supplied and the level of employment. Frame (c) shows the aggregate goods market with aggregate demand and aggregate supply for goods plotted against the price level.

First, pretend that there are no curves in frame (a) at all. Instead of using frame (a), recall the diagram for the labor market that was employed in the classical theory of aggregate supply [frame (a) of Figure 14.6]. You will recall that in that frame, we plotted the level of employment against the *real* wage. Where the supply of labor curve cuts the demand for labor curve, the equilibrium real wage and the level of employment are determined. Let us suppose that the level of employment determined in that frame is the value n^* plotted on the horizontal axis of frame (a) of Figure 17.1. That is, we have determined n^* from the classical analysis of Chapter 14.

You can now determine the level of output that will be produced with the level of employment n^*. Following the dotted line from frame

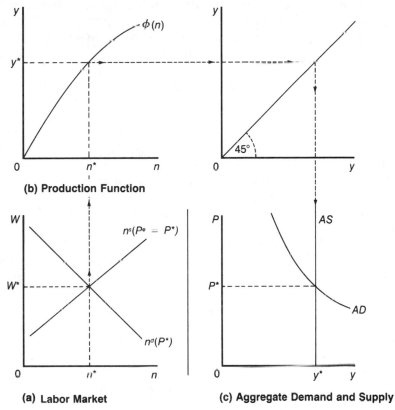

(b) Production Function

(a) Labor Market

(c) Aggregate Demand and Supply

**Figure 17.1
Full-Employment
Equilibrium**

Where the aggregate demand curve cuts the classical aggregate supply curve [frame (c)] determines the full-employment equilibrium price level P^*. When the supply of labor and demand for labor curves are plotted in frame (a) against the money wage for an actual and expected price level of P^*, they intersect at the full-employment level of employment n^* and determine the full-employment level of money wage W^*.

(a) to frame (b), you see that the level of output associated with n^* is equal to y^*. Transferring this level of output (following the dotted line) to the aggregate supply and demand diagram [frame (c)] generates the classical aggregate supply curve shown as the vertical line labelled *AS*.

From the *IS-LM* analysis of aggregate demand (recall Chapter 13), we may obtain the aggregate demand curve. This is shown in frame (c) as the curve labelled *AD*. Where the aggregate demand and aggregate supply curves intersect determines the equilibrium price level P^*.

Now that the equilibrium price level P^* has been determined, it is possible to work backwards to determine the equilibrium money wage. This could not have been done before determining the equilibrium price level because you would not have known where in frame (a) to plot the labor supply and demand curves. Recall that although these curves are fixed when graphed against the real wage, they shift with the price level when plotted against the money wage. The demand for labor curve depends on the actual price level, and we can draw this as the curve labelled $n^d(P^*)$. This is the demand for labor curve plotted against the money wage rate when the price level is equal to the equilibrium price level P^*. The supply of labor curve is plotted against the expected price level.

Since the diagram is characterizing full-employment equilibrium, the supply of labor curve is drawn for an expected price level equal to the actual price level, which in turn is equal to P^*. The labor supply curve is shown as the curve labelled $n^s(P^e = P^*)$. This supply curve cuts the demand curve at the level of employment n^*. This follows directly from the fact that the demand and supply curves are fixed when plotted against the real wage and shift proportionately to each other as the price level varies when plotted against the money wage. It follows that if the supply and demand curves are plotted against the money wage, but for the same price level, then these curves must cut at the full-employment level of employment n^*.

You can now read off, finally, the money wage that is associated with an equilibrium in the labor market at the given actual and expected price level P^*. This money wage is denoted in frame (a) as W^*.

This completes the characterization of full-employment equilibrium.

C. Effects of a Change in Aggregate Demand with a Fixed Expected Price Level

Suppose that the expected price level P^e is equal to P^* and is fixed at that value. In the next chapter we shall inquire what determines the expected price level and how it might change. It will be clearer, however, if we proceed in steps, and the first step is to examine what happens to the levels of output, employment, and unemployment, the real wage, and the price level when the economy experiences a change in aggregate demand but the expected price level does not change.

(i) The Expectations-Augmented Aggregate Supply Curve

The starting point for the analysis is the expectations-augmented aggregate supply curve discussed at length in the previous two chapters. Either the new Keynesian or new classical version of the *EAS* curve could be employed. The treatment here uses the new classical version. You may find it a useful exercise to carry out a parallel exercise using the new Keynesian version. Figure 17.2 summarizes the derivation of the new classical aggregate supply curve. You will recall that the supply of labor curve shown in frame (a) depends on the expected price level. Since the expected price level is being held constant at P^*, the supply of labor curve is $n^s(P^e = P^*)$. You will also recall that the demand for labor curve depends on the *actual* value of the price level. The demand curve labelled $n^d(P^*)$ is drawn for a level of prices equal to P^*. Where that curve intersects the supply of labor curve determines the full-employment equilibrium money wage W^* and employment level n^*. The production function in frame (b) shows that the employment level n^* will produce a level of output

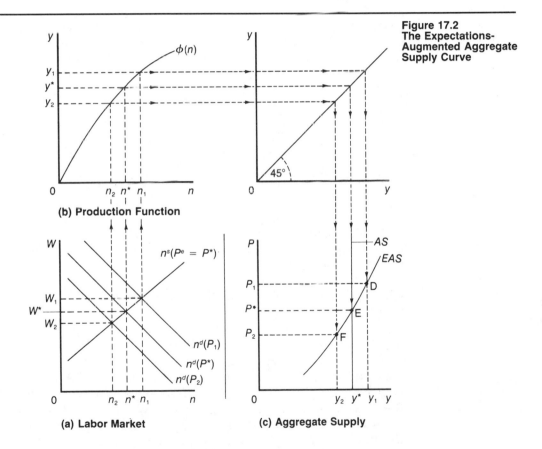

Figure 17.2
The Expectations-Augmented Aggregate Supply Curve

(b) Production Function

(a) Labor Market

(c) Aggregate Supply

As the actual price level varies between P_1 and P_2 [frame (c)], the demand for labor curve shifts between $n^d(P_1)$ and $n^d(P_2)$ [frame (a)]. With the expected price level fixed at P^*, the supply of labor curve does not shift. In frame (a) equilibrium employment and the money wage vary between n_1 and n_2 and W_1 and W_2, generating output fluctuations between y_1 and y_2 [frame (b)]. Thus, as the price level moves from P_1 to P_2, output moves from y_1 to y_2 along the curve *EAS*.

equal to y^*. Following the dotted line from frame (b) to frame (c), you arrive at point A, which represents the full-employment equilibrium point where P^*, the actual price level, is equal to the expected price level.

If the price level being considered is at a higher value than P^*, say P_1, as shown on the vertical axis of frame (c), then you have to replot the demand for labor curve, showing it to have shifted upwards. This is shown as $n^d(P_1)$ in frame (a). This determines a new higher money wage and employment level (W_1 and n_1) and, through frame (b), a higher level of output y_1. If this output level is transferred (following the dotted line) to frame (c), we see that at the price level P_1, the output level will be y_1 and the economy will operate at the point marked B.

Now consider the price level as being less than P^*, say, at P_2, as marked on the vertical axis of frame (c). In this case, the labor demand curve has to be shifted downwards. This is shown as $n^d(P_2)$ in frame (a). This labor demand curve intersects the fixed labor supply curve to determine the lower money wage and employment levels W_2 and n_2. At the employment level n_2, the economy will produce an output level of y_2. Transferring the output level y_2 (following the dotted line) to frame (c) shows us that the economy will produce at the point marked C where the price level is P_2 and the output level is y_2. Joining up all the points C, A, and B generates the expectations-augmented aggregate supply curve marked *EAS*.

Now that your knowledge of the expectations-augmented aggregate supply curve has been reviewed, it is a very simple matter to see how changes in aggregate demand affect output, employment and unemployment, the real wage, and the price level. First of all, the effects on prices and output will be considered and then subsequently the effects on the labor market.

(ii) The Effects of a Change in Aggregate Demand on Output and the Price Level

Figure 17.3 summarizes the effects of a change in aggregate demand on the price level and output. The starting point, A, is a full-employment equilibrium. Here the price level, P^*, and output level, y^*, are determined by the intersection of the aggregate demand curve, AD^*, and the aggregate supply curve, AS, as well as by the intersection of the expectations-augmented aggregate supply curve, EAS. The point A is the full-employment equilibrium as defined above, in the sense that the expected price level that underlies the EAS curve equals the actual price level P^*.

Hold the expected price level constant at P^* and ask what happens if the level of aggregate demand changes. You can think of aggregate demand changing because of a change in the money supply, government spending or taxes, or there is a shift in the demand for investment goods.

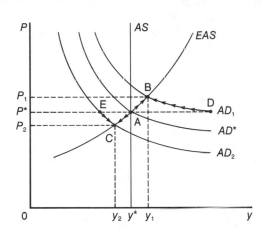

Figure 17.3
The Effects of a
Change in Aggregate
Demand with Fixed
Price Level Expectations

If the expected price level is fixed at P^*, the *EAS* curve does not move. When aggregate demand is AD^*, the actual price level is P^*, and the economy is at full employment. If aggregate demand rises to AD_1, the equilibrium is at point B with a higher price level and output level (P_1, y_1). If aggregate demand falls to AD_2, then the price level and output fall to P_2 and y_2 at point C. Fluctuations in aggregate demand when the expected price level is constant produce procyclical movements in output and the price level.

Depending on which of these shocks occur, the rate of interest, which is simultaneously determined with the variables being considered here, will either rise or fall. It is a fairly straightforward matter to work out the implications for the rate of interest by going back to the *IS-LM* analysis of Chapter 13.

Suppose that for whatever of the above reasons, the aggregate demand curve shifts from AD^* to AD_1. It is clear that with this new higher level of aggregate demand, there is only one point where the economy can come to an equilibrium, and that is the point marked B. At point B, output is y_1, and the price level is P_1.

How does this new equilibrium point B come about? The economy started out in the full-employment equilibrium at point A and then that aggregate demand suddenly increased from AD^* to AD_1. At the new higher level of aggregate demand, but with the price level remaining at P^*, there would be an excess demand for goods equivalent to the distance AD in Figure 17.3. This excess demand would generate rising prices, as people who sought to increase their purchases of goods and services would find it necessary to offer higher prices in order to acquire the goods that they were demanding. As the price level was forced upwards, the quantity of goods demanded would decline. This is shown in Figure 17.3 by the arrows moving up the expectations-augmented aggregate demand curve.

There would also be a response on the supply side of the economy. As the prices of some goods began to increase, firms, being well informed about the markets in which they operate and observing the rising price of their output, would start to increase their supply of goods and services. With a fixed expected price level the economy slides up the expectations-augmented aggregate supply curve from A to B, as shown by the arrows in Figure 17.3. As the price level increases, excess aggregate demand is choked off, and the economy comes to rest at point B, with firms satisfied that they are supplying the profit-maximizing quantity and households satisfied that they are buying the right quantity of goods.

Next, consider what would happen if aggregate demand falls. Specifically, suppose aggregate demand falls from AD^* to AD_2. This aggregate demand curve cuts the expectations-augmented aggregate supply curve at C. This is the new equilibrium point, with the price level P_2 and y_2. To see how this equilibrium comes about, perform a conceptual experiment similar to that which you have just performed in the case of a rise in aggregate demand. The price level is initially at P^* and aggregate demand falls to AD_2. In such a case, there is a cutback in demand, and there is an excess of supply over demand equal to the distance AE in Figure 17.3. This excess supply causes prices to fall. As prices begin to fall, firms reduce their supply of goods and services. As the expected price level remains constant the economy travels down along the expectations-augmented aggregate supply curve from A to C, as shown by the arrows. As the price level falls, households move along their demand curves, resulting in a movement along the aggregate demand curve from E to C. At point C there is a balance between supply and demand, and there is no further tendency for the price level or the level of output to change.

Although the above analysis was not explicit as to which theory of aggregate supply generated the expectations-agumented aggregate supply curve, the same broad predictions are generated in both the new classical and the new Keynesian cases. However, the amounts by which output and the price level move is different in each case. In the new Keynesian case the output movements are greater and the price level movements less than in the new classical case. You can easily verify this by checking back to the comparison of the new Keynesian and new classical expectations-augmented aggregate supply curves. Since the Keynesian curve is flatter than the classical curve, swings in aggregate demand have bigger output and smaller price level effects in the new Keynesian case than in the new classical case.

(iii) Key Assumption of Equilibrium Analysis

We assume that the equilibrating processes just described that move the economy from position A to position B when aggregate demand rises and from position A to position C when aggregate demand falls occur quickly enough for points A, B, and C to be the only points observed.

(iv) Summary of Effects of a Change in Aggregate Demand on Output and Price Level

We can now summarize the effects of a rise or fall in aggregate demand on output and the price level:

1. If the expected price level is constant and aggregate demand rises, then output and the price level will both rise.
2. If the expected price level is constant and aggregate demand falls, then output and the price level will both fall.

(v) Effects of a Change in Aggregate Demand on Employment and Wages

The effects on the level of employment and unemployment, the money wage, and the real wage will now be analyzed. Because of the way in which the aggregate demand experiment has been set up, these effects can immediately be read off by referring back to Figure 17.2.

First, consider the case of a rise in aggregate demand. This moves the economy, as you saw in Figure 17.3, to position B. Position B is also shown in Figure 17.2, so that you can easily see the effects on the labor market. At the price level P_1, which is the consequence of a rise in aggregate demand to AD_1, the demand for labor curve will shift to the right and be in the position shown as $n^d(P_1)$. This produces a higher money wage, W_1, and a higher employment level, n_1. It also produces a lower real wage. The real wage falls because the money wage rises by less than the rise in the price level. (Refer back to Chapter 15, Figure 15.1, and the associated discussion if you cannot see that this is true.) Indeed, it is the fall in the real wage that induces a higher level of employment. Firms, seeing that the real wage has fallen, find it profitable to hire additional workers. Households, on the other hand, having a fixed expectation of the price level, think that the real wage has increased and therefore are willing to supply more labor. The rise in employment lowers the level of unemployment to below the natural rate.

Next, consider the case of a cut in aggregate demand. If aggregate demand is cut to the curve AD_2, it will intersect the expectations-augmented aggregate supply curve at point C in Figure 17.3. Point C is also shown in frame (c) of Figure 17.2. You can see that at this price level, the demand for labor curve is shown as $n^d(P_2)$, and the equilibrium levels of the money wage and employment are W_2 and n_2. Thus a cut in aggregate demand leads to a cut in the money wage and in the level of employment. In this situation, real wages will have increased. This occurs because the price level will have fallen by more than the money wage has fallen. Firms, knowing this, will cut back on their demand for labor. Households will not resist this cutback in the demand for labor because as far as they are concerned, the real wage that they expect to receive has fallen. This arises because the money wage has fallen while the expected price level has remained constant. The fall in the level of employment produces a rise in the level of unemployment to above the natural rate.

Although the above effects have been stated in terms of the new classical theory, similar effects occur in the new Keynesian case. The key difference between the two is that in the new Keynesian case, households are knocked off the supply of labor curve. When aggregate demand increases to AD_1, the money wage remains constant, the price level rises, and the real wage falls. This induces an increase in the demand for labor that is not matched by an increase in the supply of labor. Nevertheless, workers, because of the assumed nature of the contract they have with their employers, are required to supply the extra labor even though this is in excess of their labor supply.

In the reverse case, when aggregate demand falls to AD_2, workers are knocked off their supply curves in the opposite direction. In this case, the price level falls, so that with a fixed money wage, the real wage rises, thereby lowering the demand for labor. Firms now hire less labor than would like to work.

In the new Keynesian case, the money wage is fixed and so the change in the real wage resulting from a change in the price level is always larger than that in the new classical case where any price level change is accompanied by a change in the money wage, in the same direction. Since the fluctuations of the real wage in these two cases are different, so too are the fluctuations in employment and unemployment. These fluctuations are also larger in the new Keynesian case than in the new classical case.

(vi) Summary of the Effects of a Change in Aggregate Demand with a Constant Expected Price Level

To summarize, the effects of a rise in aggregate demand with a fixed expected price level are as follows:

(1) With a fixed expected price level, a rise in aggregate demand will raise output, raise the price level, raise the level of employment, and lower the real wage. Unemployment will fall below the natural rate of unemployment.

(2) With a fixed expected price level, a cut in aggregate demand will lower the level of output, lower the price level, lower the level of employment, and raise real wages. It will also create unemployment in excess of the natural rate of unemployment.

This completes the formal analysis of the effects of a change in aggregate demand on the levels of output, employment, the real wage, and the price level — when price expectations are fixed.

Although positions B and C (Figure 17.3) in this economy are equilibrium positions, they differ from equilibrium A in a fundamental respect. That is, they cannot be sustained forever, whereas position A can. To see why they cannot be sustained forever takes us into a discussion of how expectations are formed and changed, and this will be the subject of the next chapter. Before turning to that, however, let us deal with the final task of this chapter.

D. Effects of a Change in the Expected Price Level with Constant Aggregate Demand

Although the title of this chapter is "Equilibrium with Fixed Expectations," it will be useful if we analyze what happens to output, employment, unemployment and the real wage if the expected price level changes when aggregate demand is constant. Let us start the economy out at full-employment equilibrium such as that depicted by P^* for the price level and y^* for output, in Figure 17.4. These points lie at the intersection of the aggregate demand curve, AD, and the expectations-augmented aggregate supply curve, EAS, and are also on the aggregate supply curve, AS. The expected price level evidently is P^*, the same as the actual price level.

Hold the level of aggregate demand constant at AD, but now imagine that the expected price level for some reason rises to P_1^e. What are the effects of such a change? You already know that lying behind the

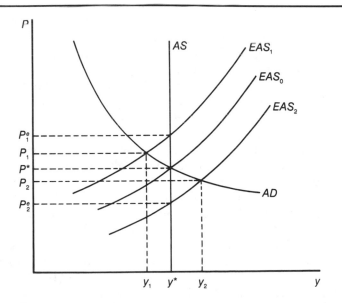

Figure 17.4
The Effects of a Change in the Expected Price Level with Constant Aggregate Demand

If aggregate demand is fixed, then the AD curve does not move. When the expected price level rises, the EAS curve moves to EAS_1, so that the price level rises to P_1, and output falls to y_1. If the expected price level falls to P_2^e, the actual price level falls to P_2, and output rises to y_2. Changes in the expected price level with constant aggregate demand lead to countercyclical movements in output and the price level.

EAS curve is a supply of labor curve that itself depends on the expected price level. A rise in the expected price level shifts the supply of labor curve upwards and by the same percentage amount as the rise in the expected price level. This in turn shifts the *EAS* curve upwards to become the curve labelled EAS_1 in Figure 17.4. We know this because we know that the *EAS* curve cuts the *AS* curve at the expected price level. The new *EAS* curve intersects the fixed *AD* curve at the price level P_1 and the output y_1. This position is the equilibrium when the expected price level is P_1^e and aggregate demand is given by the curve *AD*. In this situation, the economy is producing less than its full-employment output level. The actual price level is below the expected price level. Notice that this situation (P_1, y_1) in Figure 17.4 is comparable to point C in Figure 17.3.

Returning to Figure 17.4, let us next suppose that the expected price level was to fall from P^* to P_2^e. In this case, the *EAS* curve shifts downwards to become the curve labelled EAS_2. Again, we know this because the *EAS* curve cuts the *AS* curve at the expected price level. As before we shall hold the level of aggregate demand constant at *AD*. The new *EAS* curve cuts the *AD* curve at the price level P_2 and output level y_2. In this situation output is higher than full-employment, and the price level has fallen relative to P^* but is now above its expected level. This equilibrium $(P_2, y_2$ in Figure 17.4) is comparable to position B in Figure 17.3.

You will now be able to see some clear similarities in, but also some important differences between, the effects of a change in aggregate demand when the expected price level is constant and the effects of a change in the expected price level when aggregate demand is constant. The similarities are these: only when the expected price level and actual price level are equal to each other is the economy at full employment. If the actual price level is below the expected price level, then output is below its full-employment level. This can come about either because of a rise in the expected price level with constant aggregate demand or because of a drop in aggregate demand with a constant expected price level. In the opposite case, if the actual price level is greater than the expected price level, then output will be above its full-employment level. This can arise either because of a rise in aggregate demand with a constant expected price level, or because of a fall in the expected price level with a constant level of aggregate demand. The differences between the two experiments in the preceding section and this one are the following: a rise in aggregate demand with a fixed expected price level raises both output and the price level, and a fall in aggregate demand lowers both output and the price level, so that output and prices move in the same direction as each other. That is, movements in output and the price level and procyclical. A change in the expected price level with a constant level of aggregate demand leads to changes in output and in the price level that move in opposite directions to each other. That is, movements in output and the price level are counter-cyclical.

Aside from these differences in the directions of movement of output and prices between the two cases, all other properties of the equilibria analysed are the same. The detailed story concerning how the economy moves from one position to another, told in the previous section, applies with equal force here.

The analysis of the effects of a change in price level expectations on real wages and other labor market variables are easy to figure out. You know that anything that lowers output below its equilibrium level must also lower employment. You also know that anything that lowers employment must also raise the real wage. From this you can immediately figure out that a rise in the expected price level must lead to a rise in the money wage that exceeds the rise in the price level, and a drop in the expected price level must cut the money wage by more than the cut in the price level.

We also know, however, if the labor market is to be in equilibrium (continuing to operate with the new classical model), that anything that lowers the equilibrium level of output and employment must lower the expected real wage. Conversely, anything that raises output above its full-employment level must raise the expected real wage. From this we can immediately figure out that a rise in the expected price level must raise the money wage by more than it raises the actual price level, but by less than it raises the expected price level. The effect of this is to raise the actual real wage but lower the expected real wage. Conversely, a cut in the expected price level must lower the money wage by more than it lowers the price level, but by less than the amount by which the expected price level falls. In this case, the actual real wage falls, but the expected real wage rises.

You have now seen how changes in aggregate demand affect output and prices when the expected price level is constant and, also, how *changes* in the *expected* price level affect the *actual* price level as well as the level of output. Evidently, expectations of the price level are of crucial importance in influencing the behavior both of the actual price level and other real variables in the economy. It is the task of the next chapter to investigate more thoroughly how expectations of the price level are themselves formed and what factors lead to changes in those expectations.

Summary

A. Full-Employment Equilibrium

Full-employment equilibrium values of output, employment, unemployment, and the real wage occur when the expected price level is equal to the actual price level. The unemployment present at full-employment equilibrium is called the *natural rate of unemployment*.

B. A Simple Diagram to Characterize Full-Employment Equilibrium

Figure 17.1 is a diagram of full-employment equilibrium, and you should be thoroughly familiar with it.

C. Effects of a Change in Aggregate Demand with Fixed Expected Price level

If the expected price level is fixed, a rise in aggregate demand raises the level of output, employment, and the price level. It also lowers the real wage and makes unemployment fall below its natural rate. When the expected price level is fixed and aggregate demand falls, there is a fall in output, in employment, and in the price level. The real wage rises, and unemployment rises above its natural rate.

A rise in aggregate demand when the expected price level is fixed produces procyclical movements in output and the price level.

D. Effects of a Change in the Expected Price Level with Constant Aggregate Demand

If aggregate demand is fixed, a rise in the expected price level raises the actual price level but by less than the expected price level increases, and it lowers output. Real wages and unemployment rise, and employment falls. Money wages rise by more than the price level but by less than the expected price level. When aggregate demand is fixed and the expected price level falls, the actual price level falls, and output rises. The fall in the actual price level is less than the fall in the expected price level. Real wages fall, but expected real wages rise. Unemployment also falls below its natural rate.

A rise in the expected price level when aggregate demand is fixed produces counter-cyclical movements in output and the price level.

Review Questions

1. Define *full-employment equilibrium*.

2. Explain why there will be some unemployment at full-employment equilibrium.

3. Define the *natural unemployment rate*. Is the natural unemployment rate affected by the price level? Why or why not? Explain.

4. Characterize full-employment equilibrium in a diagram like that shown in Figure 17.1.

5. Consider Figure 17.2. Suppose the expected price level was to rise to P_1. What would happen to the *EAS* curve? Draw a new curve to illustrate your answer.

6. Why does the *EAS* curve slope upwards?

7. What happens to the levels of: (a) output, (b) employment, (c) unemployment, (d) the money wage, (e) the real wage, and (f) the price level if the money supply rises but the expected price level remains constant?

8. What happens to all the variables listed in (a) to (f) of Question 7 if the expected price level falls, while the money supply remains constant?

9. What happens to all the variables listed in (a) to (f) of Question 7 if both the expected price level and aggregate demand rise by the *same* percentage amount?

10. Review the following terms or concepts: *rational maximizing behavior* and *full-employment equilibrium*.

18

Price Level Expectations

We saw, when we examined the connection between real and market interest rates, the importance of the *expected* rate of inflation. We have also seen, in the new theories of aggregate supply that the expected price level plays a crucial role in influencing the behavior of the economy. So far, however, we have made no attempt to explain where the expected price level, or the expected rate of inflation, comes from or what causes it to change. It is certain that both the expected price level and the expected rate of inflation do change and it is clear, therefore, that we need a theory of expectations.

Not only does the *expected* inflation rate or *expected* price level play an important role in our theory of macroeconomics, it also is featured in much of the more popular (if imprecise) discussions on inflation. We often hear, for example, that there is an "inflation psychology" that is considered to be one of the major causes of inflation.

Thus, both in our theory and in popular discussion, the role played by expectations is central. The time has come to examine the determination of expectations more closely, and to move beyond the assumption that they are exogenous. The two central questions that this chapter deals with are, what determines the expected price level, and what factors lead to changes in the expected price level? You are going to discover that, paradoxical though it may seem, there is no rational basis for a view that inflation can be *caused* by an "inflation psychology" — by inflation expectations. Rather, the very things which generate inflation also generate inflation expectations. The chapter is organized around six tasks, which are to:

a) Understand the relationship between the expected price level and expected rate of inflation.
b) Understand the distinction between a subjective expectation and a conditional mathematical expectation.
c) Understand why wrong expectations are costly.
d) Understand the concept of a rational expectation.
e) Understand the concept of the rational expectation of the price level.
f) Know how to work out the rational expectation of the price level.

A. The Expected Price Level and Expected Rate of Inflation

You are already familiar with the distinction between inflation and the price level. You know that inflation is the percentage rate of change in the price level. You also know that in the analysis that we are doing in this chapter, we are abstracting from inflation. That is, we are conducting an analysis that presumes that the average rate of inflation is zero. This means that the price level is fluctuating around some constant value. Nevertheless, even though we are abstracting from inflation, it is important that you know the connection between the expected rate of inflation and the expected price level. That connection follows directly from the definition of actual inflation and its relation to the actual price level. Equation 18.1 defines the rate of inflation (π) at a particular point in time (t) as:

$$\pi_t = \left(\frac{P_t - P_{t-1}}{P_{t-1}} \right) \times 100 \tag{18.1}$$

Here, P_t is the price level at date t, and P_{t-1} is the price level at day $t - 1$. The rate of inflation at t is the change in prices from $t - 1$ to t, expressed as a percentage of the prices that prevailed at the previous point in time. For example, if the previous price level was 95 and the current price level is 100, the rate of inflation will be given by

$$\pi_t = \left(\frac{100 - 95}{95} \right) \times 100$$

$$= 5.2\%$$

The expected rate of inflation and the expected price level are related to each other by an equation similar to the above, that is,

$$\pi_t^e = \left(\frac{P_t^e - P_{t-1}}{P_{t-1}} \right) \times 100 \tag{18.2}$$

This says that the expected rate of inflation is equal to the expected price level minus the previous period's price level, expressed as a percentage of the previous period's price level. As before, suppose the previous period's price level was 95, but the expected price level is 99. Then,

$$\pi_t^e = \left(\frac{99 - 95}{95} \right) \times 100$$

$$= 4.2\%$$

Notice that the expected rate of inflation is the expected percentage change in the price level and not the percentage change in the expected price level. In fact, the change in the expected price level is not a very interesting concept. You could calculate the change in the expected price level if you wished. It would be this period's expected price level minus the previous period's expected price level, expressed as a percentage of that previous period's expected price level.

It is clear from the above that there is a close connection between the expected inflation rate and the expected price level. The key thing to note for current purposes is that in order to calculate the expected inflation rate, you need to calculate the expected price level. It is expectations about the price level that we shall focus on in the rest of this chapter. We are going to get to that, however, by a slightly roundabout route and shall not reach a good understanding of how the expected price level is determined until later in this chapter.

Let us now begin the first of three preliminary tasks that will lead us to an understanding of how price level expectations are formed.

B. The Distinction Between a Subjective Expectation and a Conditional Mathematical Expectation

(i) Subjective Expectation

The term *expectation* has two distinct meanings. In ordinary speech it is used to describe a more or less *vague feeling* about some future event. This is a subjective expectation. For example, we might be planning to travel by car along a congested highway and expect that it will take an hour to complete our journey, or we might be planning to travel by bus and expect the bus to be running 10 minutes behind schedule because of bad weather. Another example concerns the expectations of a skilled pool player. Such a person might have an expectation as to what will happen when the cue is aligned in a particular direction and applied to the cue ball with a particular direction of spin and force. That expectation may be, for example, that the second ball is dispatched to the center-right pocket and that the cue ball comes to rest lined up for an easy next shot.

Typically, we do not explicitly analyze the reasons why we hold the expectations that we do. We have subjective feelings which, on the average, seem to be right, and we do not consciously examine the sources of these feelings. The pool player, for example, does not ask himself from where his expectation comes. He simply knows how to play the game and uses a well-developed instinct and skill to achieve the appropriate movements of the balls.

A subjective expectation, then, is simply a feeling that an individual has about the likely consequences of some particular action or as to the likely outcome of some particular event.

(ii) Conditional Mathematical Expectation

There is a more precise usage of the term expectation — a conditional mathematical expectation. A mathematical expectation is nothing other than an *average*. An example will make it easy to understand this. Suppose we have 3000 cards: 1000 of them are printed with the number 4 on one side, another 1000 with the number 5, and another 1000 with the number 6. These cards are put into a bag and are shaken up so that they are thoroughly mixed. Then, 300 cards are drawn from the bag at random. You are asked to predict what the average of the numbers drawn will be. You know that there are three kinds of cards in the bag, and that one-third of them have the number 4, one-third have the number 5, and one-third the number 6. Since the cards have been shuffled very thoroughly and they have been drawn at random, you will predict that, on the average, out of 300 cards drawn, 100 will have the number 4, 100 the number 5, and 100 the number 6. You calculate the average of this and you arrive at a prediction that the average of all the cards drawn will be 5. You have just calculated a mathematical expectation.

A conditional mathematical expectation is a mathematical expectation calculated when some information is already given. For example, suppose in the numbered card game described above, you were told that of the 300 cards drawn, 200 were numbered 6. (This would be an improbable, although possible, outcome.) You are now asked to predict the average value of all 300 cards drawn. You know that there are as many 4's as 5's in the bag, so you will expect that, of the remaining cards, 50 will be 4's and 50 will be 5's. The average which you will calculate from 200 6's, 50 4's, and 50 5's is

$$\left(\frac{200}{300}\right) \times 6 + \left(\frac{50}{300}\right) \times 4 + \left(\frac{50}{300}\right) \times 5 = 5.5$$

You have now calculated a conditional mathematical expectation, or more simply, a conditional expectation. You have calculated the expected average value (expected value) of the cards, *given* that 2/3 of them are 6's.

Let us go back to those earlier examples of subjective expectations and see whether we can think of a mathematical expectation interpretation of them.

Consider first of all your car journey along a congested highway. Many factors will determine the number of minutes that it will take for you to arrive at your destination. It will depend on the number of cars on the road ahead of you, whether there are any road works that have closed one or more of the lanes, whether or not there are any accidents blocking the road, and perhaps a thousand other difficult to enumerate things. Suppose, however, that you have travelled this particular part of this highway many times in the past. You have a stock of experience from those previous journeys concerning the length of time that it takes. If you had actually kept a written record of the number of minutes it took each time you went on this particular journey, then you could calculate the average journey time. That calculation would be a mathematical expectation.

You may, however, be able to do better than that. It may be that you know that in certain circumstances the journey is quicker than others. Perhaps you know that if you begin your journey between 8:00 a.m. and 9:00 a.m. or between 5:00 p.m. and 6:00 p.m. it takes longer than if you set out at other times of the day. You might also know that the journey typically takes less time on Tuesdays, Wednesdays, and Thursdays than it does on Mondays and Fridays or that it takes longer in rainy or icy weather than on a sunny day. Given all this extra information, you could calculate the average number of minutes it takes you to complete this particular journey at different times of the day, on different days of the week, in different weather conditions and allowing for other factors that you have noticed affect the outcome. These averages would be conditional expectations. They would be conditional on the information concerning the time of day, day of the week, state of the weather, and so on.

We could tell an identical story concerning the number of minutes that you expect to have to wait for a bus.

In the case of the pool player, if the pool player could solve complicated geometrical problems in a very short span of time in his head and program himself to carry out the instructions implied by those solutions, he could make the cue ball follow exactly the trajectory and with exactly the force required to achieve his objective. This would be a rather complicated mathematical expectation calculation; it would be the calculation of a mathematical expectation of the paths of (at least) two balls. Of course, just as in the case of the numbered cards in the bag, there will be no certainty as to the outcome in any of these examples. Unless we were to pull all 3000 cards from the bag, we would not be able to predict for sure the average value of the cards drawn. Likewise, going back to the car journey example, unless we knew absolutely everything about the conditions of the road ahead of us, we would not be able to make an exact prediction concerning the time which it would take to arrive at our destination. We would, nevertheless, be able to calculate a mathematical expectation. That is, we would be able to calculate the expected value of the relevant variable conditional on all the information available.

C. Why Wrong Expectations Are Costly

Although expectations are sometimes formed purely for fun, so that wrong expectations have very little consequence other than generating mild displeasure or surprise, you will be able to think of many examples, especially those that impinge on economic behavior, where forming a wrong expectation will lead an individual to incur costs that would be better avoided. The costs arising from wrong expectations come in a variety of sizes and forms.

Consider the examples that were introduced in the previous section when we looked at the distinction between subjective and mathematical expectations. Forming an inaccurate assessment of how long a particular journey would take could have a variety of consequences. Suppose that you expected a journey to take one hour, but in fact it turned out to take an hour and a half. It may be that this is of very little consequence, causing you perhaps simply to have a half an hour less time for shopping, sitting on the beach, or doing whatever it is that you are planning to do at the end of your journey. At the other extreme, it could be very costly indeed. It could cause you to miss the departure time of an airplane on which you have a non-refundable ticket, or to miss the beginning of a play or concert. Of course, the more serious the consequences of mis-estimating the length of the journey, the more time you are likely to allow yourself. Even that, however, is not costless. It might involve forcing yourself out of bed at an earlier hour than seems to you ideal, or missing out on some other pleasurable or profitable opportunity.

Next, consider the numbered card game example that we used in the previous section. This is a simplified version of many games that form the backbone of the economy of Las Vegas. Suppose that you are running a casino in that town, and that in the operation of your roulette wheel you offer the same odds on red as on black. You do this because on most roulette wheels the number of red spots and number of black spots are equal, so that there is an equal chance that a ball will land on one color or the other. Further suppose, though, that someone has tampered with your roulette wheel and, in fact, 55 percent of the spots are black and 45 percent are red. Let us further suppose that you did not bother to inspect the wheel too carefully, and are operating on the *expectation* that the wheel is a standard one with half the spots red and half the spots black. It will not be long before astute investors are putting money on the black spots, thereby making an enormous profit and leaving you rushing for a lawyer and seeking to declare bankruptcy.

This is an example which illustrates rather nicely a further important distinction. It is the distinction between being wrong about an *individual event* and being wrong *on the average*. There is no way in which a casino operator can be right about every single event. Sometimes a client gets lucky and wins an enormous amount of money. Events that have a low probability do happen sometimes. It is possible, nevertheless, to avoid being wrong on the average. That is, it is possible to form expectations such that if we took the average of all our expectations over a period of time and compared them with the average of the events that occurred over that same period of time, although each individual event would not have been correctly predicted, on the average, the outcome and the prediction agree. In the case of the casino operator, on the average, black was coming up 55 percent of the time and red was coming up 45 percent of the time. The roulette wheel operator was working on the presumption that the two colors would come up 50 percent of the time each, which meant he was wrong on the average.

There is, of course, nothing we can do about being wrong in the case of individual events. We simply have to take random things as they come. What we can do, however, is to try to avoid being wrong on the average. By so doing we shall minimize the errors that we make in particular cases. We will not eliminate the errors, but we will be reducing their consequences to the smallest possible level.

All the examples of costs that have been discussed above have been in areas other than those with which macroeconomics is centrally concerned. Let us now consider some macroeconomic examples. Expectations have arisen in our model because of their effects on the supply of labor. Suppose a household has formed an expectation of the price level and makes a labor supply decision on the basis of it, and then discovers that the expectation was wrong. If too high a price level was expected, then too low a real wage would have been calculated, and too little work will be done. The household will wind up having consumed more leisure than is now regarded as ideal and will have a lower income to spend on consumption goods than is regarded as ideal. Conversely, if the expectation of the price level was too low, then the calculated real wage would be too high, and the household would wind up doing more work and having a larger income and more consumption goods but less leisure than seems, from the perspective of the individual, ideal.

More important economic examples in terms of costliness of errors arise in the area of capital investment decisions. Firms making multimillion- or even billion-dollar investment decisions have to form expectations about the future demand for particular products, the costs of labor and other inputs. Errors made in such expectations can have enormous costs.

Notice that in the labor supply example (and if we had developed it more fully, the same would apply to the capital investment examples) costs of wrong expectations are symmetric. Expecting a higher price than occurs is just as bad as expecting one that is too low. Also notice that the economic example is like the casino example — one in which it is quite impossible for expectations to be always correct but one in which expectations are correct on the average.

If wrong expectations inflict costs on individuals, it seems reasonable to suppose that they will try to avoid those costs. Of course, the bigger the costs, the harder people will try to avoid making mistakes. We could summarize this by saying they will try to form their expectations rationally.

Let us now go on to apply the ideas of a subjective expectation — a vague feeling about some likely event — and a mathematical expectation — a precise calculation of the expectation of some outcome based on all the information that is relevant and available — and make more precise the concept of a rational expectation.

D. Rational Expectation

(i) Definition

The definition of a rational expectation is as follows.[1] An expectation is said to be rational when the subjective expectation coincides with the conditional mathematical expectation based on all available information. Notice that the definition says that when a mathematical and a subjective expectation coincide, *then* the expectation is rational. It does not say that a rational expectation is arrived at by performing all the complicated calculations which it would be necessary to perform in order to arrive at the appropriate conditional mathematical expectation. As in the example given above, an expectation about the length of time it would take to complete a particular journey would be rational if the expectation arrived at by instinct, intuition, or judgment, based on casual observation, turned out to coincide with the expectation based on a careful and systematic recording of previous experience and on the calculation of a conditional expectation from those data.

An alternative way of thinking about a rational expectation is to regard it as implying the absence of *systematic* error. If people formed expectations that repeatedly and systematically led them astray in an avoidable way, then those expectations would not be rational.

(ii) Some Further Intuition on the Meaning of Rational Expectations

In order to get a better feel for what a rational expectation is, it might be helpful to consider expectations of a particular variable in which man has always been interested, namely, the future state of the weather.

---

[1] The concept of rational expectations presented here is that of John F. Muth, "Rational Expectations and the Theory of Price Movements," *Econometrica*, 29 (July 1961), 315-35. This concept was first introduced into macroeconomics by Robert E. Lucas, Jr. in "Some International Evidence on Output-Inflation Tradeoff," *The American Economic Review*, 63 (September 1973), 326-34.

There are many ways in which we can arrive at an expectation of the future state of the weather. One would be to turn on the appropriate TV channel and read the latest forecasts being put out by the meteorological bureau. Another would be to watch the squirrels and observe how many nuts they are stockpiling. Yet a further method would be to recall the various traditional sayings, such as the proposition about the remaining length of winter and the behavior of groundhogs, or the proposition about March beginning like a lion and ending like a lamb, or vice versa. All of these would be methods of forming a view about some future state of the weather.

At the present time and in the present state of knowledge, it is clear that the rational expectation of the future state of the weather is obtained by employing the first of these devices — the forecasts of the weather bureau. Expectations based on the other procedures, unless they are based on well-established empirical regularities, would not be rational. It may be, of course, that the squirrel actually does have some antennae that enable it to know what the likely future winter length is going to be and to react accordingly by stockpiling the appropriate quantity of nuts. In that event, it would be rational to base an expectation of the likely future winter length on the basis of that observed behavior. This simply says that a rational expectation can be based on any information, provided that information can be demonstrated to be *relevant* to the forecasting of the future value of the variable of interest.

Although, in the current state of knowledge, forming a rational expectation of the weather involves the taking of meteorological observations followed by the use of meteorological theory to generate inferences concerning the implications of those observations for the future course of the weather, such predictions are not exact. This inexactness arises from the fact that meteorological information collection is far from total. It would cost an infinite or close to an infinite amount of resources to collect enough information to make predictions about the state and movement of every last molecule of air. Rather than do that, we invest a smaller amount of resources in sampling the atmosphere at various levels and in various places and make inferences concerning the behavior between those points. Further, we do not evaluate intricate, complicated meteorological models involving millions and millions of differential equations. Rather, the meteorologists rely upon simpler theories, which, on the average, work out all right, although they do not work out in every case. So, in the area of the weather, a rational expectation is an expectation that is based on all the information that is available, even though that information is far from the total set of information that one could imagine being available. This means that a rational expectation will not always be right. It will only be right *on the average*.

Notice, that in this meteorological example, we do not require that each and every individual be an expert meteorologist and be able to work out the weather forecast for himself. All that is necessary is that there be a body of science, and a systematic observation process to inform that body of science, to enable the scientific community to make the relevant predictions. The rest of us can then consume the fruits of that scientific activity.

E. Rational Expectation of the Price Level

(i) The Concept of Rational Expectation Applied to the Price Level

A rational expectation of the price level follows very directly from the examples that have been introduced so far. The rational expectation of the price level is the price level that is predicted on the basis of *all* the available information at the time at which the expectation is formed. Such information might include all the past history of the key economic variables, such as the price level itself, output, the real wage, the money wage, the money supply, and many other economic variables.

Expectations (forecasts) concerning economic variables are typically made available to the general public by the economics profession in much the same way as weather forecasts are made available by the meteorological profession. Such journals as *The Financial Post*, *The Wall Street Journal*, and *The Economist* bring together and appraise forecasts of diverse groups of economic analysts. Of course, economic science is less settled than is meteorology. There are, as you were made aware of in Chapter 1, a variety of schools of thought concerning the way the economy works. In the present state of economic knowledge it is necessary, therefore, for each individual, in forming a rational expectation, to weigh the "economic weather forecasts" that are put out by the economics profession against his or her own personal knowledge, information, and experience. Each individual's expectation will be arrived at using a large variety of inputs. That expectation will be a rational expectation if it coincides with the conditional expectation based on all the information that is available.

(ii) A More Precise Definition of the Rational Expectation of the Price Level

We can make the definition of the rational expectation of the price level (or the inflation rate) more precise in a way that utilizes the brilliant insights of John F. Muth.[2] The ideas advanced by Muth are fairly deep and apparently difficult to grasp. Let us proceed with some care. First, let us remind ourselves (and keep on reminding ourselves) that a rational expectation is just an average. Second, consider the question (which seems at first thought totally irrelevant to what we have just been discussing) "What is theory?". Theory is, of course, a set of propositions designed to make predictions about the behavior of some variable or variables. A theory of the price level (or the inflation rate) for example, is designed to make predictions about the price level. Now no theory, of course, is exact. The best that we can expect of any theory is that it will be right on the average. This can be put more directly: all theories are designed to make predictions about the average behavior of the phenomena that they address. Realizing that theories are designed to make predictions about averages, and also realizing that a rational expectation is nothing other than an average, led John Muth to a neat and powerful operational definition of a rational expectation. That definition states that a *rational expectation is the same thing as the prediction of the relevant theory*. Thus, the rational expectation of the price level is the same thing as the prediction of the relevant theory for determining the price level.

This is not, of course, to say that the rational expectation of the price level is the prediction of *any* theory of the price level. Theories that are clearly wrong would not yield predictions that coincided with the rational expectation. Only a theory that is not wrong would do so.

Now, of course, in the current state of knowledge we do not know, at least not with any certainty, what the relevant theory for predicting the price level is. We are still in that stage of scientific inquiry of advancing alternative hypotheses and determining which, if any, of these alternatives are compatible with the facts. Although we do not know for sure that any particular theory is the correct theory, each time we advance a theory we do so in the hope that it will turn out to be the right one. Where that theory contains as part of its structure people's expectations of magnitudes predicted by the theory, the only internally consistent assumption that we can make concerning the way in which those expectations are formed is to postulate that they are formed in the same way as that particular theory says the variable is determined. In so doing, we have a very powerful technique for developing, testing, and usually though hopefully not always, rejecting a succession of alternative hypotheses concerning the determination of the macroeconomic variables.

---

[2] *Ibid.*

You may be suspecting that to assume that people form their expectations in the same way that a particular theory says the variables in question are determined somehow stacks the cards in favor of the theory by making the predictions self-fulfilling. Nothing could in fact be further from the truth. A moment's reflection will convince you of the reason for this. Suppose that we allowed ourselves the freedom to propose any hypothesis we like about expectations formation. We could invent all kinds of *ad hoc* theories linking expectations of inflation to past values of actual inflation, to past values of the money supply, or to just about anything else that came to mind. We would then be able to assume that the expected rate of inflation had changed for no reason other than that we need this assumption in order to make a particular theory fit the facts. We can put this slightly differently by saying that we would be in a position of having one theory telling us how the inflation rate (or price level) evolved for a given expected rate of inflation and then another theory generating inflationary expectations. It is immediately obvious that if we develop theories in that way, we give ourselves sufficient "degrees of freedom" to be able to make any theory fit any set of facts. In contrast, if we restrict ourselves by insisting that the expectations of inflation not be allowed to conveniently change so as to "fit the facts" but evolve to coincide with the predictions of the theory, then we would be giving ourselves no additional "degrees of freedom" with which to explain the facts. By insisting that expectations be formed in such a way that they coincide with the predictions of the model places greater demands on the model and forces us to work harder to find the right one.

In the next section we shall go on to employ these ideas to calculate the rational expectation of the price level. Specifically, we shall use the theory developed in the previous three chapters that makes predictions about the price level, and we shall assume that people's expectations of the price level coincide with the prediction of the theory.

F. How to Work Out the Rational Expectation of the Price Level

(i) The Boot-Laces Problem!

There is a preliminary problem which needs some discussion, arising from a key difference between the rational expectation of the price level and the rational expectation of something like how hot the summer will be or the amount of rain that is going to fall tomorrow. Tomorrow's weather is not going to be affected, at least as far as we

**Figure 18.1
The Effect of the
Expected Price Level
on the Actual
Price Level**

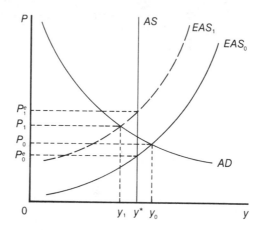

Aggregate demand is held constant at the curve *AD*. If the expected price level is P_0^e, then the expectations-augmented aggregate supply curve is EAS_0, and the actual price level is P_0 (and income y_0). If the expected price level was P_1^e, then the *EAS* curve would be EAS_1, and the actual price level would be P_1 (and income y_1). Thus holding everything else constant, the higher the expected price level, the higher will be the actual price level.

know on the basis of existing information, by our expectations of what it will be.

From the work already done in Chapter 17, however, you know that this is *not* true of the price level. The price level next year, according to our theory, will depend on our expectation of the price level next year. To see this more clearly, consider Figure 18.1. It shows the goods market as described by the theory developed in Chapter 17. The vertical axis measures the price level, and the horizontal axis measures the level of output. The curve *AD* is the aggregate demand curve, and *AS* is the aggregate supply curve derived from the labor market equilibrium conditions and the production function. The curve EAS_0 is the expectations-augmented aggregate supply curve drawn for an expected price level equal to P_0^e. Notice that the curve EAS_0 cuts the aggregate supply curve *AS* at the price level P_0^e. If the expected price level is P_0^e, so that we are on EAS_0, and if aggregate demand is *AD*, then the intersection of EAS_0 and *AD* will determine the actual price level as P_0 and the level of output as y_0. If, however, the expected price level was higher than P_0^e at, say, P_1^e, then the expectations-augmented aggregate supply curve would become the curve shown as EAS_1, which cuts the aggregate supply curve *AS* at P_1^e. In this case, with the aggregate demand curve held constant, the actual price level will be determined as P_1 and the level of output as y_1.

From this exercise you see that the actual price level is not independent of the expected price level. All that has been done in Figure

18.1 is to consider two alternative expectations for the price level, with everything else the same. Reading off the equilibrium solutions shows that there is a direct relationship between the expected and actual price levels. The higher the expected price level, the higher will be the actual price level, given a constant money supply

How then can economic theory be used to determine the expected price level when the actual price level depends on the expected price level? It is rather like asking the question, how can we lift ourselves off the ground by pulling at our own boot laces? We can pull as hard as we like, but no matter how hard we pull we shall stay put on the ground and make no progress. It looks a little bit as if the same is true concerning the use of economic theory to generate a prediction about the expected price level. If the expectation of the price level is necessary for forecasting the actual price level, how can the predictions of economic theory be used to form an expectation about the price level? How can we get off the ground?

(ii) Working Out the Rational Expectation of the Price Level

It turns out that we can solve this problem. The way in which it is solved is illustrated in Figure 18.2. Remember that what we want to do is to form an expectation of the price level that will prevail in a *future* period, and we want that expectation to be the prediction of the theory of the actual price level that will prevail in that future period.

The starting point has to be to form an expectation of the position of the aggregate demand curve. Suppose that we have done this and that the aggregate demand curve that we expect in the following period is shown as AD^e. What this means, of course, is that we have formed an expectation of the value of the money supply, government expenditure, and taxes in the next period and have figured out what they imply for the position of the aggregate demand curve in the next period. Let us also put in the diagram the classical aggregate supply curve, the vertical line labelled AS, with the full-employment output level y^*.

Now let us perform a purely conceptual experiment. Let us suppose that we start out with an entirely arbitrary expectation of the price level for the next period equal to P_0^e, as shown on the vertical axis of Figure 18.2. This means that we can now locate an expectations-augmented aggregate supply curve based on that expected price level. This is shown as $EAS(P_0^e)$. If P_0^e is the expected price level, then we see, given our expectation of the position of the aggregate demand curve for the next period, that we would be forecasting a price level higher than the expected price level P_0^e. In fact, we would be forecasting a price level equal to P_1^e. It is clear that we have a conflict. We started with a purely arbitrary expectation, P_0^e, and we see that if P_0^e is our expectation of the price level our theory does not lead to

**Figure 18.2
Calculating the
Rational Expectation
of the Price Level**

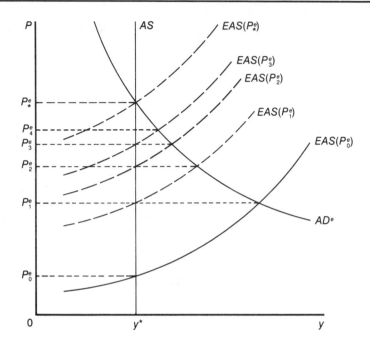

The starting point for the calculation of the rational expectation of the price level is the formation of an expectation of aggregate demand. This requires that an expectation be formed of the values of the variables that determine aggregate demand as well as their influence upon demand. The curve AD^e denotes the expected aggregate demand curve. The rational expectation of the price level can be calculated by performing a conceptual experiment. Try P_0^e as the expected price level. This cannot be the rational expectation because the predicted price level, P_1^e, is different from that initial trial value. The expected price level P_1^e in turn predicts P_2^e as the actual price level. Then P_2^e in turn predicts P_3^e, and so on. Only the expected price level P_*^e predicts an *actual* price level equal to P_*^e. This is the rational expectation of the price level. It is the price level at which the expected aggregate demand curve (AD^e) cuts the full-employment aggregate supply curve (AS).

a prediction that the price level will in fact be the value that we are expecting. Therefore, the expectation P_0^e is not a rational expectation. It is not the conditional expectation of the price level that is generated by our theory.

Suppose, continuing to perform the conceptual experiment, we now try a different expected price level. In particular, let us try P_1^e as the expected price level. This is the price level predicted by the first experiment conducted. With this higher expected price level, we now have a different expectations-augmented aggregate supply curve, namely, $EAS(P_1^e)$. (Recall that EAS cuts AS at the price level equal to the expected price level.) This higher expected price level, P_1^e, generates, as we see, a forecast for the price level next period of P_2^e. That is the price level at which the expectation of the aggregate demand curve cuts the expectations-augmented aggregate supply curve EAS_1. Again, we have a conflict. The forecast of our theory is different from the expectation P_1^e, which we arbitrarily assumed. Also, the theory leads to a prediction of the price level that is higher than the assumed expectation.

Still continuing with the conceptual experiment, let us now try a yet higher expected price level, namely, P_2^e. With this expected price level, the expectations-augmented aggregate supply curve becomes $EAS(P_2^e)$. This curve cuts the expected aggregate demand curve at the price level P_3^e. Yet again there is a conflict.

You can now see what is happening. Each time we use a trial value for the expected price level, we are generating a prediction for the actual price level that is higher than the expected price level. However, you will notice that the gap between the initially assumed expected price level and the conditional prediction of the price level is becoming smaller. Can we bring this process to an end? The answer is that we can, and we do this by predicting that the price level will be equal to that value generated by the intersection of the expected aggregate demand curve and the aggregate supply curve AS at P_*^e.

Suppose we started out with that expectation for the price level. The expectations-augmented aggregate supply curve that passes through the AS curve at that point is $EAS(P_*^e)$. That is the expectations-augmented aggregate supply curve based on an expected price level of P_*^e. The theory now predicts that the price level in the next period will also be P_*^e. Notice that we are not saying that the price level next period will actually turn out to be P_*^e. Rather, we are saying that the prediction of our theory concerning the price level is that it will be P_*^e, given that our expectation of aggregate demand is AD^e.

This leads to a very important proposition. The rational expectation is that the price level will be equal to its expected full-employment value. This is the only expectation of the price level that is consistent with the prediction of our theory concerning what the price level will be. You should not confuse this with the statement that "everyone expects full employment always to prevail." People know that random shocks will be hitting the economy and that we may *never* have full employment. They do the best they can, however, before the event, to form an expectation about the price level that, should this expectation turn out to be correct, will ensure full employment.

You now know how to determine the rational expectation of the price level in the context of the new theories of aggregate supply and the *IS-LM* theory of aggregate demand.

(iii) Individual Thought Experiments

The hypothesis about individual economic agents is that they behave on the basis of a subjective expectation of the price level that coincides with a conditional mathematical expectation of the price level, given the available information. That is, they behave on the basis of a rational expectation of the price level. That is not to say that everybody knows the same piece of economic theory that you know and that they are capable of calculating the rational expectation from this model or any other particular model. Rather, it is to say that people form their expectations of the price level in much the same way as the pool player forms his expectation of the trajectories of the balls. Just as the pool player follows instinctive and subjective calculations of the appropriate angles and forces and degrees of spin, so economic agents form their price expectations on the basis of ill-articulated thought processes. Of course, not everyone is a good pool player and not everyone is good at forming expectations of future levels of prices. Those who are good pool players, however, typically play a lot and are paid for their skills. Likewise, those who are good at making price level expectations (and who approximate to making rational expectations) typically make the expectations on which the rest of us base our behavior. They also get paid for their special skills!

Summary

A. Expected Price Level and Expected Rate of Inflation

The expected rate of inflation is equal to the expected price level minus the previous price level expressed as a percentage of the previous price level. It is not the percentage change in the expected price level but rather the expected percentage change in the price level.

B. Distinction Between a Subjective Expectation and Conditional Mathematical Expectation

A subjective expectation is a vague intuitive feeling about the likely value or outcome of some future event. A conditional mathematical expectation is the true average value of the outcome of a future event conditional on (i.e., given) whatever are the known actual values of all the relevant variables.

C. Why Wrong Expectations Are Costly

Actions are based on expectations, and wrong expectations lead to actions that may turn out to be inappropriate. If the price turns out to be higher than was expected, real wages will turn out to be lower than was expected, and people will have ended up doing more work and consuming less leisure than they would have liked to have done had they known the correct real wage ahead of time. A symmetric cost applies to an error in the opposite direction. It is important to distinguish between being right every time (which in general is impossible) and being right on the average. The casino example in the text illustrates that distinction.

D. Rational Expectation

A rational expectation of a variable is a subjective expectation that *coincides* with the conditional mathematical expectation of that variable, given the available information.

E. Rational Expectation of the Price Level

The rational expectation of the price level is the prediction of the price level that is based on all the available information at the time at which the expectation is formed. This information includes the body of economic theory relevant for predicting the price level.

F. How to Work Out the Rational Expectation of the Price Level

The rational expectation of the price level in the context of the new theories is the price level at which the expected aggregate demand curve cuts the aggregate supply curve. (The conceptual experiment whereby this expectation is worked out is discussed in the section on rational expectations and illustrated in Figure 18.2 and should be thoroughly understood.)

Review Questions

1. What is the connection between the expected price level and expected rate of inflation?

2. Define a *subjective expectation*.

3. Define a *conditional mathematical expectation*.

4. Give some examples of the costs of wrong expectations.

5. Give the definition of a *rational expectation* and explain the relationship between a rational, a conditional mathematical, and a subjective expectation.

6. What are the key distinguishing features of a rational expectation?

7. What basic postulate concerning economic behavior suggests that individuals would form expectations rationally?

8. Give some examples of economic agents (firms, individuals, etc.) who are "in the business" of providing forecasts and selling other informational services. How do individuals benefit from these services?

9. What factors govern the degree to which the expectation of the price level affects aggregate supply? Under what circumstances will an increase, for example, in the expected price level have the greatest effect on aggregate supply?

10. What factors would you expect to determine the expected price level? How responsive might the expected price level be to observations on past prices?

11. Illustrate diagrammatically the derivation of the expected price level.

12. What relationship does the rational expectation of the price level bear to the full-employment price level?

Appendix:

The Signal Extraction Problem

In Chapter 15 when we derived the new classical expectations-augmented aggregate supply curve, we supposed that people formed expectations about the average price level, ignoring the knowledge that is readily available to them concerning the price of the output of their own industry. In this chapter, we have calculated the rational expectation of the price level using only an expectation of the level of aggregate demand. We have again ignored any current information that might be available concerning the prices of some limited range of goods and services.

This appendix extends those analyses to the case in which people do use currently available information concerning the price in their own sector of the economy.[3] The level of analysis in this appendix is more demanding than that in the text. To follow everything in this appendix you need to know a small amount of statistics and calculus. You will probably, however, be able to obtain a good feel for what is going on even if you do not have that background.

The starting point is to imagine that the economy comprises many "islands" of information. Individuals (firms and their employees) know the prices on their own island, but do not know the prices on any other. Imagine that the individual firms and workers on a given island that we shall call island i observe their price to be P_i. Then let us suppose that everyone knows that the price on island i deviates from the economy average price, P, by a random amount, R_i, which itself is not observed. In other words, everyone knows that

$$P_i = P + R_i \qquad (18A.1)$$

The price P_i on the left-hand side of Equation (18A.1) is observed, but the economy average price, P, and the deviation of the individual island price from the economy average price, R_i, are not observed.

Rational people would like to use the information that they have on P_i to make the best inference possible concerning P and R_i. Let us suppose that people know that, on the average, R_i is zero. Let us also suppose that people know that the relative price on island i deviates from the economy average price by a random amount that is drawn from a normal distribution that has a fixed amount of dispersion, which we will measure by its "variance." Let us denote the variance

---

[3]The analysis presented in this appendix is a simplified version of that developed by Robert E. Lucas, Jr., in "Some International Evidence on the Output-Inflation Tradeoff," *The American Economic Review*, 63 (September 1973), 326-34.

of the distribution of R_i as τ^2. A small value of τ^2 would mean that the relative price deviated very little from the economy average price (such as the distribution labelled A in Figure 18A.1). A large value of τ^2 would mean that the relative price was drawn from a distribution that varied widely around the economy average price (such as curve labelled B in Figure 18A.1.)

Next, let us suppose that people have formed an expectation of the economy average price just prior to observing the price on their own island. Call that expectation P_0^e. You can imagine that P_0^e has been calculated in exactly the same way as was done in the body of this chapter.

Suppose that everyone knows from past experience that the actual economy average price deviates from the prior expectation by some random amount that we will call U (for unexpected price fluctuations), so that the actual price is equal to the sum of the expected price and the unanticipated component. That is

$$P = P_0^e + U \qquad (18A.2)$$

This equation contains no variables that people observe, although P_0^e is known to them because it is their prior expectation. Let us suppose that U, the unexpected portion of economy average price, has an average value of zero, but it too is drawn from a normal distribution and that it has a dispersion measured by its variance which we shall call σ^2.

An economy that has little variability of prices will have a small variance to the unexpected component of the economy average price and will look like the distribution labelled A in Figure 18A.1. An economy that has very volatile or noisy prices will be one in which people's expectations frequently deviate substantially from the actual economy average price, so that the distribution of U will be like that labelled B in Figure 18A.1.

Now it is possible to combine Equations (18A.1) and (18A.2) by noticing that we can replace P in Equation (18A.1) with the right-hand side of Equation (18A.2). This gives

$$P_i = P_0^e + U + R_i \qquad (18A.3)$$

If we subtract P_0^e from both sides of Equation (18A.3), we obtain

$$P_i - P_0^e = U + R_i \qquad (18A.4)$$

Notice that what is on the left-hand side of this equation is something that is known to everyone on island i. It is the difference between the price that they have just observed on their own island and the price that, prior to that observation, they expected would prevail on the

Figure 18A.1
The Dispersion of Prices

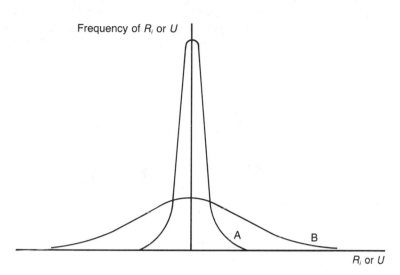

An economy that has low variability of prices will have a small variance to the unexpected component of prices (like the distribution labelled A) and an economy that has very volatile or noisy prices will have a large variance to the unexpected component of prices (like the distribution labelled B).

average in the economy as a whole. They also know that $P_i - P_0^e$ is equal to the sum of two random variables — their error in forecasting correctly the economy average price, U, and the random price on their own island relative to the economy average price, R_i.

Their task is to decompose the observed sum of these two variables into their separate components so that a better expectation of the economy average price may be calculated. It is important to notice that prior to observing the price on their own island, they expected that both U and R_i would be zero. Now that they know the sum of these two random variables, unless that sum happens to be zero (which is a possibility, although not a very likely one), they will now want to revise their estimate of the values of these variables.

We could say the same thing slightly differently. That is, the people on island i had a prior expectation about the economy average price, P_0^e; they have now observed a new piece of information, the price on their own island, and they now want to use the new information to revise their expectation about the economy average price.

To do this they can use the so-called *Law of Recursive Projection*. The law is easily stated and intuitively appealing. In order to state the law, we need one small piece of notation. Let us agree that the expectation of a random variable (x) given the piece of information (I) will be called $E(x|I)$. We can use this notation to express the expectation of the economy average price that the people on island i originally had before observing the price on their island as

$$P_0^e = E(P|I_0)$$

Here, I_0 stands for all the information originally available before observing the price on island i. What the people on island i are going to calculate is the expectation of the average price in the economy as a whole, given that initial information, I_0, and the observation of the price on island i. That is, they are going to calculate

$$E(P|I_0,P_i)$$

To perform this calculation, they are going to use the law of recursive projection, which is as follows:

$$E(P|I_0,P_i) = E(P|I_0) + E([P - E(P|I_0)][P_i - E(P_i|I_0)]) \quad \textbf{(18A.5)}$$

This looks much more formidable than it is. The left-hand side is simply the revised expectation that the agents want to make, namely, their expectation of the economy average price, given all the information that they now have available to them. The starting point for the calculation is given by the first term on the right-hand side of Equation (18A.5) and is nothing other than their original expectation. The second term on the right-hand side is the adjustment that is going to be made to the original expectation of the economy average price. It too is an expectation. It is the expectation of the error made in originally predicting the economy average price,

$$P - E(P|I_0)$$

This expectation itself is going to be calculated, given the information

$$P_i - E(P_i|I_0)$$

What is this information? Evidently it is the difference between the actual price observed on island i and the expectation of this price given the initial information. In other words, it is the error in forecasting the price on island i.

You can now interpret Equation (18A.5) in the following way. It says that the expectation of the economy average price, given the original information and the new information about island i's price, will be equal to the original expectation made prior to knowing island *i*'s price plus the expectation of the error made in forecasting the economy average price, given knowledge of the error that has been made in forecasting the island's own price. If you inspect Equation (18A.2), you will see that

$$P - E(P|I_0) - U$$

Therefore, we can replace $P - E(P|I_0)$ with U in Equation (18A.5). Also, by examining Equation (18A.3), you will see that the expectation of the price on island i prior to observing this price must have been the same as the expected average price in the economy as a whole, P_0^e, since the expectation of the random variables U and R_i are both zero. Thus, the difference between P_i now observed and its prior expectation must be the sum of the two random variables, $U + R_i$. We can use that sum therefore to replace $P_i - E(P_i)$ in Equation (18A.5). Making these adjustments gives

$$E(P|I_0, P_i) = P_0^e + E(U|U + R_i) \qquad \textbf{(18A.6)}$$

What the people on island i need to do, then, according to Equation (18A.6), is to figure out as best they can the likely value of U, given that they know $U + R_i$.

A natural way to do this is to imagine that some fraction of the sum of U and R_i is to be treated as being generated by U and one minus that fraction by R_i. Of course, if a particular fraction of $U + R_i$ is assigned to U, in general, an error will be made. Call the fraction in question a. Then the following equation can be defined to be true

$$U = a(U + R_i) + Error \qquad \textbf{(18A.7)}$$

What this says is that the random variable U that people would like to observe but have not observed is equal to some fraction a of the random variable $U + R_i$ that they have observed plus some error. Equivalently, we could say that the error that they will make in estimating the value of U as a fraction a of $U + R_i$ is given by

$$Error = U - a(U + R_i)$$

How can a value for a be chosen to make this into an operational estimation procedure? Clearly, the *expected* error is equal to zero since the expectation of each of U and R_i is equal to zero. Any value of a would deliver an expected error of zero. What people care about presumably is not just having an expected error of zero but in some sense making the least possible errors. Since positive errors and negative errors will cancel out, a useful way of giving weight to the errors is to consider the square of the error made. This renders all the errors positive and gives symmetric weights to both positive and negative errors. Let us square the error and see what we get. Evidently, squaring the error gives

$$Error^2 = U^2 + a(U^2 + R_i^2) - 2aU^2 - 2aUR_i$$

Of course, no one knows the actual error at any point in time. It is possible, nevertheless, to calculate the *expected* squared error. Calculating the expectation of the squared error gives

$$E(Error^2) = E(U^2) + a^2E(U^2 + R_i^2)) - 2aE(U^2) - 2aE(UR_i)$$

The expectation of $E(U^2)$ is the variance of the distribution of U which we are calling σ^2, and the expectation of $E(R_i^2)$ is simply the variance of the distribution of R_i that we are calling τ^2. The expectation of the product of U and R_i is, by assumption, zero. That is, we are supposing that the random shocks hitting the individual island's relative price are independent of the random shocks that hit the economy average price. With this assumption, it is evident that

$$E(Error^2) = \sigma^2 + a(\sigma^2 + \tau^2) - 2a\sigma^2 \qquad \textbf{(18A.8)}$$

What the people on island i would like to do is find a value for a that minimizes this expected squared error. In so doing they will reduce to a minimum the costs of having wrong expectations. They can do this by differentiating Equation (18A.8) with respect to a and setting the result equal to zero, and then finding the value of a that satisfies that equation. Evidently, the required value for a is

$$a = \frac{\sigma^2}{\sigma^2 + \tau^2}$$

This can now be used to calculate the expectation of U, given an observation of $U + R_i$. This expectation from Equation (18A.7) is

$$E(U|U + R_i) = a(U + R_i)$$

But, we know from Equation (18A.2) that $U = P - P_0^e$ and from Equation (18A.3) that

$$(U + R_i) = (P_i - P_0^e)$$

Using these two equations enables us to write the revised expectation of the economy average price by people on island i [Equation (18A.6)] as

$$E(P|I_0,P_i) = P_0^e + a(P_i - P_0^e)$$

or, equivalently,

$$E(P|I_0,P_i) = aP_i + (1 - a)P_0^e \qquad \textbf{(18A.9)}$$

You can now perhaps see more clearly why the calculation just performed is called the law of recursive projection. A projection is made — P_0^e; new information arrives — P_i; the old projection and the new information are then combined to arrive at a new projection. The weights attached to the original expectation $(1 - a)$ and the new information a depend on the quality of the new information.

Let us try to make the notion of the "quality of the new information" a bit more precise. You know that

$$a = \frac{\sigma^2}{\sigma^2 + \tau^2} \qquad \textbf{(18A.10)}$$

and therefore that

$$1 - a = \frac{\tau^2}{\sigma^2 + \tau^2}$$

You can think of σ^2 as measuring the amount of aggregate noise in the economy. A large value of σ^2 signifies a very noisy economy, that is, an economy whose average price is very hard to forecast. You can think of a large value of τ^2 as indicating considerable randomness in relative prices, that is, an economy in which relative prices are hard to forecast. Evidently, the bigger is σ^2, the bigger will be the value of a; and the bigger is τ^2, the smaller will be the value of a. Since a is the weight that we attach to the new information, we could equivalently say that the noisier is the economy average price, the bigger the weight we attach to the new piece of information, and the noisier are relative prices, the smaller the weight we attach to the new piece of information. This seems to be natural enough.

If the economy is subject to very large random fluctuations in the average price, then an observation on one price that is very different from what was previously expected will be interpreted as indicating that what was previously expected was wrong and is in need of major revision. Thus, the weight attached to the new piece of information will be large. Conversely, if relative prices are exceedingly random, then observing the price on an individual island is not going to be giving very much information concerning movements in the economy average price. Hence, a small weight would attach to the current piece of information in that case. The precise way in which aggregate noise and relative price noise are combined is given by Equation (18A.10) that defines a.

So far we have only talked about one island, island i. Let us suppose that the economy is made up of many such islands. Furthermore, suppose that all the islands are similar in the sense that they all are bombarded by random shocks to their own price that come from the same distribution as the one that we have just analyzed. Different islands get different values of the random shock R_i at each moment in time, but they all come from the same distribution with the same amount of dispersion τ^2 around a zero mean. In this case, the expectations of the economy average price on each island are going to be determined by an equation like Equation (18A.9).

We may aggregate these price expectations over all the islands to arrive at the economy average expectation of the economy average price. This economy average expectation is given by

$$P_t^e = aP_t + (1 - a)P_0^e \qquad \textbf{(18A.11)}$$

We are calling P_t^e the economy average expected price at time t. It will be a weighted average of the actual price, P_t, and the prior expectation of the economy average price, P_0^e. The weights will be the same as the weights attaching to each individual island's price expectations. It is important to remind yourself that no individual knows the economy average price, P_t, and no individual knows the economy average of the expectations of the economy average price, P_t^e. On each island there is a different expected price as described by Equation (18A.9). Equation (18A.11) is something that the economist analysing this economy can construct, but it is not something that people in the economy observe at the time at which the events that we are analyzing are occurring.

Let us now see how these considerations affect the labor market and the *EAS* curve. Figure 18A.2 is the vehicle for our analysis. First identify, in Figure 18A.2, Figure 18.2. Notice that the upward-sloping curve n^s is the same labor supply curve as that shown in Figure 15.2 and the three labor demand curves are the same as those in Figure 15.2. The supply curve is drawn for a value of a equal to zero. In other words, everyone ignores the information contained in their own price and sticks to their prior expectation of the economy average price regardless of what they observe.

Let us go to the opposite extreme. Imagine that $a = 1$. We will examine below precisely what that would mean. For the moment simply assume that a is 1. This means that in observing their own island price, P_i, people assume that the entire movement in their own island's price reflects a movement in the economy average price, and they revise their expectations accordingly. Thus, if the economy average price was P_1, moving the demand for labor curve to $n_1^d(P_1)$, and

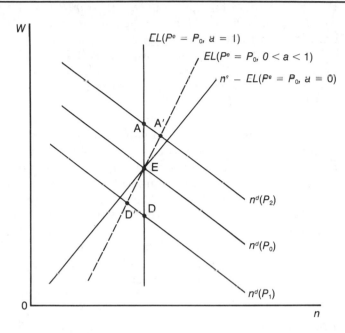

Consider what happens when the actual economy average price fluctuates between a low level of P_1 and an upper level of P_2. The demand for labor curve fluctuates between $n^d(P_1)$ and $n^d(P_2)$. Individual prices fluctuate, and the amount of information extracted from those individual prices concerning the economy average price affects the supply of labor. If individual prices fluctuate so widely around the economy average price that they give no information, then the supply of labor curve will remain fixed at n^s, and the equilibrium locus, $EL(P^e = P_0, a = 0)$, is the same as n^s. If individual prices never deviated from the economy average price, so that the observation of an individual price gives complete information about the economy average price, then the equilibrium locus would become $EL(P^e = P_0, a = 1)$. In general, observations of individual prices will contain *some*, although incomplete, information about the average price. In this case, equilibrium locus will be one such as that labelled $EL(P^e = P_0, 0 < a < 1)$. The more information that individual prices contain, the smaller the fluctuations in employment and output, and the larger the fluctuations in money wages and prices.

if everyone on seeing their own island's price revises their expectation in accordance with their observed own price, the average expectation in the economy as a whole would move in exactly the same way as the actual price had moved.

You know from the analysis lying behind Figure 15.1 that a change in the actual price that is expected will move the supply and demand curves for labor in exactly the same way. The supply of labor curve, instead of staying at n^s, would now move up parallel to itself to pass through the point marked A. Conversely, if the price level was to fall to P_2, so that the demand for labor curve fell to $n^d(P_2)$, and again if everyone seeing their own price, inferred that the economy average price had changed in exactly the same way as their own price had, the supply curve of labor would shift down parallel to itself to pass through the point D. The line AED is the equilibrium locus when a weight of one is placed on current price information that is observed. This vertical line is, therefore, labelled $EL(P^e = P_0, a = 1)$.

It is easy to see that if a was something greater than zero but less than one, the equilibrium locus would slope upwards and would lie somewhere between the labor supply curve (for $a = 0$) and the vertical line (for $a = 1$). Passing through a point like A', there would be a supply of labor curve parallel to the curve n^s. This curve would have shifted upwards as a result of the revised expectations of the economy average price but not by as much as the actual price had increased. Likewise, there would be a supply curve passing through the point D' that would represent a downward revision of the expectations of the economy average price resulting from an actual price of P_2.

You can see then that the slope of the equilibrium locus will depend on the extent to which people revise their current economy average price expectations in the light of their current observation of the particular price in their own sector (island) of the economy. The more these price expectations are revised, the closer is a to unity, and the steeper will be the equilibrium locus. The special case discussed in Chapter 15 is for $a = 0$.

Evidently, by tracing through the implications of this analysis in Figure 15.3, the slope of the *EAS* curve will also depend upon the value of a. The *EAS* curve shown in Figure 15.3 is for $a = 0$. If $a = 1$, evidently the *EAS* curve would become the same curve as *AS*. It too would become vertical. For intermediate values of a, the *EAS* curve will lie somewhere between the *AS* and *EAS* curves in Figure 15.3 — being closer to the *AS* curve, the closer a is to one; and being closer to the *EAS* curve, the closer a is to zero.

We have seen that the value of a will in fact depend on how "noisy" the economy is at the aggregate level and how big the relative price shocks are that hit the individual "islands." An economy that is subject to a large volume of aggregate noise, (large σ^2)will be one that has a high value of a. This means that such an economy will have a steep *EAS* curve compared with an economy that has a small amount of aggregate noise.

Relative price "noise" works the other way. The bigger is the source of "noise" (the larger is the value of τ^2), the smaller is a. Thus, an economy with highly variable relative prices will have a flat *EAS* curve compared with an economy that has a small amount of relative price noise.

The key conclusion of the analysis that we have just conducted is that the slope of the *EAS* curve is not independent of the amount and sources of noise in the economy.

19

Equilibrium with Rational Expectations

This chapter takes the next step in completing the rational expectations theory of the determination of the price level and real economic activity. From what you have learned so far you will almost be able to guess what this chapter deals with. You know that the expected price level is determined by expected aggregate demand. You also know, from your analysis of the determination of output and prices with a fixed price level expectation, that the actual price and output levels are determined where the actual demand curve cuts the expectations-augmented aggregate supply curve. All that now needs to be done, therefore, to complete our analysis is to explore the full implications of the distinction between expected (or anticipated) and unexpected (or unanticipated) changes in aggregate demand. Three tasks in this chapter will achieve that. They are to:

a) Understand the distinction between an anticipated and unanticipated change in aggregate demand.

b) Understand how output, employment, unemployment, the real wage, money wage, and the price level are affected by an *anticipated* change in aggregate demand.

c) Understand how output, employment, unemployment, the real wage, money wage and the price level are affected by an *unanticipated* change in aggregate demand.

A. Anticipated and Unanticipated Changes in Aggregate Demand

(I) Definition of Anticipated and Unanticipated Changes in Aggregate Demand

The level of aggregate demand in any particular year (say, year t) may be thought of as being equal to aggregate demand in the previous year (year $t - 1$) plus the change in demand over the year (Δy^d). That is

$$y_t^d = y_{t-1} + \Delta y_t^d \tag{19.1}$$

Notice that since actual output is always equilibrium output, actual output in year $t - 1$, y_{t-1}, is equal to y_{t-1}^d (aggregate demand in year $t - 1$). As soon as year $t - 1$ is past, the value of output at that date becomes known. (Actually it's a little bit strong to say that this becomes known *as soon as* the year is past. It takes a short while for the data to be accumulated.) The level of aggregate demand for year t, however, will not be known. Since rational economic agents need to form an expectation of the price level, and since the price level will depend upon the level of aggregate demand, it is necessary, in order to form a rational expectation of the price level, to form a rational expectation of the level of aggregate demand. It is necessary, therefore, to forecast the change in aggregate demand so that its future value may be predicted.

The predicted component of the change in aggregate demand is referred to as the *anticipated change* in aggregate demand, and the unpredicted component is known as the *unanticipated change* in aggregate demand.

The actual change in aggregate demand is made up of these two components. That is

$$\Delta y_t^d = \Delta y_t^{de} + \Delta y_t^{du} \tag{19.2}$$

The superscript e denotes the expected or anticipated part of the change in aggregate demand, and the superscript u, the unanticipated or unexpected part. There is not, in general, any reason why the expected and unexpected components of the change in aggregate demand should be of the same sign. They may be, in which case they will each be a fraction of the actual change. It is possible, nevertheless, for the anticipated change to be greater than the actual change so that the unexpected change is negative.

Four examples give the range of possibilities. They are set out in Table 19.1. The first example is of a correctly anticipated change in aggregate demand. The actual change is 100, and the expected change is 100. The second example is one in which the change in aggregate demand is entirely unanticipated. The expected change is 0, but the actual change is 100. The third example is one in which the actual change in aggregate demand is divided between an anticipated and unanticipated component. This example may be thought of as the most likely case. In the particular example, the division is 50/50, although in general, of course, it would not be so evenly split. The fourth and final example is one in which the actual change is less than the anticipated change, so that there is a negative unexpected component. (These are all examples of a rise in aggregate demand. Aggregate demand could actually fall and be expected to fall.)

(ii) Measurement of the Anticipated and Unanticipated Changes in Aggregate Demand

In order to actually measure the anticipated and unanticipated changes in aggregate demand, it is necessary to divide the changes in the variables that determine aggregate demand into their anticipated and unanticipated components. One such variable is the change in the money supply.

What determines the division of the actual change in the money supply between its anticipated and unanticipated components? This is not a settled matter. Robert Barro of the University of Rochester has conducted the pioneering studies on this question, using United States money supply data.[1] He has attempted to decompose the actual money supply growth into its anticipated and unanticipated components. Gillian Wogin has done comparable work using Canadian data.[2] However, this work is by no means uncontroversial, and matters are not yet settled.

The way in which this research has proceeded is to search for statistical regularities in the past history of money supply growth and then to suppose that rational agents would exploit those statistical regularities in forming a rational expectation of money supply growth. Specifically, it has been discovered that the money supply growth rate tends to be faster:

(1) The faster the money supply growth has been in the preceding two years.

---

[1] The most comprehensive account of Barro's work is Robert J. Barro and Mark Rush, "Unanticipated Money and Economic Activity," Chap. 2 in Stanley Fischer, ed., *Rational Expectations and Economic Policy*, National Bureau of Economic Research Conference Report (Chicago and London: University of Chicago Press, 1980).

[2] See Gillian Wogin, "Unemployment and Monetary Policy under Rational Expectations: Some Canadian Evidence," *Journal of Monetary Economics*, 6 (January 1980), 59-68.

(2) The bigger is the level of federal government expenditure relative to its trend.

(3) The higher was the level of unemployment in the previous year.

These findings are more than statistical patterns. They also make good intuitive sense. The proposition that money supply growth will be faster, the faster the previous two years' money supply growth has been, reflects the fact that the Bank of Canada exhibits some inertia in its decision making. It does not change course suddenly and rapidly in a zigzag fashion; rather, it changes course gradually. This means that the behavior of the Bank can, on the average, be described by a version of the formula that says that tomorrow will be very much like today.

The proposition that money supply growth increases when federal government expenditure is below its trend level is a natural consequence of the fact that money printing is a form of taxation. When there is a burst of government expenditure or a sharp drop in government expenditure, it is much easier to vary the rate at which money is printed than it is to vary such things as, for example, the sales tax, income tax, or capital gains tax. Hence, the efficient financing of government expenditure will entail varying the growth rate of the money supply to cover unusually large changes in expenditure.

The responsiveness of the money supply to the previous year's unemployment or output growth reflects a widespread belief on the part of governments that they can manipulate the economy by activist monetary policies. The old-fashioned idea that stimulating demand in times of depression and holding demand back in times of boom will moderate the business cycle lies behind this kind of monetary policy action.

The propositions just discussed can be given a precise numerical form by the use of statistical techniques that lie outside the scope of this book. From those statistical exercises it is possible to make a

TABLE 19.1
Examples of Divisions of the Actual Change in Aggregate Demand Between Anticipated and Unanticipated Changes

EXAMPLE	Δy_t^a	=	Δy_t^{ae}	+	Δy_t^{au}
1	100	=	100	+	0
2	100	=	0	+	100
3	100	=	50	+	50
4	100	=	200	−	100

forecast of what the money supply will be in the subsequent year (or in distant future years for that matter) conditional on information about the previous two years' money supply growth, the behavior of government expenditure, and the recent history of unemployment. Such a forecast becomes the anticipated change in the money supply. A movement in the actual money supply which is different from the calculated anticipated change becomes the calculated value of the unanticipated change in the money supply.

The above discussion concerning the decomposition of changes in the money supply into anticipated and unanticipated components applies in principle to changes in government expenditure, taxes, or any other variables which influence aggregate demand.

Now that the distinction between anticipated and unanticipated changes in aggregate demand is understood, and we have seen how in practice it is possible to distinguish between them, it will be useful to go on to analyze the way in which these two components of the change in aggregate demand influence the key macroeconomic variables.

B. Effects of an Anticipated Change in Aggregate Demand

The effects of an anticipated change in aggregate demand are analyzed first. This is an extreme case, but it is the clearest and simplest case with which to begin.

The analysis will be illustrated using Figure 19.1. You will recognize this as the diagrammatic summary of the theory of the determination of output (real income) and the price level. Suppose that you are looking at an economy at a particular time, called period 0. At that time the money supply is equal to M_0. The aggregate demand curve is the curve labelled AD_0. Suppose that period 0 is one of full-employment equilibrium. This is simply a convenient reference point. With period 0 being one of full-employment equilibrium, you know that the expectations-augmented aggregate supply curve, the aggregate supply curve, and the aggregate demand curve all intersect at the same point. (If you do not understand why this is so, review Chapter 15.) Thus, the actual price level and the expected price level equal each other at P_0 and P_0^e.

Now imagine that you are looking forward one year and are trying to form a view about the price level in that period. Suppose that you expect aggregate demand to rise, so that the aggregate demand curve is expected to be the curve labelled AD_1^e. This is where you expect the aggregate demand curve to be next year. You can now calculate the rational expectation of the price level, which is equal to P_1^e. (If you

Figure 19.1
The Effect of an
Anticipated Change in
Aggregate Demand on
the Price Level and
the Level of Output

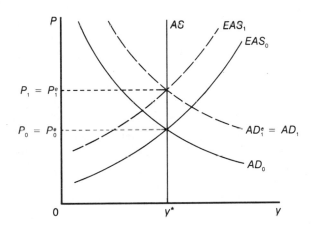

The economy is initially at full employment equilibrium where AD_0 intersects EAS_0 at output y^* and price level P_0. Aggregate demand increases in an anticipated way from AD_0 to $AD_1(= AD_1^e)$. The new expected price level is P_1^e and the expectations-augmented aggregate supply curve shifts to become EAS_1. The actual price level is determined at P_1 and output at y^*. An anticipated rise in aggregate demand raises the price level but leaves output unaffected.

are not sure as to the reason for that, check back with Chapter 18, Figure 18.2.) The expected price level P_1^e is the only expected price level which is consistent with the prediction of this model, given that expected aggregate demand is AD_1^e. This means that the expectations-augmented aggregated supply curve for period one will be located as shown by the curve EAS_1.

Next, suppose that aggregate demand actually increases by exactly the amount expected, so that the aggregate demand change is anticipated. This means that the *actual* aggregate demand curve will be the same as the *expected* aggregate demand curve. To remind you of this, the aggregate demand curve has been labelled twice as $AD_1^e = AD_1$. This is to emphasize that the actual aggregate demand curve is the same as the expected aggregate demand curve.

What is the new equilibrium level of output and prices in this economy? Recall that equilibrium occurs at the point at which the aggregate demand curve cuts the expectations-augmented aggregate supply curve. The expectations-augmented aggregate supply curve is EAS_1 — the aggregate supply curve when the expected price level is P_1^e, based on the expected aggregate demand curve AD_1^e.

You can now read off the new equilibrium. The aggregate demand curve AD_1 cuts the aggregate supply curve EAS_1 at the full-employment output level y^* and at the price level P_1. Thus the price level rises, and the level of output remains unchanged.

This is the first proposition concerning the effect of an anticipated change in aggregate demand. An anticipated rise in aggregate demand raises the price level and leaves output unchanged.

What happens to the remaining variables in the economy? Specifically, what happens to employment, unemployment, the real wage, and money wage?

You will recall that the diagram displayed in Figure 19.1 was derived originally (in Chapter 17) from an analysis of the labor market and the production function. It is convenient now to recall Figure 17.2. (Refresh your memory by turning back to it.) Starting from the fact that output has not changed, you can travel back (reversing the arrows in Figure 17.2) through the production function and immediately establish that the level of employment has not changed. If the level of employment has not changed, then firms must be willingly hiring the same quantity of labor as they were hiring before. This immediately implies that the real wage has not changed. Furthermore, if the level of employment has not changed, the level of unemployment is also unchanged — unemployment remains at its natural rate. Finally, since the real wage has not changed, but the price level has risen, it follows that the money wage must also have risen and by the same percentage amount as the price level has risen.

It is now possible to summarize all the consequences of an anticipated change in the aggregate demand: an anticipated change in aggregate demand changes the price level and the money wage by the same percentage amount as each other. It has no effects on any of the real variables in the economy, i.e., on output, employment, unemployment, and the real wage.

It is not difficult to understand the reason for these results. An anticipated change in aggregate demand shifts the expected and actual aggregate demand curves and also the expectations-augmented aggregate supply curve by the same amount. This leads to no change in the level of output and thus in all the other variables. The full effect of the change in aggregate demand comes out on the price level and since real wages are constant the money wage rises by the same percentage as the rise in the price level.

Let us now go on to analyze the opposite extreme.

C. Effects of an Unanticipated Change in Aggregate Demand

Figure 19.2 will be used to illustrate the effects on the price level and output of an unanticipated change in aggregate demand. Suppose that the economy is initially in exactly the same situation as that depicted in Figure 19.1 for period 0. That is, the aggregate demand curve is AD_0, and the expectations-augmented aggregate supply curve is EAS_0. These curves intersect at a price level of P_0, which is also the expected price level P_0^e. Output is at the full-employment level, y^*.

Unlike the previous example, suppose that everyone expects that in period 1 aggregate demand will remain at AD_0. This aggregate demand curve is marked $AD_0 = AD_1^e$ to remind you that aggregate demand expected in period 1 is the same as actual aggregate demand in period 0. From this, the rational expectation of the price level in period 1, P_1^e, remains at P_0^e. The expectations-augmented aggregate supply curve for period 1 is the same as EAS_0, and this curve is marked EAS_1 to remind you of that.

Now suppose that instead of remaining constant at AD_0, actual aggregate demand rises in period 1 to become AD_1. You can read off the equilibrium price and output levels in period 1, given that the expected price level P_1^e is constant but that actual aggregate demand has increased above the level that was expected. Equilibrium will now be at the point at which the expectations-augmented aggregate supply curve EAS_1 cuts the *actual* aggregate demand curve AD_1. The price and output levels determined by this intersection point are P_1 and y_1 respectively.

Notice that in this experiment we have an *unanticipated rise* in aggregate demand. Anticipated aggregate demand remains constant, but actual aggregate demand rises, so the unanticipated rise in aggregate demand is exactly equal to the actual rise in aggregate demand.

The effects of this unanticipated rise in aggregate demand are as follows: the price level is above its expected level and output is above full-employment output. The percentage by which the price level rises above its expected level is less than the percentage unanticipated rise in aggregate demand. This occurs because part of the unanticipated rise in aggregate demand raises real income, and part of it raises the price level. Any given percentage unanticipated rise in aggregate demand will result in the combination of a rise in real income and a rise in the price level, which, in percentage terms, sum to the percentage change in aggregate demand. How much of the unanticipated aggregate demand rise goes into output and how much into the price level depends on the steepness of the EAS curve. A very steep EAS curve will result in a large price level and small output rise. A flat EAS curve will produce the reverse allocation of the effects of the

Figure 19.2
The Effect of an
Unanticipated Change
in Aggregate Demand
on the Price Level
and the Level of
Output

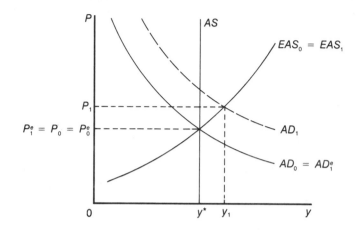

An initial equilibrium at P_0, y^* (exactly as in Figure 19.1) is disturbed by an unanticipated shift in aggregate demand to AD_1. There is no change in the expected price level so that the expectations-augmented aggregate supply curve EAS_1 remains fixed at EAS_0. The new equilibrium price and output are where the new aggregate demand curve AD_1 cuts the original EAS curve at P_1, y_1. An unanticipated rise in aggregate demand raises output and the price level but raises the price level less than proportionately to the rise in aggregate demand.

unanticipated demand increase with a large output rise and a small price rise.

What are the effects on the other variables in the economy? (Again recall Figure 17.2). Since you know from Figure 19.2 that output has risen, you also know that it must be the case that employment has also risen. How does this come about? For employment to have increased there must have been a rise in the demand for labor. You can easily verify that this indeed will have happened. The unanticipated rise in the price level will have produced an upward shift in the demand for labor curve, but since the expected price level is constant, there will have been no change in the position of the supply of labor curve. As a result, the money wage will have increased. Its increase, however, will be less than the percentage rise in prices, so that the real wage has fallen, and firms are therefore demanding more labor. With a rise in the money wage but no change in the expected price level, the expected real wage has increased, and thus households slide along their labor supply curve and willingly supply the additional labor demanded.

It is now possible to summarize the effects of an unanticipated change in aggregate demand: an unanticipated rise in aggregate demand raises the price level, but by a smaller percentage amount than the unanticipated rise in aggregate demand. It also produces a rise in the money wage, but by an even smaller percentage than the percentage rise in the price level. It causes a fall in the real wage and a fall in unemployment below the natural rate. It also produces a higher level of employment and output than the full-employment levels. The above can be readily restated for an unanticipated fall in the money supply.

Summary

A. Anticipated and Unanticipated Changes in Aggregate Demand

The change in aggregate demand may be decomposed into its anticipated or expected component and its unanticipated or unexpected component. The anticipated change in aggregate demand may be greater or smaller than the actual change. When the anticipated change is exactly the same as the actual change we speak of an anticipated change in aggregate demand. The unanticipated change in aggregate demand is simply the difference between the actual and anticipated changes. Since the change in actual aggregate demand is determined by changes in the money supply, government spending, and taxes, decomposing the change in aggregate demand into its expected and unexpected components involves decomposing the changes in these determinants of aggregate demand into their anticipated and unanticipated components.

B. Effects of an Anticipated Change in Aggregate Demand

An anticipated change in aggregate demand has the effect of changing the price level and the money wage by exactly the same percentage amount as each other and by the same percentage as the rise in aggregate demand. It has no effects on any of the real variables. Specifically, it has no effect on output, employment, unemployment, or the real wage.

C. Effects of an Unanticipated Change in Aggregate Demand

An unanticipated change in aggregate demand has both real and nominal effects. It raises the price level, but by a smaller percentage amount than the unanticipated rise in aggregate demand, and it raises the money wage by an even smaller percentage amount than it raises the price level. It thus lowers the real wage, raises the level of employment, raises the level of output, and lowers the level of unemployment.

Review Questions

1. What is the distinction between anticipated and unanticipated changes in aggregate demand?

2. What factors determine anticipated changes in aggregate demand?

3. What factors determine unanticipated changes in aggregate demand?

4. In what ways do the effects of anticipated changes in the money supply differ from the effects of unanticipated changes in the money supply?

5. Illustrate diagrammatically the effects of:
   (a) an anticipated increase in the money stock,
   (b) an unanticipated increase in the money stock,
   (c) an increase in the money supply — part of which was anticipated and part of which was unanticipated,
   (d) an anticipated rise in the money stock which turns out to be the opposite of the actual change.

6. "Whereas an unanticipated increase in the money supply lowers the real wage paid by firms, it increases the perceived real wage received by employees." Is this statement true or false? Explain.

7. "Only anticipated increases in the price level have output effects, since in order for producers to increase production during times of high prices, such increases must be anticipated." Within the context of the model we have developed, explain what is wrong with this statement.

Appendix:

The Algebra of Rational Expectations Equilibrium

This appendix sets out the simple algebra of a rational expectations equilibrium model. It presents the simplest example of a rational expectations equilibrium so that you may see the connection between this equilibrium and the equilibrium of the fixed price *IS-LM* analysis of aggregate demand. There is nothing of substance in this appendix that does not appear in the preceding chapters. As with the other algebraic appendices, if you feel comfortable with this kind of treatment, you will probably find this a convenient, compact summary of the material presented in words and diagrams in the text of the chapter.

The starting point is the *IS-LM* analysis of aggregate demand. Recall, or check back if necessary to Equation (13A.11) from the Appendix to Chapter 13, that the level of real income as determined in the *IS-LM* analysis is:

$$y = \frac{a + i_0 + g - bt + \dfrac{h}{\ell}\left(\dfrac{M}{P_0} - m_0\right)}{1 - b + (kh/\ell)} \tag{19A.1}$$

This will be the level of real income (y) if the price level is *fixed* at P_0. You may think of Equation (19A.1) as determining *aggregate demand* by allowing the price level to *vary*. The level of real income at each price level (P) is the level of aggregate demand (y^d). To emphasize this, Equation (19A.1) is modified as follows:

$$y^d = \frac{a + i_0 + g + bt + \dfrac{h}{\ell}\left(\dfrac{M}{P} - m_0\right)}{1 - b + (kh/\ell)} \tag{19A.2}$$

Notice that the difference between Equations (19A.1) and (19A.2) is that Equation (19A.1) tells us the actual level of y for a given level of P (that is, P_0), whereas Equation (19A.2) tells us what the level of aggregate demand (y^d) will be as the price level (P) varies.

We can rewrite Equation (19A.2) with a different emphasis as

$$y^d = \left[\frac{a + i_0 + g - bt - \dfrac{h}{\ell}m_0}{1 - b + (kh/\ell)}\right] + \left[\frac{\dfrac{h}{\ell}}{1 - b + (kh/\ell)}\right]\left(\frac{M}{P}\right) \tag{19A.3}$$

Calling m, the logarithm of M, and p the logarithm of P, we may write an approximation to the above as

$$y_t^d = \alpha_t + \beta(m_t - p_t), \quad \beta > 0 \tag{19A.4}$$

In Equation (19A.4), α represents the first term in brackets in Equation (19A.3), and $\beta(m - p_t)$ is a logarithmic approximation to the second term. The subscript t is added to each variable in Equation (19A.4) to remind us that these magnitudes vary over time. Thus, t represents a given point in time. Evidently, α stands for all the things that cause aggregate demand to vary, other than the real money supply. It incorporates, therefore, government expenditure, taxes, and any shifts in the investment function or the demand for money function. The money supply (m) and the price level (p) are expressed as logarithms, so that $m - p$ is the same as log M/P. (This formulation, which is linear in the logarithm of real money balances rather than the level of real money balances, makes the explicit calculation of expectations more straightforward.) The parameter β is the multiplier effect of a change in the logarithm of real money balances on aggregate demand.

We can represent the expectations-augmented aggregate supply curve in equation form as:

$$y_t^s = y^* + \gamma(p_t - p_t^e), \quad \gamma > 0 \tag{19A.5}$$

where y^* represents full employment output and p and p^e are the logarithms of the actual and expected price level, respectively. This is just a convenient translation into equation form of what you already know. To convince yourself of this, notice first that if the price level was equal to its expected value ($p = p^e$), then aggregate supply would be equal to full-employment aggregate supply y^*. As the actual price level exceeds the expected price level, so output rises above y^*. The positive parameter γ captures this. The only difference (in this simple treatment) between the new classical and new Keynesian approaches to the aggregate supply curve is that the value of γ would be different in the two theories. Because the new Keynesian aggregate supply curve is flatter than the new classical curve that would be represented by a larger γ.

Next, equilibrium prevails, in the sense that aggregate supply equals aggregate demand, and actual output y is also equal to demand and supply. We can write this as two equations. That is

$$y_t = y_t^d = y_t^s \tag{19A.6}$$

The first step in finding the rational expectations equilibrium of this model is to calculate the expected values of output and prices, *given* the expected values of α and m. (A full treatment would also have an explicit theory for the determination of α and m. We shall not make that extension here.) Calculating the expected values of y and p, given the expected values of α and m, simply involves taking the expectations of Equations (19A.4) and (19A.5) and using the fact that actual output is the same as aggregate demand and supply. Letting the superscript e stand for the expected value of a variable, you can immediately see that this implies

$$y_t^e = \alpha_t^e + \beta(m_t^e - p_t^e) \qquad \textbf{(19A.7)}$$

and

$$y_t^e = y^* \qquad \textbf{(19A.8)}$$

Equation (19A.7) follows directly from Equation (19A.4). If Equation (19A.4) describes what determines the actual level of aggregate output demanded and if demand equals actual output, then expected output must be equal to the expected value of α plus β times the expected value of real balances. That is all that Equation (19A.1) says. Equation (19A.8) follows directly from Equation (19A.5). It says what you already know, namely, that expected output will be equal to full-employment output since the expected price level is the rational expectation. That is, p_t^e is the same thing as the expectation of p_t, and so the second term in Equation (19A.5) is expected to be zero.

You can now solve Equation (19A.8) for the expected price level. Substitute Equation (19A.8) into Equation (19A.7) and rearrange it to give

$$p_t^e = m_t^e - \frac{1}{\beta}(y^* - \alpha_t^e) \qquad \textbf{(19A.9)}$$

Recall that p and m are logarithms, so that this says that the expected price level is proportional to the expected money supply.

To calculate the actual levels of output and prices, first of all, substitute Equation (19A.8) into Equation (19A.7) and subtract this equation from Equation (19A.4). Also subtract y^* from both sides of Equation (19A.5). The results are

$$y_t^d - y^* = (\alpha_t - \alpha_t^e) + \beta(m_t - m_t^e) - \beta(p_t - p_t^e) \qquad \textbf{(19A.10)}$$

$$y_t^s - y^* = \gamma(p_t - p_t^e) \qquad \textbf{(19A.11)}$$

Equation (19A.10) says that output will deviate from its full-employment level by the amount that α deviates from its expected level, plus the parameter β times the amount that the money stock deviates from its expected level minus the amount by which the price level deviates from its expected level, multiplied by the same parameter β. It is, in terms of the concepts discussed in the chapter, the unexpected component of aggregate demand. Equation (19A.11), in effect, is simply a rearrangement of Equation (19A.5). It says that deviations of aggregate supply from its full-employment level will be proportional to deviations of the price level from its expectation.

We may now solve these two equations [Equations (19A.10) and (19A.11)] for the *actual* levels of output and prices. Using Equations (19A.10) and (19A.11) with (19A.6), these solutions are

$$y_t = y^* + \frac{\gamma}{\gamma + \beta} [\alpha_t - \alpha_t^e + \beta(m_t - m_t^e)] \qquad \textbf{(19A.12)}$$

and

$$p_t = m_t^e - \frac{1}{\beta}(y^* - \alpha_t^e) + \frac{1}{\gamma + \beta} [\alpha_t - \alpha_t^e + \beta(m_t - m_t^e)] \qquad \textbf{(19A.13)}$$

The output equation says that output deviates from its full-employment level by an amount that depends on the unexpected components of α and the money supply. The price level deviates from its expected level — the first two terms in Equation (19A.13) — by an amount that depends on the deviations of α and the money supply from their expected levels.

Thus, you can see that it is only unanticipated shifts in aggregate demand that affect output, and it is both the anticipated and unanticipated shifts in aggregate demand that affect prices. The multipliers of the *IS-LM* analysis tell us about the distance of the horizontal shift of the aggregate demand curve. Equations (19A.12) and (19A.13) tell us that to the extent that this horizontal shift is anticipated, it will do nothing but raise the price level. To the extent that it is unanticipated, it will raise both output and the price level and will distribute its effects between output and the price level in accordance with the slope parameter γ, the slope of the *EAS* curve. You can see, as a matter of interest, that if γ was infinitely big, the effect of an unanticipated shift in aggregate demand would be exactly the same as the *IS-LM* analysis says, and it would have no effect on the price level. You can see this immediately for the price level in Equation (19A.13). For output, divide the top and bottom of $\gamma/(\gamma + \beta)$ by γ to give $1/[1 + (\beta/\gamma)]$. You now see that as γ approaches ∞, so $1/[1 + (\beta/\gamma)]$ approaches 1, so that Equation (19A.12) becomes the level of real income in the *IS LM* analysis.

IV

UNDERSTANDING THE FACTS

20

Inflation

You are now approaching the most interesting part of your study of macroeconomics. You are familiar with the questions that macroeconomics seeks to answer; with the main facts about Canada's macroeconomic history; and with key elements of the theory of macroeconomics — the theory of the determination of output, the price level, employment, wages, and interest rates.

This and the following three chapters will extend and apply the analysis that you have studied in the previous part of the book and show you how it is possible to make sense of the macroeconomic phenomena described in Chapter 2. Specifically, you will come to understand the phenomena of inflation, unemployment, output growth, and fluctuations in these and other variables in the form of the business cycle.

This and the next two chapters will focus on *trends*. They will abstract from the fluctuations in economic activity that characterize the business cycle. In other words, the first three chapters of this part of the book will focus on long-run relationships and patterns in the data. Chapter 23 will abstract from these long-run patterns and will focus on the cyclical fluctuations — on the departures or deviations from the trends.

You are already aware that when aggregate demand is at its anticipated (or expected) level the economy is in a state of full-employment equilibrium. When aggregate demand deviates from its expected level then output, employment, and other variables depart from their full-employment equilibrium levels. Therefore, in our study of long-term relationships and trends we shall find it useful to focus exclusively on situations in which aggregate demand fluctuations are anticipated (or expected). This will enable us to obtain a clear understanding of trends in inflation, interest rates, unemployment and employment, and output. When we have applied our theories and extended them to show how the trends may be explained we shall then come back to the case in which fluctuations in demand are unanticipated. This will enable us to study the cyclical patterns in the macroeconomic variables.

For emphasis and in order to be absolutely clear you should note that we are not saying, in this and the next two chapters, that fluctuations in aggregate demand that are unanticipated are unimportant. We are simply narrowing our vision and focussing only on the trends for the long-term averages. We shall then come back and look at a case in which we abstract from those trends and focus exclusively on the unanticipated shocks to aggregate demand that generate the ebb and flow of economic activity around the long-term trends.

The central focus of this first chapter is inflation and interest rates. The question of what causes inflation and what can be done to control it is one that has occupied the minds of some of the best economists. It is also a question that is surrounded by a great deal of mythology as well as sheer nonsense. The material that is presented in this chapter is designed to help you to arrive at a clear understanding of what does and does not cause inflation and also to help you understand and avoid some of the principal errors that are made in popular discussion — in the popular press and by political commentators — on this topic.

The chapter will take you through five tasks. These tasks are to:

a) Review the distinction between a once-and-for-all rise in the price level and inflation.

b) Understand how a once-and-for-all rise in the money stock or a once-and-for-all cut in aggregate supply raises the price level.

c) Understand how continuing growth in the money supply leads to inflation and to a gap between the market and real rates of interest.

d) Understand how a change in the growth rate of the money supply leads to a change in inflation and to more volatile inflation than money supply growth.

e) Examine the relationship between money supply growth and inflation in Canada's recent macroeconomic history.

A. Once-and-for-All Price Level Rises and Inflation

Inflation is an on going process whereby prices are rising persistently year after year. A once-and-for-all rise in the price level occurs when the economy experiences a price level that is generally stable but occasionally jumps to a new level. Recall Figure 5.1 in Chapter 5. Two economies are illustrated. One had a price level that increased from 100 to 200 over a period of 4 years. In the other economy, the price level suddenly rose from 100 to 200, and for the rest of the time prices were stable. The first economy has experienced inflation. The second economy experienced a once-and-for-all price rise. This distinction is important in analyzing the effects of various shocks on prices.

Let us now go on to study the forces that can generate once-and-for-all changes in the price level and those that can produce inflation.

B. Once-and-for-All Changes in the Price Level

We shall study the factors that produce a once-and-for-all change in the price level by combining the *IS-LM* analysis of aggregate demand that you studied in Chapter 13 with the full-employment theory of aggregate supply that you met in Chapter 14. (A reminder: we are not saying that the new theories of aggregate supply are irrelevant. We are abstracting from the effects of unanticipated shocks so as to get the clearest possible picture of the consequences of anticipated shocks.)

Figure 20.1 illustrates the determination of the price level. Notice that frame (a) contains the *IS-LM* analysis, and frame (b) contains the aggregate supply and demand analysis. The level of real income is measured on the horizontal axis of each frame and the scale on each axis is the same.

Begin by focussing on an initial full-employment equilibrium at the price level P_0. This equilibrium is depicted in frame (a) at the intersection of the curve $LM_0(P_0)$ and the IS curve. That is, the income level is y^* and the interest rate is r_0. The same equilibrium is depicted in frame (b) as the point at which the aggregate demand curve labelled $AD(M_0,g,t)$ intersects the aggregate supply curve AS. The price level is P_0 and the output level is y^*.

Now imagine that the money supply rises from M_0 to some higher level, say, M_1. If the price level remained at P_0, the LM curve with a money stock of M_1 and the price level of P_0 would be to the right of the original LM curve. This LM curve is shown in frame (a) as that labelled $LM_1(P_0)$. It intersects the IS curve at the point A. The effect of this higher money stock (M_1) in frame (b) is shown by an aggregate demand curve that is wholly to the right of the original aggregate demand curve. Such an aggregate demand curve is shown as that labelled $AD(M_1,g,t)$. Notice that the point on this aggregate demand curve marked A in frame (b) corresponds to the point A in frame (a). It is at the same price level P_0 as the initial equilibrium, but is displaced horizontally to the right and is at a higher level of real income.

Figure 20.1
The Effect of a Once-
And-For-All Rise in the
Money Supply on
Output and the Price
Level

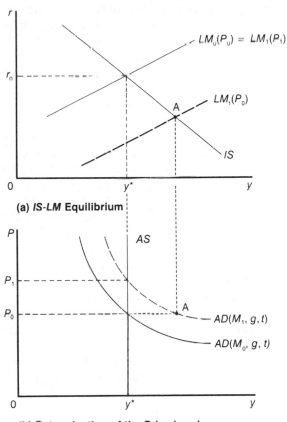

(a) *IS-LM* Equilibrium

(b) **Determination of the Price Level**

At full employment a rise in the money supply produces a proportionate rise in the price level. The initial equilibrium (y^*, r_0, P_0) shown is the intersection of *IS* and *LM* in frame (a) and the intersection of *AD* and *AS* in frame (b). This equilibrium is disturbed by a rise in the money stock. If the price level stayed constant, the *LM* and *AD* curves would shift to the right, and the economy would move to the position A. But at A the economy cannot be in equilibrium because output cannot exceed y^*. This excess demand leads to a rise in the price level. The price level rises to P_1 [frame (b)], and the *LM* curve shifts back to its original position [frame (a)].

This level of real income corresponds to the intersection of the *IS* and $LM_1(P_0)$ curves in frame (a).

It is evident that a position like A cannot be sustained. At point A there is an excess demand for goods. There is also excess demand for labor. Such a situation would produce higher prices and higher wages. How much higher? The answer can be seen by looking in frame (b) at the point at which the new aggregate demand curve, $AD(M_1, g, t)$ [the line drawn for a money stock of M_1] cuts the aggregate supply curve AS. This point is at the price level indicated in frame (b) as P_1. It is the price level that is higher than P_0 by the same percentage amount that the money stock M_1 exceeds the money stock M_0. At this higher price level, the LM curve would not be the curve shown as $LM_1(P_0)$ but rather would be the curve $LM_1(P_1)$. This LM curve is identical to the curve $LM_0(P_0)$. (If you are not sure about this, check back to Chapter 12, where the LM curve was derived and where the factors that cause the LM curve to shift were analyzed.)

You have now analyzed the effects of a once-and-for-all rise in the money stock at full employment. These effects are so simple and yet so important that they are worth emphasizing and highlighting. In frame (a) of Figure 20.1 the initial equilibrium is r_0 and y^* on the IS curve and on the LM curve labelled $LM_0(P_0)$. Now there is a one-shot rise in the money stock, from M_0 to M_1. If the price level remained constant, the LM curve would move to the dashed LM curve, $LM_1(P_0)$. The price level will not, however, remain constant at full employment. It rises, and by an amount such that the LM curve shifts back to its original position, so that it becomes the same curve as before, re-labelled $LM_1(P_1)$.

What are the effects of this one-shot rise in the money stock? The answer is very clear from the figure. There is no effect on the rate of interest and no effect on output. The price level rises proportionately to the one-shot rise in the money stock.

Let us now analyze a different once-and-for-all shock to the economy — a drop in aggregate supply. You are aware from your study of the determination of aggregate supply that shifts in the production function lead to shifts in the aggregate supply curve. (You will meet some further potential shocks to aggregate supply in the next chapter when you study unemployment. They too can be thought of as being relevant to this case and we will remind you of this in the next chapter.) Imagine that for some reason, such as a production function shock, the aggregate supply curve shifts to the right. What happens to output, interest rates and, more importantly for present purposes, the price level? Figure 20.2 illustrates the analysis of this case. Imagine that the economy starts out in exactly the same situation as it did in Figure 20.1. There is a full-employment equilibrium with an output level y_0^*, an interest rate of r_0, and a price level of P_0. That is, the economy is at the point of intersection of the IS curve and LM curve labelled $LM_0(P_0)$ and at the point of intersection of the aggregate demand curve and the aggregate supply curve AS_0.

Now we have a shock to aggregate supply which causes the aggregate supply curve to shift leftwards to the curve labelled AS_1. What now happens? Clearly the economy cannot simply stay at the old price level P_0. If it did it would be at the point marked B in frame (b) and this is not a sustainable position because at this point there is excess demand. This excess demand would raise the price level.

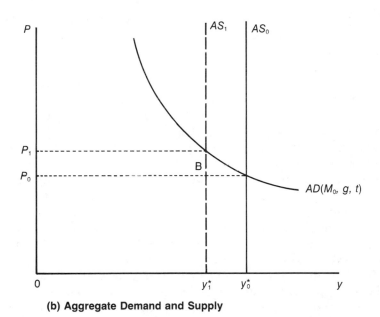

**Figure 20.2
The Effect of a Once-And-For-All Drop in Aggregate Supply on Output and the Price Level**

(a) *IS-LM* Analysis

(b) Aggregate Demand and Supply

An initial equilibrium (y_0^*, r_0, P_0) is shown at the intersection of the *IS* curve and LM_0 (P_0) in frame (a) and of the AD curve and AS_0 in frame (b). A technology shock lowers aggregate supply to AS_1. This fall in aggregate supply means that, at the old price level P_0 there is excess demand. This excess demand leads to a rise in the price level to P_1. At P_1 the real money supply declines so that the *LM* curve becomes $LM_0(P_1)$. The interest rate rises to r_1. The drop in aggregate supply leads to a higher price level, a higher real interest rate and lower output.

This happens and the price level rises until it reaches the level P_1. With a price level of P_1 the real money supply has declined so the *LM* curve moves to the left. Such an *LM* curve is shown as that labelled $LM_0(P_1)$ in frame (a). The equilibrium rate of interest has risen from r_0 to r_1. The reason why the rate of interest rises is that at a lower level of income, less will be saved. Since savings plus taxes must equal investment plus government spending the level of investment will also have to decline. Investment will only decline if the interest rate rises and that is precisely what happens in equilibrium.

You can now see that the effects of a once-and-for-all drop in aggregate supply are not entirely the same as the effects of a once-and-for-all rise in the supply of money. In the first case, that of the monetary shock, the only thing that happens is that the price level rises by the same percentage amount as the rise in the money supply. Nothing real changes. In the second case, that of a technology shock, there are real effects. This is not surprising since the shock is a real shock. A drop in aggregate supply represents a real change — a change in the economy's real productive potential. The price level rise is similar in the two cases but there the similarity ends. In the case of the technology shock, output falls and the real rate of interest rises.

Within the framework of this model there are two other types of shocks that we could analyze that would have the effects of changing the price level in a once-and-for-all fashion. We shall not work through these in detail but leave them as exercises that you may find interesting to undertake in order to reinforce your understanding of the work that you have just done. One such shock is a shock to the *IS* curve. Suppose that there was an anticipated rise in government spending or cut in taxes that shifted the *IS* curve to the right. You should be able to work out that the effects of this shock are a rise in the real rate of interest and a rise in the price level in a once-and-for-all fashion. Output remains constant.

The second kind of shock that you can analyze is one to the demand for money function. Suppose that the propensity to hold money changed in a predictable but sizeable way (for example, such as appears to have happened in the Canadian data in the early 1980s — check back to Chapter 11). Typically, suppose the propensity to hold money declined. You should be able to figure out that this would produce a rightward shift in the *LM* curve which in turn should lead to a rise in the price level. In this case, like the case of a rise in the money supply, the only thing that happens is that the price level changes. There are no change in the real variables.

You have now reviewed all the shocks that are capable of generating a once-and-for-all change in the price level. (The analysis that we have conducted looked at the case of a rise in the price level. You can reverse the exercises to produce once-and-for-all drops in the price level.) It is now time to move on to consider the perhaps more interesting case of the factors that can produce a continuously rising price level — inflation.

C. How Inflation is Generated

We shall discover how inflation is generated most effectively by taking a slightly roundabout route. The starting point for our analysis is to recall that the demand for money depends on the rate of interest that is available on other financial assets. That is, the demand for money varies inversely with the *market* rate of interest. The market rate of interest is equal to the real rate of interest when there is no inflation. In an inflationary world, however, you have already discovered that the market rate of interest is higher than the real rate of interest by precisely the same amount as the expected rate of inflation. That is,

$$r_m = r + \pi^e \qquad\qquad (20.1)$$

Since the demand for money depends on r_m and not on r, it is necessary to be rather careful in figuring out how to determine equilibrium at full employment when the expected inflation rate is not zero. Figure 20.3 will help you understand how to determine the full-employment equilibrium with inflation that is not zero.

First of all, notice that the vertical axis of Figure 20.3 measures two rates of interest, the real rate, r, and the market rate, r_m. The

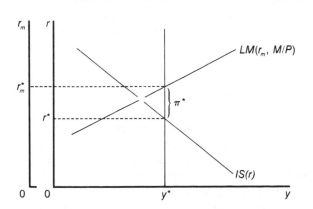

**Figure 20.3
The Effect of a
Continuously Rising
Money Supply**

A continuously rising money supply drives a wedge between the real rate of interest and market (or money) rate of interest equal to the inflation rate. The *IS* curve is drawn against the real rate of interest r, and the *LM* curve is drawn against the market rate of interest r_m. The real interest rate r^* is determined where *IS* cuts the full-employment line, and the market rate of interest r_m^* is determined where *LM* cuts the full-employment line. The vertical distance between the *IS* and *LM* curves at full employment is the rate of inflation, π^*.

diagram also shows the full-employment output level y^*. We are considering only anticipated changes in the money supply so conduct the analysis entirely in terms of the economy being at that output level. Since the demand for money depends on the market or nominal rate of interest, it is necessary to plot the *LM* curve against the market rate of interest. You should be careful to remember that the *LM* curve is indeed plotted against the market rate of interest.

The position of the *LM* curve depends, as you know, on the real money supply, M/P. We are going to analyze a situation in which both M and P are rising. As a result, it will be evident that the *LM* curve will be continuously shifting unless M and P are growing at the same rate. When M and P are growing at the same rate, M/P will be constant, and as a result the *LM* curve will be stationary.

To remind you that the *LM* curve is plotted against the market rate of interest, r_m, and that it depends on the real money supply M/P, the *LM* curve has been labelled $LM(r_m, M/P)$.

The *IS* curve, defined as it is by the equality of investment-plus-government spending with savings-plus-taxes, depends on the real rate of interest. To remind you of this, we have labelled the *IS* curve $IS(r)$. Notice that the *IS* and *LM* curves have been drawn with a break in them. The break coincides with the point at which those two curves would have intersected if they had been drawn continuously. This has been done to remind you that the point at which those two curves cut in this figure is irrelevant. (Strictly speaking, there is no point at which these two curves cut because one of them is plotted against the market rate of interest and the other against the real rate of interest. So, in effect, the two curves are not drawn in the same space at all.) You may perhaps find it helpful to think of there being two diagrams, one with an *IS* curve plotted against the real interest rate and another one with an *LM* curve plotted against the market rate of interest. Nevertheless, it is useful to draw the two curves in the same picture because we do know that there is a simple link between the two interest rates. This link, of course, is the expected rate of inflation. The market rate of interest is equal to the real rate of interest plus the *expected* rate of inflation.

Since we are focussing on situations in which there are no "surprises" — no unexpected changes in the money supply — the expected rate of inflation and the actual rate of inflation will be equal to each other. This means that the gap between the market rate of interest and the real rate of interest is also equal to the actual rate of inflation. If we are at a given level of income (marked on the horizontal axis of Figure 20.3), and if we are on both the *IS* and *LM* curves, then we can think of the vertical gap between the two curves as measuring the (expected equals actual) rate of inflation. Such an inflation rate is shown as the distance π^* in the figure, when income is at y^*.

Figure 20.3 now can be interpreted as characterizing full-employment equilibrium with an expected and actual inflation rate of π^*. The real interest rate is r^*, and with the income level y^* this puts the economy on the *IS* curve, so that there is an equality between the expenditure and income flows in the goods market. The market interest rate is the real interest rate r^* plus the inflation rate π^*, which equals r_m. This market rate of interest along with an income level of y^* puts the economy on its *LM* curve, so that there is an equality between the supply of and demand for money.

You have now reached the point at which you can almost see what is generating the ongoing inflation. If the price level is rising at a rate π^*, other things being equal, the *LM* curve would be moving leftwards. If the *LM* curve is not moving, there must be something else happening that is just offsetting the pressure to move the *LM* curve as a result of rising prices. It is rather clear what this is; it is a continuously rising money supply. Underlying the *LM* curve, when inflation is proceeding at the rate π^*, there is a rising money supply *and* a rising price level. Each is rising by precisely the same percentage amount so that the real money supply is unchanged. That is, a continuously rising money supply (that is anticipated) generates an anticipated inflation and a gap between the market rate of interest and the real rate of interest.

The precise quantitative relationship between the growth rate of the money supply and the inflation rate needs to be elaborated a little. In the example that we have just worked through we have pretended that output is held constant at y^*. In this particular case, the growth rate of the money supply and the rate of inflation are identical to each other. What would happen, however, if real income was, on the average, growing? We know that real income is trended upwards. This is obviously an important, practical question. You can answer this question very directly by extending the analysis that we conducted in the previous section concerning the effects of a once-and-for-all drop in aggregate supply on the price level. There we discovered that a cut in aggregate supply leads to a rise in the price level. Reversing this analysis would reveal that a once-and-for-all rise in aggregate supply leads to a drop in the price level. It follows immediately from this line of reasoning that an ongoing rise in aggregate supply — a continuous and steady rightward drift in the aggregate supply curve — leads to continuously falling prices (other things being equal). The precise quantitative amount by which the price level declines depends on the income elasticity of the demand for money. Let us see why this is so.

If the demand for money is unit elastic with respect to real income an X percent rise in real income leads to an X percent rise in the demand for money. Simultaneously the rise in real income lowers the price level so that if the money supply itself was constant, the real money supply rises at a rate equal to the rate of decline of prices. To attain equilibrium, the real money supply needs to rise by X percent — the same percent rise in real income that we imagined as initiating this process of adjustment. This requires that the price level fall by X percent.

If the demand for money is less than unit elastic — say, has an elasticity of 1/2 — then a rise in real income of X percent will lead to a rise in the demand for real money of less than X percent — 1/2 of X percent in the special case that we are assuming. This means, if the money supply is constant, that real money has to increase by 1/2 of X percent to maintain equilibrium and this occurs as a result of the price level falling by 1/2 of X percent.

You can now see that a continuous rise in real income, other things being equal, leads to a continuously falling price level equal to the rate of growth of real income multiplied by the income elasticity of the demand for real money balances.

You can now bring these two ideas together. You have seen that a continuously rising money supply, other things being equal, leads to a continuously rising price level with the rate of growth of the money supply equal to the rate of price increase — the rate of inflation. You have also seen that a continuous rise in real income leads to a continuous decline in the price level equal to the real income growth rate multiplied by the income elasticity of demand for real money.

Bringing these two ideas together enables us to write what might be called the *fundamental steady-state inflation equation* which is

$$\pi = \mu - \alpha\rho \qquad\qquad (20.2)$$

where, as before, π is the rate of inflation, μ is the growth rate of the money supply, ρ is the growth rate of real income and α is the income elasticity of demand for real money balances.

Shortly we are going on to analyze what happens to inflation if the growth rate of the money supply *changes*. Before we do that let us ask the question, is there anything else that can produce continuous inflation? We have studied the things that can influence the price level in a once-and-for-all fashion. We have examined the effects of a change in the money stock, a change in income, and in less detail, the effects of shifts in the *IS* curves and in the propensity to hold money — shifts in the *LM* curve induced by things other than a change in the money stock. Could these same factors generate ongoing inflation? To put this question slightly differently, could the *IS* curve continuously shift and could the *LM* curve continuously shift even if the money stock was not growing?

It seems hard to imagine a situation in which the *IS* curve would continuously shift to the right thereby generating continuous upward pressure on the price level. There are natural limits to all the things that underlie the *IS* curve and, while it is imaginable that over prolonged periods sizeable rightward shifts could occur in the *IS* curve, this does not appear to be a potential source for ongoing inflation. For example, a period during which government expenditure was increasing rapidly thereby leading to an ongoing rightward shift in the *IS* curve would produce a temporary period of perhaps quite serious rising prices. Such a process would, however, come to a natural end since there are limits to the volume of government expenditure and capacity to tax. This is not to say that there are not some important connections between fiscal policy and inflation. These connections will be explored in the policy chapters toward the end of this book.

What about continuing changes in the propensity to hold money? Wouldn't forces such as those generate an ongoing inflation? There seems to be more potential here. Improvements in the technology of the financial sector — the application of computers and mechanized record-keeping methods — do seem to lead to ongoing reductions in the amount of real money demanded. Imagine, as a result of the greater use of credit cards and other devices, that people continuously reduce, year after year, their desired holdings of real money balances; then, even if real income was constant, and even if the money supply was not growing, there would be inflation. There would be inflation because people would be trying to reduce the amount of real money they hold and, with income and the nominal money supply constant, the only way in which this could occur would be for prices to rise, thereby eroding the real value of money. In terms of Figure 20.3 the *LM* curve would be continuously shifting to the right if the price level was constant. Since this could not be an equilibrium the price level would have to be rising by exactly the correct amount to offset the tendency for the reduced demand for money to shift the *LM* curve.

You can capture these ideas by introducing a new concept that is very closely related to the propensity to hold money — the concept of the velocity of circulation of money. A given amount of money, M, can support a given flow of expenditure, Py, if the money is circulating at a given speed. We call this speed the velocity of circulation. The velocity of circulation is simply defined as the ratio of expenditure to the money stock. You will recognize immediately that this is precisely the inverse of the propensity to hold money — the ratio of the stock of money to the flow of expenditure.

Using the idea of the velocity of circulation we can capture the ideas expressed above concerning innovation in the use of money with a modified fundamental inflation equation that reads as follows:

$$\pi = \mu - \alpha\rho + \Delta v \qquad \textbf{(20.3)}$$

where Δv stands for the rate of change in the velocity of circulation of money.

You can think of the effects on inflation of ongoing real income growth and of ongoing changes in the demand for money (changes in the velocity of circulation) as being technologically driven and, in a fundamental sense, uncontrollable. However, you can see from the fundamental inflation equation that, nevertheless, the monetary authority has a weapon with which it can control the trend rate of inflation very precisely. This weapon is the trend growth rate in the money supply. Furthermore you can see that even though there are some complexities in the link between real income growth and inflation, the link between money growth and inflation, on the average, is direct and one-for-one. If the monetary authority wishes to slow the trend inflation rate it has to deliver a lower trend growth rate for the money supply. In this sense, therefore, anti-inflation policy is trivially simple to design and execute. However, there are complexities associated with implementing a policy that delivers a very predictable money supply growth rate, and also with interactions between unanticipated changes in the money supply and the level of real economic activity, such as employment and unemployment. We shall explore some of these linkages in subsequent chapters. However, these complexities should not be allowed to cloud the main issue. The main issue is revealed with crystal clarity from the foregoing analysis and in the fundamental inflation equation set out above.

Let us now go on to consider one other complication in the link between money and inflation and analyze what happens to the inflation rate when the money supply growth rate is *changed*.

D. Inflation and a Rise in the Money Supply Growth Rate

You can think of the analysis that we have conducted in the preceding section as telling us about inflation and money supply growth in an economy in which the money supply growth rate is constant. You could think of the analysis also as being relevant to a comparison of two economies, one that has a high money supply growth rate and one that has a low money supply growth rate. It does not tell us, however, what happens when the growth rate of the money supply is changed — say increased. This is what we shall now go on to examine. What would happen to the equilibrium depicted in Figure 20.3 if there was a rise in the growth rate of the money supply? The answer is illustrated in Figure 20.4.

The starting point is the full-employment equilibrium shown with an inflation rate of π_0. This equilibrium is now disturbed by a rise in the growth rate of the money supply. An increase in the growth rate of the money supply, other things being equal, would tend to make the *LM* curve move to the right. If the inflation rate stayed constant at π_0, this would lower the market rate of interest and the real rate of interest and would generate a higher level of aggregate demand. Remember that the level of aggregate demand and the interest rates are determined where the vertical gap between the *IS* and *LM* curves equals the inflation rate π_0. This rise in aggregate demand would create excess demand for goods. The excess demand for goods would put upward pressure on the inflation rate, and the rising inflation rate would offset the rightward movement of the *LM* curve and start the *LM* curve moving in the opposite direction. Where is the new equilibrium? The only new equlibrium that is possible is the one that arises when the *LM* curve has shifted, not to the right at all, but to the left and by enough to have raised the market rate of interest above the real rate of interest by the amount of the new, higher rate of money growth and rate of inflation. By the time the economy settles down on the *LM* curve labelled $LM_1(r_m,(M/P)_1)$, such a situation will have arisen. In this situation, the real interest rate is unaffected and the output level is unaffected; but the market rate of interest is higher, the inflation rate is higher and the money supply growth rate is higher, all by the same amount as each other.

Why does the *LM* curve move from the curve LM_0 to LM_1? The answer must be that the real money supply has fallen between these two situations. How could this have happened? The answer essentially is that at the moment in which the money supply growth rate increases there are two forces working on the inflation rate. One of these forces is the higher money supply growth rate, the other is a fall in the demand for money. How does this fall in the demand for money come about? You already know that a rise in the money supply growth rate which raises the inflation rate also raises the market rate

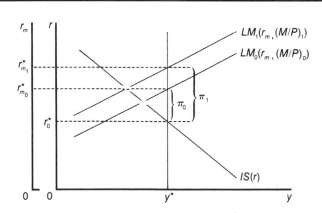

Figure 20.4
The Effect of a Rise in the Money Supply Growth Rate

The initial equilibrium (subscripted 0) is disturbed by making the money supply grow at a faster rate. This produces a faster rate of inflation that is initially greater than the growth rate of the money supply. This lowers the stock of real balances and shifts the *LM* curve to the left. The new equilibrium, subscripted 1, is one in which the inflation rate (π_1) equals the new higher money supply growth rate.

of interest. This means that the opportunity cost of holding money increases and as a result people will try to economize on their money holdings, thereby reducing their demand for money. This drop in the demand for money induced by a higher market interest rate also puts additional excess demand pressure on the markets for goods and services and this raises the price level yet further.

If everything works out smoothly and instantaneously the extra effect on the price level would occur at the point in time at which the money supply growth rate was increased. The paths of the money supply and the price level would be as depicted in Figure 20.5. The way to read Figure 20.5 is as follows.

First, the vertical axis measures the logarithms of the price level and the money supply. The horizontal axis measures time. This means that we can depict a continuous growth rate in the money supply or the price level as a straight line. If the growth rate is positive then the line slopes upwards such that the slope of the line equals the growth rate — the steeper the line, the faster the growth rate. Imagine that between period 0 and period z the money supply and the price level were growing at the same constant rate as depicted in the figure. Then imagine that at point z the money supply growth rate increases (doubles from, say, 5 percent to 10 percent). The dashed line shows what happens to the price level. At time z the price level jumps. Immediately thereafter the price level continues to rise but at the

**Figure 20.5
The Price Level and
the Money Supply**

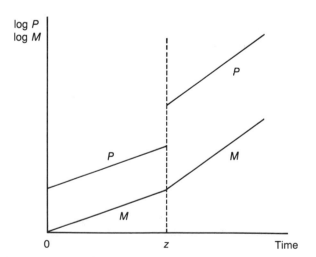

As the money supply growth rate is increased at time z there is a rise in the inflation rate. The higher inflation rate raises the market interest rate and lowers the demand for money. This drop in the demand for money adds additional excess demand pressure and this produces a once-and-for-all rise in the price level at time z.

same rate as the money supply is growing. In terms of inflation, there is a spike in the inflation rate for an instant at time z and thereafter the inflation rate is equal to the money supply growth rate. This jump in the price level is what makes the level of real money balances decline and what makes the *LM* curve shift to the left from the curve labelled LM_0 to the curve LM_1.

The particular relationship between prices and money supply shown in Figure 20.5 is not likely to be seen in any real world data. The hypothetical experiment that we have conducted to generate this change is very special. Strictly speaking, the experiment requires the following conditions. First, before the point in time z, everyone expected that the money supply growth rate would remain at its low level forever. At the moment z when the money supply growth rate was increased people were caught by surprise, but immediately thereafter they came to believe, and correctly, that the money supply growth rate would now forever be at its new higher rate. In any real-world economy this example is not going to occur. Rather, when the money supply growth rate changes it will, to some extent, be regarded as a permanent change in the trend growth rate and, to some extent, be suspected as being temporary. This means that instead of a clean jump in the price level at the point in time at which the money supply growth rate changes there will be a tendency for the price level to rise but in a steady fashion and at a somewhat higher rate than the growth rate of the money supply. This is illustrated in Figure 20.6.

You will find Figure 20.6 is identical to that presented above but the effects, rather than being concentrated on the particular point z, are distributed over time. In more intuitive, if somewhat looser terms, we can describe the process illustrated in Figure 20.6 as follows: first, when the money supply growth rate is increased from 5 percent to 10 percent, people are not sure whether that increase is permanent or temporary. To the extent that they believe it to be a temporary increase they do not revise their long-term inflationary expectations and market rates of interest do not increase. As a result the demand for money does not decline by very much and so not much additional pressure is placed upon the inflation rate. Thus, at the point in time z, the only force working on the inflation rate is the growth rate of the money supply itself. The inflation rate rises to equal the new higher growth rate of the money supply.

The longer the new higher growth rate of the money supply is maintained the more people come to realize that this higher growth rate is permanent. They increase, therefore, their long-term inflation expectations, and these expectations get incorporated into higher market rates of interest. The higher interest rates induce further reductions in the demand for money. This decline in the demand for money added to the increase in supply of money force the inflation rate up even higher. The inflation rate follows the path marked π

which overshoots the growth rate of the money supply μ but which approaches the money supply growth rate gradually from above.

You can now see that although the appropriate policies for avoiding inflation are clear and straightforward, policies for lowering the inflation rate are not so straightforward. If you reverse the analysis that we have just conducted you would see a sudden cut in the growth rate of the money supply by the monetary authority in order to achieve a lower rate of inflation produces a fall in the inflation rate that undershoots the new lower growth rate of the money supply. This could, if pursued vigorously enough, even produce falling prices for a period. Therefore, the best way to slow down inflation requires some analysis of various forces that we have studied here.

There is one very important implication of the analysis that we have just conducted that you should notice. This implication is that it is not possible for the monetary authority to permanently lower the market rate of interest by increasing the money supply. We have seen that a once-and-for-all rise in the money stock produces a once-and-for-all rise in the price level with no change in the market rate of interest. We have also seen that a rise in the growth rate of the money supply produces, in equilibrium, a rise in the market rate of

Figure 20.6
The Overshooting
Proposition

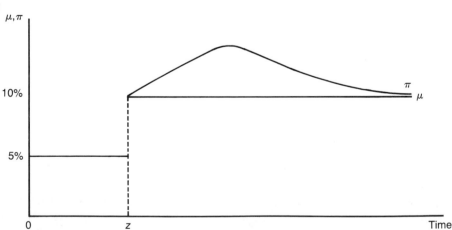

When the money supply growth rate is increased, if that increase is not initially expected to be permanent, interest rates will not rise by enough to cause an instantaneous jump in the price level. Instead the inflation rate will rise by only the amount of the rise in the money supply growth rate. If the higher growth rate of money is maintained and people come to regard it as permanent, then expectations of inflation will be increased and so market interest rates will rise. The resulting drop in the demand for money causes the inflation rate to rise even higher, thus overshooting the growth rate of the money supply.

interest and a rise in the rate of inflation. Initially, it is possible that a rise in the growth rate of the money supply would create a fall in the market rate of interest, but such a fall could only be temporary.

You now have a much richer understanding of the theory of inflation and of the inflation process. Let us now turn to our final task and see how the principles that we have learned in this chapter apply in the Canadian data.

E. Canadian Money Supply Growth and Inflation

The money supply growth rate in Canada may be measured either by the growth rate of M1 or the growth rate of some broader aggregate. Although there is no longer any official monetary target in Canada the Bank of Canada did use M1 as its monetary target during the period of official monetary control. (See Chapter 39 for more details.) We shall, therefore, use the M1 aggregate for present purposes. The growth rate of M1 is set out in Table 20.1 and charted in Figure 20.7. It is immediately clear that the money supply growth rate has been erratic over this almost twenty-year period. Starting out in 1967 with a fairly high growth rate, there was a sharp reduction in 1968, a sharp rise in 1969 and then a very severe cutback in 1970. After that there was a sudden burst of monetary expansion in 1971 to 1973 with the growth rate moving into the teens. From 1973 to 1982 the money supply growth rate has been pulled back, although in 1975 there was a short-lived return to a low teens growth rate. In 1983, there was also a temporary burst of high money growth.

TABLE 20.1
Money Supply (M1) Growth Rate in
Canada 1967–1984

YEAR	M1 GROWTH RATE
1967	9.8
1968	4.3
1969	7.1
1970	2.3
1971	12.7
1972	14.3
1973	14.4
1974	9.5
1975	13.8
1976	8.0
1977	8.3
1978	10.1
1979	6.9
1980	6.4
1981	3.6
1982	0.7
1983	10.2
1984	3.2

Source. Bank of Canada Review, November 1978 and July 1985, Table 1, column (1).

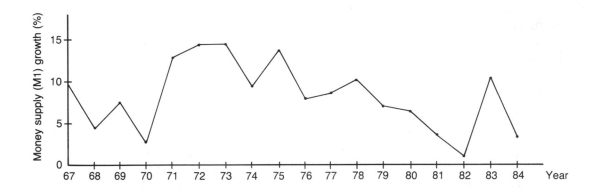

Figure 20.7
Canadian Money Supply (M1) Growth 1967-1984

Money supply growth has been erratic. The strongest burst of monetary growth was in the period 1971-1973. Before then the money growth rate was more moderate, and after that it declined through to 1982. In 1983 there was a temporary burst of high money growth.

Source: Table 20.1

Up to 1975 the Bank of Canada had no targets for money supply growth. From 1975 to 1982 targets were adopted. The target growth rate was gradually reduced and, broadly speaking, the Bank of Canada kept the money supply growth inside its target range. What is the relationship between the money supply growth rate and inflation? You will recall that the theory that we have developed says that provided the growth rate of the money supply is steady, inflation will be equal to the rate of growth of the money supply minus the rate of growth of real income plus an allowance for the change in the velocity of circulation (or the propensity to hold money). The growth rate of money supply has not been steady; on the contrary it has been highly erratic. The theory, in this case, tells us that the rate of inflation should also be erratic, and from the overshooting proposition, the rate of inflation should be more erratic than the rate of money supply growth: the rate of inflation is predicted to rise faster than money supply growth when the money supply growth has been increased, and predicted to fall more quickly than money supply growth when the money supply growth has been decreased. Further, the overshooting proposition states that the change in inflation will overshoot the change in the money supply growth rate immediately as the money supply growth rate changes.

Figure 20.8 charts the movements in inflation and money supply growth. The line marked π measures the rate of inflation. The other

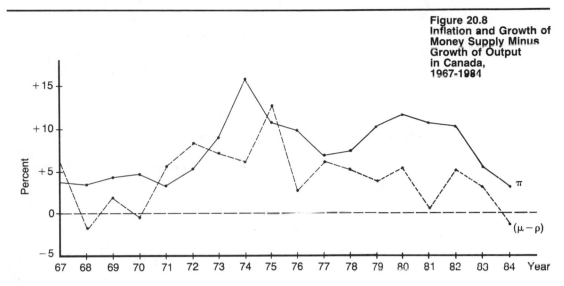

**Figure 20.8
Inflation and Growth of
Money Supply Minus
Growth of Output
in Canada,
1967-1984**

Inflation (π) and the money supply growth minus output growth ($\mu - \rho$) follow the same broad pattern. Also, inflation tends to overshoot money supply growth in the rise to the 1974 peak. Contrary to the prediction of the theory, there is a considerable time lag in the relation between inflation and money growth.

Source: Appendix to Chapter 2 and Table 20.1

line, marked $\mu - \rho$, measures the rate of growth of the money supply minus the rate of growth of real income. This is the variable which, in a steady state, would equal the rate of inflation (if the income elasticity of the demand for money was 1). It is evident that the trends in the rate of inflation are similar to the trends in the excess of monetary growth over real income growth. From 1968 to 1975 these two variables have a rising trend and since 1975 both have a declining trend. There is also an apparent tendency for some overshooting. The inflation rate overshoots the excess of monetary growth over real income during 1973 and 1974 following the money supply growth increase from 1971 to 1972. There is, however, contrary to the predictions of the theory, a considerable time lag in that relationship. Also, it is clear that as money supply growth rate was reduced in 1976 there was no tendency for the inflation rate to undershoot the money supply growth rate, as would be predicted by the theory. The trends in inflation, however, are reasonably well explained by the theory, but the timing of inflation is badly explained, and there is little tendency for inflation to undershoot the growth rate of the money supply when it is lowered. The overshooting proposition, which predicts that inflation will immediately change when the money supply growth rate changes, is strongly rejected.

Summary

A. Once-and-for-All Price Level Rises and Inflation

Inflation is an ongoing process of persistently rising prices. A once-and-for-all rise in the price level occurs when the price level moves from one steady-state level to another steady-state level.

B. Once-and-for-All Changes in the Price Level

A once-and-for-all rise in the money supply, a once-and-for-all cut in output, a once-and-for-all shift in the *IS* curve to the right, or a once-and-for-all drop in the propensity to hold money all lead to a once-and-for-all rise in the price level.

C. How Inflation is Generated

Inflation is generated by an ongoing increase in the money supply. The fundamental inflation equation states that the rate of inflation equals the rate of growth of the money supply minus the rate of growth of real income (multiplied by the income elasticity of demand for money) plus the rate of change in the velocity of circulation.

D. Inflation and a Rise in the Money Supply Growth Rate

A change in the growth rate of the money supply leads to a change in the rate of inflation. The inflation rate change will be greater than the change in the growth rate of the money supply. In other words, inflation will overshoot the money supply growth rate.

E. Canadian Money Supply Growth and Inflation

Although there is far from a perfect link between the year-to-year changes in money growth and inflation there is, in broad terms, a remarkable formation of the basic theory of inflation in the Canadian data. Figure 20.8 illustrates that relationship. Inflation and the excess of monetary growth over output have a rising trend from 1968 to 1975 and a falling trend since 1975. The overshooting proposition which states that the change in inflation will overshoot the change in the excess of monetary growth over output immediately seems to be strongly rejected by the Canadian data.

Review Questions

1. From the following, label those that are a once-and-for-all rise in the price level and those that are inflation:
    (a) The price of beef this week rose by 10 percent.
    (b) The Consumer Price Index, after having been steady for one year, jumped 10 percent at the beginning of last winter but has been steady ever since.

(c) Over the past decade the Consumer Price Index has gradually and consistently increased, so that today it is double what it was a decade ago.

(d) Over the last decade the Consumer Price Index doubled but this is the result of two big jumps, one in 1974 and one in 1979.

2. Imagine an economy that has been experiencing stable prices for as long as anyone can remember. Suddenly there is a doubling in the quantity of money. The money supply then remains constant at its new level. What happens in that economy to output, employment, real wages, and the price level? Why? Trace out all the effects and fully set our your reasoning.

3. Does the price level "overshoot" the money supply in the situation described in Question 2? If so, why? If not, why not?

4. Imagine an economy that has experienced 10 percent inflation for as long as anyone can remember. Output has been constant, and the money supply has grown at the same 10 percent rate as inflation. Suddenly there is a doubling in the growth rate of the money supply, after which the new higher (20 percent) growth rate is maintained. What happens in this economy to output, employment, real wages, and inflation?

5. Does the inflation rate "overshoot" the money supply growth rate in the economy described in Question 4? If so, why? If not, why not?

6. Describe what would happen to interest rates in the event of monetary shocks such as those set out in Questions 2 and 4 above.

7. Analyze the effects on the price level of a rise in government spending, and a once-and-for-all drop in the demand for money.

8. Does the fact that output growth and ongoing changes in the demand for money affect the rate of inflation mean that the monetary authories have no tools with which to manipulate the inflation rate?

9. Review the connection between the rate of inflation and the real and nominal rates of interest. What policy actions could the government take that would lower real rates of interest? What actions could they take that would lower nominal interest rates? Are there some policies that might raise real interest rates and lower nominal interest rates?

21
Unemployment

You do not need reminding that unemployment is an important problem in Canada today. In the winter of 1983 its rate reached more than 13 percent. Since the early 1950s, when unemployment was less than 4 percent, there has been a clear and persistent upward trend in its rate. The objective of this chapter is to help you to understand some of the reasons why unemployment exists, why it persists, and why it has followed a persistent upward trend.

As in the case of the previous chapter we shall focus here on fluctuations in unemployment that do not arise from "surprise" fluctuations in aggregate demand. The economy will be at full employment even though we are studying the factors that cause unemployment! This sounds paradoxical but a moment's reflection will tell you that it is not. You will recall that the definition of full employment is nothing other than a situation in which expectations are realized. There can be, and as you will see there often is, a sizeable amount of unemployment even in such a situation and its rate can fluctuate as a result of forces that we are now going to analyze.

In particular we shall look at the effects of five types of things: minimum wage laws; the actions of labor unions; the effects of unemployment insurance benefits; the effects of uneven pace of technical change in different sectors of the economy leading to changes in the amount of reallocation of labor between the sectors; and finally, the effects of taxes. We will also examine the importance of these factors in Canada's recent macroeconomic history.

The rest of this chapter will help you to understand some of the reasons why unemployment arises and what leads to variations in its rate by pursuing six tasks, which are to:

a) Understand how minimum wage laws create unemployment.
b) Understand how labor unions raise wages and create unemployment.
c) Understand how job search causes unemployment.
d) Understand how unemployment insurance programs create unemployment.
e) Understand how taxes affect unemployment.
f) Evaluate the importance of these influences on unemployment in Canada's recent macroeconomic theory.

A. Minimum Wage Laws and Unemployment

Every province in Canada has minimum wage regulations. In Ontario it is illegal to employ a person for a wage rate of less than $4 per hour, unless that person is a student under 18, in which case it is illegal to employ such a person for less than $3.15 per hour. (The figures vary somewhat across the provinces.)[1]

What are the effects of minimum wages? To answer this question the starting point is to recognize that minimum wages are determined by government regulation at a level *higher* than that which would prevail in unregulated labor markets. The minimum wage is set in terms of so many dollars per hour — that is, it is set as a *money* wage. The money wage is revised from time to time, however, and it is clear that what the legislators have in mind is the establishment of a minimum real wage which is above the competitive equilibrium real wage.

It is also clear that a very large fraction of the labor force is not directly affected by minimum wages. Minimum wages impinge directly only upon those workers who would otherwise have been paid a wage below the minimum. However, *minimum wages do affect* the *economy average real wage*, and for two reasons. First, since the economy average real wage is an average of all the individual real wages, the introduction of minimum wages results in a rise in the economy average real wage as a consequence of chopping off the bottom end of the wage distribution (those wages that would be lower than the minimum wage). Second, there will be a rise in the economy average real wage as a result of competitive pressures. If the lowest wage workers are paid a higher rate than an unregulated market would pay, there will be pressure to raise other wages as well. On the supply

---

[1] These figures refer to the time of writing — September 1985.

side, there will be a tendency for people to try to substitute away from slightly higher paid but more demanding jobs and enter those jobs that now attract the minimum wage rate. On the demand side, firms will substitute more expensive but more highly skilled labor for those whose wages have been increased by the minimum wage regulation. These shifts of supply towards lower productivity jobs and of demand towards more highly skilled labor will put upward pressure on real wages all the way up the scale (with the pressure of course diminishing as you move further up the income scale).

For these two reasons, then — (1) chopping off the bottom end of the wage distribution, and (2) the competitive pressures pushing up the real wages in substitute activities — the imposition of a minimum wage will raise the economy average real wage above the competitive equilibrium level. Furthermore, the higher the minimum wage relative to the competitive equilibrium wage, the bigger will be the rise in the economy average real wage relative to its competitive equilibrium.

It is now possible to analyze the effects of minimum wages. In conducting our analysis we shall find it convenient to use the classical theory of the labor market since we are focussing on the situations in which there are no discrepancies between actual and expected aggregate demand and, therefore, no discrepancies between the actual and the expected price level. We may conduct the analysis in Figure 21.1. The vertical axis of Figure 21.1 measures the economy average real wage, and the horizontal axis measures the aggregate level of employment, n. The curves labelled n^d and n^s are the labor demand and supply curves respectively. The competitive equilibrium in this labor market is the real wage $(W/P)^*$ and the employment level n^*.

Now suppose that a minimum wage is established that has the effect of raising the economy average real wage to the level marked in Figure 21.1 as $(W/P)_{min}$. What is the effect of this minimum wage law?

In a market economy in which all exchange is voluntary, no one can compel employers to hire more workers than they choose to hire. At the higher economy average real wage, $(W/P)_{min}$, the demand for labor is less than the supply of labor. It is, therefore, the demand for labor curve that will determine how much labor is employed. The level of employment will be n_1^d. This is the amount read off from the demand curve at the economy average real wage induced by the minimum wage legislation. The supply of labor at that real wage will be n_1^s.

The gap between the supply of labor n_1^s and the demand for labor n_1^d represents the number of people who will be unemployed, u_1. If you recall the definition of unemployment and the way in which unemployment is measured in Canada, you will verify that the people in the group u_1 will be recorded as unemployed. When surveyed, they

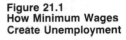

**Figure 21.1
How Minimum Wages
Create Unemployment**

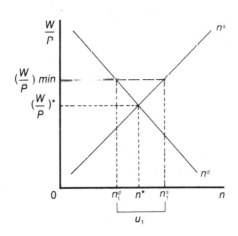

A minimum wage set higher than the competitive equilibrium wage raises the economy average real wage $(W/P)_{min}$ above the competitve equilibrium $(W/P)^*$. This creates a regulated equilibrium at which the quantity of labor employed is equal to the quantity demanded n_1^d, which is less than the quantity supplied n_1^s. The gap between the quantity supplied and demanded, u_1, measures the quantity of unemployment.

will show up as being available for work, willing to work and able to work, but not having work. The higher the economy average real wage relative to the competitive equilibrium wage, the greater will be the reduction in employment, the larger will be the number of people willing to work (the labor force) and the greater will be the amount of unemployment created.

The economy will now be in a regulated equilibrium. It is important to realize that an equilibrium is nothing more than a state of rest or, equivalently, a state in which all the forces acting on a variable exactly offset each other. One of the forces acting on the economy in this case is the minimum wage regulation, and so the real wage and employment level come to rest at a point different from the competitive equilibrium that would be reached in the absence of the regulation.

If you recall the water-level analogy (Chapter 13), minimum wage regulation is like a dam that alters the equilibrium levels of water on either side of it.

To summarize: minimum wages raise the economy average real wage above its competitive equilibrium level and generate a regulated equilibrium in which there is lower employment, a larger labor force and persistent unemployment.

B. Labor Unions and Unemployment

Labor unions are a dominant institution in the labor market. They act as an agent for households in the negotiation of employment and wage contracts. However, a much larger fraction of the labor force works on contracts negotiated by unions than are members of unions. In analyzing the effects of unions on the macroeconomic variables we shall pretend that there is a single economy-wide union — one that embraces the entire labor force.

The economy will be described using Figure 21.2. First, focus your attention on the competitive equilibrium. The curves labelled n^d and n^s are the demand and supply of labor curves (identical to those in Figure 21.1), and the economy-average real wage $(W/P)^*$ and the employment level n^* are the competitive equilibrium values for those variables. Now suppose that all the workers in this economy join an economy-wide labor union which seeks to raise real wages.

There are two types of things that the labor union could do in order to raise the real wages of its members. One possibility would be to declare that no one may work for less than the union real wage, and then to enforce this rule either by having some sort of legal protection or by using more indirect pressures. The introduction of the union real wage, like a minimum wage law raises the economy average real wage to, say $(W/P)_u$. Alternatively, the union could restrict the supply of labor by, for example, defining minimum acceptable qualifications for particular jobs such that the number of people able to meet the minimum qualifications was less than the labor supply in the absence of the union. In that event, supply would be artificially restricted, and the supply curve would move to the left of the non-union supply curve.

Either way, the result would be a higher economy average real wage and a lower level of employment. Figure 21.2 illustrates this. In examining Figure 21.2, keep the competitive equilibrium firmly in mind as a reference point. We can illustrate what happens if the union declares a *minimum wage* below which no one may be employed by recording the union-induced economy average real wage, say, $(W/P)_u$, on the vertical axis of the figure. This wage is above the competitive equilibrium real wage. Then, simply by reading off from the demand for labor curve, you can see that at the real wage $(W/P)_u$, the level of employment is n_u. This is less than the competitive employment level n^*. At the union-induced economy average real wage n_u^s people would like to have a job, and the difference between n_u^s and n_u represents the level of unemployment induced by this economy-wide labor union.

If, alternatively, the union enforced *minimum qualifications* that had the effect of shifting the labor supply curve to the left — to a position such as that shown as n_r^s — the effect would be an increased economy average real wage and lower employment. (The diagram is drawn so that the same effect arises from either of these policies. This has been done only to simplify the diagram. There is no presumption that both union strategies would have exactly the same effect.)

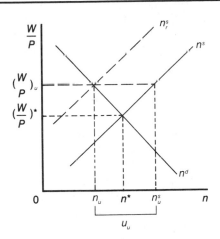

**Figure 21.2
Labor Market
Equilibrium with an
Economy-Wide Union**

An economy-wide union either restricts the supply of labor, n_r^s below the competitive supply n^s or raises the wage level $(W/P)_u$ above the competitive equilibrium rate, $(W/P)^*$. The effect is the same in either case. It lowers the employment level from n^* to n_u but raises the labor force from n^* to n_u^s. The gap between the labor force and the employment level is the amount of union-induced unemployment u_u.

In this case, the people unemployed are unemployed because they do not meet the minimum qualification standards for the job. This can often be made to look semi-respectable, for example, by dressing up the restriction as "protecting the consumer," and is therefore a much more commonly employed practice among labor unions than that of simply declaring that no one may work for less than a certain wage. It is especially widely practiced by professional labor unions such as those in the legal and medical industries. It is an easier restriction to enforce.

Either way, whether it sets union wages or introduces minimum qualifications, an economy-wide labor union will have the same kind of effect on employment and the economy average real wage as would a government-enforced minimum wage law. The economy-wide union will raise the economy average real wage above its competitive equilibrium level, will lower the level of employment, raise the quantity of labor supplied (the labor force), and will generate unemployment. The greater the ability of the union to raise the economy average real wage above the competitive equilibrium level, the bigger these effects will be.

C. Job Search and Unemployment

People allocate their time to three major economic activities: work, leisure, and job search.

Jobs cannot be found without search, and search is costly. It is useful to think of job search as being an investment. It has a cost and an expected return. The higher the cost, the smaller the amount of job-search activity undertaken. The higher the expected return or payoff, the bigger the amount of job-search activity undertaken.

Much job searching is done on a casual basis while a person is employed. Some job searchers, however, specialize in searching; that is, they cease to be workers for a period in which they spend all their non-leisure time in job-search activities. These job searchers are interesting from a macroeconomic point of view for they will be recorded as unemployed.

For a given cost of job search, it seems reasonable to suppose that the number of people engaged in full-time job search will depend on two main factors. They are: the size of the labor force and the spread between the highest and the lowest wages that are available. First, consider the relationship between full-time job search and the size of the labor force, holding the spread between the highest and lowest available wages constant at some level D_0. As you already know, the higher the economy average real wage, the bigger is the labor force. This would lead us to suppose that the supply of job search would increase as the economy average real wage increases. We need to be careful, however, before we accept this conclusion. Caution is needed because increases in the economy average real wage will also affect the costs and benefits of job search.

You can think of the wage as being part of the opportunity cost of job search. That is, over and above the direct costs involved (phone calls, travel, etc.), there is the cost of foregone earnings measured by the wage that would have been obtained from accepting the first job that came along. The higher the economy average real wage, the higher would be that portion of the opportunity cost of job-search activity. On the other side of the calculation, the real wage obtained from the best job that could be found after an appropriate search process is part of the benefit from job search. Again, the higher the economy average real wage, the higher this benefit will be on the average. Thus, the higher the economy average real wage, the higher are both the cost and expected benefit from job-search activity.

It will be assumed that these two forces, working in opposite directions to each other, are approximately offsetting each other, so that, as real wages rise, the ratio of costs to benefits stays fairly constant, and the *fraction* of the labor force engaging in full-time job-search activity remains constant. This implies that the *number* of people involved in job-search activity will rise as the labor force rises, which in turn means that the number of people engaged in job-search activity will rise as the economy-average real wage rises.

The supply of job search embodying the above considerations is shown in Figure 21.3. If, with a wage differential of D_0 the average economy real wage was $(W/P)_0$, there would be J_0 full-time job search-ers recorded as unemployed (equivalently shown as the distance AB).

Next consider the relationship between wage differentials and job search, given an economy average real wage of $(W/P)_0$. Suppose there is no wage differential so that all jobs paid the same wage. In such a case, as people retire and as new people enter the labor force some job-search activity would take place but it would not be search con-nected with finding a good wage. Rather it would be search for a job that had other desirable characteristics such as, for example, location, compatibility, and the individual's talents and abilities. It seems clear, however, that as the spread between the highest wage available and the lowest wage on offer becomes larger, so it would pay more and more people to engage in the activity of searching out the more highly paid jobs. This idea is illustrated in Figure 21.4. The vertical axis in this figure measures not the level of money wages but the wage dif-ferential — the gap between the highest money wage available (W_{max}) and the lowest money wage (W_{min}) on offer. As this gap gets larger, but holding the economy average real wage constant at $(W/P)_0$, the supply of job search increases. This is shown as the upward-sloping line labelled supply of job search. The line indicates that, even with no wage differential there would be a supply of job search of J_T and this captures the notion that demographic change and labor turnover would produce some job search even if there was no wage differential. If, with an economy average real wage of $(W/P)_0$, the gap between the highest and lowest wages was the amount labelled D_0 on the vertical axis, then the amount of job-search activity would be J_0 or, equiva-lently, the distance marked **AB**.

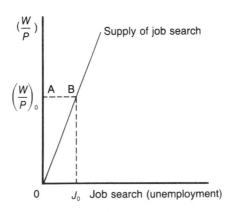

$\left(\frac{W}{P}\right)$

Supply of job search

$\left(\frac{W}{P}\right)_0$ A   B

0   J_0 Job search (unemployment)

Figure 21.3
The Supply of
Job Search

Job search is an alternative activity to working and taking leisure. The higher the economy average real wage, the more people will join the pool of job searchers. At the real wage $(W/P)_0, J_0$ workers will join the labor force and search for jobs.

Figure 21.4
The Supply of Job Search
and Wage Differentials

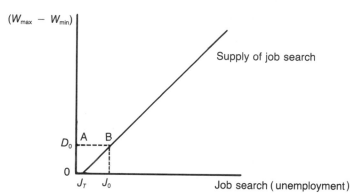

The larger is the gap between the highest and lowest wages available ($W_{max} - W_{min}$), the bigger the inducement to undertake job search in order to try to find one of the higher paying jobs. This is shown as the upward-sloping curve. At a wage differential of zero there will be some minimal job search (J_T). At the wage differential of D_0 job search will be AB (or J_0).

Notice that the distance AB in Figure 21.4 is identical to the distance AB in Figure 21.3. You should think of these curves not as two different theories of the supply of job search. Rather each shows us one aspect of the forces determining the amount of job search. If the wage differential was D_0 in Figure 21.4 and if the economy average real wage was $(W/P)_0$ in Figure 21.3 then the supply of job search would be J_0. If we vary the wage differential but hold the average real wage constant then we can think of what is happening as travelling up the curve in Figure 21.4 and rotating the curve in Figure 21.3. Conversely, if we hold the wage differential constant and raise the economy average real wage then we travel up the curve in Figure 21.3 and we shift to the right the curve in Figure 21.4.

For the most part it will be convenient to work with the supply of job search as pictured in Figure 21.3. This means that as the wage differential varies so the supply of job-search curve rotates. A larger wage differential rotates the curve to the right and a smaller wage differential rotates the curve to the left. Figure 21.5 illustrates this. This figure shows three supply of job-search curves, one for a large wage differential, one for an average wage differential and one for a small wage differential. At the average differential and at the economy average real wage of $(W/P)_0$ the supply of job search is J_0 (the distance AB) as in Figure 21.3. At this same real wage but with a small difference between the highest and lowest available wages the amount of job search would be J_S or the distance AC. With a large gap between the highest and lowest available wages the amount of job search would be J_L or the distance AE.

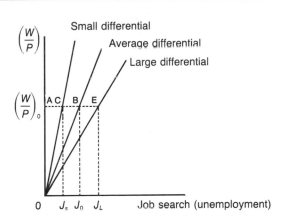

**Figure 21.5
Job Search,
Real Wages,
and Wage Differentials**

This figure is like Figure 21.3 except that it shows the supply of job search against the economy average real wage for three different levels of wage differentials. On the average, at the real wage $(W/P)_0$ job search is J_0. If wage differentials are unusually small job search will decline to J_s and if wage differentials become larger than usual, job search would rise to J_L.

Next, let us distinguish between the supply of labor and the labor force curve. The *labor force curve* is defined as the supply of labor plus the supply of job search. The supply of labor is defined as the number of people who, at a given real wage, are willing to supply their labor services to a full-time job immediately without further search.

Figure 21.6 shows how these magnitudes are related to the economy average real wage for a constant wage differential. The curve n^s is the supply curve that was used in the above analysis of Chapter 14. It shows the number of people immediately available for work without further search at each real wage. Adding horizontally to this curve the amount of job search that would be undertaken at each real wage gives the labor force curve (the curve ℓf). This shows at each real wage the total number of people available for work right now, plus the total number of people who are still searching for a job. The distance AB in Figure 21.6 is equivalent to the distance AB in Figure 21.3. Thus, the labor force curve, ℓf, simply adds the supply of job-search curve to the supply of labor curve. At the real wage $(W/P)_0$, the quantity of labor supplied is n_0, and the labor force is ℓ_0.

The vertical distances AC and BD are interesting economic magnitudes. The marginal person in employment is the last person employed at the employment level n_0. At the economy average real wage, $(W/P)_0$, this person is on the margin of indifference between accepting a job and continuing to search for a job. If the real wage was marginally below $(W/P)_0$, this person would quit and start to search for a new job. The distance AC measures the value that this marginal

**Figure 21.6
Equilibrium
Employment,
Unemployment,
and Real Wage**

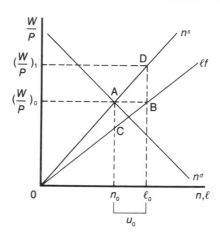

If the supply of job search is added to the supply of labor n^s, the labor force curve ℓf is derived. (The distance AB in Figure 21.6 is the same as the distance AB in Figure 21.3.) With the demand curve n^d, the equilibrium is at $(W/P)_0$ and n_0. The labor force at this equilibrium average real wage is ℓ_0, and the number of unemployed (job searchers) is u_0. The distance AC measures the value placed on job search by the last person to be employed. The economy average real wage would have to drop by AC to induce that person to leave the labor force. The distance DB measures the value placed on job search by the last person to join the labor force. The economy average real wage would have to rise by DB to $(W/P)_1$ to induce this person to take a job.

worker places upon job search. This value is the difference between the real wage at which this worker would take a job and the real wage at which this worker would join the labor force and search for a job.

There is another margin, that between being in the labor force and not being in the labor force. This individual is the last person to join the labor force of ℓ_0. At a real wage $(W/P)_0$, such an individual feels that it is just worthwhile searching for a job. A real wage equal to $(W/P)_1$ would be necessary to induce this marginal member of the labor force to actually accept a job instantaneously with no further search. The value that this individual places upon job search is the distance BD, the difference between the real wage at which this individual would take a job and the real wage at which this individual is willing to join the labor force and search for a job.

Given the demand curve n^d, the real wage $(W/P)_0$ is the competitive equilibrium real wage. The economy is in an equilibrium characterized by less than complete knowledge about job opportunities, so that there is always a certain number of people searching for jobs. The labor force is ℓ_0, the employment level n_0, and there are u_0 unemployed job searchers.

It is important that you realize that the labor market as depicted in Figure 21.6 is not in a static state, with a certain number of people being permanently employed and another group being permanently unemployed. Rather, there is a continuous turnover, with people quitting jobs to search for new ones, other people entering the labor force to search for jobs, others leaving the labor force, and still others being hired. Thus, the flows of hires and quits will be matched, and the flows of people into and out of the labor force will be balanced, so that the individuals involved are continuously in a state of flux, although the economy, on the average, is in the position shown in Figure 21.6.

It is also important to realize that the labor market theory that we have just reviewed in no way predicts that the level of search and employment will be constant. This is going to depend on, among other things, the wage differential between the highest and lowest wages of the economy. In some periods of time the differential will be large and in others small. One of the key factors likely to produce movements in this differential is the uneven pace of technical change across different sectors of the economy. Let us pursue this idea a little bit more deeply.

Imagine, for simplicity, that the economy is divided into two sectors. The labor force is allocated between these two sectors and, initially, there is no wage differential between the sectors. Figure 21.7 illustrates such an economy. Frames (a) and (b) represent the two sectors of the economy. The curves labelled n_0^d are the initial demand curves for each sector. The economy demand curve is the horizontal sum of the two individual sector demand curves. This is n_0^d in frame (a). The aggregate employment level is n_0^* [as shown in frame (c)] and this is allocated across the two sectors in the amounts n_0^1 and n_0^2 as shown in frames (a) and (b). The real wage is $(W/P)_0$ in both sectors.

Now imagine that there is a technical advance in Sector 1 that leads to a rise in the marginal product of labor in this sector and thus shifts the demand for labor curve to n_1^d. There are no other shocks. This is the only thing that happens. How does the economy adjust in this new situation? It is helpful to begin by noticing that since the marginal product of labor curve has shifted in one sector of the economy it must also have shifted for the economy as a whole. The curve n_1^d in frame (c) reflects this fact. These figures have been drawn on the presumption that Sectors 1 and 2 are initially of equal size so that the shift in frame (c) (which is drawn on one-half the scale of the other two frames) is equal to one-half of the shift in Sector 1. Now look at the new equilibrium for the economy as a whole, frame (c). The higher demand for labor produces a higher equilibrium real wage, $(W/P)_1$ and this encourages more people to join the labor force (n_1^*). Labor also reallocates between the two sectors. Employment in Sector 2, frame (b), declines from n_0^2 to n_1^2 while Sector 1 employment increases from n_0^1 to n_1^1, frame (a). This is the new equilibrium.

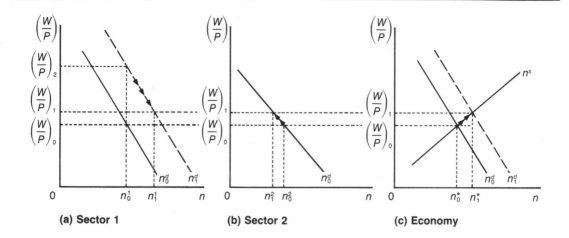

Figure 21.7
Sectoral Reallocation and Job Search

The economy has two sectors initially of equal size shown as Sector 1 and Sector 2 in frames (a) and (b). The aggregate economy is shown in frame (c). The scale on the horizontal axis in frame (c) is half of that in frames (a) and (b). The equilibrium is at $(W/P)_0$, n_0^*, n_0^1, n_0^2. Technical progress in Sector 1 raises the marginal product of labor and raises the demand for labor to n_1^d in frame (a). It raises the aggregate demand for labor accordingly in frame (c). Initially wages are bid up in Sector 1 to $(W/P)_2$. This creates a wage differential between the two sectors and increases the economy average real wage. This wage differential and rise in the average wage available induce job-search activity. New workers enter the labor force and workers leave Sector 2 to find better jobs in Sector 1. The economy gradually moves to a new equilibrium where there is no wage differential and no further (unusual rise in) job-search activity. The equilibrium is $(W/P)_1$, n_1^1, n_1^2, n_1^*. This single shock will have produced a cycle in unemployment.

It does not mean, however, that this new equilibrium is instantly reached. Rather, there could, quite reasonably, be an equilibrium path from the initial position to the final position. We can see this by looking at the state of the economy at the instant the productivity shock hits. At this point in time there are n_0^1 workers in Sector 1. Firms in this sector will probably find it most natural, initially, to compete among themselves to attract workers already in this sector — or to prevent their own workers from leaving. Wages in Sector 1 will, therefore, be bid up to $(W/P)_2$. Thus there will be a large wage differential — a gap between the wages being paid in Sector 2 ($W/P)_0$, and those being paid in Sector 1 $(W/P)_2$. This gap will induce an increase in job-search activity. Also, this large wage differential and the higher economy real wage will attract new workers to join the labor force. A large number of people will withdraw themselves from work in Sector 2 in order to search for jobs in Sector 1 and also people who have not previously been in the labor force will begin full-time job search. As a consequence of this job-search activity, people will gradually find jobs in the higher paying sector and wages in Sector 1 will decline — firms will move down their demand for labor curves. Also, as workers withdraw from Sector 2 both to search for jobs and to accept jobs in Sector 1, wages in Sector 2 will rise — firms will move up their demand for labor curves. The gradual changes that will take place are shown as the arrowed lines in Figure 21.7. Lying behind these arrows are gradual processes through which individuals will have been temporarily full-time job searchers or, in other words, temporarily unemployed.

There will be times in economic history when the amount of technical change is slow and even across the sectors of the economy. Such will be times in which the supply of job search is low and, therefore, the natural rate of unemployment will be low. There will be other times when technical progress is either rapid or very different across the different sectors of the economy — indeed the world economy — thereby leading to massive amounts of job-search activity.

Returning to Figure 21.6 you can imagine what is going on in the actual world as being described by the equilibrium adjusting as the demand for labor curve continuously shifts around. As the demand for labor curve shifts to the right and to the left, the equilibrium real wage and employment level rises and falls, as read off from the n^s curve. The labor force also rises and falls, as read off the ℓf curve. In addition, the gap between the labor force and the employment level, as read off from the figure as the horizontal distance between the ℓf and n^s curves, widens and narrows, thereby raising and lowering the equilibrium full-employment rate of unemployment.

One interesting implication of the foregoing is worth emphasizing. It is very likely that the forces that we have just been describing and analyzing will lead to fluctuations in the rate of unemployment and output. This, even within the context of the simplest theory of aggregate supply — the classical theory that ignores discrepancies between actual and expected prices — which is based on the notion that the aggregate supply curve is vertical, is capable of generating cyclical movements in the rate of unemployment and the level of output.

There is a further potentially important influence on the unemployment rate that we shall now analyze.

D. Unemployment Insurance Benefits and Unemployment

Suppose the government introduces an unemployment insurance program which makes it possible for people, while searching for a new job, to receive an income from the government equal to some fraction of the wage that they had previously been earning while employed. What effects would this have?

   It is immediately clear that such a policy would lower the cost of job search. It would therefore make job-search activity, at the margin, more attractive. You have already seen that there are two relevant margins of job search. One is the margin between search and employment, the other is the margin between employment and complete leisure (withdrawal from the labor force). Improving unemployment insurance benefits would alter both of these margins. There would be a tendency for people to search longer before accepting employment, thereby lowering the amount of work that people in aggregate would be willing to do at any given real wage. This would have the effect of rotating the labor supply curve n^s upwards. This is shown in Figure 21.8 as the movement from n_0^s to n_1^s. Additionally, people who previously were not in the labor force would now be induced to enter the labor force and take a temporary job to qualify for unemployment insurance benefits, and then later search for a more acceptable long-term job. There will, therefore, be a rotation of the labor force curve in a rightward direction. This again is illustrated in Figure 21.8 as the movement from ℓf_0 to ℓf_1.

   The curves n_0^s and ℓf_0 and the equilibrium $(W/P)_0$, n_0 represent the economy with no unemployment insurance program and are the same as those illustrated in Figure 21.6. The curves n_1^s and ℓf_1 represent the new labor supply and the labor force curves induced by an unemployment insurance program.

**Figure 21.8
How Unemployment
Insurance Benefits
Increase
Unemployment**

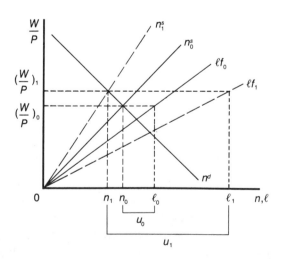

Unemployment insurance benefits lower the cost of job search and, therefore, make job search a more attractive activity relative to either working or consuming leisure. The supply of labor falls from n_0^s to n_1^s and raises the labor force supply curve from ℓf_0 to ℓf_1. The real wage rises, the employment level falls, the labor force rises and the number unemployed rises.

It is now possible to read off the effects of an unemployment insurance program on the variables. The labor market will now be in equilibrium at the real wage $(W/P)_1$ and employment level n_1. The labor force will rise to ℓ_1, and unemployment will be u_1 which is $\ell_1 - n_1$. Thus, an unemployment insurance program raises the real wage, lowers the level of employment, raises the size of the labor force, and increases the level of unemployment.

The analysis that has just been conducted has ignored the question of who pays the taxes that provide the unemployment insurance benefit. The next section of this chapter will go on to analyze the effects of employment taxes and income taxes on the level of employment, unemployment and real wages. This analysis applies more generally than just to those taxes used to pay unemployment insurance benefits. It applies to any taxes. The analysis just conducted may be augmented by the analysis of effects of taxes, to which we shall now turn.

E. Taxes and Unemployment

It will be convenient, in analyzing the effects of taxes, to abstract from the considerations of job search that were the central feature of the analysis of the previous section. This is not to say that the above analysis is irrelevant when considering the effects of taxes. It is simply a convenient way of considering one thing at a time. Once you have thoroughly mastered the material in this and the preceding sections, it will be a straightforward matter for you to consider both effects simultaneously. There is no gain, however, from presenting them as a simultaneous analysis.

The questions that we want to address now are first, what are the effects of income taxes — taxes on labor income — on the real wage, and the level of employment and unemployment? Second, what are the effects of employment taxes — taxes on firms that vary with the number of workers they employ — on the level of employment, unemployment and the real wage? And third, what are the effects of expenditure taxes — taxes on consumption — on the level of employment, unemployment and the real wage?

As a starting point, let us begin with an economy that has no taxes and then consider what happens as we introduce these alternative taxes first separately and secondly simultaneously. Figure 21.9 will illustrate the analysis. The curves labelled n^s and n^d are the supply and demand curves for labor in a world in which there are no taxes. The competitive equilibrium in this economy is at point B, where the real wage is $(W/P)^*$ and the employment level is n^*. This is exactly the position shown as the competitive equilibrium in Figure 21.1, with which we started this analysis of the labor market.

There is one additional thing which you can work out about the economy, to which attention has not previously been drawn but which is of some interest for the purpose of the present exercise — that is,

Figure 21.9
The Effects of Taxes
on the Labor Market

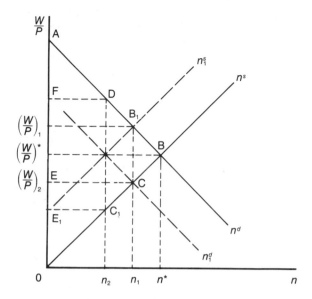

A competitive equilibrium is shown at the real wage $(W/P)^*$ and employment level n^*. This equilibrium is disturbed by the introduction of a tax on labor income or by a tax on consumption that shifts the labor supply curve to n_1^s. The real wage rises to $(W/P)_1$, and employment falls to n_1. The after-tax real wage falls. Alternatively, the equilibrium is disturbed by the introduction of an employment tax that shifts the labor demand curve down to n_1^d. Again the level of employment falls to n_1, and the real wage becomes $(W/P)_2$, equivalent to the after-tax wage level of E in the previous experiment. Both sets of taxes introduced together lower the level of employment to n_2. As taxes on employment are successively increased, labor's share of national income (defined to include the taxes) increases, while the share accruing to the owners of capital decreases.

the distribution of national income between labor and the owners of capital. Labor income will be equal to the rectangle $0(W/P)^*Bn^*$. You can readily verify that this is so by noting that the number of workers is n^*, and the wage per worker is $(W/P)^*$ so that labor income, being the product of employment and wages, is given by the area of that rectangle.

The income accruing to the owners of capital is the triangle $(W/P)^*AB$. This is a less obvious proposition than the previous one. You may, however, verify that this triangle represents the part of total product not paid to labor. To do this, begin by recalling that the demand for labor curve measures the marginal product of labor. Thus, the first worker hired would produce a marginal product of A (that is, where the demand curve hits the real wage axis). As more and more workers are hired, the marginal product declines until the final worker is hired at the equilibrium level of employment n^*, by which time the marginal product has fallen to B. For each extra worker hired, the extra output produced is equal to the marginal product, and the total product accruing to the producer is given by the entire area underneath the marginal product curve all the way up to the level of employment n^*. Total product in the economy, then, is the trapezium $0ABn^*$. That which is paid to labor is $0(W/P)^*Bn^*$, and that which is paid to the owners of capital is $(W/P)^*AB$. (In the economy shown in Figure 21.9, labor gets two-thirds and capital one-third of the economy's output.)

Now consider the introduction of an income tax. Instead of keeping all the wages they earn, workers now have to pay some fraction of their labor income to the government in the form of a tax. This means that the wage received by workers is less than the real wage paid by employers. Assuming, as we are, that the supply of labor curve is not vertical so that a higher real wage always increases the quantity of labor supplied, this implies that for any given real wage paid by the employer, there will now be a smaller supply of labor. This can be represented by shifting the labor supply curve to the left. For simplicity, the figure has been drawn on the presumption that the labor supply curve shift is a parallel one, so that the new curve after allowing for taxes is the one labelled n_i^s. The way to read n_i^s is as follows: for any given level of employment, without taxes, the wage that would have to be paid is read off from the n^s curve; with the taxes in place, however, the wage that would have to be paid to call forth the same level of employment is read off from the higher curve n_i^s. The vertical gap between n_i^s and n^s is the level of taxes.

To determine the equilibrium in this case, we have to find the point where the new effective labor supply curve n_i^s intersects the demand for labor curve n^d. This occurs at the point B_1, with a real wage equal to $(W/P)_1$ and an employment level n_1. Thus, the real wage has risen and the employment level has fallen as a result of the introduction of a tax on labor income. The after-tax income of workers will have fallen from a real wage of $(W/P)^*$ to a real wage given by the position E on the vertical axis. In fact, total wages will be $0ECn_1$. The tax receipts of the government will be $E(W/P)_1B_1C$, and the income accruing to capital will be the triangle $(W/P)_1AB_1$. The overall effects, then, of the imposition of a tax on labor income are a drop in after-tax real wage, a rise in pre-tax real wage, a fall in labor income, a rise in the government's revenue, and a fall in the income accruing to the owners of capital. There is also a fall in the level of employment.

The drop in employment from n^* to n_1 cannot, properly speaking, be regarded as unemployment. Although there are fewer people in employment in the situation n_1 as compared with n*, the situation that prevails is a competitive equilibrium. Nevertheless, it may be the case that the workers who withdraw from the labor force as the after-tax real wage falls from $(W/P)^*$ to E will be entitled to unemployment insurance benefits and will, therefore, appear to swell the ranks of the unemployed job searchers — if not forever, at least for a period. In this limited sense, an increase in taxes on labor income can be said to "create unemployment."

Next consider the effects of imposing a tax on the other side of the labor market — on the employers. Imagine that firms have to pay a tax on each worker that they employ. This will mean that the firm no longer regards the marginal product of labor as being equivalent to the value of labor. Rather, firms will regard labor as being worth its marginal product minus the tax that it has to pay on each worker employed. This means that the demand for labor curve will shift downwards. The curve n_1^d in Figure 21.9 illustrates such a demand curve.

What will be the effect of this tax on employment, unemployment, and the real wage? Let us first answer this question in the absence of income taxes. In this case, the new equilibrium will be where the curve n_1^d cuts the original supply curve n^s. This occurs at the real wage rate $(W/P)_2 = E$ and at the employment level n_1.

Notice that this experiment has been set up so as to yield an identical amount of revenue for the government as the income tax did in the previous experiment. In principle, we could analyze cases where different amounts of revenue are raised. It does, however, seem to be more instructive to hold the government revenue constant for the purpose of comparing the effects of alternative taxes.

It is now possible to read off all the effects of this employment tax on the level of employment and wages. These effects are, evidently, exactly the same as in the previous case. Employment falls from n^* to n_1; labor's share of national income falls to the same level as before, namely, $0ECn_1$; and the government revenue is exactly the same as before, as is the share of income accruing to the owners of capital. The only difference between the two cases is that the wages paid by firms fall, and firms pay the taxes to the government. In the first experiment conducted, the wages paid by firms increased, but after workers had paid their taxes the net of tax wage decreased. Workers had exactly the same net of tax income in the previous situation as they do in this one.

Next, consider what happens when taxes are imposed on the expenditure on consumer goods by workers. From the perspective of the analysis conducted here, this will have identical effects to the first tax analyzed — a tax on labor income. The easiest way to see this is to see the way in which both income taxes and expenditure taxes affect the relative price between labor and consumption. Equivalently, we may ask how income taxes and expenditure taxes affect the relative price of labor with respect to consumption goods. The wage that a worker receives is equal to the gross wage paid, scaled down by the income taxes levied by the government. Suppose that we call the income tax rate t_y. Then, the after-tax wage is $W(1 - t_y)$. When a worker purchases consumer goods, the price paid is equal to the price received by the producer, P, plus any taxes levied by the government. Call the rate of tax on expenditure t_c. This means that the price paid by the consumer will be equal to $P(1 + t_c)$. Evidently, the ratio of the price received by the worker to the price paid for goods by the worker is equal to:

$$\frac{W(1 - t_y)}{P(1 + t_c)} \qquad (21.1)$$

You may think of the expression $(1 - t_y)/(1 + t_c)$ as the wedge which taxes drive between the price that firms have to pay for their labor, W, and the price that they receive for their output, P. From the household's point of view, for any given real wage, W/P, the bigger the tax wedge, the smaller will be the supply of labor. Thus, you may think of the shift in the labor supply curve from n^s to n_1^s, analyzed in the first experiment conducted above, as arising from either the imposition of an income tax or an expenditure tax having an equivalent total yield.

Finally, consider what happens when all of these tax measures are introduced simultaneously. In this case, the relevant supply curve is n_1^s, and the demand curve is n_1^d. The equilibrium employment level falls still further to n_2, but by the construction of the example, the real wage remains at the no-tax equilibrium level of $(W/P)^*$. [To avoid having too many equilibrium positions on the one figure, we have caused these two curves to intersect at the original real wage, $(W/P)^*$.] Workers' incomes will now be $0E_1C_1n_2$, the government's tax receipts will be E_1FDC_1, and the income accruing to capital owners will be FAD. Employment will have fallen from n^* to n_2.

It is worth highlighting what is happening to the relative shares of labor and capital in national income as we move from the initial no-tax equilibrium to the after-tax equilibrium. To do this, it will be most convenient to use the accounting conventions employed in the national income accounts. In these accounts labor income is defined to include the payments of employment taxes by firms to the government. The fiction is that this is really part of the wages of the workers that is being deducted as a tax at source and handed over to the government in much the same way as the workers' income taxes are also withheld by the employer and paid to the government.

Thus, in the no-tax situation, labor income is $0(W/P)^*Bn^*$ and in the after-tax situation (after all taxes), labor income is $0FDn_2$. Using this accounting convention it is evident that as taxes are increased, the share of national income accruing to labor increases. You can see this visually in Figure 21.9. In the initial situation, labor income was equal to two-thirds of total income, whereas in the after-tax situation it is equal to six-sevenths. What is happening as taxes are increased is that although the number of workers employed declines, the average wage per worker (defined in the gross sense in which it is being defined here) increases. Total product, of course, declines in the experiment conducted here.

The experiments just reviewed have started with an economy that had zero taxes and then introduced some positive taxes. The same results could have been generated, however, starting out with an economy with a given level of taxes and then raising those taxes. Thus, if taxes on labor (whether paid by workers or employers) are increased, the prediction is that there will be a drop in the level of employment, a rise in labor's share in the national product, and a temporary rise in the measured rate of unemployment.

F. Unemployment in Canada

We have reviewed the forces that can influence unemployment (abstracting from surprise changes in the level of aggregate demand) and are now ready to examine the extent to which these various forces have been at work in Canada's recent macroeconomic history. We shall begin by examining minimum wages, labor union wages, and unemployment compensation arrangements. We shall then go on to look at some recently developed ideas about how sectoral reallocation of labor induced by differential technical change and other factors move the rate of unemployment.

Consider minimum wages. Minimum wage legislation in Canada is primarily a provincial matter. There is a vast amount of detail in the various arrangements which will not be described here. Rather, the minimum wages in one province only, Ontario, will be used as an example of what has been happening to minimum wages in Canada

Table 21.1
General Hourly Minimum Wage Rates for
Experienced Adult Workers

REGION	MINIMUM WAGE
Federal	3.50
Newfoundland	3.75
Prince Edward Island	3.75
Nova Scotia	3.75
New Brunswick	3.80
Quebec	4.00
Ontario	4.00
Manitoba	4.00
Saskatchewan	4.25
Alberta	3.80
British Columbia	3.65
Northwest Territories	4.25
Yukon	3.60

Source: Labor Standards in Canada, Ministry of Supply and Services, 1984, p 32.

as a whole. The differences across regions have not changed dramatically over this period.

It will be worthwhile, however, to take a brief look at minimum wages across Canada as a whole, and this can be done in Table 21.1. You see in Table 21.1 that there is some variability of minimum wages across the provinces, but there is a tendency for them to cluster around the same level.

Let us look at what has happened over a longer period of time to the level of minimum wages in our sample province, Ontario. The figures for Ontario set out in Table 21.2, show that the minimum wage has increased in this province fairly systematically, from $1 per hour in 1965, up to $4 per hour in 1985. However, our theoretical analysis of the effects of minimum wages examined the effects of changing the real minimum wage. It is necessary therefore to look at this minimum real wage. This is done by converting the dollar value of the minimum wage (the minimum money wage) into constant dollars, by deflating it with the *GNE* Deflator. This is done in Table 21.3.

It is immediately evident from inspecting Table 21.3 that although the minimum money wage (column 1) has increased nearly fourfold over the eight years from 1966 to 1984, the minimum real wage has increased by much less. Evaluated in 1971 dollars, the minimum real wage increased from $1.21 an hour in 1966 up to $1.28 an hour in 1984. The major movements took place in the periods 1966 to 1971 and 1976 to 1983. During that first period, there was an overall growth in the minimum real wage rate of 33 percent. (This is an average annual growth rate of approximately 5.9 percent.) However, during that same period, average weekly real earnings in the economy as a

Table 21.2
Minimum Wages (Ontario)

DATE		MINIMUM WAGE
December 27	1965	1.00
January 1	1969	1.30
October 1	1970	1.50
April 1	1971	1.65
February 1	1973	1.80
January 1	1974	2.00
October 1	1974	2.25
May 1	1975	2.40
March 15	1976	2.65
August 1	1978	2.85
January 1	1979	3.00
October 1	1981	3.50
March 1	1984	3.85
October 1	1984	4.00

Source: Ontario Statistics, 1984, p. 430.

Table 21.3
Minimum Real Wages

YEAR	MINIMUM WAGE IN CURRENT DOLARS	GNE DEFLATOR	MINIMUM REAL WAGE IN 1971 DOLLARS
1966	1.00	82.6	1.21
1967	1.00	85.9	1.16
1968	1.00	88.7	1.13
1969	1.30	92.6	1.40
1970	1.35	96.9	1.39
1971	1.61	100.0	1.61
1972	1.65	105.0	1.57
1973	1.79	114.6	1.56
1974	2.06	132.1	1.56
1975	2.35	146.2	1.61
1976	2.60	160.4	1.62
1977	2.65	172.3	1.54
1978	2.73	183.8	1.49
1979	3.00	202.7	1.48
1980	3.00	225.8	1.33
1981	3.13	249.7	1.25
1982	3.50	275.5	1.27
1983	3.50	290.1	1.21
1984	3.83	298.3	1.28

Sources and Methods: (a) *Ontario Statistics*, 1984, p. 430; (b) See Appendix to Chapter 2; (c) Minimum wage in current dollars is the average minimum wage for the year. Real minimum wage is minimum wage in current dollars divided by the GNE Deflator, i.e., column (1) divided by column (2) (times 100).

whole grew at only 3.6 percent per annum. It is clear, therefore, that in the period 1966 to 1971 the minimum real wage was rising relative to the average real wage. Through the period from 1971 to 1976, when minimum real wages were virtually constant, the average real wage in the economy as a whole increased at a rate of 2.5 percent per annum, or an approximate 16.5 percent rate overall. From 1976 to 1982 the minimum real wage fell nearly each year, with the overall decline of 22 percent. During this same period the average real wage in the economy continued to increase in 1977 and then began to decline such that the overall decline to 1982 was 0.2 percent. For the sixteen years ending 1982, the overall growth of the minimum real wage was 5 percent, while that of the average weekly real earnings in the economy as a whole was almost 22 percent. Despite the differences in the growth patterns, the minimum real wage rose over the sixteen years by 17 percent less than did the average weekly real earnings in the economy.

Let us now turn to examine the behavior of labor union wages. It is difficult to obtain comprehensive data on union wages. Purely as an example, this chapter looks at the behavior of some union wages in the construction sector. In addition to examining union real wages it is also interesting to examine what has happened to the fraction of the labor force that is unionized.

Table 21.4 summarizes some information concerning unions. The first column of Table 21.4 gives you a measure of the degree of union involvement in the economy as measured by the percentage of the labor force unionized. You will see that almost one-third of the Canadian labor force is currently unionized, and that the rate has been relatively steady throughout the last eighteen years, starting at just over one-quarter and ending at 31 percent of the labor force. It appears, at least on the basis of union-membership figures, that unions have not, over this period, expanded their sphere of influence. An alternative indicator of the growth of union influence would be the percentage of all labor contracts negotiated by unions, rather than negotiated privately. However, such information does not seem to be available.

Table 21.4
Union Membership and Wages

YEAR	PERCENTAGE OF LABOR FORCE UNIONIZED (1)	REAL WAGE GROWTH OF UNIONIZED CON-STRUCTION WORKERS (2)	REAL WAGE GROWTH IN ECONOMY AS A WHOLE (3)	DIFFERENCE BETWEEN CONSTRUCTION UNION AND ECONOMY AVERAGE REAL WAGE GROWTH (4) = (2) − (3)	RATIO OF UNION TO AVERAGE WAGE 1971 = 1.00 (5)
1967	26.1	7.0	2.7	+4.3	0.91
1968	26.6	6.6	3.7	+2.9	0.93
1969	26.3	4.6	2.8	+1.8	0.96
1970	27.2	8.8	3.0	+5.8	0.96
1971	26.8	9.3	5.4	+3.9	1.00
1972	27.8	5.8	3.4	+2.4	1.03
1973	29.2	−1.3	−1.6	+0.3	1.05
1974	29.4	−4.1	−4.3	+0.2	1.04
1975	29.8	4.0	3.4	+0.6	1.04
1976	30.6	3.9	2.5	+1.4	1.06
1977	31.0	4.3	2.2	+2.1	1.07
1978	31.3	−0.2	−0.5	+0.3	1.08
1979	—	−4.2	−1.6	−2.5	1.05
1980	30.5	−3.6	−1.3	−2.3	1.03
1981	30.6	−1.4	1.4	−2.8	1.00
1982	31.4	−1.0	−0.3	−0.7	1.00
1983	30.6	6.9	—	—	—
1984	30.6	0.4	—	—	—

Sources and Methods: (a) *Directory of Labour Organizations in Canada*: Labour Canada 1984, p. xxvi. There was no survey conducted in 1979.
(b) *Construction Price Statistics*, Statistics Canada: 1978, 1976, 1985. Table 2.2, Column 2 is the change in the Construction Wage Index minus the GNE Deflator.
(c) Cansim Series D90989 gives Average Hourly Earnings and the inflation rate of the GNE Deflator is given in the Appendix to Chapter 2. Column 3 is the growth of Average Hourly Earnings minus the inflation rate of the GNE Deflator. The earnings series was terminated in 1982.

The second column of Table 21.4 shows the rate of growth of the real wages of unionized construction workers through this period. Column 3 shows the economy's average real wage growth, and column 4 shows the difference between union and economy average real wage growth. It is immediately evident from inspecting these figures that (at least in the construction sector), union real wages ran substantially ahead of average real wages during the period 1967 to 1978 but since then have declined somewhat. The growth rate of union wages has exceeded the growth rate of average wages by 1.1 percent per annum on the average, and over the sixteen years the difference has accumulated to a 17.1 percent lead. Whether or not this simply reflects market forces that would have been present in the absence of a union, or whether it reflects an increasing tendency on the part of the construction sector unions to drive a harder bargain and raise their real wages further above the level at which they otherwise would have been, it is not possible to say for sure. However, it does seem likely that such strong increases as took place in the late 1960s and in the period 1970 to 1972 did represent an attempt by the unions to gain a real advantage vis-à-vis the average Canadian worker. From 1973 to 1978 there was a continuation of the earlier gain, but at a slower pace as the growth in the construction-union wage was just a little ahead of the economy average wage. Since 1978 real wages have fallen, with construction-union wages falling faster than the economy average wage. Column 5 shows the level of the construction-union wage relative to the economy average wage as a whole (calling 1971 = 1.00). You can see more clearly from these figures that unionized construction wages rose relative to the economy average wage, becoming by 1978, 15 percent higher than they had been in 1968. The higher relative wage slipped slightly in 1974 but only by a small amount. From 1975 to 1978 unionized construction wages rose 4 percent relative to the economy average, but then declined relative to the economy average until 1982 when it was again at its 1971 relative level.

Consider the unemployment compensation arrangements in place in Canada in recent years. The first *Unemployment Insurance Act* in Canada was passed in 1940. Amendments to this Act have taken place from time to time, and one minor amendment occurred in 1968 and a major revision in 1971. Up to 1968 the unemployment compensation arrangements applied to all wage earners, but only to those salary earners whose incomes were below $5460 per annum. This ceiling was increased to $7800 per annum in June 1968, increasing the number of workers eligible for unemployment insurance from 4.7 million to 5.1 million.

The first major overhaul of the *Unemployment Insurance Act*, however, took place in 1971 (following recommendations of the Unemployment Insurance Commission). The major changes in the 1971 Act were as follows:

(a) COVERAGE

Universal coverage was introduced. (Previously teachers, civil serv-ants, members of the armed forces, and salaried workers earning over $7800 per year had been excluded.)

(b) BENEFITS

Eligibility and Duration of Benefit. Prior to 1971 the duration of ben-efits was determined by the previous length of employment. The longer a person had worked, the longer was the period over which benefits were paid. This connection was broken with the 1971 Act. Regular benefits could be claimed up to a maximum of 51 weeks, provided that the claimant had at least eight weeks of continuous contributions to the insurance program in the previous 52 weeks and satisfied the conditions of being available for, capable of, and searching for work. In addition, eligibility conditions for sickness and maternity benefits were relaxed.

Benefit Rates. The benefit rate for all claims was set at two-thirds (three-quarters for claimants with dependents) of the average insured earnings in the qualifying period (generally the 52 weeks immediately preceding the benefit period) up to a maximum of $100 per week, with a minimum of $20 per week. Prior to 1971 benefits ranged from $14 per week to $56 per week.

Further amendments to the Act were made in January 1976 and December 1977. These amendments represented a partial return to the pre-1971 arrangements in that the maximum number of weeks for which benefits could be claimed was related again to the number of weeks of previous insurable employment.

The 1977 amendment tied the number of weeks required to qualify for benefits to the regional unemployment rate. Thus, regions with a high unemployment rate required a small number of weeks of pre-vious work to qualify for benefit, while those with a low unemploy-ment rate required a longer number of weeks to qualify.

(c) SUMMARY

In broad terms, then, there was a sizeable improvement in the quality of unemployment insurance benefits in 1971 and a slight reduction in the equality of benefits in 1976-77.

The tax wedge in 1970 is 40 percent. It remains fairly stable until 1974 when it rises slightly to 42 percent. It then declines in 1975 and remains fairly stable until 1981 when it rises to 42.75 percent. Since 1981 it has remained fairly stable at this higher level.

How do these labor market conditions relate to the unemployment rate? All four of the labor market variables which we have considered are brought together, along with the unemployment rate, in Figure 21.10. It is immediately evident that the strong rise in unemployment between 1967 and 1971 might well have been caused (at least in part) by movements of legislated minimum wages and union wages during that period. However, as the chart makes clear, after 1971 minimum real wages remained fairly steady throughout the entire period, up to 1978 but union wages continued to rise relative to average wages. Further, in 1971, unemployment compensation scales were improved, so that after 1971 the cost of job-search unemployment was lowered. This probably explains why the unemployment rate remained high over the next few years. Since 1978, both the minimum real wage and the union wage relative to the average wage have declined. The

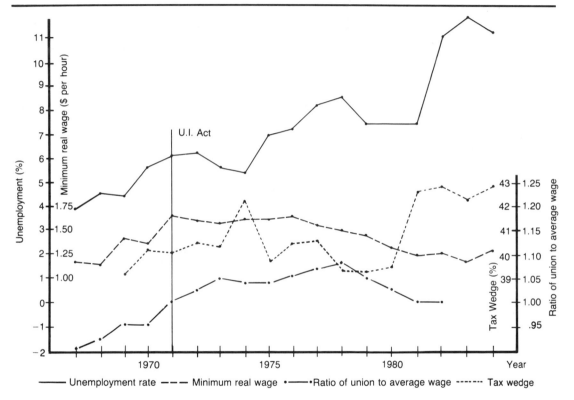

Figure 21.10
Canadian Unemployment

Minimum wages, union wages and unemployment all trended upward between 1967 and 1971. In 1971 the *Unemployment Insurance Act* extended the scale and scope of benefits available. After 1971 minimum wages and union wages remained steady; unemployment fell slightly through 1974 but after that rose persistently again. The rise in minimum and union wages before 1971 may help to account for the rise in unemployment of that period. The improved unemployment insurance may help to explain the higher average unemployment rate since 1971. The tax wedge seems unrelated to the movements in unemployment. The continued rise in unemployment after 1974 cannot be explained by any of these factors.

Sources: Unemployment rate: Appendix to Chapter 2. Minimum real wage: Table 21.5. Ratio of union to average wage: Table 21.4. Tax wedge: *National Income and Expenditure Accounts 1969–1983* and First Quarter, 1985. The tax wedge is $(t_c + t_y)/(1 + t_c)$ where t_c is total expenditure taxes divided by personal consumption expenditure net of expenditure taxes and t_y is total direct taxes paid by people divided by total employment income. Personal consumption expenditure is Table 2, line 1, total employment income is Table 4, the sum of lines 1 to 4, total direct taxes is Table 16, the sum of lines 1 to 3, total expenditure taxes is Table 16, the sum of lines 9 and 10.

movements in these two variables seem unable to explain the rise in unemployment since 1978, the tax wedge especially — its two big jumps seem to have had little impact on the path of unemployment.

Let us now turn to examine some recent and quite ingenious work that has looked at the effects of sectoral labor force reallocations on the average rate of unemployment. David Lilien[2] has proposed that it should be possible to measure variations in the amount of job-search activity by calculating the gross flows of labor across the various sectors of the economy. Specifically, Lilien proposed a measure that calculates the change in employment in an individual sector of the economy relative to the change in employment in the economy as a whole averaged across the whole economy. (The precise details of Lilien's method of calculation need not concern us here.) Applying his ideas to United States data since 1947, Lilien showed that fluctuations in the amount of labor force reallocation and the average rate of unemployment were very highly correlated. Using techniques similar to Lillien's but overcoming some of the shortcomings in his work, Lucie Samson[3] has performed similar calculations for Canada (and, in fact, for the United States, the United Kingdom, Japan and France) and obtained similar findings.

Lucie Samson's findings are summarized in Figure 21.11. The dashed line in this figure shows fluctuations in the unemployment rate that arise exclusively from fluctuations in the amount of reallocation of the labor force across the sectors of the economy and from a time trend. Movements in the unemployment rate represented by the dashed line do not measure fluctuations in aggregate demand nor do they measure fluctuations arising from "surprise" changes in aggregate demand. This dashed line measures fluctuations in the natural rate of unemployment. Plotted in the same figure, alongside the measured unemployment rate arising from sectoral reallocation is the actual average rate of unemployment. The correspondence between these two series is remarkable. Though by no means final proof, and although interpreting these figures is still a controversial matter, it appears as if fluctuations in job-search activity associated with sector reallocation of the labor force is a major factor in explaining fluctuations in the rate of unemployment. Some unemployment is left over to be explained by other things, although not much. We shall examine the forces that explain the additional ripples in unemployment in Chapter 23 when we study cycles. Notice though that most of the cycles as well as trends in unemployment are tracked by Samson's sectoral reallocation variable.

---

[2] See David Lilien, "Sectoral Shifts and Cyclical Unemployment," *Journal of Political Economy* (August 1982), pp. 777-93.

[3] See Lucie Samson, "A Study of the Impact of Sectoral Shifts on Aggregate Unemployment in Canada," *Canadian Journal of Economics* (August 1985), pp. 518–30.

Figure 21.11
The Sectoral Reallocation
and Unemployment

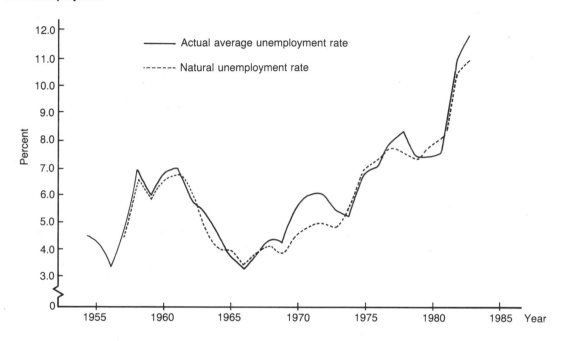

A measure of the scale of reallocation of labor across the major sectors of the economy (the dashed line) tracks the average unemployment rate (the solid line) remarkably closely. Thus most of the fluctuations in unemployment in Canada can, according to these figures, be interpreted as fluctuations in the full-employment rate of unemployment.

Source: Lucie Samson. "A Study of the Impact of Sectoral Shifts on Aggregate Unemployment in Canada," *Canadian Journal of Economics*, XVIII, 3 (August 1985) p. 527.

Summary

A. Minimum Wage Laws and Unemployment

Minimum wage laws raise the economy average real wage above the competitive equilibrium level. With voluntary exchange, this means that the number of people employed will be less than the competitive equilibrium quantity, and the number of people who would like jobs will be greater than the competitive equilibrium quantity. There will, therefore, be a rise in the real wage, a fall in employment, a rise in the labor force, and a rise in unemployment.

B. Labor Unions and Unemployment

An economy-wide labor union has exactly the same kind of effects as a government-enforced minimum wage law. The introduction of a union or the raising of minimum qualifications raises the real wage, lowers employment, increases the labor force and raises the level of unemployment.

C. Job Search and Unemployment

People allocate time to three activities: leisure, job search and work. The lower the cost of job search, the higher the economy average real wage, and the larger the gap between the highest and lowest wages available, the larger will be the equilibrium amount of job-search activity, and since job searchers are counted as unemployed, the larger the equilibrium level of unemployment. The factor influencing the gap between the highest and lowest wages available is the sectoral incidence of technical change. When technical change is rapid in some sectors relative to others, wage differentials will open up and induce increased job-search activity as new workers enter the labor force and other workers switch from the lower to the higher paid sector.

D. Unemployment Insurance Benefits and Unemployment

The introduction of an unemployment insurance program lowers the cost of job search and makes job search more attractive than work and more attractive than leisure at the margin. Therefore, it raises the labor force and cuts the supply of labor; the equilibrium real wage rises, employment falls, the labor force rises, and unemployment rises.

E. Taxes and Unemployment

If the level of taxes is increased, there will be a fall in the level of employment and a rise in labor's share of national income. The fall in employment will manifest itself as measured unemployment if the workers who withdraw their labor supply remain in the labor force.

F. Unemployment in Canada

Apparently, to some degree, movements in minimum real wages, relative union wages and changes in unemployment compensation arrangements can explain some of the movements in the rate of unemployment. Movements in the tax wedge seem to be unrelated to the path of employment. By far the most important force, however, appears to be the scale of sectoral labor force reallocation which has fluctuated and has induced unemployment fluctuations that are highly correlated with the scale of sectoral reallocation. The fluctuations in unemployment not accounted for by this factor appear to be slight.

Review Questions

1. Suppose the labor market in some particular industry is described in the following way. The demand for labor is

$$n^d = 100 - 5 \, (W/P)$$

the supply of labor is

$$n^s = 5\ (W/P)$$

(a) Plot the demand curve and state in words what the demand equation means.

(b) Plot the supply curve and state in words what the supply equation means.

(c) Calculate (either algebraically or graphically) the equilibrium real wage and level of employment.

(d) How much unemployment is there in the equilibrium calculated in (c)?

(e) If the price level is 1.2, what is the equilibrium money wage?

(f) If a minimum wage of $15 is set in this industry, what is the new equilibrium real wage, and how much unemployment is created in this industry?

(g) Suppose that all the workers in this industry become unionized, and the union sets its wage at $18. What is the real wage that is paid, and how many workers are now employed and how many cannot find work in this industry?

2. An economy consisting of 1000 firms has a labor demand given by

$$n^d = 4000 - 0.5\ (W/P)$$

and a labor supply given by

$$n^s = 3000\ (W/P) - 2000$$

(a) What is the equilibrium real wage?

(b) If the price level is 2, what is the money wage?

(c) If a minimum wage is legislated such that the economy average money wage becomes $5, how many workers are employed and how many unemployed?

(d) If there is no minimum wage, but half of all the firms become 100 percent unionized and the union sets the union wage at $5, what is the average money wage paid in this industry, and how many unionized workers are employed and unemployed, and how many non-union workers are employed and unemployed?

(e) Assume that there is no minimum wage and no unionization of labor but that the government introduces an unemployment insurance scheme which compensates any unemployed worker 75 percent of the money wage paid to employed workers. Using a diagram, show the impact of this program on the money wage paid, the number of workers employed, the number of workers unemployed, and the cost to the government of this scheme.

3. An economy with a competitive labor market has a demand curve given by

$$n^d = 1008 - 4(W/P)$$

and a labor supply given by

$$n^s = 960 + 2(W/P)$$

(a) What is the equilibrium real wage?

(b) Assume the price level to be 1, so that the equilibrium real wage is the equilibrium money wage. Now assume that the government imposes an employment tax of $1 per worker. Calculate the new equilibrium level of employment and the money wage.

(c) Calculate the level of real national income and the share of national income accruing to labor, the government, and the owners of capital.

(d) Now suppose that the government introduces a tax on labor income that shifts the labor supply curve to
$$n^s = 954 + 2(W/P)$$
What is the new equilibrium real wage, employment level, and share of national income accruing to labor, government, and owners of capital?

4. Why would we suppose that the wage differential (between highest and lowest wages) will influence the amount of job-search activity?

5. Suppose that there is a rise in the marginal product of labor in one sector of the economy and no change in the marginal product in the other sector. Trace the events that follow such a shock. Pay attention to the amount of job-search activity and unemployment. Is the unemployment generated by such a shock permanent or temporary?

22

Output Growth

We saw in Chapter 2 that the most dominant feature of the path of output is its long-term growth trend. Average output in Canada has grown at 4 percent per annum since 1926. Population has grown during that same time period at 1.8 percent per annum, so that per capita income has grown at 3.2 percent per annum. This is eqivalent to a doubling of per capita income every 22 years. The theories that you have studied so far in this book have abstracted from these long-term trends in output growth. Understanding what determines the trend will be the subject of this chapter.

The subject of this chapter is enormous. To do full justice to it would require another book at least as long as this one. Economists have been interested in the questions concerning long-term growth for as long as there has been a subject of economics. The founder of economics as we know it today, Adam Smith, wrote at length on the subject in his famous book, *On the Nature and Causes of the Wealth of Nations*, published in 1776. In the period since then, the topic has exercised the talents of the giants in our discipline such as Thomas Malthus and David Ricardo, and in more recent years, James Meade of Cambridge University, Trevor Swan of the Australian National University, Robert Solow of M.I.T., and James Tobin of Yale University.[1] These scholars have made their major contributions to the ab-

---

[1] Some of the seminal contributions to this topic are: James Meade, *A Neoclassical Theory of Economic Growth* (London: George Allen and Unwin, 1960); Trevor Swan, "Economic Growth and Capital Accumulation," *The Economic Review*, 32 (November 1956), 334-61; Robert M. Solow, "A Contribution to the Theory of Economic Growth," *Quarterly Journal of Economics*, 70 (February 1956), 65-94; and James Tobin, "A Dynamic Aggregative Model," *Journal of Political Economy*, 63 (April 1955), 103-15.

stract analysis of the determinants of economic growth. In addition, many scholars have undertaken careful measurement and empirical investigation, the most notable of these being Edward F. Denison, of the U.S. Department of Commerce and Brookings Institution.[2]

In view of the enormous volume of literature on the topic of economic growth, this chapter cannot pretend to do any more than provide an account of the highlights of the subject, and we shall concentrate on matters of principle rather than on empirical issues. Thus this chapter is somewhat different from the other three in this part of the book.[3]

You will be taken through five principal tasks, which are to:

a) Understand the concept of the per capita production function.
b) Know how to represent per capita output and savings in a simple diagram.
c) Understand the concept of the steady-state investment rate.
d) Know how to find the equilibrium values of per capita output, capital, consumption, savings and investment.
e) Understand what determines the trend rate of growth of output.

A. The Per Capita Production Function

You are already familiar with the concept of the production function. You met it in Chapter 14 when dealing with aggregate supply and the labor market. As you discovered there, a production function is simply a statement about the maximum output that can be produced with a given list of inputs and, more than that, a statement of how that maximum level of output will vary as the inputs themselves are varied. The maximum output of some particular good that can be produced will depend on the amount of capital employed, the state of technology, the amount of land resources used, and the number and skill of the workers employed. In Chapter 14, where we were concerned only with the short run, we supposed that all of the inputs into the production process with the exception of the number of workers employed, were fixed. In this chapter however, we want to focus on the process of growth itself and to allow for variations in inputs other than labor.

---

[2] Edward F. Dennison, *Accounting for the United States Economic Growth 1929-1969* (Washington, D.C.: The Brookings Institution, 1974).

[3] There are many excellent, although advanced, treatments of this topic that cover the subject in a comprehensive way. Perhaps the best introductory collection of readings of some of the major contributions to this topic is *The Modern Theory of Economic Growth* edited by Joseph E. Stiglitz and Hirofumi Uzawa (Cambridge, Mass.: M.I.T. Press, 1969). In addition to presenting the original contributions by James Meade, Robert M. Solow and Trevor W. Swan on which this chapter is based, this book also contains a seminal contribution that integrates monetary and growth theory by James Tobin, as well as much other material. The level of difficulty of the essays in this work is, however, substantially higher than the presentation given in this chapter.

It will be a useful approximation to imagine that total land resources are fixed and that, over the long run, what may be varied in order to vary output are the amounts of labor and capital employed and the state of technology that is utilized. The larger the number of people employed or the larger the stock of capital equipment used, the greater will be the volume of output. As labor and capital inputs are increased, output will increase, but by diminishing amounts — the law of diminishing returns will apply both to labor and capital. However, as technology advances over time, the amount of output that will be attainable from any given amount of labor and capital will increase.

Since the focus of our attention in this chapter is going to be on long-term trends in output, it turns out to be useful to consider the *per capita* (per head) production function rather than the aggregate production function. The previous paragraph has talked about the relationship between aggregate output and the amount of labor and capital employed in the production process. The per capita production function is a statement about how output per head varies as we vary the inputs per head as well as the state of technology. It turns out to be extremely convenient to assume that output per head varies as capital per head is varied and in a similar way to the way in which total output varies as the capital input is changed. Thus, as capital per head is increased, output per head increases but in successively diminishing amounts — the law of diminishing returns again.

In general, it is possible that output per head will depend both on capital per head and on the number of people employed — the scale of output. By assuming that output per head depends *only* on capital per head, we are assuming that there are constant returns to scale. This is an important, though probably not violent, simplification. There is a great deal of evidence to the effect that real-world production functions are characterized by constant returns to scale.

B. Per Capita Output and Savings

The per capita production function can be represented in a diagram to look much like the short-run production function with which you are already familiar (Figure 14.2). Figure 22.1 illustrates this same type of relationship but in per capita terms. As you see, we measure the amount of capital per head (k/n) on the horizontal axis in Figure 22.1, whereas in Figure 14.2 we measured the number employed n. On the vertical axis in Figure 22.1 we measure output per head (y/n) whereas, in contrast, in Figure 14.2 we measured aggregate output (y). The production function is the line labelled $f(k/n,t)$. This line shows that as capital per head is increased, so output per head increases. The curvature of the function shows that as capital per head is increased so output per head increases but by decreasing amounts.

Figure 22.1
Per Capita Production
and Savings Functions

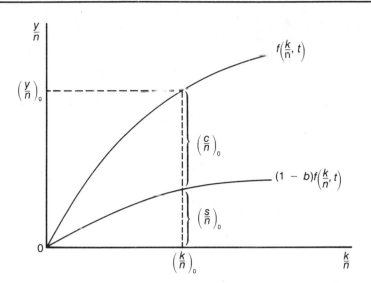

Per capita output will be an increasing function of the capital-labor ratio and will be subject to diminishing marginal productivity of capital — the curve labelled $f(k/n,t)$. Per capita savings will be a fraction of per capita output — the curve labelled $(1-b)f(k/n,t)$. At the capital-labor ratio $(k/n)_0$, output per head is $(y/n)_0$, consumption per head is $(c/n)_0$ and savings per head is $(s/n)_0$.

The curve is labelled $f(k/n,t)$ to remind you that there are two things that affect output per head. The first of these is capital per head, and we measure the effect of it on output per head as movements along the per capita production function. The second variable that affects output per head is the state of technology represented by the letter t. At any given point in time there will be a given state of technology and a given per capita production function. However, as time progresses and technology changes, in general, the per capita production function will shift upwards indicating that, at a given level of capital per head, output per head will increase.

The term *capital per head* is a slightly clumsy one and is replaced by the equivalent term, the *capital-labor ratio*.

As you already know, both from the discussion of flows and stocks in Chapter 3 and from our analysis of investment demand in Chapter 9, there are some important linkages between investment, savings and the stock of capital. The capital stock changes as a result of investment activity. In our analysis of fluctuations of economic activity around its trend, we found it convenient to ignore the ongoing effects of investment on capital accumulation and proceeded on the simplifying (although strictly untenable) assumption that the capital stock was constant. Now that we are analyzing the determinants of the long-term trends in output, we need to focus explicitly on the effects of ongoing savings and investment on the rate of capital accumulation.

In the most basic terms, you can think of the rate at which capital is being accumulated as the difference between the rate at which goods are being produced and consumed. You need to be careful to include in your definition of consumption the consumption of capital goods through their wear and tear and depreciation, what is called *capital consumption*. Provided this consumption is measured to include capital consumption it will be clear to you that the change in the capital stock is identical to income minus consumption. You know, however (ignoring government and international economic activity for simplicity) that income minus consumption is savings. You also know that a reasonable proposition about savings is that, in the long run, it is equal to some constant fraction of income. Let us, as we did in Chapter 8, call the fraction of income consumed b, so that the fraction of income saved is $1 - b$.

We can represent the amount of income saved in the same figure as our per capita production function (Figure 22.1). This is the lower line labelled $(1-b)f(k/n,t)$. It is simply the production function scaled down by the fraction $1-b$, so that it shows the amount of per capita income that is not consumed — in other words, that is saved — at each capital-labor ratio. For example, if the capital-labor ratio was $(k/n)_0$, then per capita income would be $(y/n)_0$, as indicated on the vertical axis of the figure, and that income would be divided between consumption of $(c/n)_0$ and capital accumulation — savings — of $(s/n)_0$.

What Figure 22.1 now shows us are the amounts of output per head and savings per head — capital accumulation per head — that will be achieved at each possible capital-labor ratio. The figure has an interesting feature that has not been met before in this book. It is that one of the variables that has been measured on the vertical axis represents the amount by which the variable on the horizontal axis is *changing*. That is, if we were to pick a particular capital-labor ratio again, say $(k/n)_0$, then a certain amount of output would be produced, a certain fraction of this output would be consumed and the rest would be added to the stock of capital. Thus, the stock of capital will be changing. If the labor force is also growing (if n is rising), then the capital-labor ratio will either rise, fall or stay constant depending on whether the rise in the labor force exceeds, falls short of or happens to just equal the growth of the capital stock.

The next section will analyze the process whereby the actual rates of savings, investment, and output are determined.

C. Steady-State Investment Rate

There is one and only one rate of investment that is compatible with the economy being in a steady state. By *steady state* we mean nothing other than a situation in which the relevant variables are constant over time. The relevant variables for the present are per capita output and capital stock and the rates of consumption, savings and investment. To figure out what the steady-state rate of investment is we want to work out that rate of investment that maintains the capital-labor ratio at some given constant level. To work this out, let us begin with the obvious proposition that the rate of savings (s) is equal to the change in the stock of capital or investment; that is,

$$s = \Delta k \qquad (22.1)$$

We can divide savings and the change in the capital stock by the population to give per capita savings that are equal to per capita capital accumulation; that is,

$$\frac{s}{n} = \frac{\Delta k}{n} \qquad (22.2)$$

Let us now do something that at first seems pointless but which turns out in fact to be very useful. That is, let us multiply and divide the right-hand side of Equation (22.2) by the capital stock. This, of course, multiplies the right-hand side of the equation by one, leaving it unchanged. If we do this, we obtain

$$\frac{s}{n} = \frac{\Delta k}{k}\frac{k}{n} \qquad (22.3)$$

This is still nothing other than a definition. It tells us that per capita savings are equal to the growth rate of the capital stock ($\Delta k/k$) multiplied by the capital-labor ratio (k/n).

Now, in order that the economy be in a steady state, the capital-labor ratio (k/n) must be a constant. This can only occur when the stock of capital is growing at the same rate as the labor force is growing. If, for example, neither was growing at all, then the capital-labor ratio would be constant. Equally, the capital-labor ratio would be constant provided each was growing at the same rate. Thus, the condition for the steady state is that

$$\frac{\Delta k}{k} = \frac{\Delta n}{n} \qquad (22.4)$$

Equation (22.3) above is simply a definition, and Equation (22.4) is the condition that, if satisfied, gives rise to a steady state. We can combine these two propositions to give

$$\frac{s}{n} = \frac{\Delta n}{n}\frac{k}{n} \qquad (22.5)$$

What this says is that in the steady state, per capita savings will be equal to the growth rate of the population multiplied by the capital-labor ratio. The growth rate of the population is treated as being exogenous — that is, it does not vary as a consequence of variations in any of the variables whose values we are determining in the analysis. (This assumption of modern growth theory contrasts with that of the earlier economists such as Thomas Malthus and David Ricardo who viewed the population growth rate as one of the factors that adjusted to the underlying economic conditions.)

We can represent the steady-state rate of capital accumulation in a simple diagram such as Figure 22.2. This figure, like Figure 22.1, measures the capital-labor ratio on the horizontal axis and measures the rate of savings (capital accumulation) per head on the vertical axis. The slope of the line, as is readily seen from Equation (22.5), is equal to the (exogenous) population growth rate, $\Delta n/n$. Figure 22.2, like Figure 22.1, has the interesting property that the value of the variable measured on the vertical axis is the change in the variable on the horizontal axis for a given value of n. The line plotted in Figure 22.2, however, traces all those values of s/n that deliver a constant k/n. If the economy was above that line with s/n greater than the steady-state value, the capital stock would be growing faster than the population, and k/n would be rising. At points below the ray in Figure 22.2, the rate of capital accumulation would be less than the rate of population growth, and the capital-labor ratio would be falling. The points on the line are those at which the capital stock and the labor force are growing at the same rate and therefore deliver a constant capital-labor ratio.

**Figure 22.2
Steady-State
Investment Ray**

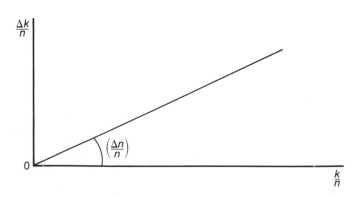

The rate of per capita capital accumulation that will maintain the capital-labor ratio intact is shown as the ray having a slope equal to the growth rate of the population.

D. Equilibrium Per Capita Output, Capital, Consumption, Savings and Investment

It is now a relatively simple matter to bring together the analyses of the two preceding sections and determine the equilibrium levels of per capita output, consumption, savings, investment and capital. This is done in Figure 22.3. A preliminary examination of this figure will reveal that it is nothing other than a combination of Figures 22.1 and 22.2. The curve labelled $f(k/n,t)$ is the per capita production function. That labelled $(1 - b)f(k/n,t)$ is the savings rate as a function of the capital-labor ratio, and the ray having the slope $\Delta n/n$ is the steady-state investment ray.

To get a feel for how the figure works and how it determines the equilibrium, let us imagine initially that the economy has a capital-labor ratio of $(k/n)_0$ as marked on the horizontal axis of Figure 22.3. The level of output per head is immediately determined as $(y/n)_0$. How much capital accumulation is taking place in this situation? Is it more or less than that required to maintain the capital-labor ratio at its constant $(k/n)_0$ level? You know that the amount of actual capital accumulation is read off from the savings line $(1 - b)f(k/n,t)$. You also know that the amount of capital accumulation required to maintain

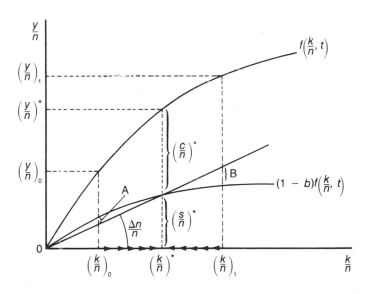

Figure 22.3 Equilibrium Per Capita Output, Capital, Investment and Savings

The per capita production and savings functions are combined with the steady-state investment ray to determine the steady-state capital-labor ratio and output per head. In a situation like $(k/n)_0$, capital grows at a faster rate than the steady-state requirement so that the capital-labor ratio rises. In a situation like $(k/n)_1$ the capital stock grows at a slower rate than that required for the steady state, so that the capital-labor ratio falls. At $(k/n)^*$, the savings rate equals the steady-state investment rate and the capital-labor ratio remains constant.

the capital-labor ratio at a constant is read off from the steady-state investment ray. At the capital-labor ratio of $(k/n)_0$, there is evidently a gap between these two amounts — labelled A in the figure. Evidently, at the capital-labour ratio $(k/n)_0$, actual capital accumulation exceeds that required to maintain a constant capital-labor ratio by the amount A. This means that the capital-labor ratio will not remain constant at $(k/n)_0$. Instead it will be rising.

Next consider what will be happening if the economy had a capital-labor ratio $(k/n)_1$ on the horizontal axis of Figure 22.3. In this case, output per head would be $(y/n)_1$. Conducting exactly the same type of exercise as that above, you can now see that there is a gap between the amount of capital that will be accumulated and the steady-state investment line of the amount labelled B in the figure. This time, however, there is less capital being accumulated than that required to maintain a constant capital-labor ratio. That is, the steady-state investment line lies above the savings function. This means that the capital-labor ratio $(k/n)_1$ is not a steady state because if the economy started out in this position, capital would be growing at a slower rate than the labor force, so that the capital-labor ratio would be falling. You can now immediately see that there is one, and only one, capital-labor ratio that is consistent with a steady state, and it is that labelled $(k/n)^*$.

This capital-labor ratio generates an output rate of $(y/n)^*$ and a savings rate equal to the steady-state rate of capital accumulation. That is, at $(k/n)^*$, the savings function intersects the steady-state investment line. There is no gap between the rate at which capital is in fact being accumulated and the rate at which it needs to be accumulated in order to maintain a constant capital-labor ratio. Thus, $(k/n)^*$ and $(y/n)^*$ represent the equilibrium capital-labor ratio and output per head in the economy. The output is divided between consumption and savings (capital accumulation) with $(c/n)^*$ being consumed and $(s/n)^*$ being saved and added to the stock of capital. In this economy, the long-term trend in output will have the same growth rate as that of the population $(\Delta n/n)$.

E. Determinants of the Trend Rate of Growth of Output

In the analysis of the preceding section, you have seen that the trend growth rate of output will be equal to the population growth rate, since there is a built-in equilibrating mechanism that ensures that the capital-labor ratio approaches its steady-state rate, thereby producing a fixed output per head. The diagrams used to characterize the solution in the previous section use a per capita production function that itself does not move. If, however, as a result of technical change, the production function is continuously shifting upwards, then output per head will grow at a rate over and above the population growth rate. This growth rate, however, will depend only on the rate at which the production function is shifting upwards and will have to be added to the basic growth rate of output — the growth rate of the population.

What this says is that the trend growth rate of output is determined by the trend growth rate in the population and the trend growth in output per head made possible by the trend in technology. Specifically, the growth rate of output does not depend on the rate of saving. A change in the rate of saving would affect the level of output per head and the capital-labor ratio but would not affect the growth trend.

You can see this very clearly by considering the analysis in Figure 22.4 which, again, abstracts from changing technology and analyzes the situation for a given production function at a given moment in time. The initial equilibrium depicted in Figure 22.3 is reproduced as the equilibrium labelled $(k/n)^*_0$ and $(y/n)^*_0$. This is an equilibrium associated with a given population growth rate $(\Delta n/n)$ and a savings rate equal to $(1 - b_0)$. Now imagine that the savings rate was to increase to $(1 - b_1)$. This would result in an upward shift in the savings function as shown in Figure 22.4. Starting out at $(k/n)^*_0$, the savings rate will now be higher than that required to maintain a constant capital-labor ratio. As a consequence, the capital-labor ratio will rise, and as it does so, output per head will also rise. The higher

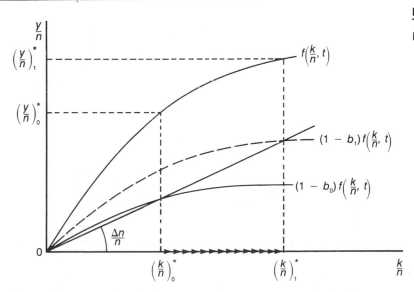

**Figure 22.4
The Effect of a Change
in the Savings Rate**

If the savings rate rises from $(1-b_0)$ to $(1-b_1)$ the savings function shifts upwards. At $(k/n)^*_0$, the rate of capital accumulation exceeds that necessary to hold the capital-labor ratio constant. Thus the capital-labor ratio rises and continues to do so up to $(k/n)^*_1$ when a new steady state is reached.

is the capital-labor ratio, the higher will be the rate of saving needed to maintain a given constant capital-labor ratio (we move along the steady-state investment ray).

Eventually, we reach the capital-labor ratio $(k/n)_1^*$, which produces the income level $(y/n)_1^*$ that is a steady state. At this capital-labor ratio, the steady-state investment ray intersects the savings function, so that the capital-labor ratio remains constant. During the transition from the initial to the new capital-labor ratio, the growth rate of output will have exceeded the growth rate of the population. This is obvious because the ratio (y/n) has increased, so that y must have been growing faster than n. However, once the new steady state is reached, the rate of growth of output will again equal the rate of population growth.

Thus, except for the process of adjustment from one steady state to another, the growth rate of output is independent of the savings rate. A different way of putting this would be to say that the growth rate of output does not depend on the savings rate but does depend on *changes in* the savings rate.

Although the savings rate does not affect the growth rate of output, it does affect the level of output per head. You can see immediately from Figure 22.4 that the higher the rate of savings, the greater will be the levels of capital and output per head.

Figure 22.5
The Effects of a Change in the Population Growth Rate

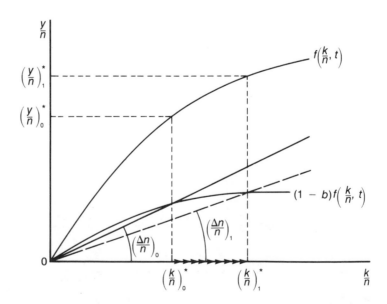

The population growth rate decreases from $(\Delta n/n)_0$ to $(\Delta n/n)_1$. At the initial equilibrium $(k/n)_0^*$, the savings rate is bigger than that required to maintain the capital-labor ratio constant. The capital-labor ratio, therefore, increases and continues to do so until it reaches $(k/n)_1^*$, its new steady state.

Although the savings rate does not affect the growth rate of output, the population growth rate does. It also influences the level of output per head in a way that you can readily see. Figure 22.5 illustrates the analysis this time. Again, the initial equilibrium as depicted in Figure 22.3 is reproduced in Figure 22.5 as $(k/n)_0^*$ with per capita output at $(y/n)_0^*$. This is the equilibrium associated with the population growth rate of $(\Delta n/n)_0$. Now imagine that the population growth rate declines to $(\Delta n/n)_1$. This will have the effect of rotating the steady-state investment ray downwards as shown in Figure 22.5. At the initial capital-labor ratio $(k/n)_0^*$ there will now be a level of savings and capital accumulation that exceeds the steady-state investment requirement. This means that the capital-labor ratio will rise. It will do so until it reaches $(k/n)_1^*$, at which point the new steady-state investment line intersects the savings function. During the process, the capital-labor ratio will have increased from $(k/n)_0^*$ to $(k/n)_1^*$ and per capita output will have grown from $(y/n)_0^*$ to $(y/n)_1^*$. In the new steady state, the growth rate of total output will have declined by exactly the same amount as the growth rate of the population. In the transition to the new steady state, output will have grown at a faster rate than the population growth rate.

You have now seen that the *level* of output per head depends on both the population growth rate and the savings rate. The lower is the population growth rate or the higher is the savings rate, the higher the output per head, and the higher the capital-labor ratio. The growth rate of output, except for transitions arising from changes in the savings rate or the population growth rate, depends only on the population growth rate and the rate of technical change.

We have focussed on the effects of the population growth rate and the savings rate on per capita output and the capital-labor ratio. It is now of some interest to examine how the rate of per capita consumption is influenced by these factors. Let us examine the possible steady-state per capita consumption levels. Figure 22.6 shows these possibilities. The figure contains the production function and the steady-state investment line. The gap between these two lines indicates the steady-state consumption possibilities. Of course, to realize any one of these possibilities, the actual savings behavior of the population would have to be appropriate.

Let us suspend consideration of what this savings behavior needs to be for a moment and simply look at the amounts of consumption per capita that are available in different steady states. Visual inspection of Figure 22.6 reveals that as the capital-labor ratio increases from zero, per capita consumption at first increases. A point is reached, however, at which per capita consumption is at a maximum. This is at the capital-labor ratio marked in Figure 22.6 $(k/n)^*$. At capital-labor ratios greater than $(k/n)^*$, consumption per capita declines as the capital-labor ratio increases. You can see, as a result of the line

**Figure 22.6
Per Capita
Consumption and the
Golden Rule**

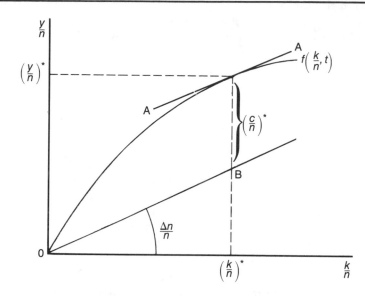

Possible steady-state values of consumption per capita are shown by the vertical distance between the per capita production function $f(k/n,t)$ and the population growth rate ($\Delta n/n$). Evidently consumption per capita is at a maximum at $(k/n)^*$. At this capital-labor ratio the marginal product of capital which is the slope of the line AA is equal to the population growth rate. That is the "Golden Rule." If the savings function passes through B, then per capita consumption will in fact be maximized. Savings may be either too great or too small to maximize per capita consumption.

labelled AA in Figure 22.6, that the slope of the production function at the point of maximum per capita consumption is equal to the slope of the steady-state investment line. This slope you know to be the growth rate of population.

What does the slope of the per capita production function measure? A moment's reflection will convince you that it measures the marginal product of capital. Think of increasing capital per head by a small amount and ask how much extra output per head do we get; the answer is that it depends on the slope of the per capita production function. At very low capital-labor ratios, we get a large amount of extra output, whereas at very high capital-labor ratios we get very little. The slope of the per capita production function thus measures the (diminishing) marginal productivity of capital. The slope of the line AA measures the marginal product of capital at the point of maximum per capita consumption.

You have just discovered what is known as the "golden rule." The golden rule states that per capita consumption is maximized when the marginal product of capital is equal to the growth rate of population.

To achieve the golden rule it would be necessary that the savings fraction be such as to pass the savings function through the point marked B in Figure 22.6. Savings rates larger than that would imply a higher capital-labor ratio than $(k/n)^*$, a higher output level than $(y/n)^*$, but a smaller consumption rate than $(c/n)^*$. Savings rates lower than that necessary to pass the savings function through B would be associated with lower output per head, lower capital per head, and lower consumption per head.

You have now seen that the growth rate of output depends on the growth rate of population and on the rate of technical change. You have also seen that the level of output per head and the capital-labor ratio depend both on the population growth rate and the savings rate. You have also seen, however, that the ultimate objective of economic activity, consumption, at any given point in time in a given state of technology has a well-defined maximum. There is thus a unique per capita consumption-maximizing rate of saving which, if achieved, would deliver not the maximum possible output per head and capital stock per head, but the optimum values of those variables.

Over time output per head and consumption per head will increase if technical change is shifting the production function upwards. There is no "free lunch" in this direction, however, because more rapid technical change would require devoting more resources to research and development and less resources to consumption. Just as there is a per capita consumption-maximizing rate of saving, so also there will be an optimum rate at which to devote resources to research and development. Like all other economic activities, this too is subject to the laws of diminishing returns.

Summary

A. The Per Capita Production Function

The per capita production function shows the maximum amount of per capita production obtainable as the capital-labour ratio is increased. The per capita production function will shift over time as a result of technical change.

B. Per Capita Output and Savings

Per capita savings (which is the same thing as per capita capital accumulation) will be some fraction of per capita output. Thus, the rate of per capita capital accumulation depends upon the level of capital per head.

C. Steady-State Investment Rate

Because the per capita rate of capital accumulation depends upon the capital-labor ratio, it follows that, in general, at any given capital-labor ratio there will be a tendency for the capital-labor ratio to either rise or fall. The steady-state investment rate is the rate of investment (of capital accumulation) that maintains the capital-labor ratio constant. The investment rate that maintains the capital-labor ratio constant is the capital-labor ratio multiplied by the population growth rate.

D.Equilibrium Per Capita Output, Capital, Consumption, Savings and Investment

The equilibrium value of the capital-labor ratio is determined as that capital-labor ratio that generates a volume of savings per head equal to the steady-state rate of investment per head. When savings per head equal steady-state investment per head, the capital-labor ratio, output per head, consumption per head and savings per head are all constant.

E. Determinants of the Trend Rate of Growth of Output

The trend rate of growth of output is determined by the population growth rate and the rate of technical change. It does not depend on the savings rate. If the savings rate changes, however, there is a transition from one level of output per head to another that involves a change in the growth rate. Specifically, a rise in the savings rate raises the capital-labor ratio and output per head. A fall in the population growth rate also has those same effects. Per capita consumption is maximized when the marginal product of capital equals the population growth rate. This is known as the "golden rule." There is a unique saving rate that will deliver the golden rule. Too much savings relative to the golden rule produces a higher output per head but a lower consumption per head than the golden rule value.

Review Questions

1. What is a per capita production function? How does it differ from an ordinary aggregate production function? Does it still possess the property of diminishing returns?

2. What happens to the per capita production function if there is technical progress? Illustrate in a diagram.

3. How does savings per head vary as output per head varies?

4. You are given the following information:

k/n	0	1	2	3	4	5	6	7	8	9	10
y/n	0	2.0	3.7	5.0	6.2	7.2	8.0	8.6	9.1	9.5	9.8

Plot the per capita production function. If the fraction of income consumed is 0.8, plot the relationship between capital per head and savings per head.

5. What is the meaning of the concept the steady-state rate of investment?

6. What determines the steady-state rate of investment?

7. Show in a diagram how the equilibrium values of output per head, consumption per head, savings per head and investment per head are determined. Analyze the forces that would act on these variables if they were not at their equilibrium values.

8. Review what happens to the four variables referred to in the previous question if there is a rise in the production function generated by technical progress.

9. Analyze the effects on the four variables set out in Question 7 in the event of a rise in the growth rate of population.

10. Does capital accumulation cause a growth in the standard of living? If not, what does?

23

Business Cycles

In the last three chapters you have studied the forces that generate trends in inflation, trends and cycles in unemployment, and trends in output. In studying each of these features of the world we have abstracted from unanticipated or "surprise" changes in aggregate demand. Now it is time to focus on these surprises and analyze how they modify the behavior of the economy compared with what would have happened in their absence. You can think of what we are going to study here as adding noise — and persistence — to the trends and unemployment cycles (generated in the preceding chapters).

The chapter will take you through six tasks, which are to:

a) Understand how unanticipated changes in aggregate demand generate procyclical co-movements in prices.

b) Understand how a combination of unanticipated and anticipated changes in aggregate demand generates surges in inflation that are independent of output and also generates procyclical co-movements in prices.

c) Know how the rational expectations theories explain the autocorrelation of output and employment.

d) Understand the implications of the rational expectations theories for interest rate behavior.

e) Understand how the rational expectations theories explain the business cycle.

f) Understand the nature of the hypothesis-testing problem posed by the rational expectations theories.

A. Procyclical Co-Movements in Prices

You have seen in Chapter 19 how an anticipated change in aggregate demand affects only the nominal variables of the economy, and how an unanticipated change in aggregate demand has both nominal and real effects. It is now possible to use this analysis to understand how the swings in economic activity that are characterized by procyclical co-movements in prices occur.

For illustrative purposes it is going to be easiest to assume that the expected aggregate demand curve does not change. Equivalently, this implies that the expected money supply and expected government expenditure and taxes are constant. (It would be possible to assume that the expected *growth rate* of the money supply was constant, so that the expected level of the money supply was increasing by a constant percentage amount each period. In this case, the aggregate demand curve would be shifting upwards at a constant percentage rate, and there would be a trend rate of inflation. We would then analyze variations in aggregate demand around its rising trend position. However, such an exercise would complicate the analysis without adding any insights and will not be pursued here.)

In order to fix our ideas, let us suppose that the level of aggregate demand that actually occurs differs from that which is expected because the actual money supply is randomly fluctuating around its anticipated level. Sometimes it is above and sometimes it is below its anticipated level. Figures 23.1 and 23.2 will illustrate what is going on. Figure 23.1 shows a hypothetical random path for the money supply. (These illustrative numbers are random drawings from a normal distribution with a mean of 100 and a standard deviation of 2.) The average value of the money supply is 100; therefore, the rational expectation of the money supply is also 100. The maximum value of the money supply in this example, 104, occurs in period 5 and is marked A. The minimum value, 95.8, occurs in period 9 and is marked B.

Figure 23.2 shows the aggregate demand and aggregate supply curves. The curve $AD(M^e = 100)$ is the aggregate demand curve drawn for the expected value of the money supply. The expectations-augmented aggregate supply curve, EAS_0, is drawn for an expected price level equal to its rational expectation, P_0^e. The vertical curve, AS, is the full-employment aggregate supply curve.

If the money supply behaves as shown in Figure 23.1, then the economy will, on the average, be at the price level P_0^e and, on the average, will be at the full-employment level of output y^*. There will, however, be fluctuations around these points. When the money supply is at A, its maximum value in this example, the aggregate demand curve will be the curve shown as $AD(M = 104)$. This determines output as y_a and the price level as P_a. When the money supply is at B, its minimum value in this example, the aggregate demand curve will be at the position shown as $AD(M = 95.8)$. In this case, output will be y_b,

**Figure 23.1
Hypothetical Money
Supply Path**

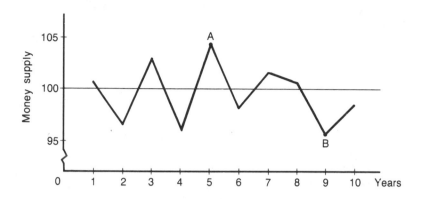

A hypothetical path for the money supply is generated by drawing random numbers from a normal distribution that has an average value of 100 and a standard deviation of 2. The path plotted was generated by taking ten drawings from such a distribution.

and the price level will be P_b. For intermediate values of the money supply (periods 1 to 4, 6 to 8, and 10), output and the price level will be determined at points in between these two extremes and along the EAS_0 curve. The thickened portion of the curve traces out the range of values of y and P generated by this hypothetical money supply path.

Although random variations in the money supply about the anticipated level have been stylized as random variations around a *constant* anticipated money supply, as noted above, it would not be difficult to generalize this analysis. If the anticipated money supply was growing, then the expected aggregate demand curve and, therefore, the expectations-augmented aggregate supply curve would also drift upwards. The actual variations in the money supply, however, would fluctuate around the rising trend, so that the actual aggregate demand curve would fluctuate around the expected curve. We would, therefore, still generate procyclical co-movements of prices, although the amplitude of the price movements would be accentuated, and those of the output movements would be smaller than those illustrated.

The predicted procyclical co-movements of prices shown in Figure 23.2 can easily be translated into a predicted negative relationship between inflation and unemployment. When output is above its full-employment level, unemployment will be below its natural rate, and vice versa. When the price level is higher than expected, the inflation rate will also be higher than expected. Therefore, procyclical co-movements of prices automatically imply a negative correlation between inflation and unemployment — the Phillips relation of Chapter 6.

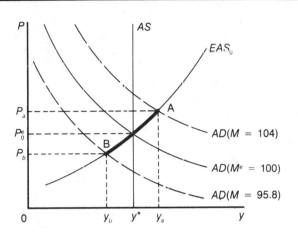

**Figure 23.2
Procyclical
Co-Movements
of Prices**

If the money supply was equal to its average value (and rationally expected value) of 100, the aggregate demand curve would be the solid line $AD(M^e = 100)$, output would be y^*, and the price level P_0^e. Actual movements in the money supply will shift the demand function as shown between the limits $AD(M = 104)$ and $AD(M = 95.8)$. With a constant expected price level, the expectations-augmented aggregate supply curve remains at EAS_0, and the actual levels of output and prices are generated along the thick line AB. This thickened line traces out the generally procyclical movement of prices.

You have now seen how unanticipated shocks to aggregate demand generate one aspect of the facts that need to be explained — the sometimes observed, systematic, procyclical co-movements of prices. Let us now move on to review our understanding of the sources of independent movements (countercyclical movements) in output and prices.

B. Independent Movements in Output and Prices

To see how the rational expectations theories are capable of accounting, in principle, for all the patterns that we observe in the co-movements of output and prices, let us consider separately the effects of anticipated, unanticipated, and combined monetary shocks to the economy.

Suppose first, as described in detail in the previous section, that there is an unanticipated rise in aggregate demand. We know that this will raise the price level (and the inflation rate) and will raise output. Thus, from this source of shock there will be a procyclical co-movement in prices. Suppose, at the opposite extreme, that there is a rise in aggregate demand that is anticipated. This will lead to a rise in the price level (inflation rate) with no corresponding movement of output (recall Chapter 19). Now combine these two effects. There are two interesting cases. One is where aggregate demand increases by an amount that is partly anticipated and partly not. In this case, there will be a rise in both output and prices, but the rise in prices will be greater than if the rise in the money supply was unanticipated. Let us translate this into a prediction about inflation and unemployment rather than about prices and output.

In the experiment just reviewed, a higher output level is associated with a lower unemployment rate, and a higher price level is associated with a higher observed rate of inflation. This means that a rise in aggregate demand that was partly anticipated and partly not would generate a rise in inflation and a drop in unemployment. The amount by which prices rise depends on the anticipated and unanticipated components of the rise in the money supply. The amount by which unemployment falls depends only on the unanticipated change in aggregate demand. What this implies is that the slope of the Phillips relation of Chapter 6 will not be constant and will, in general, depend on the decomposition of the change in aggregate demand between its anticipated and unanticipated components.

We can see this in a more extreme case by considering a second example. Suppose that aggregate demand *is anticipated* to grow at a high rate. In this situation, suppose further that aggregate demand actually increases at a slow rate. This is a situation in which there is a rise in anticipated aggregate demand but negative unanticipated aggregate demand. In such a situation, output falls, and unemployment rises. The inflation rate may either rise or fall, depending on the strength of the two offsetting effects on it. The effect of a high anticipated growth of aggregate demand will be to keep inflation high, whereas the effect of a negative unanticipated change in aggregate demand will be to lower inflation. We cannot say, a priori, which of these two effects will dominate. It is possible, however, for the first to dominate, thereby producing a higher rate of inflation with a higher unemployment rate and an output rate that is below trend. This would correspond with the case observed on several occasions in the 1970s when there was a tendency for both inflation and unemployment to rise together. Some aspects of the behavior of Canadian unemployment and inflation in the 1970s may potentially be accounted for by this line of reasoning.

The crucial thing to emphasize and reiterate is that the way in which a change in aggregate demand is divided between a change in output and a change in prices depends on the extent to which that change in aggregate demand is anticipated. On the average, output and prices will move in the same direction as each other, since swings in actual aggregate demand are likely to have greater amplitude than swings in expected aggregate demand. From time to time, however, there may be large shifts in anticipated aggregate demand, usually less than, but occasionally greater than, the change in actual aggregate demand. These occasional strong changes in expected aggregate demand will produce co-movements that are opposite to those normally observed, and when they occur, they will be associated with the appearance of badly deteriorating (or, although it did not happen in the 1970s, of miraculously improving) macroeconomic performance.

The discussion in this section and in the preceding one has focussed on the way in which the price and output co-movements might be understood. There is one further feature of the behavior of output, however, on which this discussion has not touched and to which we now turn.

C. Autocorrelation of Output and Employment

There are two distinct, although not mutually exclusive, explanations for autocorrelation of output and employment. One is based on costs of adjustment of labor and is employed in the new classical analysis. The other is based on overlapping contracts and is used in the new Keynesian theory. Let us look at each of them in turn.

(i) Adjustment Costs

The theory of profit-maximizing firms' demand for labor and supply of output as developed in Chapter 14, which underlies all the theories of aggregate supply, implicitly assumes that firms can vary their output and labor inputs instantly and costlessly. This is a reasonable assumption to make for the purpose of getting some theoretical principles straight. It is not a good assumption, however, if we want to explain the facts as they appear in actual economies. It is costly for firms to hire and fire labor and it is costly for households to search out desirable employment opportunities. In the event of a change in demand, labor inputs and outputs will only gradually adjust to meet the new demand conditions. Therefore, when the price level rises, instead of the demand for labor curve instantly shifting to reflect the new higher price level, it will move only gradually. Thus, if the economy experienced an unanticipated (say) rise in the money supply, then, although the response to this rise will be a higher price level and higher levels of output and employment, it will take firms some time to raise their output and employment levels by the amounts suggested by the theories developed in this book. Instead of the demand for labor curve suddenly shifting, it will gradually move to the right, thereby leading to a gradual change in employment and output rather than a sudden jump.

To make things clearer, suppose that after a period in which there had been an unanticipated rise in the money supply, there was a subsequent unanticipated fall. Firms will already have hired additional labor and be producing additional output, having moved some way toward satisfying the demand associated with the previously unanticipated rise in the money supply. Now that they are confronted with an unexpected fall in the money supply (and therefore an unexpected fall in the price level), they will not suddenly jump to the new lower employment and output position. Rather, they will, *starting from where they are*, gradually move toward the new lower output and employment position. This is not to say that firms are irrational and are not maximizing profits. On the contrary, it is precisely because they are maximizing profits that their adjustments will be gradual. They have to take account, not only of the cost of labor and capital and the price of output in their profit-maximizing decisions, but also of the costs of *changing* their output and employment. Thus, the costs of hiring and firing labor make the demand for labor curves move slowly, and this imparts gradual adjustment to output and employment.

Gradual adjustment may be described as *autocorrelation*. If output and employment adjust gradually, then where they will move to in the current period depends on where they started out from in the previous period, and where they will go to in the next period depends on where they are now. This can be described by saying that the values of output and employment in period t depend in part on the values of those variables in period $t - 1$.

The explanation for autocorrelation just presented is the one that is incorporated in the new classical theory of aggregate supply. A second way in which autocorrelation of output and employment can arise is emphasized in the new Keynesian theory and comes from the fact that contracts in the labor market are long and overlapping. Let us now look more closely at this explanation of autocorrelation.

(ii) Overlapping Contracts

It is not the case that everyone negotiates a labor contract on the same day of each year for the coming year. Some labor market contracts run for less than a year, some for a year, some for more than a year. The fact that labor market contracts overlap has important implications for the amount by which wages will change.

These implications are most easily seen in a simplified framework in which we imagine that contracts run for two years and that one-half of them are renegotiated each year. Figure 23.3 illustrates this setup. There are two groups: Group 1 negotiates contracts in odd-numbered years and group 2 in even-numbered years. In 1983, group 2's wages were W_0 (fixed in 1982), and group 1 negotiated a wage of W_1 to run for 1983 and 1984. In 1984, group 1's wages were predetermined at W_1 and group 2 set its wages at W_2 to run for 1984 and 1985. The pattern repeats forever. Now when group 1 is deciding on the appropriate level of wages in 1983, it will have to take some

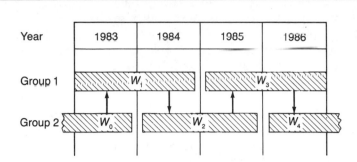

Figure 23.3
Overlapping
Contracts

Wages set in 1983 (W_1) are influenced by wages already determined (W_0) and in turn influence wages that will be set in 1984 (W_2). The pattern repeats, so that wages set in 1986 (W_4) are indirectly influenced by all earlier set wages.

account of the wages that group 2 is receiving, W_0. How much influence group 2's wage will have on group 1's decision will depend on how substitutable the labor is between the two groups. If it is not very substitutable, then the wages of one group will not be a major factor influencing the wages of the other. If, on the other hand, the two groups are very close substitutes for each other, then the wages of one will have a major influence on the wage level of the other. Why is this?

Recall that the basic assumption of the new Keynesian analysis is that money wages are set to achieve an expected equilibrium in the labor market. When just one group of workers is negotiating wages in their own sector, they have to take account of the fact that the demand for their services will depend both on their own wages and on the wages of alternative substitute labor. There is also substitutability on the supply side. The higher are the wages of one group relative to another, the more people would want to supply their services to the activities of this group. We see, then, that the expected equilibrium wage for one group depends on the wage level of the other group. The closer substitutes that the two groups are for each other, the more sensitive will the equilibrium wage of one group be to the wage of the other group.

In terms of Figure 23.3, the wages set in 1983, W_1, will be influenced by the wages that already prevail in this year (W_0). The arrow indicates the line of influence going from W_0 to W_1. Likewise, in 1984 when group 2 sets its wages, it would be influenced by the wages that have been set by W_1. Again, the arrow illustrates this line of influence. The same pattern repeats in 1985 and 1986 and so on. This means that the wages that are being set at any particular date will be influenced directly by the wages that already prevail at this date, and will be influenced indirectly by all the wages that have been set at all previous dates. Thus, the wages at any particular point in time will be influenced by wages at all past points in time.

Wages will adjust more gradually as a result of overlapping contracts than they would if all contracts were renegotiated on the same day. This is because even though demand conditions might have changed, the movement of one wage too far out of line with other wages in competing activities would not be compatible with an expected full-employment equilibrium in the relevant labor market.

The fact that wages set at any particular point in time depend on the wages set at all previous points in time means that, when setting a wage today, it is known by the parties agreeing to the wage that the decision being made will itself have an influence on decisions that are going to be made in the future.

Since future wages will be influenced in part by wages that are being fixed today, it is important in fixing today's wages to take account of likely future demand conditions. This means that rational wage setters in an economy in which contracts overlap will want to look as far into the future as they can in assessing the likely future course of both aggregate demand and demand in their own particular sector. They will seek to form rational expectations not just about the immediate future period but about all future periods.

There is a second important implication of overlapping contracts. It is that contracts in existence in any particular year, having been negotiated at different dates in the past, will incorporate expectations that were formed in the past, and, therefore, based on old information — information available at the past dates on which wages currently enforced were set. Thus, what was unanticipated when one set of contracts was written some time in the past, might already have occurred and, therefore, be part of the information on the basis of which some other, more recent contracts were written. This means that a monetary (or other aggregate demand) shock that occurs after a contract has been written, and which was unanticipated when the contract was written, will continue to have effects on output and employment until that particular contract is replaced with a new one. Furthermore, those effects will persist long beyond the date on which all existing contracts have been replaced with new ones.

To see this, you simply have to recall that wages currently being set are influenced by wages already in place. This means that if the wages set last year (to run for two years) were set at a level that is now known to have been inappropriate in the light of changes that have occurred in aggregate demand, the fact that those wages are going to remain in place for another year means that wages being set this year, while taking some account of the new information about the change in aggregate demand, also have to be set such that they do not get so far away from the wages already set that they create an excess supply or demand in the part of the market whose wages are currently being determined. Also, when the wages set last year are reset next year, they will be influenced by the wages that have been set this year and, therefore, they too will incorporate all the new knowledge about current demand conditions but will also continue to be influenced in part at least by their own previous value.

Thus, random shocks that bombard the economy will have effects that persist from period to period over the indefinite future. Their effects will die away gradually but not instantly.

You will recognize fairly readily that the behavior of wages in an economy with overlapping contracts may be described as displaying autocorrelation — that is, wages today depend on wages in some previous period. What we are seeking to understand, however, is not autocorrelated wages but autocorrelated output and employment. It is, however, only a short step from the behavior of wages to the behavior of employment and output. If wages are autocorrelated, so will employment and output be. To see this, you simply have to recall that the level of employment depends on the level of wages (real wages). The gradual adjustment of money wages takes account of the expected price level and is, in effect, an attempt to gradually adjust expected real wages. A gradual adjustment of real wages would automatically imply a gradual adjustment of the profit-maximizing level of employment and, therefore, of the level of output. Thus, overlapping labor market contracts lead not only to autocorrelated wages but to autocorrelated output and employment as well.

An Analogy: The idea that costly labor input adjustments and overlapping long-term contracts can generate autocorrelation in output, employment, and prices has a vivid physical analogy that perhaps will make things clearer. Suppose one was to hit a rocking chair at random.[1] The chair is sometimes hit frequently and sometimes infrequently, sometimes with a hard knock and sometimes with a gentle one. Within wide limits, the chair will rock in a very systematic and persistent fashion regardless of how hard or often it is hit. It will swing to and fro much more systematically than the shocks that are being imparted to it by the person who is rocking it. It is much the same with the economy. The adjustment costs in labor markets and the negotiation costs in setting up new contracts mean that when unexpected events occur, there is sufficient inertia in the economy to ensure that it does not radically alter its course as a result of the random shock. Rather, its course is much more systematic and smooth than the path of the shocks themselves.

---

[1] The rocking analogy was first suggested as long ago as 1907 by the brilliant Swedish economist, Knut Wicksell, and was elaborated upon in 1933 by Ragnar Frisch: "If you hit a wooden rocking horse with a club, the movement of the horse will be very different to that of the club." Quoted from Ragnar Frisch, "Propagation Problems and Impulse Problems in Dynamic Economics," *Economic Essays in Honour of Gustave Cassell* (New York: Augustus M. Kelley, 1967), p. 158; this was originally published in 1933.

D. Interest Rate Behavior

Although, in the presentation of the rational expectation equilibrium analysis in Chapter 19, we did not explicitly analyze the determination of the rate of interest, there are strong implications for interest rate determination in the rational expectations theories. To explore these implications fully and completely would require more time and space than is available here and, in some respects, would take us into a level of analysis that is substantially more demanding than would be appropriate. Nevertheless, it is possible to obtain a good understanding of the general implications for interest rate determination in the rational expectations theories. This brief section will pursue that task.

You already know that the market rate of interest deviates from the real rate of interest because of expected inflation. Let us recall why this is so. People borrow and lend for future periods of different lengths. That being so, the real rate of return that they obtain on a loan will be equal to the market rate of interest on the loan minus the actual rate of inflation that emerges over the term of the loan.

At the time the loan is contracted, this actual rate of inflation is unknown. The only substitute for the actual rate of inflation that both borrowers and lenders can use is their anticipation of the inflation that will occur over the term of the loan. Lenders will demand a premium on the interest rate to compensate for their anticipation of the inflation that is going to occur over the term of the loan, and borrowers will willingly pay a premium equal to their anticipation of inflation. Since both borrowers and lenders occupy the same economic environment and form their expectations in the same rational manner, there should be a consensus as to what the anticipated rate of inflation is. This amounts to saying that the market rate of interest that we observe is equal the equilibrium real rate of interest (itself a variable), plus the rational expectation of the rate of inflation *over the term of the loan in question*. Thus, for three-month loans, this means that the anticipated three-month rate of inflation will be added to the real rate of interest; similarly, for 15-to-20-year loans, the rate of inflation expected over the long term, on the average, will be added to the real rate of interest.

The anticipated rate of inflation (the rational expectation of the future price level expressed as a percentage change over the current known price level and converted to an annual rate of change) will be determined by the expectations of those things that determine the actual rate of inflation. Since the actual rate of inflation is determined by the growth rate of the money supply and the trend growth rate of output, the expected rate of inflation will depend on the expected growth rate of the money supply and expected output growth. In general, we would expect the actual growth rate of the money supply (and the actual growth rate of aggregate demand) to be more volatile than movements in the expected growth rate of the money supply and expected growth of aggregate demand. This is precisely the consideration that led to the prediction of procyclical co-movements in prices as discussed above.

Further, in general, we would expect fluctuations in the expected long-term average growth rate of the money supply to be much smaller than fluctuations in expectations of, say, the next three-months' growth rate of the money supply or the next twelve months' growth rate. Recall that the rate at which prices change depends on *both* the anticipated and unanticipated changes in the money supply. Movements in the interest rate, however, will depend only on the anticipated inflation rate and, therefore, only on anticipated movements of the money supply. This implies that fluctuations in prices (inflation) will have greater amplitude and be more erratic than fluctuations in interest rates. Further, because fluctuations in the expected long-term average money supply growth rate will be smaller than fluctuations in the expected money supply growth rate over the short term, fluctuations in short-term interest rates will have greater amplitude than fluctuations in long-term interest rates.

It is an implication of the rational expectations theories that, like prices, interest rates will display procyclical co-movements. Interest rates, however, will have fluctuations of smaller amplitude than prices, and the longer the term of the interest rate, the smaller will be the amplitude of the fluctuation. You will recognize these predictions as being in accord with the facts if you recall the information on Canadian interest rates presented in Chapters 2 and 6 of this book.

E. The Business Cycle

This section does little more than bring together and consolidate what has already been said above.[2] The first feature of the business cycle that was identified in Chapter 6 was the description of the movements of real economic activity (as measured by output) as a low-order stochastically disturbed difference equation. Specifically, we saw that it was possible to describe real *GNP* by an equation that says that deviations from trend in real *GNP* in year *t* is equal to 0.88 of its value in the previous year plus a random component. You can now

---

[2]For a much fuller treatment of this topic and more — indeed with the entire subject matter of this book — you will want to read two brilliant papers by Robert E. Lucas, Jr., "Understanding Business Cycles," *Journal of Monetary Economics*, vol. 5, supp. 1977, Carnegie-Rochester Conference Series on Public Policy; and "Methods and Problems in Business Cycle Theory, "*Journal of Money, Credit and Banking*, 12, pt. 2 (November 1980), 696-715. For a thoughtful critique, you will also want to read James Tobin's discussion paper of the second cited Lucas paper, on pp. 795-99 of the same journal.

see how the rational expectations theories explain this simple description of the evolution of real *GNP*. The autocorrelation component (the persistence effect) is rationalized either in terms of costly adjustment of inputs of labor or in terms of overlapping wage and employment contracts. The sources of randomness that hit the economy are identified as the unanticipated components of monetary and fiscal changes as well as, implicitly, randomness in decisions concerning private expenditure and money holding. A further and important source of random shocks is technological shocks to the production function, described in Chapters 14 and 21.

The second feature of the business cycle described in Chapter 6 and identified as being present in Canada is the procyclical co-movement of prices and interest rates. We have seen in this chapter how the normally observed procyclical co-movements of prices are to be explained as the consequence of fluctuations in actual aggregate demand having greater amplitude than the fluctuations in anticipated aggregate demand. We have also seen that the procyclical co-movements of interest rates, smaller in amplitude than the fluctuations in prices and of even smaller amplitude in the case of long-term interest rates, are all explicable in these same terms. Basically, fluctuations in expected values of variables are (usually) less marked than fluctuations in actual values, and the longer the period over which an average expectation is being formed, the smaller will be the amplitude of the fluctuations in this expectation.

The key ingenuity of the rational expectations theories lies in their ability to account for the autocorrelated movements of output and the procyclical co-movements of prices and interest rates, while at the same time being able to account for the infrequent but, when they occur, important independent movements of inflation and output. You have seen in this chapter how this explanation is achieved. The final task of this chapter is to set out a few problems that arise in the area of testing the explanation just advanced.

F. The Hypothesis-Testing Problem Posed by the Rational Expectations Theories

This chapter has tried to show you how the rational expectations theories of income, employment, and prices are capable, *in principle*, of explaining the facts. This exercise should not be confused with one of actually explaining the facts — a task that is much more difficult and requires careful, indeed, painstaking measurement and statistical inference.[3] Testing the explanations advanced in this chapter is

---

[3] A useful overview and survey of this topic may be found in Stanley Fischer, ed., *Rational Expectations and Economic Policy*, National Bureau of Economic Research Conference Report (Chicago and London: University of Chicago Press, 1980), esp. pp. 49-70.

something that is only in its infancy and is going to occupy a great deal of time and energy in the coming years.[4] This section merely reviews some of the highlights of the problems that arise for that activity.

The first problem that has to be solved is that of finding a plausible, a priori defendable, and, ideally, non-controversial way of decomposing changes in money, government spending, taxes (and perhaps other exogenous variables) into their anticipated and unanticipated components. This involves studying the *processes* that describe the evolution of these variables and finding ways of forecasting them that mimic reasonably well the ways in which agents in the real world might go about that task. In the example of the money supply, referred to in Chapter 19, the money supply process was described as a low-order autoregression that reacts to unusually large fluctuations in government spending and to unemployment. This seems like a promising hypothesis for explaining how anticipations of monetary growth are formed.

The second major problem arises in discriminating between the new Keynesian and new classical theories. As you saw, these two theories are very similar, but they differ in three respects. First, they imply different slopes for the expectations-augmented aggregate supply curve, and second, one theory implies that households will always be "on" their labor supply curve, whereas the other implies that they may at some stages be "off" this curve. From an observational point of view it is very difficult to discriminate between these two differences since we do not know, *a priori*, what the slope of the expectations-augmented aggregate supply curve is, nor would it be very easy, *a priori*, to identify whether or not individuals were "on" or "off" their labor supply curves.

The third source of difference does provide a potential way of discriminating, but it will not be easy to exploit. It is the difference between the two theories arising from the overlapping nature of labor market contracts emphasized by the new Keynesian theory. The difference in question is the way in which the random shocks combine to affect the current value of output, employment, and prices. According to the new classical theory, the current random shock combined with the previous actual value of output is all that is required to explain what is happening in the current period, whereas for the

[4]Three good examples of such work, though much more demanding than the level of this book, are Robert J. Barro and Mark Rush, "Unanticipated Money and Economic Activity," in Stanley Fischer, ed., *Rational Expectations and Economic Policy, ibid.,* pp. 23-54; Thomas J. Sargent, "A Classical Macroeconomic Model for the United States," *Journal of Political Economy*, 84 (June 1976), 207-37; and John B. Taylor, "Estimation and Control of a Macroeconomic Model with Rational Expectations," *Econometrica*, 47 (September 1979), 1267-86. The work of Barro and Sargent is new classical, and that of Taylor is new Keynesian.

new Keynesian approach, the shocks from previous periods explicitly have to be combined with the current period shock to generate the current period output, employment, and price level.

There is a third problem known as "observational equivalence."[5] This is a problem that arises from the fact that it is always possible to introduce *ad hoc* modifications to theories not based on rational behavior such that the non-rational "theory" makes the same "predictions" as the rational theory. The words "theory" and "predictions" have been placed in quotation marks to raise alarm bells that the predictions that come from *ad hoc* modifications to a model do not provide a basis for testing that model. The ultimate test of any theory is its ability to predict the future, not the past!

Summary

A. Procyclical Co-Movements in Prices

Generally, the swings in the actual values of variables that determine aggregate demand (for example, the money supply) are bigger than the swings in the anticipated values of these variables. This means that the aggregate demand curve fluctuates with greater amplitude than the expectations-augmented aggregate supply curve. The consequence of this is procyclical co-movements of prices in general.

B. Independent Movements in Output and Prices

Anticipated changes in aggregate demand move the price level but leave output undisturbed, whereas unanticipated changes in aggregate demand move the price level and output. By combining anticipated and unanticipated movements in aggregate demand (generated by anticipated and unanticipated movements in monetary and fiscal policy variables) we are able, in principle, to account for the facts about output and prices (or, equivalently, unemployment and inflation). As a general rule, prices are procyclical (inflation and unemployment are negatively related) for the reasons summarized above. Occasionally there will be a surge in inflation that is independent of, or even sometimes goes in the same direction as, the unemployment rate. This will arise because the anticipated rise in the money supply is high, whereas the unanticipated change in the money supply is negative.

---

[5] This problem is explained in Thomas J. Sargent, "The Observational Equivalence of Natural and Unnatural Rate Theories of Macroeconomics," *Journal of Political Economy*, 84 (June 1976), 631-40.

C. Autocorrelation of Output and Employment

Output is autocorrelated even though the shocks that hit the economy are purely random because the costs of changing labor inputs and overlapping labor contracts impart inertia into firms' adjustments of employment and output.

D. Interest Rate Behavior

Money rates of interest exceed real rates of interest by an amount equal to the anticipated rate of inflation. The term over which inflation has to be anticipated is the same as the term over which a loan is made. For three-month loans, the relevant anticipated inflation rate is that over the next three months. For twenty-year loans, the average anticipation of average inflation over the next twenty years is required. Anticipated inflation depends only on anticipated money growth, whereas actual inflation depends on both anticipated and unanticipated money growth. Interest rates fluctuate in a generally procyclical manner but with less amplitude than prices because the anticipated money supply growth rate fluctuates with a smaller amplitude than the actual money supply growth rate. Longer term interest rates have an even smaller amplitude of fluctuation because fluctuations in the anticipated long-term average money supply growth rate have smaller amplitude than those of short-term anticipations.

E. The Business Cycle

The first feature of the business cycle, the autocorrelation of output, is explained by the costs of adjusting labor input and the costs of overlapping labor market contracts. The procyclical co-movements of prices and interest rates are explained by the tendency for the actual variables that generate aggregate demand (monetary and fiscal policy variables) to fluctuate with bigger amplitude than their expected values. The non-universality of the procyclical co-movements of prices arises from the occasional jump in the anticipated money supply growth rate (sometimes in excess of that which actually occurs).

F. The Hypothesis-Testing Problem Posed by the Rational Expectations Theories

A major problem is that of finding a convincing and non-controversial way of decomposing changes in the actual values of exogenous variables into their anticipated and unanticipated components. Discriminating between the new Keynesian and new classical theories will be difficult because they are almost equivalent from an observational point of view. Further, discriminating the rational expectations theories from non-rational theory purely on the basis of the past will be difficult since it is always possible to patch up the traditional theory with *ad hoc* adjustments so that the theory yields identical predictions to rational theories. The ultimate test of any theory lies in its ability to predict the future rather than the past.

Review Questions

1. Explain how, in general, procyclical co-movements in prices and output are explained by the rational expectations theories.

2. Show how the rational expectations theories explain the fact that, on occasion, there is a strong rise in inflation accompanied by low output and high unemployment.

3. Do the new Keynesian and new classical theories differ as regards their explanation of the phenomenon described in Question 2? If so, how?

4. What is the explanation offered by the new classical theory of autocorrelation of output or employment?

5. What is the explanation offered by the new Keynesian theory of autocorrelation of output or employment?

6. What is the explanation given by the rational expectations theories of interest rate behavior? Why do long-term interest rates fluctuate with smaller amplitude than short-term rates and why do short-term rates fluctuate with smaller amplitude than inflation?

7. Review the explanation offered by the rational expectations theories of the business cycle.

8. Assess the assertion that the rational expectations theories are non-scientific because they can never be falsified.

9. (Similar to 8!) Assess the assertion that since we can decompose the changes in monetary and fiscal variables into anticipated and unanticipated components so as to make the rational expectations theories fit the facts, any such theory will suffer from the ultimate weakness of being capable of explaining everything and predicting nothing.

10. State succinctly why the assertions in Questions 8 and 9 are wrong.

V

CANADA IN THE WORLD ECONOMY

24

Canada's Economic Links with the Rest of the World

The Canadian economy has extensive economic links with the rest of the world (mainly from the United States). In 1984, of every dollar spent in Canada almost 26 cents represented expenditure on goods imported from other countries. Similarly, of every dollar's worth of goods produced, 30 cents worth was sent abroad as exports. In the five-year period from 1980-1984, Canada had an overall deficit in its trading and capital transactions with the rest of the world of a little more than $1 billion. During that same five-year period, the value of the Canadian dollar in terms of the U.S. dollar rose and then sank by almost 11 percent to 77 U.S. cents.

The chapters in this part take a broader view of the problems of macroeconomics so as to enable you to understand why Canada has experienced balance of payments problems in recent years and why the foreign exchange value of the Canadian dollar has fluctuated so much. It will also show you how shocks emanating from other countries affect the Canadian economy. This brief chapter will get you started on this process by clarifying some basic concepts and definitions.

This chapter pursues two tasks, which are to:

a) Know the definitions of the current account, the capital account, the official settlements account, and the balance of payments.

b) Know the definitions of a foreign exchange rate, an effective exchange rate, a fixed exchange rate, a flexible exchange rate, and a managed floating exchange rate.

A. Definitions of the Balance of Payments

(i) The Current Account

The current account of the balance of payments is the account in which the values of the flows of goods and services and other *current* receipts and payments between residents of Canada and residents of the rest of the world are recorded. Specifically, the current account contains the items shown in Table 24.1. The values of the items for 1984 are indicated to give you a feel for the orders of magnitude involved.

The receipts by Canadian residents come from exports of goods and services, dividend and interest payments from non-residents, and a small item — unilateral payments.

The big item, exports of goods and services, is the sum of value of all the goods and services purchased by non-residents from residents of Canada. Examples include the export of pulp, minerals, and manufactures; it also includes the spending by non-residents on vacations in Canada.

Dividends and interest received from abroad are payments by non-residents of interest and dividends due on investments made by residents of Canada in the rest of the world. Examples include the dividends paid by IBM in the United States to Canadian stockholders and interest paid by the U.S. government on U.S. Treasury bills held by the Bank of Montreal.

Unilateral transfers from abroad are receipts from abroad and are mainly made up of the funds brought to Canada by newly arriving immigrants.

On the outgoing side, the major item is imports of goods and services. This consists of purchases by Canadian residents of goods and services made in the rest of the world. This includes, for example, oranges from Florida, cars and television sets from Japan, cotton goods from Hong Kong and Taiwan, and also spending by Canadian residents on vacations in the rest of the world.

Dividends and interest paid abroad is now becoming quite a large item. This is the payment of dividends and interest by Canadian residents to non-residents who have bought Canadian securities. The biggest single item in this category is the payment by provincial governments to foreign residents who are major holders of provincial government debt.

Unilateral transfers paid abroad are primarily payments made by residents of Canada to friends and family in the rest of the world. Remittances by immigrants to members of their family in the home country are the bulk of this item. Aid to less-developed countries is also in this category.

The difference between the total receipts on the current account and the total expenses on the current account is called the current account balance. The current account is said to be in surplus when the receipts exceed expenses, and in deficit when the expenses exceed the receipts.

It is useful to think of an individual analogy to the country's current account balance. The exports of goods and services of a country can be thought of as being analogous to an individual's labor income. That is, from the viewpoint of the country as a whole, exports of goods and services are similar to the receipt of wages and salaries and other fees for labor services from the viewpoint of an individual. Dividends and interest received are analogous to income from investments made by an individual, and unilateral transfers are analogous to gifts. On the outgoing side, the imports of goods and services are analogous to an individuals's expenditures on consumption goods and capital goods. Dividends and interest paid abroad are analogous to an individual's payment of interest on loans made to him by, for example, banks and mortgage companies; unilateral transfers are the equivalent of gifts made by the individual to others.

A moment's reflection will reveal that for an individual the current account balance just described represents the net addition to (surplus) or subtraction from (deficit) his wealth. If an individual has a current account surplus, he is becoming wealthier in the sense that assets are being acquired and/or liabilities are being paid off. It is exactly the same for a country. If a country has a current account surplus, its residents in aggregate have become wealthier in the sense that

Table 24.1
The Balance of Payments, 1984

	ITEM	$ MILLION	
	1. Exports of Goods and Services:	126 212	
plus	2. Dividends and Interest Received from Abroad:	5 097	
plus	3. Unilateral Transfers from Abroad:	3 316	
equals			134 625
less	4. Imports of Goods and Services:	109 589	
less	5. Dividends and Interest Paid Abroad:	20 107	
less	6. Unilateral Transfers Paid Abroad:	2 376	
equals			132 072
equals	7. Current Account Balance:		2 553

Source: *Bank of Canada Review*, July 1985, Table J2.

Notes: 1 is the sum of exports and receipts from other services;
2 is total receipts of investment income;
3 is the sum of total transfer receipts;
4 is the sum of imports and payments of other services;
5 is total payments of investment income;
6 is total transfer payments and withholding tax;
7 is the current account balance.

their assets have increased (and/or their liabilities have decreased). Conversely, if a country has a current account deficit, it has become poorer in the sense that it now has fewer assets or more liabilities than previously.

(ii) The Capital Account

The capital account records the receipts from non-residents and payments made to non-residents arising from the issuing of new debt or the repayment of old debt. For example, if the province of Ontario sells bonds, some of which are bought by residents of other countries, the money that the government of Ontario receives on the sale of these bonds to non-residents would appear as an import of capital into Canada. It would, therefore, be recorded as a receipt in the Canadian capital account. On the other side of the capital account, if a foreign corporation or government issues new debt, some of which is bought by Canadian residents, then the payment to those foreign corporations and governments will appear as an export of capital from Canada. Equivalently, if a resident of Canada buys an apartment in Florida for $50 000, using (say) a Canadian bank deposit, when the apartment is paid for there will be a capital outflow of $50 000 from Canada and this too will be recorded in the capital account as a capital export.

The difference between capital imports and capital exports represents a country's capital account balance. In 1984, the Canadian capital account balance was a surplus of a little more than $2 billion. That is, in 1984, capital imports of Canada exceeded its capital exports by a little more than $2 billion.

Another individual analogy may be helpful. The capital account of an individual is a statment of the receipts of the individual arising from the negotiation of new loans minus the outlays for paying off old loans. Thus, for example, if an individual negotiated a bank loan for $10 000 and a mortgage for $40 000 and repaid a charge card account outstanding of $2 000, that individual would have a capital account surplus of $48 000.

(iii) The Official Settlements Account

The official settlements account records the net receipts and payments of gold and foreign currency that result from the current account and capital account transactions just described. The balance on the official settlements account, known more simply as the *official settlements balance*, is the change in the foreign exchange reserves less the change in official borrowing of the country. It is, if everything is accurately measured, exactly equal to the sum of the current account balance and the capital account balance. By accounting convention, the official settlements balance is defined as the negative of the sum of the current account and capital account balance so that when the balances on all three accounts are added together the resulting sum is always zero.

Another individual analogy might be helpful here. Suppose an individual had a current account deficit of, say, $50 000 in some particular year in which perhaps a house and some furnishings and other durable goods had been bought. That is, in the particular year, the individual received, from the sale of labor and in interest and dividends and gifts, $50 000 less than was spent on goods and services. Suppose further that the individual negotiated loans such that there was a net capital account surplus of $40 000. If the individual spent $50 000 in excess of income and received $40 000 from new loans, where did the difference of $10 000 come from? It must be the case that the individual used $10 000 of the cash balances that were previously being held. If this were not so, the individual's expenditure could not have exceeded total receipts by the $10 000 that they did. Thus, the individual analogy of the official settlements balance is simply the change in the individual's cash balances — bank account and currency holdings.

Although the individual's cash holdings have fallen in this example by $10 000, this would be recorded (using the accounting convention noted above) as a positive balance on the individual's equivalent of the official settlements account.

(iv) The Balance of Payments

In Chapter 26 you will study the theory of the balance of payments. It will be convenient, and more natural, when studying this theory if you think of the balance of payments simply as the sum of the balances on the current and capital accounts and not as the official settlements balance. The magnitude of the balance of payments, so defined, will be the same as the official settlements balance but its algebraic sign will be reversed. Thus, when the sum of the current and capital accounts is positive we shall call that a balance of payments surplus, even though, as measured by the balance of payments accountants, the official settlements balance is negative.

The Canadian Balance of Payments, 1973-1984   The Canadian balance of payments accounts — current account, capital account, and official settlements account — for the years 1973-1984 are set out in Table 24.2. As you can see, Canada has typically experienced a deficit on its current account, although the last three years shown and 1973 are an exception to this. The capital account of Canada is almost always in surplus. The only year in which a deficit was recorded was in 1982. This means that non-residents of Canada are constantly investing more in Canada than Canadian residents are investing abroad.

Table 24.2
The Canadian Balance of Payments, 1973–1984 ($ million)

YEAR	CURRENT ACCOUNT	CAPITAL ACCOUNT	NET ERRORS AND OMISSIONS	OFFICIAL SETTLEMENTS BALANCE
1973	108	75	−650	467
1974	−1 460	2 351	−867	−24
1975	−4 757	5 555	−1 203	405
1976	−4 109	8 398	−3 767	−522
1977	−4 334	5 174	−2 261	1 421
1978	−4 917	4 744	−3 126	3 299
1979	−4 840	9 161	−2 630	−1 689
1980	−1 114	941	−1 323	1 497
1981	−6 065	16 532	−9 253	−1 215
1982	2 665	−1 558	−1 802	695
1983	1 686	4 429	−5 566	−548
1984	2 553	2 132	−5 773	1 089

Source: *Bank of Canada Review*, July 1985, Table J1.

Notes: The official settlements balance is a negative of the difference between Not Official Monetary Movements and allocations of Special Drawing Rights.

The magnitude of the capital account surplus fluctuates but has, on the average since 1973, been almost $5 billion and, in the record year of 1981, reached $16.5 billion.

The official settlements balance (column 4 of Table 24.2) has to be read carefully. Remember that a positive amount means a deficit on the official settlements account, and a negative amount means a surplus. Evidently Canada's overall balance of payments has fluctuated between deficit and surplus and has, on the average, been in a deficit.

The theoretical concepts of the current account, capital account, and official settlements balance add up to zero. In practice, however, there are problems of measuring international transactions. In recent years these measurement problems have become very serious. The third column of Table 24.2 shows the extent of the measurement error by recording net errors and omissions. This is the discrepancy between the sum of the three accounts as measured by the national accounting statisticians. The net errors and omissions arise from the mismeasurement of the current account and private capital account transactions. There is no way of knowing the extent to which this error should be allocated to each of those two accounts, and so it is left as a separate item. It is somewhat disquieting to note that in several years the error has been as big or even bigger than either the official settlements balance or the current account balance, and it has been, on the average since 1973, just over −$3 billion. It may be inferred from this that there is considerable uncertainty concerning the facts about Canada's balance of payments. The fourth column, however, the official settlements balance, may be regarded as known with certainty, since this represents transactions that go through the official books of the Bank of Canada and the central banks of other countries. The official settlements balance is, therefore, a firm number.

B. Exchange Rate Definitions

(i) Foreign Exchange Rate

A foreign exchange rate is the relative price of two national monies. It expresses the number of units of one currency that must be paid in order to acquire a unit of some other currency. There are two ways in which a relative price may be defined. It may be expressed as so many units of *a* per unit of *b*, or as so many units of *b* per unit of *a*. For example, the average exchange rate between the Canadian dollar ($C) and the United States dollar ($U.S.) in 1984 was $1.29 $C. This may be expressed equivalently as 77 U.S. cents per Canadian dollar.

It is always necessary to be precise as to which way around the exchange rate is being defined. When the value of a currency *rises* (called *appreciation*), the exchange rate when expressed as units of domestic currency per unit of foreign currency, *falls*; but if it is expressed as units of foreign currency per unit of domestic currency, the exchange rate *rises*. Conversely, when the value of a currency *falls* (called *depreciation*), the exchange rate, when expressed in units of domestic currency per unit of foreign currency, *rises*; but if it is expressed as units of foreign currency per unit of domestic currency, the exchange rate *falls*. Think carefully about these distinctions and work out one or two simple numerical examples.

(ii) An Effective Exchange Rate

There is not, of course, only one foreign exchange rate. Rather, there are as many foreign exchange rates as there are foreign currencies. The more commonly encountered exchange rates are those between the Canadian dollar and the currencies of the major trading partners of Canada such as the U.S. dollar, the British pound, the French franc, the German mark, and the Japanese yen. So as to be able to measure the value of one currency in relation to an average of other currencies the concept of the *effective exchange rate* is used.

The effective exchange rate is an index number, just like the Consumer Price Index, for example. This index number is calculated as a weighted average of the value of one currency in terms of all other currencies where the weights reflect the importance of each currency in the exports and imports of the country in question.

If we denote the effective exchange rate in some period, t, by EER_t, the formula with which EER_t may be calculated is

$$EER_t = \frac{aE_{1_0} + a_2E_{2_0} + \cdots + a_nE_{n_0}}{a_1E_{1_t} + a_2E_{2_t} + \cdots + a_nE_{n_t}} \cdot 100 \qquad \textbf{(24.1)}$$

In this formula, the a's represent weights — the fraction of Canadian international trade with country 1 is a_1, the fraction with country 2, a_2, and so on. The E's represent exchange rates between the Canadian dollar and each other currency — E_1 being the number of Canadian dollars per unit of the currency of country 1, E_2 being the number of Canadian dollars per unit of the currency of country 2, and so on. The subscript t denotes the current period and the subcript 0 denotes the base period — the period for which the effective exchange rate is, by definition, 100.

The effective exchange rate of the Canadian dollar is calculated by the International Monetary Fund using this type of formula. You should be careful to note that the effective exchange rate will behave in the same way as a measure of a single exchange rate expressed as the number of units of foreign currency per unit of domestic currency. That is, when the effective exchange rate falls in value the domestic currency depreciates. Conversely, when the effective exchange rate rises in value the domestic currency appreciates.

Instead of calculating an effective exchange rate using Equation (24.1) — the type of calculation performed by the International Monetary Fund — we could alternatively calculate an effective exchange rate E which represents the number of units of domestic currency per unit of foreign currency. Such a calculation would be performed by using Equation (24.2).

$$E_t = \frac{a_1E_{1_t} + a_2E_{2_t} + \cdots + a_nE_{n_t}}{a_1E_{1_0} + a_2E_{2_0} + \cdots + a_nE_{n_0}} \qquad \textbf{(24.2)}$$

As you will see by comparing Equation (24.2) with Equation (24.1) the effective exchange rate E is equal to 100 divided by EER. The effective exchange rate measured by E behaves in the opposite way to EER. When the value of E rises the domestic currency depreciates and when the value of E falls the domestic currency appreciates. When EER is equal to 100, E is equal to 1.

The effective exchange rate expressed as E is a more natural definition to use for the purposes of conducting macroeconomic analysis. If a foreign price index is multiplied by the effective exchange rate E it becomes, in effect, a domestic price index. That is, a price expressed in foreign currency units is converted into a price expressed in domestic currency units by multiplying that price by E. It is the definition of the exchange rate based on Equation (24.2) that we shall use in subsequent chapters when analyzing the behavior of an open economy.

The Canadian Effective Exchange Rate, 1973–1984   The effective exchange rate *EER* of the Canadian dollar since 1973 is set out in Table 24.3. Alongside it is the effective exchange rate defined as *E*. The index is normalized as 100 in 1980 (1 for the *E* definition). The effective exchange rate has varied between a low of 99.8 in 1979 and a high of 125.6 in 1976. Between 1973 and 1976 there was a near 4.5 percent effective depreciation of the Canadian dollar. It then gradually appreciated by about 20 percent over the next four years. There then followed a depreciation of about 8 percent in the period between 1980 and 1983. In 1984, the Canadian dollar appreciated by almost 2 percent.

Chapter 26 will present an analysis of the forces that influence the course of the exchange rate. Before proceeding with this task, however, three more definitions are needed.

(iii) A Fixed Exchange Rate

A fixed exchange rate regime is one in which the Bank of Canada declares a central or par value at which it will act to maintain the value of its currency. It also usually involves declaring what is known as an *intervention band*. That is, in declaring a fixed exchange rate, the central bank announces that if the exchange rate rises above the par value by more than a certain percentage amount, then it will

Table 24.3
The Effective Exchange Rate of the Canadian
Dollar 1973–1984

YEAR	EER	E
1973	120.3	0.83
1974	124.3	0.80
1975	118.4	0.84
1976	125.6	0.80
1977	116.1	0.86
1978	103.9	0.96
1979	99.8	1.00
1980	100.0	1.00
1981	102.9	0.97
1982	104.9	0.95
1983	108.3	0.92
1984	106.3	0.94

Source: *International Financial Statistics Yearbook,*
        1984, p. 207. International Financial Statistics,
        September 1985, p. 140.

intervene in the foreign exchange market to prevent the rate from moving any further away from the par value. Likewise, if the rate falls below the par value by a certain percentage amount, the central bank declares that it will intervene to prevent the rate from falling any further.

In order to maintain a fixed exchange rate, a central bank stands ready to use its stock of foreign exchange reserves to raise or lower the quantity of money outstanding so as to maintain its price relative to the price of some other money.

From 1945 to 1972 the Western World operated on a fixed exchange rate system sometimes called the Bretton Woods system. This name derives from the fact that the plan for the world monetary system, which survived for thirty years after the war, was negotiated at Bretton Woods, near Washington, D.C., by John Maynard Keynes and Harry D. White. This system pegged the world's monetary system to gold. This was achieved by the United States declaring that one fine ounce of gold was worth $35 U.S. Each country then defined its own currency value in terms of the U.S. dollar. Under the Bretton Woods fixed exchange rate system, the United States took no responsibility for maintaining the exchange rates between the U.S. dollar and other currencies. Its job was to maintain the price of gold at $35 U.S. per ounce. Each of the other countries was then left to worry about its own exchange rate against the U.S. dollar. Thus, for example, if the Canadian dollar began to fall in value to the lower limit or rise in value to the upper limit of the exchange rate band, the Bank of Canada would intervene in the foreign exchange market, exchanging U.S. dollars from its foreign exchange reserves for Canadian dollars, or exchanging Canadian dollars for U.S. dollars, in order to keep the value of the Canadian dollar inside the target band.

(iv) A Flexible Exchange Rate

A flexible exchange rate — sometimes also called a *floating exchange rate* — is one which is determined by market forces. The central bank declares no target value for the exchange rate and has no direct interest in the value of the exchange rate. The central bank holds a constant stock of foreign exchange reserves — or even a zero stock — and does not intervene in the foreign exchange market to manipulate the price of its currency.

(v) A Managed Floating Exchange Rate

A managed floating exchange rate is one in which the exchange rate is manipulated by the central bank, but is not necessarily being held constant. Usually a managed floating regime is one in which the central bank announces that it is floating, but the bank does not give any indication to the market concerning the course that it would like to see the exchange rate follow. It does, however, have a view about the appropriate behavior of the exchange rate, and it intervenes in order to achieve its desires. This method of operating the foreign exchange market is one that gives the most difficulty to speculators. They not only have to speculate on what other private individuals on the average will be doing, but they also have to make predictions about central bank intervention behavior.

Summary

A. Definitions of the Balance of Payments

(i) The *current account* is the account which records the values of current goods and services sold abroad, and purchases of goods and services from abroad, debt interest receipts and payments, and unilateral transfers received from and paid abroad.

(ii) The *capital account* records the receipts and payments between residents and non-residents arising from the issue of net debt or the retirement of old debt.

(iii) The *official settlements account* records the movements in gold and foreign currency reserves (adjusted by any official borrowing) resulting from the net of the balances on the current and capital accounts. By accounting convention it is measured as the negative of the sum of the current and capital account balances so that the sum of the balances on all three accounts is always zero.

(iv) The *balance of payments* is defined as the sum of the balances on the current and capital accounts or, equivalently, as the negative of the official settlements balance.

B. Exchange Rate Definitions

(i) A *foreign exchange rate* is the relative price between two national currencies.

(ii) An *effective exchange rate* is an index representing the relative price between one national currency and an average of other national currencies. The weights on other currencies on the average reflect the importance of each currency in the international trade of the country in question.

(iii) A *fixed exchange rate* is one which takes on a value declared by and maintained by the active intervention of the central bank.

(iv) A *flexible exchange rate* is an exchange rate, the value of which is determined purely by market forces, with no direct central bank intervention.

(v) A *managed floating exchange rate* is one that is manipulated by the central bank but it is not manipulated according to any pre-announced rules.

Review Questions

1. Divide the following items into four categories: those items that belong in (a) the current account, (b) the capital account, (c) the official settlements account, and (d) none of the balance of payments accounts:

  1. Your summer vacation expenses in Europe.
  2. The government of Quebec's receipts for the sale of bonds to U.S. residents.
  3. The Bank of Montreal's purchase of U.S. dollar Travellers' Cheques from the American Express Company in New York.
  4. The transfer by the Bank of England to the Bank of Canada of 1,000 ounces of gold.
  5. Canadian imports of Japanese cars.
  6. Canadian exports of wheat.
  7. The takeover of a Canadian corporation by a U.S. corporation.
  8. The payment of interest on its bonds by the U.S. government to Canadian residents.
  9. The money brought to Canada by newly arrived immigrants.
  10. Canadian aid to poor countries.

2. Using the following items and numbers, construct the balance of payments accounts of the hypothetical economy:

Item	$m
Capital imports	2000
Debt interest received from abroad	800
Exports of goods and services	1000
Capital exports	1800
Gifts made to non-residents	100
Imports of goods and services	1100
Debt interest paid abroad	700
Rise in gold and foreign exchange reserves	400

  (a) What are the errors and omissions?
  (b) What is the current account balance?
  (c) What is the capital account balance?
  (d) What is the balance on the official settlements account?
  (e) What is the balance of payments?

3. What is a foreign exchange rate?

4. What is an effective exchange rate?

5. What is a fixed exchange rate. How is it kept fixed?

6. What is a flexible exchange rate?

7. What is a managed floating exchange rate? How is it "managed"?

25

The *IS-LM-BP* Analysis of the Open Economy

We are now ready to start studying macroeconomic theory in the open economy. Your study of open economy macro theory will parallel that for the closed economy. We shall begin by examining the way in which aggregate demand is determined in the open economy.[1]

Aggregate supply in the open economy is exactly the same as in the closed economy case. We shall, therefore, move on to consider equilibrium in the open economy once we have studied the determination of aggregate demand. We shall round off our study of the open economy by returning to the facts and examining how open economy macro theory enables us to understand the facts.

It will be convenient to approach aggregate demand in the open economy in two stages. This chapter will extend the *IS-LM* framework to the open economy by introducing the open economy extensions of the *IS* and *LM* curves. It will also introduce a new relationship known as the *BP* curve. After these basic open economy tools of analysis have been developed we shall go on in Chapter 26 to study the determination of aggregate demand in the open economy under two alter-

---

[1] The material presented in this chapter was developed primarily by Robert Mundell and J. Marcus Fleming. The two most important papers by these two outstanding scholars are: Robert A. Mundell, "The Appropriate Use of Monetary and Fiscal Policy Under Fixed Exchange Rates," *IMF Staff Papers*, 9 (March 1962), 70-77; and J. Marcus Fleming, "Domestic Financial Policies Under Fixed and Floating Exchange Rates," *IMF Staff Papers*, 9 (March 1962), 369-77. The material in the chapter is often called the Mundell-Fleming analysis.

native exchange rate regimes — fixed exchange rates and flexible exchange rates. We will study how output would be determined at a given fixed price level under these two exchange rate regimes. We shall then go on in Chapter 27 to study open economy equilibrium under the two alternative exchange rate regimes.

The chapter pursues its objectives by taking you through five tasks, which are to:

a) Know how to derive the *IS* curve for an open economy.
b) Know the definition of the *BP* curve.
c) Know how to derive the *BP* curve.
d) Understand what makes the *IS* and *BP* curves shift.
e) Understand what makes the *LM* curve shift.

A. Derivation of the *IS* Curve for an Open Economy

You already know the meaning of the *IS* curve for an economy which has balanced trade or, equivalently, a closed economy. It is the relationship between the rate of interest and level of income at which savings-plus-taxes are equal to investment-plus-government expenditure. In the open economy there are two additional expenditure flows to be taken into account in defining and deriving the *IS* curve. They are exports and imports of goods and services. In a closed economy, aggregate demand is the sum of consumption plus investment plus government spending; whereas in an open economy, aggregate demand is equal to the sum of these three items plus net foreign demand or, equivalently, exports minus imports. That is, defining exports as *ex* and imports as *im*, aggregate demand in an open economy is

$$y = c + i + g + ex - im \qquad (25.1)$$

Subtracting consumption from both sides of Equation (25.1) gives

$$y - c = i + g + ex - im \qquad (25.2)$$

The left-hand side of the above equation $(y - c)$ is simply savings-plus-taxes. We could equivalently, therefore, write this equation as

$$s + t = i + g + ex - im \qquad (25.3)$$

Adding imports to both sides of the above equation gives

$$s + t + im = i + g + ex \qquad (25.4)$$

This is the condition which, for the open economy, must be satisfied at all points on the *IS* curve. That is, savings-plus-taxes-plus- imports must equal investment-plus-government spending-plus-exports.

To derive the open economy *IS* curve, we need some propositions about how imports and exports are determined. Let us now proceed to do this.

First, consider exports. Two key variables determine a country's exports. The first is the total level of income of the people who are demanding these exports. This income level is, of course, the aggregate income of the rest of the world. It is the sum of the gross domestic products of all the countries in the world other than the country whose economy we are analyzing. The second variable that influences exports is the price of the goods produced in the domestic economy relative to the prices ruling in the rest of the world. This relative price, expressed as an economy-wide average, could be stated precisely as

$$\theta = \frac{EP_f}{P} \tag{25.5}$$

The price of foreign goods is P_f, the domestic price level is P, and the effective exchange rate (as defined in Chapter 24) is E. Thus, θ (the Greek letter theta) may be thought of as the price of foreign goods relative to the price of domestic goods. This ratio is sometimes called the *real exchange rate*. That is, the real exchange rate is the effective exchange rate E multiplied by the ratio of foreign to domestic prices (P_f/P). The bigger the value of θ, the bigger is the volume of exports. That is, the higher the foreign price level relative to the domestic price level, the bigger is the rest of the world's demand for domestically produced goods.

We can summarize these propositions about exports as follows: the volume of exports is higher, the higher is the rest of the world income and the higher is the real exchange rate.

Next, consider the factors that determine imports. Again, there are two key variables which may be isolated as having important effects on imports. The first is the level of domestic income (real GNP). The higher the level of domestic real income, the larger is the volume of imports. The other influence is the same real exchange rate variable that influences exports. This time its effect is opposite in sign. That is, a rise in rest of world prices relative to domestic prices — a rise in the real exchange rate — leads to a reduction in imports. To summarize: the volume of imports is larger the higher the level of real income, and the volume of imports will be smaller the higher the real exchange rate.

We may now proceed to derive the *IS* curve for an open economy. Figure 25.1 illustrates this derivation. Frame (d) of this figure shows an *IS* curve labelled *IS*(*C*) — *C* standing for closed economy — which is identical to the *IS* curve derived in Figure 10.4. The *IS* curve for the open economy is also shown in frame (d) and is labelled *IS*(*0*) — *0* standing for open economy. To see the differences between the *IS* curve of the closed economy and that of the open economy, begin by recalling that the condition for flow equilibrium in the goods markets of a closed economy is $i + g = s + t$, whereas for an open economy it is $i + g + ex = s + t + im$. Let us look at frame (c) of Figure 25.1. There, on the horizontal axis, we are measuring investment-plus-government spending-plus-exports. For given values of world income and the real exchange rate, exports will be constant. We may, therefore, add exports to investment-plus-government spending by drawing a line parallel to the $i + g$ curve, the new curve representing $i + g + ex$. The horizontal distance between $i + g + ex$ and $i + g$ in frame (c) represents the volume of exports ex.

The second change occurs in frame (a) of Figure 25.1. There we are measuring savings-plus-taxes-plus-imports on the vertical axis, and investment-plus government spending-plus-exports on the horizontal axis. The 45° line defines the open economy equilibrium condition for the *IS* curve.

The third change comes in frame (b). In this frame we measure savings-plus-taxes-plus-imports on the vertical axis. It is necessary, therefore, to add imports to the previously derived savings-plus-taxes schedule. To do this, recall that imports depend on the level of domestic real income and the real exchange rate. As in the case of exports, hold the real exchange rate at some fixed value. That done, the level of imports will depend solely on the level of domestic real income. We can show this in frame (b) by drawing the line $s + t + im$ above the savings-plus-taxes line and also steeper than the $s + t$ line. The vertical distance between these two lines in frame (b) measures the volume of imports. To derive the *IS* curve for the open economy, we proceed in the same way as for the closed economy but use the $i + g + ex$ and the $s + t + im$ lines instead of the $i + g$ and $s + t$ lines. Following exactly the same procedure as in Chapter 10, you can readily verify that the curve $IS(O)$ — O for open — is the open economy *IS* curve. Notice that it is steeper than that for the closed economy and that it cuts the closed economy *IS* curve at the level of income that generates a volume of imports exactly equal to the fixed volume of exports.

Since, in deriving the *IS* curve, we hold the real exchange rate fixed, it follows that at each different exchange rate there will be a different open economy *IS* curve. Precisely how the *IS* curve shifts as the real exchange rate (and other variables) change will be explored below. Before that, let us go on to define and derive a new curve — the *BP* curve.

B. Definition of the *BP* Curve

The *BP* curve is a relationship between the rate of interest and level of income such that at all points on the *BP* curve there is a balance

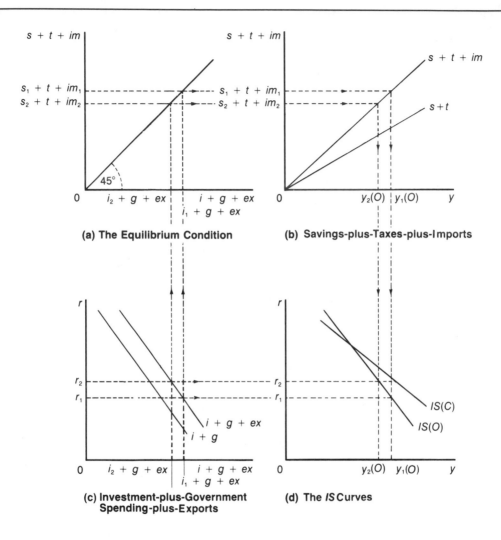

**Figure 25.1
The Derivation of the *IS* Curve
for an Open Economy**

Frame (a) shows the flow equilibrium condition that defines the *IS* curve in an open economy — the equality of savings-plus-taxes-plus-imports with investment-plus-government spending-plus-exports. In frame (c), exports are added to investment-plus-government spending to give the $i + g + ex$ line. In frame (b), imports are added to savings-plus-taxes to give the steeper $s + t + im$ line. In frame (d), the *IS* curve, *IS(C)*, is that for a closed economy (ignoring exports and imports) and that labelled *IS(O)* is for the open economy. The two curves intersect at the real income level that generates a volume of imports equal to the fixed volume of exports. A rise in exports shifts the $i + g + ex$ line and shifts the open economy *IS* curve. The relationship between these two shifts depends on the slope of the $s + t + im$ curve. The steeper the slope of the $s + t + im$ line, the smaller the shift of the *IS* curve for a given shift in $i + g + ex$.

of payments equilibrium. Put differently, at all points on the *BP* curve, the balance of payments is zero, i.e., balanced. Equivalently, there is a capital account surplus that exactly matches the current account deficit (or capital account deficit that exactly matches the current account surplus).

C. Derivation of the *BP* Curve

The starting point for deriving the *BP* curve is the balance of payments equilibrium condition that states that the sum of the current account balance and the capital account balance is zero. The prices at which a country exports and imports goods and services is determined by the world price level P_f, converted into domestic money units at the exchange rate E, so that the current account balance is $EP_f ex - EP_f im$. Dividing this by the domestic price level, P, and remembering that EP_f/P equals θ, gives the real current account balance as $\theta(ex - im)$. Adding the real capital account surplus denoted by *kas* gives the condition for the *BP* curve as

$$\theta(ex - im) + kas = 0 \qquad (25.6)$$

This says that the balance of payments (*BP*) is equal to the *value* of exports minus the *value* of imports (of goods and services) plus the capital account surplus (denoted as *kas*). We have already discussed the determinants of the *volume* of exports and imports and the real exchange rate θ, and need now only concern ourselves with the things that determine the capital account surplus.

The capital account of the balance of payments depends primarily on rates of return on investments that are available in the domestic economy compared with rates of return available in the rest of the world. As a general proposition, the higher the rates of return available in the domestic economy relative to those available in the rest of the world, the greater will be the tendency for domestic capital to stay at home and for foreign capital to be sucked into the domestic economy. Conversely, the lower are domestic rates of return relative to foreign rates of return, the greater will be the tendency for domestic capital to seek the higher returns available in other countries, and the greater will be the tendency for foreign capital to stay at home.

Relevant rates of return that have to be compared in the two countries are the *real* rates. Thus, the basic hypothesis is that the net inflow of capital into a country increases as the differential between the domestic real rate of interest and the rest of world (foreign) real rate of interest increases. The variety of risk factors could make this differential either positive or negative (or zero) in equilibrium. Whatever the equilibrium value of the differential, net capital inflows will rise as this differential rises. We can write this as a simple equation such as

$$kas = f(r - r_f) \tag{25.7}$$

We are now in a position to derive the *BP* curve. Figure 25.2 illustrates the derivation. First, it will be useful to familiarize yourself

**Figure 25.2
The Derivation
of the *BP* Curve**

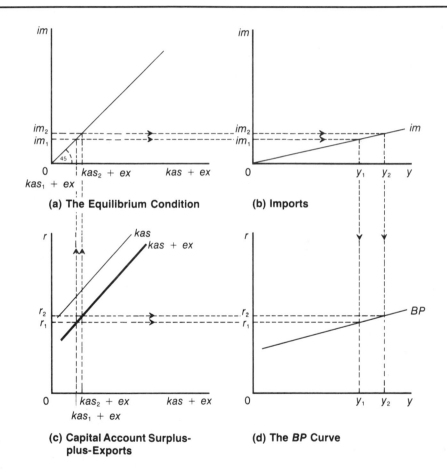

(a) The Equilibrium Condition

(b) Imports

**(c) Capital Account Surplus-
plus-Exports**

(d) The *BP* Curve

Frame (a) contains the condition that defines the *BP* curve — the equality of imports, *im*, with the capital accounts surplus plus exports, *kas* + *ex*. Frame (c) shows the capital account surplus rising with the rate of interest. Exports are added to the capital account surplus in frame (a) to give the line *kas* + *ex*. Frame (b) shows imports rising with income. Frame (d) shows the *BP* curve as the relationship between the interest rate and real income that satisfies the three lines in the other frames. The *BP* curve will shift if there is a rise in exports. The distance of the horizontal shift of the *BP* curve relative to the shift in *kas* + *ex* curve depends solely on the slope of the import function. The flatter the *im* curve, the greater will be the shift of the *BP* curve for any given change in exports, *ex*, in the *kas* + *ex* curve.

with what we are measuring on the axes of the different frames: frame (d) is going to show the *BP* curve and measures the rate of interest against the level of income; frame (c) measures the rate of interest against total receipts from the rest of the world — exports-plus-capital account surplus; frame (b) measures imports against the level of income; and frame (a) measures imports on the vertical axis and exports-plus-capital account surplus on the horizontal axis. The line in frame (a) defines the balance of payments equilibrium condition. It is a 45° line indicating that when imports equal exports-plus-capital account surplus, then there is a zero balance on the balance of payments. In frame (c), the upward-sloping line *kas* denotes the capital account surplus. It slopes up, indicating that the higher the domestic rate of interest, other things being equal, the larger will be the capital account surplus. In drawing this line, the foreign rate of interest and the expected change of the exchange rate are being held constant. The other line *kas* + *ex* in frame (c) results from adding the fixed volume of exports (for constant world real income and real exchange rate) to the capital account surplus to denote the total inflow of money from the rest of the world. In deriving the *BP* curve it will be convenient to assume that the real exchange rate is one. Later in this chapter we shall examine what happens to the *BP* curve when the value of θ changes.

Frame (b) shows the import function — the relationship between imports and real income. In drawing the line *im* in frame (b), as in frame (c), the real exchange rate is being held constant. To derive the *BP* curve, select a rate of interest r_1 and notice that in frame (c), at the interest rate r_1, there is a capital account surplus of kas_1 and a total inflow of money from the rest of the world of kas_1 + *ex*. Tracing up from frame (c) to frame (a), we know that if there is to be a balance of payments equilibrium, the level of imports must equal im_1. Taking that import level across to frame (b), we discover that in order for the import level to equal im_1, it will be necessary for domestic income to be y_1. Transferring this income level down to frame (d), and transferring the initially assumed rate of interest r_1 across to frame (d) gives one point on the *BP* curve. The income level y_1 combined with the interest rate r_1 generates a level of imports and a capital account surplus such that given the volume of exports there is a zero balance on the balance of payments. By selecting other interest rates, it is possible to derive other income levels that also give a zero balance on the balance of payments, and by joining all these various points you can generate the entire line labelled *BP*.

The *BP* curve slopes upwards in general, but could, in a particular and important circumstance, be horizontal. This circumstance would be one of perfect capital mobility. Perfect capital mobility means that any interest differential between the domestic economy and the rest of the world would automatically and instantly bring in, or drive out, funds, so that the domestic interest rate is always at a level such that the *real* rate of return on domestic investments equals the *real* rate of return available in the rest of the world. In that case, the domestic real rate of interest would always be equal to the foreign real rate and the *BP* curve would be a horizontal line at this rate of interest. As a general matter, the *BP* curve slopes up, as shown in the figure. It may be presumed, however, that it is not a very steep relationship since modest interest differentials seem to be sufficient to induce large international movements of capital. (The perfect capital mobility case will feature prominently in the next two chapters.)

Let us now go on to consider the things that make the open economy *IS* and *BP* curves shift.

D. Shifts in the *IS* and *BP* Curves

Recall that when we derived the *IS* curve, we held constant the level of world income, which influences exports, and the real exchange rate, which influences both exports and imports. What happens to the *IS* curve if either of these variables change? If world income rises, exports rise. This has the effect of shifting the *IS* curve to the right. If the real exchange rate rises, this also raises exports and lowers imports. This, too, shifts the *IS* curve to the right. The real exchange rate might rise because of a rise in the exchange rate (depreciation), a rise in the foreign price level, or a fall in the domestic price level.

Next, consider the factors that shift the *BP* curve. In drawing the capital account surplus line in frame (c) of Figure 25.2, we held constant the world real rate of interest and the expected rate of change of the exchange rate. A rise in either the world real rate of interest or the expected rate of depreciation of the domestic currency will shift the *kas* line to the left (or upwards). The factors that determine exports and imports have already been discussed in the above discussion of the factors which shift the *IS* curve. Changes in world income or the real exchange rate that shift the *IS* curve will also, necessarily, shift the *BP* curve. Anything that raises exports or lowers imports will shift the *BP* curve to the right. Thus, a devaluation of the currency (a higher value of *E*), a rise in foreign prices, a rise in world real income, or a fall in the domestic price level will all have the effect of shifting the *BP* curve to the right.

You have now seen that some factors shift the *IS* curve and the *BP* curve simultaneously. It is of some importance to establish which of these two curves shifts more in the event of a change that shifts them both. There is no ambiguity about this when the factor leading to a shift in both curves is a change in world income. In this case, both curves will shift in the same direction, but the *BP* curve will shift by more than the *IS* curve. To see this, all that you need do is to examine Figures 25.1 and 25.2 again. Consider the effect of a rise in world income, which raises exports. In Figure 25.1, this would shift the investment-plus-government spending-plus-exports line to the right, and also the *IS* curve to the right. The amount by which the *IS* curve shifts depends solely on the initial change in $i + g + ex$ and on the slope of the savings-plus-taxes-plus imports line in frame (b). The steeper this line, the smaller will be the shift in the *IS* curve.

Now consider what happens to the *BP* line. In frame (c) of Figure 25.2, the $kas + ex$ line would shift to the right. Also, the *BP* curve in frame (d) would shift to the right. The amount by which the *BP* curve shifts depends solely on the initial shift in $kas + ex$ and on the slope of the import line in frame (b). The flatter this line, the bigger will be the shift in the *BP* curve. The initial change in exports recorded in frame (c) of both figures is identical, of course. Since we know that the slope of the savings-plus-taxes-plus-import line is steeper than the slope of the imports line (convince yourself of this by noting that savings also rise as income rises), we also know that the *BP* curve must shift to the right by more than the *IS* curve shifts.

A change in world real income is not the only factor that leads to shifts in both the *IS* and *BP* curves. A change in the real exchange rate (a change in the exchange rate or the domestic or world price level) will also shift both curves. In this case, there is a potential ambiguity as to which of the two curves shifts more. The ambiguity arises from the fact — apparent by comparing Equations 25.4 and 25.6 above — that the definition of real expenditure that underlies the *IS* curve is one based on a constant (base period) real exchange rate — refer back to Chapter 3 and Equation (3.6) — whereas the definition of the balance of payments that underlies the *BP* curve is one based on the current real exchange rate. Thus, when analyzing a change in the real exchange rate, it is necessary to work out its effects on the *volume* of exports and imports in order to calculate t' *IS* curve shift, and its effect on the real *value* of exports and im in order to calculate the *BP* curve shift. To avoid a lengthy tr of all possible cases, we shall *assume* that a change in change rate has the same type of effect on the *IS* an the effect of a change in world real income that we b That is, we shall assume that a rise in the real in $\theta = EP_f/P$) raises both the volume and va' shifts both the *IS* and *BP* curves to the right. 1 to shift further to the right than does the *IS* cu.

It will be useful for the subsequent analysis to

Figure 25.3
The *IS-BP* Locus

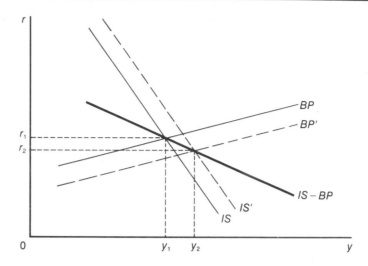

Because a shock that influences both the *IS* and *BP* curves shifts the *BP* curve by more than the *IS* curve, the intersection points of successive *BP* and *IS* curves fall on a downward-sloping line *IS-BP*.

curve that summarizes the shifts of the *IS* and *BP* curves. Let us call this curve the *IS-BP* curve. Figure 25.3 illustrates its derivation. Imagine that the economy starts out on the *IS* and *BP* curves at the interest rate r_1 and income level y_1. There is then some shock that shifts both the *IS* and *BP* curves to *IS'*, *BP'*. The new income level is y_2 and the interest rate is r_2. The line traced by the intersection points of the *IS* and *BP* curves will be called the *IS-BP* curve. It slopes downwards because we know that the *BP* curve shifts by more than the *IS* curve following any shock that shifts both of these curves. The *IS-BP* curve will be useful for analyzing the effects of changes in rest of world variables and in the exchange rate, all of which shift both the *IS* and *BP* curves in the manner illustrated in Figure 25.3.

E. The *LM* Curve in the Open Economy

The *LM* curve in the open economy is exactly the same (at least in the presentation given here) as that of the closed economy. As in the case of the closed economy, the only thing that shifts the *LM* curve is a change in the stock of money. There is an important difference between the open and closed economies, however, concerning the sources of variation in the quantity of money. To understand this, it is necessary for us to digress slightly and examine the balance sheet structure of the banking system in an open economy. In doing this we shall be drawing on the broader framework of aggregate balance sheets presented in Chapter 4.

The key thing that you need to understand is the connection between the money supply and a country's stock of foreign exchange reserves. This connection is most readily seen by considering the items in the balance sheets of the Bank of Canada and the chartered banks and the consolidated balance sheet of the banking sector. The balance sheets of the Bank of Canada and the chartered banks were first introduced in Chapter 4 (columns 3 and 4 of Table 4.2). The *consolidated banking sector* is the Bank of Canada and the chartered banks viewed as a whole.

(i) The Banking Sector and the Balance Sheets

Table 25.1 sets out the relevant balance sheets. (You might like to refer back to Chapter 4 on aggregate balance sheet accounting to see how these balance sheets fit in with those in the other sectors of the economy.)

First consider the balance sheet of the Bank of Canada, the first part of Table 25.1. Its assets are aggregated into two items: gold and

TABLE 25.1
Banking System Balance Sheets

BANK OF CANADA			
ASSETS		LIABILITIES	
Gold and foreign exchange reserves	F	Monetary base	MB
Domestic credit	DC_c		
CHARTERED BANKS			
ASSETS		LIABILITIES	
Notes and coins plus deposits at the Bank of Canada	MB_b	Deposits	D
Domestic credit	DC_b		
CONSOLIDATED BANKING SECTOR			
ASSETS		LIABILITIES	
Gold and foreign exchange reserves	F	Notes and coins in circulation with the public $(MB - MB_b)$	MB_p
Domestic credit $(DC_c + DC_b)$	DC	Deposits	D
Money Supply	M	Money Supply	M

foreign exchange reserves, and domestic credit. The gold represents actual gold in the vaults of the Bank of Canada. The foreign exchange reserves are either bank accounts that the Bank of Canada maintains with other central banks (i.e., central banks of other countries) or highly liquid foreign currency denominated securities. From the point of view of the country as a whole, the stock of gold and foreign exchange reserves serves the same purpose as notes and coins and a checking account do for you as an individual. Denote the stock of gold and foreign exchange reserves as F.

The second item in the Bank of Canada's balance sheet is the stock of government securities that it has purchased. You will recall that the Bank of Canada creates monetary base by buying government securities, either from the government directly or from the general public, and makes the purchase with newly created money. The whole collection of securities held by the central bank is called *domestic credit*. Denote the domestic credit of the Bank of Canada as DC_c.

Apart from miscellaneous items such as real estate, which may be ignored, these two items — gold and foreign exchange reserves, and domestic credit — constitute the entire stock of assets of the Bank of Canada.

The liability of the Bank of Canada is the monetary base. This is the stock of notes and coins that have been issued and are held either by the general public or in the tills of chartered banks, together with the stock of bank deposits maintained by the chartered banks at the Bank of Canada. Denote the monetary base as MB.

The Bank of Canada's balance sheet balances, so that

$$MB = F + DC_c$$

Next, consider the chartered banks. As in the case of the Bank of Canada, it is useful to distinguish between two sets of assets. First, the chartered banks hold reserves in the form of notes and coins as well as deposits with the Bank of Canada. Denote chartered bank reserve assets as MB_b.

Notice that the same letters are being used to denote the chartered banks' reserves as those used to denote monetary base because they are in fact the same thing. Part of the monetary base, MB, which is a liability to the Bank of Canada, is held as an asset by the chartered banks.

The other assets of the chartered banks have all been grouped into a single item — domestic credit of the chartered banks. This item consists of all the securities held by chartered banks, including any loan obligations that private individuals and firms have to the banks. Denote domestic credit of the chartered banks as DC_b.

Apart from some real estate, which may be neglected, these two items — reserve assets and domestic credit — constitute the entire assets of the chartered banks.

The liabilities of the chartered banks consist of the deposits that have been placed with them by households and firms. (You can think of deposits as checking account deposits only, and you can think of domestic credit as being net of savings deposits.) Denote these bank deposits as D.

The balance sheet of the chartered banks balances, so total deposits are equal to the stock of reserves plus domestic credit. That is,

$$D = MB_b + DC_b$$

Next consider the consolidation of these two balance sheets. A consolidated balance sheet is simply the balance sheet that arises from adding together individual balance sheets and netting out any items that appear as an asset in one balance sheet and as a liability in another. To consolidate the two balance sheets of the Bank of Canada and the chartered banks, first notice that gold and foreign exchange reserves appear only once in the Bank of Canada's balance sheet and, therefore, will appear in the consolidated balance sheet. Domestic credit appears twice, as DC_c and DC_b. If these two items are added together, the domestic credit of the economy as a whole is obtained. Denote domestic credit as DC. So that you are absolutely clear what domestic credit is let us elaborate a little. Domestic credit is the total of all the assets held by the Bank of Canada and by the chartered banks — other than the holdings of gold and foreign exchange reserves by the Bank of Canada. These assets include holdings of government securities by the Bank of Canada and by the chartered banks as well as private securities held by and loans made by the chartered banks.

On the liability side of the consolidated balance sheet, notice that the monetary base, MB, is partly held as the reserve asset of the chartered banks, MB_b. In the consolidated balance sheet, the difference between these two items is recorded. This difference is notes and coins in circulation with the public (denoted MB_p).

Bank deposits appear just once, in the chartered banks' balance sheet, and therefore appear again in the consolidated balance sheet.

The total liabilities of the consolidated banking system now have a familiar look. The total liabilities of the consolidated banking system consist of notes and coins in circulation plus bank deposits. This total is precisely the definition of money.

Since the two underlying balance sheets balance, so also the consolidated balance sheet will balance. From this fact it is clear that the money supply can be defined either as notes and coins in circulation plus bank deposits, a definition with which you are already familiar, or alternatively, as gold and foreign exchange reserves plus domestic credit. That is,

$$M = MB_p + D$$

or

$$M = F + DC$$

These are simply definitions. The second definition, however, is a useful one in helping us to organize our thinking about the sources of variation of the money supply in the open economy.

(ii) Changes in Reserves, the Money Supply, and Domestic Credit

The next step is to recognize that the relationship between the money supply and the stock of foreign exchange reserves and domestic credit holds each and every year, and therefore, the change in the money supply from one year to the next is equal to the change in foreign exchange reserves plus the change in domestic credit. That is (using Δ to denote change),

$$\Delta M = \Delta F + \Delta DC \tag{25.8}$$

This is a very important equation because ΔF is the balance of payments. That is, the change in the stock of foreign exchange reserves is what we mean by the balance of payments. Thus, the balance of payments is related to the change in the money supply and the change in domestic credit. The change in domestic credit, ΔDC, is usually called *domestic credit expansion*.

It will be convenient for the next step of the story to look at the equation that describes the change in reserves, in the money supply, and in domestic credit in terms of growth rates, or proportionate rates of change, rather than in terms of absolute changes. To convert the equation into growth rates, first divide both sides of the Equation (25.8) by M. This gives

$$\frac{\Delta M}{M} = \frac{\Delta F}{M} + \frac{\Delta DC}{M} \tag{25.9}$$

Terms like $\Delta F/M$ and $\Delta DC/M$ do not have immediately obvious meanings. They become much clearer if the first term is multiplied and divided by F and if the second term is multiplied and divided by DC. (Be sure that you understand how the equation below was obtained.)

$$\frac{\Delta M}{M} = \left(\frac{F}{M}\right)\frac{\Delta F}{F} + \left(\frac{DC}{M}\right)\frac{\Delta DC}{DC} \tag{25.10}$$

Equation (25.10) can be interpreted very easily. First notice that the first term $\Delta M/M$ is the growth rate of the money supply, which we have been calling μ. Next, define $F/M \equiv \psi$ so that $DC/M = (1 - \psi)$. The symbol ψ (the Greek letter psi) is the fraction of the money supply that is held by the banking system in foreign exchange reserves, and $1 - \psi$ is the fraction of the money supply held by the banking system in domestic assets. (Check that $F/M + DC/M = 1$ from $F + DC = M$.)

Also define $\Delta F/F$ as f and $\Delta DC/DC$ as dc. The letter f is the rate of change of foreign exchange reserves, and dc is the rate of change of domestic credit.

The somewhat cumbersome Equation (25.10) may, with the new definition, be written as the simpler equation

$$\mu = \psi f + (1 - \psi)dc \qquad \textbf{(25.11)}$$

This is a fundamental relationship between the rate of growth of the money supply, the rate of change of foreign exchange reserves, and the rate of growth of domestic credit. It says that the growth rate of the money supply, μ, is a weighted average of the growth rates of the stock of foreign exchange reserves and domestic credit. The weights, which add up to one, are the fraction of the total money supply backed by holdings of foreign exchange reserves, ψ, and the fraction of the total money supply backed by domestic credit $(1 - \psi)$.

This relationship may be used in order to determine how the *LM* curve shifts in the open economy. If domestic credit is held constant, which would be the natural way of interpreting a neutral domestic monetary policy, then unless the economy is on the *BP* curve, the quantity of money will be changing. Specifically, at all points above the *BP* curve, the quantity of money is rising, and at all points below it, the quantity of money is falling. This means that if the economy is above the *BP* curve, it is experiencing a balance of payments surplus, and the *LM* curve is shifting to the right. Conversely, if the economy is below the *BP* curve, it is experiencing a balance of payments deficit, and the *LM* curve is shifting to the left.

An alternative domestic monetary policy would be to stabilize the quantity of money regardless of the state of the balance of payments. This would involve changing domestic credit by an equal but opposite amount to the change in foreign exchange reserves resulting from the balance of payments deficit or surplus. Such an action is known as *sterilizing* the balance of payments. Such a policy can be undertaken, but only for limited periods of time, since, in general, sterilization actions accentuate the balance of payments problem. Pursuing tighter and tighter domestic monetary policies in the face of the balance of payments surplus tends to make the surplus bigger, and pursuing slacker and slacker monetary policies in the face of the balance of payments deficit tends to make the deficit worse. A situation in which the quantity of money changes by the same amount as the change in foreign exchange reserves is, therefore, an interesting one to analyze since it represents the only policy action that can be sustained over an indefinite period. Sterilization cannot.

These shifts of the *LM* curve arising from a balance of payments deficit and surplus can only occur in a fixed exchange rate world. In a flexible exchange rate regime there is no change in the stock of foreign exchange reserves since the balance of payments is always zero. That is, the *LM* curve in the flexible exchange rate world is identical to that in the closed economy and shifts in that curve result only from changes in domestic monetary policy.

Summary

A. Derivation of the *IS* Curve for an Open Economy

The *IS* curve for an open economy shows the relationship between the rate of interest and level of real income at which savings-plus-taxes-plus-imports equals investment-plus-government spending-plus-exports. It is steeper than the *IS* curve for a closed economy and intersects the latter at the real income level and interest rate at which imports equal exports.

B. Definition of the *BP* Curve

The *BP* curve shows the relationship between the rate of interest and level of real income at which the sum of the current account and capital account and thus the balance of payments is zero.

C. Derivation of the *BP* Curve

For a given real exchange rate (i.e., a given level of domestic and foreign prices and nominal exchange rate) and a given level of world real income, exports are fixed. The capital account surplus depends on the domestic rate of interest, and imports depend on domestic income. By finding the level of real income that generates an import volume equal to the exports-plus-capital account surplus generated by a given interest rate, it is possible to trace out the *BP* curve. The curve slopes upwards, except in the case of perfect capital mobility, in which case it is horizontal.

D. Shifts in the *IS* and *BP* Curves

In addition to the factors that shift the *IS* curve in a closed economy, a change in world real income, the exchange rate, or the foreign price level shifts the *IS* curve in an open economy. A rise in world real income, a rise in the world price level, or a depreciation of the domestic currency shifts the *IS* curve to the right. The *BP* curve shifts as a result of changes in world real income, the exchange rate, the world price level, or the world real rate of interest. A rise in world real income, a rise in the world price level, a fall in the world real rate of interest, or a depreciation of the currency shifts the *BP* curve to the right. A change in world income that shifts both the *IS* and the *BP* curves shifts both curves in the same direction but shifts the *BP* curve by more than it shifts the *IS* curve. A change in the real exchange rate also shifts both the *IS* and *BP* curves, and we assume that the *BP* curve shifts by more than the *IS* curve.

E. The *LM* Curve in the Open Economy

In the open economy the money supply is, by definition, the sum of foreign exchange reserves and domestic credit. The *LM* curve shifts because of changes in the money supply. In an open economy, when the exchange rate is fixed, this occurs if the balance of payments is other than zero. A balance of payments surplus is associated with a rising money supply and a balance of payments deficit with a falling money supply. Thus, if the economy is off the *BP* curve, the *LM* curve is shifting. This can only happen if the exchange rate is fixed.

Review Questions

1. What is the equilibrium condition that an open economy satisfies as it moves along the *IS* curve?

2. How does the *IS* curve of an open economy differ from that of a closed economy?

3. What determines the *slope* of the open economy *IS* curve?

4. What makes the open economy *IS* curve shift, and in what direction?

5. What is the equilibrium condition that is satisfied as the economy moves along its *BP* curve?

6. What determines the slope of the *BP* curve?

7. What makes the *BP* curve shift, and in what direction?

8. Explain how a rise in world real income shifts the *IS* and *BP* curves. Which shifts by more? Why?

9. Explain what the equation means:

$$\Delta M = \Delta F + \Delta DC$$

10. Illustrate your answer to Question 1 by showing what happens to the Canadian money supply, the stock of foreign exchange reserves, and domestic credit in the event that:

(a) The Bank of Canada buys British Government bonds with its reserves of pound sterling.

(b) The Bank of Canada buys U.S. dollars with new Canadian dollars.

(c) The Bank of Canada buys Canadian federal government bonds with new Canadian dollars.

11. What happens to the *LM* curve if the economy is (a) above, (b) below, and (c) on its *BP* curve?

26

Aggregate Demand in the Open Economy

You are now in a position to discover how the aggregate demand curve of the open economy differs from that of the closed economy. There will be two cases: one for a fixed exchange rate regime and one for a flexible exchange rate regime. It will be convenient to approach the aggregate demand curve in two steps. First, we shall study the determination of output and the rate of interest at a given price level. Then once we have understood this we shall move on to derive the aggregate demand curve under the two alternative exchange rate regimes but for the particular case in which capital is perfectly mobile.

There are some challenging problems in achieving a completely satisfactory analysis of the open economy. In the open economy, there are more variables to be determined and more sources of shocks than in the closed economy, and this raises the dimensionality of the problem which has to be solved. It makes it harder to arrive at simple, intuitive, easily grasped models. In this chapter and the next one, we are going to try to give you a feel for how the open economy operates using two alternative assumptions about capital mobility. When we study the determination of output and interest rates at a given price level we shall permit capital to be imperfectly mobile (though it could easily be regarded as being perfectly mobile as a special case). When we come to study the derivation of the aggregate demand curve and the interactions between aggregate demand and aggregate supply in the next chapter, we shall only look at the case of perfect capital mobility. Our own judgment is that this is only a slightly extreme assumption. It is not quite the way the world is but it is very close.

The virtue of making this assumption, aside from the fact that it does not strike us as being wildly at odds with the world, is that it simplifies the analysis considerably. It makes it possible to gain insights about issues that otherwise would be hard to understand.

There is an alternative extreme assumption that also yields a much simplified analysis, but that yields very different conclusions. This is the opposite extreme to perfect capital mobility — zero capital mobility. This alternative strikes us as being so violently at odds with the world as to be uninteresting and not worthwhile analyzing. Both perfect capital mobility and zero capital mobility simplify the task of analysis. One of them does it in a way that only mildly violates the facts while the other does it in a way that renders the analysis utterly pointless. By way of an analogy, assuming perfect capital mobility seems to us to be quite analogous to assuming there to be no atmosphere (a vacuum) for the purpose of calculating the length of time it would take for a 5 kilogram rock to fall from the top of the CN Tower and hit the ground. The atmospheric resistance may be presumed to be negligible and, hence, the calculations simplified considerably by assuming it to be zero. The answer obtained will be wrong, but not misleadingly wrong. The alternative assumption of zero capital mobililty strikes us as being analogous to simplifying the calculation of the power required to put a satellite into earth orbit by assuming zero gravity. The assumption would be so wildly at odds with the facts that the rocket would never leave the launching pad!

Let us now, with these preliminary justifications for the underlying assumptions about capital mobility, proceed to the main tasks of this chapter. These tasks are to:

a) Know how to determine the levels of output, interest rates, and the balance of payments in a fixed exchange rate regime at a given price level.

b) Know how to determine the levels of output, interest rates, and the exchange rate in a flexible exchange rate regime at a given price level.

c) Know how to derive the aggregate demand curve when capital is perfectly mobile.

A. Determination of Output, Interest Rates, and the Balance of Payments in a Fixed Exchange Rate Regime at a Given Price Level

Let us now determine the equilibrium values of output, the interest rate, and the balance of payments when the exchange rate is fixed and for a given domestic price level. We shall do this for given levels of world income, interest rates, and the price level; for the given fixed exchange rate; and for fixed levels of domestic government spending and taxes. The equilibrium levels of output, the rate of interest, and the balance of payments is determined at the triple intersection point of the *BP, LM*, and *IS* curves as shown in Figure 26.1. The *IS* and *BP* curves are exactly the same as those derived in Figures 25.1 and 25.2. The *LM* curve is exactly the same as the curve derived in Chapter 12.

(i) Equilibrium

The way the model works to determine the equilibrium is slightly more complicated than the standard closed economy variant of the *IS-LM* analysis. The idea is that income and the rate of interest are determined at each instant by the intersection of the *IS* and *LM* curves, as they were before in the closed economy analysis. This is not, however, the end of the story. If the intersection of the *IS* and *LM* curves is above the *BP* curve, then there is a balance of payments surplus, and the money supply is rising. A rising money supply means that the *LM* curve is shifting to the right, so that income is rising and the rate of interest falling (the economy is sliding down the *IS* curve). Such a process would continue until the *LM* curve came to rest where the *IS* curve intersects the *BP* curve. At such a point, the balance of payments is zero and the money supply constant, so that the *LM* curve is no longer shifting.

Conversely, if initially the *IS* and *LM* curves cut each other below the *BP* curve, then there is a balance of payments deficit. The money supply is falling, and the *LM* curve is moving to the left. In the process, the level of income falls, and the interest rate rises (the economy slides up the *IS* curve). This process continues until the *LM* curve

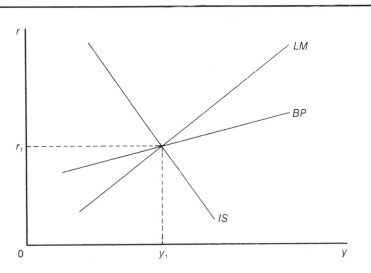

**Figure 26.1
Equilibrium with
Fixed Exchange Rates**

Equilibrium output and interest rate are determined at the point of intersection of the *IS* and *BP* curves. The *LM* curve also passes through this intersection point because the money supply adjusts to ensure that this happens.

goes through the intersection point of the *IS* and *BP* curves. At this point, the balance of payments deficit has disappeared and the money stock is constant.

You will probably get a better feeling for what is going on here by working through a series of experiments that result from the economy being shocked by a variety of domestic and foreign disturbances. We shall now turn to such an exercise.

(ii) Fiscal Policy

First, consider the effects of an expansionary fiscal policy. Figure 26.2 illustrates. The economy is at an initial equilibrium exactly like that depicted in Figure 26.1, with the interest rate at r_1 and real income at y_1. There is then a rise in government spending or a cut in taxes that shifts the *IS* curve to *IS'*. The impact effect of this fiscal policy action is to raise the rate of interest and the level of income to r_2 and y_2 respectively. The economy would now, however, be experiencing a balance of payments surplus since it is operating at a point above the *BP* curve. With a balance of payments surplus, the money supply is rising, so the *LM* curve is shifting to the right. As this happens, the succession of *LM* curves intersect the curve *IS'* at lower and lower interest rates but at higher and higher income levels (along the arrowed path). The economy finally settles down at the interest rate r_3

**Figure 26.2
The Effects of an
Expansionary Fiscal
Policy under Fixed
Exchange Rates**

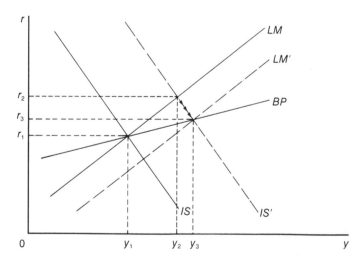

An initial equilibrium y_1, r_1 is disturbed by a rise in government spending or tax cut that shifts the *IS* curve to *IS'*. The impact effect of this is to raise the interest rate and income to r_2 and y_2. In this situation, there is a balance of payments surplus that raises the money supply, thereby shifting the *LM* curve to the right. The final equilibrium is the interest rate r_3 and real income y_3 where *IS'* intersects the *BP* curve. The *LM* curve will by then have become *LM'*. The adjustment process takes the economy down the *IS* curve.

and income level y_3. The effect, then, of an expansionary fiscal policy in an economy with a given price level and a fixed exchange rate is to raise interest rates and the real income level. A balance of payments surplus brings an inflow of money that subsequently lowers interest rates, but not to their initial level,[1] and raises income still further.[2]

(iii) Monetary Policy

Second, consider the effects of an expansionary monetary policy. Again, let the economy start out at the initial equilibrium level r_1, y_1 depicted in Figure 26.1. Figure 26.3 shows the effect of a monetary disturbance. Imagine raising the quantity of money (by raising domestic credit) in a once-and-for-all manner, so that the *LM* curve shifts to *LM'*. Initially, the interest rate drops to r_2 and real income rises to y_2. Clearly, with a higher income level bringing in more imports and a lower interest rate lowering the capital account surplus, there is a balance of payments deficit. In this situation, the money supply falls, and the *LM* curve moves to the left. As it does so, it intersects the *IS* curve at higher and higher interest rates and at lower and lower real income levels (the arrowed path). Eventually, the quantity of money returns to its initial level, and the economy returns to its initial interest rate and income position. All that has happened is that the quantity of money is backed by a higher amount of domestic credit and a smaller amount of foreign exchange reserves in the final situation than initially. This is the only change between the initial and final situation. Thus, in a fixed exchange rate economy, monetary policy has no permanent effects on aggregate demand.

The analysis that we have just conducted implicitly assumes that the country has a sufficiently large stock of foreign exchange reserves to permit the initially assumed expansion of the domestic money supply. Of course, if the country did not have sufficient foreign exchange reserves, then the experiment could not be conducted. If the country attempted to increase its money supply in a situation in which it had insufficient foreign exchange reserves, it would cease to be a fixed exchange rate country. It would find itself forced off the fixed exchange rate when its foreign exchange reserves fell to such a low level that it was unable to intervene in the foreign exchange market to maintain the value of its currency. One possibility in such

---

[1] In the special case of perfect capital mobility internationally, the interest rate will return to its initial level.

[2] There is a possible, although most unlikely, case that would arise if the *BP* curve was steeper than the *LM* curve. In this case, the impact effect of the expansionary fiscal policy would be to produce a balance of payments deficit. Money would flow out of the economy, thereby shifting the *LM* curve leftwards, raising the rate of interest, and lowering the level of real income. The new equilibrium would be one in which both interest rates and real income had increased above their initial levels.

Figure 26.3
The Effects of a
Rise in the Money
Supply under Fixed
Exchange Rates

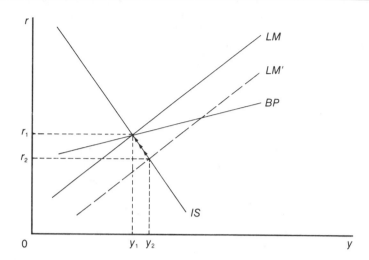

An initial equilibrium at y_1, r_1 is disturbed by a once-and-for-all rise in domestic credit that shifts the *LM* curve to *LM'*. The impact effect of this is to lower the interest rate to r_2 and raise real income to y_2. A balance of payments deficit results, and this leads to an outflow of money. As the money supply falls, the *LM* curve shifts back to the left and settles eventually at the initial equilibrium y_1, r_1.

a situation would be for the country to devalue its currency. Let us now analyze this case along with the effects of foreign shocks.

(iv) Devaluation and Foreign Shocks

Third, consider the effect of a devaluation of the currency. A devaluation is a once-and-for-all rise in the value of the exchange rate, E. Again, suppose the economy starts out at the real income and interest level y_1, r_1, as depicted in Figure 26.4. Then imagine that there is a once-and-for-all rise in the value of the exchange rate (devaluation). This raises exports and lowers imports, thereby shifting both the *IS* curve and *BP* curve to the right. The new curves are shown as *IS'* and *BP'* and are drawn to reflect the fact that the *BP* curve shifts further to the right than does the *IS* curve. The initial impact of the devaluation is to take the economy to the equilibrium y_2, r_2, where the original *LM* curve intersects the new *IS* curve. In this situation, there is a balance of payments surplus since the economy is above the new *BP* curve (*BP'*). The balance of payments surplus leads to a rise in the money supply and the *LM* curve starts to shift to the right. As the *LM* curve shifts to the right, it intersects the *IS* curve at lower and lower interest rates and higher and higher real income levels (along the arrowed adjustment path). Eventually income rises to y_3 and the interest rate falls to r_3. The final effect of a devaluation,

Figure 26.4
The Effect of a
Devaluation

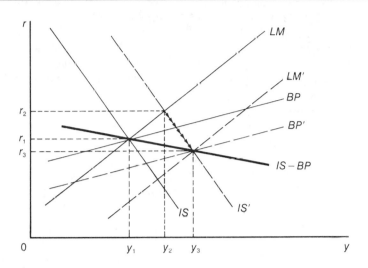

The initial equilibrium y_1, r_1 is disturbed by a devaluation of the currency. This raises exports and lowers imports, shifting the *IS* and *BP* curves to the right. The impact effect of this is to raise the level of real income to y_2 and the interest rate to r_2 and to create a balance of payments surplus. The balance of payments surplus leads to a rising money supply. The *LM* curve shifts to the right producing a falling rate of interest and a continuing increase in real income. The resting point is where the curve *IS'* intersects the curve *BP'*. The *LM* curve will by then have become *LM'*. The adjustment process takes the economy down the curve *IS'*.

therefore, is to raise real income and lower interest rates. The balance of payments is in surplus during the adjustment process, but it is in equilibrium at the end of the process.

It should be emphasized that these responses to a devaluation are all conditional on the price level remaining constant. If the price level was to rise by the same percentage amount as the devaluation, then the real exchange rate would not be affected, and the economy would remain at its initial equilibrium level. Alternatively, if the price level *initially* remained constant, the path described in Figure 26.4 would be set up, and the economy would move from y_1, r_1, to y_2, r_2, and then start to proceed towards y_3, r_3. If, during this process the price level began to rise and eventually rose all the way to full proportionality with the devaluation, then instead of continuing to travel down the curve *IS'*, both the *IS'* and *BP'* curves would shift leftwards, and the economy would gradually move back to y_1, r_1.

Other shocks emanating from the rest of the world have effects similar to a devaluation. A rise in world income or a rise in the world price level have exactly the same effects as a devaluation. Conversely, a fall in the world real rate of interest, which shifts the *BP* line but not the *IS* curve, has no impact effect on real income and the interest rate. It does, however, set up a process in which the balance of payments is in surplus, and so the *LM* curve starts moving to the right. Real income rises, and the interest rate falls until the point of intersection of the original *IS* curve with the new *BP* curve is reached.

This completes our analysis of the effects of domestic policy and foreign shocks on output, interest rates, and the balance of payments in a fixed exchange rate regime at a given price level. Let us now turn to examine a flexible exchange rate economy.

B. Determination of Output, Interest Rates, and the Exchange Rate in a Flexible Exchange Rate Regime at a Given Price Level

Analyzing a flexible exchange rate economy is slightly harder than the fixed exchange rate case. The problem arises because the *IS* and *BP* curves have three variables in them — real income, the rate of interest, and the exchange rate — all of which we want to determine, and it is, therefore, hard to construct diagrams in two dimensions that have the simplicity of those in the fixed exchange rate case. In order to make the analysis of the flexible exchange rate economy as comparable as possible with that of the fixed exchange rate economy, we shall use a series of diagrams (Figures 26.5 to 26.7) drawn in interest rate real income space, as we did before when analyzing the fixed exchange rate case. This means that the exchange rate will not appear explicitly on one of the axes of the picture. It will be possible, nevertheless, to work out directions of change of the exchange rate when various shocks are administered to the economy. This is analogous to the way in which the balance of payments was determined in the previous section.

(i) Equilibrium

It will be useful, as a starting point, to reinterpret Figure 26.1 as a flexible exchange rate equilibrium rather than as a fixed exchange rate equilibrium. Under flexible exchange rates, the quantity of money (both the stock of foreign exchange reserves and domestic credit) is determined by the central bank. The position of the *LM* curve is therefore bolted down, so to speak, by monetary policy. If the point of intersection of the *IS* and *BP* curves is not on the *LM* curve, something has to adjust. The adjustment that occurs is in the exchange rate. Since domestic and foreign prices are constant, different values of the exchange rate E generate different values of the real exchange rate θ. Different values of θ generate different values of exports and imports and, therefore, produce different *IS* and *BP* curves.

Since the *IS* curve slopes downwards and the *BP* curve slopes upwards, there is one, and only one, point (a real income level y, and interest rate r) at which they intersect and at the same time falls on the *LM* curve. The value of the exchange rate that underlies the *IS* and *BP* curves when they cut the *LM* curve is the equilibrium exchange rate. Thus, you may interpret Figure 26.1 as a flexible exchange rate equilibrium in the sense that the exchange rate has to be the particular value that causes the *IS* and *BP* curves to intersect each other at a point on the *LM* curve. This contrasts with the fixed exchange rate interpretation of Figure 26.1, which is that the *IS* and *BP* curves are fixed in position, while the *LM* curve takes up the slack — the money supply varies to ensure that the *LM* curve is located at the point of intersection of the fixed *IS* and *BP* curves.

To repeat for emphasis, in a fixed exchange rate world the *IS* and *BP* curves are fixed in position and determine the steady-state equilibrium, while the quantity of money and, therefore, the *LM* curve arc dragged along to this fixed intersection point. In the case of the flexible exchange rate economy, the *LM* curve is fixed in position, while the exchange rate is free to move, thereby shifting the *IS* and *BP* curves to an intersection point on the *LM* curve.

(ii) Fiscal Policy

Let us now proceed to analyze the effects of the same set of policy and foreign shocks that were analyzed in the preceding section in the flexible exchange rate case. First, consider the effect of an expansionary fiscal policy. The economy is initially in an equilibrium, such as that shown in Figure 26.5, at y_1, r_1. There is then expansion of government spending or a tax cut that shifts the *IS* curve from *IS* to *IS'*. The impact effect is to raise the income level to y_2 and the interest rate to r_2. In this situation, if the exchange rate was fixed, there would be a balance of payments surplus. With a flexible exchange rate, however, the balance of payments surplus is not allowed to occur. The central bank simply does not stand ready to take in foreign exchange at a pegged exchange rate. Instead, the exchange rate adjusts. In this case there is an excess supply of foreign currency, so its price falls or, alternatively, the domestic currency appreciates. This lowers the real exchange rate, thereby raising imports and lowering exports. In this process, the *IS* and *BP* curves shift to the left. Since we are assuming that the *BP* curve shifts by more than the *IS* curve, as they move they intersect along the line marked *IS'-BP*. They will eventually come to rest intersecting the *LM* curve at the interest rate r_3 and real income level y_3. The exchange rate at this point is lower than the initial exchange rate (the currency has appreciated). Thus, the effects of an expansionary fiscal policy in a flexible exchange rate economy are to raise real income and the rate of interest and to appreciate the currency.

The rural sector of the economy may be hostile towards such an outcome and may complain about the difficulty of doing profitable

Figure 26.5
The Effects of an
Expansionary Fiscal
Policy under Flexible
Exchange Rates

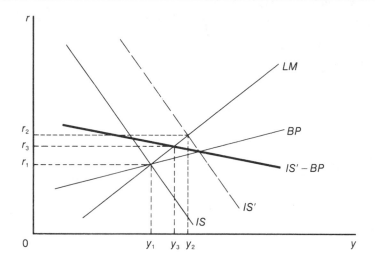

An initial equilibrium y_1, r_1 is disturbed by a rise in government spending or a tax cut that shifts the *IS* curve to *IS'*. If there was no change in the exchange rate, real income would move to y_2 and the interest rate to r_2, thereby producing a balance of payments surplus. With a flexible exchange rate, this does not happen. Instead the exchange rate falls (the currency appreciates), thereby lowering exports and raising imports. Both the curve *IS'* and the *BP* curve shift to the left. The equilibrium is at the point at which the *IS'*-*BP* locus intersects the *LM* curve, at the interest rate r_3 and real income y_3. Thus, the effect of an expansionary fiscal policy is to raise income, raise the rate of interest, and appreciate the currency.

business in foreign markets. In effect, what is happening is that because the government has increased its spending, real resources have to be diverted from the rest of the economy to the government, and this is accomplished by making total world demand for domestic goods decline and domestic demands for rest of world goods increase. The appreciation of the currency is the mechanism whereby this happens. It is not the *cause* of problems perceived by domestic farmers and manufacturers.

(iii) Monetary Policy

Next, consider the effects of an expansionary monetary policy. Again, start the economy out at the equilibrium (y_1, r_1) shown in Figure 26.6. This is at the triple intersection of *IS*, *BP*, and *LM* curves. Then let there be a rise in the quantity of money. This shifts the *LM* curve to *LM'*. The new equilibrium clearly has to be somewhere on the curve *LM'*. At the initial exchange rate, the *IS* and *BP* curves intersect on the old *LM* curve. There must be another exchange rate (a higher value) at which the *IS* and *BP* curves intersect on the new *LM* curve, *LM'*. The *IS-BP* curve traces out the intersection points of the *IS* and *BP* curves as the exchange rate changes. The intersection of the *IS*-

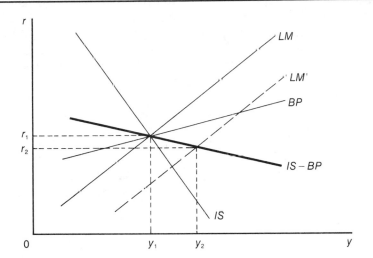

Figure 26.6
The Effects of
an Expansionary
Monetary Policy
under Flexible
Exchange Rates

An initial equilibrium at y_1, r_1 is disturbed by a rise in the money supply that shifts the *LM* curve to *LM'*. This leads to a higher exchange rate (devaluation), which shifts the *IS* and *BP* curves along the *IS-BP* locus until they intersect the new *LM* curve at y_2, r_2. Thus, the effect of an expansionary monetary policy under flexible exchange rates is to lower the interest rate, raise real income and depreciate the currency

BP curve and the *LM'* curve determines the new equilibrium level of real income y_2 and the interest rate r_2. We know that the exchange rate is higher than the initial one because we know that it is associated with a higher level of exports and lower level of imports than prevailed initially. Recall that a higher value of the exchange rate implies a depreciation of the currency.

The effects of expansionary monetary policy in a flexible exchange rate economy with a given price level may be summarized as follows: a rise in the money supply leads to a lower rate of interest, a higher level of real income, and a depreciation of the currency.

(iv) Foreign Shocks

Finally, consider the effects of a change in world income. Imagine that the economy is at (y_1, r_1) in Figure 26.7 and that the rise in world real income shifts the *IS* and *BP* curves to *IS'* and *BP'*. These curves necessarily intersect along the line *IS-BP*. Varying the exchange rate changes exports and imports, thereby shifting the *IS* and *BP* curves. Varying foreign real income (the shock that we are considering here) also changes exports and shifts the *IS* and *BP* curves. Since the *LM* curve has not changed (the domestic money supply being held constant), we know that the final equilibrium must be at a point on the *LM* curve. We further know that it has to involve the intersection of

IS and *BP* curves. We can see that there is only one such point, and that is the initial equilibrium income and interest rate level (y_1, r_1). What happens is that the exchange rate has to change (appreciate in this case) so as to return the *IS* and *BP* curves from their shocked positions *IS'*, *BP'* to their initial positions. The initial *IS* and *BP* curves then describe the initial exchange rate and the initial level of world real income and also the new higher level of world real income and lower value of the exchange rate (appreciated currency).

Comparison of Fixed and Flexible Exchange Rate Economies   It is of some interest to compare the responses of the economy under fixed and flexible exchange rate regimes. You can do this by comparing Figure 26.2 with Figure 26.5 (fiscal policy), Figure 26.3 with Figure 26.6 (monetary policy), and Figure 26.4 (interpreted as a foreign shock) with Figure 26.7 (for a rise in world real income). Expansionary fiscal policy has a bigger output effect but smaller interest rate effect under fixed exchange rates than under flexible exchange rates. Expansionary monetary policy raises real income and lowers the interest rate under flexible exchange rates, but it has no effect, in the steady state, under fixed exchange rates. A rise in world real income raises domestic real income and lowers domestic interest rates under fixed exchange rates, but it has no effect on interest rates and real income, in the steady state, in a flexible exchange rate economy.

Figure 26.7
The Effects of a
Rise in World Income
under Flexible
Exchange Rates

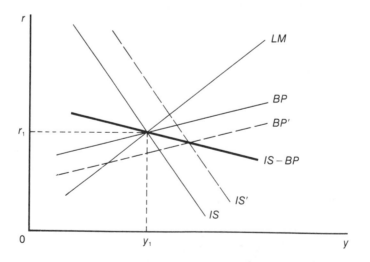

An initial equilibrium y_1, r_1 is disturbed by a rise in world real income that shifts the *IS* and *BP* curves to *IS'* and *BP'*. The currency appreciates to produce an equivalent shift of these curves back to their initial positions, so that the real income level and interest rate are undisturbed. Thus, the effect of a rise in world real income under flexible exchange rates comes out entirely as a change in the exchange rate.

This completes our analysis of the determination of output and interest rates under both fixed and flexible exchange rates when the price level is fixed. We shall now go on to see how we may derive an aggregate demand curve for an open economy under both fixed and flexible exchange rates when capital is perfect mobile internationally.

C. Aggregate Demand when Capital is Perfectly Mobile

In order to develop a rational expectations equilibrium theory of the open economy we need to see how expected aggregate demand determines the rational expectation of the price level and how actual aggregate demand, interacting with the expectations-augmented aggregate supply curve, determines the actual levels of output and prices. We further need to work out, under a fixed exchange rate regime, how the balance of payments is determined, and how, under flexible exchange rates, the exchange rate is determined.

The first thing to establish is that if capital is perfectly mobile, the domestic *real* rate of interest, r, will be equal to the world *real* interest rate, r_f. Why will the domestic and world real interest rates be equal? Since capital is perfectly mobile there will be no impediments preventing people from obtaining the highest possible returns on their investments. If real interest rates were not equal it would pay to move funds from those countries where the yields were low to countries where the yields were high. You already know from studying investment in Chapter 9 that the higher the capital stock, the lower the marginal product of capital. This force will be at work when captial is moved from a low yield country to a high yield country. The country losing capital will have a rising real interest rate and the country receiving capital will have a falling real interest rate. Only when the real interest rates are equal will the process of moving capital from one country to another stop. If capital is perfectly mobile, any discrepancy between real interest rates will immediately set up a capital flow that is sufficient to eliminate the discrepancy. Thus, with capital perfectly mobile internationally, the domestic and world interest rates are equal. The *BP* curve will be horizontal at this real rate of interest.

The exogeneity of the real rate of interest has powerful simplifying implications for the analysis. In the analysis of the two preceding sections we had to determine the values of three variables — output, the rate of interest, and either the balance of payments (under fixed exchange rates), or the exchange rate (under flexible exchange rates). By assuming perfect capital mobility and, therefore, the exogeneity of the real rate of interest, the problem reduces to that of determining two variables, namely, the level of real income, and either the balance of payments (under fixed exchange rates) or the exchange rate (under flexible exchange rates).

The analysis of the two preceding sections did hold the price level constant. This is a central variable of interest that we shall want to determine in our study of macroeconomic equilibrium. That being so, although we have eliminated from consideration the determination of one variable (the real rate of interest), we want to bring into focus the determination of another variable — the price level. This is a lot easier to do in the case where the real interest rate is fixed than where we simultaneously seek to determine the real interest rate as well as all the other variables of concern.

(i) Aggregate Demand with a Fixed Exchange Rate

With these preliminary remarks in mind, what we now want to do is to use the *IS-BP-LM* analysis to develop a theory of aggregate demand for the open economy under fixed and flexible exchange rates. The two exchange rate regimes give rise to different propositions about aggregate demand in a rather interesting way. First, recall what the aggregate demand curve is. It is the relationship between the price level and the quantity of output that will be demanded such that the economy is on the *IS* and *LM* curves. Let us derive the aggregate demand curve for an open economy under both fixed and flexible exchange rates in the case where there is perfect capital mobility internationally.

First, consider the fixed exchange rate economy. Figure 26.8 illustrates the analysis. Frame (a) contains the *IS*, *BP* and *LM* curves, and in frame (b) we will generate the aggregate demand curve. The *BP* curve is horizontal at the world rate of interest, r_f. Imagine first, that the price level is arbitrarily given as P_0, marked off on the vertical axis of frame (b). With the price level at P_0, the *IS* curve would be the curve labelled $IS(EP_f/P_0)$. We know that under fixed exchange rates, the money supply is endogenous and has to be equal to whatever quantity is demanded at the level of income generated by the intersection of the *IS* and *BP* curves. Thus, the *LM* curve will automatically pass through the intersection of *IS* and *BP* at the world interest rate r_f and the income level y_0. Call the money supply in this case M_0, so that the *LM* curve is $LM(M_0/P_0)$. Point A in frame (b) at (y_0, P_0) is one point on the aggregate demand curve.

Next, consider raising the price level to P_1. In this case, the *IS* curve becomes $IS(EP_f/P_1)$ to the left of the original *IS* curve. Why does this happen? It happens because world prices have fallen relative to the domestic price level, thereby lowering the net demand for domestic output in the rest of the world and raising domestic demand for world output. This leftward shift of the *IS* curve intersects the *BP* curve at the income level y_1. Again, the money supply will adjust through the balance of payments to ensure that the *LM* curve passes through this point. Call the new money supply M_1, so that the *LM* curve is that labelled $LM(M_1/P_1)$. Point B in frame (b) at the income level y_1 and price level P_1 is another point on the aggregate demand curve.

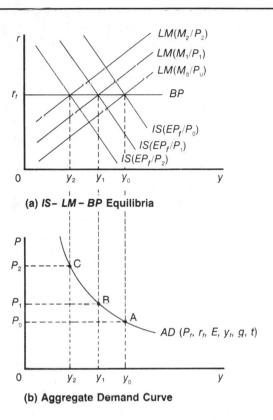

Figure 26.8
The Aggregate
Demand Curve
under Fixed
Exchange Rates
and Perfect
Capital Mobility

(a) *IS- LM - BP* Equilibria

(b) **Aggregate Demand Curve**

With perfect capital mobility, the *BP* curve is horizontal [frame (a)]. Where the *IS* curve cuts the *BP* curve determines the level of aggregate demand. As the price level rises, the *IS* curve shifts to the left with aggregate demand falling. The curve ABC traces out such an aggregate demand curve. The *LM* curve shifts as a result of a change in the money supply via the balance of payments to ensure money market equilibrium at each point along the aggregate demand curve. Aggregate demand depends only on the factors that underlie the *BP* and *IS* curves, that is, the exchange rate, the world price level, the world rate of interest, world real income, government expenditure and taxes.

Consider a still higher price level, P_2. This shifts the *IS* curve further to the left to $IS(EP_f/P_2)$, which determines the income level y_2. The money supply falls even further through a balance of payments deficit, so that the *LM* curve becomes $LM(M_2/P_2)$. Point C at the income level y_2 and price level P_2 is yet another point on the aggregate demand curve. Joining up the points A, B and C generates the aggregate demand curve.

You will notice from the way in which the aggregate demand curve has been derived that the exogenous variables that determine the position of the aggregate demand curve are entirely in the *BP* and *IS* curves. The *LM* curve is a slack relationship that automatically adjusts (via a balance of payments adjustment of the money supply) to ensure an equilibrium money supply to support the interest rate, real income, and price level generated by the *IS-BP* intersection. The position of the aggregate demand curve, therefore, depends only on those things that influence the position of *IS* and *BP* curves. These variables are the world price level, real income, and rate of interest; government spending and taxes; and the exchange rate. These are shown in parentheses on the label of the aggregate demand curve to remind you that the curve will shift as a result of changes in these variables. The money supply does not in any way determine the position of the aggregate demand curve in the fixed exchange rate, perfect capital mobility, open economy.

To summarize: for a fixed exchange rate open economy with perfect capital mobility, the aggregate demand curve is determined by the intersection of the *IS* and *BP* curves and in no way depends on the *LM* curve. This does not mean that the *LM* curve is irrelevant. Rather, it means that the *LM* curve determines the quantity of money, but not the level of aggregate demand.

(ii) Aggregate Demand with a Flexible Exchange Rate

Let us now go on to consider the derivation of the aggregate demand curve in a flexible exchange rate, perfect capital mobility economy. Figure 26.9 illustrates this. For the moment ignore frame (c) of this figure. Frame (a) contains the *IS*, *BP* and *LM* curves, and frame (b) derives the aggregate demand curve. Again, the *BP* curve is horizontal at the world real rate of interest, r_f. Recall that in the flexible exchange rate case, the exchange rate that underlies the position of the *IS* curve is determined in the analysis, whereas the money supply that underlies the position of the *LM* curve is exogenously determined by the monetary policy actions of the central bank.

To derive the aggregate demand curve, again pick a price level (initially P_0) marked on the vertical axis of frame (b). With a fixed money supply (M_0) and the price level at P_0, the *LM* curve will be $LM(M_0/P_0)$. The level of aggregate demand y_0 is determined where this curve intersects the *BP* curve. The *IS* curve will pass through the point of intersection of the curves $LM(M_0/P_0)$ and *BP* because the exchange rate adjusts until the change in the real exchange rate generates sufficient domestic demand to ensure that the *IS* curve passes through precisely this point. Indeed, this is how the exchange rate is determined. The output level y_0 determined by the intersection of the *LM* and *BP* curves, along with the price level P_0, marked as point A in frame (b), represents one point on the aggregate demand curve.

Next, consider a higher price level P_1, marked on the vertical axis of frame (b). At this higher price level, while maintaining the money supply at M_0, the *LM* curve shifts to the left to become $LM(M_0/P_1)$. This intersects the *BP* curve at the lower income level y_1. The income level y_1 with the price level P_1 [marked as point B in frame (b)] represents another point on the aggregate demand curve. The *IS* curve

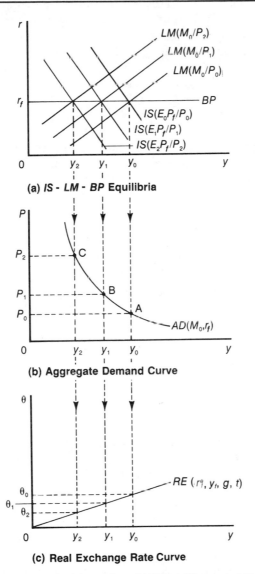

Figure 26.9
The Aggregate
Demand and
RE Curves in a
Flexible Exchange
Rate, Perfect Capital
Mobility Economy

(a) *IS - LM - BP* Equilibria

(b) Aggregate Demand Curve

(c) Real Exchange Rate Curve

Under flexible exchange rates, the intersection of *LM* and *BP* curves determines aggregate demand. As the price level rises from P_0 through P_2, real money balances fall and aggregate demand falls along the line ABC. Where the *IS* curve cuts the intersection of *LM* and *BP* curves is determined the real exchange rate. The lower the level of real income, the further to the left must the *IS* curve be, and the lower must be the net demand for domestic goods. The real exchange rate must fall, therefore, as real income falls.

will pass through this point because the exchange rate adjusts to E_1, giving the *IS* curve $IS(E_1 P_f/P_1)$.

Finally, suppose the price level was P_2, so that the real money supply was reduced still further, and the *LM* curve shifted yet further to the left to $LM(M_0/P_2)$. This would generate a real income level of y_2, shown in frame (a). Again the IS curve would shift to the left with an adjustment in the exchange rate to E_2 to ensure that the real exchange rate moved by exactly the amount required to put the IS curve at the point of intersection of LM and BP curves. The income level y_2 at the price level P_2 [point C in frame (b)] represents another point on the aggregate demand curve.

The points A, B, and C in frame (b) trace out the aggregate demand curve for an economy under flexible exchange rates when capital is perfectly mobile internationally. Notice that in the derivation of this aggregate demand curve, it was purely the intersection of the LM and BP curves that determined the level of aggregate demand. This curve is therefore labelled as $AD(M_0, r_f)$ to remind you that it is the variables that underlie the LM and BP curve, namely, the money supply and the foreign interest rate, that determine the position of the aggregate demand curve in a flexible exchange rate economy, with perfect capital mobility internationally.

To summarize: under flexible exchange rates with perfect capital mobility internationally, aggregate demand is determined by the intersection of the LM and BP curves, and the position of the aggregate demand curve depends only on the world rate of interest and the domestic money supply. It in no way depends on world real income or prices or domestic fiscal policy. The IS curve is not irrelevant in the flexible exchange rate economy; it determines the exchange rate but not aggregate demand.

(iii) Aggregate Demand: Summary

Under both fixed and flexible exchange rates when capital is perfectly mobile internationally the aggregate demand curves slope downwards, and both curves depend on the world rate of interest. A higher world rate of interest would shift the fixed exchange rate aggregate demand curve to the left and the flexible exchange rate aggregate demand curve to the right. You can easily see why this is so. Under fixed exchange rates, it is the IS-BP intersection that determines aggregate demand, so that a higher world interest rate would mean a lower level of aggregate demand; whereas, under flexible exchange rates, it is the LM-BP intersection that determines aggregate demand, so that a higher world interest rate would give a higher domestic velocity of circulation of money and a higher level of aggregate demand for a given money supply. Aside from the world rate of interest, the two aggregate demand curves have no other variables in common. Under fixed exchange rates, it is the exchange rate, the world price level, world real income, and domestic fiscal policy variables that affect domestic aggregate demand; whereas under flexible exchange rates, it is the domestic money stock only that affects aggregate demand.

(iv) The Real Exchange Rate

The concept of the real exchange rate has already been introduced in Chapter 25. It is, you will recall,

$$\theta = EP_f/P$$

In the next chapter we are going to analyze the determination of the real exchange rate and the way in which it interacts with other variables in the model. One of those other variables is, of course, the exchange rate E. Sometimes, for emphasis, or in order to avoid confusion between θ and E the term *nominal exchange rate* will be used to refer to the exchange rate E. Thus, the term "real exchange rate" will always refer to θ and two alternative terms "exchange rate" and "*nominal* exchange rate" will be used to refer to E.

It is convenient to begin by examining how the real exchange rate varies with real income. Figure 26.9 [frame (c)] shows this relationship. It plots the real exchange rate (θ) on the vertical axis and real income (y) on the horizontal axis. This curve is called the *real exchange rate curve* and is labelled RE. Why does the RE curve slope upwards? The answer to this question is found in the properties of the IS curve. Indeed, the RE curve in effect shows the value of the real exchange rate that ensures that the IS curve passes through the intersection point of the LM and BP curves. As the price level is raised from P_0 to P_1 and P_2, so the nominal exchange rate moves from E_0 to E_1 to E_2 to ensure that the real exchange rate equals θ_0, θ_1, and θ_2, the values that make the level of real income read off from the IS curve equal to the level of aggregate demand determined by the LM-BP intersection. That is, as the price level is raised, both real income (y) and the real exchange rate (θ) fall. The RE curve slopes upwards.

The variables that make the RE curve shift are the same as those that make the IS and BP curves shift. They are world real income and interest rates and domestic fiscal policy variables. The RE curve does not shift as a result of any monetary action. It is, as its name suggests, entirely a real curve. The RE relationship will be important in the subsequent analysis of the behavior of a flexible exchange rate economy.

Summary

A. Determination of Output, Interest Rates, and the Balance of Payments in a Fixed Exchange Rate Regime at a Given Price Level

At each instant, the real income level and interest rate are determined at the point of intersection of the IS and LM curves. If this intersection point is off the BP curve, the LM curve is shifting. The steady state occurs where the *IS* and *BP* curves intersect. The *LM* curve intersects this point as a result of the money supply adjusting, while the balance of payments is out of equilibrium.

Expansionary fiscal policy raises output and interest rates and leads to a temporary balance of payments surplus. Expansionary monetary policy leads to a temporary balance of payments deficit and no steady-state change in real income or the rate of interest. A devaluation initially raises the rate of interest and real income level, but it eventually lowers the rate of interest below its initial level and raises income still further. In the process, the balance of payments will have been in surplus. A rise in world real income has a similar effect to that of a devaluation.

B. Determination of Output, Interest Rates, and the Exchange Rate in a Flexible Exchange Rate Regime at a Given Price Level

Under flexible exchange rates, the *LM* curve is fixed in position. The positions of the *BP* and *IS* curves depend on the value of the exchange rate. As the exchange rate varies, these curves shift to intersect each other along a downward-sloping *IS-BP* locus. The equilibrium exchange rate is the exchange rate that locates the *BP* and *IS* curves at an intersection point along the *LM* curve. In a flexible exchange rate economy, expansionary fiscal policy raises real income and the rate of interest and appreciates the currency. Expansionary monetary policy lowers the rate of interest, raises the level of real income, and depreciates the currency. A rise in world income leads to an appreciation of the domestic currency but no change in real income or the rate of interest.

C. Aggregate Demand when Capital is Perfectly Mobile

If capital is perfectly mobile, the rate of interest is determined exogenously in the rest of the world. In a fixed exchange rate economy, aggregate demand is determined purely by the *IS* curve and the world rate of interest. Shifts in aggregate demand, therefore, depend on changes in the world price level, world real income, world interest rates, and domestic fiscal policy. In a flexible exchange rate world, aggregate demand is determined solely by the domestic demand for money, supply of money, and world interest rates. Changes in aggregate demand in this case, therefore, depend only on the world rate of interest and the money supply. In the fixed exchange rate setting, the *LM* curve determines the money supply via the balance of payments, and in the flexible exchange rate setting, the *IS* curve determines the nominal exchange rates, and both the *IS* and *BP* curves determine the real exchange rate.

Review Questions

1. Work out the effects on all the relevant variables, under fixed exchange rates, of the following shocks:
  (a) a rise in government spending
  (b) a rise in domestic credit
  (c) a rise in the exchange rate
  (d) a rise in world real income
  (e) a rise in world prices
  (f) a rise in the world real rate of interest
How do the effects depend on the degree of capital mobility internationally?

2. Work out the effects on all the relevant variables, in a flexible exchange rate regime, of the six shocks listed in Question 1. How do the effects depend on the degree of capital mobility?

3. On the basis of your answers to Questions 1 and 2, how would you choose between the two alternative exchange rate regimes?

4. What determines aggregate demand in an open economy that faces perfectly mobile international capital flows:
  (a) under fixed exchange rates?
  (b) under flexible exchange rates?

5. Why does the exchange rate regime make a difference to the determinants of aggregate demand?

6. What determines the real exchange rate?

27

Trends in the Open Economy

You are now ready to bring together the various components of the open economy and study equilibrium. You will study the determination of output, prices, interest rates, the balance of payments and the foreign exchange rate and examine how these variables are affected by domestic and foreign shocks.

We shall tackle these problems in two stages much as we did when studying the closed economy. First, in this chapter, we will take you through some analysis of the effects of expected or anticipated changes in variables so that we shall be analyzing an economy that remains at full employment. We shall study the determination of trends in prices, exchange rates, the balance of payments and interest rates. Secondly, we shall go on in the next chapter to the more complicated analysis of the effects of unanticipated disturbances to the economy.

You are going to discover that there is a great deal of myth and sheer nonsense talked about the factors that determine the foreign exchange rate and the balance of payments. You are going to discover precisely what the Bank of Canada can and cannot do to achieve independence in its monetary policy actions from the United States. You are going to equip yourself with some basic tools that will enable you to interpret some of the turbulent occurrences in Canada's international economic relations in recent years, such as its weak dollar vis-à-vis the U.S. dollar and its high interest rates.

The chapter will take you through four tasks. Those tasks are to:

a) Understand the "law of one price" — (i) purchasing power parity (PPP), (ii) interest rate parity (IRP).

b) Understand how the balance of payments is determined at full employment when the exchange rate is fixed.

c) Understand how the exchange rate is determined at full employment in a flexible exchange rate regime.

d) Understand how the balance of payments and the exchange rate are linked, at full employment, in a managed floating regime.

A. The "Law of One Price"

A fundamental law of economics that is of great use in understanding the forces that determine the balance of payments and the exchange rate is the "law of one price."

The law of one price is a proposition concerning the effects of arbitrage. Arbitrage is the buying of a commodity at a low price and simultaneously contracting to sell it for a higher price, thereby making a profit in the process. If it is possible to buy a particular good for some price, say, p_b, and sell the good for a price p_s, then it is possible to make a profit at a rate given by:

$$\text{Arbitrage Profit Rate} = \frac{(p_s - p_b)}{p_b}$$

If such a situation exists, individuals who see the profit opportunity available will increase their demand for the good whose price is p_b. They also increase their supply of the good at the price p_s. This arbitrage activity of increasing demand at the price p_b and increasing supply at the price p_s will put upward pressure on the buying price — that is, p_b will rise — and downward pressure on the selling price — that is, p_s will fall. Arbitrage will continue to the point at which one price prevails, that is, $p_s = p_b$, until there are no arbitrage profits to be made.

This is the law of one price, namely, that arbitrage will compete away all price differences between identical commodities. If there are transport costs between two locations, or tariffs and impediments to trade are imposed by the government, or there are costs of acquiring information about the prices of alternative sources of supply, arbitrage will not compete price differentials all the way to zero. It will, however, compete differentials down to the level such that the only remaining price difference reflects underlying real technological- or government-induced barriers to further price gap reductions.

The law of one price has two important implications that are useful for understanding the determination of the balance of payments and exchange rates: namely, the purchasing power parity and interest rate parity theorems.

(i) Purchasing Power Parity (PPP)

The purchasing power parity theorem states that the price of a good in one country will be equal to the price of this same good in another country where the prices are expressed in units of local currency and converted at the current exchange rate. (This would have to be modified to allow for any tariffs and transportation costs.)

As an example, if a car in the United States costs $U.S. 5000, that identical car (trade barriers and transport costs absent) would, at an exchange rate of $C 1.25 per $U.S., cost $C 6250 in Canada. Even allowing for transport costs and tariffs, if these factors were *constant*, then, although the *level* of prices in the United States might be different from the *level* of prices in Canada, the *rate of change of prices* in the two countries would be linked to each other by the relation:

> percentage change in $C price
> *equals*   percentage change in $U.S. price
> plus   the percentage rate of depreciation of the $C
> in terms of the $U.S.

To go back to the car example, suppose that car prices in the United States are rising by 5 percent per annum. This means that the car that sells for $5000 this year will sell for $5250 next year. Further, suppose that the $C appreciates from $C 1.25 per $U.S. to $C 1.1875 per $U.S. — a five percent appreciation — then the purchasing power parity theorem states that the price of a car in Canada next year will remain at $C 6250. That is, car prices in Canada will change by the percentage change of car prices in the United States, 5 percent, plus the percentage depreciation of the value of the $C – 5 percent.

(ii) Interest Rate Parity (IRP)

The interest rate parity theorem is a close cousin of the purchasing power parity theorem. It arises from arbitrage activities in asset markets. The interest rate parity theorem states that, provided capital is free to move internationally (and abstracting from political risk differences) the market (or nominal) rate of interest available in one country will be equal to the market rate of interest available in another country adjusted for the expected rate of change of the exchange rate between the currencies of the two countries.

Thus, suppose, for example, that the market rate of interest in the United States is 10 percent, and the market rate in Canada is 12 percent. Then, if it is expected that the $C is going to depreciate by 2 percent, the rate of interest that would be obtained by an American investing in a Canadian security will be the 12 percent interest on Canadian bonds minus the expected depreciation of the $C of 2 percent, which would equal 10 percent, the same as he could obtain in the United States. Conversely, a Canadian investing in the United States would obtain 10 percent interest on the U.S. security plus a 2 percent gain from the appreciation of the $U.S. vis-à-vis the $C, totalling 12 percent. This would be equivalent to what could be obtained in Canada.

As another example, if the rate of interest in Canada was greater than 12 percent, the rate of interest in the United States was 10 percent, and the expected rate of depreciation of the $C was 2 percent, there would be gains to be made from investing in Canada. As investors sought to exploit these gains, they would increase the demand for Canadian securities and lower the demand for U.S. securities. This would raise the price of and lower the rate of interest on Canadian securities and would lower the price of and raise the rate of interest on U.S. securities.

If there were flexible exchange rates, the flow of funds into Canada would also lead to an immediate appreciation of the $C. This would mean that the expected rate of future depreciation of the $C would increase. The combination of a higher U.S. interest rate, a lower Canadian interest rate, and a rise in the expected rate of depreciation of the $C would restore the interest rate parity relation. That is, the interest rate in Canada would equal the interest rate in the United States plus the expected rate of depreciation of the $C.

These two propositions may now be used to enable you to understand the basic forces that determine the balance of payments and the exchange rate at full employment.

B. Determination of the Balance of Payments at Full Employment Under a Fixed Exchange Rate

The starting point for an analysis of the balance of payments[1] is the discussion in Section E of Chapter 25 concerning the links between the money supply and the level of foreign exchange reserves. Recall Equation (25.11). This equation states that

$$\mu = \psi f + (1 - \psi)dc \qquad \textbf{(27.1)}$$

The rate of change of foreign exchange reserves, f, is the balance of payments (expressed as a proportion of the existing stock of reserves). The factors that determine f are, therefore, exactly the same as the factors that determine the balance of payments. It is tempting to rearrange the above equation so that the variable in which we are interested, f, appears on the left-hand side. If you divide the Equation

---

[1] The origins of this theory, a theory that has not changed much in more than two hundred years, is David Hume, "Of the Balance of Trade," *Essays: Moral, Political and Literary* (London; Oxford University Press, 1963) pp. 316-33; first published in 1741. An excellent modern restatement of Hume's theory, in slightly more general terms than that given in this chapter, is Harry G. Johnson, *Further Essays in Monetary Economics* (London: George Allen and Unwin Ltd., 1972), pp. 229-49.

(27.1) by ψ and then subtract $[(1 - \psi)/\psi]dc$ from both sides of the equation, you obtain

$$f = \frac{1}{\psi}\mu - \left(\frac{1-\psi}{\psi}\right)dc \qquad \textbf{(27.2)}$$

This equation says that the percentage change in the stock of foreign exchange reserves — the balance of payments expressed in percentage terms — depends on the rate of growth of the money supply and the rate of growth of domestic credit. If it is possible to work out what determines these two factors, then we shall have a theory that explains the balance of payments.

(i) Domestic Credit Expansion

Let us deal first with domestic credit expansion, *dc*. In an open economy with a fixed exchange rate, domestic credit growth is the variable that the monetary authorities can control by their monetary policy actions. If the Bank of Canada wants to see the growth of domestic credit increased, then all it has to do is buy bonds from individuals, thereby increasing its own stock of domestic securities. This also makes more reserves available to the chartered banks and encourages them to acquire more domestic securities. Conversely, if the Bank of Canada wants to reduce the amount of domestic credit, it can do so by selling government securities, thereby reducing its own holdings of those items. This will also encourage the chartered banks to sell securities since the availability of reserves to these banks will have been lowered.

Thus, *the Bank of Canada controls the growth rate of domestic credit.* This is an exogenous variable. Under fixed exchange rates, however, the Bank of Canada cannot control the money supply. The very act of pegging the foreign exchange rate means that the Bank of Canada must always be willing to buy and sell foreign exchange. That is, the Bank of Canada must always be willing to raise or lower its own stock of foreign exchange in order to preserve the fixed value of its currency in terms of foreign currencies. Thus, although the Bank of Canada can decide how many domestic assets to buy and hold, it has no control over the gold and foreign exchange reserves that it holds. It follows, therefore, that it cannot control the money supply since the money supply is the sum of domestic credit (which the Bank of Canada can control) and foreign exchange reserves (which it cannot control).

Now note that Equation (27.2) above tells us that the balance of payments depends *both* on the growth rate of the money supply and the growth rate of domestic credit. Although the growth rate of domestic credit may be treated as being under the control of the Bank of Canada, the money supply growth rate may not be regarded as being controlled by the Bank of Canada, so it is necessary to enquire what does determine its value.

(ii) Growth Rate of Money Supply

When the Bank of Canada is pegging the foreign exchange rate and is, as a result, unable to determine the supply of money, the quantity of money in existence will be determined by the amount of money demanded. We have already discovered, in Chapter 11, what determines the demand for money — it depends on the price level, the level of real income and the rate of interest. The demand for money will change, therefore, as the price level changes, as real income changes and as the interest rate changes. In a steady state, when the rate of interest is constant, the growth rate of the money supply is equal to the rate of inflation plus the rate of growth of output. That is,

$$\mu = \pi + \rho \tag{27.3}$$

Now recall that the rate of output growth depends on such things as demographic trends, capital accumulation and technical progress, all of which are being treated as exogenous to, and independent of, the processes that are being analyzed here (these were analyzed in Chapter 22). The rate of output growth, then, may be taken as given. This still leaves two variables — the rate of inflation and the rate of money supply growth — which have to be determined.

The theory of inflation developed in Chapter 20 (which dealt only with a closed economy) used Equation (27.3) to determine the steady-state rate of inflation. In the closed economy, the Bank of Canada can control the growth rate of the money supply (μ) and with a given output growth rate Equation (27.3) determines the steady-state rate of inflation. In a fixed exchange rate open economy, however, it is not possible for the Bank of Canada to decide what the money supply growth rate will be since it has no control over one of the components of the money supply, namely, the stock of the foreign exchange reserves. Equation (27.3), therefore, cannot be regarded as determining the rate of inflation. Rather, given the inflation rate and the growth rate of output, and given a fixed exchange rate this equation determines the growth rate of the money supply. Thus, the growth rate of the money supply is determined by the growth rate of the demand for money.

If the growth rate of the money supply is determined by the growth in the demand for money, what determines the rate of inflation in a fixed exchange rate economy? The answer is the law of one price.

(iii) The Law of One Price

The next step in the story is to recall the law of one price and its implication — the purchasing power parity proposition. You will recall that the law of one price says that the rate of change of prices in one country (where the prices are expressed in the currency of that country) will be equal to the rate of change of prices in another country (expressed in units of currency of that other country) plus the rate of depreciation of the first country's currency against that of the second country. In other words, calling the rate of inflation in the rest of the world π_f and the rate of depreciation of the currency, $\Delta\varepsilon$, we have

$$\pi = \pi_f + \Delta\varepsilon \qquad (27.4)$$

This equation may be better understood with an example. Suppose that inflation in the rest of the world was running at 10 percent per annum and that the domestic currency was appreciating at 2 percent per annum. This would imply that the rate of inflation in the domestic economy would be 8 percent per annum. Thus, there is a relationship between inflation rates in different countries and exchange rates arising from arbitrage operations in the markets for goods and services.

Now, recall that the analysis being conducted refers to an economy with a fixed exchange rate. If the exchange rate is fixed, then the rate of change of the exchange rate will be zero. From this it follows that in a fixed exchange rate economy, the domestic rate of inflation, π, will equal the inflation rate in the rest of the world, π_f. That is,

$$\pi = \pi_f \qquad (27.5)$$

This is a fundamental proposition concerning the behavior of the rate of inflation in an open economy operating under a fixed exchange rate. It does not hold exactly because there are other real disturbances going on that change *relative* prices in the world. How useful an approximation to reality it is, we shall see later in this chapter.

You can think of the rate of inflation in the rest of the world as being independent of the behavior of the domestic economy that is being analyzed. You may think of the world inflation rate as being determined by world aggregate money supply growth in exactly the same way as it was in Chapter 20. It is as if the whole world has one money, since all monies can be converted into any money at a known fixed exchange rate. The relevant money supply, therefore, is not the national money supply, but the sum of all the national money supplies (converted into a common unit). Its growth rate is the growth rate that determines the world inflation rate.

With domestic inflation being determined by world inflation, it is now clear that in a fixed exchange rate economy, the fundamental inflation equation becomes an equation that tells us about the rate of growth of the money supply rather than about the rate of inflation itself. That is, the equation

$$\mu = \pi_f + \rho \qquad (27.6)$$

determines μ. The rate of inflation π_f is determined in the rest of the world, and the rate of output growth ρ is determined by long-run forces that are exogenous. What this says is that in a fixed exchange rate open economy, the rate of growth of the money supply will be equal to the rate of growth of the demand for money. More money is demanded if prices become higher, and more money is demanded if output increases. The growth in the demand for money is equal to $\pi_f + \rho$. Money is supplied to meet this demand automatically as a result of the central bank's intervening in the foreign exchange market to maintain the fixed value of the exchange rate. If, when there was a rise in the demand for money, the central bank did not supply the extra money needed, the currency would tend to rise in value. To prevent this from happening, the central bank would have to take in additional foreign exchange reserves and supply additional domestic money in exchange for the foreign money taken into its reserves.

(iv) The Balance of Payments

It is now possible to see what determines the balance of payments at full employment. The balance of payments (expressed as a proportion of the stock of reserves) is equal to

$$f = \frac{1}{\psi}\mu - \left(\frac{1 - \psi}{\psi}\right)dc$$

Also, the money supply growth rate is given in Equation (27.6):

$$\mu = \pi_f + \rho$$

By combining these two propositions, we have

$$f = \frac{1}{\psi}\pi_f + \frac{1}{\psi}\rho - \left(\frac{1 - \psi}{\psi}\right)dc \qquad \textbf{(27.7)}$$

This equation is a fundamental proposition concerning the determination of the balance of payments at full employment under fixed exchange rates. It says that if a country at full employment has a fixed exchange rate, it may have either a balance of payments surplus or a deficit or an equilibrium, and that it is a simple matter to achieve whichever of these outcomes is desired.

The one policy variable that determines the overall balance of payments at full employment is the rate of growth of domestic credit. By selling government securities from its portfolio and tightening reserves which also encourages chartered banks to sell securities from their portfolios, the central bank can achieve a surplus on the balance of payments. By doing the contrary, that is, buying domestic securities from the general public and giving the chartered banks enough reserves to increase their holdings of domestic securities, the central bank can generate a deficit on the balance of payments.

The balance of payments is fundamentally a monetary phenomenon caused by the monetary policies of the central bank. As a first approximation, the balance of payments is independent of the trade flows and capital flows that underlie it.

(v) Aggregate Demand and Supply

Since the money supply is endogenous and not subject to control, you may be wondering what has become of our theory of aggregate supply and aggregate demand in an open economy at full employment with a fixed exchange rate. Figure 27.1 illustrates what is going on. This is a standard aggregate supply, aggregate demand diagram. If the rate of growth of output is zero, then y^*, full-employment output, is constant. Also, if the level of foreign prices is held constant, the inflation rate will be zero. Suppose the foreign price level is P_f, so that the domestic price level implied by that foreign price level is P_f converted into domestic currency at the exchange rate E. This is marked as EP_f on the vertical axis. The aggregate supply curve is shown as AS. These two curves intersect at the point A. This is the equilibrium point for the economy.

You may now ask the question, what if the aggregate demand curve does not pass through the point A? The answer is that the aggregate demand curve cannot avoid passing through the point A because the money supply, which determines the position of the aggregate demand curve, is determined by the demand for money. The demand for money at point A is an amount such that the aggregate demand curve evaluated for a money supply equal to this amount passes exactly through A.

Figure 27.1
Output, the Price
Level and Aggregate
Demand in a Fixed
Exchange Rate
Open Economy

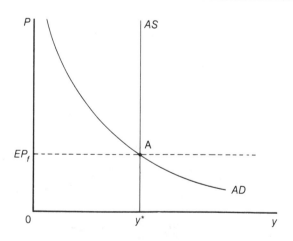

The aggregate supply curve *AS* determines full-employment output, *y**. The foreign price level *P_f*, when converted to domestic prices at the exchange rate *E*, determines the domestic price level as *EP_f*. Position A denotes the equilibrium. Aggregate demand *AD* will automatically pass through this point because the supply of money that influences the position of the aggregate demand curve is determined by the demand for money and, therefore, by the price level and real income level at the point A (rather than being determined exogenously as in the case of the closed economy).

If you conduct a thought experiment, you can see that the economy can only be at point A. Such a thought experiment was conducted in 1741 by David Hume and is still relevant today.

> Suppose four-fifths of all the money in Great Britain is to be anni-hilated in one night, and the nation reduced to the same condition, with regard to specie [money supply] as in the reigns of the Harrys and Edwards, what would be the consequence? Must not the price of all labour and commodities sink in proportion, and every thing be sold as cheap as they were in those ages? What nation could then dispute with us in any foreign market, or pretend to navigate or to sell manufactures at the same price, which to us would afford sufficient profit? In how little time, therefore, must this bring back the money which we had lost, and raise us to the level of all the neighbouring nations? Where, after we have arrived, we immediately lose the advantage of the cheap-ness of labour and commodities and the farther flowing in of money is stopped by our fulness and repletion.
>
> Again, suppose that all the money of Great Britain were multiplied fivefold in a night, must not the contrary effect follow? Must not all labour and commodities rise to such an exorbitant height, that no neighbouring nations could afford to buy from us — while their com-modities, on the other hand, became comparatively so cheap, that, in spite of all the laws which could be formed, they would be run in upon us, and our money flow out — till we fall to a level with foreigners, and lose that great superiority of riches, which had laid us under such disadvantages?
>
> Now it is evident, that the same causes, which would correct these exorbitant inequalities, were they to happen miraculously must prevent their happening in the common course of nature, and must for ever, in all neighbouring nations, preserve money nearly proportionable to the art and industry of each nation. All water, wherever it communicates, remains always at a level. Ask naturalists the reason: they tell you, that, were it to be raised in any one place, the superior gravity of that part not being balanced, must depress it, till it meet a counterpoise; and that the same cause, which redresses the inequality when it hap-pens, must for ever prevent, without some violent external operation.[2]

This completes the basic theory of the balance of payments in a fixed exchange rate economy. Let us now go on to see how, with a flexible exchange rate regime, the exchange rate itself is determined.

C. Determination of the Exchange Rate at Full Employment Under a Flexible Exchange Rate Regime

(i) Fundamental Inflation Equation Again

The starting point in understanding what determines the exchange rate at full employment is to recall the factors that determine trend movements in inflation. You will recall from Chapter 20 that provided the rate of money supply growth is steady, the rate of inflation will

---

[2] David Hume, "Of the Balance of Trade," pp. 318-19.

settle down at a rate equal to the difference between the growth rate of the money supply and the growth rate of full-employment output. That is, the fundamental inflation equation is

$$\pi = \mu + \rho \tag{27.8}$$

Recall why this relationship holds. If the rate of money supply growth (less the growth rate of output) is higher than the rate of inflation, then real money balances will be increasing faster than the demand for money is increasing, and the aggregate demand for goods curve will shift outwards, thereby raising the rate at which prices rise. If the rate of money supply growth (less the growth rate of output) is slower than the rate of inflation, then real money balances will be declining faster than the demand for real money balances is declining. As people attempt to restore their money balances to the desired level, the level of demand for goods will be cut, and this in turn will slow the rate at which prices rise. These forces will always operate when the rate of inflation is different from the money supply growth rate less the growth rate of output.

(ii) What is True for One Country is True for Another

The fundamental inflation equation used above, Equation (27.8)

$$\pi = \mu - \rho$$

is not a proposition that is true for only one country. It is true for all countries. Consider some other country, called f for foreign. The fundamental inflation equation must also be true for the foreign country. That is,

$$\pi_f = \mu_f - \rho_f \tag{27.9}$$

This simply says that in the foreign country the rate of inflation will be equal to its rate of money supply growth minus its rate of full-employment output growth.

(iii) Purchasing Power Parity Again

Next recall the important proposition that arbitrage in goods generates purchasing power parity. You will recall that although tariffs, transport costs, and other impediments to trade may drive a wedge between the level of prices in one country and the level in another, arbitrage will ensure that for given levels of trade distortions, the rate of change of prices in one country will be brought to equality with the rate of change of prices in the other when adjusted for any change in the exchange rate. This was stated in Equation (27.4) as:

$$\pi = \pi_f + \Delta\varepsilon \tag{27.4}$$

This says that the rate of inflation in the domestic economy (π) will be equal to the rate of inflation in the foreign economy (π_f), plus the rate at which the currency of the domestic economy is depreciating against the currency of the foreign economy ($\Delta\varepsilon$).

(iv) Movements in the Exchange Rate

The above propositions may now be brought together to work out what determines the foreign exchange rate at full employment. Combining the domestic forces which make for domestic inflation with the international arbitrage forces that ensure that purchasing power parity is, on the average, maintained produces a theory of the trend movements in the exchange rate. To see this, first of all notice that the purchasing power parity relationship, Equation (27.4) may be rewritten using the two fundamental inflation Equations (27.8) and (27.9). Since the domestic inflation rate π is equal to the domestic money supply growth rate (μ) minus the rate of output growth (ρ), the left-hand side of the purchasing power parity Equation (27.4) — π — may be replaced with $\mu - \rho$. The same is true of π_f. Notice that π_f is equal to the rate at which the money supply is growing in the foreign country (μ_f) minus the rate of output growth in that country (ρ_f). Let us, therefore, replace π_f on the right-hand side of Equation (27.4) by $\mu_f - \rho_f$. Making both of these substitutions results in:

$$\mu - \rho = \mu_f - \rho_f + \Delta\varepsilon \qquad \textbf{(27.10)}$$

This is nothing other than the purchasing power parity proposition [Equation (27.4)] combined with the fundamental inflation equation for each country [Equations (27.8) and (27.9)]. This equation may now be rearranged so that it provides an explicit statement as to what is happening to the exchange rate ($\Delta\varepsilon$). That is,

$$\Delta\varepsilon = (\mu - \mu_f) - (\rho - \rho_f) \qquad \textbf{(27.11)}$$

This is the *fundamental exchange rate equation*. It says that

	The rate of change of the foreign exchange rate between the currencies of two countries
equals	The difference between the money supply growth rates in the two countries
minus	The difference between the output growth rates in the two countries

This equation also says that:
(1) The faster is the money supply growth rate in the domestic economy, the faster will the domestic currency depreciate against the foreign currency (the bigger will be ($\Delta\varepsilon$).
(2) The faster is the money supply growth rate in the foreign country, the faster will the domestic currency appreciate in terms of the foreign currency.
(3) The faster is the growth rate of output in the domestic economy, the stronger will be the domestic currency relative to the foreign currency ($\Delta\varepsilon$ will be smaller).
(4) The faster is the rate of growth of output in the foreign economy, the weaker will be the domestic currency relative to the foreign currency.

(v) Supply and Demand Yet Again

The factors which determine the exchange rate in the above analysis are nothing other than the forces of supply and demand. The exchange rate is a price like any other price. It is the relative price of two national monies. The exchange rate is determined by the supply of and the demand for domestic money relative to the supply of and demand for foreign money. (Remember that money is a stock, not a flow.)

Look again at the fundamental exchange rate equation — Equation (27.11). The first part of this equation tells us about the growth rate of the relative supplies of two monies ($\mu - \mu_f$). If $\mu - \mu_f$ is positive, the domestic money supply is growing at a faster rate than the foreign money supply, then the domestic money supply is rising relative to the foreign money supply. The second part of the equation, ($\rho - \rho_f$), tells us about the growth rate in the relative demands for the two monies. If the growth rate in output is greater in the domestic economy than that in the foreign economy, then the demand for domestic money will grow at a faster rate than the demand for foreign money.

Now, if the growth in the relative supplies of money ($\mu - \mu_f$) is just equal to the growth in the relative demands for money ($\rho - \rho_f$), the exchange rate will not change, i.e., $\Delta\varepsilon$ will be zero. This means that there is a critical growth rate for the domestic money supply (let us call it μ^c) at which the exchange rate will be steady. To find the growth rate μ^c, simply solve the fundamental exchange rate equation — Equation (27.11) — for the μ that is associated with $\Delta\varepsilon = 0$, i.e.,

$$\Delta\varepsilon = (\mu - \mu_f) - (\rho - \rho_f) = 0 \qquad \textbf{(27.12)}$$

so,

$$\mu^c = \mu_f + (\rho + \rho_f) \qquad \textbf{(27.13)}$$

If the money supply grows at a rate faster than μ^c, the currency will depreciate ($\Delta\varepsilon$ will be positive), and if the money supply grows at a rate slower than μ^c, the currency will appreciate ($\Delta\varepsilon$ will be negative).

Therefore, the key thing that a country can control to influence its exchange rate is its money supply growth rate. Other things being equal, the faster the money supply grows, the faster will the currency depreciate (or the slower will it appreciate). The exchange rate will only be steady if the money supply grows at the critical rate that equals the foreign money supply growth rate plus the difference between the domestic and foreign output growth rates.

(vi) Does a Depreciating Currency Cause Inflation?

There is a popular view which says that inflation is caused by a depreciating currency and that a country can be trapped in a vicious circle of inflation and depreciation about which nothing can be done.

You now know enough to know that this is not true. A depreciating currency is a symptom of inflation and is caused by the same thing that causes inflation. You know from the fundamental inflation equation that, other things being equal, inflation is higher the higher the money supply growth rate. You also know from the fundamental exchange rate equation that the currency depreciates faster ($\Delta\varepsilon$ is positive and increasing) the bigger the growth rate of money supply (μ). Thus both inflation and a depreciating currency are caused by too high a growth rate of the money supply.

If a country wants to maintain a steady exchange rate, it is necessary for the country to achieve a money supply growth rate relative to the growth rate of the money supply in the rest of the world that exactly offsets the difference in the growth in demands for domestic and foreign money arising from any differences in output growth rates. This being the case, with a steady exchange rate, the country must accept the inflation rate that is generated in the rest of the world. If, on the other hand, a country wants to achieve a zero rate of inflation, it becomes necessary for the country to make its own money supply grow at the same rate as its own output growth. That is, set μ equal to ρ. This will not ensure a constant value for the exchange rate, however, since the exchange rate will depend on both domestic monetary policy and the monetary policy of the rest of the world. If the rest of the world is inflating, whereas the domestic economy is maintaining stable prices, then the domestic currency will appreciate ($\Delta\varepsilon$ will be negative). If, however, the foreign economy is deflating — that is, has falling prices — while the domestic economy is maintaining steady prices, then the domestic currency will depreciate ($\Delta\varepsilon$ will be positive).

(vii) Stable Exchange Rates vs. Stable Prices

The above remarks serve to emphasize that a country cannot choose both its inflation rate and the behavior of its exchange rate simultaneously. A country must make a choice as to whether it wants to achieve stable prices, thereby allowing its exchange rate to adjust from time to time to reflect the difference between domestic and foreign inflation; or whether it wants to achieve a fixed exchange rate with the rest of the world, in which case it will have to allow the foreign inflation rate to be fully reflected in the domestic inflation rate.

You now have an understanding of the factors that determine the long-term movements in exchange rates. You see that there are no effects on the exchange rate in the long run arising from such things as import and export demands and the flow of goods and services across national boundaries. In the long run, the exchange rate is determined by monetary equilibrium. With a fixed exchange rate, the country abdicates control over its money supply. The automatic changes in the stock of foreign exchange reserves ensure that the growth rate of the money supply is exactly equal to the growth rate of the demand for money, the latter being equal to the world rate of inflation plus the domestic output growth rate. In the case of a flexible exchange rate, the domestic monetary authority controls the stock of foreign exchange reserves and the domestic money supply, thereby forcing the adjustment onto the exchange rate itself. It is movements in the exchange rate that ensure that the stock of money that has been determined by the Bank of Canada is willingly held by private economic agents.

D. Determination of the Balance of Payments and the Exchange Rate at Full Employment in a Managed Floating Regime

The theory of the determination of the exchange rate under a floating exchange rate regime and of the balance of payments under a fixed exchange rate regime at full employment may be combined in a fairly natural way to determine the fundamental constraints on the actions of a central bank seeking to pursue a managed floating exchange rate policy. To see these constraints, we simply need to combine three bits of information that have already been examined in the previous sections of this chapter. The first is the relationship between the growth of the money supply, the growth of foreign exchange reserves, and the growth of domestic credit. This is Equation (27.1) which says that

$$\mu = \psi f + (1 - \psi)dc \qquad \textbf{(27.1)}$$

The second ingredient is the steady-state relation between the money supply growth, inflation and output growth, Equation (27.3), which says that

$$\mu = \pi + \rho \qquad \textbf{(27.3)}$$

The final ingredient is the purchasing-power parity proposition, Equation (27.4), which says that

$$\pi = \pi_f + \Delta\varepsilon \qquad \textbf{(27.4)}$$

Combining these three propositions — substituting for the inflation rate in Equation (27.3) by using Equation (27.4) and then substituting this for the money supply growth rate in Equation (27.1) — gives

$$\pi_f + \Delta\varepsilon + \rho = \psi f + (1 - \psi)dc$$

If you subtract the foreign inflation rate from both sides of this equation, and also subtract ρ and ψf from both sides, you obtain

$$\Delta\varepsilon - \psi f = (1 - \psi)dc - (\pi_f + \rho) \qquad \textbf{(27.14)}$$

The left-hand side of this equation contains the rate of change of the exchange rate ($\Delta\varepsilon$) minus the rate of change of foreign exchange reserves (weighted by the fraction of the money stock backed by those reserves, ψ) that is ψf. Let us give a name to the left-hand side of Equation (27.14): *exchange market pressure*.[3] The right-hand side is simply the growth rate of domestic credit (weighted by the fraction of the money supply backed by domestic credit, $1 - \psi$) minus the foreign rate of inflation (π_f) and minus output growth (ρ).

All Equation (27.14) says is that for a given foreign rate of inflation, a given π_f, the greater the rate of domestic credit expansion and the lower the output growth, the stronger will be the exchange market pressure. Exchange market pressure will have to be reflected in either the exchange rate or the stock of reserves. Either the exchange rate will have to rise (the currency will have to depreciate) or reserves will have to fall (the balance of payments will be in deficit). Some combination of these two things cannot be avoided. If the central bank wants to manage the exchange rate and keep the exchange rate from falling, then it will have no alternative but to accept a balance of payments deficit with the resultant drop in its foreign exchange reserves.

The converse of all this is that the lower the domestic credit growth and the higher the output growth relative to the foreign rate of inflation, the less will be the exchange market pressure. This would imply that the lower the growth rate of domestic credit, the more the foreign exchange reserves would rise and/or the stronger would be the rate of appreciation of the currency ($\Delta\varepsilon$ negative). In other words, a central bank wishing to pursue tight domestic credit policies (low dc) but at the same time to prevent the currency from appreciating (prevent a high negative value of $\Delta\varepsilon$) would have to be willing to allow the foreign exchange reserves to rise (a surplus on the balance of payments). Equation (27.14) states the fundamental constraint on the freedom of the central bank to pursue a managed floating policy.

A fixed exchange rate is the special case of Equation (27.14) where the central bank manages the value of $\Delta\varepsilon$ equal to zero, permitting all of the exchange market pressures to come out in the stock of foreign exchange reserves — in the balance of payments.

A flexible exchange rate regime is the other opposite extreme, where f is set equal to zero (foreign exchange reserves are constant or the balance of payments is zero), and all exchange market pressures are felt by the exchange rate itself.

---

[3]The term was first suggested by Lance Girton and Don Roper in "A Monetary Model of Exchange Market Pressure Applied to the Postwar Canadian Experience," *The American Economic Review*, 67 (December 1977), 537-48.

A managed float is simply a linear combination of these two extremes determined by the political and other pressures that operate on the conduct of monetary policy.

We have now completed our analysis of the effects of anticipated shifts of aggregate demand in the open economy. We have studied how the price level, the exchange rate, and the balance of payments are determined at full employment in the event of various anticipated shocks. It is now time to broaden our view and consider how the open economy reacts to unanticipated disturbances originating both in the domestic economy and in the rest of the world. This is the subject of the next chapter.

Summary

A. The "Law of One Price"

The law of one price asserts that arbitrage will reduce price differentials to the minimum consistent with transport costs, tariffs, and other physical barriers and impediments to trade.

The purchasing power parity theorem states that the price of a particular good in one country will be the same as the price in another country (when the prices are converted at the current exchange rate). This proposition does not strictly apply to price levels, since tariffs and transportation costs drive a wedge between price levels. However, it does apply to price *changes* expressed in percentage terms. That is, the percentage change in the price of some commodity in Canada will be equal to the percentage change of the price of the same commodity in the United States (say) plus the percentage rate of depreciation of the Canadian dollar in terms of the U.S. dollars.

The interest rate parity theorem is an application of the law of one price to asset markets. It states that the rate of interest in Canada will be equal to the rate of interest in the United States plus the expected rate of depreciation of the Canadian dollar.

B. Determination of the Balance of Payments at Full Employment Under a Fixed Exchange Rate

In an economy at full employment with a fixed exchange rate, the balance of payments (as a first approximation) is determined by the domestic credit policies of the central bank. If the central bank creates too much domestic credit, there will be a balance of payments deficit. If the central bank creates too little domestic credit, there will be a balance of payments surplus. The central bank can always achieve a zero balance by permitting exactly the right amount of domestic credit to be created.

C. Determination of the Exchange Rate at Full Employment Under a Flexible Exchange Rate Regime

When the exchange rate is flexible and the economy is at full employment, the money supply and its growth rate are controllable by the central bank. Inflation is determined in such a case in exactly the same way as it is in the closed economy, by the growth rate of the money supply. The exchange rate is determined by differences in money supply growth rates and output growth rates between countries. Specifically, the exchange rate, being a price like any other price, is determined by supply and demand. Since the exchange rate is the relative price between two national monies, it is determined by the relative supplies (stocks) of the two monies and the relative demands for them. There is a sense in which the exchange rate is unlike any other price in that its value depends directly on the relative monetary policies of the two countries.

D. Determination of the Balance of Payments and the Exchange Rate at Full Employment in a Managed Floating Regime

For a given foreign rate of inflation, the faster the growth rate of domestic credit, the greater will be the amount of exchange market pressure. Exchange market pressure must come out either in a depreciation of the currency or a loss of foreign exchange reserves (a balance of payments deficit). The central bank can select a policy that favors smoothing exchange rate adjustments by permitting reserves to take the strain, or may select a policy which favors a steady stock of foreign reserves by permitting the foreign exchange rate to take the strain. The central bank cannot choose both the exchange rate and the stock of foreign exchange reserves.

Review Questions

1. What would be the price of jelly beans in Canada if the U.S. price was $U.S.5 per kilogram and if there were no tariffs or taxes on jelly beans, and if the Canadian dollar was worth 81¢ U.S.? Suppose, one year later, that jelly beans cost $U.S.5.50 per kilogram and the Canadian dollar was worth 85¢ U.S. What is the percentage change in the Canadian price? What is the percentage change in the U.S. price? What is the percentage change in the exchange rate? How do these variables relate to each other?

2. You have $10 000 to invest for one year. If you buy a U.S. government bond, it will give you a sure return after one year of 10 percent.

If you convert your $10 000 into U.S. dollars, you will do so at an exchange rate of 83¢ U.S. per $C. You can buy a Canadian government bond that will give a sure return after one year of 13 per cent.

   (a) What would the exchange rate between U.S. and Canadian dollars have to be one year hence for it to be just worth buying the U.S. bond?

   (b) If you firmly expected the U.S. dollar to be cheaper than your answer to (a), what would you do?

   (c) If people generally shared your expectation, what would happen?

3. Work out the effects on the balance of payments when the exchange rate is fixed and the economy is at full employment, of the following:

   (a) a rise in the price level

   (b) a rise in interest rates

   (c) a rise in real income

   (d) a rise in domestic credit

   (e) a collapse of Canadian wheat production due to drought.

4. Work out the effects on the exchange rate, in an economy at full employment with a flexible exchange rate, of the shocks listed in Question 3 above.

5. Why can't a country pursue any balance of payments *and* exchange rate objectives it chooses? Draw parallels between a country's exchange rate policy and the price and output policies of a monopolist.

28

Fluctuations
in the
Open Economy

This chapter analyzes the effects of unanticipated domestic and foreign disturbances. It takes you through three tasks, which are to:

a) Understand how aggregate demand "surprises" affect output, the price level and the balance of payments with a fixed exchange rate regime.

b) Understand how aggregate demand "surprises" affect output, the price level and the exchange rate in a flexible exchange rate regime.

c) Understand the effects of an unanticipated real exchange rate shock on output, the price level and the exchange rate in a flexible exchange rate regime.

A. Aggregate Demand Shocks with a Fixed Exchange Rate

The theory of aggregate demand under fixed exchange rates was generated in Chapter 26 and is summarized in Figure 26.8. This aggregate demand curve may be used in an analogous way to the closed economy aggregate demand analysis to determine the rational expectation of the price level and, therefore, the position of the expectations-augmented aggregate supply curve. Figure 28.1 will illustrate the analysis. In this figure, the aggregate supply curve is shown as AS at the output level y^*. The aggregate demand curve drawn for the expected values of the variables that determine its position, $AD^e(P_f^e, y_f^e, r_f^e, E^e, g^e, t^e)$, is the aggregate demand curve that is expected on the basis of expectations of the exogenous variables that influence aggregate demand and given that the economy is operating under fixed exchange rates. The rational expectation of price level P^e is determined where this expected aggregate demand curve intersects the *AS* curve. The expectations-augmented aggregate supply curve passes through that point and is the upward-sloping curve *EAS*. The *EAS* curve for the open economy is identical to that for the closed economy. You may think of this *EAS* curve as having been generated by the new classical theory of aggregate supply (Chapter 15) or the new Keynesian theory (Chapter 16).

If the actual aggregate demand curve is in exactly the same position as the expected aggregate demand curve, then output and prices will be determined at their full-employment and expected levels respectively. The balance of payments is in equilibrium, with perfect capital mobility ensuring a capital account surplus that exactly matches whatever the current account deficit is (or capital account deficit matching the current account surplus).

If, however, the actual values of the variables that determine aggregate demand turn out to be different from their expected values, so that the actual aggregate demand curve is in a different position, say, at $AD(P_f, y_f, r_f, E, g, t)$, then actual output and prices will be determined where this actual demand curve cuts the expectations-augmented aggregate supply curve at (y_1, P_1). This is exactly the same as

**Figure 28.1
Equilibrium
with Fixed
Exchange Rates**

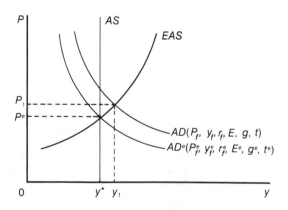

With fixed exchange rates, the expected price level is determined where the expected aggregate demand curve cuts the aggregate supply curve. This position depends on the expected values of foreign prices, foreign real income and foreign interest rates, and on the exchange rate and domestic fiscal policy variables. Actual output and prices are determined where the actual aggregate demand curve cuts the expectations-augmented aggregate supply curve. An anticipated change in any of the variables that determine aggregate demand will have price level effects only, and an unanticipated change in any of these variables will affect both output and the price level.

in the closed economy except that the factors that shift the aggregate demand curve in this case are different from those responsible for shifts in the closed economy aggregate demand curve. Random fluctuations in actual demand around its expected value will generate procyclical price and output co-movements.

The balance of payments is in equilibrium at the higher price and output levels, but the mix between the current account and capital account is different from the full-employment mix. With a fixed exchange rate and fixed world price level, the higher domestic price level means that the real exchange rate is lower, so that imports rise and exports fall. The higher real income level also raises imports. Thus, the current account of the balance of payments moves into a smaller surplus or larger deficit. This change in the current account is matched by an equal, but opposite, change in the capital account.

This is all there is to the determination of output, prices, and the balance of payments in a fixed exchange rate economy with perfect capital mobility. As in the closed economy case, anticipated changes in aggregate demand have price level effects only, and unanticipated changes have the effects traced out in Figure 28.1. Changes that are partly anticipated and partly not anticipated have effects that combine those shown in Figure 28.1 with the pure price level adjustment that occurs in the anticipated case. Notice that the domestic economy is not immune from shocks occurring in the rest of the world. Other things being equal, an anticipated change in the foreign price level or an anticipated devaluation of the currency raises the domestic price level by the same percentage amount. Fluctuations in world output, prices, and interest rates lead to fluctuations in domestic aggregate demand, and if they are not anticipated, lead to fluctuations in output in the domestic economy that are procyclical with fluctuations in the world economy.

Let us now go on to consider the more difficult, but perhaps more interesting, case of flexible exchange rates.

B. Aggregate Demand Shocks with a Flexible Exchange Rate

We shall proceed in a similar way in analyzing the flexible exchange rate economy as we did with the fixed exchange rate. The first task is to determine the rational expectation of the price level and, therefore, the position of the expectations-augmented aggregate supply curve. This is not as straightforward in the case of a flexible exchange rate as it was in the case of a fixed exchange rate. The reason for this is that the exchange rate contains information that it will be rational for people to use in forming their expectation of the price level. There is a fundamental informational difference between a fixed exchange rate and flexible exchange rate economy. Under fixed exchange rates, it is the stock of foreign exchange reserves that adjusts on a daily basis to random shocks that hit the economy. These movements in the stock of foreign exchange reserves are not continuously reported and are unknown outside the central bank. In a flexible exchange rate economy, the exchange rate itself is constantly adjusting to reflect the random forces that influence the economy and is available for all to see at almost zero cost. There is, therefore, more widespread information available in a flexible exchange rate economy than in a fixed exchange rate economy, and this information may be used in order to make inferences about the shocks that are hitting the economy. Making complete sense of this will take a paragraph or two.

(i) Pretrading Expectations

Let us begin by imagining that we are at the beginning of a trading period before any trading has begun. All the markets — labor, money, goods, and foreign exchange — are not yet open for business. We are standing at the beginning of the business "day" and trying to form expectations about all the variables in the economy. Figure 28.2 will be a useful vehicle for analyzing this situation.

Frame (a) shows the aggregate demand and supply analysis. Frame (b) is exactly the same as frame (c) of Figure 26.9. The top left frame of Figure 28.2 is simply a device for turning the price level through 90° so as to read the same price level on the horizontal axis as we are reading on the vertical axis. Frame (c) is a device for determining the exchange rate. The way to read this is as follows: Recall that the real exchange rate θ, is defined as

$$\theta = EP_f/P$$

Multiply both sides of this equation by P, so that you obtain

$$\theta P = EP_f$$

Now the foreign price level P_f is being treated as fixed, and if we hold the exchange rate constant, EP_f will be constant. This says that, for a given foreign price level, θP (the real exchange rate multiplied by the domestic price level) is equal to a constant, once we have determined the exchange rate.

For a particular exchange rate, we could draw a rectangular hyperbola in frame (c) that shows the relationship between θ and P. Thus, for some particular exchange rate, as shown in frame (c) as E^e, and for a given world price level P_f, if the domestic price level rises, then the real exchange rate θ must fall by an equal percentage amount. That is all that the curve E^e traces out.

In principle, there is a whole family of such curves, all rectangular hyperbolas and all drawn for different values of the exchange rate. We don't need the whole family of those curves for the moment (although we shall need more than one subsequently). Now that you

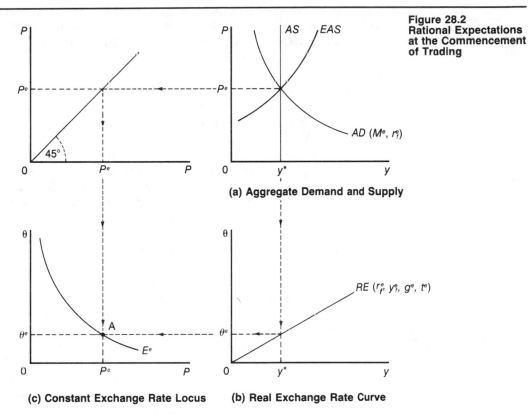

Figure 28.2
Rational Expectations at the Commencement of Trading

(a) Aggregate Demand and Supply

(c) Constant Exchange Rate Locus   **(b) Real Exchange Rate Curve**

Before any information is revealed, the rational expectation of the price level, the (nominal) exchange rate and the real exchange rate can be calculated. Where the expected aggregate demand curve (based on expected money supply and expected foreign interest rates) cuts the AS curve, the expected price level P^e is determined. Expected income is y^*, and this determines the expected real exchange rate θ^e. There will be one (nominal) exchange rate only, E^e, that is compatible with the expected price level and the expected real exchange rate. This is shown at point A in frame (c).

know how to read frame (c), the only slightly tricky part of the figure, let us proceed to use this figure to analyze the determination of the rational expectation of the price level and the exchange rate.

The starting point is in frame (a). The *AS* curve is determined by the classical model of aggregate supply and is located at y^*. The curve $AD(M^e, r_f^e)$ is the expectation of the aggregate demand curve for a flexible exchange rate economy, based on the derivation in Figure 26.9. Its position depends only on the expected money stock and expected world rate of interest. The rational expectation of the price level is determined where this curve cuts the *AS* curve. The rational expectation of output is y^*.

Next, calculate the value of the real exchange rate that is consistent with this value of output. To do this, simply read off from the *RE* curve in frame (b) the value of the real exchange rate consistent with the income level y^*. This value is θ^e. This same value may also be read off from the vertical axis of frame (c). To calculate the rational expectation of the nominal exchange rate, transfer the rational expectation of the price level from frame (a) through the 45° line to the horizontal axis of frame (c). Then join θ^e and P^e to give point A in frame (c). Point A will lie on a rectangular hyperbola, the location of which determines the nominal exchange rate. There will be a unique constant exchange rate locus, labelled E^e, that passes through point A. Any other nominal exchange rate would involve a different combination of the price level and the real exchange rate than what is implied by the rational expectations of these two variables.

Just prior to the commencement of business in this economy, the expectations of output, the price level, and the real and nominal exchange rates are those depicted in Figure 28.2. A higher expected money supply would result in a higher expected price level, no change in the expected real exchange rate, and a higher expected nominal exchange rate (a depreciated currency). You can easily work this out for yourself by considering what happens in this figure if we replace the expected *AD* curve with an equivalent curve located to the right of the existing one. There will be no change in expected output or the expected real exchange rate. There would simply be a rise in the expected price level and a rise in the expected nominal exchange rate that would be proportional to each other.

(ii) Extracting Information from the Exchange Rate

Next, imagine that this economy has just started to do business. No one knows what the money supply is that underlies the actual aggregate demand curve, so no one can do any better, on the basis of information available about the economic aggregates, than continue to expect that the aggregate demand curve is in the position shown in frame (a) of Figure 28.2. There is more information now, however, than there was before trading began. In particular, everyone now knows the actual value of the nominal exchange rate as it is determined on a minute-by-minute basis in the foreign exchange market. In other words, as soon as trading begins, it is known whether or not the exchange rate expectation was correct. If the exchange rate expectation was incorrect, then it will be immediately clear to everyone that the initial expectation of the price level must also have been incorrect.

Let us think through the consequences of this, using Figure 28.3. The starting point is the initial expected values for the price level, the nominal exchange rate, and the real exchange rate, shown as P^e, E^e, and θ^e. Suppose that the actual aggregate demand curve turned out to be not $AD(M^e,r_f^e)$ but $AD(M,r_f)$, as shown in frame (a) of Figure 28.3. According to the theory, the actual levels of output and prices are y_1, P_1, where the actual aggregate demand curve cuts the expectations-augmented aggregate supply curve. Transferring this solution for output down to frame (b) shows the actual real exchange rate as θ_1. Transferring the price solution, P_1, from the vertical axis of frame (a) through the 45° line to the horizontal axis of frame (c) gives the point B in frame (c) as the real exchange rate-price level point. Point B lies on the constant (nominal) exchange rate locus E_1 and so determines the exchange rate at this value.

Now the actual price and income levels, although determined by the analysis, are not known to the people in the economy. They only observe the prices of the small range of goods that they are currently engaged in trading, and do not know the general price level or any of the other aggregates. Everyone, however, knows the nominal exchange rate. It is observed on a continuous basis and is therefore available for all to see. In the situation depicted in Figure 28.3, everyone knows that the exchange rate is E_1 and that it is different from E^e. The economy is not at point A in frame (c), but at point B. No one would know this, however, for no one knows the *real* exchange rate. This is not a directly and instantly observed variable. People do, however, know that the nominal exchange rate is different from what they had expected it to be. That being so, everyone knows that a mistake has been made in forming expectations about aggregate demand. Aggregate demand could not be the curve $AD(M^e,r_f^e)$. If it was, the exchange rate would be E^e, and not E_1, which it has turned out to be. The price level P_1 and the income level y_1 cannot, therefore, be a rational expectations equilibrium.

If the exchange rate is higher than expected, then the aggregate demand curve must also be higher than it was previously expected to be, and the expected price level needs to be revised upwards. By how much does the expected price level need to be revised upwards? To answer this question we need to see how a change in the expected price level affects both the expected exchange rate and the actual exchange rate. Only when the expected price level is such as to generate an expected exchange rate that is the same as the actual exchange rate will the price expectation be rational. That is, only in such a situation will all the information available have been incorporated into price level expectations.

We can examine how the rational expectation of the price level will be formed when information conveyed by the exchange rate is employed if we perform a conceptual experiment. Imagine that the expectation of the price level is increased from P^e to P_1 — in frame (a) of Figure 28.3. (Be clear that this is not a description of the *process* that would go on in the world because P_1 is not observed and could not therefore be used to calculate an expected price level. This is simply an imagined experiment that will help make clear the *amount* by which the expected price level must rise and not the *process* whereby it does so.)

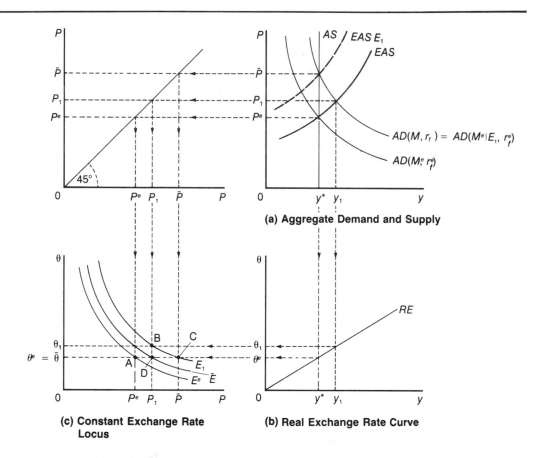

(a) Aggregate Demand and Supply

(c) Constant Exchange Rate Locus

(b) Real Exchange Rate Curve

Figure 28.3
The Information Content of the Exchange Rate Influences the Rational Expectation of the Price Level

Before trading begins, expected aggregate demand is $AD(M^e, r_f^e)$. The expected real exchange rate curve is RE. The expected equilibrium for the economy is a price level of P^e, real income of y^*, real exchange rate of θ^e and nominal exchange rate of E^e. The economy is shocked: aggregate demand turns out to be higher than expected at $AD(M, r_f)$. The real exchange rate curve remains at RE. The expected price level of P^e, generates an actual price level of P_1, an actual real income level of y_1, actual real exchange rate θ_1 and an actual (nominal) exchange rate of E_1. Since the expected exchange rate, E^e, is different from the actual exchange rate E_1, and since only the exchange rate is observed, people know that their expected price level is wrong. The price level expectation will be revised upwards so as to incorporate the new information that the exchange rate is E_1. Only if the expected price level is $\bar{P}$ will the expected exchange rate equal the actual exchange rate (at point C). In this case, the actual price level is also be $\bar{P}$, output y^* and the real exchange rate θ^e. (In this example, the equilibrium and initial exchange rates are the same — E_1. This is a special case and will not in general occur.)

What we need to do is to examine the effects of the higher expected price level on both the actual and expected exchange rate. Consider first its effects on the expected exchange rate. With an expected price level of P_1, the *EAS* curve will shift up (not shown in the figure) to intersect the *AS* curve at P_1. In other words, the expected level of aggregate demand will remain constant at y^*. In turn, the expected real exchange rate will remain constant to θ^e. To see what this implies for the (nominal) exchange rate, all we have to do is to trace through as we have done before to frame (c) of Figure 28.3. Tracing the price level P_1 and the real exchange rate at θ^e into frame (c) shows that they imply a nominal exchange rate equal to $\overline{E}$ (meeting at point D on the constant exchange rate locus $\overline{E}$). Thus, raising the expected price level raises the expected exchange rate. In fact, although not transparent from the figure, there will be a one-to-one correspondence between the change in the expected price level and the change in the expected exchange rate. If the expected price level rises by X percent, the expected exchange rate will rise by the same X percent.

Next consider the effect of a change in the expected price level from P^e to P_1. It is clear that with an expected price level of P_1 but with the actual aggregate demand curve remaining in its position, $AD(M, r_f)$, the actual price level would rise above P_1. Further, output would be above y^*. It would, however, be below y_1. (These values have not been shown in the figure.) With output between y^* and y_1, the real exchange rate would lie between θ^e and θ_1. With the price level above P_1 and the real exchange rate below θ_1, it is evident that the actual value of the nominal exchange rate could rise or fall depending on whether the price level or the *real* exchange rate effect is larger. The rise in the price level would tend to raise the nominal exchange rate, whereas the fall in the real exchange rate would tend to lower it.

Although there is ambiguity as to the direction of movement of the exchange rate, there is no ambiguity about the fact that the actual exchange rate will have moved closer to the expected exchange rate. How do we know this? We know, first, that in the initial experiment, the pretrading expected exchange rate was E^e and the actual exchange E_1. Thus, the actual exchange rate was higher than the pre-trading expected exchange rate. We also know that a rise in the expected price level raises the expected exchange rate by the same percentage amount as the rise in the price level, but it raises the actual exchange rate by less than that and could even result in a fall in the actual exchange rate. Thus, raising the expected price level to P_1 closes the gap between the actual and the expected exchange rate. We can see, however, that the expected price level P_1 cannot be the rational expectation of the price level because it does not generate an actual value of the exchange rate equal to its implied expected value. You can see this by noting that with an expected price level of P_1, the real exchange rate would lie between θ_1 and θ^e. The actual price level would be above P_1 but below $\overline{P}$. (Verify that you indeed agree with the propositions just stated.)

With the real exchange rate between θ_1 and θ^e and the price level between P_1 and $\overline{P}$, it is evident that the actual (nominal) exchange rate locus must lie between E_1 and $\overline{E}$. Thus, the actual exchange rate implied by an expected price level of P_1 is higher than the expected exchange rate implied by this expected price level. It is evident that we could repeat the experiment just conducted with a higher price level (equal to the actual price level generated by the expected price level P_1). If we did perform such an experiment, we would discover that, with one exception, we repeatedly obtained the same type of result that we have just obtained.

There is just one price level, however, that would give a different result and that is $\overline{P}$. The price level $\overline{P}$ occurs where the actual aggregate demand curve cuts the AS curve. Expected aggregate output remains y^* and the expected real exchange rate remains at θ^e. With an expected price level of $\overline{P}$, this implies an expected exchange rate of E_1 — point C in frame (c) representing the expected equilibrium. With an expected price level $\overline{P}$ the expectations-augmented aggregate supply curve shifts up to cut the AS curve at $\overline{P}$. This is the curve labelled $EAS|E_1$. With the actual aggregate demand curve intersecting the expectations-augumented aggregate supply at $\overline{P}$, the actual price level is also determined at $\overline{P}$. Thus, the actual exchange rate is also E_1. Point C becomes not only the expected but also the actual equilibrium position of the economy.

To avoid having to shift the constant exchange rate locus too many times, we have used a special set of assumptions to ensure that the final equilibrium exchange rate and the initial exchange rate implied by the initial expectation and the aggregate demand shock are the same, E_1. There is, in general, no reason why this would be so. Indeed, for it to be so the RE curve must be a straight line and the aggregate demand curve must be a rectangular hyperbola (have an elasticity of minus one).

In the setup in Figure 28.3, we have rigged things such that people are able to work out exactly what the actual aggregate demand curve is from the observation of the exchange rate. This has happened because, purely for the purpose of introducing you to the ideas involved, we have imagined that there is just a single source of random disturbance to the economy, namely, a random disturbance to aggregate demand. That being so, from observing the exchange rate it is possible to infer exactly what this random disturbance is and, as a result, to correct for it by adjusting the expectation of the price level conditioned on the knowledge of the exchange rate. The expectations-augmented aggregate supply curve conditional on the actual exchange rate, $EAS|E_1$, moves to intersect the actual aggregate demand curve, which in turn becomes the expected aggregate demand curve conditional on the exchange rate, $AD(M^e|E_1,r_f^e)$, at full-employment output. If there were additional sources of disturbance so that the aggregate demand shock being analyzed here was just one of several random disturbances affecting the economy, then it would *not* be possible to make a direct inference from the exchange rate as to the position of the aggregate demand curve. Even though people might know they had made a mistake, in the sense that the exchange rate turned out to be different from what they had expected it to be, they would not know for sure the source of that mistake. That being so, they would not be able to correctly identify the actual values of the exogenous variables that are influencing the economy.

This can be seen more clearly if we consider a case in which there are two sources of shocks — shocks to the aggregate demand curve (coming from the money supply or the world rate of interest) and shocks to the *RE* curve (coming from world real income or fiscal policy). We shall consider two experiments. Both of them are highly artificial. Despite their artificiality, however, they are useful experiments for clarifying the concepts and propositions about the behavior of a flexible exchange rate economy.

(iii) An Unexpected Change in Aggregate Demand

The first experiment imagines that the economy has always had a completely predictable level of aggregate demand, so that expected aggregate demand and actual aggregate demand have always been one and the same. This could be put more directly as saying that there have never been any aggregate demand shocks in the economy. This economy has, however, often been subjected to real exchange rate shocks — shocks from world real income or from domestic fiscal policy. In fact, the normal state of affairs is for the real exchange rate curve to be constantly bombarded in a random fashion. Imagine that in a particular period in such an economy, an aggregate demand shock in fact occurs, but no real exchange rate shock occurs. This will be a very unusual circumstance for this hypothetical economy. It will in fact be something that by the hypothetical setup assumed has never happened before. Naturally, the nominal exchange rate will respond to the shock that has occurred. It will be rational in this situation for people to infer that there has been a real exchange rate shock. It will also be rational for them to infer that there has been no aggregate demand shock. They will be wrong, but they will not be irrational. To see what happens in this situation, let us use Figure 28.4.

The setup in Figure 28.4 is comparable to that of Figure 28.3. Before trading began, people formed expectations about aggregate demand and the real exchange rate and, as a result, formed their pre-trading rational expectations of the price level, the real exchange rate, output, and the nominal exchange rate. These are shown in Figure 28.4 in the following way. The curve labelled AD^e in frame (a) is the expected

**Figure 28.4
The Effects of
an Unanticipated
Aggregate Demand
Shock**

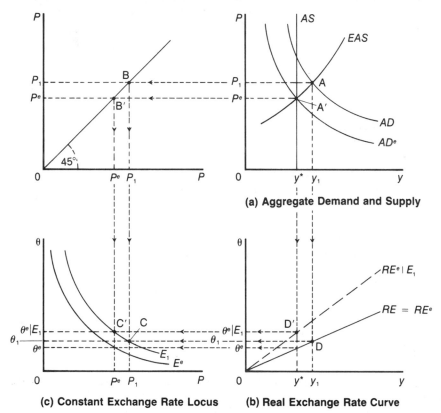

(a) Aggregate Demand and Supply

(c) Constant Exchange Rate Locus   **(b) Real Exchange Rate Curve**

The economy is initially at y^*, P^e, θ^e and E^e on the aggregate demand curve AD^e, the expectations-augmented aggregate supply curve EAS, the real exchange rate curve $RE = RE^e$ and the constant exchange rate locus E^e. There is then a completely unanticipated rise in aggregate demand to AD. This raises the price level to P_1 and raises real income to y_1. It also raises the real exchange rate to θ_1. At the price level P_1 and real exchange rate θ_1 the exchange rate becomes E_1. The higher nominal exchange rate is incorrectly interpreted as a rise in the real exchange rate to $\theta^e|E_1$. The corners of the square ABCD describe the actual situation, and the corners of the square A'B'C'D' describe the situation that agents rationally believe to be occurring. The effect of an unanticipated rise in aggregate demand is to raise prices, output, the real exchange rate and the nominal exchange rate. The higher real exchange rate tells us that the nominal exchange rate rises by more than the price level does.

aggregate demand curve. Where it intersects the AS curve determines the rational expectation of the price level, P^e. The expectations-augmented aggregate supply curve EAS passes through the point A' where the expected aggregate demand curve cuts the aggregate supply curve. The real exchange rate curve, both actual and expected, is labelled $RE = RE^e$ in frame (b). At the expected full-employment output level, the expected real exchange rate is given as θ^e on the vertical axis of frame (b). Transferring the expected price level through the 45° line to frame (c), and transferring the expected real exchange rate also across from frame (b) to frame (c), we arrive at a point in frame (c) that lies on a constant exchange rate locus that determines the expected nominal exchange rate (E^e). This is the pre-trading rational expectation for this economy.

The shock described above is an aggregate demand shock, but one that is completely misperceived. The actual aggregate demand curve that incorporates this shock is shown in frame (a) as the curve AD. Where the actual aggregate demand curve cuts the expectations-augmented aggregate supply curve (point A) determines the actual price level P_1 and output level y_1. At the output level y_1, reading from frame (b), we determine the real exchange rate as θ_1. If the price level is P_1 and the real exchange rate θ_1, transferring these two magnitudes to frame (c) takes us to point C on a constant exchange rate locus E_1. Thus, the actual exchange rate in this situation would be E_1, the price level P_1, income y_1, and the real exchange rate θ_1. People will see that the exchange rate is different from what they had expected it to be. They will not, however, see any reason to revise their expectations of the price level. As far as they are concerned, there must have been a change in the real exchange rate. This is the normal state of affairs. Aggregate demand shocks never occur, so there will be no reason based on observed regularities in the past, to revise opinions about the level of aggregate demand.

People will be able to reconcile the currently observed exchange rate E_1 with the currently expected level of aggregate demand AD^e and the currently expected price level P^e, by adjusting their expectations of the real exchange rate to fall on the line labelled $RE^e|E_1$. To see this, notice that there is a square, the corners of which are A', B', C' D', that just touches the intersection of AD^e and EAS, the 45° line, the constant exchange rate locus E_1, and the expected real exchange rate curve $RE^e|E_1$. Thus, the expected price level P^e, and the expected real exchange rate $\theta^e|E_1$, and the actual (nominal) exchange rate E_1 are all compatible with each other and with an expectation that the economy is at full-employment output y^*. The other square, ABCD, represents the actual situation. This is where the actual aggregate demand curve cuts the expectations-augmented aggregate supply curve, the economy is on the actual RE curve and again on the actual constant exchange rate locus. Both C and C' are on the same constant exchange rate locus. Thus, the actual exchange rate E_1 is compatible with the combined expectation of the price level and the real exchange rate.

In effect, people are making two offsetting mistakes. Aggregate demand is actually higher than they believe it to be, and the real exchange rate curve is actually lower than they believe it to be. In combination, these two mistakes generate the same expectation of the exchange rate as the actual exchange rate and, therefore, cannot be corrected simply by observing the exchange rate.

Before leaving this highly artificial economy that has frequently been bombarded with real exchange rate shocks, but never before with an aggregate demand shock, let us consider what would happen if there was no aggregate demand shock, but if the economy did, indeed, undergo a real exchange rate shock. Specifically, imagine that the aggregate demand curve had remained at AD^e, but that the real exchange rate had in fact changed, so that the actual real exchange rate was denoted by the line $RE^e|E_1$. If this shock had occurred, then the economy would have remained at full-employment output y^*, the price level would have remained at P^e, the nominal exchange rate would have moved to E_1, and the real exchange rate to $\theta^e|E_1$. The square A′B′C′D′ would in fact describe the actual situation. Thus, by forming expectations on the basis of what usually happens, people would have correctly inferred the real exchange rate shock by using the information given to them by the exchange rate. In the previous experiment, where there was an unanticipated change in aggregate demand leading to a rise in the price level, output, the real exchange rate, and the (nominal) exchange rate, it was the unanticipated nature of the aggregate demand change that caused the problems.

Let us now briefly turn our attention to what is happening to the current account of the balance of payments during the administration of the shock. The economy was subject to an unexpected aggregate demand shock, and there was a rise in the price level, in the output level and in the real exchange rate. The higher real exchange rate leads to a rise in world demand for domestic output (exports) and a drop in domestic demand for world output (imports). Other things being equal, this tends to raise the current account surplus (or lower the deficit). Other things are not equal, however. The higher real income level raises imports, thereby contributing to a lowering of the current account surplus (or increasing the deficit). In general, we do not know which of these two offsetting forces is the stronger and do not, therefore, know in which direction the current account balance changes. The overall balance of payments would be maintained at zero as a result of the flexible exchange rate.

C. Real Exchange Rate Shocks

Let us now leave this highly artificial economy and go on to consider another equally highly artificial situation, at the opposite extreme. Imagine an economy that is always being bombarded by aggregate demand shocks, but which has never before known a change in its real exchange rate. Imagine that in some period that we shall now analyze, the economy suffers a real exchange rate shock, but no aggregate demand shock. Just as above, this is a very unusual event — something that has perhaps never happened before. The nominal exchange rate responds to the real exchange rate shock, but people rationally attribute the nominal exchange rate adjustment to an aggregate demand shock — to something that commonly occurs — and not to the real exchange rate shock — something that has never before been known. What happens to output, prices, the exchange rate, and the real exchange rate in this case? Figure 28.5 will analyze this situation.

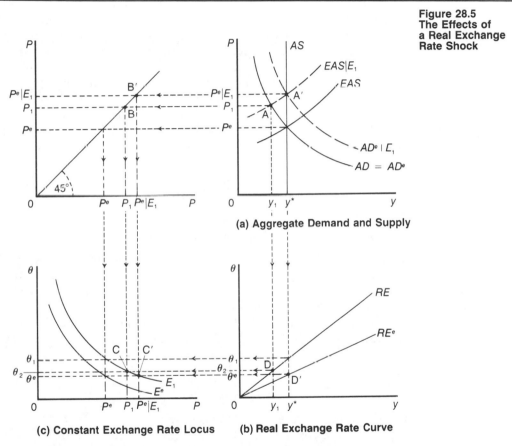

**Figure 28.5
The Effects of
a Real Exchange
Rate Shock**

(a) Aggregate Demand and Supply

(c) Constant Exchange Rate Locus

(b) Real Exchange Rate Curve

The economy is initially at P^e, y^*, θ^e and E^e on the aggregate demand curve $AD = AD^e$, the expectations-augmented aggregate supply curve EAS, the real exchange rate curve RE^e and the constant exchange rate locus E^e. There is then an unanticipat[e] in the real exchange rate to RE. With no change in income and the price level, th[e] the exchange rate to E_1 (the exchange rate compatible with the price level P^e an[d] real exchange rate θ_1). Since the real exchange rate shock is unanticipated, th[e] nominal exchange rate is read incorrectly as an aggregate demand shock. The price level is revised upwards to $P^e|E_1$, which shifts the expectations-augmented gate supply curve to $EAS|E_1$. Actual output and the price level is determined at and the real exchange rate at θ_2. The price level P_1 and the real exchange rat[e] consistent with the exchange rate E_1. The actual situation as described by the [...] the square ABCD and the expected situation by the corners of the square A'B[...] The unanticipated rise in the real exchange rate raises the price level, lowers [...] raises the nominal exchange rate. The nominal exchange rate rises by more t[han] price level does, therefore the real exchange rate rises.

(i) Pretrading Expectations

Let us first use Figure 28.5 to describe the pretrading rational expectations of the variables. The expected aggregate demand curve is AD^e in frame (a) and where this curve intersects the AS curve is determined the rational expectation of the price level P^e and the location of the EAS curve. The expectation of the real exchange rate in frame (b) is the curve labelled RE^e, so the rational expectation of the real exchange rate is θ^e. Transferring the rational expectation of the price level through the 45° line to frame (c) and transferring the expected real exchange rate to frame (c) gives a point on the constant exchange rate locus E^e. This, then, is the initial pretrading rational expectation for the economy.

Imagine that there is now a shock to the real exchange rate, and the actual real exchange rate becomes the line RE. If there was no change in the rational expectation of the price level, and if actual aggregate demand equals expected aggregate demand (as we shall assume it to be), the level of output and prices would remain constant at P^e and y^*, but the real exchange rate would rise to θ_1. At the price level P^e and the real exchange rate θ_1, the economy would be on a constant exchange rate locus E_1 shown in frame (c). Thus, the (nominal) exchange rate would be higher than expected.

(ii) Extracting Information from the Exchange Rate

Recalling that this is an economy which, by assumption, never has had a real exchange rate shock before, but often has aggregate demand shocks, it will be evident that people will read the higher (nominal) exchange rate as implying that there must have been an aggregate demand shock. As a result, they will revise their expectations of the price level upwards. Since they know the exchange rate to be E_1, and since they firmly expect the real exchange rate to remain at θ^e, they will believe the economy to be at the point C' on the constant exchange rate locus E_1. They will read off from this point on the locus E_1 the rational expectation of the price level, conditional on knowing that the exchange rate is E_1. This is labelled in frame (c) as $P^e|E_1$. That is, given that people firmly believe that the real exchange rate has remained at θ^e, but that they know the (nominal) exchange rate to be E_1, they calculate a rational expectation of the price level that is compatible with these two facts.

Now transfer the rational expectation of the price level $P^e|E_1$ from frame (c) through the 45° line to frame (a). This takes us to the point A' in frame (a). Passing through the point A' is an expectations-augmented aggregate supply curve, given knowledge of the exchange rate as E_1. This is the curve labelled $EAS|E_1$. Where this expectations-augmented aggregate supply curve intersects the actual aggregate demand curve (point A) determines the level of output y_1 and the price level P_1. With the real exchange rate actually being determined by the RE curve, the output level y_1 determines a level of the real exchange rate of θ_2. (The real exchange rate θ_1 would be associated with full-employment output y^*.)

Now transfer the price level P_1 through the 45° line to frame (c) and transfer the real exchange rate θ_2 across to frame (c). These meet at point C on the constant exchange rate locus E_1. Thus, the nominal exchange rate E_1 that gives rise to an expectation of the price level of $P^e|E_1$, and an expected real exchange rate of θ^e (point C') also gives rise to an actual price level P_1 and an actual real exchange rate θ_2 at point C. The actual equilibrium is described by the corners of the square ABCD, and the expected equilibrium by the corners of the square A'B'C'D'. The effects of this unanticipated rise in the real exchange rate curve have been to raise the domestic price level, raise the exchange rate (depreciate the currency), and lower output.[1]

(iii) Aggregate Demand Shocks

Now consider what would have happened in this economy if it had been actually subjected to the shock to which it is normally subjected, namely, an aggregate demand shock. Imagine that instead of having a real exchange rate shock, the real exchange rate remained at its normal level RE^e. Imagine further that there was a shock to aggregate demand that took the actual aggregate demand curve to the curve labelled $AD^e|E_1$. Such a shock would have raised the exchange rate, and the higher exchange rate would have been interpreted as evidence of a positive aggregate demand shock. People would have adjusted upwards their expectations of prices, thereby building into their current expectations the information being given by the exchange rate. The only equilibrium to which this economy could have come would be the one described by the corners of the square A'B'C'D'. That is, the economy would have remained at full-employment output, the price level would actually have risen to $P^e|E_1$, and the exchange rate risen to E_1. The real exchange rate would have remained at θ^e.

This serves to emphasize that the reason why the real exchange rate shock in this economy had an effect on output was because it was unanticipated. This is directly analogous to the reasons why the aggregate demand shock had output effects in the previous extreme example.

In this case of the economy that is normally subjected to aggregate demand shocks, but was unusually subjected to a real exchange rate shock, there is no ambiguity as to what happens to the current account balance. There is a fall in output and a rise in the real exchange rate.

---

[1] In order to keep the diagrammatic analysis clean, we have rigged this experiment to yield a rational expectations equilibrium in "one iteration" by selecting convenient slopes for the *EAS* and *RE* curves. In general, although the characterization of equilibrium shown in Figure 28.6 is correct, a lengthier iterative process would have to be followed in order to establish what the equilibrium is. Its defining characteristics are the two squares: ABCD, which describes the actual situation, and A'B'C'D', which describes the expected situation. The points C and C' are on the same constant exchange rate locus.

The combination of these two things is unambiguously to raise the current account surplus (or lower the deficit), since the lower real income level lowers imports, whereas the higher real exchange rate lowers imports and stimulates exports.

More General Shocks   The experiments conducted and illustrated in Figures 28.4 and 28.5 are excessively simplified. In practice, *both* the real exchange rate and aggregate demand will be shocked simultaneously, and there will be difficulty in disentangling the extent to which each of these two have been shocked. Nevertheless, the conclusions that we have reached using the simplified analyses apply to the more general case. The propositions made above concerning the effects of unexpected changes in aggregate demand and the real exchange rate, taken by themselves, apply to cases where there is a mixture of both shocks. Shocks that reveal themselves through changes in the exchange rate will, in general, be misinterpreted not completely, as in the two extreme examples used above, but partly. The more common is a particular type of shock, the more inclined will people be to infer the presence of this shock when there is a previously unanticipated change in the exchange rate. The smaller will be the real effects, and the larger will be the price level effects of such a shock. Notice that it is not possible, given that people observe the exchange rate, for there to be unanticipated changes in one variable that are not offset by unanticipated changes in other variables. At least two mistakes must be made.

Fixed vs. Flexible Exchange Rates Again   It is often said that flexible exchange rates give an economy insulation from foreign shocks. What does the above analysis say about this? Certainly we discovered when analyzing the fixed exchange rate economy that an unanticipated change in foreign prices, real income, or interest rates would produce a change in domestic output and prices. Does the same apply in the flexible exchange rate case? The answer is clearly yes.

Foreign interest rate shocks affect the position of the aggregate demand curve; foreign real income shocks affect the position of the real exchange rate curve; and foreign price level shocks affect the position of the constant exchange rate locus. Thus, each of these shocks will have an effect upon the exchange rate. Through their observed effect on the exchange rate they will lead to inferences about the positions of each of the aggregate demand and real exchange rate curves. If the only foreign shock that occurred was to the foreign price level and if it was known that this was the only shock that had occurred then it would be known that the change in the foreign exchange rate had arisen from this source alone and correct inferences would be made concerning the source of that shock. No other variables than the exchange rate would change and the domestic economy would be completely insulated from this foreign nominal shock.

If, in contrast, shocks occur to all three of these variables, movements in the foreign exchange rate will lead to inferences about the sources of shock that will, in general, be incorrect. Foreign shocks — even foreign price level shocks — will partly be misperceived as domestic demand shocks or as foreign real shocks (real interest rate or real income). To the extent that they are so misperceived, they will lead to real output, employment, and price effects in the domestic economy. Interestingly, a foreign shock that raises the expected price level will, other things being equal, produce a stagflation style of result comparable to that which we saw when analyzing the effects of supply shocks in Chapter 14.

What the flexible exchange rate does offer is insulation from the effect of anticipated foreign shocks. Any such shocks will come out entirely in the exchange rate and leave the domestic price level and output level undisturbed. Such shocks, of course, will be pretty hard to imagine occurring uncontaminated by unexpected components. Nevertheless, it is important to note that flexible exchange rates *do* give insulation from ongoing, anticipated, trend changes in prices in the rest of the world.

Summary

A. Aggregate Demand Shocks with a Fixed Exchange Rate

The expected values of fiscal variables and foreign variables determine the expected aggregate demand curve, which in turn determines the rational expectation of the price level. The actual aggregate demand curve intersecting the expectations-augmented aggregate supply curve determines actual output and the price level. Anticipated changes in fiscal policy or foreign variables have price level effects only; unanticipated changes affect both output and the price level. Fluctuations in the current account of the balance of payments are countercyclical and domestic output is procyclical with world output. An anticipated foreign inflation or depreciation of the currency raises the domestic price level proportionately.

B. Aggregate Demand Shocks with a Flexible Exchange Rate

With flexible exchange rates, the continuous information given by the exchange rate has to be used to form a rational expectation of the shocks influencing the economy. If there was one, and only one, source of shock, then knowledge of the exchange rate would enable a perfect inference to be made and would ensure that the economy always operates at full-employment equilibrium.

If there is more than one source of shock — in this case an aggregate demand shock and a real exchange rate shock — then observation of the nominal exchange rate does not enable a complete inference to be made concerning the magnitudes of those shocks separately. As a result unanticipated fluctuations in aggregate demand lead to pro-cyclical co-movements in output and prices as they did in the closed economy case.

C. Real Exchange Rate Shocks

An unexpected (and misperceived) rise in the real exchange rate leads to a rise in the nominal exchange rate. If this is perceived as having arisen from a domestic aggregate demand shock it leads to a rise in the expected price level shifting the *EAS* curve upwards. The result is a rise in prices and a drop in output — stagflation.

Review Questions

1. How is the rational expectation of the price level determined when the exchange rate is fixed and capital is perfectly mobile internationally?

2. Work out the effects on the rational expectation of the price level (with fixed exchange rates and perfect capital mobility internationally) of the following:

    (a) an anticipated rise in the world price level of 10 percent
    (b) an anticipated rise in world income
    (c) an anticipated rise in domestic credit
    (d) an unanticipated devaluation
    (e) an anticipated devaluation of 10 percent
    (f) an unanticipated rise in domestic credit
    (g) an unanticipated tax cut
    (h) an anticipated rise in government spending.

3. Work out the effects on output, the price level, and the current account balance (with fixed exchange rates and perfect capital mobility) of the eight shocks listed in Question 2.

4. What is the fundamental difference between a fixed and a flexible exchange rate regime? Which generates the most information?

5. How is the rational expectation of the price level determined when the exchange rate is flexible and when capital is perfectly mobile:

    (a) before the markets being trading?
    (b) when trading is taking place?

6. How is the rational expectation of the price level affected by the eight shocks listed in Question 2, when the exchange rate is flexible and capital is perfectly mobile?

7. How are output, the price level, the exchange rate, and the current account balance affected by the eight shocks listed in Question 2, when the exchange rate is flexible and capital is perfectly mobile?

8. Do flexible exchange rates provide better insulation from foreign shocks than do fixed exchange rates?

29

Canada
in the
World Economy

One of the most labored excuses for Canadian macroeconomic performance is that "it is all the fault of the rest of the world in general and the United States in particular." It is especially fashionable to blame high inflation and high interest rates on the policies being pursued by countries other than Canada. This chapter is going to take you through the highlights of the facts about world macroeconomic developments since 1970 and, using the insights made available by macroeconomic theory, analyze the ways in which the Canadian economy has been influenced by events in the rest of the world. It will also briefly ask what Canada can do to attain the most effective insulation from shocks emanating from the rest of the world. The chapter will take you through four tasks, which are to:

a) Know the main patterns of world output, prices, interest rates, and exchange rates since 1970.
b) Understand the causes of world output, prices, interest rate, and exchange rate movements since 1970.
c) Understand how Canada has been influenced by world macro-economic developments since 1970.
d) Understand the nature of Canada's macroeconomic policy choices.

A. World Output, Prices, Interest Rates, and Exchange Rates

There is a mass of information available on macroeconomic developments in the rest of the world, and it would be quite impossible to do more than scan the highlights in this chapter. Excellent summary sources of information that you will probably find useful, mainly as reference sources, are the publications of the International Monetary Fund (IMF) and the Organization for Economic Cooperation and Development (OECD). The International Monetary Fund publishes each year *International Financial Statistics, Yearbook*. This contains a wealth of macroeconomic data on most of the 140 countries that are members of the International Monetary Fund. In addition, the IMF provides up-to-date information on the macroeconomic developments in its member countries with the monthly publication of *International Financial Statistics*. The OECD publishes a series of "country reviews" at periodic intervals. It also publishes an excellent semi-annual (in July and December) appraisal of the world economy called *Economic Outlook*. You will find these publications of the IMF and OECD in the government publications section of your university library and in the major public libraries.

(i) Output Growth

In viewing the highlights of the macroeconomic developments since 1970, it will be convenient to consider the four groups of variables, output, prices, interest rates, and exchange rates, one at a time. Let us first consider output developments. Figure 29.1 illustrates the growth rate of output (measured by GNE or GDP) for three different aggregate entities, Canada, the United States of America and the world. The striking pattern in the growth rates shown in Figure 29.1 is their similarity as we move from the small Canadian economy to the larger United States economy to the even larger economy of the world. There is a general boom in world economic activity in the opening years of the 1970s, reaching a peak in 1973. The period 1974-75 sees the world plunging into recession, and 1976 sees the whole world recovering. From 1976 to 1982, output growth falls to a recession in 1982. In 1983-84, output growth strenghtens each year.

Canada's growth performance departs from that of the rest of the world in some interesting details. It is higher than that of the United States all the way through to 1976, but then falls below the U.S. rate for two years. Canada's growth for 1979 to 1981 again exceeds that of the United States but then falls below the U.S. growth rate for the next three years. Although experiencing the general world recession of 1974-75 and 1982, Canada feels the 1974-75 recession with less severity, but the 1982 recession with more. There are some small independent movements in Canada's output growth rate, the most notable being in 1972 and 1978, when Canada briefly, and to a small degree, runs against the major world tide.

(ii) Prices

Figure 29.2 sets out the inflation rates of Canada, four other countries, and a world average. The four countries (Germany, Japan, United

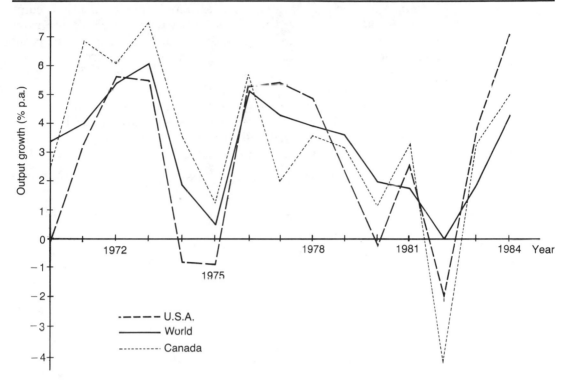

Figure 29.1
Real Output Growth, 1970-84

The output growth rates of Canada, the United States and the world have been remarkably similar since 1970. A boom in 1972-73 was followed by a deep recession in 1974-75, a recovery in 1976, output growth falling through to the recession of 1982 and a recovery in 1983–84.

Source: Canada, Appendix to Chapter 2; Other Countries, *International Financial Statistics, Yearbook*, 1985, p. 130–131.

Kingdom, and United States) have been selected because they are the dominant countries in the world economy, viewed from Canada's perspective. The world average is an average of the 140 countries that are members of the International Monetary Fund. Each country is weighted by its share in world gross output (converted into U.S. dollars). The most striking contrast between the inflation paths shown in Figure 29.2 and the output growth rates shown in Figure 29.1 is the way in which inflation rates diverge through the decade of the seventies. As the decade opens, the five inflation rates shown in this chart are all clustered together lying between a little over 3 percent per annum and about 7.5 percent per annum. This 4 percentage point spread between the highest and lowest is roughly maintained through 1972. The divergence then begins. By 1974, the spread between the lowest and highest inflation rate is more than 17 percentage points (Japan being 24.4, and Germany 7.0). The inflation rates stay very far apart for the rest of the decade, although they do begin to come closer together again by 1979. This return to similar inflation rates gradually continues until, in 1983, there is only a 4 percentage point spread between the highest and the lowest of the five inflation rates. Is is also worth noting that world inflation by 1981 is higher than that of each of the five countries shown.

The second feature of these inflation rates that is noteworthy is the common cyclical pattern. All countries' inflation rates accelerate between 1972 and 1974-75, all fall through 1978, all rise again through to 1980-81 and all fall again through 1984.

Figure 29.2
World Inflation of
Consumer Prices,
1970-84

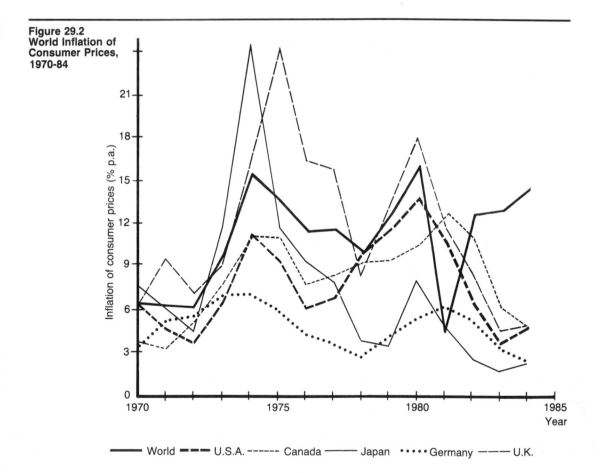

Inflation exploded in all countries in 1973–74. After a brief recovery there was a further rise towards the end of the seventies with all inflation rates peaking in 1980–81. Having been very similar to each other, inflation rates diverged after 1973, but by 1983 they were once again very similar.

Source: International Financial Statistics, Yearbook, 1985, p. 104–105.

Canada's inflation performance through this decade looks very average when compared with the other major countries and with the world aggregate measure. Compared with Germany, however, and compared with Japan since 1978, Canada's inflation performance is a poor one. At the beginning of the 1970s, Canada, along with Germany, is inflating at the lowest rate of all the major countries and little more than half of the world average rate. By 1981 Canada's inflation peaks and is running at twice that of Germany (and Japan) and at slightly less than ninety percent of the world average rate.

Although macroeconomics is concerned with broad averages of prices, there is a particular price which took on a special significance in the 1970s, namely, the price of oil. The causes of that oil price rise and its consequences for Canada cannot be ignored even in a brief examination of world macroeconomic influences since 1970. Let us, therefore, examine what happened to the price of oil since 1970.

There are several alternative measures of the price of oil, and one only has been selected as being fairly representative, namely, the U.S. dollar price of Saudi Arabian crude oil (Saudia Arabia is the biggest producer in the world). Table 29.1 sets out the U.S. dollar price (column 1) of a barrel of Saudi Arabian crude oil on the average for each year since 1970. The second column shows the percentage rate of change in this price over the previous year. After opening the decade with a modest inflation rate, there is a tendency for the oil price to move upwards more quickly in 1971, 1972, and 1973. There is, in 1973-74, what can only be described as an explosion — a near quadrupling of the price. Between 1975 and 1978, oil prices rose only

Table 29.1
World Oil Price 1970-84

YEAR	SAUDI ARABIA CRUDE $ U.S. PER BARREL	PERCENT RISE OVER PREVIOUS YEAR
1970	1.30	1.6
1971	1.65	26.9
1972	1.90	15.2
1973	2.70	42.1
1974	9.67	258.1
1975	10.72	10.9
1976	11.51	7.4
1977	12.40	7.7
1978	12.70	2.4
1979	17.26	35.9
1980	28.67	66.11
1981	32.50	13.36
1982	33.47	2.98
1983	29.31	−12.43
1984	28.47	−2.87

Source: *International Financial Statistics Yearbook*, 1985, p. 141, line 76aa.

modestly and especially so when viewed against the average rises in other prices. In 1979-80 there is another large increase, but since then the inflation rate has moderated such that by 1983 oil prices were actually falling. We shall return to an examination of these oil prices when analyzing the causes of world macroeconomic activity. It is important to take careful note of the timing of the movements in oil prices. The key explosion occurs at the end of 1973 and is partly reflected in the 1973 price rise (42.1 percent), but mainly in the 1974 rise (258.1 percent). The second jump in oil prices occurred in 1979 and is party reflected in the 1979 price rise (35.9 percent) and partly in the 1980 price rise (66.11 percent).

(iii) Interest Rates

Let us now turn to examine the developments in world interest rates since 1970. It will be convenient to focus on those same countries whose inflation performances were highlighted in the previous section. Figure 29.3 shows both short-term [frame (a)] and long-term [frame (b)] interest rates in the five major countries.

The pattern in interest rate movements shown in this figure reflects one of the stylized facts about the business cycle which you have already viewed in the specifically Canadian context. That is the tendency for long-term rates of interest to fluctuate less than short-term rates. Aside from this key difference between the movements of short- and long-term rates, the movements of both rates reflect the same pattern. Rates fall slightly from 1970 through 1973, then rise very sharply to a peak in 1974, fall to a new trough in 1977-78, and rise again through to 1980-81 then fall gradually. National differences in interest rates reflect the national differences in inflation rates that we looked at in the previous subsection. The countries experiencing the highest inflation rates are those whose interest rates are highest in these years. The sharp decline in Japanese and German interest rates (both short- and long-term) between 1975 and 1978 is a clear example of this. Also, the sharp and persistent rise in United Kingdom and Canadian interest rates in the period 1980-81 is another example at the other end of the spectrum.

(iv) Exchange Rates

Finally, let us examine the behavior of exchange rates among the major currencies since 1970. Focussing on these same major economies, Figure 29.4 shows the value of the Canadian dollar against the German mark — the deutsche mark (DM), the Japanese yen (¥), the United Kingdom pound — the pound sterling (£UK), and the United States dollar ($U.S.). Between 1970 and 1976, the Canadian dollar remained fairly stable against the U.S. dollar and depreciated slightly against the Japanese yen and German mark. Valued against the pound sterling, the Canadian dollar appreciated markedly, especially between 1975 and 1976. The value of the Canadian dollar

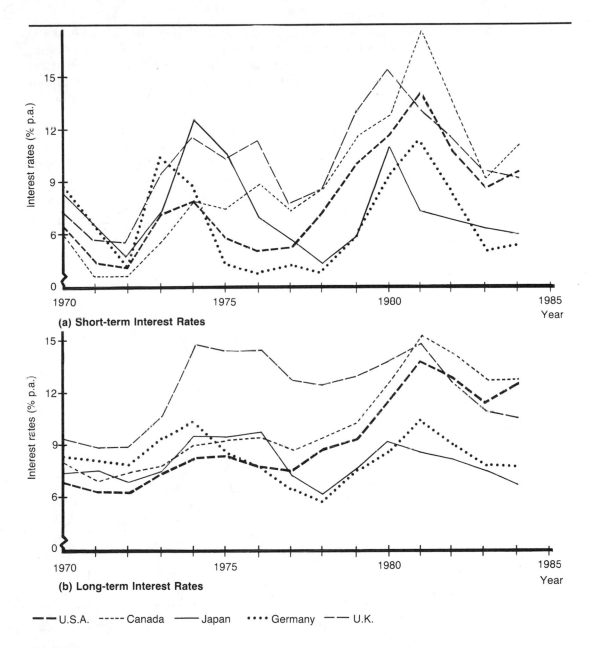

(a) Short-term Interest Rates

(b) Long-term Interest Rates

— ■ —U.S.A.   ----- Canada   —— Japan   • • • Germany   — — U.K.

Figure 29.3
World Interest Rates, 1970-79

Movements in interest rates broadly reflect movements in inflation. Short-term rates, frame (a), fluctuate with greater amplitude than long-term rates, frame (b). Countries whose inflation rates are highest are those whose interest rates are also the highest. Like inflation, interest rates diverge after 1973. By 1983 the similarity of interest rates is also restored.

Source: *International Financial Statistics Yearbook,* 1985. Short-term interest rates: U.S.A., Canada, U.K., 3-month Treasury Bill Rate, line 60c. Germany, Japan call money, line 60b. Long-term interest rates for all countries is that on a long-term government bond, line 61.

since 1976 stands in marked contrast to that of the first half of the decade. Between 1976 and 1978 the Canadian dollar depreciated substantially against all four currencies shown here. It continues to depreciate against the U.S. dollar, but appreciates against the German mark and the pound sterling through to 1984. The Canadian dollar is fairly stable against the Japanese yen.

This completes our brief discussion of the macroeconomic developments in the major countries of the world, as well as in Canada, since 1970. Let us now turn to the task of explaining and understanding the sources of these movements and also of assessing the influence of the rest of the world on Canada.

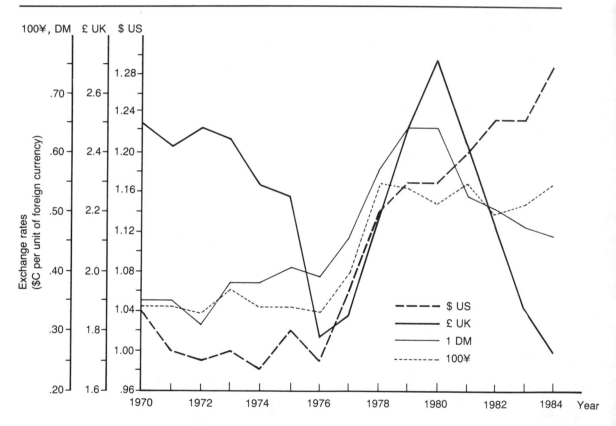

Figure 29.4
The Value of the Canadian Dollar in Terms of Four Major Currencies

Up to 1976 the Canadian dollar was remarkably stable in value against the U.S. dollar. It depreciated slightly against the deutsche mark and the yen and appreciated strongly against the pound sterling. From 1976 to 1980, the Canadian dollar depreciated against all four currencies. After 1980 the Canadian dollar depreciated against the U.S. dollar, appreciated against the pound sterling and the German mark and was relatively steady against the Japanese yen.

Source: Bank of Canada Review, May 1981, Table 65, and July 1985, Table I1.

B. Explanation of World Macroeconomic Developments

First let us try to understand the *world averages* of output growth and inflation. How can we account for the movements in the world averages of output and inflation set out in Figures 29.1 and 29.2?

Let us use the above interpretation to account for the movements in output and prices since 1970. The slight drop in inflation in the first two years and the slight drop in output are seen as the consequence of tightening money growth in the late 1960s. This slowdown in money growth is interpreted as being initially unanticipated, but one which was subsequently, though only gradually, incorporated into inflation expectations. The surge of money growth in 1971 and 1972 is interpreted as having been initially unanticipated and the source of rising output with steady inflation. Eventually, the higher money growth rate was built into price expectations and, by 1973, it was producing a strong inflation acceleration.

By 1974 the inflation acceleration is very strong. This year very rapid inflation coincides with a deceleration in money growth. By 1974 money supply growth actually falls. It may be reasonably conjectured that the drop in money supply growth in 1974 was unanticipated. It is even plausible to suggest that the slowdown of money growth in 1973 had also, to some extent, been unanticipated. This is seen as a principal determinant of the deep recession in world economic activity in 1974 and 1975. It is also seen as the source of falling inflation in 1975 and 1976. The renewed burst of money growth from 1975 through 1976 — largely unanticipated — generates the big world recovery of real activity into 1976. That higher money growth rate of 1976 was built into peoples' expectations and reflected in a shortening of contracts and the speeding up of the effects of a change in money growth on output and prices. The renewed acceleration of inflation towards the end of the 1970s is also the consequence of this higher money growth rate. Slowing money growth in 1980-81 brings a quick slowdown of output growth, moderating inflation in 1981-82. The higher money growth after 1982 is accompanied by a rise in output growth and persistent inflation.

From this account of the world economy since 1970, it is evident that although in principle it would be desirable to know what was happening to world fiscal policy variables through this period, movements in world money growth alone seem to have been a dominant influence on the course of world output and inflation.

The other feature of world macroeconomic activity since 1970, evident in Figures 29.2 and 29.3, is the divergence in inflation and interest rates across the major countries from 1973 to 1980. Why did these divergences occur? In a deep sense, we do not know the answer to this question, for it resides in some as yet not well-understood differences in national tendencies to inflate. We do know that those tendencies have been present for many years. They were not, however, permitted to have full reign until the fixed exchange rate system established after World War II finally collapsed in 1972. We can say that the proximate cause of the spreading out of world inflation and interest rates through the second part of the 1970s and the early 1980s was the consequence of this collapse. As countries one after another abandoned the commitment to maintaining a fixed exchange rate against the U.S. dollar and gold, so national monetary policies became more diverse, and national inflation and interest rate experiences diverged from each other.

As we discovered in Chapter 27, under fixed exchange rates, purchasing power parity and interest rate parity keep one country's inflation and interest rates broadly in line with those in other countries. (They will not, of course, be exactly equal, for differences reflecting differences in national risk and changes in the real terms of trade will be reflected in the aggregates.) The details shown in Figures 29.2 and 29.3 for the early 1970s are an interesting reflection of these propositions.

We further discovered, in Chapter 27, that when the exchange rate is flexible, trends in the exchange rate and trends in interest rates all must be compatible with each other, and that all are generated by trend movements in national money supply growth rates relative to each other. Thus, an economy that is pursuing a high money supply growth rate relative to the rest of the world will be a country whose currency is becoming cheaper, whose inflation rate is higher, and whose interest rates are higher than the world average. These patterns are clearly discernible in the figures presented in the preceding section. The countries with low inflation, Germany and Japan, are also the countries with low interest rates and strong currencies. The countries with high inflation, the United Kingdom, the United States and Canada, are also the countries with high interest rates and weak currencies. Study the patterns shown in Figures 29.2, 29.3, and 29.4. They provide a remarkable cross-country confirmation of the prediction that trends in interest rates, inflation rates and exchange rates line up with each other.

In approaching this question it is helpful to begin by realizing that the world is closer than any national economy to approximating a closed economy, the behavior of which we have analyzed in the bulk of this book. It would seem instructive, therefore, to examine the forces which, according to closed economy macroeconomic analysis, are the principal determinants of output and price movements. According to this theory, aggregate demand is determined by the money supply, government spending, taxes, and other factors that influence the scale of investment spending. It would be a massive undertaking to compile world aggregate measures of all these variables. In principle, we would like to know what happened to world aggregate government spending and taxes as well as to factors influencing world aggregate investment spending. Such an exercise has not, as far as we are aware, been undertaken. What has been undertaken is the compilation of world money supply growth. The International Monetary Fund has constructed a world aggregate index of money and the growth rate of money (based on national money supply growth rates weighted by the share of each country in world output). It is possible, therefore, to examine the influence, if any, of world money supply growth on world economic activity. Although not a substitute for a careful and detailed statistical analysis, Figure 29.5 provides an overview of this relationship.

The world money supply growth rate is shown in Figure 29.5, along with world inflation and output growth. We will return to those other two series below. First, focus on the movements in world money growth over the period after 1968. As the figure shows, there is a steady decline in world money growth between 1968 and 1970, followed by three years in which the growth rate accelerates. Although money supply growth accelerates between 1970 and 1973, the rate of acceleration itself slows down. That is, the 1973 growth rate is bigger than that of 1972, but by a smaller increment than that by by which 1972 exceeds 1971, which, in turn, is smaller than the increment by which 1971 exceeds 1970. By 1974 the world money supply growth rate is cut, and rather substantially so, to a rate less than that which prevailed three years earlier. After 1974 money supply growth fluctuates, rising to a peak in 1976, falling to a trough in 1981 and rising again in 1983, but it remains in the same high range as it had moved into in 1972-73.

According to the theory of output and inflation, anticipated changes in the money supply growth rate lead to changes in the rate of inflation and to no change in output. Further, the inflation rate overshoots the money supply growth rate during the transition process to the new higher inflation rate. Further, according to the theory, an unanticipated change in the money supply growth rate leads to a change in both output and inflation.

Effects comparable to the predictions of the theory can be seen by examining the movements of output and inflation shown in Figure 29.5. The way that inflation and output growth have been plotted involves some adjustments in the *timing* of the variables. Instead of plotting inflation and output growth in each year corresponding to the growth rate of the money supply in that same year, the timing of inflation and output growth has been adjusted in the following way. First, up to 1975, money growth in each year is lined up with output one year later and inflation two years later. After 1975, the time lag is compressed. Money growth in each year is lined up with output growth in the same year and inflation one year later.

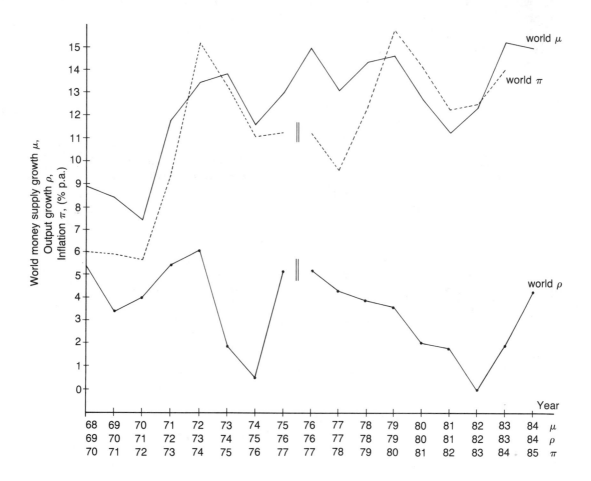

Figure 29.5
World Money Supply
Growth, Output Growth,
and Inflation, 1970-84

World money growth, inflation, and output are closely related. Before 1975 changes in the money supply growth rate preceded changes in output growth by one year, and inflation by two years. After 1975, changes in money supply growth were contemporaneous with changes in output growth and preceded inflation changes by one year.

Source: International Financial Statistics, Yearbook, 1985, pp. 80–81, 104–105, 130–31, line 1.

These data may be interpreted as saying that when a change in the money supply growth rate occurs, it is largely unanticipated and has its impact on output. Only after a period is the change in the money supply growth rate perceived to be of sufficient durability for inflationary expectations to be revised upwards. The patterns revealed in Figure 29.5 suggest that a change in the money supply growth rate has a strong effect on output, with about a one-year time lag, and on inflation, with about a two-year lag. After 1975, the lags are shorter. The output lag is now less than one year, and the inflation lag about one year. The shorter lag may be interpreted as the consequence of people paying more attention to inflation when its rate is high than when it is low. At higher rates of inflation, and higher rates of money growth, the consequences of misjudging the inflation rate are more serious than at lower rates. It is, therefore, rational to pay more attention to, and become more responsive to, changes in money supply growth rates. According to the new Keynesian interpretation of the aggregate supply response (recall Chapter 16), contracts would get shorter and/or would tend more to be indexed to the cost of living in high-inflation situations than in low-inflation situations. This would shorten the time lag in response of both output and prices to a change in money growth.

You may by now be saying to yourself, "This all sounds very well, but what about the price of oil? Don't we all know that the world's macroeconomic problems of the 1970s, the inflation, as well as the recession of the middle 1970s, were caused by movements in world energy prices in 1973? Don't we also know that the renewed burst of inflation at the end of the decade, as well as the recession of 1980-82, is also the consequence of a subsequent rise in the price of oil?" These are certainly fashionable propositions. They also almost certainly contain an element of truth. The burst of inflation in 1974, the recession of 1975, and the renewed inflation of 1979-80 were all made more severe than they otherwise would have been as a result of the *timing* of the oil price changes.

It is of some interest and importance to notice, however, that we have been able to explain the broad movements in world output and inflation, both on the average and across individual countries, without any need to refer to the price of oil as a separate item. It is also of some importance to note the *timing* of the movements of world money supply growth, output, and inflation. In the early 1970s, changes in the money supply growth rate *preceded* changes in the output growth rate by one year, and changes in the inflation rate by two years. Since 1976, changes in the output growth and inflation rate continued to follow changes in the money supply growth rate, but the time lag has shortened substantially.

While knowing that something happens *after* something else does not constitute proof that the former causes the latter, when combined with a body of detailed analysis as to *how* one causes the other, it amounts to fairly impressive evidence that a causal relationship is at work. The macroeconomic theory reviewed in this book sets out the links whereby changes in money supply growth influence output and prices. The combination of this theory with the facts shown in Figure 29.5, simple and highly aggregative though they are, seems to constitute fairly powerful evidence for the proposition that variations in world money supply growth have been a primary cause of variations in world output growth and inflation.

There are some further aspects of the oil price rises of the 1970s that reinforce this conclusion and that are worth considering here. The first of these arises from the fact that the price of oil is a relative price, while inflation is the change in the absolute price level. It is true that oil is an important commodity, and a large change in its relative price will have important consequences. It is also true that the relative price of oil changed dramatically in the early part of the 1970s. What is remarkable about the behavior of the price of oil is not that its price has risen relative to the prices of other goods, but that the rise came so suddenly, rather than gradually, over a longer period. Table 29.2 gives some information about long-term developments in the price of oil. Interestingly, as shown in the first column, the U.S. dollar price of oil fell between 1950 and 1970. In the same period, as shown in the second column, world prices measured by the IMF World Consumer Price Index more than doubled. Between 1950 and 1970, the real price of oil (the dollar price divided by the world Consumer Price Index) fell to little more than one-third its 1950 level. In the next decade, the real price increased more than nine-fold. The change between 1950 and 1980, not quite a tripling of the real price of oil, represents a 3.4 percent annual growth in the real price of oil. If oil prices had increased at this steady trend rate throughout the 30 years between 1950 and 1980, the real prices in 1960 and 1970 would have been $14.61 and $20.47 a barrel, as shown in the fourth column in Table 29.2. If this trend had been followed throughout the thirty-year period, the prices of the 1970s would have been entirely unremarkable, and the *macro*economic effects of the oil price changes would have been negligible or even non-existent.

The theory of relative prices (microeconomics) predicts that the price of an exhaustible resource will rise at a rate equal to the real rate of interest. The real rate of interest is the money or market rate of interest minus the rate of inflation, and generally is seen to lie between 2 and 3 percent per annum. The prices of exhaustible resources are predicted to rise at the real rate of interest because, were this not so, it would not pay anyone to own the reserves of those resources. Rather, it would pay to extract them from the ground and consume them instantly.

Table 29.2
The Price of Oil, 1950-1980

YEAR	SAUDI ARABIAN CRUDE $ U.S. PER BARREL	WORLD CPI	REAL PRICE OF OIL	TREND OF REAL PRICE
1950	1.71	16.4	10.43	10.43
1960	1.50	23.0	6.52	12.11
1970	1.30	35.4	3.67	14.05
1980	28.67	100.0	28.67	16.31
1984	28.47	164.5	17.31	17.31
			Annual Growth Rate 1.5%	

Source and Methods: *International Financial Statistics Yearbook* 1985, col. 1 is pp. 130-131, line 76aa; col. 2 is pp. 138-139, line 64; col. 3 is col. 1 divided by col. 2 multiplied by 100; col. 4 is the trend between the 1950 and 1980 points.

You can see this by considering the choice between investing in, say, an oil well and investing in some other profit-seeking activity. A dollar invested in the oil well today will yield a rate of return only if the oil can be sold later at a higher price than it could be sold for today. If the rate at which the price of oil is predicted to rise exceeds the rate of return on other activities, then it will pay to invest in oil wells. This would drive up the price and drive down the rate of return on oil wells. Conversely, if the price of oil is expected to rise less quickly than the rate of return on other activities, then it will pay to try to sell oil wells. This will drive down their price and raise the rate of return on them. The price of an oil well today is nothing other than the price of oil today (adjusted for extraction costs). It is evident, then, that the equilibrium price of an oil well, which will determine the current price of oil, will be such that the expected future price of oil will rise at a rate equal to the real rate of interest.

In looking back over any particular historical episode, it will not be the case that the price of oil has behaved exactly as predicted by the theory. The theory concerns expectations about future price changes, not realizations of past price changes. Nevertheless, it would be surprising if over very long periods of time, the price of oil behaved differently from the predictions of the theory.

Over the decades of the fifties and sixties the price of oil did behave very differently from what the theory predicts. The real price of oil fell successively through that twenty-year period. Why it did so constitutes an interesting fact, requiring an explanation. The explosion in the price of oil relative to the price of other commodities in the early seventies can be viewed as an adjustment in the price of oil to place the price level on the track that it ought to have been on during the fifties and sixties. Thus, an explosion in the price of oil in the early seventies may be viewed as a sudden (and perhaps surprising) adjustment in the real price (relative price) of oil to place the price back on the trend that it would have been on by then had the price increased each and every year by an amount roughly equal to the real rate of interest.

Noting that the change in the price of oil was a relative price change, not an absolute price change, does not mean that it might not have been responsible for triggering the worldwide inflation explosion in the later part of the 1970s and into the early 1980s. If the rise in the price of oil generated additional money growth, then it would generate additional inflation. To some extent, on the average, this may well have happened. It has not, however, happened everywhere. The cross-country experience set out in Figure 29.2 shows that not all countries experienced high and accelerating inflation after the oil shock of 1973-74.

Indeed, two countries, Germany and Japan, each of whom had very different impact effects of the oil shock on their inflation rates, pursued policies which almost completely eradicated inflation by 1978. Furthermore, these are two countries who rely more than any others do on imported oil for their energy requirements. In the Japanese case there was a very big impact effect of the oil shock on inflation, while in the German case the impact effect was milder. In both cases, however, the subsequent trend in inflation was downwards.

If the oil shock of 1973-74 was the primary cause of the inflation of the second half of the 1970s, it surely would have to be the case that the inflation rates of all countries would have been broadly similar to each other, and if anything, these countries with the greatest reliance on imported oil should surely have experienced the greatest inflation. What we see is almost the exact reverse of this. First, national inflation developments become more different from each other after the oil shock than before it, and second, the countries that rely most on imported energy have the lowest inflation. The conclusion to which this leads is that national monetary policies (trend growth rates in national money supplies) are, as they always have been, the principal causes of trends in national inflation rates in the 1970s and early 1980s. Furthermore, changes in world average money growth, preceding as they did by almost two years the world oil shock, were as they always have been the major causes of the explosion of world inflation since 1970.

C. World Macroeconomic Influences on Canada

First, let us recall the movements in Canadian output, inflation, interest rates, and the exchange rate since 1970. Referring back to Figure 29.1, it is evident that Canada had a growth rate of output that closely matched those of other countries. Canada's output grew faster than the world average between 1970 and 1975, slower between 1976 and 1980, and except for 1982, faster in the early 1980s, but not by much. Canadian inflation was typical of world inflation. (Refer back to Figure 29.2.) Canada was inflating at a slower rate than the rest of the world throughout the 1970s and early 1980s, and slower than the United States for most of this fifteen-year period, though Canada's inflation and that of the United States were very similar. Movements in both short- and long-term interest rates in Canada have been close to those in the United States, although Canadian interest rates are consistently higher than U.S. rates. The exchange rate was fairly constant against the U.S. dollar, the Japanese yen, and the deutsche mark between 1970 and 1975, but appreciated against the pound. Between 1976 and 1984 the Canadian dollar depreciated against all these currencies except the pound. The Canadian dollar depreciated against the pound from 1976 to 1980, but since then it has appreciated. Why have these patterns in Canadian macroeconomic activity occurred? Let us now try to answer that question.

In answering this question it will be convenient to split the period into two parts, pre-1975 and post-1975. Up to 1975, although there were some movements in the exchange rate, Canada was, *de facto*, operating on a fixed exchange rate against the U.S. dollar. Recalling the theory of fixed exchange rates as developed in Chapters 26, 27 and 28 and presuming Canada to be operating in a perfect capital mobility world, we know that aggregate demand is determined by world income, interest rates, prices, and by domestic fiscal policy. Anticipated changes in these variables would lead to changes in Canadian prices (and world prices) and have no output effects. Unanticipated changes in these variables would move both output and prices in a procyclical manner. The interpretation of the movements of inflation and output in Canada in the period up to 1975 is essentially the same as the interpretation of movements in those variables in the rest of the world during that period. Initially, the explosion of world money growth was unanticipated, and this initially produced a boost of world output and, subsequently, the explosion of inflation. The world monetary contraction of 1974 was largely unanticipated and was responsible for producing the world and Canadian contraction of output in 1975. This same reduction of world money growth which became incorporated into expectations by 1975 and 1976 brought the inflation rate down during those two years.

Since 1975, Canada has been a flexible exchange rate economy pursuing monetary targeting. In such an economy, aggregate demand depends upon the domestic money supply. The expected price level, however, depends both on the process generating domestic money and on the observed exchange rate. Observing the exchange rate is the same thing as being given information about the joint effects of monetary policy and aggregate real shocks (as described in Chapter 28). Since 1976, the continuing weakness of the Canadian dollar is clearly being read in part as a real shock and in part as a monetary shock. Other things being equal, the higher the exchange rate (the larger the depreciation of the currency), the higher will be the expected price level (and expected inflation rate). This, in combination with tight monetary policies (which are not perceived as being as tight as they are), will lead to low output growth and a poor inflation performance, as well as to high rates of interest.

There are some interesting interactions between the world oil price shock and macroeconomic policy in Canada which are worth reviewing. When the world oil price increased in 1973-74 and again in 1979-80, the Canadian government sought to shelter Canadians from these shocks by pegging the domestic price of oil substantially below the world price. As a result of this, Canadian oil production did not rise, and oil consumption did not fall, by as much as each would have done had the Canadian price been permitted to move to the world price. This meant that Canada had an increased import bill for oil and an increased government subsidy for oil consumption. The effects of this on the Canadian balance of payments and on the Canadian government budget deficit are such as to engender an expectation of higher money growth in Canada in the future. Thus, although the rise in the relative price of oil is not in and of itself the cause of inflation, if the oil price rise is not permitted to be translated immediately into a domestic oil price rise, but rather to generate a balance of payments deficit and a government budget deficit, the consequences for inflation, interest rates, and exchange rates can be serious. It is interesting to contrast the Canadian and Japanese performances in this respect. In Japan, where no oil is produced and almost all energy needs are imported, the relative price of energy was permitted to rise immediately as the world oil price rose. The impact of this was to take the Japanese inflation rate into the middle twenties for a brief period. This done, however, the Japanese balance of payments and budget deficit (large though each became) did not have to continue to support the burden of subsidizing the consumption of oil.

D. Canada's Macroeconomic Policy Choices

The macroeconomic policy choices which face Canada fundamentally boil down to choosing an exchange rate or money supply growth rate. That is, at the extremes, Canada could have rigid monetary targeting (cause the Canadian money supply to grow at a known, pre-determined rate) and have a flexible exchange rate determined on the foreign exchange market, or Canada could peg its foreign exchange rate (to the United States dollar, any other individual currency, or a basket of currencies) and let the domestic money supply and price level be determined by the rest of the world. Some combination of these two extremes could be achieved by some pre-determined mechanism for a managed float of the Canadian dollar. None of these policies avoids world shocks to the Canadian economy. You have seen *why* this is so in Chapter 28, and *that* it is so in the two preceding sections of this chapter.

It is commonly believed that monetarists advocate fixing the money supply growth rate and floating the exchange rate and that to advocate a fixed exchange rate is the ultimate in interventionism and, therefore, an extreme form of Keynesianism. Nothing, in fact, could be further from the truth. A fixed exchange rate policy *is* a monetary policy and often is the best monetary policy. The open economy version of monetarism says that for big countries there is really no alternative but to control the growth rate of the money supply, but for smaller countries there always is the alternative of pegging the value of domestic money against the value of some other money. In selecting a currency against which to peg, it is of some importance to pay attention to the monetary policies that will govern the value of that currency in terms of goods. Fixing the value of the Canadian dollar against, say, the deutsche mark, would produce a very different behavior for the Canadian price level than would fixing it against the U.K. pound.

The lesson that we learn from economic theory and from the brief consideration of the facts in the previous parts of this chapter is that it seems to be very hard to insulate against real fluctuations (fluctuations in output growth). They are shared more or less uniformly by all countries regardless of the policies they have pursued. They are shared by countries with high inflation and by countries with low inflation, by countries whose currencies have been strong and those whose currencies have been weak, by countries with high interest rates and countries with low interest rates. The other lesson that is clear from theory and the facts is that it is possible to insulate a country from inflation arising in the rest of the world. By pursuing firm-enough domestic monetary policies (which also are credible and engender a rational expecation of future firm monetary policies), low inflation, low interest rates and a strong currency can be achieved. Furthermore, they can be achieved even in the face of massive relative price changes such as occurred in the price of energy in the middle 1970s. Yet further, low inflation does not seem to require low growth.

In order to achieve low inflation and low interest rates, it is necessary to float the exchange rate and permit an appreciation of the value of the currency against those of countries whose inflation rates are higher than that being attained domestically. Whether or not that worsens macroeconomic fluctuations of real variables, such as output and unemployment, it is not possible to say in the current state of knowledge. Certainly, we know that aggregate demand is insulated from foreign shocks (provided capital is perfectly mobile) in the flexible exchange rate case. We also know, however, that rational expectations of the price level will be influenced by observations of the exchange rate, which will in turn be influenced by shocks arising in the rest of the world. Whether these shocks will translate into domestic output and employment movements that have bigger amplitude than those that would arise under a fixed exchange rate cannot be said on the basis of what we now know. For the time being, however, the gains to be had on the inflation front from pursuing a flexible exchange rate would seem to be so worthwhile as to push us very strongly in the direction of choosing the money supply rule, flexible exchange rate extreme.

Summary

A. World Output, Prices, Interest Rates, and Exchange Rates

World output growth went into a boom in 1972-1973 and a deep recession in 1974-75. It recovered in 1976, but fell through 1982. In 1983-84 output growth began to recover.

World inflation exploded in 1973-1974, moderated markedly in 1975-1976, but then accelerated again until 1980-81 and then declined through 1984. Interest rates followed the inflation pattern very closely. The Canadian dollar was fairly steady against the U.S. dollar, depreciated slightly against the deutsche mark and the yen, and appreciated against the British pound in the first half of the 1970s. It depreciated substantially against all major currencies in the second half of the seventies. In the period 1980-84 the Canadian dollar continued to depreciate against the U.S. dollar, but appreciated against most other major currencies. Growth rates in output have been remarkably similar in all countries throughout the 1970s, while inflation and interest rates have diverged markedly, especially after 1974.

B. Explanation of World Macroeconomic Developments

The macroeconomic theory of the closed economy may be used to understand the movements of world average output and prices. While, in principle, world aggregate fiscal policy variables play a role, it turns out that movements in world money supply growth are well capable of explaining the main trends in both output and inflation. It is necessary to interpret the data as there being about a two-year lag before money growth is fully incorporated into inflation in the first half of the 1970s, and approximately a one-year time lag since 1975. The divergence of inflation and interest rates across the major countries in the second half of the decade of the seventies is seen as arising from the pursuit of diverging monetary policies in a world of flexible exchange rates.

C. World Macroeconomic Influences on Canada

Up to 1975, Canada was, for all practical purposes, operating on a fixed exchange rate against the United States. The movements of world money growth which influenced world aggregate output and prices can be interpreted as having influenced those same Canadian variables, and for the same reasons. The transmission mechanisms are set out in Chapters 27 and 28. After 1975, Canada was a flexible exchange rate economy pursuing an independently targeted monetary policy. Assuming Canada to be an economy with perfect capital mobility, aggregate demand would be determined purely by domestic monetary policy. The expected price level (and therefore the expectations-augmented aggregate supply curve) would, however, be influenced by shocks arising in the rest of the world, for the reasons outlined in Chapter 28. Such shocks would influence the exchange rate, which would, in part, be misinterpreted as being domestic monetary shocks. The combination of a depreciating exchange rate with tight monetary policy would lead to depressed output growth and only a moderate reduction in inflation. Canada's post-1974 energy policy may be predicted to have accentuated the tendency for output to be depressed and inflation to fall slowly, since it imposes larger balance of payments and government deficits than would otherwise arise.

D. Canada's Macroeconomic Policy Choices

At the extremes, Canada may choose a flexible exchange rate with monetary targeting or a fixed exchange rate, with the money supply and inflation being determined by the country (or countries) against whom the exchange rate is fixed. In the present state of knowledge we cannot say definitively that one of the extremes is better than the other. It is possible to say, however, that world inflation may be avoided by firm domestic monetary policies which are pursued with long-term credibility. This requires that the exchange rate be flexible.

Review Questions

1. Review the major movements in world income, prices, interest rates, and exchange rates since 1970.

2. Compare the performance of Canadian output growth, inflation, and interest rates with those of Germany, Japan, the United Kingdom, and the United States since 1970.

3. What are the broad facts about world money growth, output growth, and inflation since 1970? How might the fluctuations in output and prices be explained?

4. Why did national inflation rates and interest rates diverge in the second half of the 1970s?

5. Why do countries with high inflation also have high interest rates and depreciating currencies?

6. Did the rise in world money growth in the 1970s occur before, during, or after the oil price shock? What bearing does your answer have on interpreting the causes of the inflation explosion in 1973-74 and 1979-80?

7. Can the different national inflation experiences in the post-oil-shock period be explained? What are the implications of this explanation for the widely held view that Canada's inflation in the 1970s and early 1980s was caused by the two world energy shocks and was inevitable?

8. What, according to the prediction of the rational expectations theory, were the main foreign influences on the Canadian economy during the 1970s?

9. How may Canada attempt to insulate Canadian output movements from those occurring in the rest of the world? How successful was Canadian policy in this respect since 1970?

10. What contribution did Canada's energy policy make during the second half of the 1970s to the reduction of inflation and interest rates in Canada? Why would it be *de*flationary to allow the Canadian price of energy to *rise* to world levels?

VI

MACROECONOMIC POLICY

30

Introduction to Macroeconomic Policy

You have now completed your study of macroeconomic theory — the problem of explaining macroeconomic phenomenon — and are ready to examine the implications of that theory for the formation and conduct of macroeconomic policy. There has been a good deal of policy discussion implicit in the presentation of the theory itself, but it is now time to address the policy issues more directly and systematically. This brief introductory chapter will enable you to start on this process by doing three things. It will enable you to:

a) Know what macroeconomic policies seek to achieve.
b) Know the highlights in the evolution of the policy debate.
c) Understand the idea that policy is a process and not an event.

A. What Macroeconomic Policies Seek to Achieve

There is little disagreement among economists concerning what an ideal macroeconomic performance would look like. There might be some arguments of detail, but these are insignificant compared with the broad agreement on two matters. First, it would be ideal if unemployment, except for that associated with job searching and normal labor turnover, could be entirely eliminated. That is, it would be ideal if unemployment could be kept at its "natural" rate. Equivalently, it would be ideal if output could be maintained at its full-employment equilibrium value on a continuous basis. Second, it would be ideal if inflation could be held at a steady, constant, low (perhaps,

568

ideally, zero) rate. Associated with this would be the ideal that the market rate of interest would be equal to the real rate of interest. Third, it would be ideal if the balance of payments could be zero and if the foreign exchange rate was steady and predictable. Recognizing that perfection is impossible, the objective could be expressed slightly more generally as that of minimizing the deviations of: (1) unemployment from its natural rate, (2) output from its full-employment rate, (3) inflation from zero, (4) market interest rates from real interest rates, (5) the balance of payments from zero, and (6) the exchange rate from some fixed level.

It is worth emphasizing that the specification of the unemployment objective is that of keeping unemployment as close to its natural rate as possible and *not* that of lowering the natural rate to as low a level as possible. It is important to understand that too little unemployment can have serious consequences for the economic welfare of all, even those who are from time to time unemployed. Job search and job changing are productive activities. Further, even if it is judged that the natural rate of unemployment is, in fact, too high, then the only policy measures that can be taken to influence this rate are microeconomic (relative price) policies. It would be necessary to change the unemployment insurance arrangements, methods of taxing income from employment, or some other similar matter such as was discussed in Chapter 21. In other words, the natural rate of unemployment is not itself a variable that can be influenced by the macroeconomic policy instruments of aggregate government spending, taxes, or monetary growth.

The *objectives of macroeconomic policy*, then, are to minimize the variability of unemployment and output about their natural rates and to minimize the variability of inflation around some low, possibly zero, value.

B. Highlights in the Evolution of the Policy Debate

In the nineteenth and early twentieth centuries, the general feeling was that the fluctuations in economic activity that characterized the business cycle were natural phenomena that simply had to be put up with. They were in the same class as storms, floods, and tempests. They buffeted human societies in a serious and sometimes devastating way but simply had to be accepted as one of the harsh facts of life. The Keynesian revolution, which began in the middle 1930s, but didn't achieve its full influence until the 1950s and 1960s, radically changed that view. The business cycle was seen as being controllable. It was widely believed that monetary and fiscal policy could and should be used to manipulate aggregate demand to ensure the achievement of full employment and stable prices. Some believed that monetary and fiscal policies could achieve the objective of high employment and output but not that of price stability; they were nevertheless undaunted in their pursuit of both objectives and regarded the implementation of direct controls on wages and prices or, more euphemistically, "incomes policies," as the appropriate additional instrument for achieving price stability.[1]

As we moved into the 1970s, it became increasingly apparent that macroeconomic policy was not delivering the promised stability. Inflation rates accelerated, and this despite the fact that unemployment rates were historically high and output growth sagging. Coincidental with this dismal macroeconomic policy performance there emerged a radically new view of how economic fluctuations are generated and what might be done to moderate them. The centerpiece of the new view is the hypothesis that expectations are formed rationally.[2] This hypothesis not only leads to a radical transformation in the explanation of the phenomenon of the business cycle, but also leads to a radically different view of policy.

The business cycle is viewed as the outcome of shocks to the economy that are either not correctly foreseen or not fully perceived. Policy influences the cycle in that the *unanticipated* variations in policy instruments lead to variations in output and prices. According to this view, policy is a process that has to be decomposed into an anticipated and unanticipated component. By minimizing the unanticipated variations in policy, the business cycle will be smoothed as much as is possible. There may be a case for having a pre-announced, countercyclical policy response, but there will never be a case for random, haphazard "discretionary" policy intervention. The cycle will not go away, and it may sometimes be quite severe. But ad hoc, previously unexpected attempts to intervene and boost aggregate demand can only be more destabilizing on the average than doing nothing other than pursuing a previously announced policy strategy.

It is this new view of policy that you will be introduced to in the remaining chapters of this part of the book. Before moving on to them, it will be worthwhile spending a moment or two on the final topic of this chapter.

---

[1] For a superb account of this view, see Franco Modigliani, "The Monetarist Controversy or, Should We Forsake Stabilization Policies?" *American Economic Review*, 67 (March 1977), 1-19.

[2] A very good presentation of this view, which does not explicitly introduce the rationality of expectations, but which is clearly groping in that direction, is Milton Friedman, "The Role of Monetary Policy," *American Economic Review*, 58 (March 1968), 1-17. The best discussion in the context of an explicit rational framework is Thomas J. Sargent and Neil Wallace, "Rational Expectations and the Theory of Economic Policy," *Journal of Monetary Economics*, 2 (April 1976), 169-84.

C. The Idea that Policy is a Process and Not an Event

The old-fashioned way of analyzing macroeconomic policy was to ask questions like, What will happen if the level of government spending is raised by 10 percent or if the money supply growth rate is cut from 7 percent to 4 percent? What will happen if taxes and spending are cut by the same amount? Questions of this kind are questions that treat policy as an *event*, in the sense that a certain well-defined policy action occurs. The idea, then, is to trace out the effects of this policy shock on output, prices, interest rates, employment, etc. You now understand that accepting the hypothesis that expectations are formed rationally implies that such exercises are meaningless.

It is simply not possible to analyze the effect of a single-event policy change without knowing whether or not that change was anticipated or unanticipated. Once that is known, it is possible to analyze the effects on output, prices, and the other variables in the economy. *It is not possible, however, to know whether or not a particular policy event was anticipated or unanticipated by considering that event in isolation.* It is, necessary to have a model of the evolution of the policy instruments that enables the policy instruments at any particular time to be decomposed into their anticipated and unanticipated components.

It is unavoidable that the entire policy process be analyzed so that a particular policy event may be identified as anticipated, unanticipated, or partly one and partly the other. It is also necessary to examine the broader institutional and political settings within which policies are being made, for it is the entire policy process that influences the quality of macroeconomic performance. Work of this kind is only in its infancy. It will, however, become a major part of the next generation of research in understanding and improving macroeconomic policy.

The remaining chapters in this part of the book are first of all going to examine the links between monetary and fiscal policy. This will show you that when viewing the entire monetary and fiscal policy processes, these two sets of policies are inextricably linked together. Next, we shall examine the way in which the Bank of Canada conducts its policies for achieving a particular path for the money supply. After these two preliminary chapters we shall move to the substance of the policy debate and analyze the key reasons for the differences in policy views that were set out in Chapter 1 of this book.

Summary

A. What Macroeconomic Policies Seek to Achieve

Macroeconomic policies seek to minimize fluctuations of unemployment and output about their natural rates and to minimize the variability of inflation around some low, possibly zero, value. Other objectives, such as lowering the natural rate of unemployment, are not, strictly speaking, *macroeconomic* policies. They involve *microeconomic* intervention to change relative prices.

B. Highlights in the Evolution of the Policy Debate

The pre-Keynesian view of macroeconomic policy was that nothing could be done. Fluctuations simply had to be lived with in the same way as other natural disorders. The Keynesian revolution led to the optimistic view that by manipulating monetary and fiscal policy, aggregate demand could be controlled in such a way as to achieve full employment and price stability. The new view is that because expectations are formed rationally, the best that policy can do is to avoid injecting uncertainty into the economy. Fully predictable policy is therefore required. It may be possible to achieve the best outcome with a pre-announced policy-feedback rule, but it will not be possible to do better with *ad hoc* discretionary intervention.

C. The Idea that Policy is a Process and Not an Event

If expectations are formed rationally, analyzing the implications of a policy change requires that it be decomposed into an anticipated and unanticipated component. Only by analyzing the entire process of policy is it possible to say whether a particular event was anticipated or unanticipated.

Review Questions

1. What are the objectives of macroeconomic policy?

2. Review your understanding of the three main stages in the evolution of ideas on the proper role of macroeconomic policy.

3. What does it mean to say that "policy is a process and not an event"?

31

The Constraints on Monetary and Fiscal Policy

Although governments are sovereign (within the limits of the constitution) even they must obey certain economic laws. The most fundamental of these laws, to which even governments are subject, is the law of opportunity cost or, equivalently, the principle that "there is no such thing as a free lunch."

A government cannot command use over real resources without taking them from private individuals and firms. Like private individuals and firms, the government has a budget that must be balanced, in the sense that, in the short run, the government must either tax or borrow to cover its spending. In the long run, its loans have to be repaid, so that in some fundamental sense, the government must raise taxes in an amount sufficient to cover its expenditure. This places some important limitations on the conduct of fiscal and monetary policy and introduces some important linkages between these two areas of policy.

Let us go on to explore these linkages and examine the constraints on government by pursuing three tasks, which are to:

a) Understand the nature of the government budget constraint.
b) Understand the implications of the government budget constraint for the conduct of monetary and fiscal policy.
c) Understand the implications of the government budget constraint for the formation of rational expectations.

A. Government Budget Constraint

Let us begin by examining the main items in the government's budget. Table 31.1 summarizes the government's payments and receipts. The first payment listed is government expenditure on goods and services. This is the variable that appears in the national income accounts as one of the aggregate expenditure items; it also features prominently in the theory of aggregate demand. The second item is transfer payments. These are the direct payments by the government to households and firms under various income-support programs. The third item is the interest that the government has to pay on outstanding debt. These three items added together constitute the total payments made by the government. They must be matched by government receipts.

The first item listed under receipts is legislated taxes. The prefix "legislated" is there to alert you to the idea that there are some receipts by the government that are in the nature of taxes but are not explicitly legislated. (More of this in a moment.) The legislated taxes are those on incomes, expenditure, wealth, foreign trade, and a variety of specific activities. The second receipt item is net issues of debt. Like any large organization, the government is constantly borrowing and repaying debt previously contracted. The net issue of debt constitutes the excess of newly issued debt over loans repaid. The final receipt is the net issue of currency. In a sense, this is not really a receipt. In effect, the government mints new currency simply by stamping the appropriate images on the appropriate bits of metal. Nevertheless, in terms of the government's accounts, this has to be reckoned as a receipt, since, from the point of view of the government, it is one of the things the government can use to cover its expenditure.

TABLE 31.1
The Government's Payments and Receipts

	ITEM
	Payments
	Government expenditure on goods and services
plus	Transfer payments
plus	Debt interest payments
	——————————————
equals	Total payments
	Receipts
	Legislated taxes
plus	Net issues of debt
plus	Net issue of currency
	——————————————
equals	Total Receipts

The debt issued by the government is not all bought by the general public. Some of it is bought by the Bank of Canada. Although the Bank is an independent agency, its profits, nevertheless, are paid to the federal government. This being so, it is of some importance to consider separately what happens in the Bank of Canada when new debt issues of the government are purchased by the Bank rather than by the general public. Equally important is to examine what happens inside the Bank when it buys existing debt from the public. We can examine these Bank of Canada transactions very straightforwardly by considering the changes in the Bank's balance sheet that occur in any period of time. Table 31.2 summarizes these changes.

Table 31.2 is very closely related to Table 4.2, which you studied in Chapter 4. In effect, it is the change in any given period in the items in the fourth column (the Bank's balance sheet) shown in that table. The first item is the change in the Bank's holdings of gold and foreign exchange reserves. The second item is the change in government security holdings by the Bank. These represent the changes in the Bank's assets. The next two items — change in chartered bank deposits with the Bank of Canada, and net issue of new bank notes — constitute changes in the Bank's liabilities. The difference between the change in its assets and liabilities constitutes the Bank's profit, or the change in the Bank's net worth. You can see by checking back to the fourth column of Table 4.2 (Chapter 4) that these balance sheet changes agree with the balance sheet levels set out in that table. The importance of changes in government security holdings by the Bank (minus Bank profits) is that they are equivalent to changes in the two components of the economy's monetary base — chartered bank deposits with the Bank of Canada, and bank notes.

We gain useful insights if we consolidate the government's receipts and payments with the changes in the Bank of Canada's balance sheet. This is done in Table 31.3. The first two items in Table 31.3 are exactly the same as in Table 31.1 — government expenditure on goods and services, and transfer payments. The next two items appeared in Table 31.1 as a single item. Debt interest paid by the government has now been divided into two items, that paid to the public and that

TABLE 31.2
Changes in the Bank of Canada's Balance Sheet

	Change in gold and foreign exchange reserves
add	Change in government securities
less	Change in chartered bank deposits with the Bank of Canada
less	Net issue of new bank notes
	————————————
equals	Bank of Canada's Profit

paid to the Bank of Canada. Total payments, then, in Table 31.3 are exactly the same as those in Table 31.1, but with debt interest payments separated into those paid to the Bank and those paid to the general public.

The receipts shown in Table 31.3 are more detailed than those in Table 31.1. The first item, legislated taxes, is exactly the same as before. The next item shown in Table 31.1 has been split into two parts: net issue of debt to the public and net issue of debt to the Bank of Canada. The first of these appears as the second receipt in Table 31.3. The net issue of debt to the Bank of Canada may be expressed more conveniently by using Table 31.2. Notice that the net issue of debt to the Bank (called "change in government securities" in Table 31.2) is equal to the Bank's profit, plus the change in chartered bank deposits with the Bank of Canada plus the net issue of new bank notes minus the change in gold and foreign exchange reserves. These four items appear in Table 31.3 to represent the net issue of government debt to the Bank. The next item, net issue of currency, is exactly the same as that in Table 31.1.

Now focus on the column on the right-hand side of Table 31.3. It provides a summary of the payments and receipts by the consolidated government-central bank sector. Government expenditure is called G, transfer payments TR, and debt interest paid to the public DI. Debt interest paid to the Bank is not given a symbolic name, nor are

TABLE 31.3
Consolidation of Government and the Bank of Canada

	ITEM	
	Payments	
	Government expenditure on goods and services	G
plus	Transfer payments	TR
plus	Debt interest paid to public	DI
plus	Debt interest paid to the Bank of Canada	
equals	Total payments	
	Receipts	
	Legislated taxes	TAX
plus	Net issue of debt to the public	ΔD
plus	Profits of the Bank of Canada	
plus	Change in chartered bank deposits with the Bank of Canada	
plus	Net issue of bank notes	ΔDC_c
less	Change in gold and foreign exchange reserves	
plus	Net issue of Currency	
equals	Total Receipts	

profits received from the Bank. Assuming that the Bank's operating costs are small relative to the total interest payments received by the Bank, these two items may be regarded as approximately offsetting each other because there is a receipt and a payment that are of approximate equal magnitude.

On the receipts side of the account, legislated taxes are labelled *TAX*, and the net issue of debt to the public is labelled ΔD. The final four items — the change in chartered bank deposits with the Bank of Canada, the net issue of bank notes, and net issue of currency, and the negative of the change in gold and foreign exchange reserves — are lumped together as a single item. You will recognize that item (referring back if necessary to Chapter 4 and to Chapter 25) as the change in the monetary base, ΔMB, less the change in reserves ΔF or, more simply, the change in central bank domestic credit, ΔDC_c. In what follows, we shall suppose that we are studying an economy whose exchange rate is flexible and whose reserve changes are zero (or negligible) so we shall use ΔMB and ΔDC_c interchangeably.

The sum of the receipts by the government must exactly equal the sum of the payments made by the government. This is the government budget constraint:

$$G + DI + TR - TAX - \Delta D - \Delta MB = 0 \qquad (31.1)$$

This says that the government must raise taxes or borrow or create money on a scale exactly equal to the volume of its purchases of goods and services and its payments of debt interest and transfer payments. Let us now move on to consider some of the implications of this government budget constraint.

B. Government Budget Constraint and the Conduct of Monetary and Fiscal Policy

The government's budget constraint with which we ended the last section may be rewritten in the following form:

$$\Delta MB + \Delta D = G + DI + TR - TAX \qquad (31.2)$$

This emphasizes that the expansion of the stock of monetary base and of government debt will necessarily be equal to the difference between the government's total spending and its legislated tax receipts. This immediately places a link between monetary policy and fiscal policy. You can think of monetary policy as the rate at which the money stock grows. You can think of fiscal policy as the scale of government spending and the scale of taxes. The government budget constraint says that there is a connection between these two. It also says, however, that so long as the government is able or willing to issue debt (ΔD) and pay interest on it (DI), there is no hard-and-fast link between the two branches of macroeconomic policy. In any given short-term period (a year or two, or perhaps even five years or so), the government may issue debt to loosen the link between monetary and fiscal policy. You are now going to discover, however, that on the average and over the long run, this cannot be so.

To get a feel for why this is, imagine what would happen if you spent more than your income. For the first year you could perhaps go to the bank and get a loan to cover the deficit. You might even be able to do that for two years, or if you had a very indulgent bank manager, perhaps for a third year. At some stage, however, the day of reckoning would arrive. It would be necessary to tighten the reins, lower consumption, and start to pay off the loans that have accumulated. Although the details differ, exactly the same constraints necessarily apply to the government. To see why this is so, it is necessary to understand that when the government issues debt, it is doing nothing other than deferring taxes.

The government issues all kinds of debt. Some of it is long-term debt, with twenty-five or more years to run to the date at which the government will redeem it. Some debt is medium-term, with ten to fifteen years to run to the redemption date; and some is short-term debt, with up to five years to run to the redemption date. In addition, the government issues very short-term debt in the form of three-month treasury bills. Further, some government debt is non-marketable and takes the form of savings bonds. This type of debt is redeemable on demand, but at a penalty to the holder.

Although the government issues many different kinds of debt, it is sensible to think of government debt as if it was a *perpetuity*. A perpetuity is a bond that will never be redeemed by the issuer. The British government issued such bonds in the eighteenth and nineteenth centuries. They are called *consols*. Although the government of Canada does not issue such bonds, it is nevertheless sensible to think of all Canadian government debt as perpetual debt. The reason why this is so is that although the particular bonds issued by the government will be redeemed, when they are redeemed they will be replaced by new bonds. Thus, the debt is continuously turned over, with new bonds being issued to replace the old bonds that are retired. We can therefore think of government debt as perpetual debt rather than as debt that will be repaid.

A perpetuity is a bond that promises to pay a certain sum of money each year forever. Call that amount $c. The bond will never be redeemed, so that it has no redemption price. However, it can be sold to someone else, and the new owner will receive the $c per annum while in possession of the bond. How much would a person be willing to pay for a bond that promised to pay $c per annum in perpetuity? Let us call the price that a person would be willing to pay $V. If you invested $V in the best alternative asset, say a corporate bond or some physical capital or a private business, you would make a rate of return of, let us say, r percent per annum. Clearly, you would not be interested in buying a government bond that promised to pay $c per annum unless the rate of return on that bond was at least as great as the r percent per annum that you could obtain from some other activity.

Expressed as an equation — with the price of the bond $V and the payment by the government $c per annum — the rate of return on the bond is as follows:

$$\text{Rate of Return} = \frac{\$c}{\$V} \cdot 100$$

If

$$\frac{\$c}{\$V} \cdot 100 > r\%$$

then you would be interested in buying government bonds. But if

$$\frac{\$c}{\$V} \cdot 100 < r\%$$

then you would want to buy government bonds. Indeed, anyone holding a government bond in such a situation would want to sell it. In the first situation everyone would be wanting to buy government bonds and in the second situation everyone would be wanting to sell them. With everyone buying government bonds their price would rise and with everyone selling government bonds their price would fall. Thus, government bonds will have an equilibrium price when

$$\frac{\$c}{\$V} \cdot 100 = r\%$$

From this, it is clear that the price of the government bond will be

$$\$V = \frac{\$c}{r\%} \cdot 100$$

For example, if a bond promised to pay $5.00 per annum, and if the rate of interest was 5 percent per annum, then the price of the bond would be $100. The price of a government bond could be written equivalently as

$$\$V = \frac{\$c}{r}$$

where r is the rate of interest expressed as a proportion of 1 (i.e., $r\% \div 100$).

Now suppose the government issues a bond and receives $V. So that you can see the value of this to the government, let us isolate the bond sale and subsequent interest payments on the bond from the other receipts and expenditure of the government. To do this we must assume that the government is not going to change its expenditure on goods and services or transfers, nor change the taxes that it legislates, nor create any new money. It is simply going to issue its

bond and allow the bond to be completely self-financing. You can think of this as meaning that when the government receives the proceeds from its bond sale, V, it has to set aside a fund that will generate sufficient interest income to enable it to meet the interest payments on the bond of c per annum in perpetuity.

Let us suppose, then, that the government has sold a bond for V (which is equal to c/r, where c is the number of dollars per annum that the government will pay out on the bond). How much must the government set aside to be able to meet these interest payments? At the end of the first year the government will need c from its fund. If it set aside a sum of money a_1 such that a_1 plus the interest received on a_1, namely $r\$a_1$, was equal to c_1, then it would have enough money to pay out c at the end of the first year. For example, if the rate of interest is 5 percent and the government is committed to paying $5 on the bond at the end of one year, it will need to set aside approximately $4.76 at the beginning of the year. The $4.76 invested at 5 percent would yield a 24¢ interest income which, when added to the $4.76 investment, would give the government the $5 that it needs to meet its bond-interest payment. To meet its bond-interest payments in two years time, it needs to set aside a sum of money such that the interest on the sum plus the interest on the first year's interest would add up to a suffucient sum to pay the bond interest. Call this sum of money a_2. It would be a sum such that $a_2(1 + r)^2 = c$. In general, then, in order to meet *all* its interest payments out into the future, the government would need to set aside sums of money as shown in Table 31.4. Thus, if the government is going to have enough funds to meet the interest payments on its bond over the infinite life of the bond, it will need a fund equal to $a_1 + \$a_2 + \$a_3 + \cdots + \$a_i + \cdots$. (The dots "$\cdots$" stand for all the terms not written explicitly.) We can work out the value of each a_i from Table 31.4: if you divide c by $(1+r)$, then you get a_1; if you divide c by $(1+r)^2$, then you get a_2; if you divide c by $(1+r)^i$, then you get a_i.

Thus, the amount that the government will have to set aside (S) to meet *all* the future interest payments on its bonds is

$$S = \frac{\$c}{1+r} + \frac{\$c}{(1+r)^2} + \cdots + \frac{\$c}{(1+r)^i} + \cdots$$

TABLE 31.4
The Funds Needed to Pay Interest on a Perpetuity

To pay $c in one year you need	a_1 now such that	$a_1 (1+r) = \$c$
To pay $c in two years you need	a_2 now such that	$a_2 (1+r)^2 = \$c$
To pay $c in three years you need	a_3 now such that	$a_3 (1+r)^3 = \$c$
To pay $c in i years you need	a_i now such that	$a_i (1+r)^i = \$c$

or, equivalently,

$$S = \left[\frac{1}{1+r} + \frac{1}{(1+r)^2} + \cdots + \frac{1}{(1+r)^i} + \cdots \right] \$c \qquad \textbf{(31.3)}$$

To figure out how much this is, we need to add up the infinite sum inside the brackets in Equation (31.3) above. To do this, multiply both sides of Equation (31.3) by $1/(1+r)$.
This will give

$$\frac{1}{(1+r)} S = \left[\frac{1}{(1+r)^2} + \cdots + \frac{1}{(1+r)^i} + \cdots \right] \$c \qquad \textbf{(31.4)}$$

All the missing terms in Equation (31.3) represented by the dots will be identical to the missing terms in Equation (31.4), except for the last term in Equation (31.4). That last term in Equation (31.4) will equal the last term in Equation (31.3) multiplied by $1/(1+r)$. However, as you go further and further into the future, the terms $1/(1+r)^i$ become very very small and can be ignored. So, ignoring the last term in Equation (31.4), you can subtract Equation (31.4) from Equation (31.3) to obtain

$$S - \left(\frac{1}{1+r} \right) S = \left(\frac{1}{1+r} \right) \$c \qquad \textbf{(31.5)}$$

Then multiply both sides of Equation (31.5) by $(1+r)$ to give

$$S(1+r) - S = \$c \qquad \textbf{(31.6)}$$

or

$$S + rS - S = \$c \qquad \textbf{(31.7)}$$

Or, more simply,

$$S = \frac{\$c}{r} \qquad \textbf{(31.8)}$$

So, S, the sum that the government would need to set aside in order to meet the interest payments on its bond, is equal to $\$c/r$. But this is exactly the sum the government receives when it sells the bond. *It would be necessary, therefore, if the government is to make its bond self-financing, to set aside all the receipts from the bond to meet future interest payments.* Thus, when proper accounting is made for the future interest payments that a bond will generate, the government gets precisely nothing when it sells a bond. You can think of selling a bond as simply putting off the evil day of raising taxes — or cutting spending. It is possible for the government to increase its revenue in any one year by selling more bonds, but it cannot increase its revenue indefinitely by selling bonds since it immediately commits itself to an interest stream that exactly offsets the receipts that it obtains from its bond sales. The implication of this for the government's budget constraint is very important. It means that *the government cannot regard bond financing as anything other than deferred taxes.*

It may have occurred to you that there is a possibility of the government avoiding eventually having to raise taxes to pay for its current bond financing by always selling bonds to pay the future interest commitment on its current bonds. In effect, the government could put off the evil day forever by always borrowing more. A moment's reflection will lead you to the conclusion that if the government did pursue this course, and if — aside from borrowing to cover debt interest — the government had a balanced budget, the stock of government bonds outstanding would grow at a rate equal to the rate of interest on bonds.

You can see this directly by considering a situation in which the government initially had a stock of bonds outstanding of, say, $100, and in which the rate of interest was, say, 10 percent per annum. In year two the government would sell $10 worth of bonds to pay the interest on the initial $100 worth. Its outstanding stock of bonds would then be $110. The next year the government would issue $11 worth of bonds to pay the $10 interest on the original $100 worth plus the $1 interest on the $10 bond issued in year two. This process would continue forever with the stock of bonds outstanding growing at 10 percent per annum. Of course, since the rate of interest on bonds represents in part the real rate of interest and in part an inflation component, the real stock of government bonds outstanding would not be growing at that same rate of interest. The real stock would in fact grow at a rate equal to the real rate of interest. Provided the economy is growing — the population, the stock of capital equipment, and wealth in general — the government can get away with this device of always borrowing to pay interest on its debt but only to the extent that it permits its stock of bonds outstanding to grow at the same rate as the economy as a whole.

Now consider what would happen if the government tried to issue new bonds to pay interest on its old bonds, but at a rate that involved the stock of government bonds growing faster than the growth rate of total wealth in the economy. In such a situation the fraction of government bonds held in the portfolios of households and firms would be continuously rising. There would come a point at which the total amount of private sector assets consisted of nothing other than government bonds. There would be no space in people's balance sheets to hold physical capital and corporate debt. Government debt would be the only debt in existence.

Of course, real capital generates a real rate of return and is itself the source of economic growth. In contrast, government debt does not generate any real return for the economy as a whole. The interest payments on government debt simply constitute a transfer of wealth from taxpayers to bondholders. Thus, an economy in which the government had attempted to increase its outstanding debt to pay interest on old debt at too fast a rate would be one in which the stock of capital had declined and general economic decline had set in.

It is clear from these considerations that the maximum long-run sustainable growth rate of government debt is equal to the growth rate of the overall stock of real wealth in the economy. In what follows we shall abstract from such long-term growth considerations. You should be careful to note, therefore, that the analysis that follows would need to be modified slightly to allow for the case where the economy was growing at some positive steady rate. In effect, you would need to add to the government's revenue sources the possibility of obtaining revenue in perpetuity by allowing the stock of its bonds outstanding to grow at the same rate as the economy as a whole. Let us now return to the case where there is no ongoing growth and the government cannot regard its bond financing as a permanent source of revenue but rather as deferred taxes.

We can use the result that we obtained above to condense the government budget constraint into a more fundamental statement. First, let us consolidate taxes, *TAX*, and transfers, *TR*, into a single item — *NET TAX* equals *TAX* less *TR*. Second, since the receipts from bond sales less the debt interest paid on outstanding bonds generate a future tax liability, let us also combine those items with *NET TAX* to obtain a single item $\overline{T}$ equal to *NET TAX* plus ΔD less *DI*. Be careful to notice that this is an unconventional definition of taxes. It includes all *current* taxes minus all *current* transfers plus the *future* taxes that are implied by the *current* difference between bond sales and interest payments.

The government budget constraint may now be collapsed into the simpler statement, namely,

$$G - \overline{T} = \Delta MB \tag{31.9}$$

In the next chapter, the connection between the monetary base and the money supply itself will be explored. For the rest of this chapter, let us agree to take on trust the proposition that, on the average, the growth rate of the monetary base and the growth rate of the money supply will be the same. Equivalently, we could say that the change in the monetary base will be some fraction of the change in the money supply. Let us call that fraction q. In this case,

$$\Delta MB = q\Delta M \tag{31.10}$$

We could now use Equation (31.10) to replace the change in monetary base with the fraction q of the change in the total money supply to obtain

$$G - \overline{T} = q\Delta M$$

However, it may be more instructive to view this government budget constraint in *real terms* — the real government budget constraint. We can do this by dividing through the budget constraint by the price level. Let us divide the above equation by the *GNP* Deflator P to obtain

$$\frac{G}{P} - \frac{\bar{T}}{P} = \frac{q\Delta M}{\bar{P}}$$

Now define $G/P = \bar{g}$ and $\bar{T}/P = \bar{t}$. This means that

$$g - \bar{t} = \bar{q}\left(\frac{\Delta M}{P}\right) \tag{31.11}$$

Next multiply and divide the right-hand side of this equation by M, i.e.,

$$q\left(\frac{\Delta M}{P}\right) = q\left(\frac{\Delta M}{P}\right)\cdot\left(\frac{M}{M}\right)$$

This leaves the value of the equation undisturbed. However, you can now see, changing the order of the variables, that

$$q\left(\frac{\Delta M}{P}\right) = q\left(\frac{M}{P}\right)\cdot\left(\frac{\Delta M}{M}\right)$$

Also, you will recall that $\Delta M/M = \mu$, the growth rate of the money supply. Therefore,

$$q\left(\frac{\Delta M}{P}\right) = q\left(\frac{M}{P}\right)\cdot\mu$$

Using this equation to replace the right-hand side of Equation (31.11) gives

$$\bar{g} - \bar{t} = q\left(\frac{M}{P}\right)\mu \tag{31.12}$$

This is the *fundamental government budget constraint equation*. This equation cannot be violated. It tells us that whenever the government changes its expenditure, it must change at least one other variable. It must either change taxes or change the growth rate of the money supply.

Another instructive way of looking at the government's fundamental budget constraint equation is one that emphasizes the nature of money creation as a tax. When the government creates new money (monetary base) it is able to use that money to acquire goods and services, or make transfer payments, in exactly the same way as it does when it spends the revenue collected in legislated taxes. Thus, money creation is like a tax. Part of the money creation tax is available purely as a consequence of real economic growth. As real incomes grow so also the demand for money grows and the government can obtain resources by spending the new money that is created merely to meet the growing demand for money. This part of the tax from money creation is known as the growth tax.

If the government creates money at a rate in excess of that needed to meet the demands of a growing economy it is still able to use that additional money to acquire goods and services. As a consequence, however, inflation will ensue. The part of the tax from money creation over and above that needed to meet the demands of a growing economy is called the inflation tax.

The rate of economic growth tends to be rather constant so the growth tax is not highly variable. Rather, variations in the tax from money creation are primarily reflected in variations in the inflation tax. To summarize: the government must raise taxes to cover its spending. There are two sources of taxes — legislated taxes, $\bar{t}$, and the money creation tax $\mu q(M/P)$. The latter comprises the growth tax (which does not vary much) and the inflation tax. There is no restriction on the government as to the extent to which it uses either of these sources of revenue. The restriction is that it must raise a large enough total from both of them, taken together, to cover its expenditure.

C. Government Budget Constraint and Formation of Rational Expectations

The government budget constraint has dramatic implications for the formation of rational expectations. It will not be rational to expect a monetary and fiscal policy that violates the government's budget constraint. To expect a violation of that constraint is to expect something that cannot happen. Such an expectation would not be rational. This means that if at some time a government is running a large current deficit and issuing a larger quantity of bonds, then the rational expectation will be that at some future date, government expenditure is going to be cut, or legislated taxes are going to be increased, or the rate of money printing and, therefore, of inflation, is going to be increased. Based on the best analysis available of the constraints operating upon the government and its likely course in the future, individuals will rationally assign weights to these alternative future changes in government actions. A government, or more generally, a political system, that has a long-run track record of repeatedly inflating its way out of short-run financial problems will rationally be expected to pursue such policies again in the future. A government that has heavily constrained itself from using the inflation tax by, for example, setting up a highly independent central bank with extensive powers to control the growth rate of the money supply independently of the short-term wishes of the government will be one that will rationally be expected to correct any short-term deficit by either raising legislated taxes or cutting spending rather than by increasing the inflation tax.

There will no hard-and-fast, simple-to-state rule that will enable individuals to make the correct inferences concerning future monetary and fiscal policy. The hard fact of the government budget constraint must, however, be taken into account in forming a rational expectation as to likely future changes in the direction of policy. Only if the government is currently running a deficit that is being financed by its current rate of money printing is it pursuing a policy that can be pursued on the average over the long term. The pursuit of such a policy will simplify the task faced by individuals in forming rational expectations, but it will by no means eliminate the problem.

Summary

A. Government Budget Constraint

The government budget constraint states that total government expenditure on goods and services, transfers to individuals, and debt interest must equal receipts from legislated taxes, the sales of new debt, and the creation of new money.

B. Government Budget Constraint and the Conduct of Monetary and Fiscal Policy

Although the government can issue debt, thereby weakening the link between monetary and fiscal policy in the short run, on the average over the long term, debt interest has to be paid that exactly offsets the receipts from debt sales. This means that, in effect, issuing debt is the same thing as deferring taxes. The long-term average government budget constraint does not give the government the option of raising debt. There is, therefore, on the average, a fundamental connection between fiscal policy and monetary policy. Conventionally, legislated taxes together with the creation of new money must raise sufficient funds to cover the government's expenditure. Monetary policy and fiscal policy, on the average, are interdependent.

C. Government Budget Constraint and Formation of Rational Expectations

It will not be rational to form an expectation of long-term money growth and inflation that is based on a violation of the government's budget constraint. In a situation in which the government is currently running a deficit or surplus, and issuing (or retiring) large volumes of debt, individuals will have to form a rational expectation concerning which of the variables in the government's budget constraint will be varied in order to satisfy the long-term average budget constraint. In some situations it will be rational to expect a future burst of inflation, whereas in others it will be rational to expect continued mild inflation and adjustments of legislated taxes or expenditure.

Review Questions

1. Review the items that appear in the government's budget constraint.

2. Sort the following items into the three items in the government's budget constraint (i.e., expenditure on goods and services, taxes, and money creation):

    (a) welfare payments

    (b) the purchase of a typewriter financed by printing $100

    (c) the purchase of a foreign security (be careful here)

    (d) social security payments and receipts

    (e) national defense expenditure.

3. Why are "legislated" taxes so-called?

4. Explain why transfer payments may (as a first approximation) be treated as negative taxes.

5. Review the links between the government and central bank and explain how the "change in the monetary base" gets into the government's budget constraint.

6. What is the relationship between the price that someone will pay for a bond and the stream-of-interest payments on that bond?

7. Calculate the equilibrium market price of a perpetuity that promises to pay $1 per annum, given that interest rates on alternative available assets are currently 8 percent.

8. "The present value of a bond is always zero." Explain.

9. If the price for which a bond can be sold is exactly the same as the present value of the future stream-of-interest payments, why would anyone issue bonds?

10. Explain why bond sales are deferred taxes.

11. If the government can issue money on which it does not have to pay interest, why do you suppose we observe governments issuing debt on which they do have to pay interest?

12. Explain why, on the average, the government must finance its expenditure with either legislated taxes or the inflation tax.

13. Review your understanding of why it would be irrational to expect the government to be able to issue debt on an increasing scale indefinitely.

14. Looking at Canadian monetary policy and fiscal policy since 1970, what conclusions do you reach concerning a rational expectation about future monetary and fiscal policy changes in Canada?

32
Control of the Money Supply

The quantity of money in existence — the money supply — features prominently in macroeconomic theory as a major influence on aggregate demand and the price level. The anticipated level (and growth rate) of money is the single most important factor determining the price level (and the rate of inflation). Unanticipated changes in the money supply are a major source of fluctuations in output and employment.

The final thing that we need to do before getting on with the substance of analyzing macroeconomic stabilization policy is to examine how the money supply is determined and controlled. In the last chapter we asked you to take on trust the proposition that, on the average, the monetary base and the total money supply stand in some constant relationship to each other. This chapter will explain why this is a reasonable proposition. It will look at the detailed linkages between the money supply and the monetary base, and at the way in which the Bank of Canada has, in the past, conducted monetary policy with a view to achieving a target growth path for the monetary aggregate M1. The chapter will *not* present a comprehensive description of the Bank's operations, however.

The chapter contains two tasks, which are to:

a) understand the links between the monetary base and the money supply

b) understand how the Bank of Canada has operated to achieve a target growth path for the money supply and how the money supply is influenced by the Bank's targeting of the exchange rate.

A. The Links Between the Monetary Base and the Money Supply

The starting point for understanding the links between the monetary base and money supply is two definitions. Both definitions are implied in the economy balance sheet structure that you studied in Chapter 4. The first is the definition of the money supply. It is convenient when analyzing the determinants of the money supply to decompose it into two parts — the monetary base held by the public and the bank deposits held by the public. (Which bank deposits we would count would depend on which monetary aggregate we were dealing with. We are going to deal with M1 in this chapter, although we shall use the symbol M to denote this aggregate.) Let us write the definition of the money supply as follows:

$$M = MB_p + D \qquad\qquad (32.1)$$

In this definition, M stands for the money supply, MB_p for the notes and coins held by the public, and D for bank deposits.

The next definition concerns the monetary base itself. The monetary base consists of the notes and coins held by the public (MB_p), which is already in the above definition, and the notes and coins together with deposits at the Bank held by the chartered banks, which we will call MB_b. The monetary base, then, is allocated across the two holders — the public and the banks — so that

$$MB = MB_p + MB_b \qquad\qquad (32.2)$$

These are just definitions and they don't tell us anything about what determines either the money supply or the monetary base.

The first behavioral hypothesis that we need is one concerning the general public's allocation of money between notes and coins and deposits. The general idea is that in conducting our everyday transactions, there is a fairly stable fraction of those transactions that we would customarily undertake with notes and coins. This means that we would want to hold a fairly stable fraction of our total money holdings in the form of currency. Let us call that fraction v. This means that we could say that

$$MB_p = vM \qquad O < v < 0 \qquad\qquad (32.3)$$

This simply says that v is some fraction, and the amount of monetary base (notes and coins) that people on the average hold is equal to that fraction v of their total money holdings. There is an equivalent proposition which is that bank deposits are equal to one minus the fraction v times total money. That is,

$$D = (1-v)M \qquad \qquad (32.4)$$

Although this is a pretty mechanical proposition about how people allocate their money between currency and bank deposits, provided the bank deposits are non-interest bearing, it seems to be a reasonable hypothesis and one that adequately describes the facts.

The next thing that we need to consider is how the banks decide how much monetary base to hold. That is, what is the demand for monetary base by the banks? This question is a lot like the question, What determines the demand for money by households and firms? Why do the banks hold monetary base? That is, why do they hold notes and coins and deposits with the Bank of Canada? The answer is that they hold notes and coins in order to be able to meet demands for currency on the part of their customers. They also hold deposits at the Bank of Canada so that they can make payments to other banks. They need to do this when the total value of all the checks paid by their customers in any one trading period exceeds the value of checks paid to their customers during that same period. As a general rule, it will be obvious that the bigger the volume of bank deposits that a bank has accepted, the bigger the size of currency reserves and Bank of Canada deposits the bank will need to keep on hand. The volume of bank deposits, then, is the first determinant of the demand for monetary base by the chartered banks.

When studying the demand for money by individuals, we discovered that at high rates of interest (and high rates of inflation), there is a bigger incentive for people to try to economize on their holdings of money than when interest rates (and inflation) are low. The market rate of interest was seen as the opportunity cost of holding money. Similar considerations apply to the decision by a chartered bank on how much of its deposits to hold in the form of monetary base reserves. Deposits placed with a bank can be used by that bank for two kinds of purposes. One is to hold monetary base. The other is to acquire interest-earning assets of various kinds, including making loans to households and firms. Clearly, the bank makes no money on its holdings of monetary base. Profits for a bank are obtained by making loans and buying interest-earning securities. Just as households economize on their holdings at high interest rates, so also will banks. The higher the rate of interest on loans and securities, the more will banks economize on their holdings of monetary base, and the smaller will be the fraction of their deposits held as reserves and the larger the fraction that will be lent.

There are two factors, then, that determine the bank's demand for monetary base. One is the total volume of deposits that the bank has accepted. The larger the volume of deposits, the bigger the amount of monetary base required. The other is the level of interest rates. The higher the interest rate, the more will the bank seek to economize on its monetary base and, therefore, the lower will be its holdings of monetary base.

We can summarize all this in a very simple equation that looks a lot like the demand for money function of households and firms. This equation says that

$$MB_b = zD + mb_0 - \ell_b r_m \qquad 0 < z < 1; \; mb_0, \; \ell_b > 0 \qquad \textbf{(32.5)}$$

What this equation says is that, other things being equal (for a given market rate of interest), the higher the level of bank deposits, the more monetary base banks will hold. For a $1 million rise in deposits, they would hold a fraction z of $1 million in extra monetary base.

The fraction of total deposits z that the banks will want to hold in the form of monetary base represents two kinds of influences: one imposed on the bank, and the other, part of its voluntary behavior. Imposed on the bank is a minimum required reserve holding below which the bank is not permitted to let its monetary base holdings fall. Over and above this, on the average the bank will find it prudent to hold a certain level of reserves in excess of the required reserves. The fraction z represents the sum of both of these influences.

In addition to the effect of deposits on monetary base holdings of the bank, there is the influence of interest rates. Let us suppose that the term $mb_0 - \ell_b r_m$, on the average, is equal to zero. That is, if interest rates are at their long-run average level, the demand for monetary base by the banks would be completely described by the fraction z of total deposits. If, however, interest rates go above their average level, then the banks will seek to economize on monetary base holdings; and if interest rates go below their average level, then the banks will be less eager to make loans and economize on monetary base. This is what the second two terms in the above equation are saying.

In order to derive the supply of money in the economy, all that is necessary is to examine the equilibrium in the market for monetary base itself. The supply of money function is not like an ordinary supply function. Like the aggregate supply and aggregate demand functions, it is an equilibrium locus. The market that is in equilibrium on the money supply function is the market for monetary base. By setting the supply of monetary base equal to the demand for monetary base, we can find the quantity of money that will be supplied. To do this, we need the following equation:

$$MB = vM + z(1-v)M + mb_0 - \ell_b r_m \qquad \textbf{(32.6)}$$

The left-hand side of this equation is the supply of monetary base. The right-hand side is the demand for monetary base by the public and by the banks. The term (vM) is the demand for monetary base by the public (fraction v of the total money supply). The remaining terms represent the demand for monetary base by the banks. The first of these is z times bank deposits. Bank deposits are represented as $(1-v)M$; we know this from Equation (32.4) above. The final two terms represent the interest-sensitive component of the demand for monetary base by the banks, which, on the average, we are taking to be zero. You can now collect together the first two terms that multiply M and obtain

$$MB = [v + z(1-v)]M + mb_0 - \ell_b r_m$$

Then divide both sides of this equation by $[v+z(1-v)]$, to give

$$M = \frac{1}{v + z(1-v)} \{MB - mb_0 + \ell_b r_m\} \qquad \textbf{(32.7)}$$

What this says is that the money supply will be some multiple of the monetary base — (the multiple being $1/[v +z(1-v)]$ on the average — but will deviate from that in the same direction as variations in the interest rate. The higher the market rate of interest, other things given, the higher would be the money supply.

You are now in a position to summarize the links between the monetary base and the money supply. When the demand for monetary base equals the supply of monetary base, there is a direct relationship between the supply of money and the supply of monetary base. Other things being equal, a \$1 million rise in the monetary base will produce a rise in the money supply of $1/[v +z(1-v)]$ million dollars. For a given monetary base, the higher the market rate of interest, the greater will be the money supply. This arises because banks will seek to economize on their use of monetary base at higher interest rates.

We can link the above discussion with that in the previous chapter by noting that, on the average, the money supply and money base will be linked by the simpler relation

$$M = \frac{1}{v+z(1-v)} (MB) \qquad \textbf{(32.8)}$$

or, more compactly, definining $v + z(1-v) = q$, we have

$$M = \frac{1}{q} (MB) \qquad \textbf{(32.9)}$$

The fraction q in this equation is exactly the same fraction as q introduced in the previous chapter.

The link that we have established between the monetary base, interest rates, and the money supply is not to be confused with a statement that says the money supply is determined by the monetary base and the rate of interest. It could well be that the monetary base itself responds to interest rates and the money supply in such a way that the actual path of the money supply is determined by some exogenous policy decision, and the monetary base and interest rates are the variables that do the adjusting to make that path possible.

To emphasize this possibility, consider the above relationship between the money supply and the monetary base written in the following way:

$$MB = qM$$

(This is exactly the same as Equation (32.9) except that both sides have been multiplied by q and the two sides of the equation have been reversed). If the money supply itself was determined by the factors that influence the demand for money, then the monetary base would be indirectly determined by the demand for money. Thus,

$$MB = qM^d$$

This alternative way of looking at the link between the money supply and the monetary base is, in fact, one that better describes the way in which the money supply and monetary base have been determined by the policy actions of the Bank of Canada. This is what we are now going to examine.

B. The Bank of Canada's Control of the Money Supply

If the relationship between the monetary base and the money supply which we have just examined was a very precise one, it would be possible for the Bank of Canada to exploit the relationship in order to achieve the desired path for the money supply. The Bank would simply have to manipulate the monetary base from day to day in whatever way was required in order to make the money supply grow at the desired growth rate. The Bank of Canada believes, however, that the relationship between the monetary base and the money supply is not a very precise one and, in fact, is insufficiently precise to give predictable control over the money supply. Whether or not the Bank is correct in that belief is a question of some controversy, and it would not be possible to settle the matter here.

As a matter of fact the Bank has had a variety of alternative attitudes towards controlling the money supply. We are already aware that there have been periods in Canada's history when the foreign exchange rate has been fixed. You know from your study of the links between reserves, the money supply, and the exchange rate that in such a situation the Bank has in effect abdicated control of the money stock, allowing it to be determined purely by forces outside its control. There have also been periods during which, although the Bank has not in a formal sense been pursuing a fixed exchange rate, its foreign exchange rate targeting policies have been so heavy-handed as to in effect preclude any independent monetary control. Such appears to be the behavior of the Bank of Canada in the middle 1980s following the abandonment of money supply control.

There was a period, however, between 1975 and 1980 when the Bank of Canada did pursue explicit money supply targeting. During this period the Bank sought to achieve target growth paths for the M1 monetary aggregate. The technique of monetary control employed during that period is an interesting one and worth examining. It did not exploit directly the link between the money base and the quantity of money for the reasons noted above (the Bank having sufficient faith in the predictability of the multiplier linking those two magnitudes). Rather the Bank approached the task of monetary control in an indirect manner. It started out with the demand for money function rather than the supply of money function as the first input into its monetary control exercise. Recall that the demand for money function says that the demand depends on real income and the market rate of interest. That is, writing the demand for money function as we did in Chapter 11,

$$\frac{M^d}{P} = ky + m_0 - \ell r_m$$

In effect, the way the Bank proceeded was to estimate, using statistical techniques, the values of the parameters of the demand for money function (k, m_0, ℓ). It then selected its target for the money supply — we shall call that monetary target M^*. It then forecasted the price level and the income level that it thought would prevail on the average over the coming months. Let us call the Bank's forecasted values of the price level and real income, respectively, P^f and y^f. The Bank then "solved" the demand for money function for the market rate of interest that would be required in order to make the amount of money demanded equal the money supply *target*, given the forecast of prices and income. We can obtain that solution simply by rearranging the demand for money function in the following way. First of all, set the demand for money M^d equal to the target money supply M^* and set the levels of income and prices equal to their forecasted values y^f and P^f. That is,

$$\frac{M^*}{P^f} = ky^f + m_0 - \ell r_m$$

Now rearrange this equation to "solve" for the market rate of interest. That is,

$$r_m = \frac{1}{\ell} \{ky^f + m_0 - \frac{M^*}{P^f}\}$$

This equation tells us the market rate of interest which, if the Bank achieves it and if the Bank's forecasts of income and prices are correct, will on the average make the money supply equal to M^*, the target money supply.

The way in which the Bank actually got the interest rate to move up or down to the desired level is by tightening or loosening its hold over the monetary base. If the Bank wants to make interest rates rise, it sells government securities from its own portfolio to the general public. As people pay for these securities, so the monetary base falls, and the banks find themselves short of reserves. To replenish their reserves the banks start to sell their short-term securities, thereby putting further upward pressure on market rates of interest. The Bank would hold conditions tight in the credit markets until the market rate of interest has risen to the level the Bank wishes to achieve in accordance with the above equation, a level that it is hoped will achieve the monetary target. If the Bank wants to lower the rate of interest, then it would go into the marketplace and buy government securities, paying for them, in effect, with newly created monetary base. In this event, the banks would find themselves with surplus reserves, would seek to lend those reserves, and in the process, would put downward pressure on interest rates. Again, the Bank would keep credit market conditions loose until interest rates had fallen to the level that it felt appropriate for the achievement of its monetary target.

This technique of monetary control which was employed by the Bank of Canada in the late 1970s and early 1980s is far from perfect. The Bank could be considerably wrong in its forecasts of prices and income and, to the extent that it is wrong, it will miss its money supply target. You can see this very easily if you perform the following exercise. Use the equation that we solved above for the Bank's chosen rate of interest and substitute that back into the demand for money function. You will then obtain the following equation:

$$\frac{M^d}{P} = ky + m_0 - \frac{\ell}{\ell}\{ky^f + m_0 - \frac{M^*}{P^f}\}$$

Notice that this equation simplifies considerably to the following:

$$\frac{M^d}{P} = \frac{M^*}{P^f} + k(y - y^f)P$$

which may be further rearranged by multiplying through by the price level to give

$$M^d = M^*\frac{P}{P^f} + k(y - y^f)P$$

Let us pause and see what this equation is telling us. Given the technique of control of the money supply used by the Bank of Canada, it is the demand for money that will determine how much money is in existence. The left-hand side of the equation therefore tells us what the quantity of money will be. It will be the same as M^d. How will that relate to the Bank's target? The answer is that it will deviate from the target in general. In order to be bang on target, the Bank would have to forecast the price level correctly. That is, the actual price level (P) would have to equal the forecasted price level P^f. Furthermore, the forecast of income would have to be equal to actual income. If the actual price level turned out to be bigger than the forecasted price level, then, with a correct income forecast, the money supply would exceed the desired money supply by the same percentage as the price level exceeds the forecasted price level. If the level of income turned out to be higher than the forecasted level of income, then the money supply would exceed its target by an amount equal to the excess of actual income over forecasted income multiplied by the price level and by the parameter k.

Imperfect though this technique of monetary control is, the Bank of Canada gave itself a target range of plus or minus two percentage points and, on the average, did manage to achieve an actual money supply growth path that was inside that target range. (There were two brief exceptions, during postal strikes in 1975 and 1978, when the money supply strayed above the target range, and occasional periods when the money supply has gone below the target range.)

Since 1982 the Bank of Canada has been pursuing no announced money supply targets. It is not clear from the Bank's pronouncements precisely what their monetary policy has been. It is possible, nevertheless, to make inferences about what that policy has been by studying the behavior of interest rates, the exchange rate, and other magnitudes. The consensus view is that in this post-monetary targeting period the Bank has been, in effect, targeting the foreign exchange rate. The Bank has taken a view on what the appropriate value for the exchange rate is and has attempted to manipulate domestic interest rates in order to achieve this objective rather than a money supply objective. In terms of the analysis that we conducted in Chapter 27 the Bank has been pursuing a managed floating exchange regime.

In the subsequent chapters we are going to go on to analyze the effects on output and prices (and other variables) of macroeconomic stabilization policies. We shall study the effects of monetary and fiscal policies. In our study of monetary policy we shall presume that we are dealing with an economy in which the monetary authority is in fact controlling the money supply and pursuing a policy of flexible exchange rates. The analysis can, however, be interpreted differently. Instead of imagining that the monetary authorities are trying to achieve a particular level of aggregate demand by manipulating money supply you could imagine them attempting to achieve the same objective by manipulating the foreign exchange rate. Thus, either of the two theories of aggregate demand developed in Chapter 26 could be regarded as relevant for the exercises that will be conducted. If the economy has a flexible exchange rate with money supply targeting, then it is policy changes in the money supply itself that are seen as the instruments through which aggregate demand is affected. If, in contrast, the exchange rate is being targeted, then the fixed exchange rate theory of aggregate demand is the relevant one and policy induced changes in the exchange rate that would shift the aggregate demand curve are regarded as the monetary policy being analyzed.

Sight should not be lost, however, of a central confusion that emerges from the material presented in this chapter and that contained in Chapter 27 where we studied the links between the exchange rate and the domestic monetary policy. This implication is that if the monetary authority so chooses it does have sufficient instruments to control the money supply and to treat the money supply as a direct instrument of aggregate stabilization policy.

Summary

A. The Links Between the Monetary Base and the Money Supply

The money supply function is, like the aggregate supply function, an equilibrium locus. The market that is in equilibrium along the money supply function is the market for monetary base. The demand for monetary base by the public (the demand for currency) may be presumed to be a fairly stable fraction of the demand for money in total. The demand for monetary base by banks will depend partly on the level of deposits and partly on the market rate of interest. The greater the level of deposits, the more monetary base demanded by banks; the higher the market rate of interest, the smaller the monetary base demanded by banks.

Other things being equal, the higher the monetary base, the higher the money supply, and the higher the market rate of interest, the higher the money supply. On the average, the money supply will be a fairly stable multiple of the monetary base, though over shorter periods there will be independent fluctuations in the two variables associated with movements in market rates of interest.

B. The Bank of Canada's Control of the Money Supply

The Bank of Canada has had varying attitudes towards control over the money supply. Between 1975 and 1982 the Bank sought to achieve a target growth path for the money supply by operating on the demand side of the money market. The Bank "solved" the demand for money function for that level of interest rates that would induce the amount of money demanded to equal the target value of the money supply, given the Bank's own forecasts of the price level and the level of real income. That technique of control was imperfect. Deviations of prices or income from their forecasted levels led to deviations of the money supply from its target. Despite these obvious imperfections the Bank did manage to stay within a target range of 4 percentage points (except for brief periods). Since 1982 the Bank has not had a money supply target but has been pursuing exchange rate targets.

Review Questions

1. What is the monetary base? Who issues it (whose liability is it) and who holds it (whose asset is it)?

2. What determines the demand for currency by households and firms?

3. What determines the demand for monetary base by the commercial banks?

4. What is the money supply function?

5. What markets are in equilibrium when the economy is "on" the money supply function?

6. What would lead to a shift in the money supply function?

7. Does the money supply function imply that the monetary base determines the money supply?

8. Does the Bank of Canada exploit the money supply function to control the Canadian money supply or does it ignore it?

9. How does the Bank of Canada manipulate the monetary base in order to change the supply of money?

10. How did the Bank of Canada use the demand for money function in its old method of controlling the supply of money?

11. What are the main potential sources of error, or looseness, in the Bank's old method of monetary control?

12. What are the main potential sources of error, or looseness, in the Bank's current monetary control procedures?

33

Monetary Policy I: Aggregate Demand Shocks

You already know that monetary policy is of central importance for influencing the rate of inflation. You saw in Chapter 20 how an ongoing growth rate of the money supply generates ongoing price increases — inflation. You also saw that although there are many other factors that can influence the inflation rate, by setting an appropriate long-term growth trend to the money supply the monetary authority can offset those factors and achieve any desired trend rate of inflation. You did note, however, when we studied trends in the inflation rate that there are important interactions between unanticipated demand shocks and the price level that modify the course of inflation. We also learned, when we studied macroeconomic equilibrium with rational expectations, that unanticipated shocks to aggregate demand will produce not only departures of the inflation rate from its steady-state path but also fluctuations in output and employment.

What we are now going to do in this chapter is to focus on a central macroeconomic policy question, namely, what can and should monetary policy do to offset cyclical aspects of macroeconomic performance — to control the business cycle? This is a controversial question. There are two broad views concerning its answer, and this chapter, along with the next, is designed to help you understand the nature of the controversy. The material presented in these two chapters will take you right to the frontiers of the current debate in economics.[1] However, nothing that will be dealt with in these chapters is inherently more difficult than the material that you have handled so far.

The chapter will help you with five tasks. They are to:

a) Know the key difference between the monetary policy advice given by monetarists and that given by Keynesians.

b) Know what aggregate demand shocks are and how they affect the aggregate demand curve.

c) Understand the consequences of following monetarist monetary policy advice in the face of aggregate demand shocks.

d) Understand the consequences of following Keynesian monetary policy advice in the face of aggregate demand shocks.

e) Understand why monetarists and Keynesians offer conflicting monetary policy advice.

A. Monetarist and Keynesian Monetary Policy Advice

For present purposes, monetary policy will mean manipulating the money supply. The procedures described in the previous chapter, whereby the Bank of Canada could achieve money supply control, are understood to be capable of delivering whatever supply of money the Bank chooses. This chapter will be concerned with the effects of the Bank achieving alternative targets for the money supply rather than with the ways in which those targets are achieved.

The monetary policy advice given by Keynesians is:

(1)   Raise the money supply to a higher level than it otherwise would have been if output is (or is forecast to be) below its full-employment level.

(2)   Lower the money supply below what it otherwise would have been if output is (or is forecast to be) above its full-employment level.

The precise amount by which the money supply should be moved in order to achieve the desired level of output is a technically complex matter, but one that Keynesians believe they can handle with the help of large-scale econometric models.

---

[1] The leading articles on this topic are much more demanding than the simplified presentation given in this and the next two chapters. On the monetarist side, the leading pieces are: Thomas J. Sargent and Neil Wallace, "Rational Expectations and the Theory of Economic Policy," *Journal of Monetary Economics*, 2 (April 1976), 169-84; and Robert E. Lucas, Jr., "Rules, Discretion and the Role of the Economic Advisor" in *Rational Expectations and Economic Policy*, Stanley Fischer, ed., National Bureau of Economic Research (Chicago and London: University of Chicago Press, 1980), 199-210. On the Keynesian side, the best pieces are: Edmund Phelps and John B. Taylor, "Stabilizing Powers of Monetary Policy Under Rational Expectations," *Journal of Political Economy*, 85 (February 1977), 163-89; and Stanley Fischer, "Long-term Contracts, Rational Expectations, and the Optimal Money Supply Rule," *Journal of Political Economy*, 85 (February 1977), 191-206.

The monetarist policy advice contrasts very sharply with the Keynesian advice and is as follows:

If output is below its full-employment level so that there is a recession, monetarists advise holding the money supply on a steady course that is known and predictable, rather than raising the rate of growth of the money supply above that known and predictable path. Conversely, when the economy is in a boom, with output above its full-employment level, the monetarist advice is again to hold the money supply growing at a steady and predictable rate rather than to reduce its growth rate.

Thus, Keynesian advice is to manipulate the money supply growth rate, raising it in a depression and lowering it in a boom; the monetarist policy advice is to keep the money supply growth rate steady, regardless of whether the economy is in a boom or a slump.

To see *why* each group of economists gives the advice that it does and to see precisely why there is a disagreement, it is necessary to analyze how the economy reacts to shocks that do not themselves stem from the actions of monetary policy. It is then necessary to ask how monetary policy can be used to counter the effects of these shocks. There are two broad sources of shocks — one on the aggregate demand side, and the other on the aggregate supply side of the economy. The aggregate demand shocks are considered in this chapter, and the aggregate supply shocks in the next one.

B. Aggregate Demand Shocks and the Aggregate Demand Curve

The *IS-LM* analysis of aggregate demand, developed in Chapters 8-13 for the closed economy and Chapters 25 and 26 for the open economy, did not explicitly contain aggregate demand shocks. It was presented as if the level of aggregate demand would be determined *exactly* once the value of the money supply and the fiscal policy variables were set. This was an oversimplification, and one that it is now necessary to relax. In this chapter, we relax this simplification on the demand side of the economy.

You will recall that the theory of aggregate demand was developed from a theory of consumption, investment, and the demand for money and international trade and capital flows. A moment's reflection will tell you that by holding the money supply and fiscal policy variables constant, the position of the aggregate demand curve will be fixed and predictable only if the consumption function, investment function, demand for money function and the international flows of goods and capital are fixed and predictable. If a significant group of individuals decided in one particular year that they would manage with a smaller ratio of money balances to income than normal, then in that particular year there would be a surge of expenditures. This would happen as this group of individuals put into action their decisions to lower their money balances below their normal level in relation to their incomes. Conversely, if a significant group of individuals decided in a particular year that they wanted a higher ratio of money balances to income than normal, they would cut back on their expenditures as they put their decisions into effect.

There are many factors that could lead individuals to vary, over time, their consumption, investment, and demand for money and international transactions. On the average, such factors would cancel out and for most of the time, when aggregated over all the individuals in the economy, would not be very important. From time to time, however, such factors could be important and might knock the economy significantly away from its *normal* equilibrium position.

Perhaps some examples will be helpful. Suppose it is widely believed that there is going to be a major drought. This might lead people to invest in a stockpile of food and to lower their average money holdings for a period. While this stockpiling was going on, there would be an increase in the level of aggregate demand as people attempted to put through their increased expenditure plans. In the opposite direction, suppose that it was widely believed that there was going to be a major technical innovation in, say, automobiles, such that the current year's model will be quickly superseded by a vastly superior technology. In such a case, the sales of cars in the year in question would be unusually low, and people would hold on to their money balances in readiness for a subsequent increase in expenditures. In this case, there would be a retiming of expenditures, with sales in one year being unusually low, and sales in some subsequent year, or years, being unusually high.

These are simply examples; you can probably think of many more. Most of the examples which you will think of will turn out to involve *randomness in the timing of people's expenditures in acquiring either durable goods, capital goods, or other goods to store. Random fluctuations in the composition of people's assets — between money holdings on the one hand and real asset holdings on the other hand — lead to random fluctuations in aggregate demand.*

You can think of the aggregate demand curve that we have been working with in the earlier parts of this book as being the level of the aggregate demand curve *on the average*. This curve is reproduced in Figure 33.1 as the solid line labelled $AD(M_0)$. It is labelled in this way to remind you that the position of the AD curve depends on, among other things, the money supply, M. The subscript on M is there to denote the initial value of the money supply, M_0. Later we shall analyze what happens when we change M, holding everything else constant.

Now allow also for random shocks arising from the considerations just described to affect the position of the aggregate demand curve.

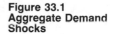

Figure 33.1
Aggregate Demand
Shocks

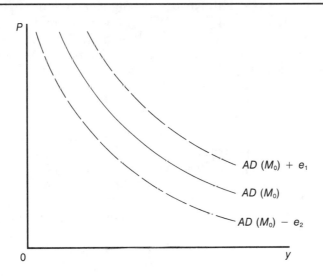

Random fluctuations in consumption, investment, and the demand for money summarized as the shock e shifts the aggregate demand curve around its average position, even though the money supply is fixed. On the average, the shocks will be zero. The shock e_1 is an example of a positive shock and minus e_2 is a negative shock.

Sometimes aggregate demand will be higher than its average value, and sometimes lower than its average value. We can capture such random shocks as an addition to or subtraction from the average position of the aggregate demand curve. Let us call the aggregate of all the random shocks to demand e. On the average, e is equal to zero. It will, however, take on large positive or negative values. If e took on a positive value, say, e_1, then the aggregate demand curve would move to the right, such as the curve shown as the broken line $AD(M_0) + e_1$. If there was a negative random shock, say, *minus* e_2, then the aggregate demand curve would move to the left, such as that shown as the broken line labelled $AD(M_0) - e_2$. At any particular point in time the aggregate demand curve might lie anywhere inside the range of the two broken-line curves. On the average, the aggregate demand curve would be located in the middle of this range at $AD(M_0)$.

Thus, for any given level of the money supply you can think of there being a whole set of possible aggregate demand curves. The *actual* position of the aggregate demand curve depends on the size of the random shock, e, and on the money supply.

C. Consequences of Monetarist Policy

Let us now analyze what happens when there is an aggregate demand shock and when the monetary policy pursued is that advocated by monetarists. Figure 33.2 illustrates the analysis. Let us suppose that the anticipated money supply is M_0. Recall that the monetarist policy involves making the money supply follow a totally predictable path under all circumstances. Specifically, assume the actual money supply is held constant at M_0. It will now be obvious that the actual money supply will equal the anticipated money supply. In other words, if the monetarist policy rule is followed, there will be no unanticipated changes in the money supply.

Since, on the average, the aggregate demand shock e will be zero, it will be rational to expect a zero aggregate demand shock. Thus the rational expectation of the price level P_0^e is found where the expected aggregate demand curve $AD(M_0)$ cuts the aggregate supply curve AS. This aggregate demand curve is the expected aggregate demand curve *in the double sense that it is drawn for an expected value of the aggregate demand shock equal to zero and for the money supply equal to its anticipated level of M_0.* Passing through the point P_0^e and y^* is the relevant expectations-augmented aggregate supply curve. This is the expectations-augmented aggregate supply curve drawn for the rational expectation of the price level of P_0^e.

Now suppose that there is a random increase in aggregate demand by an amount e_1 such that the demand curve *actually* moves rightwards to $AD(M_0) + e_1$. If the monetary policy advice of the monetar-

**Figure 33.2
The Consequences of
Following Monetarist
Policy Advice**

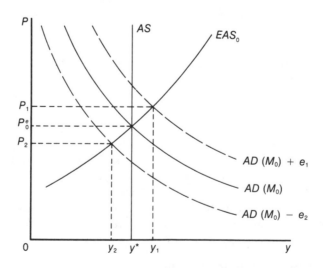

Monetarist policy holds the money shock constant. Expected aggregate demand is $AD(M_0)$, and the rationally expected price level P_0^e. Actual random fluctuations in aggregate demand generate fluctuations in output with procyclical co-movements in prices.

ists is followed and the money supply is held at M_0, its anticipated level, the result of this random shock to aggregate demand will be a rise in the price level to P_1 and a rise in output to y_1.

Next consider the opposite case. Suppose there is a negative random shock to aggregate demand — a random fall in aggregate demand — so that the aggregate demand curve shifts leftwards to $AD(M_0) - e_2$. Again, following the monetarist policy advice, the actual money supply is held steady at its anticipated level M_0. There is therefore a drop in the price level to P_2 and a drop in output to y_2.

You can now see that the consequences of following the monetarist policy advice are that the economy will experience random deviations of output from its full-employment level and random deviations of the price level from its expected level as the economy is continuously "bombarded" with random aggregate demand shocks. These shocks are not offset by changes in the money supply. There will also be fluctuations in employment, unemployment, the real wage, and money wage. You can work out the directions in which these variables will move from Chapter 19. Further, for the reasons discussed in Chapter 23, there will only be a gradual return to full employment following a shock.

Let us now examine the consequences of following Keynesian policy advice.

D. Consequences of Keynesian Policy

Let us begin with exactly the same setup as before. The anticipated money supply is M_0, and the expected aggregate demand curve drawn for an expected zero aggregate demand shock is the curve $AD(M_0)$. (For the moment ignore the other labels on that curve in Figure 33.3.) The rational expectation of the price level is P_0^e and the relevant expectations-augmented aggregate supply curve is EAS_0.

Now suppose that there is a positive random shock to aggregate demand (e_1) taking the aggregate demand curve to the higher curve $AD(M_0) + e_1$. The Keynesian policy advice in this situation is to cut the money supply. If the money supply is cut by exactly the right amount, it is possible to offset the positive aggregate demand shock, thereby making the actual aggregate demand curve the same as the curve $AD(M_0)$. Suppose that the money supply that exactly achieves that effect is M_1. Then the aggregate demand curve would be the same as $AD(M_0)$. We have given that aggregate demand curve a second label, $AD(M_1) + e_1$. This is to indicate to you that *the same aggregate demand curve can arise from different combinations of the money supply and the random aggregate demand shock*. If the aggregate demand shock was zero and the money supply was M_0, the aggregate demand curve would be the same as in a situation in which the money supply was M_1 (smaller than M_0) and the aggregate demand shock was e_1 (a positive

**Figure 33.3
The Consequences of
Following Keynesian
Monetary Policy
Advice**

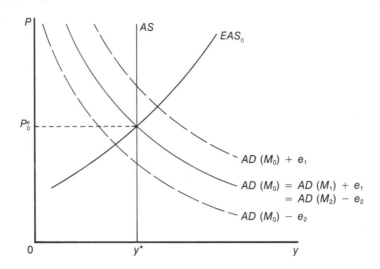

If a random shock hits the economy, thereby shifting the aggregate demand curve (with the money stock constant), Keynesian policy would change the money stock so as to offset the random demand shift. The actual aggregate demand curve would remain constant as the continuous line in the figure. Output would be stabilized at full employment and the price level at its expected level.

value). Following this Keynesian policy rule of changing the money supply to offset the aggregate demand shock gives the prediction that the level of output will stay constant at y^* and the price level will stay at its rational expectation level P_0^e.

The same conclusion would arise if the consequences of a negative aggregate demand shock were examined. If aggregate demand fell by a random amount, e_2, with a fixed money supply M_0, the aggregate demand curve would move to $AD(M_0) - e_2$. If this random shock was offset by a rise in the money supply to (say) M_2 — a value big enough to raise the aggregate demand curve back to its original level — then the aggregate demand curve would again become the same as $AD(M_0)$. The curve $AD(M_0)$ has been labelled yet a third time as equal to $AD(M_2) - e_2$ to remind you that with a higher money supply (M_2) and a negative value of the aggregate demand shock (e_2), it is possible to place the aggregate demand curve in the same place as it would have been with a lower value for the money supply (M_0) and a zero random shock to aggregate demand.

Again, following Keynesian policy advice, the economy stays at the price level P_0^e and the full-employment output level y^* where the aggregate demand curve $AD(M_2) - e_2$ cuts the expectations-augmented aggregate supply curve EAS_0.

You see then that the consequences of following Keynesian stabilization policy are to remove all the fluctuations from output and to keep the price level at its rationally expected level.

E. Why Monetarists and Keynesians Offer Conflicting Advice

(i) Comparison: Keynesian Policy Seems to be Better than Monetarist Policy

From the above presentation of the effects of following a monetarist policy rule and Keynesian policy intervention, it is apparent that monetarist policy leaves the economy contaminated by the effects of random shocks to aggregate demand, whereas Keynesian policy completely insulates the economy from these shocks by exactly offsetting their effects. It would appear, then, that monetary policy can be used to keep the economy free from random fluctuations in output and the price level, and assuming that to be a desirable end, Keynesian monetary policy should so be used. Put more directly, it would appear that Keynesian policy is better than monetarist policy.

Naturally, since there is a debate about the matter, things are not quite as simple as they have been presented in the above two sections. Let us now try to find out why Keynesians and monetarists disagree with each other.

(ii) Informational Advantages

In the two monetary policy experiments that we have conducted and compared in the preceding sections, we have not made the same assumptions concerning the information available to the Bank of Canada and to private economic agents.

When conducting the monetarist policy analysis, it was assumed implicitly — and it is now time to be explicit about the matter — that the Bank and private economic agents all had the same information. No one knew what value e would take in the coming time period. Everyone, including the Bank, expected that it would be zero.

When conducting the Keynesian policy analysis, however, it was assumed implicitly — and again it is now time to be explicit — that no private agent was able to forecast the value of the random shock e, but that the Bank knew the value of e exactly and was able to move the money supply so as to precisely offset its effects on aggregate demand. In other words, it was assumed that the Bank knew more than private economic agents concerning the position of the aggregate demand curve.

Instead of assuming that the Bank has such an informational advantage, let us analyze what would happen if the Bank had to operate a Keynesian policy with a time lag such that it could only change the money supply when it knew that there had been an aggregate demand shock that it had been able to observe. Also, however, let us recognize that what can be observed by the Bank can also be observed by anybody else. If the Bank knows that the economy is experiencing a positive (or negative) aggregate demand shock, then it seems reasonable to suppose that everyone else knows that too.

In order to make things as clear as possible, let us look at two periods of time (years). We will analyze what would happen if there was a positive aggregate demand shock (e_1) in the first period and then no aggregate demand shock in the second period. Suppose that the Bank reacts to an aggregate demand shock with a one-period lag. That is, if there has been a positive aggregate demand shock in period one, the Bank cuts back on the money supply in the second period in an attempt to offset the effects of the observed, first-period aggregate demand shock. Further, let us suppose that everyone knows as much as the Bank knows about the aggregate demand shock. Yet *further, let us suppose that everyone knows that the Bank is pursuing a Keynesian policy and will react with a one-period lag by changing the*

**Figure 33.4
The Consequences
of Following Keynesian
Monetary Policy
Advice with an
Information Lag**

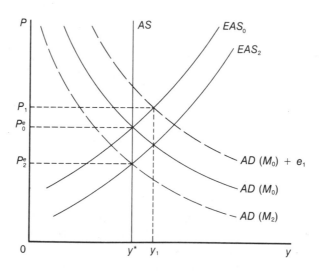

An economy initially at full-employment equilibrium (y^*, P_0^e) is disturbed by a random shock to aggregate demand (e_1). Output and prices rise to y_1, P_1 the same as they would if the monetarist rule was being pursued. The higher output level induces a monetary contraction under the Keynesian rule (lowering the aggregate demand curve to $AD(M_2)$). Since everyone knows the government is using the Keynesian rule, the expected aggregate demand curve (in the absence of random shocks) will be the same as the actual curve. The economy will return to full employment but with a lower price level. Pursuing a Keynesian rule with a one-period lag leaves output on the same path as in the case of the monetarist rule but makes prices more volatile.

money stock. Let us now work out what will happen as a result of this monetary policy response.

Figure 33.4 illustrates the analysis. The economy is initially expected to be on the demand curve $AD(M_0)$, at a price level P_0^e and an output level y^*. The relevant expectations-augmented aggregate supply curve is EAS_0. Let this be the point at which the economy starts out. Then, in period one, let there be a positive aggregate demand shock e_1. No one can predict the aggregate demand shock before it happens, and therefore, no one reacts to it until period two. However, the shock affects the actual behavior of the economy in period one, and the price level and output level settle down at P_1 and y_1, respectively. These are the values of the price level and output at which the new aggregate demand curve $AD(M_0) + e_1$ cuts the expectations-augmented aggregate supply curve EAS_0.

Now, in the next period (period two), everyone has observed that there has been a positive aggregate demand shock. Furthermore, everyone can work out the size of the shock from knowing what the actual price and output levels turned out to be. The Bank reacts to this aggregate demand shock by cutting the money supply in period two to a value of (say) M_2. Assuming that there is no aggregate demand shock in this second period, the new aggregate demand curve will be below the original curve $AD(M_0)$ since the money supply has been cut below M_0. In particular, the aggregate demand curve will be $AD(M_2)$. Private agents will expect the aggregate demand curve to be $AD(M_2)$ because they will expect the monetary authorities to cut the money stock as a reaction to the previous period's aggregate demand shock e_1. They will form a rational expectation of the price level of P_2^e, and the expectations-augmented aggregate supply curve will become EAS_2. If (as we are assuming) there is no aggregate demand shock in period two, the economy will settle at its full-employment output level of y^* and the price level of P_2^e.

Thus, following a Keynesian policy rule, but with a one-period information lag, implying that the Bank of Canada has no better information than the private sector has, leads to a movement in output that is exactly the same as that which occurs when the monetarist policy rule is followed. However, there is a difference between the two policies in the behavior of the price level. The price level fluctuates more when Keynesian policy advice is followed than it does with the monetarist rule. Output behaves exactly the same under either policy, but the price level is more variable with Keynesian than with monetarist policy.

We see, then, that following Keynesian policy advice, which has a one-period lag on information and with no informational advantage for the Bank, is exactly the same as following monetarist policy advice in its effect on output. However, it leads to bigger fluctuations in the price level than does monetarist policy.

(iii) The Essence of the Dispute Between Keynesians and Monetarists

The essence of the dispute between Keynesians and monetarists concerning the effects of monetary policy turns on the question of information and the use that may be made of new information. The monetarist asserts that the Bank of Canada has no informational advantage over private agents and that it can do nothing that private agents will not do for themselves. Any attempt by the Bank to fine tune or stabilize the economy by making the money supply react to previous shocks, known to everybody, will make the level of output behave no better than it otherwise would have done and will make the price level more variable.

Keynesians assert that there is an effective informational advantage to the Bank. They agree that individuals will form their expectations rationally, using all the information that is available to them. But they go on to assert that individuals get locked into contracts based on an expected price level that, after the fact of an aggregate demand shock, turns out to be wrong. *The Bank of Canada can act after private agents have tied themselves into contractual arrangements based on a false price level expectation* to compensate for and offset the effects of those random shocks. Figure 33.3 can be reinterpreted as showing what happens if the private sector is tied into contracts based on a wrong expected price level. In that case, if both the Bank of Canada and private agents *observe* an aggregate demand shock of (say) e_1, but if private agents are tied into contracts based on the expected price level P_0^e, *and if* the Bank can change the money supply quickly enough, then the Keynesian policy outcome shown in Figure 33.3 can be achieved.

The essence of the debate, then, concerns the flexibility of private sector responses vis-à-vis the flexibility of the Bank's responses to random shocks that hit the economy. If everyone can act as quickly and as effortlessly as everyone else, there is no advantage from pursuing Keynesian policy, and indeed, there are disadvantages because the price level will be more variable. If, however, the Bank can act more quickly than the private sector, there may be a gain in the form of reduced variability of both output and the price level from pursuing Keynesian policy.

(iv) An Unsettled Scientific Question

There is no easy way of deciding which of these two views better describes the world, and further scientific research is required before the matter will be settled.

One thing that can be said, however, is that because it is difficult to know exactly what random shocks are hitting the economy, attempts to pursue Keynesian policy will make the money supply more random and less predictable than would monetarist policy. You have seen (Chapters 19 and 23) that an unpredictable monetary policy gives rise to cycles in economic activity arising from the money supply movements themselves. Thus, Keynesian policy will necessarily impart some cyclical movements into the economy as a consequence of the fact that the money supply itself is less predictable under Keynesian policy than under a monetarist policy rule. Monetarist policy will (as far as possible) remove any fluctuations from aggregate demand that arise from the money supply itself. The only things that can lead to business cycles under a monetarist policy rule are the random fluctuations arising from private aggregate demand (or aggregate supply) shocks. The random shocks emanating from the behavior of the Bank of Canada are eliminated.

Whether random shocks that arise from the private sector are the dominant shocks is another matter of dispute. Here, however, there seems to be less room for disagreement. It is fairly well established that one of the major sources of fluctuations in economic activity in modern industrial economies is instability in monetary policy itself. Unanticipated variations in the money supply seem to account for much of the variation that we observe in the level of economic activity. However, they certainly do not account for all the observed fluctuations. To take an extreme, the Great Depression of 1929 through 1934 has not yet been satisfactorily explained by *any* theory. We must therefore remain cautious and display a certain amount of humility. This does not, however, bode well for the Keynesian policy recommendation, which, in order that it may improve matters, must be based upon the presumption that we know rather a lot about the way in which the economy behaves.

The bottom line defense of the monetarist is that we are too ignorant about the workings of the economy to be able to do any better than to remove at least those sources of fluctuation in economic activity that we *can* control, namely, those that stem from instability in the money supply. If such fluctuations were removed, the economy would behave in a more stable manner than it has in the past. Of course, it would not be perfect. Perfection, however, requires a great deal more information than we currently have available to us.

Summary

A. Monetarist and Keynesian Monetary Policy Advice

Monetarists recommend the adoption of a steady and predictable money supply growth rule. The money supply growth rate should be kept constant no matter what the current state of the economy.

Keynesians recommend the use of active variations in the money supply to offset aggregate demand shocks. They recommend raising the money supply when output is below its full-employment level and lowering the money supply when output is above its full-employment level.

B. Aggregate Demand Shocks and the Aggregate Demand Curve

Aggregate demand shocks are random variations in the level of aggregate demand that arise from random movements in the timing of expenditures and from random fluctuations in desired holdings of real assets and financial assets. If people try to hold more real assets and fewer financial assets, there will be a rise in the demand for goods — a rise in aggregate demand.

Aggregate demand shocks shift the aggregate demand curve. For any given price level, the level of aggregate demand will vary around its most likely value, depending on the size of the aggregate demand shock.

C. Consequences of Monetarist Policy

Adopting a monetarist policy permits fluctuations in output, employment, unemployment, the price level, the money wage, and the real wage. For example, in the case of a positive aggregate demand shock, output, employment, the price level, and the money wage will rise, and the real wage and unemployment will fall.

D. Consequences of Keynesian Policy

Keynesian policy is designed to isolate the economy from a random shock and eliminate fluctuations in output and the price level. In the case of a positive aggregate demand shock, Keynesian monetary policy advice is to lower the money supply so as to leave aggregate demand (and thus the position of the aggregate demand curve) unchanged. This would lead to no adjustment in the rational expectation of the price level, so that the level of output, employment, unemployment, the price level, the real wage and the money wage would remain constant.

E. Why Monetarists and Keynesians Offer Conflicting Advice

The dispute between monetarists and Keynesians rests on whether the Bank of Canada has an informational advantage over private agents in the economy. Monetarists argue that the Bank has no more information than do private agents. Any attempt by the Bank to offset *previous* random aggregate demand shocks (now known to all agents in the economy) by varying the money supply will not reduce the fluctuations in output, whereas it will increase those in the price level.

Keynesians assert that the Bank has an *effective* informational advantage over private agents because private agents get locked into contracts that cannot be revised quickly as new information becomes available. Private agents are locked into contracts based on the wrong expected price level, whereas the Bank can respond quickly to the new information (the aggregate demand shock) and can change the money supply quickly enough so that output, employment, and the price level remain steady.

The successful application of Keynesian policy would require a large amount of information on the part of the Bank of Canada and government, and there is a presumption on the part of monetarists that in the present state of knowledge they do not have sufficient information. Monetarists assert that attempts at pursuing Keynesian policies will, in the current state of knowledge, generate larger fluctuations in both output and prices than would occur with the adoption of a monetarist rule.

Review Questions

1. Summarize and contrast the monetary policy positions of Keynesians and monetarists.

2. Give some examples of factors which might cause aggregate demand shocks.

3. Work out, using the appropriate diagrams, the consequences of pursuing monetarist policy in the face of random fluctuations in aggregate demand.

4. Explain the rationale that monetarists use for permitting random aggregate demand shocks to influence aggregate output and prices.

5. Work out, using the appropriate diagrams, the Keynesian monetary policy required to stabilize the economy in the face of a positive shock.

6. Work out, using the appropriate diagrams, the effects of pursuing Keynesian policy, but with the monetary authorities reacting with a one-period lag to aggregate demand shocks.

7. Set out the major differences in the predicted consequences of pursuing monetarist and Keynesian policies in the face of random aggregate demand shocks.

8. What is the primary source of disagreement between Keynesians and monetarists which causes each group of economists to give the advice that it does?

34

Monetary Policy II: Aggregate Supply Shocks

In September 1973, the members of the Oil-Producing Exporting Countries (OPEC) announced a fourfold increase in the price of crude oil. At the same time they announced an embargo on the shipment of oil to certain countries and a decision to cut back their production levels. In a single afternoon, the OPEC decision delivered a *supply shock* to the Western world which has only been matched by the events of major wars. The consequences of the OPEC oil price rise have been widespread and long drawn out. They also triggered a fierce debate as to what constituted the appropriate macroeconomic policy response.[1]

The supply shock administered by OPEC was an unusually large one. Supply shocks are not, however, unusual events. We saw, in Chapter 14, that supply shocks in the form of shifts in the aggregate production function arising from variations in the pace of technical change and capital accumulation as well as climatic factors can produce shifts in aggregate supply.

This chapter is going to help you to evaluate alternative policy recommendations for dealing with supply shocks. You have five tasks, which are to:

---

[1] An excellent presentation of a Keynesian view on this is Robert M. Solow, "What to Do (Macroeconomically) When OPEC Comes," in *Rational Expectations and Economic Policy*, Stanley Fischer, ed., National Bureau of Economic Research (Chicago and London: University of Chicago Press, 1980), 249-64. Also see Neil Wallace's comment on Solow on pp. 264-67 of the same volume.

a) Understand the distinction between the expectations-augmented aggregate supply curve and the expectation of the aggregate supply curve.

b) Understand the consequences of following monetarist policy advice in the event of an aggregate supply shock.

c) Understand the consequences of following Keynesian policy advice in the event of an aggregate supply shock.

d) Understand the consequences of following a Keynesian policy with an information lag.

e) Understand the essence of the dispute between Keynesians and monetarists concerning supply shock policies.

A. Expectations-Augmented Aggregate Supply Curve and the Expectation of the Aggregate Supply Curve

The starting point for your analysis of supply shocks is to recall the theory of aggregate supply presented in Chapter 14. In that chapter we analyzed the way in which production function shocks can lead to shifts in the *AS* curve. If it is a little while since you have studied that material it will probably be worthwhile refreshing your memory before going further.

The next matter to which we have to attend is an important distinction concerning the use of the word "expectation." The word "expectation" is going to be attached to the aggregate supply curve in two very different ways. First, there is the expectations-augmented aggregate supply curve (*EAS*). This is what it always has been, namely, a curve showing the level of aggregate supply for a given expected price level. Second, the concept of the expectation of the aggregate supply curve will be used. This is a new concept that has not been used before. The aggregate supply curve is the vertical aggregate supply curve *AS* — which shows the level of aggregate supply when the expected and actual price levels are equal to each other. If there are no aggregate supply shocks, the position of this curve is determined uniquely by the production function and the condition of equilibrium in the labor market. However, when random shocks affect the production function, they also affect the position of the aggregate supply function. The size and direction of random shocks to the production function cannot be known before they occur, though on the average those shocks cancel out — are zero. Thus, the aggregate supply curve based on a zero aggregate supply shock — the expected or average aggregate supply shock — will be called the *expectation of the aggregate supply curve*.

Keeping this distinction clear, and as a prelude to analyzing the effects of alternative policies towards aggregate supply shocks, let us see how each of these aggregate supply curves shifts in response to such a shock.

Figure 34.1 shows the effects of an aggregate supply shock on the aggregate supply and expectations-augmented aggregate supply curves. Suppose that initially the economy was on the curve AS_0, and the aggregate demand curve $AD(M_0)$ at a full-employment equilibrium y_0^* and P_0^e. The expectations-augmented aggregate supply curve has both a superscript and a subscript. The subscript refers to the value of the money supply, and the superscript refers to the value of the aggregate supply curve. Thus, EAS_0^0 is at the point of intersection of AS_0 and $AD(M_0)$.

Now suppose that there is a random shock in aggregate supply that cuts aggregate supply at each level of employment. This will shift the aggregate supply curve to (say) AS_1. Suppose further that the expected value of the money supply remains at M_0, so that the aggregate demand curve $AD(M_0)$ is expected to remain unchanged. Also, suppose the aggregate supply shock is unanticipated, so that the expectation of the aggregate supply curve is that it remains at AS_0. In this case, the rational expectation of the price level will remain at P_0^e. The aggregate supply curve shift is easy to work out. It simply shifts leftwards by the amount of the drop in output that results from the aggregate supply shock.

Figure 34.1
An Aggregate Supply
Shock and the
Aggregate Supply
Curves

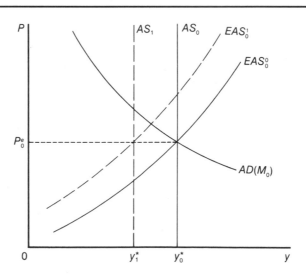

An unexpected aggregate supply shock shifts the aggregate supply curve, for example, from AS_0 to AS_1. The expectations-augmented aggregate supply curve is dragged along horizontally with the AS curve. The curve EAS_0^0 is the expectations-augmented aggregate supply curve for the expected price level P_0^e (expected money stock M_0) and an expected aggregate supply curve of AS_0. The curve EAS_0^1 refers to the same expected price level and money stock but to the lower level of aggregate supply.

What happens to the expectations-augmented aggregate supply curve? This is not as straightforward to figure out. However, a moment's reflection will tell you that that curve must also shift horizontally by the same amount as the aggregate supply curve has shifted. The expectations-augmented aggregate supply curve always cuts the *actual* aggregate supply curve at the expected price level. Since the aggregate supply shock is (by assumption) unanticipated, there is no prior knowledge about it. The aggregate supply curve has shifted, at random, from its expected position AS_0 to an unexpected position AS_1. The expectations-augmented aggregate supply curve will have been dragged along with the aggregate supply curve so as to intersect it at the expected price level P_0^e. Given the aggregate supply shock, there will now be a lower level of output available at all price levels. Nothing has happened to change the expected price level, which remains at P_0^e. That is, nothing has happened to yield new information to economic agents that would lead them to revise their price level expectation.

Thus, the effect on the aggregate supply curves of an aggregate supply shock is to shift both the aggregate supply curve and the expectations-augmented aggregate supply curve horizontally by the amount of the shock. The curve EAS_0^1 is the expectations-augmented aggregate supply curve when the expectation of aggregate demand is $AD(M_0)$ and when aggregate supply has unexpectedly dropped to AS_1.

You are now in a position to go on to compare the effects of alternative policies.

B. Consequences of Monetarist Policy

Figure 34.2 illustrates the consequences of following monetarist policy in the event of an aggregate supply shock. Suppose that there is a random drop in aggregate supply from AS_0 to AS_1 and that a monetarist policy rule of fixing the money stock at M_0 is followed, so that the aggregate demand curve remains as $AD(M_0)$. The initial equilibrium in the economy is the point A, where output is y_0^* and the price level is P_0^e. When the supply shock occurs, the aggregate supply curve shifts to AS_1, and the expectations-augmented aggregate supply curve shifts with it to EAS_0^1. There is no monetary policy reaction, and the economy settles at point B, with a price level of P_1 and an output level of y_1.

If, in the next period, the aggregate supply shock disappears, so that the economy reverts to its normal position on the aggregate supply curve AS_0, with the expectations-augmented aggregate supply curve EAS_0^0, the economy will return to the full-employment point A from which it started. Thus, following monetarist policy in the face

Figure 34.2
The Consequences of
Following Monetarist
Policy Advice in the
Event of a Supply
Shock — Stagflation

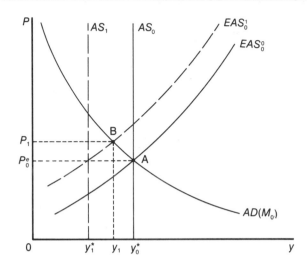

An economy initially at full-employment equilibrium (y_0^*, P_0^e) is disturbed by a negative aggregate supply shock that unexpectedly takes the aggregate supply curve to AS_1, and the EAS curve to EAS_0^1. The impact equilibrium is at y_1, P_1. Prices rise and output falls: the economy experiences stagflation.

of an aggregate supply shock leads to a movement in output and the price level in opposite directions to each other. This is the phenomenon sometimes called *stagflation*. That is, the economy stagnates and inflates at the same time. It is to avoid stagflation in the face of an aggregate supply shock that some economists advocate adjusting the money supply to accommodate the supply shock. Let us now see what would happen if we follow this Keynesian policy.

C. Consequences of Keynesian Policy

Figure 34.3 illustrates the analysis. Again, suppose the economy starts out at point A at the intersection of the aggregate demand curve $AD(M_0)$, the aggregate supply curve AS_0, and the expectations-augmented aggregate supply curve EAS_0^0. As before, let there be a shock to aggregate supply that moves the aggregate supply curve to AS_1, and the expectations-augmented aggregate supply curve to EAS_0^1. Keynesian policy would counter this drop in aggregate supply with a stimulation to the money supply. The Keynesian response would be to raise the money supply to (say) M_1, such that the aggregate demand curve shifts to the curve labelled $AD(M_1)$. The new equilibrium would then be at point C, with the output level at y_0^* as originally, but with the price level at P_1.

If, in the next period, the aggregate supply shock disappeared and the economy reverted to its normal aggregate supply curve AS_0, then

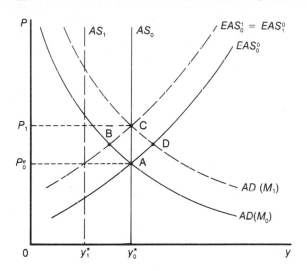

**Figure 34.3
The Consequences of
Following Keynesian
Monetary Policy
Advice in the Event of
a Supply Shock —
Avoiding Stagflation**

In the same situation as analyzed in Figure 34.2, the Keynesian advice is to raise the money supply, thereby raising aggregate demand from $AD(M_0)$ to $AD(M_1)$. This would move the economy to point C (full employment with a price level P_1). What happens in the next period depends on what the government does and what it is expected to do. An anticipated return of the money supply to its initial level will return the economy to its initial position A. An anticipated maintenance of the money supply at its new level will keep the economy at point C. If the money supply is expected to fall back to the original position but actually stays at the new position, the economy will go to D, and finally, the money supply is lowered to its original level, but unexpectedly so, the economy will go to B.

one of *four* possibilities would arise. First, if the money supply is returned to its original level M_0 and if everyone expects that to happen, the economy will return to the original position A. Second, if the money supply is kept at its higher level M_1 and, again, if everyone anticipates that that will happen, the economy will stay at point C, but the expectations-augmented aggregate supply curve EAS_0^1 will become EAS_1^0, being the expectations-augmented aggregate supply curve drawn for a value of the money stock equal to M_1 with the aggregate supply curve at AS_0. Third, and fourth, if there is confusion in the minds of economic agents as to whether the monetary authorities will revert to the original money supply or stay with the new money supply, then the expectations-augmented aggregate supply curve will be located somewhere in between positions A and C on the AS_0 curve, and the economy will experience an output boom if the money supply stays at M_1, or an output slump if the money supply is returned to M_0. The price level will be between P_0^e and P_1. At the extremes, if the money supply was expected to revert to M_0, but in fact remained at M_1, the economy would move to point D; and if the money supply was expected to remain at M_1, but in fact reverted to M_0, the economy would move to point B.

Which of the above four possibilities would in fact arise would depend on the monetary policy *process* being followed by the Bank of Canada. If the Bank had a history of responding to supply shocks with a one-period loosening of monetary policy and a subsequent reverting back to the original level of the money supply, then the first possibility analyzed above would in fact arise. If the Bank had a history of expanding the money stock in response to a supply shock and then keeping the money supply at its new level, then the second possibility would arise. Possibilities three and four would only arise if the Bank had generated confusion in the minds of economic agents as a result of its own previous random behavior.

We may now summarize the consequences of following a Keynesian policy in the face of an aggregate supply shock as follows: such a policy leads to inflation initially but with no drop in output and employment. In the next period, whether inflation falls and/or output falls, rises, or stays at its full-employment level depends on what the expected and actual money supplies are. Notice that the Keynesian policy of adjusting the money supply so as to accommodate the supply shock avoids the reduction in output generated by following the monetarist policy, but only at the expense of higher inflation.

D. Consequences of Keynesian Policy with an Information Lag

Next, consider what would happen in the case of following a Keynesian policy with an information lag. Suppose a Keynesian policy is adopted with a one-period reaction lag to the aggregate supply shock. Figure 34.4 illustrates this. Again, let the economy begin at position A on the aggregate demand curve $AD(M_0)$, the expectations-augmented aggregate supply curve EAS_0^0, and the aggregate supply curve AS_0. Then let there be an aggregate supply shock shifting the aggregate supply curve to AS_1 and the expectations-augmented aggregate supply curve to EAS_0^1. Since this is a random shock that no one has been able to predict, the economy will move to position B, with an output level of y_1 and a price level of P_2. *This is exactly the response resulting from following the monetarist policy rule.*

Next, suppose that in the following period, the Bank reacts to this cut in aggregate output by raising the money supply to M_1. Provided that everyone correctly anticipates this monetary policy reaction, this will put the economy back at the full-employment output level, but at the higher price level P_1, at position C. To help you see more clearly what is going on at the equilibrium marked C, the expectations-augmented aggregate supply curve has been given a second label — EAS_1^0. This tells you that that particular *EAS* curve describes two situations: one in which the expected money supply is M_0 and the

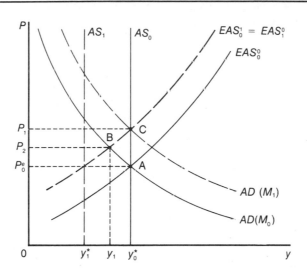

Figure 34.4
The Consequences of Following Keynesian Monetary Policy Advice in the Event of a Supply Shock with an Information Lag

The economy is subjected to exactly the same shock as in the previous figures. Since there is a one-period policy response lag, in the first period, the period of the shock, the economy behaves in the same way as it would under a monetarist rule. It moves from A to B. If the monetary authority now stimulates demand to $AD\,(M_1)$, but people know that a Keynesian policy is being pursued and, therefore, expect this policy response, the price level will rise to P_1 and output returns to y_0^* in the next period. Thus, the behavior of output is identical in the Keynesian case to the monetarist case, but the price level is more variable under Keynesian policy.

actual aggregate supply curve is AS_1; and a second situation in which the expected money supply is M_1 and the actual aggregate supply curve is at the position AS_0. Thus, with a one-period information lag, a Keynesian stabilization policy in the face of an aggregate supply shock leads to exactly the same path for output as occurs under the monetarist policy, but the price level has a different behavior. With the monetarist policy, the price level returns to its original level; but with the Keynesian policy, the price level rises to P_1.

E. The Essence of the Dispute Between Keynesians and Monetarists

Exactly the same considerations are relevant in judging the appropriateness of Keynesian and monetarist policy responses to an aggregate supply shock as were relevant in the case of an aggregate demand shock. There is now, however, an additional reason for suspecting that a Keynesian policy will be difficult to carry out. You have already seen in the previous chapter that a Keynesian policy requires a great deal of information. It requires information about the magnitude of the aggregate demand shocks. You now see that to pursue appropriate aggregate supply corrections, it is necessary to have good information about aggregate supply shocks as well. It will be apparent that if *both* of these types of shocks occur simultaneously, it will be necessary for the monetary authorities to have the ability to disentangle the separate shocks that are affecting the economy and to offset both of them in the appropriate way and with greater speed than the private sector can react to them.[2]

Further, if the private sector learns that the public sector is going to react to aggregate supply shocks and if the private sector has as much information as the Bank of Canada does concerning those shocks, then the Bank's reaction will always be built into the private sector's expectations, and the Bank's actions themselves will result exclusively in price level variability.

Thus, the monetarists' objection to Keynesian policy is that it does not improve the performance of the economy as regards the behavior of output, and unambiguously makes the price level less stable and predictable than would a monetarist policy.

Summary

A. Expectations-Augmented Aggregate Supply Curve and the Expectation of the Aggregate Supply Curve

The expectations-augmented aggregate supply curve traces the amount of aggregate supply as the price level varies for a given expected price level. The expectation of the aggregate supply curve refers to the vertical aggregate supply curve, which traces the quantity that will be supplied at each price level when that price level is fully expected. The expectation of that vertical aggregate supply curve refers to its position in normal or usual periods, when aggregate supply shocks are zero.

B. Consequences of Monetarist Policy

A random negative shock to aggregate supply with a fixed money supply will lower the level of output and raise the price level in the period in which the aggregate supply shock occurs. The level of employment will fall. The economy will experience stagflation.

C. Consequences of Keynesian Policy

Keynesian policy in the face of a negative aggregate supply shock would be to stimulate demand by raising the money supply. Perfectly conducted, this would have the effect of leaving output and employment unchanged, but raising the price level.

---

[2]A thorough (though demanding) analysis of precisely this topic is presented by Gary C. Fethke and Andrew J. Policano in "Co-operative Responses by Public and Private Agents to Aggregate Demand and Supply Disturbances," *Economica*, 48 (May 1981), 155-72.

D. Consequences of Keynesian Policy with an Information Lag

If a Keynesian policy is followed but with a one-period lag in the receipt of information concerning the aggregate supply shock, the economy would respond in exactly the same way under a Keynesian policy as it would have done under a monetarist policy in the period in which the shock occurs. If, using a Keynesian policy, the monetary authorities stimulate demand with a one-period lag and if everyone correctly anticipates this, there will be a rise in the price level but no output effect in the second period.

E. The Essence of the Dispute Between Keynesians and Monetarists

The essence of the dispute between Keynesians and monetarists concerning the appropriate response to aggregate supply shocks is exactly the same as that discussed in the previous chapter concerning aggregate demand shocks. The issue turns on who gets information fastest and who can react fastest to new information. If the Bank of Canada has no superior information, then the use of Keynesian policy to correct aggregate supply shocks will leave the behavior of output unaffected and will produce a greater degree of price level variability than will the pursuit of a monetarist policy.

Review Questions

1. What is the distinction between the expectations-augmented aggregate supply curve and the expectation of the aggregate supply curve?

2. How does the expectations-augmented aggregate supply curve shift in the event of a negative aggregate supply shock?

3. Work out, using the appropriate diagrams, the effects of pursuing a monetarist policy in the face of a temporary (one-period only), but unpredictable, drop in aggregate supply.

4. For the same shock as in Question 3, work out the effects of pursuing a Keynesian policy.

5. Contrast the output and price-level paths in your answers to Questions 3 and 4.

6. If there was a previously unpredictable but, once occurred, known to be *permanent* shock to aggregate supply, what would happen to output and the price level:
  (a) with a monetarist policy?
  (b) with a Keynesian policy?

7. If a negative aggregate supply shock was always responded to with a rise in the money supply, and a positive aggregate supply shock was responded to with an unchanged money supply, what would the path of the inflation rate be like? (This is a tougher question than the others.)

35

Fiscal Policy

This chapter examines how fiscal policy affects the level of output, employment, unemployment, the real wage, the money wage, the price level and the rate of interest. You will be aware that there is a great deal of popular discussion concerning the desirability of alternative government spending and tax policy changes. The chapter is designed to help you to understand and evaluate this discussion. Your tasks are to:

a) Understand the key differences between the Keynesian and monetarist policy recommendations concerning fiscal policy.

b) Understand the distinction between anticipated and unanticipated fiscal policy.

c) Know how output, employment, unemployment, the real wage, money wage, and price level are affected by an anticipated change in government expenditure.

d) Know how output, employment, unemployment, the real wage, money wage and price level are affected by an unanticipated change in government expenditure.

A. Keynesian and Monetarist Fiscal Policy Advice

The Keynesian and monetarist disagreement concerning the appropriate use of fiscal policy is much like their disagreement over monetary policy.

(i) Keynesian Fiscal Policy Advice

Keynesians recommend that:
1. When output is *below* its full-employment level, either
    (a) raise government expenditure, or (b) cut taxes, or
    (c) raise government expenditure and cut taxes together.
2. When output is *above* its full-employment level, either
    (a) cut government expenditure, or (b) raise taxes, or
    (c) cut government expenditure and raise taxes together.

Keynesians also tend to favor a political constitution that gives centralized fiscal control so as to facilitate active fiscal policy changes.

(ii) Monetarist Fiscal Policy Advice

Monetarists disagree profoundly with the Keynesian fiscal policy advice. They say that government expenditure should be set at a level that is determined with reference to the requirements of economic efficiency rather than with reference to macroeconomic stability.

(a) Government Expenditure Monetarists recommend that government expenditure be set at a level such that the marginal utility derived from public expenditure per dollar spent is equal to the marginal utility derived from private expenditure per dollar spent. (Recall your microeconomic analysis of the optimum allocation of a consumer's budget. Monetarists assert that the same considerations that apply to an individual's budget allocation are relevant for the allocation of resources between the public and private sector.) If the marginal utility per dollar spent on private goods is less than the marginal utility per dollar spent on government goods, then government expenditure is too low and private expenditure is too high, and there is a need to reallocate resources away from the private sector and towards the government sector — to increase public expenditure. Conversely, if the marginal utility per dollar spent on private expenditure is greater than the marginal utility per dollar spent by the government, then the government sector is too big, and there is a need to reduce government spending so that private spending may be increased.

Monetarists would therefore begin by looking at the marginal utility per dollar spent on such items as national defense, law and order, education, health services, and all the other things purchased directly by government and would compare these with the marginal utility per dollar of private expenditure. Monetarists assert that government expenditure should be set with reference to this economic efficiency criterion only.

Monetarists — or at least some of them — go on to argue that there is a problem arising from an imperfection in the political marketplace. They suggest that there appears to be a tendency for the interaction of politicians, the bureaucracy, and the electorate to generate a level of government expenditure that exceeds the efficient level. That is, there is a tendency for government expenditure to rise, relative to private expenditure, to a level such that the marginal utility per dollar spent on goods bought by the government is below that in the private sector. They therefore advocate constitutional limitations on the fraction of aggregate output which may be spent by the government.

Further, monetarists tend to favor political constitutions that have decentralized federal and local fiscal authorities, so that those who levy and spend taxes on public consumption are not too distant from the people who they represent, and also so as to encourage competition between jurisdictions.

To summarize: monetarists advocate setting the level of government expenditure on considerations of economic efficiency and independently of the state of the aggregate level of output, employment, unemployment, or prices. There is a presumption that government expenditure should be held to a steady fraction of aggregate output.

(b) Taxes Monetarists recommend that taxes be set at a level which enables the government to buy the utility-maximizing volume of public goods and services and maintain a constant money supply growth rate.

This policy recommendation follows directly from the monetarist view about the appropriate government spending policy and money supply policy. Recall that the government is constrained by the budget equation:

$$g - \overline{t} = q\left(\frac{M}{P}\right)\mu$$

Also recall from Chapter 33 that the monetarists' advice on the money supply growth rate, μ, is that it be set at a constant and steady value. One possible value would be zero, but usually monetarists recommend that μ be set equal to the rate of growth of output, so that the level of prices (recalling the fundamental inflation equation) is constant. Since monetarists recommend that government expenditure be set equal to its utility-maximizing level (independently of the state of the macroeconomy) and that the money supply should grow at a steady rate (independently of the state of the macroeconomy), it follows that they want to see the level of legislated taxes set such that these other two objectives may be met.

In other words, for monetarists, taxes and government expenditure go together. Both need to be set at levels such that an efficient allocation of resources between the government and private sector is achieved and, further, so that the money supply growth rate stays at a constant zero-inflation rate.

You see, then, as in the case of monetary policy, that Keynesians advocate that fiscal policy be used in an active manner to raise output if it is below its full-employment level and to lower it if it is above its full-employment level, whereas monetarists recommend that policy be set steady, independently of fluctuations in the level of output and the other macroeconomic variables.

B. Anticipated and Unanticipated Fiscal Policy

The distinction between anticipated and unanticipated fiscal policy is directly analogous to the distinction between anticipated and unanticipated changes in the money supply. The level of government expenditure, g_t, in any year t is equal to the value in the previous year g_{t-1}, plus the change between the previous year and the current year Δg. That is,

$$g_t = g_{t-1} + \Delta g$$

The change in government expenditure Δg can be decomposed into the change that was anticipated Δg^a and the component that was unanticipated Δg^u. That is,

$$\Delta g - \Delta g^a + \Delta g^u$$

The same distinction applies to taxes as well.

C. Effects of Anticipated Change in Government Expenditure

(i) The Effects on Output and the Price Level

The effects of an anticipated change in government expenditure will be analyzed by working out, first of all, its effects on output and the price level. After that, the implications of these effects for changes in the labor market variables (employment, unemployment, the real and money wages and the rate of interest) will be worked out. Figure 35.1 will be used to illustrate the analysis.

Suppose that the money supply is fixed at M_0 and the level of government expenditure is initially at g_0 and taxes at t_0. This means that the aggregate demand curve will be the solid curve labelled $AD(M_0, g_0, t_0)$. The rational expectation of the price level, given this aggregate demand level, will be P_0^e. That is the price level where the aggregate demand curve cuts the aggregate supply curve. The expectations-augmented aggregate supply curve EAS_0 cuts the aggregate supply curve at the same point. The economy will initially be at full-employment equilibrium, so that the actual price level is equal to the expected price level P_0^e, and the actual level of output is y^*.

**Figure 35.1
The Effects of an
Anticipated Change in
Government
Expenditure and
Taxes on the Level of
Output and Prices**

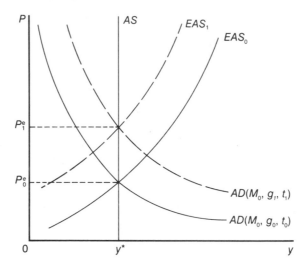

An anticipated rise in government spending and taxes with a constant money supply
raises the expected and actual aggregate demand to $AD\,(M_0, g_1, t_1)$, raises the expected
and actual price to P_1^e, but leaves output undisturbed.

Now suppose there is an anticipated rise in government expenditure. Further, suppose that there is a matching anticipated rise in
taxes, so that there is a balanced budget multiplier shift in the aggregate
demand curve. (If you are not sure about this, check back to Chapter
13.) If government spending was to rise without a rise in taxes, then
it would be necessary to raise the rate of money supply growth, and
this would generate inflation. (It would not be impossible to analyze
this case, but the balanced budget fiscal policy is easier to analyze.)

Suppose that the balanced budget increase in government expenditure and taxes is such as to shift the aggregate demand curve
to the broken line labelled $AD(M_0, g_1, t_1)$. With the money supply being
held constant at M_0, but with government expenditure and taxes
raised to g_1 and t_1 respectively, the aggregate demand curve has shifted
rightwards.

Also, recall that the rise in government expenditure to g_1 is assumed
to be anticipated. This means that all economic agents will be aware
that government expenditure has increased to g_1. Everyone will be
aware, therefore, that the price level is going to rise because the new
aggregate demand curve is to the right of the original one. The new
rational expectation of the price level will be calculated as P_1^e. This
is the price level where the new aggregate demand curve cuts the
aggregate supply curve. A new expectations-augmented aggregate
supply curve (the broken line labelled EAS_1) will be located so that

it goes through the point where the new aggregate demand curve cuts the aggregate supply curve.

You can now read off directly the effects of an anticipated rise in government expenditure on output and the price level. If the level of government expenditure and taxes *actually* rises to g_1 and t_1, so that the actual aggregate supply curve becomes the same broken curve $AD(M_0, g_1, t_1)$, then the level of prices will be equal to the rational expectation of the price level, namely, P_1^e and output will remain at its full-employment level y^*.

You can see then that an anticipated rise in government expenditure (matched by an anticipated rise in taxes) will raise the price level and leave the level of output unchanged.

(ii) The Effects on the Labor Market

It is a trivial matter to work out the effects of an anticipated rise in government spending (matched by a tax rise) on the labor market variables. Since output has not changed, neither will employment, unemployment, nor will the real wage have changed. Since the price level has gone up, so must the money wage rate have risen. The money wage rate will rise by the same percentage amount as the rise in the price level, thereby leaving the real wage unchanged. This is all there is to the effects of an anticipated rise in government expenditure.

There is, however, a very important caveat. You should be aware that the analysis that has just been performed is based on the assumption that the extra taxes raised in the experiment are non-distorting. That is, that they are of a form that does not affect the supply of, or demand for, labor. If there were changes in such taxes as income or payroll taxes, there would be further important effects on employment and on the real wage to take into account. These in turn would lead to a different response of output to that worked out above. In fact, if higher taxes shifted the labor supply curve to the left, the levels of output and employment would *fall*, and the price level would rise by even more than that shown in Figure 34.1. This is the essence of the supply-side analysis of some of the economists and other supporters of the Reagan economic program in the United States. They argue that by *cutting* taxes and government spending, in a predictable, i.e., an anticipated way, the supply of labor will rise, output and employment will rise, and the inflation rate (the price level in the analysis here) will fall. You will be taken through an analysis of this view in the next chapter.

(iii) The Effects on Interest Rates

You can work out the effects of an anticipated rise in government spending and taxes on interest rates by using the analysis developed in Chapters 10 and 13. From this analysis you know that a balanced budget rise in government spending (rise in spending matched by tax rise) will shift the *IS* curve to the right by the amount of the spending rise. This means that, at full employment, the rate of interest increases. You will recall that this occurs as part of the equilibrating mechanism whereby room is made for the extra government spending as a result of private investment decisions being cut back. This is sometimes stated as the phenomenon of a rise in government spending "crowding out" private spending.

(iv) Random Shocks and Policy Responses

If there was a random shock to aggregate demand or to aggregate supply such as those discussed in Chapters 33 and 34, it would not be possible to offset those random shocks with an anticipated change in government expenditure. Any anticipated fiscal policy action would be allowed for by private economic agents in forming their own rational expectations and would leave the level of output undisturbed. Therefore, anticipated fiscal policy changes cannot be used to stabilize the level of output, employment, and unemployment in the face of random shocks. They only have price level effects.

Let us now go on to analyze the effects of an unanticipated change in government expenditure.

D. Effects of Unanticipated Change in Government Expenditure

(i) The Effects on Output and the Price Level

To analyze the effects of an unanticipated change in government expenditure, let us again begin by working out its effects on the level of output and the price level. Figure 35.2 will illustrate the analysis. The economy initially has a money supply M_0 and government spending level g_0 and taxes t_0, so that the aggregate demand curve is the continuous line $AD(M_0, g_0, t_0)$. The aggregate supply curve is *AS*, and equilibrium is at the full-employment output level y^* and the actual and rationally expected price level of P_0^e. Also, suppose that all economic agents anticipate that government expenditure, taxes, and the money supply will be maintained at their initial levels of g_0, t_0, and M_0 respectively. Suppose, however, that instead of doing the expected, the government unexpectedly increased its expenditure and taxes by equal amounts to g_1 and t_1 respectively. With equal unexpected rises in government expenditure and taxes, the Bank of Canada will maintain the money supply constant at the initial level of M_0. The unanticipated rise in government expenditure and the equal unanticipated rise in taxes will shift the aggregate demand curve outwards to the curve $AD(M_0, g_1, t_1)$. Since this shift is unanticipated, the expectations-augmented aggregate supply curve remains the curve EAS_0. The new equilibrium is obtained at the point at which the new aggregate demand curve $AD(M_0, g_1, t_1)$ cuts the expectations-augmented aggregate supply curve EAS_0. You can read off this new solution as the price level P_1 and the output level y_1 in Figure 35.2.

You can now easily see the effects of an unanticipated rise in government expenditure (matched by an equal tax rise). An unanticipated rise in government expenditure (matched by an unanticipated tax rise to maintain a balanced budget) will raise the level of output and raise the price level.

We could easily reverse the above experiment and consider an unanticipated cut in government expenditure (matched by a tax cut to maintain a balanced budget) and this would lead to a fall in both output and the price level.

(ii) The Effects on the Labor Market

It is now possible to work out the effects of these unanticipated changes in government expenditure on the labor market variables. Let us consider for illustrative purposes an unanticipated *rise* in government expenditure. (You can work out the effects of an unanticipated *fall* for yourself.)

Since an unanticipated rise in government spending raises output, it follows immediately that it must also raise the level of employment. You can read this off by considering Figure 17.2 in Chapter 17. Further, since the level of employment rises, the level of unemployment falls below its natural level. In order to induce a rise in employment, firms must willingly hire the additional labor and still be maximizing

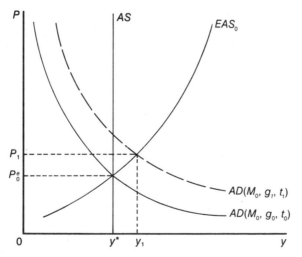

**Figure 35.2
The Effects of an
Unanticipated Change
in Government
Expenditure and Taxes
on the Level of Output
and Prices**

An unanticipated rise in government spending and taxes with a constant money supply shifts the aggregate demand to AD (M_0, g_1, t_1). This raises output to y_1 and the price level to P_1.

profits. This implies that the real wage must fall. However, the real wage falls only if the money wage rises by less than the rise in the price level. This therefore is a further implication of the analysis concerning the effects of an unanticipated change in government spending.

To summarize the effects of an unanticipated rise in government spending on the labor market variables: an unanticipated rise in government expenditure (matched by an unanticipated tax rise) will raise the level of employment, lower the level of unemployment, lower the real wage, and lead to a rise in the money wage, but by a smaller percentage amount than the rise in the price level.

(iii) Random Shocks and Policy Responses

You see, then, that an unanticipated change in government expenditure is capable of moving the level of aggregate output and employment around. It is possible to stimulate demand and raise output with an unanticipated rise in government spending and to cut back on output with an unanticipated cut in government spending.

It follows, therefore, that an unanticipated change in fiscal policy could be used to offset a random shock to either aggregate demand or aggregate supply. However, exactly the same considerations that were discussed in Chapters 33 and 34 concerning monetary policy apply here. If the government can change its expenditure (and taxes) quickly enough to offset shocks that private agents know have occurred, but which they are contractually unable to respond to, then it would be possible to use fiscal policy along the lines suggested by Keynesians to reduce the amount of variability in economic activity. However, if government expenditure and tax changes can only be engineered slowly and no more quickly than private contracts can be renegotiated, then there is no scope for government expenditure and tax variations to do anything other than lead to price level variability. Because of the legislative and bureaucratic lags in the enactment and implementation of fiscal policy changes, many Keynesians are now coming to the view that fiscal policy is not a useful stabilization weapon and are placing more emphasis on active variations in the money supply as the appropriate way of stabilizing the economy.

(iv) Fiscal Policy and Inflation

There is a further reason for concern over the use of fiscal policy as a stabilizing device. This concerns its inflationary consequences. Throughout the exercises conducted in this chapter, it has been supposed that the inflation rate was being held at zero, with the money supply growth rate held at the output growth rate (in the case of this model, both zero). If, starting from an initial situation of zero inflation, there was to be a permanent rise in government expenditure, with a permanent commitment not to change taxes, then we know that the money supply would eventually have to start growing at a faster rate. This means that the aggregate demand curve would begin to shift upwards continuously. Also, the expectations-augmented aggregate supply curve would shift upwards continuously as rational agents would continuously revise their price level expectations upwards. Provided the money supply growth was anticipated, these two curves would move up at the same pace as each other, with inflation ensuing. With an anticipated inflation, the economy would stay at full employment. It is unlikely, however, that the money supply growth rate would be precisely anticipated. The money supply growth rate could be either above or below its anticipated level. This being the case, there could either be an output boom or an output slump (stagflation) as the inflation rate increased. Either of these effects is possible, depending on whether the money supply growth accompanying a fiscal policy change is under- or over-anticipated.

Summary

A. Keynesian and Monetarist Fiscal Policy Advice

Keynesians recommend the active use of variations in government spending and taxes to raise demand when output is below its full-employment level and to lower demand when output is above its full-employment level.

Monetarists urge the maintaining of a steady fiscal policy that is dictated by resource-allocation considerations between the public and private sector, and not by economic-stabilization considerations. They advocate a level of government spending consistent with an optimal division of resources between the government and private sector, and a level of taxes such that the money supply growth target that they advocate may be achieved.

B. Anticipated and Unanticipated Fiscal Policy

Just as in the case of monetary policy, a change in government expenditure or taxes may be decomposed into the part that was anticipated and the part that was unanticipated. The unanticipated change in government spending and taxes is simply the actual change minus the change that was anticipated. When there is no unanticipated change, fiscal policy is anticipated.

C. Effects of Anticipated Change in Government Expenditure

An anticipated rise in government expenditure matched by an equal anticipated tax rise will raise the price level and raise the money wage by the same percentage amount as each other. It will leave the level of output, employment, unemployment, and the real wage unchanged. These predictions assume *neutral* tax changes.

D. Effects of Unanticipated Change in Government Expenditure

An unanticipated rise in government expenditure matched by an equal unanticipated tax rise will raise the level of output and the price level. It will also raise the level of employment and the money wage. However, the money wage will not rise by as much as the price level, and the real wage will fall. There will also be a fall in the unemployment rate.

Exactly the same considerations apply to evaluating the appropriateness of alternative fiscal policies as were discussed in Chapters 33 and 34 concerning monetary policies. That material should be studied carefully and its relevance to the fiscal policy debate understood.

Review Questions

1. Outline the key disagreements between Keynesians and monetarists regarding fiscal policy.

2. What criterion does the monetarist use for determining whether or not additional government spending is recommended? What criterion does the typical Keynesian policy advisor use?

3. Why is it that some monetarists feel there should be a constitutional limitation on the fraction of GNP which may be spent by the government?

4. What are the implications, in terms of the government's budget deficit, of following a monetarist rule of setting the rate of growth of the money supply equal to the rate of growth of real output?

5. Suppose there is a random shock to aggregate demand. Work out, using the appropriate diagrams:

    (a) the consequences for real income, the price level, and the levels of employment, unemployment and real wages of a monetarist fiscal policy

    (b) The consequences for real income, the price level, and the levels of employment, unemployment and real wages of Keynesian fiscal policy

    (c) The consequences for real income, the price level, and the levels of employment, unemployment and real wages of a Keynesian policy with a one-period lag in changing government spending and/or taxes.

6. Suppose there is an anticipated rise in government expenditure not matched by a tax rise. Suppose further that inititially the inflation rate was zero. Trace out the future time path of the inflation rate following this policy change.

7. Suppose there is a rise in government expenditure, not matched by a tax rise, that at first is unanticipated, but then is maintained and subsequently becomes anticipated. Trace out the time path which will be followed by the rate of inflation, real output, and unemployment.

36

The "Supply Side"

In recent years, and especially in the period since Ronald Reagan became President of the United States, a great deal has been heard about "supply-side" macroeconomics. Less attention has been given to "supply-side" policies here in Canada but, both the MacDonald Commission, which issued its massive report on Canada's economic prospects[1] in September 1985 and the Progressive Conservative government, elected in the fall of 1984, have emphasised the importance of paying attention to the incentive effects of government intervention and taxation. The first budget of Canada's newly elected government, introduced by Finance Minister Michael Wilson in 1985, sought to encourage innovation and employment by providing selective incentives, especially to small-scale businesses. These measures are, however, much less comprehensive and far-reaching than the extensive cuts in income tax rates that the Reagan administration has introduced in the United States. "Supply-side" macroeconomic policies are presented by proponents as some "new" magic that, in contrast to the old Keynesian policies, can cure all our ills of inflation, unemployment, and sagging productivity. As a matter of fact, the economic analysis that provides the basis for the propositions of the "supply-siders," as they are known, is not new at all. It is *pre*-Keyne-

---

[1] *The Report of the Royal Commission on the Economic Union and Development Prospects for Canada*, Minister of Supply and Services Canada, 1985.

sian. That does not mean that it is wrong. It does mean, however, that the way in which it is presented, especially by the media, is misleading. This chapter is designed to help you evaluate the claims of the supply-siders. To that end you will pursue eight tasks, which are to:

a) Understand why governments are productive.
b) Understand how productive government activity affects the production function and the demand for labor.
c) Understand how paying for government (taxation) affects the supply of labor.
d) Understand how efficient government raises output and employment.
e) Understand how overgrown government lowers output and employment.
f) Know the effects of supply-side policies on the price level.
g) Understand how the supply-side analysis can be extended to apply to savings and capital accumulation.
h) Appraise (briefly) the supply-side policies of the Reagan administration in the United States.

A. Why Governments are Productive

The easiest way to convince yourself that governments are productive is to conduct a thought experiment. Imagine a world in which there is no government. What are the most basic services provided by government that such a world would lack?

Perhaps the most fundamental service provided by government is the establishment of property rights and the enforcement of contracts. Thus government can be thought of as an economic agent that has a monopoly in the legitimate use of coercion. Governments use that monopoly power to require the rest of us to behave in certain well-defined ways. If we enter into contracts with each other, then we are required to fulfill our part of the bargain. Failure to do so may result in the injured party seeking a satisfactory settlement by appealing to the courts. Our persons and our physical property are also protected by criminal laws that automatically come into action if those rights are violated. The punishment of those convicted of crimes is the government's way of imposing a price penalty that is designed to deter such criminal activity. The provision of national defense can be thought of as a natural extension of such activity whereby the government seeks to guard the personal and physical property of its citizens against damage or theft by foreigners.

Try to imagine a world in which these services are not provided by monopoly government. How are they provided? The answer is that individuals and groups will seek to provide for their own security by carrying arms themselves or hiring others to protect them. More of human history has been characterized by such arrangements than by those with which we are familiar in the modern world. In such a world, a large volume of human and physical resources would be devoted to the provision of personal and collective security. These resources, if released from such activities, could be put to other productive use. In the absence of a government, however, private individuals are not going to see it as being in their interest to divert resources from the provision of personal security to the production of other goods and services. They will use their scarce resources in the most productive way and that will involve protecting what they have acquired rather than producing additional goods and services.

The emergence of a government with a monopoly in the use of coercion that uses this monopoly to establish and enforce property rights by operating a criminal and civil legal system confronts rational individuals with a different set of constraints. Instead of seeing it as being in their best interest to protect what they have, individuals will benefit from the collective (or shared) provision of such protection services and will enjoy a greater measure of freedom that may be employed in other productive activities.

A second activity which would not be present in a world without government is the provision of public health services. By *public* health services we mean such things as the provision of clean drinking water, sewage services, innoculation programs against easily communicated diseases, and the like. These should be distinguished from *private* health services, which deal with the prevention and treatment of conditions specific to a given individual. It is the nature of public health services (but not private health services) that their fruits may be consumed by all regardless of individual contributions. It is likely therefore that unless the government directly organizes and provides public health services, no one will see it as being in their own interest to expend such resources to provide an appropriate level of such a service. As a consequence, disease will reduce the effective productivity of the population.

Governments provide many things other than a basic legal system and public health services. Some of these are productive, although it is a controversial matter as to whether they may be more productively provided by government than the private sector. Still other activities of government are not productive at all. They involve, in effect, the replacement of private violations of property rights with public violation.

Examples of the former activities are the provision of a road system, schools and universities, and various kinds of insurance. There is no easy way of knowing whether the government provision of these activities is more or less efficient than a private provision of the same services would be. Certainly there are large variations across jurisdictions in this regard. Some countries (for example Switzerland) seek to provide almost everything they can privately, whereas others (for example the Soviet Union) have sought to shrink the private sector to provide only a narrow range of consumer goods. Although it is controversial and impossible to settle in any definitive way whether private or public provision other than in the area of a basic legal and security system and the provision of public health is the more productive, it does seem reasonable to suppose that the more things government provides, the more likely it is that it will start encroaching on areas where it is less able to produce efficiently than the private sector would be.

Examples of activities indulged in by modern governments that appear to have no productivity at all involve the massive income and wealth redistributions that take place. Macroeconomics is not the part of the subject that deals in detail with this topic. We may note, however, that if it is desired to redistribute income and wealth in an efficient way, there exist well-defined so-called negative income tax schemes that could achieve this with vast reductions in the volume of bureaucracy required as compared with the schemes that most modern governments, including that in Canada, pursue at the present time. It is also transparently obvious that most of the transfers that take place do not go from the rich to the poor, but go from the rich and the poor to the politically powerful middle. Thus, the political process itself may be seen as, to some degree, performing the same function as is performed by a less formal system and indeed more primitive system of property expropriations.

It is easy to summarize the above: some things that governments do they do better than any other agent conceivably could. A monopoly provider of law and order and national security together with public health is almost certainly the most efficient such provider. A government monopoly in most other activities is probably about equally efficient with private provision. However, as an agent that transfers wealth among individuals, government is fairly inefficient.

B. How Productive Government Activity Affects the Production Function and the Demand for Labor

In order to go beyond the description of government activity in the previous section and develop an analysis of how government affects aggregate economic activity, it is necessary to see how productive government activity affects the aggregate supply curve that we studied in Chapter 14.

The first effect that we shall identify is perhaps the obvious one — this is the influence of productive government activity on the short-run production function and on the demand for labor. This is illustrated in Figure 36.1. Frame (a) shows the production function for two economies. One economy has no government provision of productive services such as those described above, and its production

function is the one labelled $\phi(n,g_0)$. The other is an economy in which
the government is providing a level of activity that supports a legal
system, national defense and public health services that raise the
productive efficiency of the population and enables them at each level
of employment to produce more output than they could in the absence
of those government services. The production function that relates to
that economy is the one labelled $\phi(n,g^*)$, as representing the maximum output that can be achieved no matter what services the government provides. In other words, think of g^* as a level of government
activity that maximizes the economy's productive potential.

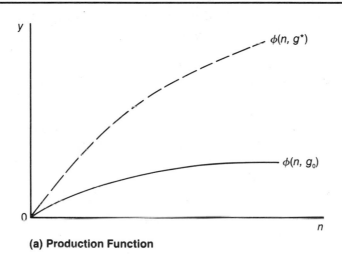

**Figure 36.1
How Productive
Government
Affects the
Production Function
and Demand for Labor**

(a) Production Function

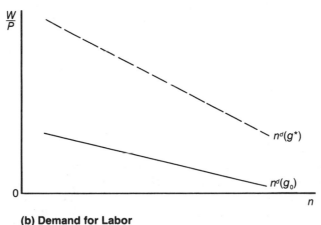

(b) Demand for Labor

An economy with no government has a production function $\phi(n,g_0)$, [frame (a)] and a
demand for labor curve, $n^d(g_0)$, [frame (b)]. If the government provides productive
services that enable individuals to pay less attention to the needs of their own security
and also provides basic public health, the production function and labor demand
function will shift upwards to the curves labelled $\phi(n,g^*)$ and $n^d(g^*)$.

We do not need to become bogged down here in the controversies as to precisely what government services are involved in that production function. Certainly included are the provision of law and order, defense and public health, in addition to some other activities provided by modern governments.

Just as the provision of productive goods and services by the government shifts the production function, so it also shifts the labor demand curve. Recall from the discussion in Chapter 14 that the demand for labor curve is nothing other than the marginal product of labor curve. In the no-government economy of frame (a), the marginal product of labor is very low. Thus, the demand for labor curve in such an economy would be a curve such as that shown in frame (b) and labelled $n^d(g_0)$. In contrast, in the economy that has a government providing the output-maximizing volume of public goods and services, the marginal product of labor is much higher. This would be depicted in frame (b) as the curve $n^d(g^*)$.

Recall that the slope of the production function measures the marginal product of labor. The slope of the production function with no government is much lower than that of the production function with productive government activity. These differences in the slopes of the production function are reflected in the levels of the demand for labor curves.

C. How Taxes Affect the Supply of Labor

Government services are paid for by taxes. Governments levy taxes on all kinds of activities, but to keep the analysis simple, we shall suppose that all taxes are levied on labor income. What do taxes on labor income do to the supply of labor? Although there are qualifications to any answer (which you will probably study in a course on public finance), the basic answer is that taxes lower the supply of labor. Figure 36.2 illustrates why this is so. In this figure the curve labelled $n^s(t_0)$ is the labor supply curve in an economy that has no taxes. Thus, if the wage rate was the amount labelled "after tax (W/P)," then the quantity of labor supplied would be the amount labelled n^*.

Suppose now that the government was to levy a tax of an amount labelled t^*. Ask the question, How much would have to be offered in order to induce n^* workers to work in this new situation? The answer presumably is that the after-tax wage would have to be the same as the wage in the no-tax situation. This could only be achieved if the before-tax wage was the amount labelled on the vertical axis as "before tax (W/P)." Thus, to induce a supply of labor n^*, the real wage would have to be higher, if taxes were t^*, by an amount t^* than they would have to be in a no-tax situation. The same would be true of any level of employment and so the entire labor supply schedule

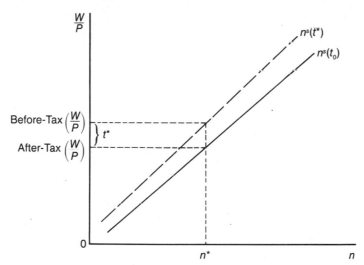

**Figure 36.2
How Taxes Affect
the Supply
of Labor**

The supply of labor depends upon after-tax real wages. Higher after-tax real wages induce a bigger labor supply. The higher the tax, the higher before-tax real wages will have to be to induce any given labor supply. Thus a tax of t^* at an employment level n^* would shift the supply of labor curve from $n^s(t_0)$ to $n^s(t^*)$.

would be shifted to the left of $n^s(t_0)$ to become the supply curve labelled $n^s(t^*)$. Clearly the higher the taxes, the further will the supply curve shift to the left.

D. How Efficient Government Raises Output and Employment

It is now possible to bring together the analysis of the two preceding sections and see how efficient government leads to a rise in both output and employment and also to a rise in real wages. There are two offsetting effects to be considered. First, the provision of government productive activities shifts the production function and demand for labor curve upwards. Second, the payment for these government activities through taxes has the effect of lowering the supply of labor. There is a strong presumption that the former expansionary activity strongly dominates the latter contractionary activity. Figure 36.3 shows how things work out.

The figure contains two frames just like Figure 36.1 did and frame (a) is identical to that in Figure 36.1. Frame (b) brings together the demand for labor — frame (b) of Figure 36.1 — with the supply of labor — (Figure 36.2). First let us consider an economy with no government. This will be an economy with a production function $\phi(n,g_0)$ and a demand for labor $n^d(g_0)$. With no government there will be no taxes and the labor supply curve would therefore be that labelled

**Figure 36.3
Efficient
Government**

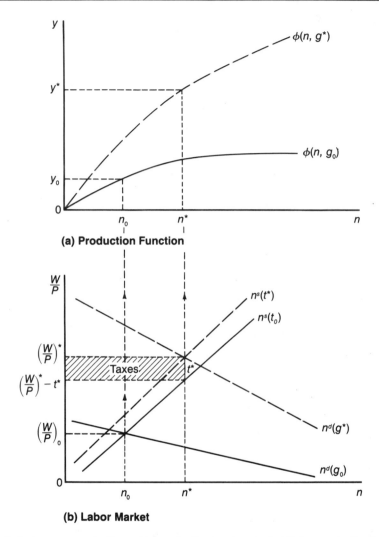

(a) Production Function

(b) Labor Market

An efficient government will provide productive services that shift the production function up from $\phi(n,g_0)$ to $\phi(n,g^*)$ [frame (a)], with an associated upward shift in the demand for labor curve $n^d(g_0)$ to $n^d(g^*)$ [frame (b)]. This government activity will be paid for by the minimum possible level of taxes, which will have a modest distorting effect in the labor market shifting the labor supply curve from $n^s(t_0)$ to $n^s(t^*)$. The resulting equilibrium will be one that has higher employment (n^*), output (y^*) and after-tax real wages $(W/P)-t^*$ than in the no-government case.

$n^s(t_0)$. Equilibrium in the labor market in this economy would occur at the employment level n_0 with the real wage $(W/P)_0$. The level of output in this economy would be read off from the production function in frame (a) as the amount y_0.

Contrast this economy with one in which there is a government that provides a level of services that makes it possible to raise output for each level of labor input, as depicted by the production function $\phi(n,g^*)$. In this case, the demand for labor would be $n^d(g^*)$. Assume that the government pays for its productive activities with the minimum possible taxes and that that level of taxes is t^* per worker. This would shift the supply of labor curve to $n^s(t^*)$. The equilibrium in this case occurs where the tax distorted labor supply curve cuts the government productivity-enhanced demand for labor curve at n^* and the real wage rate $(W/P)^*$. The level of output in this economy is that read off from the higher production function $\phi(n,g^*)$ at y^*. Thus, in this economy, government has the effect of raising employment from n_0 to n^*, raising output from y_0 to y^*, and raising real wages from $(W/P)_0$ to $(W/P)^*$. The government has to be paid for with taxes, and the tax per worker of t^* multiplied by the number of workers n^* gives a total tax bill as indicated by the shaded area in frame (b). After-tax wages are $(W/P)^* - t^*$.

In terms of real world events, in the no-government economy, a large amount of productive labor over and above n_0 will be expended on self-protection and property-protection, but only a small amount of goods and services (y_0) will be produced. People will be in a general state of belligerence and will not be very productive. In the economy with an efficient government, the government will be maintaining law and order (presumably with some equilibrium amount of violation taking place), and people will be freed from the need for self-protection and able to engage in productive work.

E. How Overgrown Government Lowers Output and Employment

It will by now be pretty obvious to you that a government that grows too big will actually lower output. This will happen because as government gets bigger and bigger, it contributes nothing extra to the productive capacity of the economy but has a negative effect on production as a result of the fact that higher taxes lower the labor supply.

Figure 36.4 illustrates an economy with an overgrown government. The equilibrium labelled y^*,n^*, $(W/P)^*$ is that for the economy with an efficient government as shown in Figure 36.3. The equilibrium marked y_0,n_0, $(W/P)_0$ is that for an economy with no government and exactly like that in Figure 36.3. Suppose that government grows bigger than the efficient size shown in Figure 36.3. Specifically, suppose the government raises taxes substantially above those levels necessary to provide a volume of government services that maximize the productive potential of the economy. It doesn't much matter what the government does with those taxes. The legislators may squander them on self-aggrandizement, they may be given to the poor, or they

**Figure 36.4
Overgrown
Government**

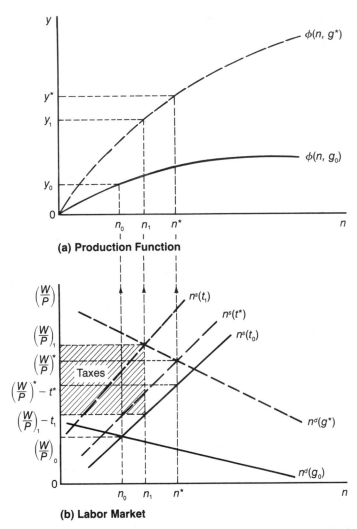

(a) Production Function

(b) Labor Market

A government that grows too big is one that raises taxes over and above the levels necessary to pay for the efficient scale of government, i.e. the tax rises from t^* to t_1. As this happens, the distorting effect of taxes shifts the supply of labor curve to the left to $n^s(t_1)$, thereby raising wages (before taxes) from $(W/P)^*$ to $(W/P)_1$ and lowering output (y^* to y_1) and employment from n^* to n_1. After-tax real wages fall from $(W/P)^* - t^*$ to $(W/P)_1 - t_1$.

may be used to provide goods and services that would otherwise have been provided privately. The point is that the taxes are not spent on any activity that can enhance the productive capacity of the economy. Thus, the production function that is relevant remains that labelled $\phi(n,g^*)$. The higher taxes shift the supply of labor curve to the left to a position such as that labelled $n^s(t_1)$. The demand for labor remains at $n^d(g^*)$. Equilibrium occurs at the employment level n_1 and the real wage $(W/P)_1$. The output level associated with that employment level n_1 is y_1. Clearly, by raising taxes above the minimum level necessary to provide the output-maximizing volume of government services, the government has introduced a distortion in the labor market that reduces overall work effort and output. Real wages exceed $(W/P)^*$ — those that occur in the economy with an efficient government (Figure 36.3). After-tax wages are lower in the economy with the overgrown government because the government takes a bigger tax bite — as shown by the shaded area in frame (b).

Figure 36.4 provides the essence of the supply-side argument. By lowering taxes and lowering the volume of unproductive government services provided with those taxes, it would be possible to raise output, raise employment and raise after-tax real wages. You can see this directly by comparing the equilibrium $y_1, n_1, (W/P)_1 - t_1$ with the equilibrium $y^*, n^*, (W/P)^* - t^*$. Clearly, if the overgrown government was to reduce its size to the efficient size, output, employment and after-tax wages would all rise.

There is in any actual real world situation disagreement and room for genuine doubt as to which government activities are productive and which unproductive. To a large degree disagreements between supply-siders and others turn not on the analysis contained in Figure 36.4 but on the empirical judgment concerning the productivity of government services. If reducing taxes involved reducing the provision of productive government services, then as taxes fell the production function would also fall, and the demand for labor curve would also shift downwards. Whether or not such a reduction in government would raise or lower output and employment would depend on which of the two effects was stronger. If, at the margin, government activity is very unproductive and the distorting effects of taxes on labor supply are very severe, then a reduction in government would raise output and employment. If, in contrast, the marginal government activities are slightly productive and the disincentive effects of taxes on labor supply only slight, then a reduction in government activity could lower output and employment. There is little agreement on which of these two effects dominate and not much in the way of solid empirical evidence that can readily settle the issue.

In the above comparison of an economy with an efficient government and an economy with an overgrown government, we have stumbled into a concept often used in discussion of supply-side matters — the so-called Laffer curve.[2] Figure 36.5 illustrates a Laffer curve. It is a curve that measures the tax rate on the vertical axis and the amount of taxes paid on the horizontal axis. The curve has the shape

---

[2] The Laffer curve is so named because it was popularized by Professor Arthur B. Laffer of the University of Southern California.

Figure 36.5
The Laffer Curve

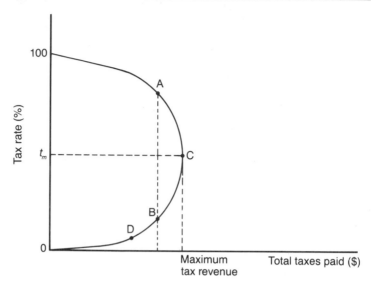

The Laffer curve shows the relationship between taxes paid and the rate of tax. At a zero tax rate no taxes are paid, and at a 100 percent tax rate no one will have any incentive to work (or do whatever other activities are being taxed), and so again no taxes will be paid. The general shape of the curve will be that shown so that at some tax rate (t_m), tax revenues are at a maximum.

shown for a reason that, if not immediately obvious, will be obvious in a moment. If the tax rate was zero, fairly clearly no taxes would be paid. Thus, the Laffer curve starts at the origin of the diagram. If the tax rate was a 100 percent then presumably nobody would do any work (or indulge in whatever other activity that tax is based on). Thus again, no revenue would be generated by the government and no taxes paid. The Laffer curve therefore bends back on itself starting at the origin when the tax rate is zero and returning to zero taxes raised when the tax rate is a 100 percent.

For intermediate tax rates there is a range over which, as the tax rate rises, tax revenues also rise. This is the portion of the curve ODBC. For tax rates above that marked t_m, as tax rates are increased, revenues fall. This happens because the activity that is being taxed will decline at a faster percentage rate than the tax rate itself increases. Figure 36.5 has been drawn such that the revenue-maximizing tax rate is 50 percent. There is, however, no presumption that this will be the revenue-maximizing rate. Such a rate would vary and depend upon the slopes of the supply and demand curves in question. The economy with an efficient government shown in Figure 36.3 might be thought of as being at a point such as D on the Laffer curve. The economy with an overgrown government might be in a position such as that depicted by B on the Laffer curve.

A government that was interested in raising taxes to the maximum possible level, presumably to further the interests of bureaucrats and legislators, would levy taxes at the revenue-maximizing rate. It has sometimes been suggested, and some of the current supply-siders in the United States have joined in this suggestion, that taxes in the United States at the present time are so high that the economy is in a position like that shown as A on the Laffer curve. A moment's reflection will suggest that, though this is a possibility, it is unlikely. If the government had raised taxes to such a high level that their revenues were the same as they would be with a much lower rate of taxes, then the government would be denying itself some revenue and at the same time would be inflicting costs on the rest of the economy over and above those that would be inflicted at a maximum revenue situation. In other words, at position A on the Laffer curve, the economy would generate an output level much below that being generated at position B on the Laffer curve.[3]

A key point to note is that it is unlikely that the economy is in a position like A and much more likely that it is in a position like B. If the economy is in a position like A, then it clearly pays to go to B, since that would involve the same tax revenues but more output and employment. However, if the economy is in a position like B, whether it would be desirable to move to a position like D depends on empirical judgments concerning the strength of supply-side effects.

F. The Effects of Supply-Side Policies on the Price Level

Not much needs to be added to the analysis that you have already conducted in Chapter 7, Section D. There we analyzed the effects of a shift in aggregate supply on the price level, showing that anything that lowered the level of aggregate supply raised the price level. Exactly the same considerations apply to the supply-side analysis. Any tax change which raises output will in effect shift the aggregate supply curve rightwards, thereby lowering the price level. This is why supply-siders believe that their policy recommendations will have advantageous effects on the inflation rate. It is important to notice, however, that even if supply-side policies were successful, they would have a once-and-for-all effect on the price level and no effect on the trend rate of inflation. This effect, as always, will be determined by the rate of growth of the money supply.

---

[3] Professor James Buchanan and Dwight Lee of the Virginia Polytechnic Institute have an ingenious argument that suggests that perhaps it would be possible for a government to get to a position like A as a result of taking too myopic a view of the consequences of increasing tax rates. See James M. Buchanan and Dwight Lee, "Politics, Time and the Laffer Curve," *Journal of Political Economy*, 90 (August 1982), 816-19.

G. Extension of Supply-Side Analysis to Saving and Capital Accumulation

The entire analysis that has been conducted in terms of a short-run production function could also be extended to apply to longer-term savings and capital accumulation. Over time, the economy's productive potential grows as a result of technical progress and capital accumulation. The amount of this activity undertaken is determined by an equilibrium process much like that that determines the level of employment. Other things being equal, the more capital the economy has, the lower will be the marginal product of that capital. The higher the marginal product of capital, the more will people seek to save and acquire capital. Taxes on the income from capital will lower the incentive to save and lower the incentive to accumulate capital. These taxes will, therefore, act in exactly the same way as taxes on labor. They will reduce the amount of economic activity that is taking place and lower the output of the economy.

H. Reagan's Supply-Side Policies

This final section will briefly examine the supply-side aspects of the Reagan economic program in the United States. It will not, however, go into great detail. It will simply help you to relate this program to the analysis that has been conducted in this chapter. (If you are interested in a more detailed description of the program, you should refer to the *Economic Report of the President* of January 1982 and 1983.)

(i) The Reagan Supply-Side Program in a Nutshell

There are four key features to the Reagan supply-side program. They are:
(1) The provision of more national defense
(2) Reductions in domestic programs
(3) Tax cuts
(4) Deregulation.

(ii) Supposed Effects (Claims by Supply-Siders)

What are the likely effects of a program having these four features? Let us examine this question not in the journalistic terms with which you are probably familiar but in terms of the analysis that we have conducted in the previous sections of this chapter.

First, a rise in defense expenditure may be thought of as a provision of a larger volume of productive government activity. How much would be contributed by additional defense expenditure depends, of course, on the marginal productivity of the additional defense services provided. Presumably, the idea of the supply-siders would be that, by providing more national defense the government is providing a greater measure of security than would otherwise be available, and that this is either desirable for its own sake (security is a good that people value) or because it will enable (and perhaps induce) a greater measure of confidence in the medium- to long-term future, thereby encouraging a greater volume of savings and investment.

The reduction in domestic programs is presumably viewed as a reduction in either low-productivity or unproductive government activity. Taken together, the rise in defense spending and the cut in other programs would be viewed by a supply-sider as releasing resources for productive use, thereby shifting the aggregate production function upwards.

The tax cuts in the Reagan program are seen as increasing both the supply of labor and the supply of savings, thereby increasing the equilibrium volumes of employment and capital accumulation.

The deregulation aspects of the Reagan supply-side program were not analyzed in the previous sections of this chapter. You may, however, conveniently think of deregulation as being equivalent to the reduction of taxes and the reduction of (unproductive?) government expenditure. If the government imposes a regulation on a private individual or firm, the effect of that is to require that individual agent to undertake actions which would otherwise not be pursued. This causes the individual to divert resources from voluntary to involuntary uses. This aspect of regulation is exactly like the imposition of a tax that also diverts resources from voluntary to involuntary uses — from voluntary consumption and saving activity to the involuntary payment of taxes.

The other aspect of regulation is that it requires government itself to employ large numbers of professional and clerical labor simply to monitor the activities of those being regulated and enforce the regulations. Thus, regulation imposes additional government expenditure and additional diversions of private resources from voluntary uses. The reduction of regulation seen in these terms would involve a reduction in both taxes and government spending. Its effects, therefore, would be exactly the same as the effects of reducing taxes and reducing government spending on unproductive activities that we have analyzed in earlier sections of this chapter.

In overall terms, the Reagan supply-side program adds up to a net increase in government spending and a net decrease in taxes. This arises because the defense-spending increases are greater than the cuts in spending on domestic programs. This means that the Reagan program has the effect of raising the federal budget deficit. Supporters of the supply-side view argue that this increase in the deficit is purely a short-run or transitory phenomenon. They predict that the supply-side policies will raise income by so much that the increase in overall tax revenues in the medium and longer term will be sufficient to offset the spending increase and put the federal budget in surplus.

These then, are the claims of the supply-siders. Are they justified?

(iii) Likely Effects of Supply-Side Programs

In evaluating the effects of supply-side programs such as those pursued by the Reagan administration, it is vital to distinguish between long-run and short-run effects. It seems likely (and is apparently confirmed by most empirical investigations) that, in the short run, the responsiveness of labor supply and the supply of savings to changes in taxes will be small. The key reason for this is that it is costly for people to change their behavior. They will be inclined to change their behavior only gradually in response to new conditions which call forth a different pattern of activity. Further, if there is some uncertainty as to the permanence of a change in policy, there will be even more reluctance to commit oneself to a change in behavior. In terms of the figures that we have used in this chapter, you can think of this as saying that in the short run, the supply curve of labor (and the supply curve of savings) is very steep. This means that, although a tax cut would indeed shift the labor supply curve (and the supply of savings curve) to the right, the amount of this rightward shift would be very small in the short run. In addition, the effect of changes in government activity on the overall productivity of the economy is likely to be slight in the short run. These two things taken together imply that the immediate and short-run effects of the Reagan supply-side policies are likely to be very small in terms of what they do to the level of employment and output.

There is an additional short-run consequence of policies such as those currently being pursued that is of considerable importance. It is the essence of the supply-side policies of the Reagan administration that labor (and other) resources be *reallocated*. In other words, certain activities will be decreased and others will be expanded. For example, less urban renewal and more defense would involve a shifting of resources away from building and civil engineering activities and into electronics and high-technology metals. These, of course, are just examples of many millions of reallocations of labor and other resources. Now when labor is reallocated, this does not take place without cost.Workers leaving one type of job have to find another job. This involves a period of job search such as that analyzed in Chapter 21. When policies are pursued that increase the amount of reallocation going on in the economy, they also increase the amount of job-search activity. This also gives rise to an increase in unemployment.

We have already seen that the advocates of supply-side policies recognize that those policies, at least as being pursued by the Reagan administration, will have the effect of increasing the government's budget deficit in the short run. The analysis that we have just conducted concerning short-run effects agrees with this but would suggest adding an additional burden to the government's budget deficit, namely, the increased expenditure on unemployment compensation that is a necessary accompaniment of the increased amount of resource and labor reallocation taking place.

The long-run effects of consistently pursuing lower taxes and lower levels of unproductive government activity will certainly, in qualitative terms, be the same as those claimed by the supply-siders. Output, employment and savings will all rise. How important this would be in *quantitative* terms is virtually impossible to say on the basis of what we currently know. Some believe that the effects would be slight; others that they would be enormous. What can be said with reasonable confidence, however, is that the long run may in fact be a very long way off. Notions of short run and long run in economic analysis are not clear statements about how long things take to happen in calendar time. Indeed, if properly understood "short run" and "long run" are not things that happen after a specified period of time at all. Rather, they are things that happen after certain adjustments have been made. By "short run" we usually mean a situation in which adjustments have taken place in response to a given shock while holding constant all the stocks of the various capital (including human capital) assets in the economy. By "long run" we mean the adjustment that will have taken place when all the capital stocks (physical and human) have adjusted to a given shock. Clearly, adjusting the stock of human capital takes at least as long as the length of time that it takes to replace a generation. Individuals typically acquire their human capital in specific form and just once in a lifetime. Long-run adjustments, therefore, can be presumed to take a very large amount of calendar time. In the intervening period the effects that will be felt will be those that pertain to the short run.

We have already seen that in the short run, it is recognized that the federal deficit will rise as a result of Reagan's supply-side programs. If that deficit increase persists for a substantial amount of time, then it will place inflationary burdens on the economy. You know this from the analysis that we conducted in Chapter 31 where we analyzed the linkages between fiscal and monetary policy. This consideration has to be added to the other predictions coming from the supply-side policies concerning the behavior of the price level. It is true, as we saw earlier in this chapter, that a successful supply-side program that lowers taxes and lowers unproductive government activity will raise the full-employment level of output. With a given money supply this will indeed lower the price level. If, however, the supply-side program adds to the federal deficit for a substantial period of time, then this in itself will put pressure on the monetary authorities to increase the *growth rate* of the money supply, thereby leading to a higher rate of inflation.

There are no easy and ready ways of deciding how successful, over the long run, programs of the type being pursued by the Reagan administration will be. What can be said fairly confidently, however, is that in the short run such policies would be much more easily pursued if the federal budget was not badly unbalanced. This would involve seeking to cut out unproductive government spending wherever it may be found, regardless of whether it is in the defense or domestic programs area and finding savings at least equal to the short-run cut in tax revenues. By combining the supply-side programs with such an overall federal budget balance, the danger of subsequent inflationary pressures would be avoided and the policies would likely be pursued with greater success.

Summary

A. Why Governments are Productive

Governments are productive because, by using their monopoly in coercion, they are able to reduce the resources involved in the protection of persons and property and able to enforce public health standards that raise the productivity of labor. Governments do many other things that are productive, but there is controversy and imprecise knowledge concerning the productivity of those additional government activities as compared with the productivity of equivalent privately provided services. In addition, governments indulge in many activities that have either low or perhaps even negative productivity.

B. How Productive Government Activity Affects the Production Function and the Demand for Labor

Productive government activity can be viewed as shifting the production function upwards, so that higher output levels are attainable at each level of labor input. Similarly, the slope of the production function is increased or, equivalently, the marginal product of labor rises. This means that the demand for labor curve shifts upwards.

C. How Taxes Affect the Supply of Labor

The higher the taxes, the lower will be the supply of labor. The supply of labor will depend on the after-tax real wage. In general, the higher the after-tax real wage is, the more labor will be supplied. Thus, a rise in taxes that lowers the after-tax wage rate will cause the labor supply curve to shift to the left.

D. How Efficient Government Raises Output and Employment

Efficient government raises output, employment and real wages as a result of the operation of two offsetting forces, one of which clearly dominates. The dominant force is the rise in the production function and the rise in the demand for labor that results from the provision of productive government activity. To some degree offsetting this, although only partially so, is the effect of the taxes levied to pay for the government services. These lower the supply of labor. Nevertheless, the two effects combined (Figure 36.3) result in higher output, higher employment and higher real wages.

E. How Overgrown Government Lowers Output and Employment

Government can grow too big in the sense that taxes continue to be increased and be spent on activities that do not raise the production function and the marginal product of labor. When that happens, all the effects of increased government size are negative, and the supply of labor curve shifts to the left, thereby producing a lower level of employment, lower output and a lower after-tax real wage (Figure 36.4).

F. The Effects of Supply-Side Policies on the Price Level

Any action that shifts the aggregate supply curve will, other things given, change the price level in the opposite direction. Thus, a rise in output (shifting aggregate supply to the right) resulting from supply-side policies lowers the price level. Supply-side policies in and of themselves have no effect on the rate of inflation, which is determined by the growth rate of the money supply.

G. Extensions of Supply-Side Analysis to Saving and Capital Accumulation

The supply-side analysis applied in this chapter to the labor market could be applied equally well to the market for capital goods and the supply of savings. Just as higher taxes on labor income are a disincentive to work, so high taxes on capital income are a disincentive to save. Lower savings result in lower capital accumulation and lower output. As an empirical matter, the importance of these effects is in dispute and is badly in need of detailed numerical measurement.

H. Reagan's Supply-Side Policies

The supply-side policies of the Reagan administration involve increasing defense spending, cutting spending on domestic programs, cutting taxes, and deregulating. In terms of the analysis of this chapter, this should be thought of as *attempting* to raise productive government spending and cut unproductive government spending, thereby shifting the production function upwards. Tax cuts are designed to shift the supply of labor (and supply of savings) curves to the right. Deregulation is like cutting both taxes and government spending simultaneously. The hoped-for effects of these policies are a rise in output and employment. It is recognized that these effects will occur in the long term and that in the short term there will be a rise in the federal budget deficit. However, there are good reasons to believe that the short term may well last for a long time, so that the hoped-for effects may be so long in coming that the short-run budget deficit triggers a renewed burst of inflation in the intervening period. The policies would be more convincingly pursued with more vigorous cutting of unproductive government activity and a balanced federal budget.

Review Questions

1. What productive services do governments provide? List five government activities that you regard as definitely productive (*productive* meaning that the government can provide the services more efficiently than could the private sector); five activities that you think are neutral (meaning that you think that the private sector could provide them about as effectively as the government can); and finally, five activites that you think are definitely wasteful (meaning that you think that the activities either should not be pursued at all or that, if they are to be pursued, should be pursued by the private sector).

2. How do productive government activities affect the production function?

3. Show the effects of a rise in the provision of some productive government service on the demand for labor.

4. What happens to the supply of labor if taxes increase? Is it always the case that the supply of labor curve shifts in the way presented in this chapter?

5. (This question should be done only by students who have studied the appropriate microeconomic theory of public finance.) Analyze the effects of a change in taxes on the supply of labor and on the demand for consumption using indifference curve analysis. What do you have to assume about the "income effect" in order to ensure that a rise in taxes lowers the supply of labor?

6. Show in a diagram how a balanced budget cut in taxes and a cut in totally unproductive government spending affects the levels of output, employment and real wage.

7. Analyze the effects of the experiment described in the previous question on the price level.

8. Suppose that a tax cut induced an additional amount of savings. What would be the effect of the increased savings rate on the economy? (This is a harder question, and a full answer requires that you refer back to Chapter 22, which analyzed long-term growth.)

9. Set out the key features of the supply-side aspects of the Reagan economic program and review their likely effects.

37

Wage
and
Price Controls

The emergence of rapid inflation combined with politically unacceptable unemployment rates has led, in the postwar years, to a search for new anti-inflation policies.

You already know from your understanding of the new theories of output and the price level that it is possible to reduce the rate of inflation by reducing the growth rate of the money supply. You also know that provided the reduction in the growth rate of the money supply is anticipated, inflation will fall without causing a recession — without causing a drop in output and a rise in unemployment. However, it is practically impossible for the Bank of Canada to engineer a cut in the money supply growth rate that is anticipated. Simply to announce a cut is not sufficient. People have to see before they believe. This means that while the Bank of Canada is convincing people of its intentions to lower the money supply growth rate, there will be a tendency for the actual money supply growth rate to be below the anticipated growth rate. In other words, the money supply will be below its anticipated level. As you know, the consequence of this is that the actual price level will be below the expected price level, and the actual level of output below the full-employment level.

It is to avoid this problem that new policies have been searched for. The major alternative "new" policy that has been widely advocated and used throughout the postwar years is that of wage and price controls — sometimes alternatively and more euphemistically called "prices and incomes policy."

The United Kingdom and other Western European countries were among the first to embark upon such policies after World War II. In the United Kingdom there have been eleven episodes of wage and price controls. The United States has had three such policies in the postwar years — the Kennedy "guideposts," the Nixon controls, and the Carter "price and pay standards." Canada has used wage and price controls just once — from October 1975 to December 1978.

Although viewed by their supporters as sophisticated "new" weapons, wage and price controls are perhaps better to be described as "blunt old instruments."

One of the earliest recorded episodes of wage and price controls was in A.D. 301, when the Roman emperor Diocletian, in his famous Edict, sought to control the prices on 900 commodities, 130 different classes of labor, and a large number of freight rates. Penalties for the violation of Diocletian's controls ran all the way to death. Controls have been used on and off ever since that time (and possibly in earlier times as well).

It is clear, then, that controls are certainly an old and not a new idea. The view that they are a blunt instrument rather than a sophisticated weapon will take the rest of this chapter to develop. However, as a prelude to this and so as to leave you in no doubt about our view of controls, let us summarize our view in the following way:

> [T]he so-called "new" policies are the oldest and crudest, best likened to medieval medicine based on ignorance and misunderstanding of the fundamental processes at work and more likely to kill the patient than to cure him.
>
> It was not until relatively recently in the long sweep of human history, in the seventeenth and eighteenth centuries, that the principles governing the determination of the general level of prices were made clear. The insights of Bodin and Hume and the refinements which have followed through the work and writings of Irving Fisher, Wicksell, Keynes and modern monetary theorists, such as Milton Friedman, are critical for understanding and influencing the monetary forces which determine the general level of prices [and] the rate of inflation.[1]

The new policies for controlling inflation, then, are monetary policies. There has been no essential technical advance in this field since the eighteenth century. There have been some refinements, but the fundamental ideas developed by Bodin and Hume remain the theoretical underpinnings of any successful anti-inflationary policy. The rest of this chapter is designed to help you understand and appreciate this.

You have five tasks. They are to:

a) Know the main features of the content of a wage and price control program.

---

[1]From Michael Parkin, *The Illusion of Wage and Price Controls* (Vancouver: The Fraser Institute, 1976), pp. 101-102.

b) Understand the distinction between a posted price and an actual price.

c) Understand why wage and price controls do not affect the expected price level.

d) Understand why wage and price controls do not affect the actual price level.

e) Understand why wage and price controls can only make matters worse.

A. Content of a Wage and Price Control Program

A wage and price control program typically has three sets of features:

(1) A set of rules about wages, prices, and, sometimes, profits.

(2) A set of penalties for a violation of the rules.

(3) A monitoring agency.

(i) Rules

The rules concerning wages center on the specification of a maximum normally allowable rate of increase of wages. Thus, for example, the policy may specify that the maximum rate of increase in wages shall not normally exceed some given percentage amount over a given specified period. There are almost always exceptions clauses built into such rules. Often, these permit higher than "normal" increases in the cases of the lowest paid workers.

The price rule sometimes takes a similar form to the wage rule. That is, a maximum allowed rate of price increase over a particular period is specified. More often, however, the price rule is couched in terms of a restriction allowing prices to rise only by an amount sufficient to cover the increased costs that arise from labor cost increases allowable under the wage rule.

Profit rules are more complex, both to state and to administer, and often are absent. When explicit profit rules are used, they are typically couched in terms of some maximum percentage of a previous period's average profits. In the Canadian case, for example, profit margins were required to be held to not more than 95 percent of the margins obtained, on the average, in the five years preceding the controls.

(ii) Penalties

Penalties for violation of the rules vary enormously. In the case of Diocletian's controls, the penalties ran all the way to death. In modern times they typically involve fines and *roll-backs* — a requirement that the wage or price be rolled back to the level that it would have been had the rules been obeyed.

(iii) Monitoring Agency

Monitoring agencies also vary enormously. Sometimes a special monitoring agency is set up. This was done in Canada, with the Anti-

Inflation Board. In other cases, existing government departments are used to provide the policing and monitoring, and the ordinary courts are used to carry out enforcement.

B. Posted Price and Actual Price

There are many dimensions to a transaction. These can be conveniently summarized under three headings: (1) a price dimension, (2) a quantity dimension, and (3) a quality dimension.

When you decide to buy something, you are buying a certain quantity of a commodity of a presumed quality for a certain price. This is true not only for commodities, but it also applies to labor services. For example, you might hire a certain quality of plumber for a certain number of hours for a certain price (i.e., wage).

A wage and price control program seeks to control directly one dimension of a transaction, namely, the price. In principle, of course, what it is trying to control is the price at which a specific quantity and quality of product or labor service is traded. It is extremely difficult, however, to monitor quantity and quality. Some examples will perhaps help to make this clear.

Suppose that the price dimension of a transaction is policed completely effectively. A good example of this would be the policing of the price of a university professor working for a Canadian university. Suppose the wage of the university professor is controlled by a wage control program and is effectively controlled to be below the market equilibrium wage. What will the professor do in that situation? It is clear that he will seek to maximize his utility by changing either the quality or the quantity of the labor that he supplies. If the wage rate being offered is below the market equilibrium wage rate, then he will lower the quantity and/or quality of work below the market equilibrium quantity/quality. Specifically, he will either take more leisure or indulge in more non-teaching, non-research, income-earning activities. The effective price of a unit of professorial services will have have been controlled. The posted price will have been controlled fully, but the actual price — the price for a specific quality and quantity — will have risen in exactly the same way as it would have done in the absence of the controls.

As another example, suppose that to perform some industrial job a certain grade of electrician is required (call it a grade-three electrician). Suppose that although a grade-three electrician is required to do this particular job, the wages of grade-three electricians have been controlled below the equilibrium wage, and a particular firm cannot hire enough of this type of labor. Clearly, what the firm will do is to hire the next, more-expensive grade of electrician (call it grade two), and, if necessary, upgrade people to that grade in order to get the job done and maximize profits. Again, the posted price —

the price of a grade-three electrician — will have been effectively controlled. However, the actual price paid to a particular individual supplier of effort will not have been controlled. People who otherwise would have been grade-three electricians now become grade-two electricians, and their wages rise in exactly the same way as they would have done in the absence of controls.

Consider a commodity market. The sticker price of a car is a posted price. However, as you know, the actual price at which a car gets traded is typically different from the sticker price, and includes a discount. Precisely what discount is offered is very hard to monitor and police. It is true that a discount is a reduction of the actual price below the posted price. However, if the posted price was controlled below its equilibrium level, then by reducing the size of the discount, the actual price could increase to achieve and maintain market equilibrium. Thus, when posted prices are controlled, the gap between posted prices and actual prices — if actual prices are at a discount — will narrow.

The distinction between posted and actual prices should now be clear from the above examples. The posted price is the visible price but not necessarily the price at which trades actually take place. It is, of course, the actual price and the average of all actual prices that constitute the general price level and not the fictitious numbers that are stuck on car windshields or attached to jobs of specific grades.

Let us now move on to examine the effects of wage and price controls on actual prices. As a prelude to this, however, it is necessary to analyze the effects of controls on *expected* prices.

C. Wage and Price Controls and the Expected Price Level

The most sophisticated advocates of wage and price controls base their belief in the potency of these measures on a view that controls can effectively lower inflationary expectations and, as a result, lower the actual rate of inflation without generating a recession. You already know that if inflationary expectations indeed can be lowered, then it is possible to lower the inflation rate and even have an output boom while the inflation rate is falling. (Go back to Chapter 17 and study the analysis shown in Figure 17.4. If the expectations-augmented aggregate supply curve can be lowered while the aggregate demand curve is held constant, then you see that the equilibrium price level falls and equilibrium output rises.)

Let us begin our analysis of the effects of wage and price controls, then, by working out what their effects on the expected price level are. *Do wage and price controls lower the expected price level and lower the expectations-augmented aggregate supply curve?*

To analyze this, consider Figure 37.1. The curve $AD(M_0, g_0, t_0)$ is the aggregate demand curve. To focus our attention exclusively on controls, let us hold the level of the money supply, government expenditure and taxes constant at the levels M_0, g_0, and t_0 and, furthermore, let us suppose that they are anticipated. You will recall that this implies that the actual position of the aggregate demand curve and its expected position are one and the same. This assumption enables us to isolate the effects of the controls.

The curve AS is the aggregate supply curve generated from equilibrium in the labor market. The expected price level P_0^e is determined by the intersection of the aggregate demand curve and the aggregate supply curve. Through this same point at which the aggregate demand curve cuts the AS curve passes the expectations-augmented aggregate supply curve EAS_0. This is the aggregate supply curve drawn for an expected price level of P_0^e which, in turn, is the rational expectation given a money supply of M_0 and a government spending level of g_0. Let us suppose that the economy is in equilibrium, with the actual price level at P_0^e and the output level at full-employment, y^*.

Now suppose the government introduces price and wage controls. Mark on the vertical axis of Figure 37.1 the price level P_c that the government is seeking to achieve with its controls. It is the price level that would emerge if the rules that specify the allowable behavior of wages and prices in the economy were effectively enforced. Thus the horizontal line at P_c represents the ceiling that the government would like to enforce on the price level.

Figure 37.1
Why Controls Do Not Lower the Expected Price Level

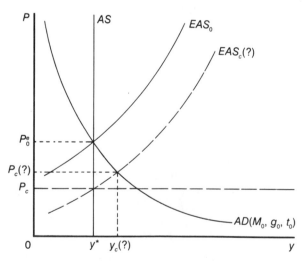

If the full-employment equilibrium is y^*,P_0^e, and a price control program seeks to maintain the price level at no higher than P_c, the expected price level will remain at P_0^e. To see this, notice that if the controlled price level was the expected price level the EAS curve would be $EAS_c(?)$. This would generate a price level of $P_c(?)$. The only expected price level that is rational (that predicts itself) is P_0^e. Thus controls do not lower the expected price level.

It is important to recognize that there is a major difference between the government attempting to impose a price ceiling on the general price level and the imposition of a price ceiling on some specific commodity such as, say, apartment or house rents. It is imaginable that sufficient resources could be devoted to monitoring and enforcing rent control regulations. This, however, is a far cry from being able to control the general price level. There are literally trillions of individual prices that make up a modern economy. To monitor, police, and effectively control the *actual* prices — the actual as opposed to the *posted* prices — on all the trillions of different kinds of commodities and factor services would require more resources than the entire gross national product.

Private individuals, maximizing their utilities and profits, will do the best they can for themselves, subject to the constraints which they face. If, by adjusting the quality dimension of transactions they can evade without detection the effects of a control on posted prices, then they will find it profitable to do so and, indeed, will do so. There is no presumption, therefore, that the actual price level in the economy will be equal to the price level that would emerge if all the rules that specified the allowable behavior of wages and prices were followed. Such rules will not be followed, and the price level will be different from the level implied by the exact adherence to those rules.

With this in mind, we now want to return to the question, What will be the effects of controls on the expected price level? Specifically, will the target price level P_c become the expected price level? Let us conduct a conceptual experiment exactly like the one we conducted in Chapter 18 when discussing the determination of the rational expectation of the price level.

Let us first suppose that the expected price level is indeed the controlled price level P_c. Would this be a rational expectation? If P_c was the expected price level, then the expectations-augmented aggregate supply curve would become the curve $EAS_c(?)$. We have put a (?) after that expectations-augmented aggregate supply curve to remind you that we are conducting a conceptual experiment and we are asking the question, Could this be the relevant expectations-augmented aggregate supply curve once the controls are imposed? You can see immediately that if the expectations-augmented aggregate supply curve is $EAS_c(?)$, and if the aggregate demand curve remains unchanged (which by assumption it does), then the price level and output level will be determined at $y_c(?)$ and $P_c(?)$. Again, we have put a (?) after these quantities to remind you that they are conceptual experimental values that we are considering and not necessarily actual values that the economy will achieve.

Now, recall the concept of a rational expectation. It is the prediction implied by the relevant theory, conditional on all the information available at the time the prediction is made. If the prediction of the theory is that the price level will be $P_c(?)$, it is clear that we cannot have P_c as the rational expectation of the price level. Further, therefore, $EAS_c(?)$ cannot be the relevant expectations-augmented aggregate supply curve. If you follow through the analysis in Section D of Chapter 18 on the determination of the rational expectation of the price level, and apply that analysis to this case, you will see that there is only one price level that will be rationally expected. That price level is P_0^e in other words, only the expected price level P_0^e leads to the prediction that the actual price level will be equal to the expected price level; and hence, only the price level P_0^e is the rational expectation. It follows, therefore, that the expectations-augmented aggregate supply curve will not move as a consequence of introducing controls and will remain at EAS_0.

Another way of thinking about the above analysis is as follows: rational economic agents will expect the price level to be determined by the forces that in fact determine the price level, namely, aggregate supply and aggregate demand. Wage and price controls (as a first approximation, to be modified in the final section) will not be expected to have much effect on aggregate supply. Further (again as a first approximation to be modified in the final section), controls will not affect the money supply or the level of government expenditure and taxes, so aggregate demand will be unaffected. Holding all these things constant, nothing that the controls have introduced would lead any rational person to expect that the actual price level would change as a result of the imposition of the controls. Hence, the rational person will expect the price level to be exactly the same with controls in place as without them.

The above remarks are to be interpreted as applying only if there is indeed no expectation that either aggregate supply AS, the money supply, government spending or taxes are going to be changed *as a consequence* of the introduction of controls. The possible effects of controls on these variables will be analyzed in the final section of this chapter.

D. Wage and Price Controls and the Actual Price Level

You have now seen that the theory of output and the price level predicts that the introduction of wage and price controls will have no effect on the expected price level and no effect on the position of the expectations-augmented aggregate supply curve. It is now a simple matter to analyze the effects of controls on the *actual* price level.

Figure 37.2 illustrates the analysis. The curves AS, $AD(M_0, g_0, t_0)$, and EAS_0 are the relevant aggregate supply, aggregate demand, and expectations-augmented aggregate supply curves in the immediate pre-control situation. The economy is at full-employment output y^*, with the actual and expected price level at P_0^e. Now suppose that wage and price controls are imposed, which would imply, if they were fully observed, a price level of P_c, as shown on the vertical axis of Figure 37.2. What happens to the actual price level in this situation?

Recall that the actual price level is determined at the point of intersection between the expectations-augmented aggregate supply curve and the aggregate demand curve. By the analysis of the preceding section, the controls will not move the expected price level and will not, therefore, move the expectations-augmented aggregate supply curve. The expectations-augmented aggregate supply curve remains at EAS_0.

Wage and price controls are not monetary policy and are not fiscal policy. As a first approximation, there will be no change in the money supply and no change in government expenditure and taxes when the controls are imposed (we will modify this in the next section). Therefore, nothing happens to the aggregate demand curve when we impose controls.

Since nothing happens to the expectations-augmented aggregate supply curve, nor to the aggregate demand curve, it is clear that the point at which these curves intersect remains unchanged. The price level remains at P_0^e and output remains at y^*. Thus, as a first approximation, controls have no effect on the actual price level. They may well control posted prices, and an index of posted prices may

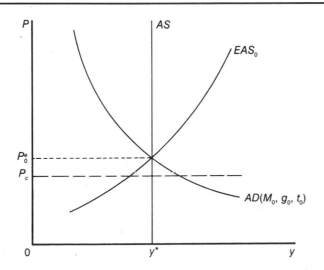

Figure 37.2
Why Controls Do Not Lower the Price Level (or the Inflation Rate)

The imposition of controls does not affect either the *EAS* curve or the *AD* curve. The equilibrium price level is determined at the intersection of those curves and, therefore, will be independent of the control price level.

not rise by as much as actual prices. Indeed, an index of posted prices may well approximate to P_c for a period. However, the actual price level in the economy will be unaffected, and if the price index is constructed from accurate price sampling, the recorded overall price index will show a price level of P_0^e rather than the controlled price level of P_c.

It is often suggested that the use of wage and price controls in conjunction with appropriate monetary and fiscal (aggregate demand) policies can lower inflation at a more acceptable price than by pursuing demand policies on their own. The analysis that you have just been through explains to you why that line of reasoning is incorrect. You know from your analysis of the effects of monetary and fiscal policy in the three preceding chapters that a reduction in aggregate demand will have both output and price level effects. The closer the demand change comes to being anticipated, the more will those effects be on the price level and the less on output. An ideal anti-inflation policy, therefore, would be one which lowered the rate of growth of aggregate demand and in an anticipated way.

You have further seen in the analysis in this chapter that introducing wage and price controls does nothing *over and above* what is being achieved by aggregate demand policy to influence the expected price level. It follows that what is required in order to make anti-inflation policies more successful and less painful is not wage and price controls but greater credibility concerning the ongoing pursuit of anti-inflationary aggregate demand policies. There are, unfortunately, good reasons for supposing that wage and price controls will actually work against the achievement of such credibility for they introduce additional problems of their own. Let us now examine these.

E. Wage and Price Controls Make Matters Worse

The conclusion of the preceding section is that wage and price controls have no effects. However, there are many reasons for supposing that they will have some effect upon the economy. It is best to regard the conclusion of the previous section as a first approximation rather than as the whole story. Let us now examine some of the possible effects.

First of all, controls divert real resources from other productive activities. The army of bureaucrats, accountants, lawyers (and even economists!) hired directly and indirectly by the wage-price monitoring agency could be employed in other productive activities. To the extent that there is a diversion of labor resources from producing goods and services (from producing y), there will be a shift in the aggregate supply available for private and government consumption.

You can think of this as a shift in the aggregate supply curve (as illustrated in Figure 37.3) from AS_0 to AS_1. Of course, in asserting that the aggregate supply curve has shifted to the left, we are asserting that the value of the output of the army of bureaucrats, accountants, lawyers, and economists employed in administering the control program is zero.

Just as the price level may very well be incorrectly measured during a period of wage and price controls, so may the value of national income. The national income statisticians would certainly impute a value of output to those employed in administering the wage and price control program equal to the factor incomes paid to them. In suggesting that income would fall in the event of the diversion of real resources away from productive activities to administering the program, we are saying that the national income accounts are incorrectly calculated and that the wages of those employed in administering the program should be regarded as a transfer payment from productive people to those who are unproductive. In this respect, it is no different from other forms of government transfer payments. (Although the remarks made here arise in connection with a discussion of wage and price controls, you may reflect on their more general applicability!)

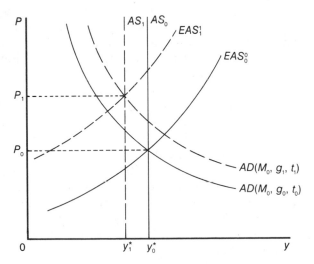

**Figure 37.3
Why Controls Can
Only Make Things
Worse**

Controls divert resources from productive activity, thereby lowering aggregate supply from AS_0 to AS_1. They also involve additional government expenditure and taxes to administer the control program. This raises the aggregate demand curve from $AD(M_0,g_0,t_0)$ to $AD(M_0,g_1,t_1)$. The consequence is a higher price level (P_1) and lower output y_1^*. These effects are probably not large, but they are certainly in the wrong direction.

Second, a wage and price control program typically involves additional government expenditure, both on the bureaucratic side and on professional labor hired on a short-term contract basis. Such a rise in government expenditure and taxes needed to pay for this expenditure would lead to a shift in the aggregate demand curve, as illustrated in Figure 37.3, from $AD(M_0, g_0, t_0)$ to $AD(M_0, g_1, t_1)$.

It is clear that the combination of diverting resources from private activities, which lowers the output supplied, and raising government expenditure and taxes, which shifts the aggregate demand curve, exerts separate but reinforcing effects on the price level. The rightward shift of the aggregate demand curve and the leftward shift of the aggregate supply curve will both tend to make the price level higher than it otherwise would have been (and the inflation rate higher than it otherwise would have been). Also, output will be lower than it otherwise would have been.

It would be wrong to suggest that these effects are likely to be of a large magnitude. However, they are certainly going to be present in the *directions* indicated in Figure 37.3, and there have been episodes in history when such effects may have been large.

There is a third possible factor to be taken into account. This is the effect of wage and price controls on monetary policy. With a wage and price control program in place to control the inflation rate, it is possible that the Bank of Canada and the federal government will become less concerned with maintaining anti-inflationary monetary policy. There also may be a temptation to use monetary policy in an attempt to stimulate aggregate demand, while using wage and price controls to keep inflation in check. If the money supply rises more quickly while the controls are in place, there will be a tendency for the inflation rate to rise even further than it would have done had there been no control program.

A fourth and major consideration concerning the effects of the controls arises from the fact that some prices are in fact controlled effectively, whereas others are not. The overall average effect of controls on the general price level of zero can be seen as hiding some effective control in some particular areas, with a tendency for demand to spill over into less controlled areas, where prices will rise to even higher levels than they would have in the absence of controls. If this happens (and there is good reason to suppose that it does because of the excessive attention paid by the wage and price monitoring board to specific sensitive sectors), then there will be some further serious economic losses inflicted.

Figure 37.4 illustrates the market for some particular good. It could be steel plate or any other highly visible commodity that the monitoring agency can effectively and fully control. The price on the vertical axis is the *relative* price of the good in question. This is equal to the money price of the good divided by the price level, that is, $p = P_i/P$. The horizontal axis in Figure 37.4 measures the quantity of the

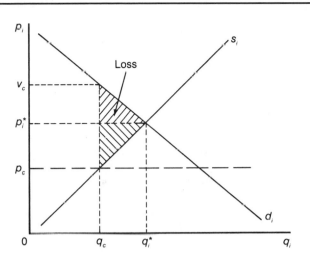

**Figure 37.4
How an Effective Price
Control Causes a Loss
of Welfare**

If a price control on some particular commodity or group of commodities is effective in holding the price below the equilibrium level, the value placed upon the commodity at the margin by the consumer (v_c) exceeds the real cost of production (p_c). A loss of producer and consumer surplus (the shaded area) results.

good. The curves d_i and s_i are the demand and supply curves (which you develop in your microeconomic theory course), and p_i^* and q_i^* are the competitive equilibrium price and quantity, respectively. Now suppose that an *effective* price control of p_c is imposed on this particular commodity. Assume that effective policing of quantity and quality ensures that p_c is the actual price and not just the posted price. It is clear that the quantity supplied will be reduced from q_i to q_c as the firms that produce this commodity seek to avoid the heavy losses that would be incurred if they maintained their output at q_i^*. The consumer places a value on the marginal quantity consumed of v_c. That is, the marginal utility of the last unit consumed exceeds the price by the distance $v_c - p_c$. The shaded triangle represents the total loss that results from the imposition of an effective price control of p_c. You can think of the shaded triangle as measuring the total difference between the value placed upon consumption of this commodity and the marginal cost of producing it as we move from the competitive equilibrium position of q_i^* to the controlled position of q_c. There will, in general, be a large number of losses of this kind arising from the unevenness with which wage and price controls are imposed upon the economy.

Overall, then, the effects of wage and price controls that we can detect are all in the direction of either raising prices or lowering output, or lowering economic welfare.

Summary

A. Content of a Wage and Price Control Program

A wage and price control program has three features:
 (1) Rules about wages, prices, and profits.
 (2) Sanctions and penalties.
 (3) A monitoring agency.

B. Posted Price and Actual Price

A posted price is the published or announced price; an actual price is the price at which a trade actually takes place for a given quantity and quality of product (or factor service).

C. Wage and Price Controls and the Expected Price Level

Since wage and price controls do not (as a first approximation) affect the level of the money supply or the level of government spending, they do not affect the level of aggregate demand. Also, as a first approximation, they do not affect aggregate supply. Since they do not therefore affect anything which determines the actual price level, it would be irrational to expect the actual price level to be affected by controls.

D. Wage and Price Controls and the Actual Price Level

The actual price level is determined at the intersection of the aggregate demand and expectations-augmented aggregate supply curves. Wage and price controls do not shift either of these curves and do not therefore affect the actual price level.

E. Wage and Price Controls Make Matters Worse

To the extent that wage and price controls divert resources from the private sector, they lower output and raise the price level. To the extent that they generate a bigger government spending level to finance the program, they raise the price level. To the extent that they encourage slack monetary policies, they raise the inflation rate. To the extent that wage and price controls are applied unevenly and made to stick in some sectors, they generate relative distortions and produce losses of economic welfare from a misallocation of resources.

Review Questions

1. What are the three features of a wage and price control program? Give an example of each of these features.

2. Distinguish between the actual price and the posted price in terms of the three dimensions of a trade outlined in this chapter.

3. Explain why wage and price controls may be used to control posted prices, but not actual prices.

4. List some products and the way in which each product's actual price can be adjusted in response to controls on its posted price.

5. Explain why wage and price controls cannot influence the rational expectation of the price level.

6. Work out, using the appropriate diagrams, the effects of expansionary monetary policy during a period of price controls.

7. Explain what is meant by the statement that "wage and price controls can only make matters worse."

8. In terms of ordinary demand and supply curves, illustrate the welfare loss associated with price controls.

9. Who benefits from wage and price controls? Why do you think they are so popular?

38

Tax Based
Incomes Policies (TIPS)

Recognizing the crudeness and ineffectivness of wage and price controls, some economists are now advocating yet another "new policy" for dealing with inflation, known as a *tax based incomes policy* or TIP. Like wage and price controls, such a policy represents an attempt to lower inflation while reducing the cost of doing so in terms of lost output and employment. In contrast to wage and price controls, however, a TIP really is a new policy. It is so new, in fact, that no one yet has tried it! It does, however, have a lot of supporters. It was first suggested in 1973 by Henry Wallich (then a professor at Yale University, now a Governor of the Federal Reserve System) and Sidney Weintraub (of the University of Texas at Austin).[1] Recently, the idea of controlling inflation by using a TIP has been strongly embraced by the economists on President Carter's Council of Economic Advisors who, in their final annual report[2] wrote on this topic in some detail. TIP has many Canadian supporters.

This chapter will help you to understand TIP. It will also reveal to you that the proposal is fatally flawed. When carefully analyzed, it becomes apparent that the effects of a TIP would be precisely the *opposite* to those claimed by its advocates. It would raise unemploy-

---

[1] See Sidney Weintraub *et al.*, *Keynes and the Monetarists and Other Essays* (New Brunswick, N.J.: Rutgers University Press, 1973), Chapter 6, "A Tax Based Incomes Policy," pp. 103-24.

[2] See *Economic Report of the President*, 1981 (Washington, D.C.: U.S. Government Printing Office, January 1981).

ment, lower employment, lower output and raise prices. This chapter will enable you to reach these conclusions by taking you through four tasks, which are to:

a) Understand the essential idea of a TIP.
b) Understand how a "reward pay" TIP affects the supply of labor.
c) Understand how a "profit penalty" TIP affects the demand for labor.
d) Understand why a TIP would lower the level of employment and output and raise the price level.

A. The Essential Idea of a TIP

The essential idea of a TIP is to use the tax system to encourage, though not to mandate, desirable inflationary behavior on the part of firms and workers. In a situation in which there is an ongoing inflation, those who raise their wages by less than some target percentage would face lower taxes than would those who raised their wages and prices by more than the target percentage. The idea is to encourage the taking of wage and price decisions that are below a target inflation rate and discourage those above the target rate. There are many varieties of TIP. First, a TIP could be applied to both wages and prices or only to wages or prices. Second, a TIP could both penalize those who raise wages and prices by too much and reward those who raise them by less than the target amount, or could either impose penalties only or give rewards only. Third, the TIP taxes could be graduated, becoming increasingly severe the higher wages and prices are increased above the target, with rewards becoming increasingly great the further a firm or group of workers deviates below the target. Such an arrangement is known as a "continuous" TIP. Alternatively there could be a flat rate penalty or reward depending on whether or not a price or wage change was above or below the target. Such an arrangement is known as a "hurdle" TIP.

Of the many varieties of TIP that are possible, it is recognized even by the most ardent TIP advocates that the administrative costs involved in operating a TIP are likely to be large. Bearing that in mind, one of the most popular TIP ideas is to focus only on wages and to have a "hurdle" TIP rather than a continuous one. In addition, because the advocates of TIP believe that, to a large degree, the problem of inflation is one that arises from a lack of social cohesion, they advocate a *pay reward* rather than *penalty* system. Thus, perhaps the most popular form of TIP among its advocates, (and that advocated by the Council of Economic Advisors to President Carter), is the *reward pay scheme with a hurdle applied* only to *wages.* Furthermore, it is usually suggested that a TIP should be a temporary program, put in place only for so long as it takes for the inflation rate to fall to some acceptable level.

Now that you are aware of the essential characteristics of a TIP, you will also be in a position to see the central idea of such a program. The idea is to discourage excessive wage and price increases, encourage moderate ones and thereby bring down the rate of inflation, by penalizing "undesirable" inflationary behavior and rewarding "desirable" behavior. The idea sounds good and it sounds right. A little digging is required in order to discover that, what appears to be a good idea on the surface is in fact severely flawed when we get underneath the surface and actually understand how such an arrangement would work. Let us now begin to do that by putting together the necessary bits of analytical apparatus.

B. Reward Pay TIP and the Supply of Labor

As a prelude to analyzing the effects of a TIP it will be helpful if we establish how the labor market will be operating in a steady-state inflation without a TIP in place. Figure 38.1 will illustrate the analysis. The vertical axis measures the *money* wage rate and the horizontal axis the level of employment. The demand and supply curves drawn in this diagram are, therefore, the same type of demand and supply curves that we used when developing the theory of aggregate supply in Chapter 15. Recall that each time the price level changes we have to shift both the supply and the demand curves when we draw them against the money wage.

We shall consider just two time periods — a time period called 0 and a time period called minus 1 (subscript -1). At time (-1) the demand and supply curves were those shown as $n^d(P_{-1})$ and $n^s(P_{-1})$ and the equilibrium level of employment was n^*_{-1} and the money wage was W_{-1}. Between period -1 and period 0 the price level rises by a steady-state inflation rate, π, to P_0. The supply and demand curves, therefore, shift upwards by that percentage amount to the curves labelled $n^d(P_0)$ and $n^s(P_0)$. The equilibrium level of employment remains the same ($n^*_0 = n^*_{-1}$) but the money wage rate rises to W_0 which represents the same rate of increase as occurred in the price level. That is

$$\frac{W^*_0 - W^*_{-1}}{W^*_{-1}} = \frac{P_0 - P_{-1}}{P_{-1}} = \frac{P^e_0 - P_{-1}}{P_{-1}} = \pi$$

We have indicated there that not only is the rate of wage change equal to the rate of price change but the expected rate of inflation is also equal to the actual rate of inflation. Let the government now wish to impose a low inflation rate on the economy and let it attempt to do this by implementing a tax based incomes policy with a hurdle rate of change of wages. Wages that change above the hurdle will be penalized and those that change below the hurdle will not. There

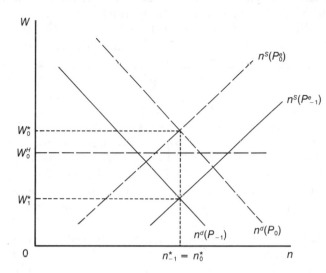

Figure 38.1
Steady-State Inflation
in the Labor Market

The expected price level rises at the steady-state rate π. The demand for and supply of labor curves both rise at this same rate, so does the rate of change of wages (from W_0^* to W_1^*). Inflation is moving at a pace faster than that which the government seeks to encourage through a TIP. A TIP would introduce a hurdle wage (W^H) so that the rate of growth of money wages is less than π.

could be a profits penalty TIP in which case firms that allowed wages to rise above the hurdle would be penalized with a higher tax rate than those who only permitted wages to rise at a rate at or below the hurdle. The rate of wage rise allowed by the hurdle H. That is

$$\frac{W_0^H - W_{-1}}{W_{-1}} = H$$

Alternatively we could represent the hurdle level of wages for period 0. This is obtained simply by rearranging the above equation and obviously is

$$W_0^H = (1 + H)W_{-1}$$

We can show W_0^H in Figure 38.1. Let us imagine that the hurdle rate of wage increases in fact less than the ongoing steady-state rate of inflation. Such a hurdle wage level for period 0 is illustrated in the figure as that marked W_0^H.

We can now go on to analyze the effects of a TIP by examining how a reward pay TIP would affect the supply of labor. In conducting our analysis it will be very convenient to abstract from the underlying ongoing inflation process and focus simply on period (subscript 0). Referring back to Figure 38.1 work with the supply curves and demand curves labelled $n^s(P_0)$ and $n^d(P_0)$. The equilibrium money wage rate would be W_0 in the absence of a hurdle but the hurdle wage rate is W_0^H. The history of the economy that led us to this point will be ignored in what follows. We shall pretend, if you like, that the government is seeking to lower the price and the wage levels from P_0 and W_0. When we say that they will try to lower the price level we simply mean lower the price level relative to where it otherwise would have been. We are not talking about cutting the absolute level of prices.

Figure 38.2 is going to be used to illustrate the analysis. As in Figure 38.1, we shall measure the level of employment (n) on the horizontal axis and the money wage rate (W) on the vertical axis. Focus first on the supply curve of labor, the solid curve labelled $n_0^s(P_0^e)$. This is the same supply of labor curve as that which you met in Chapters 15 and 16 and is identical to $n^s(P_0)$ in Figure 38.1. Recall that the supply curve depends on the expected price level (P_0^e). At each different expected price level the supply curve will shift. For the present let us hold the expected price level constant at its rational expectations level. We have to be careful in making such an assumption. If the analysis that we are about to perform makes changes that themselves affect the price level, then it would not be permissible to suppose that the expected price level is constant. If, on the other hand, it turns out that the introduction of a TIP has no effect on the actual price

Figure 38.2
A Pay Reward TIP

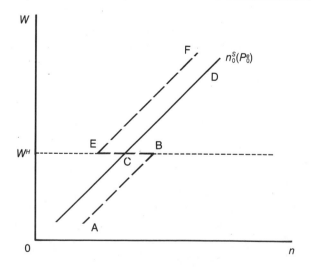

In the absence of a TIP the supply of labor is $n_0^s(P_0^e)$. A pay reward TIP shifts the supply of labor to the right at wages below the hurdle wage (W^H) to become AB. With no other changes the supply curve becomes ABCD. If the general level of taxes is increased at the same time as the TIP is introduced, the supply curve shifts to the left at wages above W^H so that the labor supply curve becomes ABEF.

level then it will have no effect on the rational expectation of the price level, and we shall be justified in making this assumption. Let us for now regard it as a provisional assumption and one that has to be checked when we have worked out the implications of the TIP that we are now examining.

Let us further suppose that the supply curve of labor as drawn in Figure 38.2 already incorporates the effects of any taxes that exist in the economy. In other words, the supply curve shown is not the supply curve that would describe an economy with no taxes. Rather, it is the supply curve that characterizes the economy as it is with its existing taxes in place.[3]

Let us now disturb this economy by introducing a *reward pay* TIP. The main feature of a reward pay TIP is a hurdle wage. The hurdle will be specified in terms of a hurdle percentage rise in wages. For any given initial level of wages, we may translate the hurdle rate of change of wages into a hurdle level of wages as we did in Figure 38.1. That is, if wages rise above a certain level from a certain initial starting point, then they will have risen by more than a certain percentage above the initial starting point. We are calling the hurdle wage W^H. This is marked on the vertical axis of Figure 38.2 and indicated by the horizontal line going from W^H.

The idea of a reward pay TIP is that if wages stay below W^H, then a reward will be paid in the form of some reduction in existing taxes paid. How would such a reward affect the supply of labor? It would raise the supply of labor at each given wage rate (holding the expected price level constant). That is, the supply of labor curve at all wages below W^H would shift to become the dashed curve labelled AB to the right of the original supply curve. What we have just done is nothing other than an application of the analysis performed in Chapter 21 where we analyzed the effects of taxes on the labor market. If no other changes were made in the tax system, the supply of labor curve would now become the disjointed curve ABCD in Figure 38.2.

It may be, however, that although the TIP program merely has a reward provision shifting the supply curve below the hurdle wage, there is, nevertheless, a rise in the general level of taxes deemed necessary by the government to maintain its budget in balance while offering rewards to those whose wages stay below the hurdle wage. If that is the case — that is if taxes in general are increased — and if some of those increased taxes fall on labor incomes, then those whose wages rise above W^H would not be confronted with the original taxes embodied in the original labor supply curve, $n_0^s(P_0^e)$. They would be confronted with higher taxes than those. This being so, their supply

---

[3] Refer back to Chapter 21 for an explanation of the effects of taxes on the supply of and demand for labor.

curve would shift to the left reflecting the higher taxes paid on incomes in excess of the hurdle wage, W^H. The combined effect of a reward for wages below W^H and additional taxes on wages above W^H would be to change the labor supply curve from the curve $n_0^s(P_0^e)$ to the disjointed curve ABEF. This curve ABEF is then the labor supply curve if the government introduces a reward pay TIP.

You have now worked out the first step in an analysis of a reward pay TIP, namely its effects on the supply of labor. It shifts the supply curve of labor to the right for wages below the hurdle level and either leaves the supply curve unchanged or shifts it to the left for wages above the hurdle level, depending on how the government adjusts the rest of its taxation policy when introducing the reward pay TIP.

Let us now go on to examine how a profit penalty TIP would operate on the demand side of the labor market.

C. Profit Penalty TIP and the Demand for Labor

An alternative form of TIP is one which, instead of directly adjusting the taxes paid by workers, influences the taxes paid by firms. Such taxes will affect the value of labor to a firm and will, therefore, affect firms' demands for labor. Let us see how this works out.

Figure 38.3 will be used to illustrate the analysis. Like Figure 38.2, it measures the level of employment on the horizontal axis and the money wage on the vertical axis. We are going to conduct the analysis using the "new classical" story, though you could readily modify the assumptions using a new Keynesian set-up and get results which, though quantitatively different, would be qualitatively identical to those that will be derived here. Employing the new classical framework requires us to take note that the demand for labor curve depends upon the actual price level. The curve labelled $n_0^d(P_0)$ is the initial demand for labor curve. At different actual price levels, different quantities of labor will be demanded, reflected in shifts in the demand curve shown. The remarks made in the preceding section concerning the assumption of a fixed expected price level apply with equal force to the *actual* price level in the analysis that we are doing here. We shall proceed on the assumption that the *actual* price level is fixed at P_0. If, as a result of the introduction of a TIP, something happens to change the price level, then we shall have to check back to see how such a change affects the conclusion that we have reached — to see whether it reinforces them or offsets them. As before, then, let us proceed on the provisional assumption that the price level is fixed and then later check to see whether that assumption was justified and, if not, how changing it affects the conclusions reached.

The profit penalty TIP, like the reward pay TIP, defines an acceptable rate of change of wages which we can translate into a hurdle level of money wages marked W^H on the vertical axis of Figure 38.3.

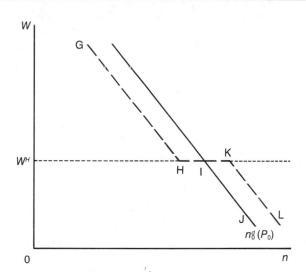

Figure 38.3
Profit Penalty TIP

In the absence of a TIP the demand for labor is $n_0^d(P_0)$. A profit penalty TIP raises the taxes paid by firms who raise wages above the hurdle level, W^H. This shifts the demand curve at wages above W^H to the left to become GH. It payroll and other taxes levied on firms are lowered on wages below W^H to offset this profit penalty tax, the demand curve at wages below W^H shifts to the right to become the segment KL. Overall, then, the demand curve with a TIP is GHKL.

If wages rise above W^H firms will be penalized by having to face a higher rate of taxes on their profits. If wages do not rise as much as W^H the firm will not have to face the additional taxes. You can think of a higher tax rate triggered by paying wages greater than W^H as meaning that the value of the marginal product of labor to a firm is lower at wages above W^H than what it is at wages below W^H. If, at wages above W^H the firm has to pay more taxes, then it will be willing to pay less for labor than it otherwise would have been. The result is that the demand for labor curve will shift to the left to become the curve labelled GH. If that is all that happens then the demand curve, instead of being $n_0^d(P_0)$ will become the disjointed curve GHIJ. As in the previous example, however, it is possible that, as part of the overall adjustment of taxes on the introduction of the profit penalty TIP, the government would see fit to lower the general level of taxes in other directions. If some of the tax reduction came in the form of lower payroll taxes or other taxes on the employment of labor, then at wage rates below W^H, it is possible that the demand for labor curve would shift to the right to become the segment KL in Figure 38.3. A combined profit penalty TIP with a general payroll tax reduction would, therefore, change the demand for labor curve to become the disjointed curve GHKL.

To summarize, a profit penalty TIP would change the labor demand curve, shifting it to the left above the hurdle wage rate and either leaving it unchanged or shifting it to the right below the hurdle wage rate depending on the overall package of tax adjustments implemented.

Let us now go onto the next step of the analysis and see how these alternative TIPs affect the equilibrium in the labor market and in the goods and money market.

D. Effects of TIP on Employment, Output and Prices

Now that we have worked out how different types of TIP affect supply and demand in the labor market, we can go on to see how they affect the equilibrium levels of employment and wages. In pursuing this exercise, we shall initially maintain the assumption that we made in the two previous sections that the expected and actual price levels remained constant. Later in this section we shall check whether or not that assumption was appropriate. We shall analyze the effects of a reward pay TIP and profit penalty TIP separately, though it is a straightforward matter to combine them, and we shall leave that as an exercise for you to conduct on your own.

First let us examine the effects of a *pay reward* TIP. Figure 38.4 will enable you to work out the effects in a fairly straightforward way.

**Figure 38.4
Equilibrium Employment
with a Pay Reward TIP**

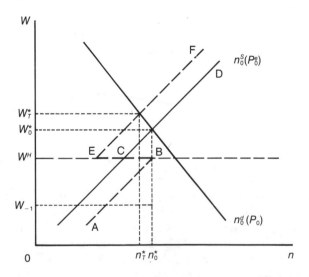

Last period the money wage is W_1 and the employment level is n_0^*. If no TIP is introduced the equilibrium this period would be W_0^*, n_0^*. The introduction of a pay reward TIP with no other tax changes this period would give a supply curve of ABCD and leave the labor market undisturbed. The TIP would have no effect. The introduction of a pay reward TIP accompanied by a general rise in taxes on labor income would shift the supply curve to ABEF. Money wages would rise to W_T^* and employment would fall to n_T^*.

Begin by familiarizing yourself with the various parts of Figure 38.4. Suppose that in the absence of a TIP the supply and demand for labor curves would be those shown as $n_0^s(P_0^e)$ and $n_0^d(P_0)$. They intersect at the employment level n_0^* and the money wage rate W_0^*. This would have been the equilibrium in the absence of a TIP. Let us suppose that in the previous period, -1, the money wage level was W_{-1}. (You can think of the price level as having been such that the demand and supply curves intersected at the employment level n_0^* at the money wage rate W_{-1} in the previous period. The price level is expected to rise and does rise by an amount such that the demand and supply curves shift to become those illustrated in Figure 38.4.)

The objective of a TIP is to make the money wage rise by less than it would have done in the absence of a TIP. A hurdle wage will be specified that is below the wage that would otherwise have occurred, W_0^*. Let us suppose that the permitted wage rise is such that the hurdle wage is at W^H. Further, suppose that there is both a reward for pay rises less than W^H and a general adjustment in the level of income taxes for all other workers so that the combined effect of the TIP and other tax adjustment is that illustrated in Section B above and results in the disjointed supply curve ABEF. You can now read off the new equilibrium. The money wage rises to W_T^* and the level of employment falls to n_T^*. This happens because the relevant part of the supply curve that intersects the demand curve shifts in the wrong direction (to the left). The rightward shift in the labor supply curve below the hurdle wage rate is simply irrelevant for determining the final outcome of the policy change.

Although those raising their wages by less than W^H would get a pay reward, no one is on this particular margin of choice. The demand curve for labor simply does not intersect this section of the supply curve of labor. Notice that for it to do so, it would be necessary that the hurdle wage be set *above* rather than below the otherwise equilibrium wage. If this was done, then the supply curve of labor would shift to the right over the relevant range and would result in a fall in money wages and a rise in employment. Such an arrangement would, however, hardly be worth calling a TIP. This could be achieved by a general cut in the level of taxes on labor income independently of the rise in individuals' wages since, in such a case, no wages would rise by as much as the hurdle level and everyone would get the tax cut. In the case where the hurdle wage rate is below the equilibrium — the formula advocated by proponents of TIPs — in effect, everyone faces a rise in taxes. Although everyone is entitled to the tax cut in the event that they take a small enough wage rise, no one takes a small enough wage rise. Everyone takes an equilibrium wage rise and this results in everyone paying more taxes.

There is the other case where the government introduces the pay reward TIP with no other changes in the tax system. In this event, the supply of labor curve becomes the disjointed curve ABCD and in this case there is no change in the levels of employment and wages from those levels that would have prevailed in the absence of the TIP program. A reward pay TIP with no other changes in taxes, therefore, and the hurdle wage set below the equilibrium wage has no effect on anything! (It does have effects arising from the diversion of scarce resources into the administration of the TIP program. It should not, however, be necessary to devote many resources to the activity since no one is on the margin at which they are being affected.)

Consider next a profit penalty TIP. The effects of this alternative TIP can be worked out in Figure 38.5. As before, the equilibrium in the absence of a TIP would have been at the employment level n_0^* and the wage rate W_0^*. Also as before, the previous period's wage level was W_{-1} and the hurdle wage rise would take the wage level to W^H. Wage rises below W^H will not be penalized and wage levels above W^H will. This means that the demand for labor curve is shifted to the left at all wages above W^H and becomes the curve GH. At wages below W^H what happens to the demand curve depends on what else happens to other tax arrangements. If no other tax changes occur then the demand for labor curve at wages below W^H does not move — it remains the curve IJ. If other payroll taxes are decreased to offset the increased tax revenues arising from the profit penalty for above hurdle wage changes then the demand curve at wages below W^H would shift to become the segment KL.

You can now immediately read off the new equilibrium with a profit penalty TIP in place. The equilibrium level of employment will fall to n_T^* and the equilibrium wage rate will fall to W_T^*. Notice that the tax arrangements for wages below W^H make no difference to the outcome. It does not matter whether the demand curve is GHIJ or GHKL. The only segment of the demand curve that is relevant is the GH segment since this is the only segment that intersects the supply curve.

Let us compare these two alternative TIPs. They have both lowered the level of employment. One of them has lowered the money wage (the profit penalty variety) and the other either leaves the wage unchanged or raises the wage depending on whether or not there is a change in the general level of income taxes introduced at the same time as the reward pay TIP. The reward pay TIP on its own leaves the levels of employment and wages unchanged. It is only the accompanying adjustment in the general level of taxes designed to pay for the reward pay TIP that could have the effects of raising wages and lowering employment. It is worth noting that since in equilibrium no rewards are actually paid out, then in equilibrium no additional tax revenues need be raised, so the most natural outcome from a reward pay TIP is the no-change result.

Let us now return to the assumption that we have been maintaining throughout that the price level is actually and is expected to remain

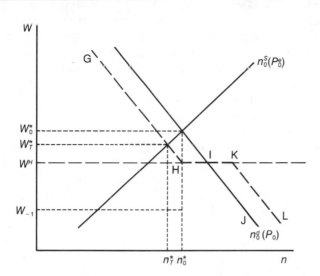

**Figure 38.5
Equilibrium, Employment
and Wages with
a Profit Penalty TIP**

In the absence of a TIP the equilibrium would be n_0^*, W_0^*. A profit penalty TIP shifts the supply curve to GHKL and lowers money wages to W_T^* and lowers employment to n_T^*. Whether the demand curve becomes GHIJ or GHKL (depending on other tax adjustments) is irrelevant.

constant. Is this assumption compatible with the conclusions that we have reached? If not, what consequences follow?

In the case where there is no change in the level of wages and employment (a reward pay TIP with no other adjustment in taxes), evidently the equilibrium levels of employment and aggregate supply remain constant. Since, in the experiments that we are conducting, we are doing nothing to influence the level of aggregate demand, it follows that we have done nothing to influence the equilibrium level of prices. The actual and rational expectation of the price level will, therefore, remain constant in that case.

In the case of a reward pay TIP with a general rise in taxes, or in the case of a profit penalty TIP, the conclusion reached is that the equilibrium level of employment falls. That being so, the aggregate supply curve will shift to the left. With a constant level of aggregate demand and a drop in aggregate supply, the actual price level will rise. It will be rational to expect such a rise so that both the actual and rational expectation of the price level will rise in this case. What are the effects of this on the outcomes that we have just analyzed?

The effect of a higher than otherwise expected and actual price level will be to shift the supply and demand for labor curves upwards by more than they otherwise would have moved. Thus, they will intersect at an even higher money wage than otherwise would have been the case. In the absence of any additional sources of confusion between actual and expected aggregate demand, there is no reason to presume that the effect on expected prices would be any different from that on actual prices. Thus, both curves will move up by the same proportionate amount intersecting at the same quantity of employment but at a higher money wage. Thus, the conclusions that we reached above when holding the actual and expected price levels constant are not seriously misleading. The actual results would involve higher wages than have been shown in Figures 38.4 and 38.5 but the same levels of employment.

It is now possible to summarize the effects of these TIP programs. Either they have no effects or their effects are perverse. When they do have effects, these effects are to lower the level of employment, lower output and raise the price level. Thus, far from easing the transition to a lower rate of inflation, they exacerbate the problems and make the transition even more painful than it otherwise would have been. If, in addition, the introduction of a TIP contaminates the signals that agents are receiving by making it harder for them to discern what policy is and, therefore, leads them to make bigger errors in judging the overall levels of aggregate supply and aggregate demand then fluctuations could occur (both up and down) in the level of activity relative to the full-employment equilibrium level.

Thus, what at first sight seems like a natural application of economic theory to the problem of encouraging slower inflation is, on deeper investigation, a fatally flawed proposal which would actually make matters worse.

Summary

A. Essential Idea of a TIP

The essential idea of a TIP is to penalize excessive wage and price increases and reward moderate ones. By so doing it is hoped to lower the rate of inflation while avoiding output losses and high unemployment in the process. The method of achieving this objective is to specify a hurdle wage such that for wages that rise above the hurdle a penalty may be imposed and for wages that rise below the hurdle a reward is offered. (Variants would offer only rewards or impose only penalties, or do both and the rewards and penalties could fall on either workers or employers.)

B. Reward Pay TIP and the Supply of Labor

A reward pay TIP would lower the taxes paid by workers if wages rose by less than the hurdle wage and might be paid for by a rise in the general level of taxes on labor that would affect those wages that rose above the hurdle wage. The effect of this on the supply of labor would be to shift the supply of labor to the right at wages below the hurdle level and to the left at wages above the hurdle level. As a result, the supply curve becomes ABEF in Figure 38.2.

C. Profit Penalty TIP and the Demand for Labor

A profit penalty TIP would affect firms' demands for labor. Wage rises to levels above the hurdle level would be met by a penalty rise in the firms' taxes, and wage rises to levels below the hurdle might be rewarded with a lowering of firms' taxes. The effect on the demand for labor curve would be to shift it to the left at wages above the hurdle level and to the right at wages below the hurdle level to become the curve GHKL in Figure 38.3.

D. Effects of TIP on Employment, Output and Prices

A reward pay TIP with no change in the general level of taxes on labor income will have no effects at all on the levels of employment and wages. The reason is that although the supply curve shifts to the right, the rightward shift is on a section of the supply curve that is irrelevant, being below a wage that itself is below the equilibrium wage.

A profit penalty TIP would lower the wage and lower the level of employment. It does this because it shifts the demand for labor curve to the left.

The variant of TIP that leaves output and employment unchanged has no effect on aggregate supply and, since a TIP policy has no effect on aggregate demand, will leave both output and the price level unchanged.

TIP programs that have the effect of lowering the level of employment will also lower aggregate supply. This makes the aggregate supply curve intersect aggregate demand at a lower level of output and a higher price level. Thus, the effects of a TIP may be summarized: either a TIP has no effect or it lowers employment, lowers output and raises the price level.

Review Questions

1. What is the essential idea of a TIP?

2. List the alternative varieties of TIPs.

3. What are the effects of a reward pay TIP on the supply of labor?

4. What are the effects of a profit penalty TIP on the demand for labor?

5. How does the introduction of a reward pay TIP affect the equilibrium levels of employment, real wages, output and prices?

6. How does a profit penalty TIP affect the equilibrium levels of employment, real wages, output and prices?

7. In this chapter, the new classical labor market has been used. Examine how the results change if a new Keynesian labor market is employed.

39

Wage Indexation

Wage indexation is the linking of *money* wages to changes in the cost of living — to changes in the Consumer Price Index (CPI). Many wage-contracts feature indexation as a means of insulating *real* wages from aggregate demand shocks. Some economists — and politicians — fear indexation for they believe it to be inflationary. They believe that with indexed wages a price rise could trigger a wage rise which would lead to yet a further price rise . . . and so on. As a consequence of this belief, it is suggested that wage indexation should be outlawed. What are the macroeconomic effects of wage indexation? That is the central question addressed in this chapter.

The chapter will lead you towards a better understanding of how wage indexation affects the economy. In particular, it will help you to see how wage indexation affects the fluctuations in output, employment and unemployment and also how it affects the price level and inflation. You will discover that while indexation certainly affects the behavior of the price level, it does not affect the trend rate of inflation — at least not directly. You will also discover that indexation has important implications for fluctuations in output, employment and unemployment — effects that are often ignored in popular discussions of this topic.

The chapter[1] will take you through seven tasks, which are to:

a) Know the different types of indexation arrangement.

---

[1] The analysis in this chapter is based almost exclusively on the work of Jo Anna Gray, "Wage Indexation: A Macroeconomic Approach," *Journal of Monetary Economics*, 2, No. 2 (April 1976), 221-35.

b) Understand how full percentage indexation fixes *real* wages.

c) Understand how employment, output and prices respond to *demand* shocks when *real* wages are fixed.

d) Understand how employment, output and prices respond to *supply* shocks when *real* wages are fixed.

e) Compare fluctuations under fixed *real* wages with those under fixed *nominal* wages.

f) Understand why indexation makes the economy more sensitive to supply shocks and insulates it from demand shocks.

g) Understand why indexation cannot cause inflation.

A. Types of Indexation

There are two main types of indexation:

(i) Full-percentage indexation

(ii) Partial-percentage indexation.

Full-percentage indexation is perhaps the most straightforward and obvious. Wages are set in dollar terms for a prespecified period of time, say, one year. It is also stipulated that as the cost of living becomes known through the year, so wages will be changed by the same percentage change as that of the cost of living at some pre-agreed intervals. Usually, this would be done every three months. Consider an example: suppose that it was agreed that the wages for some particular job would be $8.00 per hour but that, through the year, the wages would be adjusted each quarter to reflect the change in the cost of living over the previous three months. Further, suppose that as the year unfolded, the inflation rate turned out to be 2 percent in the first quarter, 3 percent in the second quarter, 1 percent in the third quarter and 2 percent in the fourth quarter. The wage paid would be $8.00 for the first quarter. In the second quarter the $8.00 would be increased to $8.16 — the 16¢ increase representing 2 percent of $8.00 — the percentage rise in the cost of living. In the third quarter the wages would be increased to $8.40, the rise of 24¢ representing 3 percent of $8.16 — a rise that again reflects the percent rise in the cost of living. In its fourth quarter wages would be increased yet again to $8.49 — a rise of 1 percent. At the end of the fourth quarter there would be a new negotiation of a new contract. Applying the cost-of-living rise of the fourth quarter — a 2 percent inflation rate — would automatically have taken the wage rate to $8.66. There is no presumption, and certainly no requirement, that the newly ne-gotiated wage for the second year be $8.66. The wage-fixing process can determine a new real wage to reflect underlying changes in supply and demand conditions.

The indexation of wages is a means of ensuring that wages adjust more frequently than new contracts are negotiated or new decisions handed down. At the point in time when a contract is renegotiated or a new decision handed down, adjustments can be made that result in wages changing by more or less than they would have changed with the straight application of the indexation adjustment.

Partial-percentage indexation is exactly like full-percentage indexation except that instead of changing wages by the full percentage amount of the change in the cost of living, some formula for discounting the cost-of-living change is applied. For example, changes in the cost of living resulting from changes in the relative price of imports or changes resulting from government policy induced relative price changes might be discounted when adjusting wages.

B. Indexation and Real Wages

How does indexation influence real wages? Suppose that wages are not indexed. In that case the money wage is fixed. That is, wages are set in terms of dollars. The real wage that results from setting money wages is simply that money wage divided by the price level. Call the money wage W_0. Call the initial price level P_0. This means that the initial real wage would be given by

$$\text{Real Wage} = \frac{W_0}{P_0} \qquad (39.1)$$

If, after the money-wage has been set, the price level rises at the rate of π per period (say per quarter), then the price level would rise to $P_0(1 + \pi)$ after one quarter. In this case the real wage would become:

$$\text{Real Wage} = \frac{W_0}{P_0(1 + \pi)} \qquad (39.2)$$

Evidently the real wage falls by the same percentage amount as the price level rises.

Now consider what would happen if wages were fully indexed. When the price level rises by the rate of π, so does the money-wage rate. That is, money wages would rise to become $W_0(1 + \pi)$. Thus, the real wage would be completely insulated from movements in the inflation rate, that is:

$$\text{Real Wage} = \frac{W_0(1 + \pi)}{P_0(1 + \pi)} \qquad (39.3)$$

Partial indexation would raise wages by some fraction of the inflation rate. Suppose that that fraction is a. In that case, wages would rise to $W_0(1 + a\pi)$ and the real wage would become

$$\text{Real Wage} = \frac{W_0(1 + a\pi)}{P_0(1 + \pi)} \qquad (39.4)$$

You can see that if the fraction a equals one, we have full indexation and real wages remain constant. If a is equal to zero we have no indexation and real wages fluctuate in the manner described by Equation (39.2). Partial indexation lets real wages fluctuate when the price level changes but by some smaller amount than they would fluctuate with no indexation at all.

The first thing that we have learned about indexation, which will be crucial to the subsequent analysis, is that the behavior of real wages depends on the type of indexation. With no indexation, real wages fluctuate in the opposite direction to fluctuations in the price level. With full percentage indexation, real wages remain constant — until the next negotiation date — and with partial indexation, real wages change but by less than they would with no indexation.

We are now going to go on to analyze the implications of these different real wage responses for the behavior of employment, output and the price level.

C. Demand Shocks with Fixed Real Wages

None of the analysis that we shall do in this and the subsequent sections of the chapter are new to you. In many ways you can regard this chapter as bringing together a diversity of analyses that have been employed in other contexts earlier in the book.

Figure 39.1 (which is closely related to Figure 14.7) provides the basis for the analysis.

First familiarize yourself with the way in which this figure works. Frame (a) shows the demand and supply curves for labor, frame (b) the production function and frame (c) the aggregate supply and aggregate demand curves. Suppose that in this economy wages are fully indexed. This means that the real wage will remain constant at the level at which it was set initially. Let that real wage be $\left(\dfrac{W}{P}\right)_0$. In this case the economy will replicate a full-employment, competitive economy and the employment level will be n^*. Given an employment level of n^*, we can discover, from the production function, that output will be y^*. Tracing this value of output through to frame (c) gives an aggregate supply of AS. It is clear that the AS curve is vertical because nothing can happen to change real wages in this economy — at least not until the next wage-setting date. If the level of aggregate demand is given by the curve AD_0, the price level is P_0 and the output level y^*.

Now we imagine that there is a demand shock. Let aggregate demand unexpectedly rise. Specifically, let it rise to AD_1. Even though the rise in aggregate demand is unexpected, the fact that wages will always adjust to reflect any changes in the price level means that real wages will remain constant. With real wages constant, employment is constant and so, therefore, is output. The AS curve, in effect, also

**Figure 39.1
Wage Indexation
and Demand Shocks**

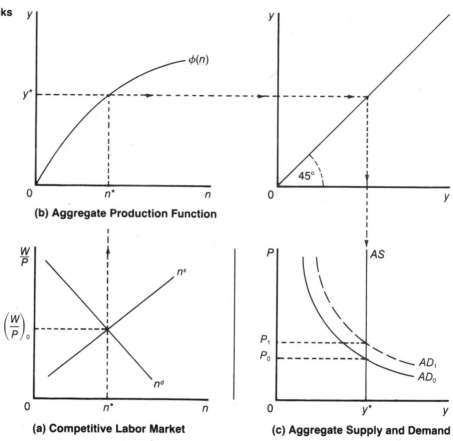

Wage indexation fixes the real wage so that the aggregate supply curve becomes vertical. Fluctuations in demand generate fluctuations in the price level and leave output constant.

becomes the *EAS* curve for the fully-indexed economy. The price level will rise to P_1 but output will not change.

Nothing would be altered in the above analysis if, instead of fixing the money wage such that the real wage equalled the competitive equilibrium real wage, wages had been set above that level. Suppose a minimum wage had been set higher than the competitive equilibrium. This would have determined a level of employment below the full-employment level and would imply that the aggregate supply curve lies to the left of the full-employment aggregate supply curve. This curve would still, however, be vertical. With a fixed real wage there would be one and only one level of employment and, therefore, only one level of output. As aggregate demand fluctuates, the price level would fluctuate and output would remain constant at its below full-employment level.

We have seen then that with fully-indexed wages, the real part of the economy is insulated from fluctuations in aggregate demand. These fluctuations change the price level but leave all the real variables undisturbed.

Let us now go on to consider what happens when there are supply shocks.

D. Supply Shocks with Fixed Real Wages

To analyze the effects of supply shocks with fixed real wages consider Figure 39.2.

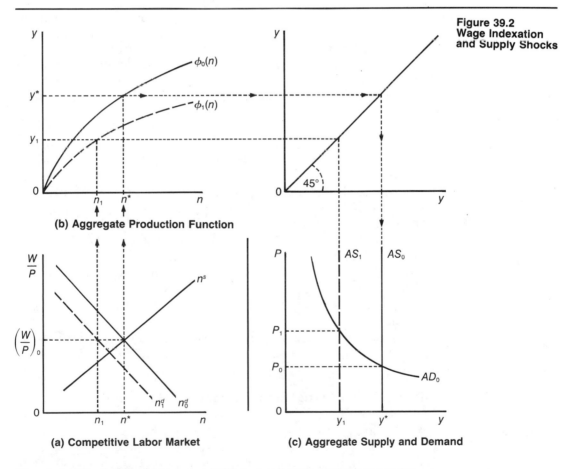

**Figure 39.2
Wage Indexation
and Supply Shocks**

(b) Aggregate Production Function

(a) Competitive Labor Market

(c) Aggregate Supply and Demand

Wage indexation fixes the real wage at $(W/P)_0$ so that if a supply shock occurs that changes the *equilibrium* real wage, the economy will be prevented from adjusting to its new equilibrium. Employment and output will fluctuate and the price level will also fluctuate but in the opposite direction to output and employment.

Again, begin by familiarizing yourself with the relevant parts of Figure 39.2. Frame (a) contains the labor market, frame (b) the production function and frame (c) the aggregate supply and aggregate demand curves. Imagine that the economy initially has the production function labelled $\phi_0(n)$. Associated with this production function is the demand for labor n_0^d. The supply of labor is n^s. The demand for labor and the supply of labor are equal to each other at n^* and at the real wage $\left(\dfrac{W}{P}\right)_0$. In this situation the aggregate supply curve is the vertical line in frame (c), AS_0. Assume that the aggregate demand curve is AD_0. Finally, suppose that wages are set and fully indexed to fix the real wage at $\left(\dfrac{W}{P}\right)_0$ — the full-employment level. (Again, note that we could have fixed the real wage above its full-employment level without affecting the substance of anything that will follow.)

Now, suppose that there is a supply shock to this economy. In particular, suppose that the production function shifts downwards to that labelled $\phi_1(n)$. At the same time, the demand for labor curve will shift to the curve labelled n_1^d. With a fixed real wage, employers will now be willing to hire labor only up to the point at which its marginal product equals this fixed real wage. This employment level is n_1. With an employment level of n_1 and with the production function $\phi_1(n)$, the level of aggregate supply would become AS_1.

If aggregate demand remained unchanged at AD_0, the consequence of this supply shock, with a fully-indexed wage, would be to lower output from y^* to y_1 and to raise the price level from P_0 to P_1.

Thus, we can see that in contrast to the case of a demand shock, wage indexation does not insulate the economy from the effects of a supply shock. When the supply shock hits, real things happen. A negative supply shock, such as that analyzed here, will lower output and raise the price level. A positive supply shock (which you can easily analyze for yourself) would raise output and employment and lower the price level.

Let us now go on to compare the performance of the indexed economy with a non-indexed economy.

E. Comparison of Fixed Money Wages with Fixed Real Wages

How does an economy with indexed wages behave in comparison with one that has non-indexed wages? This is the question that we shall address in this section. First, we need to establish how an economy with fixed money wages behaves. After a moment's reflection, you will realize that like the analyses of the two preceding sections, you have studied this matter before. You have studied an economy in which money wages are fixed when dealing with new-Keynesian theory of aggregate supply in Chapter 16, in particular, the analysis surrounding Figure 16.2. You have studied the effects of aggregate demand shocks in such an economy in Chapter 33. You have studied how aggregate supply shocks affect such an economy in Chapter 34. All that we have to do here, therefore, is to bring together the various results of these analyses and compare them with those that we have just discovered concerning the performance of an economy with indexed wages in the previous section.

First, let us look at demand shocks.

(i) Demand Shocks

Figure 39.3 is going to be used to conduct our analysis of the effects of demand shocks in an economy with a fixed money wage. Such an economy will have an *EAS* curve such as that shown in Figure 39.3 and marked $EAS(K)$. The expected price level is P_0^e and the full-employment output level is y^*. Expected aggregate demand is AD_0^e. On the average this economy would be at its full-employment level with the price level equal to the expected price level. Imagine that this economy is one that experiences demand fluctuations between the limits AD_2 and AD_1. That is, the demand curve sometimes rises and sometimes falls between those two limits. With a fixed money wage, you know that this economy will generate fluctuations in output and prices between the limits y_1 and y_2 for output and P_1 and P_2 for the price level. In other words, as the aggregate demand curve fluctuates, so the economy will travel up and down its Keynesian *EAS* curve.

Contrast this result with what would happen in the indexed economy that we studied in Section C. In this case, we discovered that with a fixed real wage the level of employment would remain constant at its full-employment level. The *AS* curve therefore becomes the relevant aggregate supply curve. With demand fluctuating between AD_2 and AD_1, the price level would fluctuate between $P_2(I)$ and $P_1(I)$.

Thus, comparing the indexed and non-indexed economy, it is clear that with demand shocks, output fluctuates more and the price level fluctuates less in the non-indexed economy than in the indexed economy. A partially-indexed economy would behave in an intermediate position between these two extremes. That is, there would be some output fluctuations in the face of a demand shock but they would be smaller than in the non-indexed case. Prices would fluctuate more than in the non-indexed case but not by as much as in the fully-indexed economy.

**Figure 39.3
Indexed and
Non-indexed Wages:
Demand Shocks**

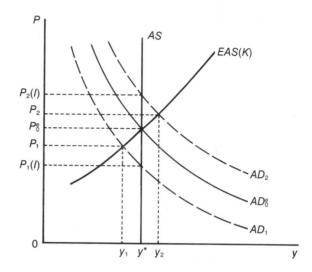

With fixed money wages the economy will operate at the intersection of the Keynesian *EAS* curve and the aggregate demand curve. Demand fluctuations will lead the economy to slide up and down the *EAS* curve. The indexed economy operates at the intersection of the vertical *AS* curve and the aggregate demand curve. Aggregate demand shocks will lead the indexed economy to slide up and down the *AS* curve. Output fluctuates more and prices fluctuate less in the non-indexed economy which is subjected to demand shocks.

Although the analysis in Figure 39.3 deals only with the goods market, it is a straightforward matter to interpret those results in terms of the labor market. When output fluctuates, so does employment (and so does unemployment). Real wages (actual real wages) also fluctuate in the opposite direction to the fluctuations in output.

Let us next consider supply shocks.

(ii) Supply Shocks

To study the effects of a supply shock, you first need to recall the analysis conducted in Chapter 34 and particularly that surrounding Figure 34.4. Figure 39.4 reproduces the relevant material (supplemented by some additional features that we need for the current analysis). First, focus on the curves AS_0, AD_0, and $EAS_0^0(K)$. This represents the initial situation in the economy. The expected price level is P_0^e and the output level is y^*. There is then a supply shock identical to that which we analyzed in Section C above. That supply shock shifts the AS curve to AS_1. For an economy with a fixed money-wage rate — an economy identical in analytical terms to the new-Keynesian economy — the EAS curve will shift to the right so that it intersects the new AS curve at the original expected price level. That is, the EAS curve becomes $EAS_0^1(K)$. (As in Chapter 34, the subscript on EAS

refers to the price expectation and the superscript refers to the production function. Thus, EAS_0^1 is the EAS curve when the expected price level is P_0^e and the production function is $\phi_1(n)$.)

What happens in this economy if the money wage is fixed following this supply shock? The answer is read off simply by noting that the equilibrium occurs at the point at which the aggregate demand curve (AD_0) intersects the new EAS curve (EAS_0^1). This equilibrium occurs at the output level marked as y_1 and the price level P_1.

Contrast this with the result that we discovered in Section D above for an indexed economy. In the indexed case, the economy moves to the output level $y_1(I)$ and to the price level $P_1(I)$. That is, with the real wage unchanged, the shift in the demand for labor curve results in a reduction in the employment level by an amount sufficient to raise the marginal product of labor with this new lower production function to equality with the fixed real wage.

Comparing the two results for a supply shock, we see that in both cases — in the case of the indexed and non-indexed economy — a negative supply shock lowers output and raises the price level. The reverse result would also hold. That is, for a positive supply shock output would rise and the price level would fall in both economies. The magnitude of the effect, however, depends on whether or not wages are indexed. If wages are indexed, the changes in output and in the price level are greater than those changes for a non-indexed economy.

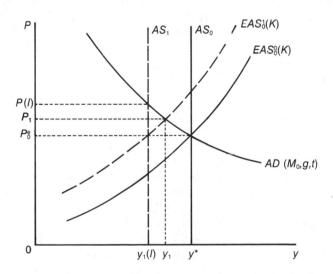

**Figure 39.4
Indexed and
Non-indexed Wages:
Supply Shock**

In the indexed economy a supply shock shifts the aggregate supply curve to AS_1. In the non-indexed economy the EAS curve shifts to $EAS_0^1(K)$. The effect of the supply shock is that output falls more and the price level rises more in the indexed economy than in the non-indexed economy.

A partially indexed economy would behave in an intermediate position. A negative supply shock in a partially indexed economy would lower output and raise the price level and a fall in output and a rise in prices would exceed those for a non-indexed economy but be less than the changes occurring in a fully indexed economy.

F. Why Indexation Makes the Economy More Sensitive to a Supply Shock and Insulates it From a Demand Shock

You have now discovered that an indexed economy is insulated from demand shocks but is more sensitive to supply shocks. Why does this happen?

In effect, a demand shock is a purely nominal shock. It is a shock that does not affect the equilibrium real wage. If some means can be found, therefore, of preventing the real wage from changing in the face of a demand shock then all subsequent real effects can be avoided. Indexation does this job. It automatically insulates the real wage from the demand shock and therefore insulates all other aspects of the economy — employment and output — from the effect of the demand shock.

In contrast, a supply shock is a real shock. It does require a change in the real wage to achieve full-employment equilibrium. Indexation pegs the real wage thereby preventing an adjustment which, if it could take place, would lessen the impact of the shock on output and employment. By fixing the money wage, the real wage is left free to move. A fixed money wage is not ideal. A flexible money wage and a flexible price level would do a better job. Nevertheless, the fixed money wage does permit some movement in the real wage, thereby preventing the supply shock from having as large an effect on employment and output as in the indexed case.

Again, partial indexation lies somewhere in between the two extremes.

It is worth summarizing the key results that we have discovered. If an economy is subjected to demand shocks, these shocks are completely avoided by the adoption of fully-indexed wages. If the economy is subjected to supply shocks, those shocks have their biggest effect in the economy with indexed wages and are moderated somewhat for an economy that has non-indexed wages. Thus, whether indexation is desirable or not depends primarily on the major sources of shocks. In an ideal sense, it would be wise to index wages when there is a demand shock and not index them when there is a supply shock. That is what partial indexation is often designed to achieve. The trouble with this is that either no one knows which shocks are which at the point in time that they occur or, if some people know, not all people do, and it is hard to get general agreement as to which type of shock has occurred. That being so, a set of arrangements have to be entered into that are suitable for the economy *on the average*. If an economy is usually subjected to demand shocks and rarely subjected to supply shocks, then indexation makes sense. In the reverse case, an economy that has extremely stable demand conditions but volatile supply (production function) conditions would be one in which indexation would be undesirable. Figuring out the appropriate degree of indexation involves trading off the gains on the demand shock side with losses on the supply shock side.

G. Why Indexation Does Not Cause Inflation

The idea that indexation causes inflation seems to be deeply ingrained in many minds. The idea seems to be that if a rise in prices triggers a rise in wages, there will be an inevitable perpetual motion mechanism set up. Wages are the biggest item of costs, so a rise in wages will raise prices. But with indexation, a rise in prices will raise wages, and so on and so on.

You know from the analysis of aggregate supply and aggregate demand that this cannot be so for it ignores the aggregate demand side of the economy. A rise in wages and prices can be thought of as a leftward (or upward) shift in the *EAS* curve. With a given level of aggregate demand, that does raise prices but it also lowers output and employment. There is a unique equilibrium level of prices that occurs at the point at which aggregate demand and aggregate supply intersect. With a fixed money supply (or a fixed growth rate of the money supply) or with a fixed exchange rate, aggregate demand and the price level are bolted down.

Only if we had a flexible exchange rate and if the Bank of Canada raised the money supply every time the price level rose, could there be a problem. In this case, the aggregate demand curve would become perfectly inelastic — a vertical curve. The economy would then have not only indexed wages but also an indexed money supply. That is, if the money supply rose by the same percentage amount as the price level had just increased, the money supply itself would be indexed to the price level. In this case, indexation would be inflationary. Indeed there would be no natural limit to either the price level or the rate of inflation. So long, however, as the Bank of Canada does not index the money supply and either pegs the money supply growth rate or equivalently, for present purposes, pegs the foreign exchange value of the Canadian dollar, there is no way in which indexation of wages can trigger a cumulative, inflationary process.

It is worth noticing, however, that in the face of either demand or supply shocks the price level fluctuates more with indexed wages than with non-indexed wages. Thus, *fluctuations* in the inflation rate around any given trend would have greater amplitude in an economy with indexed wages than one that did not utilize indexation.

Summary

A. Types of Indexation
There are two main types of indexation: full-percentage indexation and partial-percentage indexation.

B. Indexation and Real Wages
Full-percentage indexation fixes real wages for the interval between negotiations. Partial-indexation allows some movement in real wages but not as much as would occur with fixed money wages.

C. Demand Shocks with Fixed Real Wages
With fixed real wages (whether fixed at the competitive equilibrium level or higher) the aggregate supply curve is vertical (as in the basic model). Fluctuations in aggregate demand lead to fluctuations in prices but not in output and employment.

D. Supply Shocks with Fixed Real Wages
When supply shocks occur and real wages are fixed, employment and output fluctuate. The price level fluctuates in the opposite direction.

E. Comparison of Fixed Money Wages and Fixed Real Wages
Demand shocks have a larger effect on the price level and a smaller effect on output, the greater the degree of indexation of wages. Supply shocks have a larger effect on output and on prices, the greater the degree of indexation of wages.

F. Why Indexation Makes the Economy More Sensitive to a Supply Shock and Insulates it From a Demand Shock
A demand shock is purely nominal and does not require any real changes to restore equilibrium. Indexation prevents the nominal shock from disturbing real wages and therefore insulates the economy from all other real effects.

A supply shock requires a change in the real wage to achieve equilibrium. Indexation prevents that change from occurring. A fixed money wage, though not ideal, permits some adjustments of the real wage in the correct direction.

G. Why Indexation Does Not Cause Inflation
Inflation is generated by the interaction of aggregate supply and aggregate demand. So long as the aggregate demand curve does not become perfectly inelastic as a result of indexing the money supply, there will be a determinate price level and rate of inflation. Fluctuations in the price level will be larger in an indexed economy than in one without indexation.

Review Questions

1. What are the main types of indexation?

2. Use a numerical example to illustrate precisely how full-percentage indexation and partial-percentage indexation differ from each other.

3. How do real wages behave in a fully-indexed economy compared with a non-indexed economy?

4. What happens in an indexed economy to output, employment, real wages and the price level when there is a sudden drop in aggregate demand? What happens to output, employment, real wages and the price level in a fully-indexed economy if there is an upward shift in the production function?

5. Does output fluctuate more or less in an indexed economy compared with a non-indexed economy in the face of (i) an aggregate demand shock and (ii) an aggregate supply shock?

6. Why does indexation make the economy more sensitive to supply shocks?

7. Why does indexation insulate the economy from demand shocks?

8. How does indexation affect the behavior of the price level? Can wage indexation cause inflation?

40

Canadian Macroeconomic Policy Since 1975

Now that you have completed your study of the theory of macroeconomic policy you are in a good position to re-examine Canada's recent macroeconomic history and examine the possible influences of government policy on that history. In Chapter 2 you studied the course of the macroeconomic variables all the way back to the early 1920s. It would take more time and space to re-examine that entire history than is available in a single chapter so it is necessary to be selective. To give you an example of how you might proceed, we are going to focus on one short episode of Canadian macroeconomic policy, the period since 1975. This is an important and interesting episode, as you will soon discover.

You will probably find it helpful to read this chapter in conjunction with Chapter 2 as well as Chapters 20 to 23 and Chapter 29. Chapter 2 will help you to refresh your memory of the historical context in which the last decade is placed. Chapters 20 to 23 will enable you to review your understanding of the determination of the key macroeconomic variables — inflation, unemployment and output growth — and the way in which they evolve over time to give rise to business cycles. Chapter 29 will help you to review your understanding of how developments outside Canada have influenced the course of the Canadian economy. The present chapter provides you with yet a further look at all the issues raised and discussed in those earlier ones but viewed from a very specific prespective, that of Canadian macroeconomic policy. Specifically, this chapter will take you through four tasks, which are to:

a) Know the main features of monetary policy since 1975.
b) Know the main features of fiscal policy since 1975.
c) Know the main features of the 1975-78 wage and price control program.
d) Understand how each of these policies has contributed to the course of Canadian inflation, unemployment, and output growth in the period since 1975.

A. Monetary Policy Since 1975

Prior to 1975, money supply growth in Canada had become extremely rapid. In fact, between 1971 and 1975 the average (compound) growth rate of the M1 money supply was 12.9 percent per annum. In 1975 the Bank of Canada embarked upon a new approach to monetary policy making. The Bank announced a target range for the rate of growth of the money supply (defined as M1). Its initial target was cautious. It set a high target growth rate for the money supply and gave itself plenty of room to manoeuver by setting a wide range around its target. Specifically, for a three-month period centered on May 1975 to a three-month period centered on March 1976, the Bank aimed to achieve a growth rate of M1 money supply of not less than 10 percent per annum, but not more than 15 percent per annum. On several subsequent occasions, the target growth rate has been reduced. Table 40.1 sets out the targets for money supply growth, starting with the first one of May 1975 through November 1982. The Bank of Canada abandoned formal monetary targeting at this time.

The actual growth rate of the money supply over the specific target periods is also shown in Table 40.1. These money supply targets and actual growth rates are shown in Figure 40.1. The money supply growth figures presented in Table 40.1 and plotted in Figure 40.1 can

TABLE 40.1
Monetary Growth Targets and Outcomes 1975-1981

PERIOD	TARGET RANGE % p.a.	ACTUAL AVERAGE % p.a.
May 1975 — March 1976	10–15	10.7
March 1976 — June 1977	8–12	8.9
June 1977 — June 1978	7–11	8.5
June 1978 — January 1980	6–10	7.6
January 1980 — February 1981	5– 9	6.5
February 1981 — November 1982	4– 8	1.6

Source: *Bank of Canada Review*, September 1978, p. 18; January 1980, p. 27; February 1981, p. 4.

be supplemented by some additional annual growth rate figures, shown in Table 40.2. Here we have shown the annual rate of growth of the money supply from 1974 to 1984 of three definitions, the monetary base (μ_0), M1(μ_1), and M2(μ_2). The third and fourth columns of Table 40.2 show the averages, first of all, of M1 and M2 growth ($\mu_{1,2}$) and, finally, the average of all three money supply growth rates ($\mu_{0,1,2}$). We have used these additional money supply growth figures (and some averages) so as to try to present a broad picture of the movements in monetary growth without sidetracking you into a discussion of which monetary aggregate is the most appropriate.

The figures in Tables 40.1 and 40.2 and the graph in Figure 40.1 all show the same broad features of monetary policy. In 1974 and

Figure 40.1
Money Supply and
Target Growth Ranges

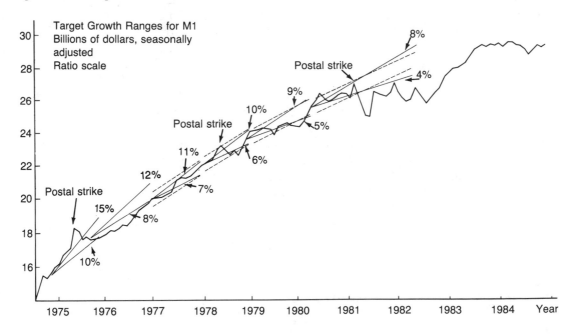

The figure shows the actual growth rate of the money supply and the target growth ranges between 1975 and 1982. For the most part, targets were achieved until 1981. After that date M1 was always substantially below target. There were erratic accelerations and decelerations in M1 growth through this period of monetary targeting. After 1982, targets were abandoned and actual M1 growth remained quite erratic.

Source: 1974–82: Bank of Canada, *Annual Report of the Governor to the Minister of Finance and Statement of Accounts* for the year 1982, p. 26; 1983–84: *Bank of Canada Review*, April 1985, Table E1.

1975 money supply growth rates were unusually high. When the first target growth range was announced in 1975, the actual growth rate of money was inside but close to the top end of the target. The target values for money supply growth have been reduced successively through each of the years since 1975, the mid-point of the target range having been halved from its 12.5 percent rate in 1975 to 6 percent in 1981. The actual growth rate of M1, broadly speaking, stayed inside its target band until 1981. It briefly went above the target range in 1975 (fourth quarter) and again in the fourth quarter of 1978. Both of these, the first being more serious, were associated with mail strikes. For a period in 1976-77 and again briefly in 1980, M1 went below its target range.

These brief and slight departures from the target range look insignificant, however, when compared with what happened in 1981 and 1982. In mid-1981 there was a massive cut in M1 that resulted in substantial undershooting of the target growth path. The M1 money supply remained substantially below its target until the targets were finally abandoned in November 1982.

A further feature of the behavior of M1, very apparent in Figure 40.1, is the erratic reversals of growth rate that are apparent. There have been periods of extremely rapid growth followed by periods of decline. The general pattern that emerges, however, is one of the steady declining trend growth rate of M1.

The growth rates of other monetary aggregates not specifically targeted by the Bank of Canada — the monetary base and M2 — though not corresponding on a year-by-year basis with the growth rate of M1 do, nevertheless, reveal similar trends in money growth.

Perhaps the closest correspondence between the growth rates of the different aggregates is that between the monetary base and M1. The growth rate of M2, at least until 1969, also responds in a similar manner to M1 and monetary base growth, although with higher absolute levels. Between 1974 and 1978 there is little difficulty in observing a tendency for money growth to slow down. Whether measured by the monetary base M1 or M2, the same conclusion is reached. In 1979 and 1980, however, M1 growth continues to slow down, the monetary base tightens very sharply in 1979, and even in 1980 is still growing at a slow rate relative to the rates experienced in the earlier part of the 1970s. M2 growth, however, begins to accelerate again and by 1980 is almost up to its 1974 level.

Is monetary policy between 1979 and 1980 becoming slack again, as indicated by M2 growth, or is it remaining tight, as indicated by M1 and monetary base growth? There can be little doubt that M2 growth is not giving an accurate reflection of the stance of monetary policy through this period. Interest rates in Canada rose substantially in 1969 and 1970, partly as a consequence of the pursuit of tight monetary policies. The higher interest rates were reflected, in part, in higher interest rates on savings deposits at banks. This led to a substitution away from currency and checking accounts and into savings accounts. The result was that M1 growth tightened substantially, while M2 growth mushroomed. The truth about the rightness of monetary policy at that time probably lies in between these two and is reasonably well indicated by the growth rate of the monetary base. On this view, monetary policy was tight in 1979 and 1980, but not as tight as would be indicated by considering M1 growth alone.

Viewed overall, there was a clear tightening of monetary policy in 1975-76 and again in 1979-80. Broadly speaking, Bank of Canada monetary growth targets were achieved, although with a great deal of irregularity in the performance of money growth inside its target range.

In the period during which targeting was breaking down, 1981-82, and the years after that, Bank of Canada monetary policy appears to have been exceedingly tight. The growth rate of the monetary base slowed down to become negative in 1984. Although it continues to be very erratic, there is an unmistakable tendency for the growth rate of M1 and M2 to be tightened substantially. The average growth rates shown in the final two columns of Table 40.2 show this tightening very clearly.

In this description of Bank of Canada monetary policy we have focussed largely on the behavior of the growth rates of monetary aggregates. There is an alternative story about Bank of Canada policy and interpretation of the Bank's policy actions that is a very interesting one. It is an interpretation that emphasizes not the growth rate of monetary aggregates but the behavior of the foreign exchange rate. As you know from your study of the international aspects of

TABLE 40.2
Money Supply Growth Rates, 1974-1984
(percent per annum)

YEAR	μ_0	μ_1	μ_2	$\mu_{1,2}$	$\mu_{0,1,2}$
1974	14.7	9.3	20.5	14.9	14.8
1975	14.2	14.0	15.2	14.6	14.5
1976	12.8	8.0	13.0	10.5	11.3
1977	13.4	8.5	14.3	11.4	12.1
1978	12.6	10.1	11.1	10.6	11.3
1979	4.3	6.9	15.7	11.3	9.0
1980	9.7	6.4	18.9	12.7	11.7
1981	8.8	3.6	15.2	9.4	9.2
1982	3.0	0.7	9.3	5.0	4.3
1983	6.5	10.2	5.7	8.0	7.5
1984	−8.3	3.2	4.4	3.8	−0.2

Sources: μ_1 and μ_2, Bank of Canada Review, July, 1985. The method and sources for μ_0 are set out in the Appendix to Chapter 40.

macroeconomics (see especially Chapters 27 to 28) monetary policy can take the form of controlling the exchange rate, thereby allowing the money supply to be determined by the demand for money, or can control the money stock leaving the exchange rate to be determined by market forces. When we studied the movements of the foreign exchange value of the Canadian dollar in Chapter 29, we saw a good deal of movement both up and down in the value of the Canadian currency in terms of other major currencies. It is very revealing, however, to look not just at how the Canadian dollar moved against individual currencies but against an average of currencies. The particular average that suggests itself is that for the ten leading western economies known as the Group of 10 (Belgium, Canada, France, Germany, Italy, Japan, the Netherlands, Sweden, the United Kingdom and the United States).

Figure 40.2
The Foreign Exchange
Value of the
Canadian Dollar

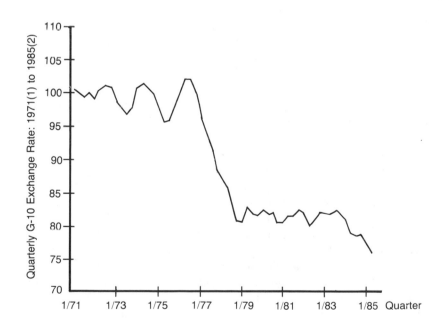

The value of the Canadian dollar (expressed as an index number) is shown against the currencies of the Group of 10. The exchange rate cycled around a constant value until 1977. It then declined precipitously but was stabilized again between 1979 and 1983. A further drop in its value occurred in 1984.

Source: *Bank of Canada Review,* September 1984, p. 22.

Figure 40.2 shows the value of the Canadian dollar (expressed as an index number) against the values of the currencies of the Group of 10 on a quarterly average basis since 1971. Examining the data shown in this figure reveals very clearly that, in the period since 1979, the Bank of Canada appears to have been very effectively stabilizing the foreign exchange value of the Canadian dollar. Although the weighted average exchange rate does fluctuate, those fluctuations are very small and not much larger than those that would be expected even under a rigid fixed exchange rate system. A further decline in the value of the Canadian dollar was permitted in 1984 but this has the appearance of a "devaluation" under a pegged exchange rate regime rather than as a market-determined exchange rate.[1]

Let us now turn to an examination of fiscal policy.

B. Fiscal Policy Since 1975

There have been some dramatic developments in fiscal policy in Canada in the past decade though there have been few dramatic changes in direction of the actual policies pursued by the government. The dramatic developments have arisen from the way in which the evolution of the economy has interacted with the government's programs for spending and tax policies.

The story of fiscal policy in Canada in the last decade is set out in the two frames of Figure 40.3. Frame (a) shows the actual paths of government spending, taxes (net of transfer payments) and the deficit, all expressed as a percentage of GNP.

Government spending on goods and services is seen as being virtually constant over the decade. It has fluctuated between 22.5 percent and close to 25 percent of GNP. Taxes (net of transfers) have, in contrast, declined sharply. As a consequence, the deficit has increased sharply. Net taxes in 1974 were almost 23.5 percent of GNP. By 1984 they had fallen to 16.25 percent. The bulk of what is going on behind this figure is that transfer payments have increased dramatically. One of the major transfer payments, the value of which has risen, is the value of interest on the national debt.

Corresponding to this sharp rise in transfer payments (and therefore decline in net of transfer tax receipts) has been the dramatically rising deficit. As you can see, the deficit has trended upwards and very strongly so, starting out at a surplus of almost 1 percent of GNP in 1974 and ending with a deficit of more than 8 percent of GNP by 1984.

---

[1] For a very useful and extensive discussion of this interpretation of Canadian monetary policy in recent years, and for the source of this idea, you should consult Peter Howitt, *Monetary Policy in Transition* (Montreal: C.D. Howe Research Institute, 1986).

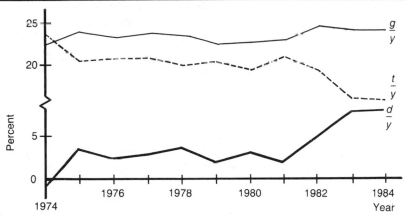

(a) Fiscal policy as percentage of GNP

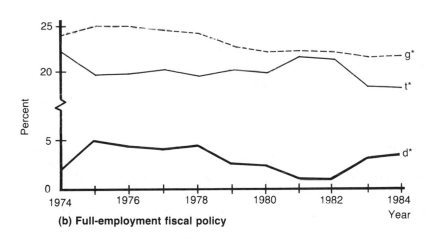

(b) Full-employment fiscal policy

**Figure 40.3
Fiscal Policy**

Frame (a) shows government spending, taxes (net of transfers) and the deficit as percentages of GNP. Government spending has remained steady, taxes dropped in 1975, held steady until 1982 and then fell again. A tax cut was responsible for this in 1975 but rising transfer payments and debt interest are the source of the later drop. The deficit grew dramatically through this period. Frame (b) tries to correct for the effects of the state of the economy and shows how these variables might have evolved if the economy had remained at full employment. The key problem seems to be that taxes are too small a fraction of GNP relative to spending. There is no trend rise in the deficit when this adjustment is made.

Sources and methods: (a) 1974–1982: *National Income and Expenditure Accounts*, 1969–1983, Statistics Canada, Catalogue 13-201 (Ottawa: 1984). Government expenditure (*g*) is Table 2, the sum of lines 2, 4 and 13; national income (*y*) is Table 2, line 19; taxes (*t*) are Table 16, the sum of lines 1 to 10 inclusive minus Table 17, the sum of lines 6 to 12 inclusive; the deficit (*d*) is government expenditure minus taxes. (b) 1983 to 1984: *National Income and Expenditure Accounts*, First Quarter 1985, Statistics Canada, Catalogue 13-001 (Ottawa: 1984). Government expenditure, national income and the deficit are the same as above; taxes are Table 6, the sum of lines 1, 7, 12, 13 and 17 minus the sum of lines 51, 57, 60 and 63.

The behavior of taxes (net of transfers) is worth examining a bit more closely. Notice that from 1975 through 1981 that variable was fairly steady (at about 20 percent of GNP). In 1974, however, there was a cut of about 3 percentage points in its value and, after 1981, a steady and persistent decline of almost 4 percentage points. The drop in this variable in 1975 was almost entirely associated with a cut in the effective average tax rate. This tax cut created a gap between government spending and government revenue. This gap remained in place throughout the second half of the 1970s and still remains in place in the middle 1980s. As a result, the total stock of public sector debt has been increasing steadily. In 1981-82, interest rates began to rise very sharply. The combination of sharply increased interest rates with a much bigger stock of government debt resulted in a sharp rise in total debt interest payments. These payments are classified as a transfer payment and so reduced sharply the value shown in Figure 40.3 for tax receipts net of transfer payments.

A good deal of the fluctuations in government spending, taxes and the deficit arise from the state of the economy. Government spending programs tend to result in a higher outlay for the government in times of economic recession. Also, tax receipts tend to decline when the economy is in a recession state. Thus the deficit is artificially swollen when the economy is in a recession. The data shown in frame (b) of Figure 40.3 attempt to correct for the state of the economy. (Precise methods whereby these corrections are made are described in the appendix to this chapter.) You can think of the data plotted in frame (b) of Figure 40.3 as showing how government spending, taxes and the deficit would have behaved if the economy had been at a constant trend value of output throughout the decade under review. These figures reveal Canada's current fiscal policy problems in a slightly different light. What they show is a situation in which government spending has been basically restrained, falling steadily and persistently, though only slightly, as a fraction of GNP. Taxes also have remained fairly constant but, crucially, have been less than government spending. Thus there has been a persistent though not rising deficit throughout this period.

These, then, are the major patterns in fiscal policy in the past decade. Let us now turn to an examination of wage and price controls.

C. Wage and Price Control Program, 1975-78

The wage and price control program — the so-called "Attack on Inflation" — was launched on October 14, 1975, and ended on December 31, 1978.[2]

---

[2]"Attack on Inflation: A Program of National Action," Policy statement tabled by Donald S. Macdonald in the House of Commons, October 14, 1975 (Ottawa: Government of Canada).

The program set out guidelines for wages, prices, and profits in the following terms:

(i) Wages were to grow at not more than 8 percent from 1975 to 1976, 6 percent from 1976 to 1977, and 4 percent from 1977-1978. There were some exceptions allowing minimum wage rises of $600 per annum and maximum pay rises of $2400 per annum regardless of the percentage rise these figures represented. There were also some allowances for productivity gains, and adjustments for previous shortfalls of wages relative to price and productivity growth. However, the basic wage norm was

1976	8%
1977	6%
1978	4%

(ii) The guidelines on prices were that "increases in prices should be limited to amounts no more than required to cover net increases in costs" (p. 16). Where it was possible to allocate costs to individual products, prices were to be controlled so as to "leave [the] percentage pre-tax net profit margin no higher than 95 percent of its average percentage pre-tax [level] in the last five completed fiscal years" (p. 17).

Thus, price rises were supposed to be in line with wage rises adjusted for productivity growth. Canadian average productivity growth has been of the order of 2 percent per annum. We can therefore view the wage guidelines, combined with the price and profit rules, as implying a targeted rate of inflation for the three years of

1976	6%
1977	4%
1978	2%

The wage and price controls were monitored by a new agency, the Anti-Inflation Board. This was a relatively expensive monitoring agency, costing $16 million in 1975-1976, $24 million in 1976-1977, and $18 million in 1977-1978, with a staff of between 856 in the first year and 598 in the final year of operation.

The Anti-Inflation Board had powers to investigate wage and price increases and to require that increases outside the guidelines be rolled back to the guideline levels.

Summary of Policy in all Three Areas, 1974-1984:
(i) Money supply growth rates were reduced sharply in 1975-76, and again, though with some divergence between the broad and narrow measures, in 1979-80. In the period 1980-84 there has been a further substantial slowing of money supply growth.
(ii) Government spending on goods and services and revenue from money creation expressed as percentages of trend output fell slightly throughout the period. Taxes fell and borrowing rose by 3.5 percent of trend in output in 1975 and remained constant thereafter.

(iii) Wage and price controls were targeted at an inflation rate of 6 percent in 1976, 4 percent in 1977, and 2 percent in 1978.

D. Inflation and Output Growth Since 1975

It is not possible to present a definitive account of the precise ways in which each of these policies has influenced the course of the Canadian economy. The basic research needed to undertake that task has not been done. Such research would have to be undertaken, published in learned journals, and subjected to the usual scholarly criticism before it could be condensed and presented to you in a form that was sufficiently non-controversial and capable of being simplified without distortion. What we can do, however, is examine the ways in which, according to the modern theories of inflation, unemployment, and output, the economy may be interpreted as having responded to the policy regime that has been in place in the last decade. By way of an analogy, if you think of the job of understanding how the economy has responded to the policy regime of the last decade as going on a tour of unknown terrain, the modern theories that we have available can be regarded as providing useful clues as to the things to look out for en route so as to pick our way through the unknown territory, rather than as a fully worked-out detailed map of the entire area under investigation.

In proceeding to analyze the effects of policy, it will be convenient to begin with the wage and price control program and then move on to consider monetary and fiscal policy taken as a package.

(i) The Wage and Price Controls, 1975-1978[3]

The wage and price control program was designed to lower the rate of inflation. The central question that we need to address here is, Did the program have that effect? Table 40.3 summarizes some relevant data for making that assessment.

The first obvious fact that is striking about Canada's inflation in the second half of the seventies is that as measured by the GNE Deflator, inflation fell each and every year while the controls were in place and then climbed back almost to the pre-controlled level when the controls were lifted. The behavior of inflation as measured by the Consumer Price Index is not quite so dramatic. This inflation rate dropped substantially in the first full year of controls, but then rose slightly in each of the remaining years of the controls, and did not show a marked explosion when the controls were lifted. Another "price"

---

[3] The best overview of the effects of the wage and price controls on Canada's inflation is *Inflation and Public Policy*, Anti-Inflation Board (Ottawa, 1979). Page 85 of that volume gives a bibliography of other AIB publications on the effects of the controls.

TABLE 40.3
Assessing the Effects of the Wage and Price Controls: 1975-1978

YEAR	INFLATION GNE DEFLATOR	INFLATION CPI	GROWTH OF AVERAGE HOURLY EARNINGS	GROWTH OF REAL WAGES	UNEMPLOYMENT RATE
1974	15.3	10.9	13.5	2.6	5.3
1975	10.7	10.8	15.7	4.9	6.9
1976	9.5	7.5	13.8	6.3	7.1
1977	7.0	8.0	10.8	2.8	8.1
1978	6.4	9.0	7.2	−1.8	8.4
1979	10.3	9.1	8.8	−0.3	7.5

Sources: GNE Deflator and CPI, Appendix to Chapter 2; average hourly earnings, *Bank of Canada Review*, May 1981, Table 1, column 18; real wages is the difference between columns 3 and 2; unemployment, Appendix to Chapter 2.

which the control program sought to influence was the price of labor (the growth rate of average hourly earnings is shown in the third column of the table). Like the growth rate of the GNE Deflator and the Consumer Price Index, earnings growth declined during the control program compared with the previous level. Its behavior looks a lot like that of the GNE Deflator, falling each and every year of the controls and then, at the end of the control program, rising, although to nothing like the pre-controlled level. Real wages (the fourth column of the table) grew strongly in the first year of the control program, but then were moderated and actually fell by almost 2 percent in the final year of the program.

Two facts are clear from this brief examination of the behavior of inflation and the prices of final output and labor. Inflation and real wages grew at a slower rate during the control period (1976-78) than they had done prior to the controls (1974-75) or than they did after the controls were lifted (1979). This much is fact. What is not fact is the proposition that the controls were effective. This has to be inferred from the appropriate evidence. All the major published studies on the subject have focussed their attention on the behavior of real wages. It is probably the case that the slowdown in real wage growth between 1976 and 1978 was not due to slack labor market conditions. The final column of Table 40.3, which shows the unemployment rate, reveals that labor market conditions did slacken during the control program. Unemployment rose from a little under 7 percent at the start of the program to almost 8.5 percent by the end of it. By studying the normal effects of slack labor markets on real wage growth, it is possible to assess the extent to which what happened during the control program was a normal response. The evidence seems to point to the conclusion that real wage growth slowed down more quickly than normally would have been the case in the event of labor markets being as slack as those observed during 1976, 1977, and 1978. This does not automatically lead to the conclusion that it is the controls that were slowing down the growth of real wages.

During that same period the composition of the labor force was changing. Women over the age of twenty-five were becoming a more important part of the labor force (up from 25 percent to 27 percent in that three-year period), and men over twenty-five were becoming a less significant part (down from 50 percent to 48 percent). More thorough investigation is still needed to examine the extent to which this changed labor force composition might have accounted for a slowing down of real wage growth. It is certain that some contribution came from this source, since women, on the average, are paid lower wages than men. An increase in the percentage of women in the labor force would automatically be associated with a decrease in the average real wage. It is the quantitative importance of this effect which needs to be worked out in order to check out further whether there is any residual lowering in real wage growth which can only be accounted for by the controls.

The effectiveness of the control program on inflation itself has not been investigated as comprehensively as have its effects on real wages. It has been observed, however, even by those who favor the use of controls, that most of the slowdown in inflation during 1975-78 was associated with a dramatic fall in the rate at which world food prices were inflating. These prices were outside the range of influence of the Anti-Inflation Board. Further, the inflation rates on items that were subject to control fell much less. This observation is entirely in line with the theoretical analysis presented in Chapter 37. That analysis concluded that the controls cannot have affected the inflation rate because they could not affect either the expectations-augmented aggregate supply curve or the aggregate demand curve (except for some second-order effects that are likely to go in the wrong direction). This is not, of course, a denial that the controls might have had some effects. It is possible that the theory itself is wrong. Possible though that is, it will be recalled that the rational expectations theory is capable of explaining the broad facts about inflation and output that we have observed in the Canadian economy (Chapter 23). Further, if that same theory which denies that the controls could have operated to lower Canada's inflation rate gives us some insights into why the inflation rate did fall between 1976 and 1978 and why it rose again in 1979 and 1980, then although less than final proof, this would certainly amount to interesting circumstantial evidence against the hypothesis that the controls were responsible for that three-year period of lower inflation.

Let us now turn to an examination of these matters by looking at monetary and fiscal policy over this period.

(ii) Monetary and Fiscal Policy[4]

As we have seen, monetary and fiscal policy are intimately linked, so it is useful to examine them together. The theory of inflation, output, and employment emphasizes that policy is a process rather than a series of disconnected events, and that it is essential, in order to understand the effects of policy, to decompose any specific policy action into an anticipated and unanticipated component. We cannot do this in any precise way, but we can be guided by these considerations in exploring the evolution of monetary and fiscal policy in the second half of the 1970s.

To start the process, let us examine the main facts about monetary and fiscal policy on the eve of the period under review. Up to 1974, fiscal policy in Canada had involved a budget that was close to being in balance. The deficit to be financed by either borrowing or money creation was always substantially less than 1 percent of Gross National Product. At the beginning of the period under review, there was a marked disruption of this previous order. In 1975, taxes fell and the deficit rose by 3.5 percent of trend GNP. This represents an enormous shock to the Canadian economy. If that deficit was to be turned into additional money — if the debt was to be financed by creating additional monetary base — then the monetary base would grow at something close to 25 percent per annum, implying an inflation rate in excess of 20 percent per annum. Of course, few, if any, believed that this would happen. An economy that has normally run along with a deficit of less than 1 percent of GNP would not be expected to suddenly and dramatically create a deficit of 3.5 percent of GNP on a permanent on-going basis and finance that deficit by money printing. On the contrary, the widely held belief in 1975 must have been that the newly emerged deficit of 3.5 percent of GNP would be a temporary matter and would fairly quickly be eradicated by adjustments to government spending and/or taxes.

Along with the small and fairly predictable deficits of the 1960s and early 1970s went a fairly predictable, low money supply growth rate at least up to 1970. Between 1971 and 1974, however, there was an unusual burst of high money growth in Canada. The year 1975 saw the adoption of the Bank of Canada's new monetary targeting policy, and in that same year money supply growth rates began to be contained and returned towards, although not to, their levels of the late sixties.

---

[4]For an excellent account of Canadian macroeconomic policy in general, and monetary policy in particular, see Thomas J. Courchene, *Money, Inflation, and the Bank of Canada* (Montreal: C. D. Howe Research Institute, 1976); *Monetarism and Controls, The Inflation Fighters* (Montreal: C. D. Howe Research Institute, 1976); and *Money, Inflation and the Bank of Canada, Vol. II* (Montreal: C. D. Howe Research Institute, 1981).

Thus, at the beginning of the period that we are reviewing, an almost unprecedented budget deficit of 3.5 percent of GNP had emerged which, it is judged, was regarded by most people as likely to be temporary. Money supply growth rates had been unusually high in the three or four preceding years, but were being lowered by 1975.

The predictions of macroeconomic theory concerning the effects of these 1975 policy actions are as follows. First, because the newly emerged fiscal deficit was believed to be temporary and because of the pursuit of lower money supply growth rates, the expected inflation rate should fall. Second, output might rise or fall relative to trend, depending on whether the reduction in inflationary expectations was greater than or less than the reduction in actual inflation. In fact, inflation began to fall and so did output. The implication is that the expected rate of inflation did not fall quite as much as did the actual rate of inflation in that year.

Moving into 1976, there was essentially no change in fiscal policy. The deficit remained at roughly its previous level, and there were no major changes in spending or tax programs leading to any expectations of a subsequent change in the deficit. By this time, a few people would have been suspecting that the deficit was not going to be quickly eradicated. At this stage, however, few would have been entertaining seriously the prospect of covering the deficit by increased money printing. In fact, monetary policy of 1976 strongly countered any such view. All the monetary aggregates grew at slower rates than they had in 1975, indicating a further consistent deflationary tightening of monetary policy. The predictions of theory concerning the developments in 1976 are that inflation should fall and, given the normal response pattern, real output should also fall relative to trend. In fact, there was a temporary burst of output growth (probably partly stimulated by the recovery of the world economy), but inflation did indeed fall as predicted by the theory.

As the economy moved into 1977, fiscal policy recorded its second year of no change. By now, important elements of the community had begun to doubt the determination of the government to bring fiscal policy back under control and remove the deficit and, on this account alone, inflationary expectations tended to increase. Such beliefs were enhanced by the performance of monetary policy in 1977 for it, too, like fiscal policy, underwent very little change. The growth rates of most aggregates stayed close to their 1976 levels. The prediction of theory is that output should fall and inflation should be fairly steady (maybe even rising slightly). In fact, output growth did fall relative to trend, but inflation moved ambiguously. The inflation rate as measured by the GNE Deflator fell, but as measured by the Consumer Price Index, it rose.

Another year of no change followed in 1978. Again, there were no major fiscal policy changes, and the deficit remained fairly steady.

Also, the money growth rates of 1978 were close to their 1977 levels. (M1 actually grew faster, but M2 slower.) By now, serious doubts concerning the intention to change spending programs and taxes and remove the deficit must have been taking hold. A more widespread belief that the deficit was here to stay and would eventually be financed by creating more money was also taking hold. In this situation, the prediction of theory is that inflation should actually begin to rise (driven up by the increased inflationary expectations), but that output should fall (since the growth of aggregate demand relative to trend had not been changed). The outcome for 1978 was almost exactly as predicted. Output growth fell, as predicted, but inflation again registered an ambiguous response, with the GNE Deflator showing a lower inflation rate and the Consumer Price Index a higher rate. The next year was one of considerable increase in confusion. For yet another year, a deficit averaging 3.5 percent of GNP had been experienced, and by now, few doubted the permanence of this deficit situation, and the likelihood of increased monetary financing of the deficit became a more widespread belief. The monetary policy developments of 1979 did not help to allay any fears for the monetary base, and M1 growth rates, although declining, were accompanied by a sharp rise in the growth rate of M2. Higher interest rates, triggered mainly by the higher inflationary expectations coming from the continued high deficit, meant that although M1 growth was slower, its velocity of circulation had increased. The main predictions of theory in this case are that inflation should rise as a result of the higher inflationary expectations and that output should fall relative to trend as a result of the maintenance or slight reduction in the overall level of demand. This actually did occur in 1979, with inflation beginning to climb on both the CPI and GNE Deflator measures. Output growth was substantially below its trend value.

By 1980 a virtual certainty seemed to have emerged concerning the permanence of the government's budget deficit. By now, after a full half-decade of deficits, with no policies being introduced to modify the situation, there was a widely held belief that the deficit was permanent and that at some stage it would be financed by an increased rate of money printing. The actual conduct of monetary policy gave no support to such a belief, at least for the immediate future. M1 growth was further tightened in 1980, although money base growth began to accelerate again, as did the growth rate of M2. The average money supply growth rates (averaged over all the aggregates) did not change much between 1979 and 1980. The predictions concerning these developments are that inflation should rise as a result of the higher inflationary expectations and that real output should decline relative to trend as a result of the continued firmness of actual monetary policy. These predictions were entirely borne out by the developments of 1980.

In 1981 and 1982 monetary policy became exceedingly tight. The money supply growth rate, regardless of how it is measured, decelerated sharply. With a large fiscal deficit remaining in place and, presumably, with continued high inflationary expectations, the rate of inflation hardly moved at all during those two years but output growth sagged severely. This again is entirely in line with the predictions of our theory. Monetary policy was loosened slightly in 1983 but then tightened again in 1984. By this time, however, inflation had begun to recede. The very tight monetary policies of 1981-82 and the deep recession that they generated seem to have broken fears of ongoing inflation despite the fact that the deficit remains in place. We cannot know why people have become more confident that inflation will be contained but that is certainly the interpretation that we have to place on the inflation of 1983 and 1984 and also the interpretation that we have to place on the recovery and output growth. It seems that this demonstration of an unwillingness to finance the deficit with money creation has been a sufficiently convincing one even though the political choices that have to be taken in order to remove the deficit remain in the future.

This brief account of the economic history of Canada in the second half of the 1970s, using the insights of the rational expectations theory of output and prices, seems to provide a good guide to what was happening. The drop in inflation during the period 1976 through 1978 and its subsequent rebound are well accounted for by the evolution of actual and expected policy based on an admittedly informal, but nevertheless reasonable, interpretation of how expectations might have evolved. There were some movements in unemployment through this period which are not directly accounted for by the movements of output that have been described in the preceding paragraphs. Those unemployment movements probably had more to do with relative price-incentive effects than with aggregate demand effects. It would nevertheless be useful if they could be explained. That task would, however, go beyond what this chapter seeks to do.

What does our theory tell us is going to happen to output and inflation in Canada during the balance of the 1980s? Rather than attempting to answer this question directly, we want to approach the answer by an interesting indirect route. Suppose we had asked the question in 1980, "What does our theory tell us is going to happen to output and inflation in Canada during the early 1980s?" What would we have said? Fortunately we know the answer to this question because the first edition of the book, published in early 1982, was written in the spring of 1980. The following words, appeared on pages 526 and 527 of that first edition:

> What does our theory tell us is going to happen to output and inflation in Canada during the early 1980s? Of course it only makes conditional predictions. It does not say what government policy will be. It does, however, say what will happen if policy pursues this or that course. We can make three fairly definite statements. If the government

cuts its present budget deficit, either by raising taxes, cutting spending, or some combination of the two, and if the Bank of Canada maintains its six year record of slowing down the growth rate of *M1*, then inflation in Canada will fall, real output will stay close to its full-employment level, and unemployment will stay close to its natural rate. All this will happen in a fairly short span of time. The reasoning that leads to this prediction is that the expected rate of inflation will fall as a result of the coherence or consistency between monetary and fiscal policy, and the actual rate of inflation will fall at approximately the same rate as the fall in the expected rate.

If the government does not take steps to change its fiscal policy and cut its deficit, and if the Bank of Canada maintains its existing monetary policy of slowing down the growth rate of *M1*, then inflation in Canada will fall, but only gradually, and rather painfully. It will be associated with a deep cut in real output growth relative to trend and a strong and fairly persistent rise in the unemployment rate. The reasoning behind these predictions is that with fiscal policy continuing to signal higher future inflation, and monetary policy continuing to deliver lower current aggregate demand, the expectations augmented aggregate supply curve will not drop fast enough to prevent a deep recession. If the Bank continues on its policy course unhindered, then the inflation rate will eventually have to fall, since the fundamental inflation equation cannot be violated, and the velocity of circulation of money will not continue to rise and rise without limit. High real rate of interest will eventually choke off the excessive spending, and inflation will eventually fall.

The third scenario is one in which the government does not cut its deficit, and the Bank of Canada abandons its disinflationary monetary policies. In that event, it is clear that real output and unemployment will stay close to their natural full-employment levels, and the inflation rate will accelerate into the high teens and perhaps low twenties. The current rational expectation is some weighted average of all three of these possible outcomes. That is why inflationary expectations are so stubborn and are remaining well in excess of 10 percent as the 1980s begin. It is also why interest rates are remaining so high.

We can make the same kinds of conditional predictions concerning the evolution of the Canadian economy during the final years of the 1980s. How the economy will evolve will depend upon the development in monetary and fiscal policy during the final years of the 1980s. The same reasoning that led to the predictions about the first half of the 1980s will apply to the second half of the decade. Only if the deficit is removed and if money supply growth is kept in check, will the economy return to a low-inflation, high-employment, steady-growth situation. The continued combination of a large fiscal deficit and tight monetary policy will probably keep inflation in check but will engender ongoing uncertainty as to the future course of inflation and the future changes to be implemented in fiscal policy. This is likely to lead to a situation of continuing high unemployment and slow output growth. Continuing with high deficits and allowing money supply growth to become more loose will do little to help the unemployment and growth situation but will add renewed inflation to the list of Canada's economic ills.

Summary

A. Monetary Policy Since 1975

Monetary policy in Canada in 1975 was inflationary. Money supply growth rates were in the range of 15 percent per annum. In that year the Bank of Canada embarked upon a new, gradualist, anti-inflationary monetary policy. It announced a target range for money supply (M1) growth which has been revised downwards each year since then. The actual M1 growth rate remained inside its target band for most of the time until 1981 when it went, and remained substantially below target. The targeting approach was abandoned in 1982. The growth rates of the monetary base and the broader monetary aggregates were in sympathy with the growth of M1 with the exception of 1979-82. In these years, M1 growth continued to slow, while the growth of the broader aggregates remained high.

B. Fiscal Policy Since 1975

Government spending on goods and services has been virtually a constant fraction of trend output over this period. Taxes (net of transfer payments) fell by 3.5 percent of trend GNP in 1975 and have remained at that new lower level since then. The deficit of approximately 3.5 percent of GNP has been financed mainly by borrowing. The fraction of GNP passing to the government through money creation has remained fairly constant.

C. Wage and Price Control Program, 1975-78

Wage and price guidelines implying an inflation rate of 6 percent in 1976, 4 percent in 1977, and 2 percent in 1978 were established with the "Attack on Inflation" of 1975. The Anti-Inflation Board set up to monitor the program had wide powers to investigate price and wage rises and roll back those in excess of the target range.

D. Inflation and Output Growth Since 1975

The effect of the wage and price control program on the course of Canadian inflation is judged to have been negligible. The main pattern of evolution of inflation and output growth since 1975 is explained by the combination of monetary and fiscal policy. Inflation fell through 1978 and then began to rise again. It remained at a level in excess of 10 percent through 1982 but then, finally, by 1983 and 1984 fell dramatically. Output growth, relative to trend, declined systematically after 1976 and reached a deep recession point by 1982. Stronger growth emerged in 1983-84.

The main forces influencing these developments have been the combination of firm monetary policies and changing beliefs about the likely future of the government's budget deficit. Through the 1970s it appears that the firm monetary policies did little to reduce fears that the government's deficit would be so persistent as to eventually signal the end of those firm monetary policies. When the monetary screws were tightened severely in 1981 and 1982, however, and the economy was put into a deep recession, it seems that the credibility of persistent anti-inflationary policies came to be more firmly established. The conditional predictions for the second half of the 1980s are that if the budget deficit is cut and if the Bank of Canada maintains firm monetary policies, then inflation will remain low and output growth will be maintained at a level in line with its longer-term average and unemployment will begin to decline. If the deficit is not reduced and if the Bank of Canada continues to maintain its firm monetary policies then inflation might remain low but output growth will be slow and unemployment will remain high. If the government does not bring the deficit under control and if the Bank of Canada abandons firm monetary policies then Canada will experience a high rate of inflation into the indefinite future and this will be added to its other underlying economic problems of slow growth and high unemployment.

Review Questions

1. Describe the main features of monetary policy in Canada since 1975.

2. What have been the Bank of Canada's monetary policy targets?

3. How close has the Bank of Canada come towards achieving its targets?

4. Review the reasons why the Bank of Canada may have had some difficulty in achieving its monetary growth targets.

5. What have been the main developments in Canadian fiscal policy since the middle 1970s?

6. To what degree does the recent pattern of Canadian government spending, taxation and money creation conform to the long-run average government budget constraint?

7. Summarize the main features of Canada's wage and price control program which operated from 1975 to 1978.

8. How may Canada's inflation and output growth during the past decade be accounted for, using the insights provided by macroeconomic theory? What must have been the main changes in anticipated policy if the theory is to fit the facts? Do these changes seem plausible?

9. What are the possible scenarios for inflation and output in Canada in the second half of the 1980s? What does government policy have to do to deliver low inflation at low cost?

APPENDIX A
Sources and Methods for Monetary Base Growth

Monetary Base Growth

YEAR	LIABILITIES OF THE BANK OF CANADA (excluding public sector deposits)	PERCENT CHANGE
1970	5 176	—
1971	5 945	14.9
1972	7 032	18.3
1973	7 994	13.7
1974	9 169	14.7
1975	10 471	14.2
1976	11 812	12.8
1977	13 394	13.4
1978	15 080	12.6
1979	15 735	4.3
1980	17 261	9.7
1981	18 773	8.8
1982	19 341	3.0
1983	20 590	6.5
1984	18 878	−8.3

Source and Method: *Bank of Canada Review*, May 1981 and July 1985. Liabilities are Bank of Canada series B200 less government deposits, B254, and government enterprise deposits, B256. In calculating the growth rate of the monetary base we have ignored coins. This exclusion makes almost no difference to the growth rate

APPENDIX B
Method of Calculating Cyclically Adjusted Values

This note describes the method used to calculate the data plotted in Figure 40.3 (b). First for the period 1974 to 1984 we ran the following regressions:

$$\text{Actual} = \text{Constant} + \text{Time Trend} + \text{Cycle} + \text{Random}$$
$$(g/y) = a_1 + b_1 \text{ time} + c_1 (y - y^*) + u_1$$
$$(t/y) = a_2 + b_2 \text{ time} + c_2 (y - y^*) + u_2$$
$$(d/y) = a_3 + b_3 \text{ time} + c_3 (y - y^*) + u_3$$

where time is a sequence 1,2,...; and $(y - y^*)$ is the deviation of real GNP from trend as listed in the Appendix to Chapter 2. To calculate the cyclically adjusted values of (g/y), (t/y) and (d/y) we subtracted the cycle components from the actual values to give:

$$\text{Cycle Adjusted} = \text{Constant} + \text{Time Trend} + \text{Random}$$
$$(g/y)^* = a_1 + b_1 \text{ time} + u_1$$
$$(t/y)^* = a_2 + b_2 \text{ time} + u_2$$
$$(d/y)^* = a_3 + b_3 \text{ time} + u_3$$

These are the values plotted in the figure.

Index